EARLY AMERICAN PATTERN GLASS

1850 – 1910

EARLY AMERICAN PATTERN GLASS

1850 - 1910

MAJOR COLLECTIBLE TABLE SETTINGS

WITH PRICES

BILL JENKS   JERRY LUNA

Wallace-Homestead Book Company

Radnor, Pennsylvania

On the cover: Rose Sprig in vaseline.

Designed by Anthony Jacobson
Manufactured in the United States of America

Library of Congress Cataloging in Publication Data
Jenks, Bill.
    Early American pattern glass, 1850–1910: major collectible table
settings with prices/Bill Jenks and Jerry Luna.
        p.   cm.
    Includes bibliographical references.
    ISBN 0-87069-545-2
    1. Pattern glass—United States—History—19th century—Collectors
and collecting—Catalogs.   2. Pattern glass—United States—
History—20th century—Collectors and collecting—Catalogs.
    I. Luna, Jerry.   II. Title.
    NK5439.P36E18   1990
    748.2913'075—dc20   89-51560
                                                              CIP

5 6 7 8 9 0   8 7 6

CONTENTS

ACKNOWLEDGMENTS

Uncovering and authenticating historical research quickly becomes a labor of major proportion that demands the cumulative knowledge and talents of many individuals and institutions. No longer can an author sit isolated at a desk. One's resources no longer lie within the realm of self creativity but among those who share a common desire to know and explore. To all who have opened their homes and shops and provided items to be photographed, personal knowledge of the glass industry, and original source materials, we thank you on behalf of tomorrow. You have broadened and enlightened many new horizons.

Of the many who have encouraged and supported our efforts, we extend a special word of thanks to Harry L. Rinker and Ellen Schroy (Rinker Enterprises, Zionsville, PA.) for their support, encouragement, and unbridled help in developing into a reality what began as a wishful desire. Without access to Harry's extensive reference library, collection of reproduction glassware, and knowledge, this book would not have been possible.

A special thank-you must be extended to Howard Glatfelter, Jr., Kingston, PA., who unselfishly transformed his happy home into the offices that housed both cameras and computers, spent endless days toting glassware back and forth (often from great distances) to be photographed, and supported and encouraged us from the beginning of this project.

Of special note, the authors wish to single out and extend their gratitude and appreciation to the following individuals for their ceaseless contributions to this book: Mrs. Linda Luna (The Glass Giraffe Antiques, Rahway, NJ.) for understanding and encouraging the persistent rigors of her husband's dream; Andrea & Alan Koppel (Iris Cottage Antiques, Canaan, NY.) and Nellie & Charlie Huttunen (Long Island, NY.) whose outstanding collections of Lion glass and inventories were always available to be photographed and studied; Lil & Bud Marchant (Lil-Bud Antiques, Yarmouthport, MA.) whose outstanding inventory and collection provided many of the photographs that would have otherwise been missing; and Harry J. Robinson (Shippensburg, PA.) who graciously entrusted us with his collection of vaseline Rose Sprig to be photographed for the cover.

Although we appreciate the help of everyone who has shared in our endeavor, the authors would like to acknowledge and express their sincere appreciation to the following individuals who came to our rescue:

John & Alice Ahlfeld
York, PA.

Mr. & Mrs. Eugene Bankert
Gene's Antiques
Hanover, PA.

Helen Baringer
Coopersburg, PA.

Roger Benett
Brimfield, MA.

Keith & Nancy Bergey
Sellersville, PA.

Mary Bertram
Lansing, MI.

Elizabeth Bixby
New Oxford, PA.

Betty Bowersox
Hershey, PA.

Nelia M. Bredehoft
Salem Antiques
St. Louisville, OH.

Scott Brown
Grand Rapids, MI.

Joyce Burn
Ontario, Canada

Jim Burns
Wycott, IN.

Cathy Chambers, Manager
Eastern National Antiques Show
Harrisburg, PA.

Henry Derby
Atlantic, VA.

Doehne's Ox Bow Shop
Harrisburg, PA.

Woodrow Dyer
North Scituate, RI.

Tom Eiserlahr
West Hartford, CN.

Gary & Catherine Etzler
Taneytown, MD.

Joan & Ron Foose
Cromwell, CT.

Helen Goldberg
Willow Antiques
Pittsboro, NC.

Golden Webb Antiques, Inc.
Wilkes Barre, PA.

Roger Graham
Pittsburgh, PA.

Bill Gross
Port Orange, FL.

Grace & Al Guido
Grantiques
Frenchtown, NJ.

Herb & Nancy Hallman
Churn Antiques
Allentown, PA.

Robert Hefenfinger
Harrisburg, PA.

Joyce Heilman
Great Eastern U.S. Antique Show
Allentown, PA.

Betsy Hewlett
Early American Pattern Glass
Yarmouthport, MA.

Rod & Chris Kaiser
Syracuse, NY.

Roberta & Mel Lader
Alexandria, VA.

Jacquelyn & Bernard Little
Littles Antiques
Littlestown, PA.

David & Wendy Loss
Piscataway, NJ.

Robert Lucas
Tarentum, PA.

Eugene F. Markle
New Oxford, PA.

George Mazeika
Storrs, CN.

Mildred Miller
Dublin, PA.

William Morrison
Lancaster, PA.

Kevin and Karen Nastos
Long Island, NY.

Shirley Olson
Pine Bough Antiques
East Hartford CN.

Mark Prime
Prime Antiques, PA.

Joan Raines Antiques
New Rochelle, NY.

Michael Rath
Williamsport, PA./Hudson, FL.

Darryl K. Reilly
Dandara's Antiques
Pepperel, MA.

Chris & Rena Reynolds
C&R Antiques
Branford, CN.

Harry & Laura Sine
Sine's Antiques
New Hope, PA.

Daniel M. Sourbeer Antiques
St. Petersburg, FL.

Miriam Stock
Stock's Antiques
Dillsburg, PA.

Sugar Hill Antiques
Washington, PA.

Suitsuss II
Granger, IN.

Dwayne Taylor Antiques
Hudson Falls, NY.

Robert & Carolyn Weikel
Weikel Antiques
Red Lion, PA.

Chub & Bette Wicker
Wicker's Antiques
Millbrook, NY.

National Archives & Records Services,
Washington, DC.

Rakow Library, Corning, NY.
Norma P.H. Jenkins, Head Librarian
Kathy Kapral, Micro Filmer
Elizabeth Hylen, Acquisition Librarian
Virginia L. Wright, Associate Librarian

Sandwich Glass Museum, Sandwich, MA.
Dorothy G. Hogan, Director
Kirk Nelson, Curator

Smithsonian Institution,
Washington, DC.

State Museum of PA., Harrisburg, PA.
James R. Mitchell, Curator of Industry,
   and Technology
Carl Tallman, Head Librarian

Sturbridge Village Museum,
Sturbridge, MA.

In researching original materials, we received cooperation and assistance from the following institutions and individuals who have proven invaluable to our study:

Bennington Museum, Bennington, VT.
Eugene Kosche, Curator of History
Ruth Levin, Registrar
Catherine Zusy, Curator of
   Decorative Arts

Commissioner of Patents & Trademarks,
Washington, DC.

Corning Museum of Glass, Corning, NY.
Dr. David Whitehouse, Chief Curator

Henry Ford Museum,
Dearborn, MI.

Metropolitan Museum of Art
New York, NY.

The authors would like to thank the entire staff of the Chilton Book Company for the support and guidance they have given us. In particular, we extend our appreciation and thanks to Troy Vozzella, (production editor), Kathy Conover (senior editor), and Anthony Jacobson (book designer) for the excellence they have demonstrated. To the late Alan Turner (former editorial director), we shall remain forever indebted to his friendship and dedication to this book.

To the fine people at PPS (Professional Photographic Services, Wilkes Barre, PA.): Edwin Mengak, Nancy Turner, and Christine Hontz. Thanks for a job well done.

Unintentionally, the contributions of many may not have been mentioned. To all, we extend our appreciation and thanks.

INTRODUCTION

Collecting and dealing in early American pattern glass for a combined total of thirty years, we have always felt the need for a reference book that contained most known data. Shuffling through countless reference works produced at best scattered results and opposing opinions. What one author christened "Feather," for example, another called "Doric," creating as many different names for a single pattern as there are authors. Separating fact from fiction became a task that boggled the imagination as many half-truths and opinions, unknowingly perpetrated by modern researchers, slipped into the realm of fact.

In researching material for *Early American Pattern Glass*, the most difficult problem encountered was uncovering factual information. Although a limited number of original glass company and general/wholesale merchandise catalogs have been uncovered and preserved, they are rare and often difficult to attain in their original form. More commonly encountered are the patent records and company advertisements illustrating the glassware of the last quarter of the 19th century. Determining by whom a specific design was first manufactured or later reissued, when a line was first introduced, and what forms and colors are original to the line, required direct access to these materials. The most striking revelation in the study of original source material was the overwhelming wealth of unpublished fact that has unwittingly been overlooked or dismissed.

Because most existent glass company catalogs are undated, assigning specific production dates from a catalog study is a slow, tedious, and often dangerous process. As patterns were added to or deleted from production, catalogs were often haphazardly revised by enterprising personnel to reflect the availability of current production by adding or removing pages. As factories merged or changed ownership, as in the case of the United States Glass Co. merger of 1891, outdated member catalogs were often pulled apart and combined by hand to form a single new catalog of active lines. More often than not, the dates we encountered in these catalogs were affixed by rubber stamp or hand dated with pen and ink and do not reflect a true production date.

Beginning in the mid 1880s, many glass factories attempted to broaden merchandising through advertising. Weekly trade journals such as *China, Glass & Lamps*, ran impressively illustrated ads with superb line drawings. These ads became a tool by which newly introduced lines were promoted, often for several months at a time. Another means of introducing and promoting new patterns to the trade was to have them reviewed in publications such as *The Crockery & Glass Journal*. When a pattern inevitably lost its popularity, general merchandise and wholesale catalogs such as *Butler Brothers* and *The Baltimore Bargain House* illustrated and sold it with the combined stock of various factories as barrel groupings, often renaming discontinued patterns. Frequently employed by contemporary writers as the only guide to attribution, advertisements alone tend to heighten the confusion as to when, where and by whom a pattern was produced.

Similarly, the use of patent dates cannot in itself be considered a failsafe method of dating glassware. Patent records indeed furnish the date, designer, original pattern name (when furnished by the patentee), and required patent specifications. Upon registration, however, a patentee's options could include the assignment of his design to a glass company for immediate manufacture, his right to hold the design for future use, or the decision to disregard the design entirely. Frequently, impressed or embossed patent dates found on items have been traced to a mechanical process or improvement having nothing to do with the article itself.

The most logical method we encountered in attributing, dating, and uncovering the number of forms for each given pattern has been a combination of all source information. All accessible company catalogs, patent records, trade journals, and company advertising has been consolidated in an effort to establish the most viable history for each pattern.

How to Use this Guide

The purpose in writing this book has been to present, in a systemized format, the most pertinent information concerning each of the patterns presented. Emphasis has been placed on the type and number of forms originally produced. For convenience, patterns have been listed by their more popular name, and major categories have been set in bold type. In many instances, the name of an author enclosed in brackets follows a pattern designating that author's use of the name.

The original manufacturer, designated as "OMN", refers to the first manufacturer responsible for the production of a pattern. Subsequent reruns or reissues refer to the continuation of a pattern by a second concern. Estimated dates of production are presented as "circa", referring to the first year in which a pattern may have been produced. In instances where an original manufacturer or estimated date of production could not be ascertained due to a lack of substantiating data, attributions have been assigned on the basis of style and period. With regard to Canadian/American patterns, we have limited attributions to recording present thought. Wherever possible, forms, colors and decorative techniques have been witnessed by the authors and verified against existing records. Measurements have been faithfully recorded from both original catalogs and existing examples.

Special comment must be made concerning the measurements of items. Without exception, every glass catalog studied, when denoting an illustration's dimensions, treated each item in terms of even measurements. Catalog sizes for any given form were illustrated by $\frac{1}{4}$ inch, $\frac{1}{2}$ inch, or inch increments. At no time could we find a single example of the off-beat sizes that plague both collectors and dealers. This leads us to believe that items ending in odd measurements, such as $\frac{7}{8}''$, $\frac{9}{16}''$ and the like, are the products of retooled molds, improper cooling procedures, or poor quality control, and not of deliberate design. Measurements recorded ending in odd increments have been taken from existing examples.

In the hope of promoting clarity, we have used the following abbreviations in the text and listings throughout the book:

AKA = also known as
h.s. = high standard
l.s. = low standard
n.o.s. = not original stopper
n.o.t. = not original top
o.s. = original stopper
P. or PP. = page or pages
Pl. or Plts. = plate or plates
R = rare
S = scarce
var. = variant
VR = very rare

A complete list of references and their corresponding abbreviations is presented in the Key to the References at the back of the book.

The most often asked question in the antiques and collectible field concerns the monetary worth or marketable price of a desired item Popularity, availability, condition, and age all combine to create value.

Values presented have been structured from a number of sources: comparative studies of sales, mail order advertising, personal interviews, current price scales, and the response to our questionnaires from hundreds of dealers and collectors nation-wide. All values are suggested retail prices for items in original, mint condition and with perfect decoration. Unless rarity dictates otherwise, the presence of chips, cracks, missing parts, and severe scratches or wear to either the decoration or item greatly reduces an item's true value.

In those geographical locations where the presence of pattern glass is limited and desirability is high, prices tend to rise at a more rapid rate. Specialized auctions, featuring major collections, represent still another source of inflated values. Thus, the prices we have recorded must be viewed solely as a guide to retail pricing and may fluctuate according to supply and demand.

By no means should the information contained herein be considered definitive or complete. Ongoing research is producing results that may add to or alter the history of a pattern, including its colors and forms. It is the wish of the authors that opposing opinions and relevant information be shared with them in an effort to record the most accurate account of the patterns treated. Please feel free to write to us at The Antique Research Center, P.O. Box 1964, Kingston, PA 18704.

A History of American Pattern Glass

Prior to 1820, the mainstay of the American glass industry consisted solely of blown wares. Influenced by continental designs and techniques, glass was of a utilitarian nature that fulfilled the basic needs of everyday life. Timely and costly to produce, a more efficient method of manufacture was born out of the necessity to compete the cheaper foreign imports that flooded the market.

By 1821, the first patents for the production of glassware by means of a mechanical press were granted in the United States. On September 9, 1825, John P. Bakewell, Pears & Bakewell, Pittsburgh, PA., was granted a patent for an improvement in making glass furniture knobs. Between 1825 and 1829, numerous other patents were granted for the improvement of the mechanical process of pressing glassware. These include Henry Whitney and Enoch Robinson (November 4, 1826), John Robinson (October 6, 1827), Phineas C. Drummer and George Drummer (October 16, 1827), John Robinson (November 14,

1827), Thomas Bakewell and John B. Bakewell (May 14, 1828), and Deming Jarves (December 1, 1828 and June 13, 1829).

It is not known where or by whom the first glass article was mechanically pressed in America. Although Deming Jarves of the Boston & Sandwich Glass Co., Sandwich, MA., has been credited for being the first, the glass industry as a whole began experimenting with the new process by the late 1820s. The new ware was first exhibited in 1829 at the American Institute of the City of New York.

Throughout the 1830s imagination and ingenuity, coupled with lower production costs and work time, produced a myriad of lacy flint patterns. These were heavily stippled and more ornate than the geometric patterns typical of the past. By 1832, pressed tableware was being manufactured for both domestic and foreign distribution and advertised by numerous glass houses. The Early Period of pressed glass had successfully begun.

Unlike earlier blown pattern, the delicate lacy effect and elaborate design elements of the new ware was quickly reflected in the high cost of mold making. By the late 1830s numerous factories, convinced of the economics of pressing tablewares, favored a return to a more simple, cost efficient design. By 1840, table settings began to reflect this cost consciousness in newly introduced fluted designs. Lacy glass became impractical and unprofitable. The introduction of firepolishing, a technique used to improve and finish the surface of pressed items, further added to the decline of the lacy motif.

The fine, feathery designs of lacy glass further waned in the early 1850s as manufacturers began to favor the heavier, more geometric patterns which resembled popular cut glass. Utilitarian in nature, public need outweighed artistic design. At this time, a new wave of realism appeared with stylized motifs seen in such patterns as Bellflower, Horn of Plenty and Ribbed Grape. Throughout the 1850s the number of forms in table sets began to increase as competition forced factories to vie for sales. This has become known as the Middle Period of pressed glass.

The 1860s witnessed a new wave of activity as the industry flourished. The discovery of natural gas in Western Pennsylvania and continued technological improvements became the natural stepping stones that revolutionized the industry. Forced to seek cheaper means of production during the Civil War, William Leighton, Sr. of J.H. Hobbs, Brockunier & Co., Wheeling, WV., experimented with the old lead glass formula. By replacing soda ash with bicarbonate of soda, Leighton's new lime formula produced a glass that was lighter in weight, more economical to produce, and viable enough to receive the most delicate of impressions. This new glass formula emerged as perhaps the single most important technological development effecting the production of pressed tablewares. Later combined with the profuse use of color and decorative applications, the introduction of lime glass provided the final momentum for factories to begin producing countless patterns and items.

After 1865 the use of lime glass so dominated the glass industry that firms refusing to use the new technique inevitably failed. At this time, realism and geometric motifs were beginning to be replaced by highly sculptured studies in design and detail. Patterns such as Lion, Frosted Flower Band, and Strawberry exemplified animals, flowers, and fruit.

Considered to be the beginning of the Late Period of pressed glass, 1870 and the years that followed produced a wealth of decorative designs. Introduced by Gillinder & Sons at the Centennial Exposition of 1876 in Philadelphia, PA., clear items, subjected to the use of hydrofluoric acid to produce a frosted or satin-like effect, were later followed by the introduction of chocolate, custard, marbleized, and ruby-stained glass, and a rainbow of rich, mellow colors that extended to as late as 1900. Between the years 1880 and 1890, many patterns contained more than 60 different items as new forms were conceived and added to lines.

Torn by labor troubles, the depletion of natural gas, and the depression, the 1890s was a time of turmoil in which many factories were forced to close or combine in an effort to survive. Both the United States Glass Company and the National Glass Company emerged, reissuing older patterns from member firms in an effort to cut costs. By early 1900, both the quality and dignity of most pressed glass tablewares had vanished. Inferior and often pretentious novelty items beckoned for the consumer's attention. Beginning in the mid 1920s, collectors and dealers of early American pattern glass have been plagued by the rash of reproduction glassware that since flooded the market. First seriously addressed by Ruth Webb Lee in her book *Antique Fakes & Reproductions* and later by Dorothy Hammond in her two volume *Confusing Collectibles* and *More Confusing Collectibles*, reproduction glassware remains a subject of great concern.

Webster's Third International Dictionary defines a reproduction as an exact copy, likeness or replica of an original. Applied to the process of pressing glass, it may then be stated that a reproduction is any object so produced, from a new mold, as to appear identical to that which has been copied.

From the early 1970s, a number of authorized reproductions of classic early American pressed glassware have been commissioned by various museums. Issued from new molds as faithful copies in both original and new colors, each has been permanently marked or embossed with the appropriate institution's insignia or initials. Less common has been the reproduction of items as limited edition color runs as represented by the Metropolitan Museum of Art's use of the Bellflower pattern.

The reproduction of classic pressed glass patterns supposedly represents a two-fold purpose. The sale of reproductions has been viewed as an additional source of revenue and as a means of making items available that would otherwise be impossible to attain. It is when unscrupulous individuals knowingly attempt to alter and sell reproductions as "old" and "original" that we begin to question the need for any reproduction. Fortunately, the reproductions faithfully representing original items are so scarce that they are easy to detect through study and comparison.

Look-alike items, more commonly known as giftware, present more of a problem. In continual production for more than half this century, a vast number of pressed glass items, vaguely resembling many of the older patterns, have been produced for the department store and gift shop trade. Created in an attempt to capitalize on the popularity of old glass, a majority of look-alike items have been produced from new molds in both new and original colors and forms. (Items which have been reissued from original molds have been cited under the appropriate pattern listing.)

Many reproduction and look-alike items have made their way into antique shops and shows, causing confusion among both seasoned and beginning collectors and dealers. As a general guideline, size, weight, and quality of workmanship should be considered when examining an item of suspect age. New items are generally lighter in weight than originals, unless the originals were produced from a lead bearing formula. New colors are harsher and more artificial than the old, which appear smooth and mellow. New glass displays a high, lustrous appearance and a somewhat oily feel. The most obvious difference between new and original pattern glass is the disregard for quality and craftmanship always displayed by authentic items.

PATTERN GLASS
FROM A TO Z

Spoonholder.

AKA: Interlocking Bands, Keyhole Band.

Non-flint. Maker unknown, ca. mid 1870s.

Original color production: Clear.

Reproductions: None.

References: Mtz-1 (PP. 128-129), Mil-1 (Pl. 174), Uni-1 (P. 124).

Items made	Clear	Items made	Clear
Butter dish, covered	45.00	Goblet	20.00
Compote, high standard ·		Pitcher, water, bulbous, applied	
Covered	45.00	handle, ¹/₂ gallon	60.00
Open	20.00	Sauce dish, flat, round	10.00
Creamer	45.00	Spoonholder	20.00
Egg cup, single, pedestaled	25.00	Sugar bowl, covered	35.00

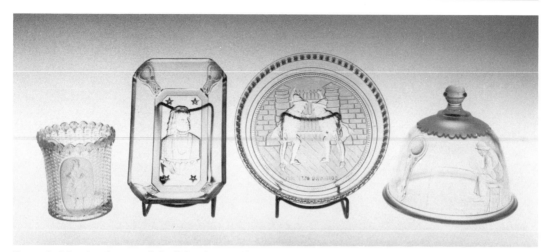

Spoonholder (variant); relish dish; cheese dish, base and cover.

OMN: Possibly Crystal's No. 350. AKA: Annie, Jenny Lind, Pinafore, Theatrical.

Non-flint. Attributed to the Crystal Glass Co., Bridgeport, OH., LaBelle Glass Co., Bridgeport, OH., and Riverside Glass Works, Brilliant, OH. ca. early 1880s.

Original color production: Clear, clear with acid finish.

Reproductions: The Imperial Glass Co., Bellaire, OH., reproduced from a new mold, the pickle jar and relish tray in amethyst, blue and clear. Reproductions are heavier in weight and lack a fine definition of detail.

References: Eige-CG WV (P. 21), Enos-MPG (Chart-2), Kam-4 (PP. 5-6), Kam-5 (P. 55), Lind-HG (PP. 423-432), McCn-PGP (P. 390), Mil-1 (Pl. 120), Mtz-1 (Pl. 80), Mtz-2 (PP. 194-195), Pet-Sal (P. 21), Rev-APG (PP.132, 227-228), Uni-1 (P. 89), Uni-2 (P. 95).

Items made	Clear	Items made	Clear
Bowl, open, footed, smooth rim		9½"d	200.00
6"d	50.00	10"d	200.00
7"d	50.00	11"d	250.00
8"d. "Miss Neilson"	80.00	12"d	300.00
9½"d	85.00	Open	
Butter dish, covered, "Fanny		High standard	
Davenport and Miss Neilson"	90.00	10"d	100.00
Cake stand, high standard, "Annie		12"d	125.00
Pixley and Maud Granger"		Low standard	
9½"d	150.00	5"d	50.00
10"d	150.00	6"d	55.00
Candlesticks, pair	250.00	7"d	85.00
Celery vase, pedestaled		Creamer, "Fanny Davenport and Miss	
"Actress Head"	125.00	Neilson"	100.00
"HMS Pinafore"	150.00	Goblet, "Kate Claxton and Lotta	
Cheese dish, covered, flat, "The Lone		Crabtree" portraits	90.00
Fisherman, Two Dromios base"	250.00	Marmalade jar, covered	110.00
Compote		Mug, "HMS Pinafore"	50.00
Covered, high standard		Pickle dish, flat, oblong, "Love's	
8"d	200.00	Request Is Pickles"	50.00

Items made	Clear		Items made	Clear
Pitcher			Shaker, original pewter lid	60.00
Milk, 1 quart, 6½"h. "HMS Pinafore			Sauce dish, round	
Fancy Davenport"	275.00		Flat	
Water, ½ gallon, 9"h. "Romeo and			4½"d	15.00
Juliet Balcony Scene"	250.00		5"d	15.00
Platter, bread			Footed	
"HMS Pinafore", 7" x 12"	90.00		4½"d	20.00
"Miss Neilson" and motto, 9" x 13"	80.00		5"d	20.00
Relish dish, flat, oblong			Spoonholder, "Mary Anderson and	
4½" x 7"	40.00		Maud Granger"	80.00
5" x 8"	40.00		Sugar bowl, covered, "Kate Claxton	
5½" x 9"	40.00		And Lotta Crabtree"	90.00
Salt			Tray, dresser, flat	75.00
Master	50.00			

ADONIS

Plate, 10"d.

OMN Adonis. AKA: Pleat and Tuck, Washboard.

Non-flint. McKee & Brothers, Pittsburgh, PA. ca. 1897.

Original color production: Blue, canary-yellow, clear. Illustrated in a full page advertisement by McKee & Brothers for 1897, and still offered in the Baltimore Bargain House General Merchandise catalogs No. 479 (August, 1903), No. 483 (December, 1903), and No. 496 (August 15, 1904).

Reproductions: None.

References: Bat-GPG (P. 163), Kam-2 (PP. 127-128), Kam-5 (P. 27), Kam-6 (Pl. 12), McCn-PGP (P. 385), Mtz-1 (PP. 142-143), Pet-Sal (P. 43), Rev-APG (P. 236).

Items made	Canary	Clear	Blue
Bowl			
Round, open, flat, beaded rim			
5"d	15.00	10.00	20.00

Items made	Canary	Clear	Blue
8″d., master berry	15.00	10.00	20.00
Oval, open, flat	15.00	10.00	20.00
Butter dish, covered	70.00	60.00	80.00
Cake plate, flat, 11″d	25.00	15.00	30.00
Cake stand, high standard, 10½″d	45.00	40.00	50.00
Celery vase, scalloped rim, collared base	35.00	30.00	40.00
Compote			
Covered, high standard, 8″d	55.00	50.00	60.00
Open, high standard			
4½″d., jelly	25.00	20.00	30.00
8″d	45.00	40.00	50.00
Creamer	25.00	20.00	30.00
Pitcher			
Milk, 1 quart	55.00	45.00	60.00
Water, ½ gallon	55.00	45.00	60.00
Plate, round			
10″d	25.00	15.00	30.00
11″d	25.00	15.00	30.00
Relish tray, flat	20.00	15.00	20.00
Salt shaker, original nickel top	25.00	15.00	25.00
Sauce dish, round, flat, beaded rim			
4″d	10.00	5.00	10.00
4½″d	10.00	5.00	10.00
Spoonholder	35.00	25.00	40.00
Sugar bowl, covered	40.00	30.00	45.00
Syrup pitcher, original pewter top	125.00	65.00	125.00
Tumbler, water, flat	20.00	15.00	25.00

AEGIS

Goblet.

OMN: Swiss. AKA: Bead and Bar Medallion.

Non-flint. McKee Brothers, Pittsburgh, PA., ca. late 1800's. Shards have been found at the site of the Burlington Glass Works, Hamilton, Ontario, Canada. Illustrated in the McKee & Brothers 1880 catalog as "Swiss".

Original color production: Clear.

Reproductions: None.

References: Kam-1 (PP. 60-61), Lee-VG (P. 79, No. 5), McCn-PGP (P.109), Mil-2 (Pl. 82), Mtz-1 (PP. 122-123), Stot-McKe (PP. 55-56), Uni-1 (P. 328).

Items made	Clear	Items made	Clear
Bowl		6″d	20.00
Covered		7″d	20.00
Collared base, 6″d	15.00	8″d	25.00
Flat, 5″d	15.00	Creamer	35.00
Open, oval, flat	15.00	Dish, open, flat, scalloped rim	
Butter dish, covered	35.00	7″d	20.00
Compote		8″d	20.00
Covered		9″d	20.00
High standard		Egg cup, single	25.00
6″d, sweetmeat, hexagonal stem	40.00	Goblet	30.00
7″d	45.00	Honey dish, flat, round, 3½″d	7.00
8″d	50.00	Pickle dish, 5″ x 7″	15.00
Low standard		Pitcher, water, bulbous, applied	
6″d	30.00	handle, ½ gallon	55.00
7″d	35.00	Salt, master, open, footed	15.00
8″d	40.00	Sauce dish, round, smooth rim	
Open		Flat, 4″d	8.00
High standard		Footed	
6″d	20.00	3½″d	8.00
7″d	20.00	4″d	10.00
8″d	25.00	Spoonholder	20.00
Low standard		Sugar bowl, covered	30.00

ALABAMA States Series

Syrup (n.o.t.) rectangular dish; creamer; Toothpick Holder.

OMN: U.S. Glass No. 15062, Alabama. AKA: Beaded Bullseye And Drape [Kamm].

Non-flint. The United States Glass Co. (pattern line No. 15,062), Pittsburgh, PA. ca. 1899. Illustrated in the United States Glass Co. 1904 catalog, the Baltimore Bargain House General

Merchandise catalog No. 479 (August, 1903) and No. 483 (December, 1903), and the Butler Brothers Spring, 1904 catalog.

Original color production: Clear. Occasional items may be found in emerald green and clear with ruby stain.

Reproductions: None.

References: Bat-GPG (PP. 136-137), Bros-TS (P. 42), Hea-1 (P. 13, Fig. 4), Hea-5 (PP. 13-14), Hea-7 (P. 65), Kam-1 (PP. 81-82), Leclr-CGD (P. 34), McCn-PGP (P. 53), Migh-TPS (Pl. 3), Mtz-2 (PP. 106-107), Pet-Sal (P. 153), Pet-GPP (PP. 181-182), Rev-APG (P. 310).

Items made	Clear	Items made	Clear
Bowl, open, flat		Dish, open, flat	
8″d., round, master berry	45.00	Jelly, single handle	20.00
Rectangular	20.00	Rectangular	20.00
Butter dish, covered, flat	60.00	Honey dish, covered, flat	65.00
Cake stand, high standard	50.00	Mustard pot, covered, notched lid	65.00
Caster set, 4 bottles, silver plated stand	125.00	Pickle dish	15.00
Celery		Pitcher, water, pressed handle, ½	
Tray	35.00	gallon	95.00
Vase	65.00	Relish tray, rectangular	20.00
Child's miniatures		Salt shaker, tall, original top	35.00
Butter dish, covered	225.00	Sauce dish, round, 4″d	
Creamer	65.00	Flat	15.00
Spoonholder	65.00	Footed	
Sugar bowl, covered	90.00	Covered, original notched lid	45.00
Compote, high standard		Open	15.00
Covered	65.00	Spoonholder	30.00
Open, 5″d, jelly	40.00	Sugar bowl	50.00
Creamer		Syrup pitcher, original lid	110.00
Individual	20.00	Toothpick holder	65.00
Table size	45.00	Tray, water, round, 10½″d	40.00
Cruet, original patterned stopper	55.00	Tumbler, water, flat	35.00

ALL OVER DIAMOND

Small cruet (o.s.); large cruet (o.s.); wine; goblet.

OMN: Duncan No. 356, U.S. Glass No. 15011. AKA: Diamond Block [Lee], Diamond Splendor [Millard], Diamond Splendour [Unitt].

Non-flint. George Duncan & Sons (pattern line No. 356), Pittsburgh, PA. ca. 1890-1891. Continued production by the United States Glass Co. (pattern line No. 15,011), Pittsburgh, PA. at Factory "D" (George Duncan & Sons, Pittsburgh, PA.), and later at Factory "P" (Doyle And Co., Pittsburgh, PA.) ca. 1892-1899. Similar to Gillinder's Westmorland pattern, All Over Diamond is illustrated in the United States Glass Co. ca. 1895, 1898, and 1907 catalogs, and by Butler Brothers in 1899.

Original color production: Clear. Clear with ruby stain or any other color is rare.

Reproductions: None.

References: Bar-RS (Pl. 14), Bred-EDG (PP. 118-120), Hea-5 (PP. 13-14), Hea-7 (P. 67), Hea-OS (Fig. 3059), Kam-3 (P. 134), Lee-VG (Pl. 66), Mil-1 (Pl. 40), Mtz-2 (PP. 170-171), Rev-APG (PP. 148, 151, 310), Uni-1 (P. 165), Wlkr-PGA (Fig. 8, No. 4)

Items made	Clear	Items made	Clear
Biscuit jar, covered		9"d	20.00
No. 1	50.00	Square, scalloped rim	
No. 2	45.00	7"	20.00
No. 3	40.00	8"	20.00
Bottle		9"	20.00
Bitters	35.00	Bowl, finger	10.00
Water	35.00	Butter dish, covered	
Bowl, open, flat		Individual	15.00
Crimped rim		Table size	45.00
5"d	15.00	Cake stand, high standard	35.00
7"d	15.00	Candelabrum	
8"d	15.00	3-arm	125.00
9"d	20.00	4-arm	165.00
Smooth rim		Celery	
Round		Tray, flat	
7"d	15.00	Crimped rim	15.00
8"d	15.00	Smooth rim	15.00

Items made	Clear	Items made	Clear
Vase	25.00	No. 2	40.00
Claret jug	50.00	No. 3	45.00
Compote, covered, high standard	40.00	No. 4	60.00
Condensed milk jar	25.00	No. 5, ½ gallon	70.00
Cordial	20.00	Lamp, bouquet	400.00+
Creamer	35.00	Pickle tray	15.00
Cruet, original cut or pressed stopper		Pitcher, water, bulbous, applied handle	
1 ounce	40.00	(6 sizes)	45.00
2 ounce	40.00	Plate, round	
4 ounce	45.00	6"d	10.00
6 ounce	45.00	7"d	10.00
Decanter, original cut or pressed		Salt shaker, original nickel plate top	20.00
stopper		Sauce dish, flat (smooth or crimped	
1 pint	45.00	rim)	
1 quart	55.00	Round	
Dish, oval		4"d	10.00
Crimped rim		4½"d	10.00
7"l	15.00	Square	
8"l	15.00	4"	12.00
9"l	20.00	4½"	12.00
10"l	20.00	Spoonholder	20.00
11"l	25.00	Sugar bowl, covered	35.00
Straight rim		Syrup pitcher, original top	40.00
5½", ice cream	15.00	Tray	
7"l	15.00	Round	
8"l	15.00	Water	35.00
9"l	20.00	Wine	35.00
10"l	20.00	Square, ice cream	40.00
11".l	20.00	Tumbler, water, flat	15.00
Egg cup, single, pedestaled.	15.00	Vase	
Goblet, round stem	25.00	7"h	20.00
Ice tub, handled	35.00	8"h	20.00
Jug		9"h	25.00
No. 1	35.00	Wine	20.00

ALMOND THUMBPRINT

Footed tumbler; goblet; covered sweetmeat; wine; open master salt.

AKA: Almond, Finger Print, Pointed Thumbprint.

Flint. Attributed to Bryce, Bakewell, Pittsburgh, PA. ca. 1865 and Bakewell, Pears & Co., Pittsburgh, PA. ca. 1860's. Reissued in non-flint by the United States Glass Co., Pittsburgh, PA. after the merger of 1891.

Original color production: Clear. Blue, milk white or any other color is rare. Edges of dishes may or may not be cable-edged.

Reproductions: None.

References: Brn-SD (PP. 32-33), Cod-OS (PP. 15, 19), Fer-YMG (P. 73), Inn-EPG (P. 53), Lee-EAPG (Pl. 154, No. 14), McKrn-AG (Fig. 210), Mil-1 (Pl. 156), Mil-OG (P. 208), Mtz-1 (PP. 44-45),Oliv-AAG (P. 58), Rev-APG (P. 86), SpilAEPG (P. 272), Thu-1 (PP. 34, 158), Uni-2 (P. 47), Wlkr-PGA (Fig. 8, Nos. 18, 48).

Items made	Flint	Non-flint
Butter dish, covered, flat	80.00	45.00
Celery vase	60.00	35.00
Champagne	65.00	35.00
Compote covered		
High standard		
4³⁄₄"d., jelly	45.00	25.00
7"d	60.00	40.00
10"d	80.00	45.00
Low standard		
4³⁄₄"d	45.00	25.00
7"d	55.00	30.00
Cordial	35.00	25.00
Creamer	65.00	40.00
Cruet, footed, original stopper (2 styles)	55.00	—
Decanter, o.s.	65.00	—
Egg cup, covered, single, pedestaled	45.00	25.00
Goblet, barrel shaped bowl	30.00	15.00
Pitcher, water, ¹⁄₂ gallon	85.00	40.00
Punch bowl	—	80.00

Items made	Flint	Non-flint
Salt		
Dip, individual	15.00	10.00
Master		
Covered, footed	45.00	25.00
Open, footed	25.00	20.00
Spoonholder, scalloped rim	20.00	15.00
Sugar bowl, covered	60.00	40.00
Sweetmeat jar, covered, high standard, 6"d	75.00	45.00
Tumbler		
Flat	40.00	20.00
Footed	40.00	20.00
Wine, 4"h	25.00	15.00

AMAZON

H.s. true open saucer bowl compote; h.s. true open deep compote.

H.s. banana stand; h.s. double bud vase; covered oval bowl (lion head handles).

OMN Amazon. AKA: Sawtooth [Lee], Sawtooth Band [Millard].

Non-flint. Bryce Brothers, Pittsburgh, PA. ca. 1890-1891. Reissued by the United States Glass Co., Pittsburgh, PA., at Factory "B" (Bryce Brothers, Pittsburgh, PA.) ca. 1891 to 1904. Amazon was advertised throughout the 1889 and 1890 issues of *Pottery and Glassware Reporter*, and illustrated in the ca. 1891 and 1898 United States Glass Co. catalogs.

Original color production: Clear (plain or engraved with engraving "B" [Fern & Berry]. Amber, amethyst, blue, canary-yellow, clear with ruby stain or any other color is rare.

Reproductions: None.

References: Bar-RS (Pl. 13), Bat-GPG (PP. 41, 43), Drep-ABC OG (P. 205), F.G. (P. 97), Hart-AG (P. 46), Hrtng-P&P (P. 6), Hea-5 (PP. 77-78), Hea-6 (PP. 17-18), Hea-7 (P. 67), Hea-OS (P. 58, No. 811), Kam-3 (Pl. 141), Kam-7 (Pl. 1), Lee-VG (Pl. 42), Mil-1 (P. 46), Mtz-1 (PP. 34, 37), Pet-Sal (p. 21), Rev-APG (PP. 86, 310), Spil-AEPG (P. 277), Wlkr-PGA (Fig. 15, No. 2).

Items made	Clear	Items made	Clear
Banana stand, high standard	65.00	6"d	60.00
Bowl, flat		7"d	65.00
Oval, covered, 6½"	50.00	8"d	65.00
Round		Open	
Covered		Flared, scalloped rim, deep bowl	
5"d	25.00	4½"d	25.00
6"d	25.00	5"d	25.00
7"d	30.00	6"d	25.00
8"d	30.00	7"d	30.00
9"d	30.00	8"d	30.00
Open, round		Round, flared bowl	
Scalloped rim		5"d	25.00
5"d	15.00	6"d	25.00
6"d	15.00	7"d	30.00
7"d	15.00	8"d	30.00
8"d	15.00	9½"d	45.00
Flared, plain rim		Saucer bowl, sawtooth rim	
5"d	10.00	8"d	30.00
6"d	15.00	9"d	30.00
7"d	15.00	10"d	45.00
8"d	20.00	Low standard, open, 4"d	15.00
Butter dish, covered	60.00	Cordial	40.00
Cake stand, high standard		Creamer, table size	30.00
8"d	30.00	Cruet, footed, original "fist" or	
9"d	30.00	"maltese cross" stopper	50.00
9½"d	35.00	Dish	
10"d	35.00	Oval	
Celery vase		Covered, flat, lion handles	
Flat	30.00	6"	25.00
Footed	30.00	7"	30.00
Champagne	35.00	8"	35.00
Child's miniatures		Open, flat, lion handles	
Butter dish, covered, flat	50.00	6"	10.00
Creamer, pedestaled	25.00	7"	15.00
Spoonholder, pedestaled, sawtooth		8"	20.00
rim	30.00	Round, open, shallow bowl, lion	
Sugar bowl, covered, pedestaled	30.00	handles	
Claret	35.00	4½"d	20.00
Compote		6"d	20.00
High standard		Egg cup, single	10.00
Covered		Goblet	
4½"d., jelly	40.00	4½"h	25.00
5"d	55.00	5"h	25.00

Items made	Clear	Items made	Clear
6"h	30.00	Handled, 4½"d	15.00
Pitcher, water, ½ gallon	60.00	Footed	
Relish tray	25.00	4"d	15.00
Salt		4½"d	15.00
Dip		Spoonholder	30.00
Individual, 1½"h	15.00	Sugar bowl, covered	55.00
Master	15.00	Syrup pitcher, original top	75.00
Shaker, tall, original top	25.00	Tumbler, water, flat, ½ pint	20.00
Sauce dish, round		Vase, flower, high standard, ruffled	
Flat		rim	
Flared bowl, scalloped rim		Double bud	30.00
4"d	10.00	Single bud	15.00
4½"d	10.00	Wine	30.00

AMBERETTE (only for items in clear with amber stained panels).

Master berry bowl; creamer with applied handle.

OMN: Ellrose. AKA: Daisy and Button-Panelled-Single Scallop, Daisy and Button-Single Panel, Paneled Daisy, and Panelled Daisy and Button.

Non-flint. George Duncan & Sons, Pittsburgh, PA., introduced in March, 1885. Reissued by the United States Glass Co., Pittsburgh, PA. ca. 1892. Reviewed in the March 5, 1883 *Pottery and Glassware Reporter,* the December 3, 1885 *American Pottery and Glassware Reporter,* and illustrated in the undated ca. 1891 and 1898 United States Glass Co. catalogs.

Original color production: Clear with amber stain. Clear, clear with ruby stain and solid colors of canary and blue. Although illustrated in the Duncan catalog with Amberette, the "ale" does not display the characteristic amber stained, vertical panels and is not part of the original set.

Reproductions: None.

Goblet.

References: Brnd-EDG (PP. 86-88), Chip-ROS (Pl. 169), Drep-FG (P. 201-"D"), Hea-3 (PP. 55, 72), Hea-5 (PP. 104-105), Hea-6 (P. 36), Inn-PG (P. 383), Kam-1 (P. 80), Kam-5 (P. 94), Kraus-EDG (P. 189), Lee-EAPG (Pl. 169), Oliv-AAG (P. 62), Pet-Sal (P. 153), Rev-APG (PP. 144-145), Uni-2 (P. 69).

Items made	Clear w/ Amber	Items made	Clear w/ Amber
Bowl		9"d	95.00
Round		Shallow bowl	
Covered collared base		8"d	85.00
7"d	110.00	9"d	95.00
8"d	125.00	Finger	55.00
Open		Oval, open, flat	
Collared base		5"	55.00
7"d	75.00	7"	75.00
8"d	85.00	8"	85.00
Flat		12"	125.00
Flared rim		Square	
8"d	85.00	Flat, scalloped rim	
9"d	95.00	5"	55.00
Scalloped rim		6"	65.00
Deep bowl		7"	75.00
8"d	85.00	8"	85.00

Items made	Clear w/ Amber	Items made	Clear w/ Amber
9″	95.00	Gas shade, 9″d	90.00
Butter dish, covered		Olive dish, scalloped rim, 6″	35.00
Flat smooth rim	125.00	Pickle dish	35.00
Scalloped rim	125.00	Pitcher, applied handle	
Butter pat, square (R)	35.00	Milk, 3 pint	200.00
Cake stand, high standard, 10″	150.00	Water, ½ gallon	225.00
Celery		Plate	
Tray	65.00	Bread, 11″l	75.00
Vase, scalloped rim	85.00	Dinner, 7″	45.00
Compote, open, high standard		Salt shaker, original top	55.00
Oval, scalloped rim, 9″	135.00	Sauce dish, square	
Round		Collared base	
Flared-scalloped rim		4″	25.00
8″d	125.00	4½″.	25.00
9″d	135.00	Flat, smooth rim	
Scalloped rim		4″.	25.00
8″d	125.00	4½″	25.00
9″d	135.00	Spoonholder, scalloped rim	65.00
Creamer, applied handle	65.00	Sugar bowl, covered	125.00
Cruet, original patterned stopper	175.00	Tumbler, water	55.00

ANTHEMION

Tumbler; spoonholder.

AKA: Albany.

Non-flint. Model Flint Glass Co., Findlay, OH. ca. 1890-1900, and the Albany Glass Co., Albany, IN. ca. 1894.

Original color production: Amber, blue, clear. The main pattern design element of Anthemion is that of a finely stippled body with a leaf in clear relief.

Reproductions: None.

References: Bat-GPG (PP. 177, 181), Bond-AG (P. 47), Hart-AOG (P. 136), Her-GG (P. 37, Fig. 330), Kam-5 (PP. 137-138), Lee-EAPG (Pl. 58, No. 3), Mtz-1 (PP. 7-77), Rev-APG (PP. 243-244), Smth-FG (P. 27).

16

Items made	Clear	Items made	Clear
Bowl, master berry, square, open, fan		Plate, square	
rim, 7″	20.00	7″	25.00
Butter dish, covered	65.00	10″	25.00
Cake plate, curled edges, 9½″d	35.00	Relish tray, triangular, flat	15.00
Cake stand, high standard	40.00	Sauce dish, flat	
Celery vase	35.00	Round	
Creamer	30.00	4½″d., plain center	10.00
Marmalade jar, covered	40.00	4½″d., oak leaf center	10.00
Pitcher		Spoonholder	25.00
Milk, 1 quart	50.00	Sugar bowl, covered	45.00
Water, ½ gallon	50.00	Tumbler, water, flat	30.00

APOLLO, Adam's

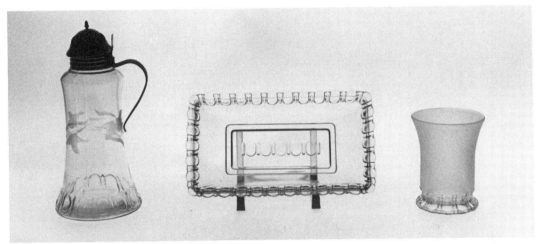

Syrup (etched); relish tray; tumbler (frosted/clear).

OMN Apollo, Adam's. AKA: Canadian Horseshoe, Frosted Festal Ball [Millard], Shield Band [Millard], Thumbprint And Prisms [Stuart].

Non-flint. Adams & Co., Pittsburgh, PA. ca. 1875. Reissued by The United States Glass Co., Pittsburgh, PA. at Factory "A" (Adams & Co., Pittsburgh, PA.) ca. 1891 to 1899. Advertised in the Butler Brothers Spring 1899 catalog, Apollo is illustrated in the Adams & Co. 1875-1885 catalog, and the undated ca. 1891, 1904, and 1915 (Export) catalogs of the United States Glass Co.

Original color production: Clear, clear with acid finish (plain or copper wheel engraved). Clear with ruby stain, clear with blue, pale yellow, dark green or any other color is rare. Originally produced in more than 65 pieces.

Reproductions: None.

References: Hea-5 (PP. 14, 65), Hea-7 (P. 67), Kam-3 (P. 6), Lee-VG (Pl. 62, No. 3), Mil-1 (Pl. 149), Mil-2 (Pl. 70), Mtz-1 (P. 146), Rev-APG (P. 18), Wlkr-PGA (Fig. 8, No. 16).

Items made	Clear	Clear / Frosted
Bowl		
Desert, oblong, scalloped rim	25.00	30.00
Open, flat		
Flared bowl		
5″d	10.00	15.00
6″d	10.00	15.00
7″d	15.00	20.00
8″d	15.00	20.00
Round bowl		
5″d	10.00	12.00
6″d	10.00	12.00
7″d	15.00	20.00
8″d	15.00	20.00
Salad, round, scalloped rim	25.00	30.00
Butter dish, covered		
Plain rim	50.00	60.00
Flanged rim	65.00	75.00
Cake stand, high standard		
8″d	35.00	40.00
9″d	35.00	40.00
10″d	45.00	55.00
12″d	45.00	55.00
Celery		
Tray, rectangular	20.00	20.00
Vase, pedestaled	30.00	35.00
Compote, round		
Covered, high standard, 6″d	65.00	85.00
Open		
High standard, smooth rim		
5″d	25.00	30.00
6″d	30.00	35.00
7″d	35.00	35.00
8″d	40.00	45.00
Low standard, smooth rim		
5″d	20.00	25.00
6″d	20.00	25.00
7″d	25.00	30.00
8″d	30.00	35.00
Creamer	35.00	40.00
Cruet, original stopper	75.00	90.00
Dish, pickle, rectangular	15.00	20.00
Egg cup, single	30.00	35.00
Goblet, 6½″h	30.00	40.00
Lamp, kerosene, 10″h., original burner and chimney	90.00	90.00
Pickle tray, oblong	15.00	20.00
Pitcher, bulbous		
Milk, 1 quart	85.00	95.00
Water		
½ gallon	65.00	80.00
1 gallon	65.00	80.00
1 gallon, tankard	75.00	90.00
Plate, square, 9½″	25.00	30.00
Salt		
Master, flat, oblong	25.00	30.00
Shaker, original top	25.00	30.00

Items made	Clear	Clear / Frosted
Shaker, original top	25.00	30.00
Sauce		
Flat, smooth rim		
Round		
3½"d	6.00	10.00
4"d	8.00	10.00
Flared		
3½"d	10.00	14.00
4"d	10.00	14.00
Footed, round, smooth rim		
3½"d	10.00	15.00
4"d	10.00	15.00
5"d	10.00	15.00
Spoonholder	35.00	30.00
Sugar bowl, covered, footed	45.00	55.00
Sugar shaker, original top	45.00	60.00
Syrup pitcher, original top	90.00	110.00
Tray, water, round	45.00	55.00
Vase	15.00	25.00
Wine	35.00	45.00

ARCHED GRAPE

Champagne; goblet

Flint, non-flint. Boston & Sandwich Glass Co., Sandwich, MA. ca. 1870s. Attributed to The Burlington Glass Works, Hamilton, Ontario, Canada.

Original color production: Clear. Finials are clusters of grapes and leaves.

Reproductions: None.

References: Hart-AG (P. 50), Lee-EAPG (P. 215), Lee-SG (P. 518), McCn-PGP (P. 317), Mil-1 (Pl. 51), Mtz-1 (P. 80), Uni-1 (P. 229), Uni-2 (P. 86), Uni/WorCHPGT (P. 37), Wlkr-PGA (Fig. 8, Nos. 4, 46).

Items made	Non-flint	Items made	Non-flint
Butter dish, covered	45.00	Champagne	50.00
Celery vase	40.00	Compote, covered, high standard	75.00

Items made	Non-flint	Items made	Non-flint
Creamer	60.00	Footed, 4″d	10.00
Goblet	25.00	Spoonholder	30.00
Pitcher, water, ½ gallon, applied handle	65.00	Sugar bowl, covered	65.00
Sauce dish, round		Wine	35.00
Flat, 4″d	10.00		

ARGUS

Champagne; spillholder; goblet; egg cup.

Celery vase; champagne.

OMN: Concave Ashburton. AKA: Argus-Creased, Argus-Faceted Stem, Argus (5-row), Barrel Argus, Hotel Argus, Master Argus, Tall Argus (bulbous stem), and Thumbprint.

Flint. Adams & Co. (Argus ½ pint tumbler only), Pittsburgh, PA. ca. 1872, Bakewell, Pears & Co., Pittsburgh, PA. ca. 1870. King, Son & Co., Pittsburgh, PA. ca. 1875. McKee & Brothers,

Pittsburgh, PA. ca. 1865. Illustrated in the Adams & Co. 1872 catalog, the Bakewell, Pears & Co. ca. 1875 catalog, and the McKee Brothers 1859 and 1868 catalogs.

Original color production: Clear. Any color is very rare. Of heavy, brilliant flint glass, the main pattern element of Argus is exactly that of Ashburton with the exception of a row of elongated thumbprints running between the upper and lower band of connected loops on Argus pieces. Produced by several factories, stems, bases and applied handles vary from one manufacturer to another.

Reproductions: The Imperial Glass Co., Bellaire, OH., reissued, from new molds, the covered butter dish (referred to as a covered nappy) in amber, heather, and verde (green). Authorized by the Henry Ford Museum, Dearborn, MI., the Fostoria Glass Co., Fostoria, OH. reissued the four piece table set in clear, non-flint, each item embossed with the museum's "H.F.M." monogram. New items are lighter in weight, lacking the conventional belltone of quality flint.

References: Enos-MPG (Chart-7), Inn-PG (P. 346), Inn/Spil-McKe (PP. 22, 49, 131), Lee-EAPG (Plts. 2, 11), McKrn-AG (Plts. 206, 208), Mil-1 P. 51), Mil-OG (P. 89), MTZ-2 (PP. 190-191), Oliv-AAG (P. 51), Pear-CAT (P. 5), Rev-APG (P. 237), Spil-AEPG (P. 5), Stout-McKe (P. 42), Uni-1 (P. 34-35), Uni/Wor-CHPGT (P. 37), Wlkr-PGA (Fig. 8, No. 24).

Items made	Flint	Items made	Flint
Ale glass, footed, 5½"h	70.00	Glass, jelly	40.00
Beer glass	75.00	Goblet	45.00
Bottle, bitters	60.00	Honey dish, flat, round	20.00
Bowl		Lamp, oil	
Open, flat, 5½"d	50.00	Collared base, 4"h	60.00
Covered, low collared base, 6"d	95.00	Footed	75.00
Butter dish, covered, footed, 8"d	85.00	Mug, applied handle (R)	65.00
Celery vase, pedestaled, scalloped rim		Paper weight	75.00
Cut ovals	80.00	Pickle jar	60.00
Pressed ovals, pattern on base	50.00	Pitcher, water, applied handle, ½	
Champagne, cut ovals		gallon, 8¼"h	200.00+
Barrel shaped bowl, knob stem, 5⅛"h	50.00	Punch bowl, pedestaled base, scalloped	
Flared bowl, knob stem, 5¼"h	50.00	rim	
Compote		11½"d	165.00
Covered		14⅛"d	175.00
High standard		Salt	
6"d	60.00	Individual, round, flat	25.00
8"d., 14⅛"h., pattern on base	100.00	Master, footed, open	30.00
9"d	100.00	Sauce dish, flat, round, 4¼"d	20.00
Low standard		Spoonholder, scalloped rim	50.00
6"d., no pattern on base	50.00	Sugar bowl, covered	65.00
9"d	90.00	Tumbler	
Open, scalloped rim, 10⅜"d	55.00	Flat	
Cordial	55.00	½ pint	60.00
Creamer, applied handle	125.00	Bar	60.00
Decanter		Ship	60.00
Pint	75.00	Whiskey, applied handle	75.00
Quart	75.00	Footed	
Egg cup, footed, open, single	55.00	4"h	40.00
Handled	55.00	5"h	60.00
Handleless	40.00	Wine, 4"h	45.00

Spoonholder; fruit basket; covered sugar bowl; creamer (all pieces are in "Regular" form).

OMN Art. AKA: Jacob's Tears, Job's Tears [Kamm], Teardrop and Diamond Block.

Non-flint. Adams & Co., Pittsburgh, PA. Introduced in 1889 with continued production by The United States Glass Co. at Factory "A" (Adams & Co., Pittsburgh, PA.) ca. 1891. Reviewed in the September 5, 1889 issue of the *Crockery and Glass Journal*, advertised in the Spring, 1899, Butler Brothers catalog. Art is illustrated in the 1874 Adams & Co. catalog in 48 pieces and in the United States Glass Co. catalogs of ca. 1891 and 1898.

Original color production: Clear, clear with ruby stain (ruby stain produced after the U.S. Glass merger of 1891). Clear with acid finish, milk white, or any other color is rare. Produced in "Regular" and hotel or "Extra Heavy" form, Art is similar to U.S. Glass Co.'s Teardrop And Thumbprint.

Reproductions: None.

References: Bar-RS (Pl.1 4), Hart-AG (P. 72), Hea-5 (PP. 14, 66), Hea-7 (P. 33), Kam-3 (P. 77), Lee-VG (Pl. 45), Mil-1 (Pl. 108), Mtz-1 (PP. 210-211), Rev-APG (P. 18), Uni-1 (P. 54), Wlkr-PGA (Fig. 8, No. 54).

Items made	Clear	Clear w/ Ruby Stain
Banana stand, high standard, 10″d	85.00	150.00
Basket, fruit, high standard, 10″d	90.00	—
Biscuit jar, covered	85.00	150.00
Bowl		
Open		
Round, flat		
Flared rim		
7″d	25.00	—
8″d	25.00	—
8½″d	35.00	—
9″d	35.00	—
10″d	40.00	—
Pointed at one end, 8″d	50.00	55.00
Collared base, flared rim		
6″d	25.00	—

Items made	Clear	Clear w/ Ruby Stain
7″d	25.00	—
8″d	25.00	—
9″d	30.00	—
10″d	35.00	—
Covered, round, collared base		
Flared bowl		
6″d	30.00	—
7″d	30.00	—
8″d	40.00	—
Belled bowl		
6″d	30.00	—
7″d	35.00	—
Butter dish, covered	55.00	100.00
Cake stand, high standard		
7¾″d	55.00	—
9″d	55.00	—
10″d	65.00	—
10½″d	65.00	—
Celery vase, flat, scalloped rim	30.00	65.00
Compote, High standard		
Covered		
6″d	55.00	100.00
7″d	55.00	185.00
8″d	65.00	185.00
Open		
Belled bowl		
6″d	40.00	—
7″d	45.00	—
8″d	50.00	—
Round bowl		
6″d	40.00	—
7″d	45.00	—
8″d	50.00	—
9″d	60.00	—
10″d	65.00	—
Scalloped rim, shallow bowl		
8″d	45.00	—
9″d	45.00	—
10″d	45.00	—
Cracker jar, covered	150.00	—
Creamer, flat, applied handle		
Hotel size		
Round, squatty	45.00	55.00
Large, round	45.00	55.00
Table size	50.00	55.00
Tankard, ⅓ pint	50.00	55.00
Cruet, (blown), applied handle, original stopper	65.00	225.00
Dish, preserve, oblong, 8″l	20.00	30.00
Dresser set	125.00	—
Goblet	55.00	75.00
Jar, cracker, covered	125.00	—
Jug, bulbous, squatty, flat, applied handle		
½ pint	85.00	—
3 pints	85.00	—
Mug	45.00	—
Pickle dish, flat, rectangular	25.00	40.00

Items made	Clear	Clear w/ Ruby Stain
Pitcher, flat, applied handle		
Milk, 1 quart	100.00	150.00
Water	85.00	125.00
Bulbous, ½ gallon	85.00	175.00
Squatty, square		
3 pint	85.00	—
2½ quart	85.00	—
Plate, round, 10″d	35.00	—
Preserve dish, oblong, 8″	30.00	—
Relish tray, 7¾″ x 4¼″	25.00	65.00
Sauce dish		
Flat		
Round		
4″d	10.00	—
4½″d	10.00	—
Pear shape (pointed at one end)		
4″d	15.00	—
4½″d	15.00	—
Footed, round, scalloped rim		
4″d	15.00	—
4½″d	15.00	—
Spoonholder, flat, scalloped rim	25.00	55.00
Sugar bowl, covered		
Hotel size	45.00	65.00
Table size	45.00	65.00
Tumbler, water, flat	45.00	55.00
Vinegar jug		
½ pint	55.00	—
3 pint	55.00	—
Wine (R)	90.00	—

ARTICHOKE

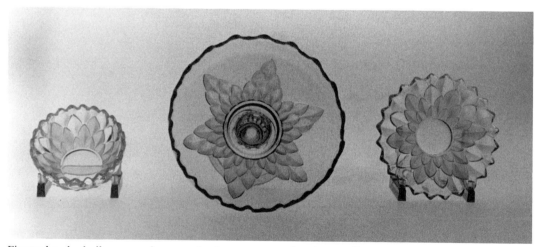

Finger bowl; shallow open low standard compote; underplate to finger bowl.

OMN: Fostoria's No. 205, Valencia. AKA: Frosted Artichoke.

Non-flint. Fostoria Glass Co. (pattern line No. 205), Moundsville, WV. ca. 1891. Illustrated in the Fostoria Glass Co. ads for 1891.

Original color production: Clear, clear with acid finish. Limited production in clear, opalescent and satin finished colors.

Reproductions: The L.G. Wright Glass Co., New Martinsville, WV. (distributed by Jennings Red Barn, New Martinsville, WV. and Carl Forslund, Grand Rapids, MI.) illustrated in the company's 1970 catalog a goblet in clear and acid finish, a form not part of the original set.

References: Bat-GPG (PP. 59-60), Kam-7 (P. 78), Lee-VG (Pl. 24), McCn-PGP (P. 421), Mry-HF (P. 38), Mtz-1 (P. 107), Mtz-2 (P. 76), Pet-GPP (P.195), Pet-Sal (P. 153), Rev-APG (P. 159), Uni-1 (P. 58), Weath-FOST (P. 3).

Items made	Clear	Items made	Clear
Bobeche	35.00	Finger bowl, 4″d., scalloped, with matching underplate	45.00
Bowl, open, round, flat		Lamp, oil, miniature, matching shade	250.00+
7″d	30.00	Pitcher, water	
8″d	30.00	Bulbous, ½ gallon	110.00
Rose	35.00	Tankard, ½ gallon	110.00
Butter dish, covered	50.00	Salt shaker, original top, (VR)	65.00
Cake stand, high standard	40.00	Sauce dish, round	
Celery vase, flat, scalloped rim	35.00	Flat	10.00
Compote		Footed	10.00
High standard		Spoonholder, flat, scalloped rim, double handles	25.00
Covered	85.00	Sugar bowl, covered, double handles	55.00
6½″d	75.00	Syrup pitcher, original top	100.00
7″d	90.00	Tray, water, round	45.00
Open, 10″d	50.00	Tumbler, water, flat	35.00
Low standard, open, shallow, 8″d	60.00	Vase	25.00
Creamer, flat, pressed handle	35.00		
Cruet, original stopper	65.00		

ASHBURTON

Egg cup; wine; covered sugar bowl; goblet; champagne.

OMN: Ashburton, Double flute. AKA: Barrel Ashburton, Chocked Ashburton, Dillaway, Double Flute, Double Knob Stem Ashburton, Flaring Top Ashburton, Giant Straight Stemmed Ashburton, Large Thumbprint, Near Slim Ashburton, Proxy Ashburton, Semi-Squared Ashburton, Short Ashburton, Slim Ashburton, and Tailsman Ashburton.

Flint, non-flint. Major production by the New England Glass Co., East Cambridge, MA. ca. 1869. Bakewell, Pears & Co., Pittsburgh, PA. ca. 1875. Bellaire Goblet Co. (reissued by the United States Glass Co., Pittsburgh, PA.) after 1891. Bryce, Richards & Co. ca. 1854. Bryce, McKee & Co., Pittsburgh, PA. ca. 1854. The Boston & Sandwich Glass Co., Sandwich, MA. Shards have been found at the site of The Burlington Glass Works, Hamilton, Ontario, Canada. Advertised by the Boston & Sandwich Glass Co. in 1848, Ashburton is illustrated in the New England Glass Co. 1868 catalog, the Bakewell, Pears & Co. 1875 catalog, and the ca. 1854-1859 Ovington Brothers catalog "Double Flute" or Ashburton pattern.

Original color production: Clear. (enameled, plain or engraved. Amber, amethyst, blue-green, canary-yellow, emerald green, milk white, opal, opaque white or any other color is very rare. Of heavy, brilliant flint glass, the main pattern element of Ashburton is a large oval above a loop, such ovals being either connected or disconnected. Produced by several factories, minor details such as bulbous or fluted stems, quality and brilliance of the metal and item size are commonplace. Early pieces are heavier and more brilliant than later issues.

Reproductions: Items in Ashburton have been reissued, from new molds, by numerous concerns in both clear and color including the Imperial Glass Co., Bellaire, OH., the L.G. Wright Glass Co., New Martinsville, WV. (most likely by the Westmorland Glass Co.), and the Westmorland Glass Co., Grapeville, PA.

The Metropolitan Museum of Art authorized the Imperial Glass Co. to reissue the following items, each marked with the museum's "M.M.A." insignia: goblet, jug (quart), lemonade glass, and covered sugar bowl. The Imperial Glass Co. also reissued the goblet in cornflower blue marked with both the company's trade mark and paper label.

The L.G. Wright Glass Co., New Martinsville, WV. (distributed by Jennings Red Barn, New Martinsville, WV., and Carl Forslund, Grand Rapids, MI.) reissued the following items in 1967 in amber, bermuda blue, clear, green: bowl (low standard, shallow, flared rim), candlestick (low), claret, compote (high standard, belled-flared bowl), creamer (pressed handle), goblet, water pitcher (pressed handle), sugar bowl (covered), tumbler (flat, termed the "iced tea").

The Westmorland Glass Co. reissued the following reproductions ca. 1977-1978: (brown, clear, olive-green, pink): goblet, sherbert, tumbler (flat, termed the "old fashion"), tumbler (footed, termed the "ice tea"), and wine (termed the "juice").

References: Inn-PG (Plts. 364-365), Lee-EAPG (Pl. 3, Nos. 1-3), Mag-FIEF (P. 23. Fig. 20). McKrn-AG (Pl. 207, No. 1), Oliv-AAG (P. 51), Spil-AEPG (P. 25, Nos. 992-994), Spil-TBV (P. 109), Uni-1 (PP. 29, 31), Uni-2 (P. 15), Uni/Wor-CHPGT (P. 16), Wat-PG (Fig. No. 9), Wat-CG (P. 99).

Items made	Clear	Items made	Clear
Ale glass		Jug, handled	
6½"h	55.00	With underplate	
Long Tom (R)	75.00	Extra large flip	250.00
Bottle		1 quart	250.00
Bitters	55.00	Without underplate	
Water or tumbleup, matching		1 pint	100.00
tumbler	60.00	3 pints	100.00
Bowl, flat, round, open, 6½"d	75.00	1 quart	100.00
Butter dish, covered (2 styles)	85.00	Lamp	90.00
Carafe	175.00	Mug	
Celery vase		Beer, 7"h, pressed handle, 6⅝"h	100.00
Scalloped rim	80.00	Pony	100.00
Smooth rim	80.00	Pitcher, water, applied handle, 6⅝"h	450.00
Champagne		Plate, 6⅝"d	75.00
Flared bowl	75.00	Sauce dish, flat, round, 4¼"d	15.00
Straight bowl, cut ovals	75.00	Spoonholder (2 sizes)	40.00
Claret		Sugar bowl, covered	
5¼"h., low stem	50.00	Large	55.00
5¾"h	50.00	Small	55.00
Compote, open, low standard, 7½"d	65.00	Toddy jar, covered, handled with	
Cordial, 4¼"h		matching underplate, extra large	
Flared bowl	85.00	glass, 1 quart	300.00
Round bowl	85.00	Tumbler	
Creamer, applied handle	175.00	Bar	75.00
Decanter		Footed	80.00
With bar lip or heavy bar collar		Handled, ½ pint	85.00
1 pint	175.00	Quart	
3 pint	175.00	Handled	85.00
Quart	250.00	Handleless	85.00
With stopper, cut or pressed		Sarsaparilla	50.00
½ pint	175.00	Ship	
1 pint	175.00	⅓ pint	45.00
3 pint	200.00	½ pint	45.00
1 quart	250.00	Soda	40.00
Egg cup		Tap	
Double, footed, open	95.00	⅓ pint	45.00
Single, footed, open	35.00	1 pint	45.00
Glass		Water, flat	60.00
Flip, handled	125.00	Whiskey, flat, applied handle	75.00
Jelly	55.00	Vase, plain rim, 10½"h	75.00
Long Tom	65.00	Wine	
Goblet		Cut design	65.00
Engraved panels	45.00	Pressed design	40.00
Flared sides	40.00	Flared bowl	40.00
Straight sides	40.00	Round bowl	40.00
Honey dish, round, flat, 3⅝"d	15.00		

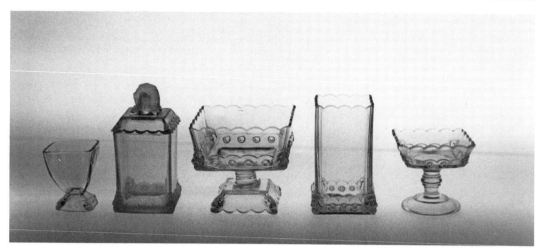

Egg Cup; covered sugar; low standard open compote; celery vase; jelly compote.

OMN: Fostoria's No. 500, Atlanta. AKA: Clear Lion Head, Frosted Atlanta, Late Lion [Peterson], Square Lion, Square Lion Heads.

Non-flint. Fostoria Glass Co. (pattern line No. 500), Moundsville, WV. ca. 1895 through 1900. Illustrated in the 1900 Fostoria Glass Co. catalog.

Original color production: Clear, clear with acid finish (plain or engraved). Odd pieces may be found in clear with ruby stain, clear with amber stain (both very rare), and camphor glass. Forms are square in shape with the exception of the tumbler and stemmed pieces. Finials are in the shape of lion heads.

Reproductions: The goblet has been reproduced in clear from a new mold ca. the early 1960s and earlier.

References: Hea-1 (P. 13), Hea-6 (P. 87), Hea-7 (P. 69), Hea-TPS (PP. 33, 60, 107), Kam-5 (Pl. 8), Migh-TPS (Pl. 4), Mil-1 (Pl. 168), Mtz-1 (P. 96), Pet-Sal (P. 33), Rev-APG (P. 157), Uni-1 (P. 185), Uni-2 (P. 217), Weath-FOST (P. 3), Wlkr-PGA (Fig. 15, No. 100).

Items made	Clear	Clear / Frosted
Banana stand, high standard, folded sides	80.00	100.00
Bowl, open, square		
Flat, scalloped rim		
6″	50.00	65.00
7″	60.00	85.00
8″	60.00	85.00
Collared base, 8″	55.00	65.00
Butter dish, covered	60.00	110.00
Cake stand, high standard, square		
9¼″	95.00	140.00

Items made	Clear	Clear / Frosted
10″	95.00	140.00
Celery vase	45.00	75.00
Compote, square		
High standard		
Covered		
4³/₄″	55.00	65.00
5″	90.00	125.00
7″	110.00	150.00
Open, scalloped rim		
4³/₈″, jelly	55.00	75.00
5″	55.00	85.00
7″	75.00	110.00
Low standard, open, scalloped rim	55.00	85.00
Creamer	50.00	65.00
Cruet, original stopper (R)	125.00	150.00
Egg cup, footed	65.00	85.00
Goblet	65.00	85.00
Marmalade jar, covered	100.00	125.00
Pitcher, water, ¹/₂ gallon	125.00	150.00
Relish dish, rectangular, 7 x 4¹/₂″	35.00	40.00
Salt		
Dip, individual	30.00	35.00
Master, flat, open	50.00	75.00
Shaker, original top (R)	85.00	100.00
Sauce dish, flat, 4″sq	15.00	20.00
Spoonholder	45.00	55.00
Sugar bowl, covered	65.00	85.00
Syrup pitcher (VR), original top	150.00	200.00
Toothpick holder	55.00	65.00
Tumbler, water, flat	35.00	50.00
Wine	85.00	100.00

ATLAS

Masterberry bowl 8″; tankard milk pitcher; h.s. open compote; celery vase; goblet.

OMN: Atlas. AKA: Bullet, Cannon Ball, Crystal Ball [Millard], Knobby Bottom.

Non-flint. Bryce Brothers, Pittsburgh, PA. ca. 1889, with continued production by the United States Glass Co., Pittsburgh, PA. at Factory "A" (Adams & Co., Pittsburgh, PA.) and "B" (Bryce Brothers, Pittsburgh, PA.) ca. 1891 to as late as 1904. Designed and patented by Henry J. Smith of Bryce Brothers (design patent No. 19,427), November 12, 1889, Atlas is illustrated in the United States Glass Co. catalogs of ca. 1891 and 1898, and advertised in the *Crockery and Glass Journal*, February 7, 1889.

Original color production: Clear, clear with ruby stain (plain or copper wheel engraved).

Reproductions: None.

References: Belnp-MG (Fig. 104), Bros-TS (P. 27), Drep-ABC OG (P. 153), Hea-5 (P. 75), Hea-7 (P. 70), Hea-TPS (P. 27), Hea-RUTPS (P. 31), Kam-2 (P. 15-16), Kam-7 (Pl. 2), Lecnr-SS (P. 12), Lee-VG (Pl. 72, No. 3), McCn-PGP (Pl. 12), Mig-TPS (Pl. 24), Mil-1 (Pl.88), Mil-2 (Pl. 9), Mtz-1 (P. 144), Pet-Sal (P. 21-"K"), Rev-APG (PP. 84, 86), Spil-AEPG (P. 280), Swn-PG (PP. 67-68), Uni-1 (PP. 76-77), Wlkr-PGA (Fig. 15, No. 5).

Items made	Clear	Clear / Ruby
Bowl, flat		
Covered		
5"d	25.00	—
6"d	25.00	—
7"d	25.00	—
8"d	30.00	—
Open		
5"d	10.00	—
6"d	10.00	—
7"d	10.00	—
8"d, Masterberry	15.00	—
Finger or waste	40.00	55.00
Butter dish, covered		
Hotel size	45.00	75.00
Table size	45.00	75.00
Cake stand, high standard		
8"d	40.00	80.00
8½"d	40.00	—
9"d	40.00	80.00
10"d	45.00	95.00
Celery vase, flat	40.00	75.00
Champagne, 5½"h	40.00	—
Compote		
Covered, high standard		
5"d	75.00	95.00
7"d	75.00	95.00
8"d	85.00	110.00
Open		
High standard, flared rim, 5"d	40.00	—
Low standard		
5"d	20.00	—
7"d	20.00	—
8"d	25.00	—
Cordial	25.00	35.00
Creamer, covered		
Hotel size	45.00	65.00
Table size	45.00	65.00
Goblet	30.00	35.00
Marmalade jar, covered	85.00	110.00
Mug	20.00	30.00

Items made	Clear	Clear / Ruby
Pitcher, tankard		
Milk, 1 quart	45.00	—
Water, ½ gallon, 10"h	45.00	—
Salt		
Dip, individual	15.00	—
Master, flat, round	20.00	—
Shaker, original top	15.00	—
Sauce dish		
Flat, round, 4"d	10.00	—
Footed		
4"d	15.00	20.00
4½"d	15.00	20.00
Spoonholder		
Hotel size	30.00	35.00
Table size	30.00	35.00
Sugar bowl, covered		
Hotel size	40.00	65.00
Table size	40.00	65.00
Syrup pitcher, original top	65.00	—
Toothpick holder	20.00	40.00
Tray, water, round	60.00	75.00
Tumbler		
Water, ½ pint	20.00	—
Whiskey, gill	20.00	45.00
Wine	25.00	—

AURORA, Brilliant's

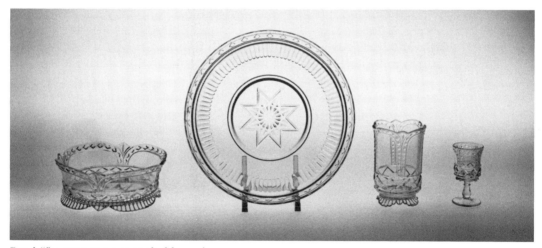

Bowl 5"; water tray; spoonholder; wine.

OMN: Aurora, Brilliant's. AKA: Diamond Horseshoe [Kamm], Diamond Horse Shoe [Metz].

Non-flint. Brilliant Glass Works, Brilliant, OH. ca. 1888-1902. Reissued by the Greensburg Glass Co., Greensburg, PA. ca. 1890 and later by McKee Brothers, Pittsburgh, PA. ca. 1902 (chocolate items only).

Original color production: Clear, plain or copper wheel engraved (engraving No. 15). Clear with ruby stained items were decorated by the Pioneer Glass Co., Pittsburgh, PA. Odd pieces may be found in chocolate.

Reproductions: None.

References: Bar-RS (Pl. 10), Bat-GPG (PP. 106-107), Boyd-GC (No. 54), Hea-7 (Figs. 822-824), Herr-GG (P. 32, Fig. 254), Kam-2 (P. 110), Kam-8 (Plts. 61-64), Lee-VG (Pl. 55), Meas-GG (P. 82), Mtz-1 (P. 194), Pet-Sal (P. 153), Rev-APG (P. 172), Uni-1 (P. 84), Wlkr-PGA (Fig. 8, Nos. 6, 18).

Items made	Clear	Clear w/ Ruby
Bowl, round, flat		
5"d	10.00	20.00
6"d	10.00	20.00
Waste	20.00	45.00
Butter dish, covered	45.00	90.00
Cake stand, high standard	40.00	80.00
Celery vase	30.00	45.00
Compote, high standard		
Covered		
6"d	65.00	95.00
7"d	65.00	95.00
8"d	85.00	125.00
Open		
6"d	20.00	30.00
7"d	20.00	40.00
8"d	25.00	45.00
Creamer	35.00	50.00
Decanter, original stopper, 11¾"h	35.00	135.00
Goblet	30.00	45.00
Mug, pressed handle	40.00	45.00
Olive dish, oblong, scalloped base	15.00	35.00
Pickle dish, fish shape	15.00	25.00
Pitcher		
Milk, 1 quart	40.00	100.00
Water, ½ gallon	55.00	135.00
Plate, bread		
10"d, plain center	30.00	35.00
10"d, star center	30.00	35.00
Relish tray, oval, scoop handled	10.00	25.00
Salt shaker	20.00	40.00
Sauce dish		
Flat, square, 4"	10.00	15.00
Footed, square, 4"	10.00	15.00
Spoonholder	25.00	45.00
Sugar bowl, covered	45.00	65.00
Tray, round		
Bread, star center, 10"d	30.00	35.00
Water	25.00	35.00
Wine	40.00	50.00
Tumbler		
Handled	20.00	35.00
Scalloped base	20.00	45.00
Wine	20.00	45.00

Wine; covered creamer; sugar bowl (lid missing) creamer; punch cup.

OMN: Indiana Glass No. 200, Federal's No. 110. AKA: Finecut Medallion [Kamm], Panelled Oval Fine Cut, Western.

Non-flint. Indiana Tumbler & Goblet Co. (pattern line No. 200), Greentown, IN., introduced in August, 1897. Federal Glass Co., Columbus, OH., ca. 1914. Indiana Glass Co., Dunkirk, IN., ca. 1907. Advertised in the August 4 and August 11, 1897 issues of *China, Glass and Lamps*, the June, 1898 issue of *Crockery, Glass and Pottery Review*, the Montgomery Ward's 1898 catalog as "Western", and the Baltimore Bargain House General Merchandise Catalog No. 496, August 15, 1904.

Original color production: Amber, canary-yellow, clear (either plain or with gilt), green. Experimental colors of cobalt blue, Nile green, opaque colors, chocolate. Not all items were made in all colors.

Reproductions: None.

References: Boyd-GC (Nos. 63-65), Enos-MPG (Chart-1), Hrtng-P&P (P. 9), Hea-1 (PP. 50-51), Hea-TPS (PP. 23, 49), Herr-GG (Figs. 45-56), Kam-2 (Fig. 43), Kam-5 (P. 124), Kam-6 (Pl. 14), Lip-GG. (PP. 26-27), Meas-GG (PP. 53-54), Mil-2 (Pl. 8), Mtz- 2 (P. 165), Rev-APG (P. 203), Uni-1 (P. 296).

Items made	Amber	Canary	Clear	Green
Banana stand, made from high standard cake stand	—	—	145.00	—
Bowl, open				
Round				
Deep, 8″d	—	150.00	55.00	—
Shallow	—	—	35.00	—
Rectangular				
7¼″ x 5″	—	—	65.00	—
8¼″ x 5¼″	—	145.00	50.00	—
Butter dish, covered	—	250.00	90.00	—
Child's miniatures				
Butter dish, covered	—	200.00	125.00	—
Creamer, 4″h.	175.00	100.00	55.00	—
Mug	—	—	45.00	—

Items made	Amber	Canary	Clear	Green
Spoonholder	—	90.00	50.00	—
Sugar bowl, covered	—	145.00	90.00	—
Compote, open				
High standard				
4¼"h	—	135.00	55.00	—
8"d	—	—	75.00	—
Low standard	—	145.00	75.00	—
Cordial	145.00	100.00	55.00	150.00
Creamer, with or without cover				
4¼"h	—	80.00	25.00	125.00
Large, rimless	—	95.00	55.00	—
Small, pedestaled base	—	85.00	40.00	—
Goblet	—	125.00	40.00	—
Nappy, covered, flat, double handled	—	135.00	55.00	—
Pitcher, water	—	350.00	125.00	—
Plate, round	—	—	55.00	—
Punch cup	—	—	—	125.00
Rose bowl				
Small	—	150.00	50.00	—
Medium	—	—	75.00	—
Large	—	175.00	75.00	—
Salt shaker, original top	—	75.00	40.00	—
Sauce dish. flat				
Round				
4¼"d	—	—	25.00	—
4⅝"d	—	50.00	20.00	—
Square	—	60.00	25.00	—
Spoonholder	—	95.00	45.00	—
Sugar bowl, covered				
2½"d	—	85.00	25.00	—
4"d	—	135.00	45.00	—
Small, pedestaled base	—	—	55.00	—
Tumbler	175.00	95.00	25.00	—
Vase				
6"h	—	135.00	45.00	—
8"h	—	175.00	55.00	—
10"d	—	225.00	75.00	—
Wine	175.00	110.00	30.00	150.00

Individual creamer; covered cracker; water bottle; goblet; champagne; wine.

OMN: Aztec. AKA: New Mexico.

Non-flint. McKee Glass Co., Jeannette, PA. ca. 1894 through 1915.

Original color production: Clear, milk white (originally termed "White Opal"). An imitation cut glass pattern, most items are marked with "Pres-Cut" in a circle in the base.

Reproductions: The punch bowl has been reissued by L.E. Smith, Mt. Pleasant/Greensburg, PA. from the original mold in clear without the original Pres-Cut trademark. Both the John E. Kemple Glass Works, East Palestine, OH and Kenova, WV and the Summit Art Glass Co., Mogadore/Rootstown, OH. also reproduced items in Aztec offering them as their own "Whirling Star" pattern.

References: Hart/Cobb-SS (P. 52), Kam-7 (PP. 43-44), Kam-8 (PP. 41-42), Pet-Sal (P. 153), Rev-APG (P. 236), Stot-McKe (PP. 114-115), Wlkr-PGA (Fig. 8, No. 28).

Items made	Clear	Items made	Clear
Bon bon dish, footed		7″	20.00
Round, 7″d	15.00	8″	20.00
Triangular, 7″	15.00	Finger, matching underplate	25.00
Bottle, water	40.00	Lemon or egg	
Bowl, open		2 part, pedestaled base, 10½″d,	
Round		2 quart	25.00
Shallow bowl, scalloped rim		2 part, flat base, 10½″d, 2 quart	25.00
7″d	15.00	Rose	
8″d	15.00	4½″d	15.00
10½″d	15.00	7″d	20.00
Deep bowl		Butter dish, covered	
Flared, scalloped rim		Round scalloped base	40.00
9″d	20.00	Square scalloped base	40.00
10½″d, lemonade or eggnog	20.00	Cake plate, tri-cornered	20.00
Regular, scalloped rim		Candlestick	30.00
7″d	15.00	Celery	
8″d	15.00	Tray, 11″l	15.00
Triangular, deep bowl, scalloped		Vase, flat, scalloped rim, 5¼″h	15.00
rim		Champagne, 5 ounce	25.00

Items made	Clear	Items made	Clear
Claret, 4 ounce	25.00	Punch bowl	
Cologne bottle		Footed	
Globular	25.00	One piece, 14″d	50.00
Tall	30.00	Two piece, 8 quart	50.00
Compote, high standard, open	30.00	Flat, two piece foot, 8 quart	65.00
Condensed milk jar, round, flat,		Punch bowl underplate (termed the	
notched lid	20.00	"sandwich plate") 21½″d	25.00
Cordial		Relish tray, flat	15.00
¾ ounce	20.00	Rose jar	25.00
1 ounce	20.00	Salt shaker, original silver plate or	
Cracker jar, covered	50.00	nickel top	
Creamer		Bulbous	15.00
Individual (referred to as the		Tall	15.00
"berry")	15.00	Spoonholder, flat, flared scalloped rim	15.00
Table size, 3¾″h	25.00	Sauce dish, flat	
Tankard	30.00	Round, scalloped rim	
Cruet, original stopper, 6 ounce	35.00	4″d	10.00
Cup, custard	8.00	4½″d	10.00
Decanter, wine, cut stopper	30.00	Heart shape	15.00
Dish, flat, handled		Triangular shape, deep bowl, 4½″	10.00
Round, 5″d	15.00	Sherbert, footed	25.00
Square, 5″	15.00	Soda fountain crushed fruit jar	55.00
Triangular, 5″	15.00	Spoonholder, 3½″h, flat, scalloped rim	15.00
Goblet, 9 ounce	35.00	Straw holder, covered, square, 12¼″h	65.00
Jar, crushed fruit, covered		Sugar bowl	
Puff, 3¼″d	15.00	Covered	
Squatty, with original spoon	45.00	Scalloped rim	25.00
Tall, with original spoon.	45.00	Smooth rim	25.00
Lamp, with matching globe, wired for		Open, flat, scalloped rim, handled	
electricity, 18¾″h	75.00	(known as "berry sugar")	15.00
Marmalade jar, covered, footed	20.00	Syrup pitcher, original nickel or silver	
Pickle jar, same as condensed milk jar		plate top	50.00
but without notched lid	20.00	Toothpick holder	15.00
Pitcher		Tray, flat	
Jug, applied handle		Olive	15.00
Squat, ½ gallon	35.00	Pickle	15.00
Tall, ½ gallon	35.00	Tumbler	
Lemonade, ½ gallon	35.00	Ice tea	20.00
Tankard, ½ gallon, pressed handle	35.00	Water	20.00
Water, ½ gallon, applied handle	35.00	Whiskey	20.00
Plate		Vase, 10″h, scalloped rim	10.00
Cake, flat, scalloped		Whiskey jug, handled, original stopper	25.00
5½″d	10.00	Wine	
9½″d	20.00	2 ounce	25.00
10″d	20.00	3 ounce	25.00
Dinner	20.00		

Goblet.

OMN: Cupid.

Non-flint. McKee & Brothers, Pittsburgh, PA., ca. 1880. Similar to George Duncan & Sons No. 400 (Three Face), Baby Face is illustrated in the McKee & Brothers 1880 catalog, and reviewed in the April 18, 1878 issue of the *Crockery and Glass Journal*.

Original color production: Clear with acid finished standards and finials, plain or copper wheel engraved (popular engravings being Nos. 147, 292, 293, 299, and 300). The main pattern design element of Baby Face consists of three "baby-like" faces on standards and finials. Limited in the number of forms originally produced, any item in Baby Face is scarce.

Reproductions: Both the goblet and wine have been reproduced from new molds from the early 1960's. Reproductions do not have the refined workmanship and detail of the old, new items displaying a too satin-like and shallow acid finish. An electrified lamp with matching ball shade was produced in the 1980s which is not original to the pattern.

References: Drep-ABC OG (P. 154), Bred-EDG (P. 29), Enos-MPG (Chart-5), Inn-EGP (P. 53), Lee-EAPG (Pl. 89, No. 40), McCn-PGP (P. 397), Mil-1 (Pl. 149), Mtz-1 (PP. 102, 105), Stot-McKe (P. 52), Uni-1 (P. 91).

Items made	Clear	Items made	Clear
Butter dish, covered	165.00	Open	
Celery		High standard, belled-flared-bowl	
Dip	35.00	scalloped rim	
Vase	75.00	7"d	55.00
Champagne	125.00	8"d	60.00
Compote		Low standard, 8"d	85.00
Covered		Cordial	100.00
High standard, belled-flared-bowl		Creamer	55.00
scalloped rim		Goblet	65.00
5¼"d	145.00	Pitcher, water, ½ gallon, pedestaled	300.00 +
6"d	160.00	Salt dip	50.00
7"d	175.00	Spoonholder	65.00
8"d	185.00	Sugar bowl, covered	100.00
		Wine	100.00

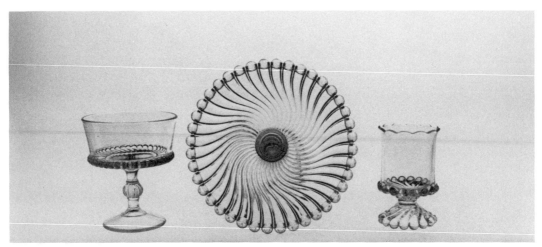

High standard open compote; high standard cakestand; spoonholder.

Covered butter dish; creamer.

OMN: Ray. AKA: Swirl And Ball.

Non-flint. McKee & Brothers, Pittsburgh, PA. ca. 1894. Illustrated as "Ray" in the McKee & Brothers 1894 catalog.

Original color production: Clear, clear with acid finish, clear with ruby stain (plain or copper wheel engraved). Originally produced in thirty five different items, Ball and Swirl is similar to Ball and Swirl Band in that Ball and Swirl has a swirled stem while the latter pattern does not.

Reproductions: The Westmorland Glass Co., Grapeville, PA. reproduced both the goblet and wine from new molds in milk white. Both the covered candy jar in milk white and round 18"d. plate in clear, reproduced during the late 1970s, are not original to the set.

References: Kam-1 (P. 110), Kam-3 (PP. 49-40), Lee-VG (Pl. 27), Mtz-1 (PP. 144-145), Rev-APG (P. 321), Stout (PP. 212, 215-216), Uni-1 (P. 77).

Items made	Clear	Items made	Clear
Bowl, finger	15.00	Pickle tray	15.00
Butter dish, covered	35.00	Pitcher	
Cake stand, high standard	35.00	Milk, tankard, 1 quart	30.00
Candlestick	40.00	Water	
Compote		¹/₂ gallon, bulbous	35.00
Covered, high standard, 9″d, 7¹/₂″h	50.00	¹/₂ gallon, tankard	35.00
Open, high standard		Plate, cake, flat	40.00
Jelly	30.00	Salt/Pepper shaker, original glass	
9″d., 8¹/₂″h., smooth rim	30.00	holder and tops	40.00
Cordial	15.00	Sauce, footed, round	10.00
Creamer	20.00	Spoonholder, footed	20.00
Decanter, wine	45.00	Sugar bowl, covered	20.00
Dish, jelly, flat, handled	15.00	Syrup pitcher, original top	45.00
Goblet	20.00	Tray, cordial	30.00
Mug		Tumbler	
Large	15.00	Water	15.00
Medium	15.00	Handled	15.00
Small	10.00	Wine	25.00

BALTIMORE PEAR

Footed honey dish; water tray; celery vase.

OMN: Gypsy. AKA: Double Pear, Fig, Maryland Pear, Twin Pear.

Non-flint. Adams & Co., Pittsburgh, PA. ca. 1874. Reissued by The United States Glass Co., Pittsburgh, PA. at Factory "A" (Adams & Co., Pittsburgh, PA.) ca. 1891. Illustrated in the United States Glass Co. ca. 1891 and 1898 catalogs.

Original color production: Clear, the main design element being that of a single or a double clear pear in high relief against a stippled background.

Reproductions: The following items have been reproduced from new molds in clear: covered butter dish, cake stand, celery vase, creamer, goblet, milk pitcher, 9″d plate, 10″d. plate, water pitcher, sauce dish, and covered sugar bowl. Reproductions are of poor quality of design, especially in the leaves which lack the fine detail of the old.

References: Drep-ABC OG (P. 40), Enos-MPG (Chart-4), Grow-GPG (P. 173, Fig. 26-"2"), Hart/Cobb-SS (P. 39), Hea-5 (P. 69, Plts. C-D), Inn-PG (PP. 353-354), Kam-1 (P. 30), Lee-EAPG (Pl. 66, No. 1), McCn-PGP (P. 313), Mtz-1 (PP. 84-85), Mil-1 (Pl. 86), Oliv-AAG (P. 59), Rev-APG (P. 20), Spil-AEPG (P. 286), Stu-BP (P. 37), Uni-1 (P. 235).

Items made	Clear	Items made	Clear
Bowl		7″d	45.00
Collared base		8″d	45.00
Covered		Open	
5″d	35.00	High standard	
6″d	40.00	5″d	30.00
7″d	45.00	6″d	30.00
8″d	50.00	7″d	35.00
9″d	55.00	8″d	35.00
Open		Low standard	
5″d	25.00	5″d	20.00
6″d	30.00	6″d	30.00
7″d	35.00	7″d	35.00
8″d	40.00	8″d	40.00
9″d	45.00	8½″d	40.00
Flat base		Creamer, 5½″h	30.00
6″d.		Goblet	35.00
Flared rim, termed "butter		Honey dish, 3½″d.	
nappy"	25.00	Octagonal, flat	15.00
Plain rim, termed "butter		Round	
nappy"	25.00	Flat	10.00
8″d., deep, octagonal, master berry	30.00	Footed	15.00
Bread plate, round, 12½″d	70.00	Pickle tray, oblong	20.00
Butter dish		Pitcher	
Covered, flat, 6⅓″d	75.00	Milk, 1 quart	65.00
Open, flat	45.00	Water, ½ gallon	95.00
Cake plate, flat, round	35.00	Plate, round	
Cake stand, high standard		8½″d	30.00
9¼″d	50.00	9″d	30.00
10″d	50.00	10″d	40.00
Celery vase	50.00	Relish tray	25.00
Compote		Sauce	
Covered		Flat, octagonal	
High standard		4″d	15.00
5″d	40.00	4½″d	15.00
6″d	40.00	Collared, round	
7″d	80.00	4″d	20.00
8″d	80.00	4½″d	20.00
8½″d	80.00	Spoonholder	40.00
Low standard		Sugar bowl, covered	55.00
5″d	30.00	Tray, water, 10½″d	35.00
6″d	40.00		

BAMBOO

Covered butter dish.

OMN: LaBelle's No. 365. AKA: Bamboo Edge.

Non-flint. LaBelle Glass Co. (pattern line No. 365), Bridgeport, OH. ca. 1883.

Original color production: Clear (plain or copper wheel engraved, including No. 225 "Wheat Sheaves" engraving).

Reproductions: None.

References: Kam-5 (PP. 21, 120), McCn-PGP (P. 347), Mtz-1 (P. 141), Mtz-2 (PP. 70-71), Rev-APG (P. 228).

Items made	Clear	Items made	Clear
Butter dish, covered	85.00	7"l	20.00
Celery vase	35.00	8"l	20.00
Compote, high standard		9"l	20.00
Covered		Salt shaker, original top (R)	35.00
7"d	55.00	Sauce dish, 4"d.	
8"d	60.00	Flat, round.	10.00
9"d	65.00	Footed	10.00
Open, oval	30.00	Spoonholder, flat	30.00
Creamer	35.00	Sugar bowl, covered	45.00
Pitcher, water, ¹/₂ gallon	75.00	Tumbler, water	35.00
Relish tray, flat, rectangular			

BANDED BUCKLE

Tumbler (Buckle variant); syrup (Banded Buckle); 6"d. l.s. covered compote (Buckle variant); wine (Banded Buckle).

OMN: Union.

Non-flint. King, Son and Co., Pittsburgh, PA. ca. 1875.

Original color production: Clear. Blue or any other color is very rare.

Reproductions: None.

References: Inn-PG (P. 301), Kam-1 (P. 9), Kam-4 (P. 9), Lee-EAPG (Pl. 102), Lee-SG (P. 536), Mil-1 (Pl. 110), Mtz-1 (PP. 122-123), Oliv-AAG (P. 51), Pet-GPP (P. 161), Pyne-PG (PP. 5, 18), Rev-APG (PP. 211, 216), Spil-AEPG (P. 276), Uni-2 (p. 120).

Items made	Clear	Items made	Clear
Bowl, open, flat, smooth rim	25.00	Pitcher, water, ½ gallon	25.00
Butter dish, covered	85.00	Salt, master	
Compote, low standard, round, 6"d.		Footed, open	25.00
Covered	45.00	Flat, oval, open, 3⅓"l	25.00
Open	45.00	Spoonholder	35.00
Cordial	35.00	Sugar bowl, covered	40.00
Creamer, footed, applied handle	85.00	Syrup pitcher, applied hollow handle	
Egg cup, single	40.00	(R), original top	175.00
Goblet	50.00	Tumbler, water, flat	50.00
Jam jar, covered	50.00	Wine	35.00
Pickle dish, oval, deep bowl	30.00		

Vase; cologne bottle (n.o.s.)

Tumbler; flat sauce; plate; 4 oz. cologne bottle (o.s.); salt shaker.

OMN: U.S. Glass No. 15,071, Virginia. AKA: Diamond Banded Portland, Maiden's Blush [Lee], Portland with Diamond Point.

Non-flint. The United States Glass Co. (pattern line No. 15,071), Pittsburgh, PA. at Factory "G" (Gillinder & Sons, Greensburg, PA.), "U" (United States Glass Co., Gas City, IN.), and "E" (Richards & Hartley, Tarentum, PA.) ca. 1901. Reviewed in the January 10, 1890 issue of the *Crockery and Glass Journal,* and illustrated in the Baltimore Bargain House catalogs No. 497 (August, 1903), No. 483 (December, 1903) and the United States Glass Co. ca. 1904 catalog.

Original color production: Clear, clear with rose blush. Odd items may be found in clear flashed with blue, green or yellow. Items were decorated by the Oriental Glass Co., Pittsburgh, PA. Produced in an extended table service.

Reproductions: None.

References: Bar-RS (P. 35), Hart/Cobb-SS (P. 69), Hrtng-P&P (P. 95), Hea-1 (P. 58), Hea-3 (P. 15, Fig. "A"), Hea-5 (p. 50), No. 236), Hea-6 (PP. 18-19), Hea-7 (P. 212), Kam-2 (P. 89),

Lee-VG (Pl. 35, No. 3), McCn-PGP (P. 581), Mtz-1 (P. 196), Migh-TPS (Pl. 3), Mil-1 (Pl. 9), Mil-2 (Pl. 9), Mur-MCO (P. 69), Pet-Sal (P. 35), Pyne-PG (P. 137), Rev-APG (P. 319), Uni-1 (P. 36), Uni-2 (P. 147).

Items made	Clear	Color Flashed	w/Rose Blush
Bon bon dish, oval, flared rim, pointed ends, 5½"l	20.00	—	30.00
Boudoir set (2 flared candle sticks, 2 covered pomade jars, 2 four ounce colognes, 1 covered puff box, 1 ring stand, 11" oval tray)	500.00	—	750.00
Bowl flat			
Covered			
6"d	40.00	—	55.00
7"d	45.00	—	65.00
8"d	50.00	—	75.00
Open			
Deep, straight-sided bowl			
6"d	25.00	—	45.00
7"d	30.00	—	55.00
8"d	35.00	—	65.00
Shallow, flared bowl			
7½"d	30.00	—	55.00
8½"d	35.00	—	65.00
9½"d	40.00	—	65.00
Butter dish, covered, flanged base	50.00	165.00	165.00
Cake stand, high standard	65.00	—	90.00
Candlestick, 9"h	55.00	—	85.00
Carafe	80.00	—	90.00
Celery			
Tray, oblong, scalloped rim, pointed ends	30.00	—	40.00
Vase	25.00	—	45.00
Cologne bottle, original stopper			
Large	45.00	65.00	85.00
Small, 4 ounce	35.00	—	65.00
Compote, high standard			
Covered			
6"d, jelly	40.00	65.00	75.00
7"d., sweetmeat	85.00	—	95.00
Open			
Flared bowl, scalloped rim			
6"d	25.00	—	40.00
7"d	30.00	—	45.00
8"d	40.00	—	50.00
Straight-sided bowl			
6"d	25.00	—	40.00
7"d	30.00	—	45.00
8"d	40.00	—	50.00
Creamer			
Individual			
Oval	25.00	35.00	45.00
Tankard	25.00	35.00	45.00
Table size, 6 ounce	35.00	45.00	50.00
Cruet, original stopper	60.00	90.00	125.00
Cup, custard or lemonade	20.00	—	35.00
Decanter, handled	50.00	—	90.00
Dish, oval, shallow, scalloped rim			
6"	25.00	—	35.00
7½"	25.00	—	35.00
9"	25.00	—	40.00
10½"	30.00	—	45.00

Items made	Clear	Color Flashed	w/Rose Blush
12½″	35.00	—	45.00
Dresser tray, flat	50.00	—	65.00
Goblet	40.00	50.00	65.00
Jar, dresser, covered	35.00	—	40.00
Lamp, oil, original burner and chimney			
Flat	45.00	—	—
Tall	50.00	—	—
Marmalade dish, footed, 4½″d.			
With original notched cover	40.00	—	55.00
Without cover	40.00	—	55.00
Match holder	30.00	—	40.00
Nappy, round, handled	20.00	55.00	65.00
Olive			
Dish, deep, scalloped, pointed ends, 5½″d	15.00	—	30.00
Tray, boat shaped	15.00	—	30.00
Pickle dish, flat	15.00	20.00	25.00
Pin tray	15.00	—	25.00
Pitcher, water, tankard, ½ gallon	75.00	90.00	225.00
Plate, 6″d	35.00	—	65.00
Pomade jar, covered (2 sizes)	35.00	45.00	50.00
Puff box, original glass cover	35.00	—	50.00
Punch bowl			
Flat, 13″	100.00	—	300.00
High standard, 15″	110.00	—	300.00
Relish tray			
6½″l	15.00	20.00	25.00
8″l	15.00	20.00	25.00
8¼″l	20.00	25.00	30.00
Ring holder, center post (R)	85.00	—	110.00
Salt shaker, original top			
Cafe, short	25.00	35.00	35.00
Hotel, tall, thin	25.00	35.00	35.00
Small, long fluted neck	25.00	35.00	35.00
Sardine box, original cover	55.00	—	65.00
Sauce dish, flat			
Oval, 4½″l	10.00	—	20.00
Round			
4″d	10.00	—	20.00
4½″d	10.00	—	20.00
Square, 4″	10.00	—	20.00
Spoonholder	25.00	—	45.00
Sugar bowl			
Individual, open, oval	20.00	—	35.00
Powdered, flat, covered	45.00	75.00	90.00
Table size, covered	45.00	75.00	90.00
Sugar shaker, original top	45.00	—	90.00
Syrup pitcher, original top	65.00	—	175.00
Toothpick holder	25.00	45.00	40.00
Tray, oval, 11″l, shallow	50.00	—	90.00
Tumbler	25.00	—	45.00
Vase			
Flared rim, tall foot			
6″h	20.00	—	40.00
9″h	35.00	—	50.00
Straight rim, short foot., 6″h	20.00	—	40.00
Wine	35.00	—	75.00

BARBERRY

Flat sauce dish; spoonholder; goblet; footed master salt.

OMN: Berry. AKA: Olive, Pepper Berry.

Non-flint. McKee & Brothers, Pittsburgh, PA. ca. 1880. The Boston & Sandwich Glass Co., Sandwich, MA. ca. 1850s through the 1860s. Shards have been found at the site of The Burlington Glass Works, Hamilton, Ontario, Canada. Illustrated in the McKee & Brothers catalog of 1880, and as "Berry" in the McKee & Brothers 1894 catalog.

Original color production: Clear. Amber, blue or any other color is rare.

Barberry was made by several factories with different variations: a) round berry clusters rather than elongated, b) heavy veined leaves with berries in high relief, the design partly covering the goblet with a wide marginal band at top, and c) a thin design on the lower portion of the goblet. Finials are in the shape of shells. A later, poor quality goblet was issued as a jelly container.

References: Bat-GPG (PP. 36-37), Brn-SD (PP. 50-51), Cod (P. 23), Enos-MPG (Chart-2), Hlms-BCA (P. 278), Kam-1 (P. 9), Lee-EAPG (Pl. 139), McCn-PGP (P. 325), McCn-EPG (Pl. 157, Mil-1 (Pl. 59), Mil-2 (Pl. 61), Mtz-1 (PP. 90-91), Oliv-AAG (P. 59), Rev-APG (PP. 235-236), Stot-McKe (PP. 63-64), Stu-BP (P. 63), Uni-1 (PP. 230-231), Uni/Wor-CHPGT (P. 39), Wlkr-PGA (Fig. 8, Nos. 19, 24, 43).

Items made	Clear	Items made	Clear
Bowl, flat		6"d	40.00
Open		8"d	45.00
Oval		Butter dish, covered, flat	
6"	20.00	Design on rim, 6"d	100.00
7"	25.00	Plain rim, 6"d	50.00
8"	25.00	Cake stand, high standard	150.00
9"	30.00	Celery vase, footed, scalloped rim	45.00
Round, shallow, smooth rim		Compote	
5"	20.00	High standard	
7"	20.00	Covered	
8"	25.00	6"d	55.00
9"	25.00	7"d	55.00
Covered		8"d	65.00

Items made	Clear	Items made	Clear
Open		Goblet (style varies)	25.00
7"d	35.00	Honey dish, flat, round	15.00
8"d	35.00	Pickle tray, oval, taped at one end, 7"l	10.00
Low standard		Pitcher, water, bulbous, applied	
Covered		handle, ½ gallon	125.00
6"d	55.00	Plate, 6"d., round	20.00
7"d	55.00	Salt, master, open	
8"d	65.00	Flat	25.00
Open		Footed	25.00
7"d	30.00	Sauce dish, round	
8"d	35.00	Flat, 4"d	10.00
Cordial	40.00	Footed, 4"d	10.00
Creamer	30.00	Spoonholder, footed, scalloped rim ...	30.00
Cup plate, 3"d	15.00	Sugar bowl, covered	55.00
Dish, flat		Syrup pitcher, original tin top, applied	
Oval, open, 8" x 5½"	15.00	handle	125.00
Round, covered, 8"d	15.00	Tumbler, water, footed	25.00
Egg cup, single, footed, open	30.00	Wine	35.00

BARLEY

Flat sauce dish; goblet; h.s. true open compote; relish tray.

AKA: Sprig.

Non-flint. Maker unknown. Attributed to Campbell, Jones & Co., Pittsburgh, PA. based on the design patented by James Dalzell (patented January 3, 1882, design patent No. 12,647, assigned to Jones, Cavitt & Co., Ltd., Pittsburgh, PA.) for a wheelbarrow master salt in the "Barley" design. To date, no positive proof has surfaced indicating that the pattern covered by the Dalzell patent covered the entire line known as Barley.

Original color production: Clear. Amber or any other color is rare.

Reproductions: None.

References: Enos-MPG (Chart-1), Kam-1 (P. 33), Lee-EAPG (Pl. 116, No. 3), McCn-PGP (P. 435), Mil-1 (Pl. 97), Mtz-1 (PP. 84-85), Rev-APG (PP. 100-101), Spil-AEPG (P. 301), Stu-BP (P. 45), Uni-1 (PP. 218-219), Wat-AGG (P. 301), Wlkr-PGA (Fig. 15, No. 10).

Items made	Clear	Items made	Clear
Bowl, flat		Goblet	25.00
Oval, 10″d	20.00	Honey dish, flat, 3½″d	10.00
Round, 8″d., master berry	15.00	Marmalade jar, covered	65.00
Butter dish, covered, 6½″d, 4½″h,		Pickle	
scalloped rim with row of		Castor, complete in original silver	
thumbprints	40.00	plate frame	90.00
Cake stand, high standard		Dish	10.00
8″d	25.00	Pitcher, water	
9″d	25.00	Bulbous, applied handle	95.00
9¼″d	25.00	Pressed handle	45.00
9½″d	25.00	Plate, 6″d., round	35.00
9⅝″d	25.00	Platter, oval, 13″l x 8″	30.00
10″d	30.00	Relish	
Celery vase	25.00	Flat, 8″ x 6″	20.00
Compote		Wheelbarrow shape, attached pewter	
Covered		wheel	
High standard		Large, 8″	65.00
6″d	45.00	Small, master salt	75.00
8½″d	60.00	Sauce dish, round	
Low standard		Flat, 4½″d., sunburst center	15.00
6″d	35.00	Footed	
8½″d	50.00	4″d	15.00
Open, high standard, 8½″d	25.00	5″d	15.00
Cordial	40.00	Spoonholder	25.00
Creamer	25.00	Sugar bowl, covered	40.00
Dish, vegetable, oval, open, flat		Tray, bread	30.00
5¼″ x 7½″	15.00	Wine	30.00
6½″ x 9½″	15.00		

BARRED OVAL(S)

Tumbler and water pitcher (both clear with ruby).

OMN: United States Glass No. 15004. AKA: Banded Portland [Unitt], Banded Portland-Frosted [Millard], Buckle [Enos], Frosted Banded Portland, Purple Block [Millard], Oval And Crossbar.

Non-flint. George Duncan & Sons, Pittsburgh, PA. ca. 1892. Reissued by the United States Glass Co. (pattern line No. 15,004), Pittsburgh, PA. at Factory "D" (George Duncan & Sons, Pittsburgh, PA). ca. 1891. Advertised in *China, Glass and Lamps* in 1891, and illustrated in the United States Glass Co. 1904 catalog.

Original color production: Clear, clear/frosted (machine ground). Clear with ruby stain (plain or copper wheel engraved).

Reproductions: The Fenton Art Glass Co., Williamstown, WV., produced from new molds, pieces in crystal and ruby. New shapes are heavier and thicker than the originals.

References: Bar-RS (Pl. 11), Bred-EDG (PP. 123-124), Enos-MPG (Chart-1), Hea-3 (P. 82), Hea-5 (PP. 44, 97), Hea-7 (P. 72), Kam-6 (Pl. 26), Lee-VG (P. 119, Pl. 41), McCn-PGP (Pl. 202), Mtz-1 (PP. 154-155), Mil-2 (Pl. 35), Pet-Sal (P. 21), Rev-APG (PP. 148-149), Thu-1 (P. 324), Uni-1 (PP. 36-37), Uni-2 (P. 57), Wlkr-PGA (Fig. 8).

Items made	Clear	Clear w/ Ruby
Bottle, water	35.00	85.00
Bowl, open, flat		
Round		
7"d	20.00	35.00
8"d	20.00	35.00
9"d	25.00	45.00
Square		
7"	20.00	35.00
8"	25.00	45.00
Butter dish, covered	45.00	125.00
Cake stand, high standard, 10"d	40.00	100.00
Celery		
Tray	35.00	75.00
Vase, footed, 6½"h	40.00	125.00
Compote, high standard		
Covered		
7"d	80.00	150.00
8"d	85.00	150.00
Open		
7"d	50.00	85.00
8"d	55.00	90.00
Creamer	45.00	75.00
Cruet, original patterned stopper	55.00	250.00
Dish, oblong, flat, open		
7"l	20.00	35.00
8"l	20.00	35.00
9"l	25.00	40.00
Goblet, 6"h	40.00	75.00
Lamp, kerosene, original burner and chimney	125.00	—
Pickle dish, rectangular, 6"	10.00	35.00
Pitcher		
Milk, 1 quart	75.00	135.00
Water, ½ gallon	100.00	185.00
Plate, cheese		
6"d	25.00	45.00
7"d	25.00	45.00
Sauce dish, flat		
Round		
4"d	10.00	20.00
4½"d	10.00	20.00

Items made	Clear	Clear w/ Ruby
Square		
4"d	8.00	20.00
4½"	8.00	20.00
Salt shaker, original top	15.00	35.00
Spoonholder	35.00	65.00
Sugar bowl, covered	60.00	110.00
Tumbler, water, flat	20.00	40.00

BASKETWEAVE

Oval dish; water pitcher; milk pitcher; goblet. All items in blue.

Non-flint. Maker unknown, ca. mid 1880s. Shards have been found at the site of the Boston & Sandwich Glass Co., Sandwich, MA., and the Burlington Glass Works, Hamilton, Ontario, Canada.

Original color production: Amber, blue, vaseline, clear, apple green. Odd pieces may be found in milk white. Some items have stippled cat's head finials.

Reproductions: The following items have been reproduced from new molds in amber, blue, clear, green and yellow: goblet, tumbler, water pitcher, and water tray, the design on new pieces being of poor quality. Stemmed pieces are thinner than the originals. Reproductions in general are smaller in size and lighter in weight. New colors are washed out, lacking the mellowness of the old.

References: Drep-ABC OG (P. 145), Drep-FR (P. 207), Enos-MPG (Chart-1), Hea-3 (P. 15, Fig. 20), Kam-5 (P. 51), Kam/Wod-Vol.1 (P. 56), Lee-EAPG (Pl. 104, No. 3), Mtz-1 (PP. 162-163), Mil-1 (Pl. 127), Stev-ECG (P. 67), Stu-BP (P. 12), Uni-2 (P. 27), Uni/Wor-CHPGT (P. 41).

Items made	Amber or Canary	Apple Green	Blue	Clear	Vas
Bowl, round, flat, smooth rim					
Covered, handled	35.00	50.00	40.00	35.00	40.00
Open					
Berry, master	25.00	40.00	30.00	25.00	30.00
Finger	20.00	35.00	25.00	20.00	25.00
Waste	20.00	35.00	25.00	20.00	25.00

Items made	Amber or Canary	Apple Green	Blue	Clear	Vas
Butter dish, covered	35.00	60.00	40.00	30.00	40.00
Compote					
Covered					
High standard, 7″d	55.00	75.00	55.00	35.00	65.00
Low standard	55.00	75.00	55.00	35.00	65.00
Open					
High standard	30.00	45.00	40.00	20.00	35.00
Low standard	30.00	45.00	40.00	20.00	35.00
Cordial	25.00	40.00	30.00	20.00	30.00
Creamer, $4^7/_8$″h	30.00	50.00	35.00	30.00	35.00
Cup	15.00	20.00	20.00	15.00	15.00
Dish, oval, open, flat	10.00	20.00	15.00	10.00	15.00
Egg cup					
Double	15.00	30.00	20.00	15.00	25.00
Single	15.00	30.00	20.00	15.00	25.00
Goblet	30.00	50.00	30.00	20.00	30.00
Mug	25.00	40.00	25.00	15.00	30.00
Pickle dish	15.00	30.00	20.00	15.00	20.00
Pitcher					
Milk, 1 quart	40.00	60.00	45.00	35.00	50.00
Water, ½ gallon	50.00	75.00	80.00	40.00	65.00
Plate, cake, handled, 11″	25.00	40.00	25.00	20.00	30.00
Salt, master, open					
Flat, oblong	—	—	—	20.00	—
Footed	—	—	—	20.00	—
Sauce, round, flat	10.00	10.00	10.00	8.00	10.00
Saucer	15.00	30.00	15.00	15.00	20.00
Spoonholder	30.00	35.00	30.00	20.00	30.00
Sugar bowl, covered	35.00	60.00	35.00	30.00	40.00
Syrup pitcher, original top	50.00	75.00	50.00	45.00	55.00
Tray, water ("rural" center)	35.00	45.00	40.00	30.00	55.00
Tumbler, water, flat	15.00	30.00	20.00	15.00	20.00
Wine	30.00	50.00	30.00	25.00	30.00

Goblet; egg cup.

AKA: Beaded Acorn.

Non-flint. Boston Silver Glass Co., East Cambridge, MA. ca. 1869. Shards have been found at the site of the Boston & Sandwich Glass Co., Sandwich, MA.

Original color production: Clear. Heavily stippled, the main pattern design element of Beaded Acorn Medallion consists of beaded ovals in which clear embossed acorns and oak leaves stand in high relief. Handles are applied and finials are in the shape of acorns.

Reproductions: None.

References: Kam-8 (P. 7), Lee-EAPG (PP. 437-438), Lee-SG (PP. 526), McCn-PGP (P. 427), Mtz-1 (PP. 72-73), Oliv-AAG (P. 59), Rev-APG (PP. 76-77), Uni-1 (PP. 142-143), Wlkr-PGA (Fig. 8, Nos. 18, 49).

Items made	Clear	Items made	Clear
Bowl, fruit	45.00	Pitcher, water, bulbous, applied	
Butter dish, covered, flat	65.00	handle, ¹/₂ gallon	95.00
Champagne	55.00	Plate, round, 6"d	20.00
Compote, covered		Relish, oval, flat, deep	
High standard, 8"d	55.00	Large	15.00
Low standard, 9"d	45.00	Small	15.00
Creamer, 5³/₄"h	40.00	Salt, master, footed, open, smooth rim	20.00
Egg cup, single	20.00	Sauce dish, flat, round, smooth rim,	
Goblet	35.00	4"d	10.00
Honey dish, flat, 3¹/₂"d	15.00	Spoonholder	30.00
Lamp, student, brass trim, original		Sugar bowl, covered	45.00
burner and chimney	100.00	Wine	35.00

Cake stand; h.s. covered compote; double relish.

AKA: Thousand Eye Band.

Non-flint. Maker unknown, ca. 1884. Shards have been found at the site of the Burlington Glass Works, Hamilton, Ontario, Canada.

Original color production: Clear. Amber or any other color is rare.

Reproductions: None.

References: Enos-MPG (Chart-3), Hlms-BCA (P. 278), Lee-EAPG (Pl. 61, No. 4), McCn-PGP (P. 342), Mil-1 (Pl. 97), Mil-2 (Pl. 151), Mtz-1 (P. 136-137), Mtz-2 (P. 130), Oliv-AAG (P. 64), Stev-ECG (P. 229), Uni-1 (P. 101), Uni-TCG (PP. 63, 221), Uni/Wor-CHPGT (P. 43), Wlkr-PGA (Fig. 8, No. 36).

Items made	Clear	Items made	Clear
Butter dish, covered	45.00	Goblet	30.00
Cake stand, high standard, $7^5/_8''$d	30.00	Pickle jar, covered	65.00
Compote		Pitcher, water, $^1/_2$ gallon	90.00
Covered		Relish tray	
High standard		Double, flat	30.00
8''d	50.00	Single, $8^1/_2''$ x $5^1/_4''$	15.00
$9^1/_2''$d	55.00	Sauce dish, round	
10''d	55.00	Flat	10.00
Low standard, 8''	55.00	Footed	10.00
Open, high standard		Spoonholder, smooth rim	25.00
$9^1/_2''$d	25.00	Sugar bowl, covered	45.00
10''d	25.00	Syrup pitcher, original top dated "June	
Creamer	25.00	29, '84"	90.00
Doughnut stand, high standard, $7^1/_2''$d	15.00	Wine	35.00

Egg cup; goblet; castor set; covered sugar bowl; spoonholder.

Flint, non-flint. The Boston Silver Glass Co., East Cambridge, MA. ca. 1869. Shards have been found at the site of the Boston & Sandwich Glass Co., Sandwich, MA. When "banded," the pattern is known as Beaded Grape Medallion-Banded.

Original color production: Clear. Designed and patented by Alonzo C. Young May 11, 1869 (mechanical patent No. 90,040). A heavily stippled pattern, the main design element consists of clear grape-filled beaded medallions, with large well defined acorn finials. Handles are applied.

Reproductions: None.

References: Brn-SD (P. 153), Chip-ROS (PP. 42, 84), Cod-OS (P. 23), Hea-OS (P. 134, No. 2552), Kam-8 (PP. 7-8), Lee-EAPG (Pl. 66, Nos. 3-4), Lee-SG (P. 536), Lee-VG (P. 261), McCn-PGP (P. 319), Mtz-1 (P. 82), Mtz-2 (PP. 767-77), Mil-1 (Pl. 85), Rev-APG (PP. 76-77), Spil-AEPG (P. 270), Uni-1 (P. 229), Wlkr-PGA (Fig. 8, Nos. 7, 14, 16, 19).

Items made	Clear	Items made	Clear
Bowl, flat, open, plain rim, 7"d	25.00	Flat, 6¼" x 9½"	60.00
Butter dish, covered, 6"d	50.00	Egg cup, footed, open	25.00
Cake stand, high standard, 11"d	150.00	Goblet	
Castor set, 4 bottles, original patterned		Stippled base	30.00
stoppers, original holder	125.00	Stippled base, 3 clear beaded ovals,	
Celery vase	50.00	grape clusters	30.00
Champagne	65.00	Stippled base, 3 small clear beaded	
Compote, oval		ovals	30.00
Covered		Honey dish, flat, 3½"d	10.00
High standard	75.00	Pickle dish, flat	20.00
Low standard	65.00	Pitcher, water, bulbous, applied	
Open, high standard, collared base,		handle, ½ gallon	125.00
8"	35.00	Plate, round, 6"d	20.00
Cordial	65.00	Relish dish	
Creamer, applied handle, 5½"h	40.00	Open, marked "Mould Pat'd May 11,	
Dish, covered		1868"	40.00
Round		Covered	140.00
Footed, vegetable	75.00	Salt	
Oval		Dip, individual, 1⅛"	20.00
Collared base, 7" x 10"	60.00	Master, open	

Items made	Clear	Items made	Clear
Flat		Sauce dish, flat, round, 4″d (2 styles)	10.00
Oval	20.00	Spoonholder	35.00
Round	20.00	Sugar bowl, covered	65.00
Footed, smooth rim	20.00	Wine	65.00

BEADED MIRROR

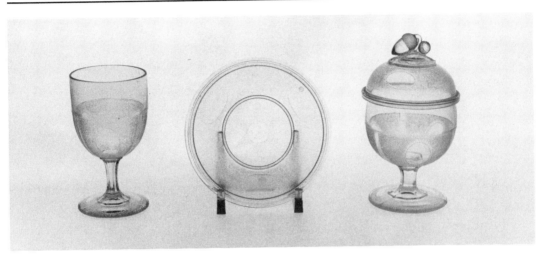

Goblet; plate; covered sugar bowl.

AKA: Beaded Medallion [Miller].

Flint, non-flint. The Boston Silver Glass Co., East Cambridge, MA. ca. 1869. Shards have been found at the site of the Boston & Sandwich Glass Co., Sandwich, MA.

Original color production: Clear. A contemporary of Beaded Grape Medallion, Beaded Mirror belongs to that group of patterns in which the main pattern element consists of heavy stippeling. Typical of the period, handles are applied and finials are acorn shaped.

Reproductions: None.

References: Cod-OS (Pl. 23), Kam-1 (P. 38), Lee-SG (PP. 520, 536), Lee-VG (Pl. 56, No. 4), Mil-2 (Pl. 10), Mtz-1 (PP. 180-181), Mtz-2 (PP. 126-127), Rev-APG (PP. 76-77), Spil-AEPG (P. 269), Spil-TBV (P. 233), Uni-1 (PP. 142), Wlkr-PGA (Fig. 8, Nos. 13, 19, 48).

Items made	Clear	Items made	Clear
Bottle		Pitcher	
Castor	15.00	Milk, tall, slender, 1 quart	55.00
Mustard	15.00	Water, ½ gallon	85.00
Oil	20.00	Plate, round, 6″d	20.00
Butter dish, covered	40.00	Relish tray	15.00
Castor set, 5 bottles in original pewter		Salt, master, footed, open	15.00
frame	100.00	Sauce dish, round	
Celery vase	35.00	Flat	10.00
Compote, covered, high standard	50.00	Footed	10.00
Creamer	40.00	Spoonholder	25.00
Egg cup, single	15.00	Sugar bowl, covered	45.00
Goblet	30.00		

BEADED SWIRL

Wine (clear); egg cup (milk white).

OMN: George Duncan's No. 335. AKA: Swirled Column.

Non-flint. George Duncan & Sons (pattern line No. 335), Pittsburgh, PA. ca. 1890, with continued production by the United States Glass Co., Pittsburgh, PA. after 1891. Reviewed in the *Crockery and Glass Journal* May 15, 1890 and the *Pottery and Glassware Reporter* February 27, 1890, and illustrated in the ca. 1891 and 1898 United States Glass Co. catalogs.

Original color production: Clear, emerald green (with or without gilt, emerald green pieces produced by the United States Glass Co.). Electric blue, clear with amber, clear with ruby, milk white, or any other color is rare. Originally produced in two forms: a) flat and b) 3-legged.

Reproductions: None.

References: Bred-EDG (PP. 113-114), Hea-5 (P. 96, Plts. A-D), Hea-6 (P. 19, Fig. 35), Kam-3 (P. 95), Lee-VG (Pl. 41, No. 1), Mur-MCO (P. 69), Rev-APG (P. 148).

Items made	Clear	Emerald Green
Bowl		
Covered, round, 3-legged		
7"d	25.00	35.00
8"d	25.00	35.00
9"d	30.00	40.00
Open		
Oval, flat		
7"	10.00	20.00
8"	10.00	20.00
9"	15.00	25.00
Round, scalloped rim		
Flat		
7"d	10.00	20.00
8"d	10.00	20.00
9"d	15.00	25.00
3-legged		
7"d	10.00	20.00
8"d	10.00	20.00

Items made	Clear	Emerald Green
9"d	15.00	25.00
Finger	15.00	20.00
Butter dish, covered		
Flat	55.00	65.00
Footed	65.00	75.00
Cake stand, high standard	65.00	75.00
Celery		
Tray		
Cupped, flat	15.00	25.00
Straight	15.00	25.00
Vase, flat, ground base	20.00	30.00
Creamer		
Flat		
Table size	20.00	30.00
Tankard	25.00	35.00
Footed, table size	30.00	40.00
Cruet, original cut or pressed stopper	35.00	225.00
Cup		
Custard, handled	5.00	10.00
Sherbert, handleless	5.00	10.00
Goblet	40.00	50.00
Pitcher, water, ½ gallon, bulbous	55.00	75.00
Plate, underplate for sherbert	10.00	20.00
Relish tray, flat	15.00	25.00
Salt shaker, original plated or nickel top		
Squatty	15.00	25.00
Tall	15.00	25.00
Sauce dish, round		
Flat		
4"d	5.00	15.00
4½"d	5.00	15.00
3-legged		
4"d	5.00	10.00
4½"d	7.00	20.00
Spoonholder		
Flat	20.00	30.00
Footed	20.00	30.00
Sugar bowl, covered		
Flat	35.00	45.00
Footed	35.00	45.00
Sugar shaker, original nickel top (VR in color)	40.00	150.00
Syrup, original plated top with ewer mouth (VR in color)	45.00	225.00
Tumbler, ground bottom	20.00	30.00
Wine	15.00	40.00

BEADED TULIP

Wine; water pitcher; creamer.

OMN: Andes. AKA: Tulip.

Non-flint. McKee & Brothers, Pittsburgh, PA. ca. 1895. Illustrated in the McKee & Brothers 1894 catalog.

Original color production: Clear. Blue, emerald green or any other color is rare.

Reproductions: None.

References: Drep-ABC OG (P. 165), Kam-3 (P. 127), Lee-EAPG (Pl. 116, No. 4), Mil-1 (Pl. 124), Mil-2 (Pl. 133), Mtz-1 (PP. 64-65), Rev-APG (P. 236), Uni-1 (PP. 194-195), Wlkr-PGA (Fig. 8, No. 37).

Items made	Clear	Items made	Clear
Bowl, oval, open, flat, 9½″d	20.00	Water, ½ gallon	65.00
Butter dish, covered, flat	50.00	Plate	
Cake stand, high standard	50.00	Bread	35.00
Champagne	35.00	Dinner, 6″d	40.00
Compote		Relish dish	20.00
Covered, 8″d	55.00	Sauce dish, round, leaf-shaped edges,	
Open, 8″d.	40.00	4″d.	
Cordial	30.00	Flat	10.00
Creamer	35.00	Footed	10.00
Dish, ice cream, oblong	25.00	Spoonholder	30.00
Goblet	35.00	Sugar bowl, covered	45.00
Marmalade jar, covered	40.00	Tray, round	
Pickle dish, oval, flat	15.00	Water	50.00
Pitcher		Wine	50.00
Milk, 1 quart	45.00	Wine	30.00

58

Vase 6½″h; celery vase; 9″ dinner plate; h.s. jelly compote.

Non-flint. Bryce, Higbee & Co., Pittsburgh, PA. ca. 1905.

Original color production: Clear.

Reproductions: None.

References: Hrtng-P&P (P. 11), Kam-2 (PP. 47-48), McCn-PGP (P. 235), Uni-1 (P. 69), War (P. 382).

Items made	Clear	Items made	Clear
Banana stand, high standard	30.00	Pitcher, water, ½ gallon	45.00
Bowl, open		Plate	
Flat, 9″d	15.00	Round	
Collared base, 9″d	15.00	Bread	15.00
Butter dish, covered	35.00	Cake, 9″d	25.00
Cake stand, high standard	35.00	Dinner	
Celery vase	20.00	8″d	15.00
Compote, high standard		9″d	25.00
Covered	35.00	11″d	25.00
Open	25.00	Square, 7″	15.00
Creamer, 5″h	25.00	Salt shaker	20.00
Cruet, original stopper	30.00	Spoonholder	15.00
Doughnut stand, high standard		Sugar bowl, covered	25.00
(referred to as child's miniature cake		Tumbler, water, flat	10.00
stand)	45.00	Vase, 6½″h	15.00
Goblet	35.00	Wine	20.00

Covered butter dish; 5 bottle castor set; octagonal covered sugar (VR).

Wine; champagne; tumbler.

OMN: R.L. Pattern. AKA: Ribbed Bellflower, Ribbed Leaf.

Flint, non-flint. Attributed to the Boston & Sandwich Glass Co., Sandwich, MA., ca. 1840s. Later production by Bryce, McKee & Co., Pittsburgh, PA.

Original color production: Clear. Amber, cobalt blue, fiery opales., green, milk white, opaque blue, sapphire blue or any other color is very rare. One of the earliest pressed glass patterns, Bellflower is illustrated in the McKee catalogs of 1864 and 1868, and the firm's illustrated price list of 1868. The main pattern design element of Bellflower consists of a clear single or double vine of bellflowers and berries upon a coarse or finely ribbed background. Quality of the glass varies from a fine silvery lustre to a dull finish, earliest pieces being pontil marked and much cruder than machine pressed items indicating such items were most likely mold-blown. Produced by numerous manufacturers for many years, finials vary from hexagonal shapes to acorn-like ornaments, stems may be knobbed or plain, and bases may be rayed, floral or of concentric ornaments. A rare variation of the pattern consists of cut rather than pressed bellflower designs.

Reproductions: The Metropolitan Museum of Art, New York, NY. authorized the Imperial Glass Co., Bellaire, OH. to reproduce, from new molds, items in lead crystal, each item embossed with the museum's "M.M.A." insignia. In 1970, the 1 quart milk pitcher in sapphire blue with applied clear handle was issued in a limited edition of 1970 copies along with the 8 ounce 6"h. clear goblet. In 1971, the 1 quart emerald green milk pitcher with applied clear handle was issued in a limited edition of 2,500. In 1972, the 1 quart canary yellow milk pitcher with clear applied handle was issued in a limited edition of 1,600 copies, and the peacock blue 1 quart milk pitcher with applied clear handle was issued in 1977 in a limited edition of 1,500 copies. In 1979 the 1 quart milk pitcher with applied handle, 8 ounce 6"h goblet, and 8 ounce, $3\frac{1}{2}$"h. water tumbler were issued in clear, and in 1981, the Peacock blue 1 quart milk pitcher with applied clear handle was reissued with the clear goblet.

References: Belnp-MG (P. 87), Chip-ROS (P. 93), Cod-OS (Pl. 21), Drep-ABC OG (P. 165), Enos-MPG (Chart-3), Fer-YMG (P. 39), Grow-GAG (P. 161, Fig. 24-"11"), Hart-AG (P. 350), Inn-EPG (P. 50), Inn-PG (P. 349), Inn/Spil-McKe (PP. 52-53), Kam-3 (P. 205), Kam-4 (P. 49), Kam-6 (P. 6), Knit-EAG (Pl. 64), Lee-EAPG (Plts. 30, 34), Lee-VG (Pl. 95), Mag-FIEF (P. 3, Fig. 2), McCn-PGP (Pl. 125), McKrn-AG (Pl. 209), Mil-1 (Pl. 94), Mil-2 (Pl. 40), Mil-OG (Pl. 130), Mtz-1 (P. 30), Mtz-2 (P. 54), Oliv-AAG (P. 57), Pap-GAG (P. 190), Phil-EOG (P. 189), Rev-APG (P. 237), Schwtz-AG (P. 120), Spil-AEPG (P. 263), Spil-CORN (Fig. 13), Stot-McKe (P. 40), Swn-PG (Pl. 13), Tas-AG (P. 54, Fig. 34), Thu-1 (P. 88), Uni-1 (P. 68), Wat-AGG (Pl. 20 "A"), Wlkr-PGA (Fig. 8, Nos. 20, 39).

Items made	Clear	Items made	Clear
		Compote	
SINGLE VINE-FINE RIB		Covered, hexagonal acorn-finial	
		High standard, 8"d	350.00
Bowl, open, flat, round		Low standard	
Plain rim, rayed base		7"d	250.00
6"d. (R)	75.00	8"d	250.00
8"d. (R)	75.00	Open	
Scalloped rim	85.00	High standard	
Butter dish, covered, hexagonal-acorn		Domed patterned base	
finial		Clear scalloped rim, 8"d	185.00
Beaded base	80.00	Rayed scalloped rim, 8"d	185.00
Flanged base	100.00	Plain base, scalloped rim	165.00
Plain base	80.00	Low standard	
Cake stand (made from footed		Domed patterned base	
compote mold) (VR)		Clear scalloped rim	
6"d., plain scalloped edge, large		7"d	150.00
sunburst in center (VR)	1000.00	8"d	150.00
8½"d., 3"h., rayed-scalloped rim,		Rayed scalloped rim	150.00
patterned base (VR)	1200.00	Plain base, scalloped rim	125.00
Oddity with design against a fine		Cordial	
diamond point background (VR)	1400.00	Barrel shaped bowl, knob stem,	
Castor, patterned bottom		rayed base	100.00
Bottle	25.00	Straight-sided bowl, plain ¼", clear	
Set, original pewter or Britannia		marginal band around bowl	125.00
standard (salt/pepper, mustard, and		Creamer, rayed foot, applied handle	125.00
vinegar)	225.00	Decanter (R)	
Celery vase, pedestaled, scalloped rim,		Heavy bar lip, quart	175.00
straight sided (VR)	185.00	Matching patterned stopper	
Champagne		Pint	225.00
Barrel shaped bowl, knob stem,		Quart	225.00
rayed base	100.00	Egg cup	
Straight-sided bowl, plain ¼", clear		Flared	40.00
marginal band around bowl	100.00	Straight-sided	40.00

Items made	Clear
Goblet	
Knob stem	55.00
Plain stem, straight-sided bowl, 1/4″	
clear marginal band around top of	
bowl	55.00
Straight stem (design to top of bowl)	40.00
Hat, made from tumbler mold (R)	350.00
Honey dish	
3″d., scalloped rim, star base (R)	40.00
3 1/4″d., plain rim, rayed base	35.00
3 1/2″d	35.00
Lamp, original burner	
All glass, coal or whale oil, scalloped	
base	175.00
Glass font, brass stem, marble base	150.00
Mug, applied handle (VR) (same size	
as whiskey)	200.00
Pickle dish, oval	35.00
Pitcher, applied handle, helmet shape	
Milk, 1 quart (ribbed to end of lip)	
(R)	450.00
Water, 1/2 gallon	250.00
Plate, round, 6″	100.00
Relish dish, open, flat, scalloped rim,	
rayed base	35.00
Salt, master, footed	
Beaded rim	
Covered	225.00
Open, scalloped rim	65.00
Scalloped edge, open	65.00
Clear scallop	65.00
Rayed scallop	65.00
Scallop and point	65.00
Sauce dish, round, flat	
Alternating large and small scallops	35.00
Flat rim, clear base	35.00
Flat scalloped rim, floral base	35.00
Scalloped rim, clear base	35.00
Spoonholder, footed	
Clear scalloped rim, short stem	40.00
Rayed to top of scalloped rim	40.00
Sugar bowl, covered	
Octagonal shape, high domed lid,	
8 1/4″h, scalloped rim, rayed base,	
mushroom finial, low foot (VR)	1200.00
Low foot, acorn finial	125.00
Syrup, applied hollow handle, original	
tin, Britannia or metal lid	
Round	555.00
Ten-sided, flared foot, 10-pointed	
rosette base (VR)	555.00
Sweetmeat, covered, high standard	225.00
Tumbler, water, flat	
Design to top	90.00
Straight-sided	
Plain base	90.00
Straight-sided, 1/4″ clear marginal	
band around rim	90.00
Whiskey, 3 1/2″h., flat	150.00

Items made	Clear
Wine	
Barrel shape bowl, rayed base	90.00
Straight-sided bowl, plain stem,	
rayed base	75.00

DOUBLE VINE-FINE RIB

	Clear
Compote, open, low standard,	
scalloped rim, 7″d	150.00
Creamer, rayed foot, applied handle	125.00
Decanter (R)	
Heavy bar lip, quart	175.00
Matching patterned stopper	
Pint	225.00
Quart	225.00
Goblet, cut bellflowers (VR)	250.00
Pitcher, applied handle, helmet shape	
Milk, 1 quart (ribbed to end of lip)	
(R)	550.00
Water, 1/2 gallon	250.00
Salt, master, open, footed	20.00
Spoonholder, footed	
Rayed to top of scalloped rim	45.00
Clear scalloped rim, short stem	45.00
Sugar bowl, covered, low foot, acorn	
finial	100.00
Tumbler, footed	125.00

SINGLE VINE-COARSE RIB

	Clear
Butter dish, flat, round	
Mushroom finial	80.00
Rose bud finial	80.00
Castor bottle	
Fluted bottom	25.00
Ribbed bottom	25.00
Champagne	
Barrel shape bowl, plain stem, 5 1/4″h	100.00
Compote Open	
High standard Scalloped rim	
Patterned base with clear marginal	
bands around top and bottom	150.00
Domed foot	
Clear scallops, 8″d	125.00
Rayed scallops, 8″d	125.00
Low standard, 9″d	125.00
Cordial, barrel shape bowl, plain stem,	
5 1/4″h	125.00
Egg cup	
Flared	35.00
Straight-sided	35.00
Goblet	
Barrel shape bowl, plain stem	45.00
Bellflower with loops, knob stem	
(VR)	250.00
Fine rib with Bellflower border (VR)	250.00
Knob stem, flared rim	50.00
Plain stem, straight-sided bowl	40.00
Rayed base	45.00

Items made	Clear	Items made	Clear
Ribbed-paneled bowl with small Bellflowers (R)	200.00	Oval Deep, scalloped rim, rayed center, 9³⁄₈"l x 6¹⁄₄"w	55.00
Stippled Bellflower.(VR)	275.00	Round Scalloped rim, 8"d	85.00
Straight stem, clear marginal band around bowl	75.00	Champagne Straight-sided, plain bowl, rayed base	125.00
Variation, 12 fluted panels around lower portion of bowl, hexagonal stem, plain foot (VR)	300.00	Cologne bottle (often marked cologne, often found in opaque green or translucent white), plain space for label	500.00 +
Lamp Bracket style, (VR)	600.00	Compote, open, high standard 9³⁄₄"d, 8¹⁄₂"h	130.00
Pitcher, applied handle Milk, 1 quart, ribbed to the top of lip	250.00	Cordial, straight-sided bowl, plain bowl, rayed base	125.00
Plate, Bellflower motif on diamond point background	125.00	Goblet (fine ribbing) Barrel shape	
Syrup, applied handle, 10 panels	650.00	Knob stem	65.00
Sugar bowl, covered Mushroom finial	100.00	Plain stem	65.00
Octagonal finial	100.00	Straight-sided bowl, ribbed to edge of rim	65.00
Tumbler, water Clear marginal band around top	90.00	Tumbler, slightly flared with two veined leaves, two three-petaled bellflowers	125.00
Straight-sided, plain base	90.00		
Whiskey, applied handle	150.00		

CUT BELLFLOWERS

DOUBLE VINE-COARSE RIB

	Clear		Clear
Celery vase, pedestaled, scalloped rim	225.00	Pitcher, water, applied handle	350.00
Champagne	250.00	Sugar bowl, covered	100.00
Decanter	250.00	Tumbler, water, flat	90.00

MISCELLANEOUS

Bowl, open, flat

BETHLEHEM STAR

Cruet (o.s.)

AKA: Bright Star, Six-Point Star, Star Burst.

Non-flint. Indiana Glass Co., Dunkirk, IN. ca. 1912. The Jefferson Glass Co., Toronto and Montreal, Canada. Illustrated in the Charles "Broadway" Rousse July-August, 1914 general merchandise catalog.

Original color production: Clear.

Reproductions: None.

References: Bond-AG (P. 77), Kam-5 (P. 97), McCn-PGP (P. 501), Mtz-1 (P. 223), Mil-2 (Pl. 104), Uni-1 (P. 289)

Items made	Clear	Items made	Clear
Butter dish, covered	35.00	Cruet, original stopper	35.00
Celery vase, handled	25.00	Goblet	30.00
Compote, covered, high standard		Pitcher, water, $\frac{1}{2}$ gallon	60.00
4$\frac{1}{2}$"d., jelly	50.00	Relish dish, flat	15.00
4$\frac{5}{8}$"d	50.00	Sauce dish, flat, round	10.00
5"d	50.00	Spoonholder	25.00
8"d	65.00	Sugar bowl, covered	40.00
Creamer, 5"h	35.00	Wine	25.00

BEVELED DIAMOND AND STAR

Cruet (o.s.); creamer; goblet; tankard water pitcher (applied handle); covered sugar bowl tumbler.

OMN: Tarentum's Albany. AKA: Diamond Prism [Millard], Diamond Prisms (Metz), Princeton.

Non-flint. Tarentum Glass Co., Tarentum, PA. ca. 1894. Illustrated in the Tarentum Glass Co. ca. 1896 catalog.

Original color production: Clear, clear with ruby stain.

Reproductions: None.

References: Bar-RS (Pl. 8), Hea-5 (P. 48, No. 207), Kam-2 (P. 74), Mil-2 (Pl. 25), Mtz-2 (P. 174), Pet-Sal (P. 156), Pet-GPP (PP. 186, 188), Uni-1 (P. 105), Wlkr-PGA (Fig. 8, No. 38).

Items made	Clear	Clear w/ Ruby
Bowl, open, flat		
7"d	15.00	30.00
8"d	15.00	35.00
Butter dish, covered, flat	40.00	100.00
Cake stand, high standard		
9"d	35.00	90.00
10"d	40.00	90.00
Celery vase	30.00	85.00
Cheese dish, covered, flat	65.00	135.00
Compote high standard		
Covered		
5"d	50.00	175.00
7"d	65.00	225.00
Open, serrated rim		
5"d	30.00	150.00
7"d	40.00	150.00
8"d	45.00	175.00
Cracker jar, covered	45.00	175.00
Creamer, tankard, 5½"h	35.00	75.00
Cruet, original patterned stopper	35.00	135.00+
Decanter, original patterned stopper, 10¾"h	60.00	150.00
Goblet	35.00	65.00
Pickle dish, flat	15.00	30.00
Pitcher		
Milk, 1 quart	40.00	125.00
Water, ½ gallon		
Applied handle	45.00	150.00
Pressed handle	55.00	150.00
Plate, round	10.00	25.00
Sauce dish, round		
Flat	10.00	20.00
Footed	10.00	20.00
Spoonholder	25.00	65.00
Sugar bowl, covered	30.00	85.00
Sugar shaker, original top	35.00	110.00
Syrup pitcher, original top, 7"	35.00	150.00
Toothpick holder	25.00	75.00
Tray, round		
Bread, 7"d	35.00	65.00
Water	35.00	85.00
Tumbler, water, flat, 3¾"h	15.00	35.00
Wine, 4"h	20.00	45.00

BIGLER

Wine; champagne; goblet; champagne; whiskey tumbler.

Flint. Attributed to the Boston & Sandwich Glass Co., Sandwich, MA. ca. 1850s. Most likely other factories.

Original color production: Clear. Amethyst, greenish-yellow or any other color is rare. Of heavy, brilliant flint glass, the main design element of Bigler is reminiscent of its contemporary "Excelsior," the Bigler pattern consisting of two rows of disconnected circles separated by a vertical band overlapping a horizontal band forming the appearance of a "cross." Unlike Excelsior, the centers of such cross bands do not display a smooth diamond ornament.

Reproductions: None.

References: Ben-CG (No. 60), Enos-MPG (Chart-4), Inn-EGP (P. 53), Inn-PG (Plts. 360, 379), Lee-EAPG (Pl. 10, No. 4), Lee-SG (P. 536), McKrn-AG (Plts. 198, 203), Mtz-1 (PP. 20-21), Sav-GW (No. 49), Spil-AEPG (P. 246), Uni-1 (P. 32).

Items made	Clear	Items made	Clear
Ale	60.00	Short stem	45.00
Bottle, bar, 1 quart	80.00	Tall stem	45.00
Bowl, open, flat, round		Lamp, whale oil, monument base,	
Flared rim, 6⅝"d	40.00	original burner	150.00
Straight-sided bowl, 10"d	40.00	Mug, applied handle	65.00
Butter dish, covered	125.00	Plate, toddy, round, 6"d	30.00
Celery vase	100.00	Sugar bowl, covered	90.00
Champagne	75.00	Salt, master, footed, open	20.00
Compote, high standard, open, 7"d	40.00	Tumbler, water, flat	55.00
Cordial	50.00	Whiskey, applied handle	100.00
Creamer	75.00	Vase, scalloped rim, square base,	
Cup plate	30.00	11⅜"h	85.00
Egg cup, double, open, footed	50.00	Wine	45.00
Goblet			

BIRD AND STRAWBERRY

High standard covered compote; water pitcher; goblet; footed oval master berry bowl.

OMN: Indiana Glass No. 157. AKA: Blue Bird, Flying Bird and Strawberry, Strawberry and Bird.

Non-flint. Indiana Glass Co., Dunkirk, IN. ca. 1914.

Original color production: Clear, clear with blue-green-red stain.

Reproductions: Flat celery vase (blue), covered high standard compote (pale green).

References: Bond-AG (PP. 94-95), Kam-2 (P. 85), Mil-1 (Pl. 75), Mil-2 (Pl. 75). Mtz-1 (PP. 104-105), Stu-BP (P. 37), Uni-1 (PP. 186-187).

Items made	Clear	Clear w/ Color
Bowl, open		
Flat, round		
5"d	25.00	45.00
9½"	45.00	85.00
10"d	55.00	95.00
10½"d, flared rim	55.00	90.00
Footed, 3-legged, oval, master berry	45.00	65.00
Butter dish, covered, flat, flanged rim	100.00	200.00
Cake stand, high standard, 10"d	55.00	125.00
Celery		
Tray, flat, serrated rim	45.00	85.00
Vase, flat base, serrated rim	85.00	125.00
Compote		
Covered, high standard		
4½"d, jelly (VR)	165.00	275.00
6½"d	125.00	200.00
Open, low standard, ruffled rim, 6"d	85.00	125.00
Creamer	45.00	125.00
Cup, punch	25.00	35.00
Hat, made from a tumbler (VR)	250.00	
Goblet		
Barrel shaped bowl	175.00	200.00
Flared bowl (VR)	225.00	275.00
Pitcher, water	250.00	350.00 +

Items made	Clear	Clear w/ Color
Plate		
Chop, round, flat		
11"d	125.00	150.00
12"d	125.00	150.00
Sandwich, 6¹/₄"d (R)	85.00	—
Relish dish, heart shaped	40.00	85.00
Sauce dish, round		
Flat	20.00	30.00
Footed, splayed legs	25.00	30.00
Spoonholder, flat	45.00	100.00
Sugar bowl, covered, double handles	65.00	125.00
Tumbler, water, flat (2 sizes)	45.00	65.00
Wine	55.00	150.00

BLACKBERRY, Hobb's

Spoonholder and celery vase (both milk white).

AKA: Messereau Blackberry.

Non-flint. Hobbs, Brockunier & Co., Wheeling, WV. ca. 1870.

Original color production: Clear, milk white. Odd pieces such as spoonholders and creamers may be found with dated bases. Designed and patented by John H. Hobbs, February 1, 1870 (patent No. 3,829).

Reproductions: The Phoenix Glass Co., Monaca, PA., acquiring the original molds to the Blackberry pattern from the Co-Operative Glass Co., Beaver Falls, PA. in 1937, reissued the following items in clear and milk white: covered butter dish, celery vase, creamer, single egg cup, goblet, covered sugar bowl and water pitcher. A comparison of original items to reissues shows new items to have a blurred design of poor quality, the new milk white color being more pearl-like in appearance than the old. Original milk white items appear near opaline when held to a bright light. Apparently two sets of molds were used in the production of the pattern: one for clear items, one for milk white items, as both forms differ.

References: Belnp-MG (PP. 33, 214), Brn-SD (PP. 48-49), Cod-OS (P. 15), Drep-ABC OG (Pl. 53), Eige-CGM WV WV (PP. 5-6), Fer-YMG (PP. 144-145), Kam-5 (P. 116), Kam-8 (P. 25), Lee-EAPG (Pl. 150-151), Lee-VG (P. 562, Pl. 6), McCn-PGP (P. 325), McKrn-AG (Plts. 210-211), Mil-1 (Pl. 132), Mil-OG (Plts. 192, 196), Mtz-1 (P. 88), Rev-APG (PP. 185-186), Spil-AEPG (P. 285), Thu-1 (P. 156), Uni-1 (P. 231), Weath-FOST (P. 144), Wlkr-PGA (Fig. 8, Nos. 18, 24, 36).

Items made	Clear	Milk White
Butter dish, covered with insert for ice	40.00	60.00
Celery vase		
High standard	60.00	90.00
Low standard	60.00	90.00
Champagne	35.00	45.00
Compote, covered		
High standard.	50.00	65.00
Low standard	35.00	45.00
Creamer, $4^3/_8''$h	55.00	65.00
Dish, oval, open, flat, $5^1/_2''$ x $8^1/_4''$	20.00	30.00
Egg cup		
Double	30.00	40.00
Single	30.00	40.00
Goblet (R)	45.00	65.00
Honey dish, flat, round	8.00	15.00
Lamp, oil, complete with original burner and chimney		
$8^1/_2''$h	100.00	—
$9^1/_2''$h	125.00	—
$11^3/_4''$h	145.00	—
Pitcher, water, bulbous, applied handle, $^1/_2$ gallon	100.00	150.00
Relish, flat	15.00	30.00
Salt, master, footed, open	20.00	30.00
Sauce dish, round, flat, $4^1/_2''$d	8.00	15.00
Spoonholder, pedestaled, scalloped rim	25.00	35.00
Sugar bowl, covered	65.00	85.00
Syrup pitcher, original top, $6^7/_8''$h (R)	150.00	225.00
Tumbler, water, flat	25.00	—
Wine	25.00	35.00

BLAZE

Goblet; footed tumbler; cologne (o.s.); champagne.

OMN: Blaze.

Flint. New England Glass Co., East Cambridge, MA. ca. 1869. Illustrated in the 1869 New England Glass Co. catalog as "Blaze."

Original color production: Clear.

Reproductions: None.

References: Bat-GPG (PP. 23, 25), Chip-ROS (P. 87), Lee-EAPG (PP. 63-64), McCn-PGP (P. 449), McKrn-AG (Pl. 208), Mil-1 (Pl. 76), Mtz-1 (P. 53), Rev-APG (P. 261), Uni-1 (P. 157), Wat-CG (PP. 100-101), Wlkr-PGA (Fig. 8, No. 45).

Items made	Clear	Items made	Clear
Bowl, flat, round		Deep bowl	
Covered		6″d	80.00
5½″d	65.00	7″d	85.00
6″d	80.00	8″d	90.00
7″d	85.00	Shallow bowl	
8″d	90.00	6″d	80.00
Open		7″d	85.00
5″d	30.00	8″d	90.00
5½″d	30.00	Low standard	
6″d	35.00	Deep Bowl	
7″d	40.00	6″d	65.00
Butter dish, covered, flat	75.00	7″d	70.00
Celery vase	80.00	8″d	75.00
Champagne	85.00	Shallow Bowl	
Cheese dish, covered		6″d	65.00
"Blaze" cover	65.00	7″d	70.00
"Plain" cover	50.00	8″d	75.00
Open, round, 6″d	30.00	Open	
Cologne bottle, o.s	65.00	High standard	
Compote		Deep Bowl	
Covered		6″d	35.00
High standard		7″d	40.00

Items made	Clear	Items made	Clear
8"d	45.00	Cup, custard, handled	20.00
Shallow Bowl		Dish, open, oval, flat	
6"d	35.00	7"	35.00
7"d	40.00	8"	40.00
8"d	45.00	9"	45.00
9"d	45.00	10"	50.00
10"d	50.00	Egg cup, applied handle	65.00
Low standard		Goblet	45.00
Deep bowl		Honey dish, 3½"d	15.00
6"d	35.00	Plate, cheese, round, 7"d	35.00
7"d	40.00	Salt, master, oblong, flat, open	30.00
8"d	45.00	Sauce dish, flat, round, 4"d	10.00
9"d	45.00	Spoonholder	35.00
10"d	50.00	Sugar bowl, covered	85.00
Shallow bowl		Tumbler, flat	
6"d	35.00	Gill	55.00
7"d	40.00	Lemonade	55.00
8"d	45.00	Water, ½ pint	55.00
Cordial	65.00	Footed	55.00
Creamer	55.00	Wine	65.00

BLEEDING HEART

Water tumbler; creamer (appied handle); egg server; creamer (pressed handle); egg cup.

OMN: King's Floral Ware, U.S. Glass Co.'s No. 85 or "New Floral".

Non-flint. King, Son & Co., Pittsburgh, PA. ca. 1875. Reissued by the United States Glass Co., Pittsburgh, PA., at Factory "C" (Challinor, Taylor And Co., Tarentum, PA.) ca. 1899. Shards have been found at the site of the Boston & Sandwich Glass Co., Sandwich, MA. and the Burlington Glass Works, Hamilton, Ontario, Canada. The Specialty Co., East Liverpool, OH. (only the goblet and mug) ca. 1888. Illustrated in the King, Son & Co. 1875 catalog.

Original color production: Clear. Milk white or any other color is rare. The main design element consists of realistic bleeding heart flowers. Water pitchers are bulbous with applied handles and low circular feet. Creamers may be found in two distinct styles: a) applied handle with pedestaled foot, and b) pressed handle with low circular foot. Standards may be straight, hexagonal or hexagonal with slightly bulbous mid sections. Finials are in the shape of large bleeding hearts. Covered items attributed to the Boston & Sandwich Glass Co. have a cable cord at the edge where the cover joins, with a row of dots on the outer underside of the rim where the cover joins on such items as compotes, sugar bowls, and butter dishes.

Reproductions: None.

References: Bat-GPG (PP. 89, 91), Drep-ABC OG (P. 161), Enos-MPG (Chart-1), Hea-5 (P. 15), Inn-PG (PP. 301, 336), Kam-1 (P. 8), Kam-8 (Pl. 82), Kam/Wed Vol. 1 (P. 87), Lee-EAPG (Pl. 128, Nos. 1-2), Lee-VG (P. 22), McCn-PGP (P. 289), Mtz-1 (PP. 58-59), Mtz-2 (PP. 74-75), Oliv-AAG (P. 59), Pap-GAG (P. 196), Pyne-PG (P. 26), Rev-APG (PP. 211-213), Spil-AEPG (P. 268), Spil-TBV (PP. 31, 318), Uni/Wor-CHPGT (P. 50), Uni-1 (P. 239), Wlkr-PGA (Fig. 8, Nos. 19, 24, 17).

Items made	Clear	Items made	Clear
Bowl, flat		Open, oval, 7³⁄₈″	30.00
Covered, round		Egg cup, footed, open	
6″	40.00	Barreled sides	40.00
9¹⁄₄″	65.00	Straight sides	40.00
Open		Egg server, footed, covered (VR)	250.00
Oval		Goblet	
5″	20.00	Barrel shaped bowl, heavy design,	
7″	20.00	knob stem	35.00
7¹⁄₄″	20.00	Jelly container, poor design, plain	
8″	30.00	stem, original tin cover	20.00
9″	35.00	Straight-sided bowl, knob stem	35.00
9¹⁄₄″	40.00	Straight-sided bowl, thin design,	
Round		knob stem	35.00
5″d	20.00	Honey dish, flat, 3¹⁄₂″d	20.00
7″d	25.00	Mug, pressed handle, 3¹⁄₄″h, original	
8″d	30.00	tin cover	55.00
Waste, flat, open	65.00	Pickle tray, oval, pear shaped, 8³⁄₄″ x 5″	40.00
Butter dish, covered, flat, 4″h.,		Pitcher	
bleeding heart finial	65.00	Milk, 1 quart, bulbous, applied	
Cake stand, high standard		handle	125.00
9″d	75.00	Water, ¹⁄₂ gallon, bulbous, applied	
10″d	90.00	handle, footed	150.00
11″d	95.00	Plate, round (R)	75.00
Compote		Platter, oval	65.00
High standard		Relish tray	
Covered, bleeding heart finial		4 divisions	85.00
7″d	85.00	Oval, 5¹⁄₂″ x 3⁵⁄₈″	35.00
8″d	90.00	Salt, master	
9″d	95.00	Flat, oval, open, smooth rim	85.00
Open, 8″d	40.00	Footed, round, open, smooth rim	50.00
Low standard		Sauce dish, flat	
Oval	100.00	Round	
Round		3¹⁄₂″d	15.00
Covered		4″d	15.00
7″d	85.00	5″d	15.00
7¹⁄₄″d	85.00	Oval	
8″d	90.00	3¹⁄₂″	15.00
Open		4″	15.00
8¹⁄₂″d	40.00	5″	15.00
Creamer		Spoonholder, pedestaled, scalloped rim	30.00
Flat, pressed handle	35.00	Sugar bowl, covered, bleeding heart	
Footed, applied handle, 5³⁄₄″h	65.00	finial	
Dish, flat		Short footed	90.00
Covered, 7″d	50.00	Tall footed	90.00

Items made	Clear	Items made	Clear
Tumbler		Footed	85.00
Flat, ½ pint	90.00	Wine	175.00

BLOCK AND FAN

Wine; ice bucket; celery vase.

OMN: Richards & Hartley's No. 544. AKA: Block with Fan [Lee], Block with Fan Border [Lee], Red Block and Fan [Millard], Romeo.

Non-flint. Richards & Hartley Glass Co. (pattern line No. 544), Tarentum, PA., ca. 1885 with continued production by the United States Glass Co., Pittsburgh, PA., at Factory "E" (Richards & Hartley, Tarentum, PA.) after 1891. Shards have been found at the site of the Burlington Glass Works, Hamilton, Ontario, Canada. Reviewed in the August 1, 1889 issue of *The Crockery and Glass Journal*, and illustrated in an undated Richards & Hartley Glass Co. catalog, and the United States Glass Co. ca. 1891 catalog.

Original color production: Clear, clear with ruby stain. Produced in an extended table service.

Reproductions: None.

References: Bar-RS (Pl. 6), (PP. 152-153), Hea-3 (P. 81), Hea-5 (P. 108, Plts. A-D), Hea-7 (Fig. 206), Kam-3 (P. 75), Kam/Wod-Vol. 1 (P. 59), Lee-EAPG (Pl. 187), Lee-VG (Pl. 41, No. 3), Luc-TG (PP. 214-220), McCn-PGP (Pl. 240), Mtz-1 (P. 154-155), Pet-Sal (P. 23), Rev-APG (PP. 286-288), Stev-ECG (P. 67), Stu-BP (P. 19), Uni-1 (P. 105), Uni/Wor-CHPGT (P. 54), Wlkr-PGA (Fig. 8, No. 43).

Items made	Clear	Clear w/ Ruby
Biscuit jar, covered	65.00	125.00
Bowl, open		
Round		
Collared base		
7"d	15.00	20.00

Items made	Clear	Clear w/ Ruby
8"d	20.00	30.00
10"d	25.00	40.00
Flat		
6"d	25.00	35.00
7"d	25.00	45.00
8"d	45.00	55.00
9½"d	45.00	55.00
10"d	45.00	55.00
Finger	55.00	55.00
Rectangular, 6" x 10"	50.00	60.00
Rose, 7"	25.00	—
Waste	35.00	—
Butter dish, covered, flat	50.00	85.00
Cake stand high standard		
9"d	35.00	—
10"d.	40.00	—
Carafe, 8½"h	40.00	95.00
Castor set tray	20.00	35.00
Celery		
Tray	30.00	60.00
Vase	35.00	75.00
Compote high standard, round		
Covered		
7"d	65.00	100.00
8"d	75.00	125.00
Open, scalloped rim		
7"d	35.00	165.00
8"d	40.00	165.00
Collared base		
4"d	10.00	—
7"d	25.00	—
8"d	30.00	—
Condiment set (under tray, salt, pepper, cruet)	100.00	-
Cracker jar, covered	85.00	145.00
Creamer, pressed handle		
Individual	25.00	35.00
Large	30.00	100.00
Small	35.00	75.00
Table size	25.00	45.00
Cruet, original stopper, 4 ounce, 8½"h	40.00	200.00
Decanter, handled	65.00	—
Dish, open, flat		
Oblong, ice cream	25.00	—
Rectangular	25.00	—
Goblet, 6"h	45.00	85.00
Ice bucket	45.00	75.00
Lamp	50.00	—
Pickle dish, oblong	20.00	35.00
Pitcher		
Milk, 1 quart	35.00	—
Water, ½ gallon, 7¾"h	45.00	125.00
Plate, round		
6"d	20.00	—
10"d	25.00	—
Relish tray, oval, flat	25.00	40.00
Rose bowl, smooth rim, flat	25.00	—
Salt shaker, tall, original top	15.00	35.00
Sauce dish, round		

Items made	Clear	Clear w/ Ruby
Flat		
4"d	8.00	20.00
5"d	8.00	20.00
Footed		
3³⁄₄"d	12.00	25.00
4"d	15.00	25.00
5"d	15.00	25.00
Spoonholder	25.00	45.00
Sugar bowl, covered	50.00	85.00
Sugar shaker, original top	45.00	125.00
Syrup pitcher, original top	65.00	150.00
Tumbler, water, flat	30.00	55.00
Wine, 3³⁄₄"h	45.00	65.00

BOW TIE

Tumbler; covered sugar; high standard compote; goblet; covered butter.

OMN: Thompson's No. 18. AKA: American Bow Tie.

Non-flint. Thompson Glass Co. (pattern line No. 18), Uniontown, PA. ca. 1889.

Original color production: Clear.

References: Hea-OS (Pl. 135, No. 2548), Kam-6 (P. 50, Pl. 17), Mtz-1 (P. 211), Mil-1 (Pl. 5), Mil-2 (Pl. 5), Mtz-2 (PP. 116-117), Pet-Sal (P. 23), Rev-APG (PP. 302-303), Uni-1 (P. 205), Wlkr-PGA (Fig. 8, No. 5).

Items made	Clear	Items made	Clear
Bowl, open		7"d	30.00
Footed, fruit, plain rim, 10"d	50.00	8"d	35.00
Flat		10¼"d	65.00
Round		10³⁄₈"d	65.00
Smooth rim		Flared rim, 8"d	35.00
6"d	30.00	Scalloped rim, 10¼"d	65.00

Items made	Clear	Items made	Clear
Rectangular, scalloped rim		Orange bowl, high standard, 10"d	85.00
4¼"x 7"	20.00	Pitcher	
5¼" x 8"	25.00	Milk, 1 quart	
5⅝" x 9"	25.00	5½"h	55.00
Butter dish, covered, flat	65.00	6½"h	55.00
Butter pat, flat, 2¾"d	35.00	Water, ½ gallon	
Cake stand, high standard, 9¼"d	85.00	7"h	75.00
Celery vase	85.00	8"h	75.00
Compote, open		9"h	75.00
High standard		Punch bowl, flat, one-piece, scalloped	
Flared-scalloped rim		rim	100.00
7"d	55.00	Relish dish, rectangular	25.00
9"d	65.00	Salt	
Smooth rim		Individual, 1⅛"h, 1½"d	20.00
5½"d	55.00	Master, round, open, smooth rim,	
8¼"d	65.00	1½"h., 3⅛"d	35.00
9¼"d	65.00	Shaker, tall, original top	65.00
10⅜"d	75.00	Sauce dish, round	
Low standard		Scalloped rim	
Smooth rim		Flat, 4"d	20.00
6½"d	45.00	Footed, 4"d	25.00
8"d	55.00	Smooth rim	
Scalloped rim		Flat, 4"d	20.00
6½"d	45.00	Footed, 4"d	25.00
8"d	55.00	Spoonholder, flat, scalloped rim, 4⅞"h	35.00
Creamer, 5"h	45.00	Sugar bowl, covered	55.00
Goblet, 5¾"h	65.00	Tumbler, water, flat, 4"h (R)	65.00
Jam jar, covered, 4½"h	55.00		

BRILLIANT

Tumbler.

OMN: Brilliant.

Flint. McKee & Brothers, Pittsburgh, PA. ca. 1864. Illustrated in the McKee & Brothers 1864 and 1868 catalogs.

Original color production: Clear.

Reproductions: None.

References: Enos-MPG (Chart-3), Inn/Spil-McKe (PP. 36-37), Lee-EAPG (Pl. 153, No. 14), Lee-VG (Pl. 95), Mil-1 (Pl. 125), Mtz-1 (Pl. 20), Rev-APG (PP. 231, 237), Stot-McKe (P. 41), Uni-1 (P. 284).

Items made	Clear	Items made	Clear
Bowl, flat, open, round	40.00	Low standard, 8″d	60.00
Butter dish, covered	65.00	Creamer, applied handle	70.00
Champagne	75.00	Egg cup	35.00
Compote		Goblet	55.00
Covered, high standard, 6″d.,		Spoonholder	45.00
sweetmeat	55.00	Sugar bowl, covered	55.00
Open		Tumbler, water, flat	75.00
High standard, 8″d	60.00	Wine	45.00

BRILLIANT, Riverside's

Water tumbler (clear with ruby stain).

OMN: Riverside's No. 436, Brilliant. AKA: Petalled Medallion [Metz], Miami.

Non-flint. Riverside Glass Works (pattern line No. 436), Wellsburg, WV. ca. 1895. Advertised in *China, Glass and Lamps* in 1895.

Original color production: Clear, clear with ruby stained (plain or copper wheel engraved). Occasional items may be found in clear with amber stain. Clear with ruby stained items are often found souvenired.

Reproductions: None.

References: Bar-RS (Pl. 13), Belnp-MG (P. 203), Boul-TPS (P. 28), Hea-1 (P. 16, Fig. 35), Hea-3 (P. 16), Hea-6 (Pl. 13), Hea-7 (P. 58, Nos. 768-771), Kam-6 (Pl. 65), McCn-PGP (P. 119), Mig-TPS (Pl. 11), Mtz-2 (PP. 154-155), Pet-Sal (P. 23), Rev-APG (P. 296), Uni-2 (P. 73).

Items made	Clear	Clear w/ Ruby
Bowl, open, flat, master berry	25.00	40.00
Butter dish, covered	40.00	100.00
Celery vase	35.00	85.00
Compote, covered, high standard	85.00	225.00
Creamer		
Individual	20.00	35.00
Table size	30.00	65.00
Goblet	35.00	65.00
Pitcher, water, ½ gallon	85.00	185.00
Salt shaker, tall, original top	25.00	40.00
Sauce dish, flat, round	10.00	22.00
Spoonholder	20.00	35.00
Sugar bowl		
Individual, true open	20.00	35.00
Table size, covered	35.00	65.00
Syrup pitcher, original top	50.00	225.00
Toothpick holder	35.00	150.00
Tumbler, water, flat	20.00	40.00
Wine	30.00	45.00

BRITANNIC

Castor set, 4 bottles (complete).

OMN: Britannic. AKA: Brittanic.

Non-flint. McKee & Brothers Glass Works (National Glass Co.), Pittsburgh, PA. ca. 1894 to after 1903. Illustrated in the McKee Glass Co. catalog of 1894 and in the McKee/National Glass Co. catalog ca. 1901. Lamps were added to the line in 1895.

Original color production: Clear, clear with ruby stain, clear with amber stain (plain or copper wheel engraved). Emerald green or any other color is rare.

Reproductions: None.

References: Bar-RS (Pl. 11), Hea-1 (P. 16, Fig. 34), Hea-2 (P. 119), Hea-6 (Figs. 20, 45), Hea-7 (Figs. 423-435), Hea-RUTPS (Fig. 230), Hea-TPS (PP. 27, 52), Kam-4 (PP. 71-72), Kam-5 (P. 27), Kam/Wod-Vol. 1 (P. 32), McCn-PGP (Pl. 234), Pet-Sal (P. 122), Stot-McKe (PP. 209,216), Thur-1 (P. 284), Uni-2 (P. 131), Wlkr-PGA (Fig. 15, No. 33).

Items made	Clear	Clear w/ Ruby
Basket, fruit	55.00	150.00
Banana stand	75.00	100.00
Bottle		
Cologne, o.s	45.00	125.00
Water	65.00	150.00
Bowl, open		
Oblong		
Crimped rim	30.00	40.00
Smooth rim	30.00	40.00
Oval, shallow bowl, serrated rim		
7″	30.00	40.00
8″	30.00	40.00
9″	30.00	45.00
Round		
Crimped rim. 8″d	25.00	35.00
Smooth rim, 8″d	25.00	35.00
Rose bowl	30.00	75.00
Square		
Cupped rim	25.00	40.00
Smooth rim	25.00	40.00
Butter dish, covered, flat	45.00	100.00
Cake stand		
Large	45.00	225.00
Small	55.00	200.00
Castor set, 4 bottle, glass holder, complete	125.00	275.00
Celery		
Tray	35.00	60.00
Vase	40.00	85.00
Compote, high standard, round		
Covered	55.00	225.00
Open		
Flared, scalloped rim		
7½″d	35.00	80.00
8½″d	40.00	85.00
10″d	65.00	90.00
Smooth rim		
5″d	30.00	70.00
6″d	35.00	80.00
7″d	40.00	85.00
8″d	45.00	55.00
Creamer, applied handle		
Bulbous	40.00	65.00
Tankard	40.00	75.00
Cruet, original stopper	50.00	150.00
Cup, custard	10.00	20.00
Dish		
Olive, handled, flat		
Crimped rim	20.00	35.00
Smooth rim	20.00	35.00
Pickle, flat		
Crimped rim	20.00	40.00
Smooth rim	20.00	40.00

Items made	Clear	Clear w/ Ruby
Goblet	35.00	50.00
Honey dish, covered, square	55.00	185.00
Jar, cracker, covered	50.00	185.00
Lamp		
Low foot, handled (2 types), original burner and chimney	65.00	—
Stand		
7½"h	95.00	—
8½"h	110.00	—
Mug, 3¾"h	15.00	25.00
Pitcher, water, applied handle		
Bulbous, ½ gallon	50.00	150.00
Tankard, ½ gallon	60.00	175.00
Salt shaker, squatty, original top	20.00	35.00
Sauce dish		
Round		
Flat	10.00	30.00
Footed	10.00	30.00
Square, flat	10.00	30.00
Spoonholder	45.00	50.00
Sugar bowl, covered	65.00	85.00
Syrup pitcher, original lid	55.00	225.00
Toothpick holder	25.00	150.00
Tray, ice cream	40.00	85.00
Tumbler, water, flat	25.00	40.00
Vase	35.00	75.00
Wine	35.00	55.00

BROKEN COLUMN

Sugar shaker; water pitcher; 8″ h.s. covered compote; celery vase; spoonholder.

OMN: U.S. Glass No. 15,021, Bamboo. AKA: Broken Column with Red Dots [Millard], Irish Column, Notched Rib [Brothers], Rattan, Broken Irish Column, Ribbed Fingerprint.

Non-flint. Columbia Glass Co., Findlay, OH. ca. 1888. Reissued by the United States Glass Co. (pattern line No. 15,021), Pittsburgh, PA. after ca. 1893 to as late as 1900 at Factory "E"

(Richards & Hartley Glass Co., Tarentum, PA.) and "J" (Columbia Glass Co., Findlay, OH.). Advertised in the Montgomery Ward's 1884 catalog, Broken Column is illustrated in the United States Glass Co. catalogs of 1892, 1895-1896, and the 1898 catalog as "Bamboo".

Original color production: Clear. Clear with ruby stain, most likely done after the U.S. Glass merger. Odd pieces may be found in cobalt blue (R). Produced in an extended table service.

Reproductions: Reissues of Broken Column have appeared from the early 1960s. These are heavier in weight than the original.

The L.G. Wright Glass Company, New Martinsville, WV. (distributed by Jennings Red Barn, New Martinsville, WV. and Carl Forslund, Grand Rapids, MI.) reissued a clear goblet from a new mold in the early 1960s which was still being illustrated in the company's 1970 catalog supplement.

Beginning in the mid 1970s, The Smithsonian Institution, Washington, D.C. (through the Imperial Glass Co.) and the Metropolitan Museum of Art, New York City, began to authorize the reissue of numerous items in clear glass from new molds, faithfully following the original design and measurements. Each item has been permanently embossed with the institution's insignia: a) "S.I." (Smithsonian Institution) and b) "M.M.A." (Metropolitan Museum of Art). The following items have been reissued: round, open, flat 8"d. and $8^{1}/_{2}$"d. bowl; 10 oz. creamer; 6"h. goblet; 9"h., 40 oz. water pitcher; 8"d. round plate; $4^{1}/_{2}$"d. round sauce dish; $4^{1}/_{2}$"h. spoonholder; $5^{1}/_{4}$"h. covered sugar bowl; and 6"h. wine. Both institutions were still offering these items for sale throughout the 1980s.

References: Bar-RS (Pl. 5), Bros-TS (P. 29), Hea-3 (P. 16), Hea-5 (P. 47, Plts. 179-183), Hea-6 (P. 96), Hea-7 (Figs. 78-87), Inn-PG (P. 381), Inn/Spil- (P. 381), Kam-4 (Pl. 116), Kam-6 (Pl. 5), Lee-VG (Pl. 71, No. 3), McCn-PGP (Pl. 204), Meas/Smth-FG (PP. 36-37), Mtz-1 (PP. 140-141), Mil-1 (Pl. 139), Mil-2 (Pl. 69), Pet-Sal (P. 55), Rev-APG (PP. 286-287), Smth-FG (PP. 36-37), Spil-AEPG (P. 311), Swn-PG (P. 69), Uni-1 (PP. 26-27), Wlkr-PGA (Fig. 8, No. 5).

Items made	Clear	Clear w/ Ruby
Banana stand		
Flat	65.00	—
High standard, 9"d	110.00	—
Basket, applied handle, 12"h, 15"l	125.00	—
Biscuit jar, covered	85.00	150.00
Bottle, water	65.00	175.00
Bowl, flat		
Covered		
Deep		
5"d	45.00	150.00
6"d	55.00	175.00
7"d	65.00	200.00
8"d	75.00	200.00
Open		
Deep		
5"d	20.00	—
6"d	30.00	100.00
7"d	35.00	100.00
8"d	40.00	125.00
Shallow		
5"d	20.00	—
6"d	30.00	100.00
7"d	35.00	125.00
8"d	40.00	—
9"d	45.00	—

Items made	Clear	Clear w/ Ruby
Finger, round	45.00	—
Bread plate	60.00	125.00
Butter dish, covered, flat, 7¹/₃"d	85.00	175.00
Cake stand, high standard		
9"d	85.00	250.00
10"d	85.00	250.00
Celery		
Tray, oval, 7"l	35.00	110.00
Vase, 6"h	50.00	135.00
Champagne	110.00	175.00
Claret	85.00	175.00
Compote		
Covered, high standard		
5"d	65.00	200.00
6"d	65.00	200.00
7"d	75.00	350.00
8"d	75.00	350.00
Open		
High standard		
Round Bowl		
5"d	35.00	90.00
6"d	35.00	90.00
7"d	45.00	125.00
8"d	55.00	145.00
Belled bowl		
5"d	35.00	90.00
6"d	35.00	90.00
7"d	45.00	125.00
8"d	55.00	145.00
Flared bowl		
5"d	35.00	90.00
6"d	35.00	90.00
7"d	45.00	125.00
8"d	55.00	145.00
Low standard, 5"d	65.00	125.00
Cracker jar, covered	95.00	—
Creamer	40.00	125.00
Cruet, 6 ounce, original patterned stopper	55.00	250.00
Cup, custard	25.00	40.00
Decanter, wine, lapidary stopper	95.00	150.00
Dish, flat, open		
Oblong		
5¹/₂", olive	25.00	65.00
7"l	35.00	75.00
8"l	40.00	85.00
9"l	40.00	90.00
Rectangular	40.00	—
Goblet	45.00	110.00
Honey dish, round, flat	10.00	25.00
Pickle		
Castor, complete with silver plate frame	100.00	350.00
Dish, oblong, flat	30.00	65.00
Jar, covered	85.00	125.00
Pitcher, water, ¹/₂ gallon, pressed handle	90.00	200.00
Plate, round		
4"d	30.00	45.00
5"d	35.00	50.00
6"d	35.00	75.00

Items made	Clear	Clear w/ Ruby
7"d	35.00	85.00
7½"d	40.00	95.00
8"d	35.00	65.00
Relish, flat, oval		
7½" x 4"	25.00	125.00
11" x 5"	25.00	125.00
Salt shaker, 3"h., original top	55.00	85.00
Sauce dish, flat, round		
4"d	15.00	30.00
4¼"d	15.00	30.00
Saucer	25.00	35.00
Spoonholder, flat, 4½"h	35.00	85.00
Sugar bowl, covered	75.00	150.00
Sugar shaker, original top	65.00	250.00
Syrup pitcher, original top	135.00	400.00
Tumbler, 4"h., water, 9 ounce	45.00	65.00
Vegetable bowl, covered, flat	90.00	—
Wine, 4"h	65.00	125.00

BUCKLE, EARLY

Wine; spoonholder; water tumbler.

OMN: Gillinder's No. 15. AKA: Buckle.

Flint, non-flint. Maker unknown. Attributed by Lee to Gillinder & Sons (pattern line No. 15), Pittsburgh, PA., ca. late 1870's. Shards have been found at the site of the Boston & Sandwich Glass Co., Sandwich, MA., the Union Glass Co., Somerville, MA., and the Burlington Glass Works, Hamilton, Ontario, Canada.

Original color production: Clear. Sapphire blue, opaque white or any other color is rare. Pieces may be found with either plain or rayed bases on goblets. The berry bowl was originally produced with a wire basket.

Produced by various factories, variations may be found with different sized points in the "buckle" design.

Reproductions: None.

References: Belnp-MG (P. 114), Brn-SD (PP. 55), Cod-OS (P. 19), Kam-5 (P. 8), Kam/Wod-Vol.11 (P. 102), Lee-EAPG (Pl. 102, No. 4), McKrn-AG (Pl. 209), Mtz-1 (PP. 122-123), Mil-1 (Pl. 110), Mtz-2 (PP. 112, 115), Rev-APG (PP. 304-305), Spil-AEPG (P. 276), Thur-1 (P. 113), Uni-1 (P. 153), Uni/Wor-CHPGT (P. 57).

Items made	Flint	Non-flint
Bowl, open, flat, smooth rim		
8¼"d, wire basket frame	60.00	50.00
9"d	60.00	50.00
10"d	65.00	55.00
Butter dish, covered	60.00	50.00
Cake stand, h.s., 9¾"d	—	30.00
Celery vase	—	30.00
Champagne	50.00	40.00
Compote		
Covered		
High standard, 6"d	95.00	40.00
Low standard, 6"d	95.00	40.00
Open		
High standard, 8½"d	45.00	40.00
Low standard, 8½"d	40.00	35.00
Cordial	75.00	—
Creamer, applied handle	110.00	40.00
Egg cup, single	35.00	25.00
Goblet	40.00	30.00
Lamp, kerosene, original burner and chimney	150.00	—
Pickle dish, flat	40.00	15.00
Pitcher, water, bulbous, applied handle	650.00+	100.00
Relish tray, oval	35.00	15.00
Salt, master, open		
Flat, oval	30.00	15.00
Footed		
Plain rim	25.00	15.00
Scalloped rim	25.00	15.00
Sauce dish, 4"d, flat, round		
Plain rim	10.00	8.00
Cable edge rim	15.00	10.00
Spoonholder, pedestaled, scalloped rim, 5½"h	40.00	35.00
Sugar bowl, covered, 8"h	75.00	55.00
Tumbler, water, flat	55.00	30.00
Wine	90.00	45.00

BUCKLE WITH STAR

Creamer; celery vase; covered sugar bowl; wine.

OMN: Bryce's Orient. AKA: Buckle And Star, Late Buckle and Star.

Non-flint. Bryce, Walker & Co., Pittsburgh, PA., ca. 1880. Reissued by the United States Glass Co. at Factory "B" (Bryce Brothers, Pittsburgh, PA.) ca. 1891. Shards have been found at the site of the Burlington Glass Works, Hamilton, Ontario, Canada. Illustrated in the 1880 Bryce, Walker & Co. catalog, and ca. 1891 United States Glass Co. catalogs.

Original color production: Clear. Covered items have a maltese cross finial.

Reproductions: None.

References: Cod-OS (Pl. 22), Hea-3 (PP. 77-78), Hea-5 (P. 85), Hlms-BCA (P. 278), Kam-1 (PP. 20-21), Kam-2 (P. 132), Kam/Wed Vol. 1 (P. 101), Lee-EAPG (Pl. 166, No. 2), McCn-PGP (P. 247), Mil-1 (Pl. 110), Mtz-1 (PP. 122-123), Rev-APG (PP. 87-88), Uni-1 (P. 539), Uni/Wor-CHPGT (P. 59), Wlkr-PGA (Fig. 8, Nos. 15, 43, 54).

Items made	Clear	Items made	Clear
Bowl, oval, flat		Mustard, covered, oval	75.00
Covered, 6"d	25.00	Pickle dish, round, flat, handled	15.00
Open, plain rim		Pitcher, water, bulbous, applied handle	75.00
7"l	15.00	Relish tray	15.00
8"l	15.00	Salt, master, open, footed	20.00
9"l	15.00	Sauce dish, round, star center	
10"l	20.00	Flat	
Butter dish, covered, flat	50.00	4"d	8.00
Cake stand, high standard	30.00	4½"d	8.00
Celery vase	30.00	Footed	
Cologne bottle, pedestaled, bulbous,		4"d	10.00
original stopper	65.00	4½"d	10.00
Compote		Spoonholder	25.00
Covered, high standard, 7"d	60.00	Sugar bowl, covered	40.00
Open, high standard, 9½"d	30.00	Syrup pitcher, applied handle, original	
Creamer, 6"h, pressed handle	35.00	Britannia or pewter lid	85.00
Goblet	30.00	Tumbler, water	
Honey dish, flat or footed, round,		Handled	55.00
3½"d	8.00	Handleless	55.00
Mug	60.00	Wine	35.00

Goblet.

Non-flint. Maker unknown, ca. 1870.

Original color production: Clear.

Reproductions: None.

References: Kam-8 (P. 6), McCn-PGP (P. 425), Mil-1 (P. 47), Mtz-1 (PP. 68-69), Lee-EAPG (Pl. 119, No. 2), Wlkr-PGA (Fig. 8, Nos. 7, 20, 27).

Items made	Clear	Items made	Clear
Butter dish, covered, flat	45.00	Relish tray	15.00
Compote, covered		Salt, master, footed, open	25.00
High standard	60.00	Sauce dish, round, 4″d.	
Low standard	45.00	Flat	8.00
Creamer, 5⅛″h, pressed handle	30.00	Footed	8.00
Egg cup, footed	25.00	Spoonholder	25.00
Goblet	30.00	Sugar bowl, covered	45.00
Pitcher, water, applied handle, ½		Syrup pitcher, original top	45.00
gallon	50.00	Wine	35.00

Wine; champagne; goblet; egg cup; tumbler.

Cologne bottle (o.s.); decanter w/bar lip.

OMN: New England Glass Co.'s Lawrence.

Flint, non-flint. Boston & Sandwich Glass Co., Sandwich, MA. ca. 1860s. New England Glass Co., East Cambridge, MA. ca. 1869. Illustrated in the 1869 New England Glass Co. catalog.

Original color production: Clear. Firey opalescent, milk white or any other color in flint is rare. Colored, non-flint items are of later production.

Reproductions: None.

References: Bat-GPG (PP. 9, 13), Drep-ABC OG (P. 177), Grow-WCG (Fig. 35), Inn-EGP (P. 53), Inn-PG (P. 418), Lee-EAPG (Pl. 49, Nos. 1-2), Lee-VG (PP. 14, 22), Mil-1 (Pl. 87), Mtz-1 (PP. 12-13), Oliv-AAG (P. 52), Rev-APG (PP. 260, 262), Uni-1 (P. 43), Wat-CG (PP. 105, 107), Wat-NEGCO Co. (P. 160).

Items made	Clear	Items made	Clear
Bottle		Plain stem	55.00
Bitters	80.00	Jar, covered, with plain stopper, 5"h	50.00
Castor	35.00	Jelly glass, flat	45.00
Cologne, original stopper	85.00	Lamp, oil	100.00
Water, tumble up	100.00	Mug, applied handle	
Butter dish, covered	150.00	3½"h	110.00
Celery vase	35.00	3⅜"h	110.00
Champagne	85.00	Pickle dish, oval	25.00
Compote, open		Pitcher, water, applied handle, ½	
High standard	75.00	gallon	200.00
Low standard	75.00	Pomade jar, covered	50.00
Cordial	75.00	Relish tray, oval	25.00
Creamer, applied handle	125.00	Salt	
Cruet, original stopper	85.00	Round	
Decanter, 1 pint		Individual	35.00
With bar lip		Master, footed	
Pint	125.00	Covered	100.00
Quart	125.00	Open	35.00
With original patterned stopper	125.00	Oblong, flat	35.00
Quart	125.00	Spoonholder	40.00
Pint	125.00	Sugar bowl, covered	125.00
Egg cup, footed		Tumbler	
Covered	165.00	Water	85.00
Open	55.00	Whiskey	75.00
Goblet		Wine	55.00
Knob stem	65.00		

BULLS EYE AND DAISIES

Wine; water pitcher; tumbler. All clear with green stained "eyes".

OMN: U.S. Glass No. 15,117, Newport. AKA: Bulls Eye and Daisy [Millard], Knobby Bulls Eye.

Non-flint. The United States Glass Co. (pattern line No. 15,117), Pittsburgh, PA. at Factory "F" (Ripley & Co., Pittsburgh, PA.) and Factory "P" (Doyle & Co., Pittsburgh, PA.) ca. 1909. Profusely illustrated throughout the Butler Brothers catalogs for 1910, 1911, and 1916, and the United States Glass Co. Factory "D" 1904 No. 111 catalog.

Original color production: Clear, clear with amethyst, blue, green and pink stained eyes, emerald green, clear with ruby stain, clear with gilt.

Reproductions: The goblet, using a paper label for identification, has been reproduced from a new mold in blue and yellow most likely for the Red Cliff Co., a Chicago distributing firm established in 1950.

References: Bat-GPG (PP. 105, 107), Hea-3 (PP. 76, 87), Hea-5 (P. 151, Plt. B), McCn-PGP (P. 311), Mil-1 (P. 166), Mtz-1 (PP. 214-215), Pet-Sal (P. 23), Uni-1 (P. 159), Uni-2 (P. 219).

Items made	Clear	Green	Clear/ Ruby
Bowl, open, flat, master berry	10.00	15.00	25.00
Butter dish, covered	25.00	30.00	90.00
Celery vase	15.00	25.00	40.00
Creamer	20.00	20.00	40.00
Cruet, original stopper	30.00	35.00	65.00
Decanter	—	100.00	—
Dish			
Jelly, round, three handled	15.00	25.00	40.00
Olive, round, flat, handled	15.00	25.00	40.00
Goblet	20.00	20.00	45.00
Pickle dish, boat shaped	15.00	25.00	40.00
Pitcher, water, $\frac{1}{2}$ gallon	35.00	40.00	90.00
Salt shaker, original top	20.00	20.00	45.00
Sauce dish, round, flat	5.00	10.00	15.00
Spoonholder, double handles	15.00	20.00	35.00
Sugar bowl, covered, double handles	25.00	35.00	55.00
Syrup, original top	35.00	40.00	150.00
Toothpick holder	20.00	30.00	50.00
Tumbler, water, flat	10.00	20.00	35.00
Wine	15.00	25.00	45.00

BULLS EYE AND FAN

Tumbler (sapphire blue); goblet (clear with gilt rim).

OMN: U.S. Glass No. 15,160. AKA: Daisies in Oval Panels.

Non-flint. The United States Glass Co. (pattern line No. 15,160), Pittsburgh, PA. ca. 1904. Illustrated in the 1904 No. 111 Factory "D" (George Duncan & Sons) catalog and the United States Glass Co. ca. 1915/1919 export catalog as No. 15,160.

Original color production: Clear, clear with amethyst, pink, sapphire blue stain, solid emerald green (with or without gilt).

Reproductions: None.

References: Bat-GPG (PP. 221, 224), Hea-1 (P. 50), Hea-5 (PP. 13, 15, 33), Hea-TPS (P. 24), Kam-1 (P. 58), Mil-2 (P. 115), Mtz-1 (PP. 216, 217), Pet-Sal (P. 158), Rev-APG (P. 317), Uni-1 (P. 159), Wlkr-PGA (Fig. 8, Nos. 55-56).

Items made	Clear	Pink Stain	Amethyst Stain	Blue Stain	Green
Bowl, open, flat					
5"d., pinched ends	—	—	—	—	18.00
8"d., master berry, round crimped sides	15.00	—	—	30.00	20.00
Butter dish, covered					
Quarter pound	45.00	—	—	—	65.00
Table-size	45.00	—	—	—	65.00
Cake stand, high standard					
8"d	25.00	—	—	—	—
9"d	25.00	—	—	—	—
Celery					
Tray	20.00	—	—	—	—
Vase	20.00	—	—	—	—
Champagne, 6 ounce	25.00	—	—	—	—
Compote, open, high standard saucer bowl, 8½"d	35.00	—	—	—	—
Creamer					
Individual	15.00	—	—	—	—
Table size, 5½"h	25.00	—	—	35.00	30.00
Cruet, 5 ounce, original stopper	35.00	—	—	—	—
Cup, custard	10.00	—	—	—	—
Goblet	25.00	25.00	25.00	45.00	45.00
Mug, lemonade, 5"h	20.00	—	—	—	—
Pitcher					
Individual, tankard	15.00	—	—	—	—
Lemonade, footed	55.00	—	—	—	—
Water, tankard, ½ gallon	40.00	50.00	55.00	100.00	100.00
Relish tray	15.00	20.00	20.00	35.00	35.00
Sauce dish, flat, round, 4"d	15.00	20.00	20.00	25.00	20.00
Spoonholder, scalloped rim	20.00	25.00	25.00	45.00	45.00
Sugar bowl, covered	35.00	30.00	40.00	35.00	50.00
Syrup, original top	35.00	40.00	50.00	75.00	75.00
Toothpick holder	35.00	65.00	—	—	45.00
Tumbler, water, flat	15.00	40.00	55.00	35.00	45.00
Vase, 11"h	20.00	—	—	—	—
Wine	20.00	40.00	20.00	25.00	40.00

Goblet; whale oil lamp; decanter; whale oil lamp.

AKA: Bulls Eye and Princess Feather, Bulls Eye with Fleur-de-Lis, Bull's Eye with Princes' Feather, Prince's Feather, Princess Feather.

Flint. Attributed to the Union Glass Co., Somerville, MA., ca. 1850s. Shards have been found at the site of the Boston & Sandwich Glass Co., Sandwich, MA.

Original color production: Clear. Amber or any color would be rare.

Reproductions: None.

References: Brn-SD (P. 53), Cod-OS (Pl. 21), Enos-MPG (Chart-4), Kam-8 (PP. 46-47), Lee-EAPG (PP. 156-158), McCln-AG (P. 39), McKrn-AG (P. 404), Mil-1 (Pl. 34), Mtz-1 (PP. 12-13), Mtz-2 (PP. 192-193), Oliv-AAG (P. 52), Pap-GAG (P. 133), Rev-APG (P. 304), Spil-AEPG (P. 216), Thu-1 (P. 92), Uni-1 (P. 43).

Items made	Clear	Items made	Clear
Ale glass, footed (R)	250.00	Stand, glass font, brass stem, marble	
Bottle, cologne	95.00	base	200.00
Bowl, fruit, open, flat, round, scalloped		Whale oil, 10"h	
rim, 8"d	85.00	All glass	150.00
Butter dish, covered	175.00	Brass stem, marble base, 10"h	100.00
Carafe	85.00	Mug, applied handle	100.00
Celery vase	85.00	Pitcher, water, applied handle, ½	
Compote, open		gallon	450.00
High standard	150.00	Salt, master, footed, open	55.00
Low standard	125.00	Sauce dish, flat, round	20.00
Creamer, 6½"h	250.00	Spoonholder	50.00
Decanter, w/bar lip		Sugar bowl, covered, 8⅝"h	125.00
1 pint	110.00	Tumbler	
1 quart	110.00	Lemonade	110.00
Egg cup, pedestaled	50.00	Water	100.00
Goblet	85.00	Whiskey	95.00
Honey dish, flat, round	20.00	Wine (2 styles)	65.00
Lamp			
Finger, small	175.00		

Whale oil lamp; goblet.

OMN: New England Glass Co.'s Union. AKA: Bulls Eye Diamond, Owl.

Flint. The New England Glass Co., East Cambridge, MA. ca. 1869. Illustrated in the ca. 1869 New England Glass Co. catalog.

Original color production: Clear. Firey opalescent, milk white or any other color is rare.

Reproductions: None.

References: Bat-GPG (PP. 9, 12), Drep-ABC OG (P. 177), Enos-MPG (Chart-1), Lee-EAPG (Pl. 49, No. 4), McKrn-AG (P. 400), McCn-PGP (P. 263), Mtz-1 (PP. 12-13), Mil-1 (Pl. 161), Oliv-AAG (P. 52), Rev-APG (PP. 260, 262), Spil-AEPG (P. 257), Uni-1 (P. 57), Wat-CG (P. 103), Wlkr-PGA (Fig. 8, No. 44).

Items made	Clear	Items made	Clear
Bottle, water	165.00	Champagne	145.00
Bowl, open, Flat		Cologne bottle, original stopper	90.00
5"d	40.00	Compote, open	
6"d	50.00	High standard	
7"d	65.00	Deep bowl	
8"d	80.00	9"d	100.00
Compote, open		10"d	125.00
High standard		Shallow bowl	
6"d	80.00	6"d	65.00
7"d	100.00	7"d	75.00
8"d	120.00	8"d	85.00
9"d	140.00	Low standard	
10"d	160.00	Deep bowl	
Low standard		9"d	100.00
6"d	70.00	10"d	125.00
7"d	90.00	Shallow bowl	
8"d	110.00	6"d	65.00
9"d	135.00	7"d	75.00
10"d	150.00	8"d	85.00
Butter dish, covered, flat	225.00	Cordial	135.00
Celery vase, pedestaled	175.00	Creamer	200.00

Items made	Clear	Items made	Clear
Decanter		Pitcher, water, tankard, applied	
Bar lip		handle, 10¼"h	300.00
1 pint	125.00	Salt, master, covered, footed	125.00
1 quart	175.00	Sauce dish, flat, round, 4"d	20.00
Original stopper		Spoonholder	100.00
1 pint	150.00	Sugar bowl, covered	175.00
1 quart	200.00	Syrup, applied handle, original top . . .	165.00
Egg cup, single, open, footed	90.00	Tumbler	
Glass, jelly, flat	125.00	⅓ pint	125.00
Goblet	125.00	Lemonade	125.00
Honey dish, flat, 3½"d	25.00	Whiskey, ½ pint	125.00
Lamp, whale oil, finger, applied handle	150.00	Tumble up, complete	165.00
		Wine	135.00

BUTTERFLY AND FAN

Covered sugar bowl; goblet.

OMN: Duncan's Grace. AKA: Bird in Ring, Butterfly with Fan, Fan [Lee], Japanese.

Non-flint. George Duncan & Sons, Pittsburgh, PA. ca. 1880.

Original color production: Clear.

Reproductions: None.

References: Bred-EDG (PP. 56-57), Kam-2 (PP. 16-17), Kam-7 (PP. 76-77), McCn-PGP (P. 399), Mil-1 (Pl. 140), Mtz-1 (PP. 106-107), Rev-APG (P. 287), Spil-AEPG (P. 297), Stu-BP (P. 57), Uni-1 (P. 205), Wlkr-PGA (Fig. 8, Nos. 17, 28).

Items made	Clear	Items made	Clear
Bowl, flat, round, master berry	30.00	Compote, high standard	
Butter dish, covered		Covered	
Flat, 6"d	55.00	7"d	95.00
Footed, 6"d	65.00	8"d	95.00
Celery vase	35.00	Open	35.00

Items made	Clear	Items made	Clear
Creamer, footed	35.00	Plate, bread	40.00
Goblet	50.00	Sauce dish, round	
Marmalade jar, covered	50.00	Flat, 4″d	15.00
Pickle jar, original silver plate frame		Footed, 4″d	15.00
with cover	80.00	Spoonholder	30.00
Pitcher, water, ¹/₂ gallon	90.00	Sugar bowl, covered	40.00

BUTTON ARCHES

Covered butter; goblet; tankard water; covered sugar bowl; creamer. All items clear with ruby stain.

OMN: Duncan No. 39. AKA: Scalloped Diamond, Scalloped Diamond-Red Top, Scalloped Daisy-Red Top.

Non-flint. George Duncan Sons & Co. (pattern line No. 39), Washington, PA. ca. 1897. Duncan & Miller Glass Co., ca. 1900. Illustrated in the George Duncan Sons & Co. 1897 catalog, and advertised in the February, 1898 *China, Glass and Pottery Review*, Button Arches was still being advertised in the Charles "Broadway" Rousse, New York, NY., general merchandise catalog for 1914 in clear with ruby stain.

Original color production: Clear, clear with ruby stain and frosted band, clam-broth, and opaque white (plain or copper wheel engraved, later souvenired). Ruby stained by the Oriental Glass Co., Pittsburgh, PA., often with a wide band of gold across the ruby stain and gilt rims or with three gold bands across the mid-section.

Reproductions: The following items have been reproduced from new molds by the Westlake Ruby Glass Works, Columbus, OH. in clear with ruby stain: butter dish (covered), cordial, creamer (individual and table size), goblet, spoonholder, sugar bowl (covered), and toothpick holder. Typical of reproductions is the mild ruby color, originally referred to as Cranberry.

References: Bar-RS (Pl. 12), Bons-BDG (P. 109), Hea-1 (P. 16, Figs. 42-43), Hea-1000TPS (PP. 51-52), Hea-3 (P. 18), Hea-6 (PP. 21, 80), Hea-TPS (PP. 39-40), Kam-1 (P. 1110), Kam-5 (P. 95), Kam-6 (Pl. 9), Kam-7 (Pl. 94), Lecnr-SS (P. 24), McCn-PGP (Pl. 6), Mig-TPS (Pl. 166), Mil-1 (Pl. 166), Mil-2 (Pl. 56), Mtz-2 (PP. 132-133), Pet-Sal (P. 24), Rev-APG (P. 148), Spil-AEPG (P. 338), Uni-1 (P. 181), Uni/Wor-CHPGT (P. 62), War-MGA (Pl. 55), Wlkr-PGA (Fig. 4, No. 59).

Items made	Clear	Clear w/ Ruby
Bowl, open, flat, master berry, 8″d	20.00	50.00
Butter dish, covered, flat, 8″d, flanged base	50.00	150.00
Cake stand, high standard, turned down rim, 9″d	35.00	175.00
Celery vase	30.00	75.00
Compote, open, high standard		
Jelly	40.00	65.00
Large, deep round bowl, flared rim	50.00	85.00
Creamer		
Individual, 2¾″h	20.00	45.00
Table size	30.00	60.00
Cruet, original stopper	55.00	165.00
Cup, custard	15.00	25.00
Goblet	25.00	40.00
Mug, handled, 4 ounce	25.00	30.00
Mustard, original notched cover with underplate	60.00	100.00
Plate, 7″d	10.00	25.00
Pitcher, tankard		
Milk, 1 quart	35.00	80.00
Water, ½ gallon	75.00	125.00
Salt		
Individual	15.00	35.00
Shaker, original plated lid, bulbous		
Short	15.00	30.00
Tall	15.00	30.00
Straight	15.00	30.00
Sauce, flat, round, 4″d	10.00	20.00
Spoonholder	25.00	40.00
Sugar bowl, covered	35.00	75.00
Syrup pitcher, glass lid, 12 ounce	—	175.00
Toothpick holder	20.00	35.00
Tumbler, water, flat, 4″h.		
Handleless	20.00	30.00
Handled	25.00	35.00
Wine, 4⅛″h	10.00	35.00

Goblet (etched fern and berry).

OMN: Wyandotte. AKA: Umbilicated Hobnail.

Non-flint. Ripley & Co., Pittsburgh, PA. ca. 1886. Reissued by The United States Glass Co., Pittsburgh, PA. at Factory "F" (Ripley & Co., Pittsburgh, PA.) after 1891.

Original color production: Clear (plain or copper wheel engraved, a conventional engraving being No. 89: "Flower And Berry").

Reproductions: None.

References: Hea-5 (P. 120, Pl. D), Kam-3 (P. 111), McCn-PGP (P. 337), Mil-2 (Pl. 9), Mtz-1 (PP. 152-153).

Items made	Clear	Items made	Clear
Bowl, open, round, flat, 10″d	20.00	Tankard	30.00
Butter dish, covered	45.00	Cruet, original stopper	30.00
Cake stand, high standard, 10″d	60.00	Goblet	25.00
Castor set, 5 bottles, original silver		Pitcher	
plate or glass holder	95.00	Milk, 1 quart	40.00
Celery vase	30.00	Water, ½ gallon	50.00
Compote, round		Plate, round	40.00
High standard		Sauce dish, round	10.00
Covered, 9″d	95.00	Spoonholder	20.00
Open, jelly	30.00	Sugar bowl, covered	30.00
Low standard, open, 9″d	45.00	Tray, water	30.00
Cordial	30.00	Tumbler, water, flat	20.00
Creamer		Wine	35.00
Legged, 5½″h	30.00		

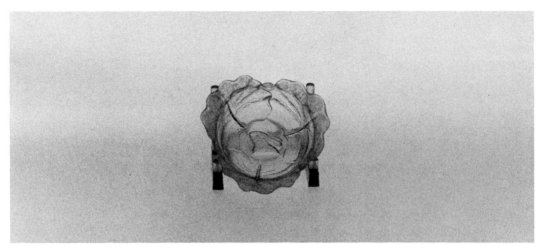

Master berry bowl.

AKA: Frosted Cabbage Leaf.

Non-flint. Original manufacturer unknown, ca. 1870s-1880s.

Original color production: Clear, clear with acid finish. Amber or any other color is rare. The main design element of Cabbage Leaf consists of finely stippled cabbage leaves and rabbits forming the body of objects into naturalistic forms. Finials are in the shape of rabbit heads.

References: Bat-GPG (PP. 77-78), Drep-ABC OG (P. 161), Lee-EAPG (Pl. 65, No. 4), McCn-PGP (P. 421), Mtz-1 (P. 107), Uni-2 (P. 219).

Reproductions: The following items have been reproduced, both in clear and clear and frosted, from new molds from the early 1960s by the L.G. Wright Glass Co., New Martinsville, WV. (distributed by Jennings Red Barn, New Martinsville, WV. and Carl Forslund, Grand Rapids, MI.) and appear in the company's 1970 catalog supplement: covered butter dish, celery vase, high standard covered compote, creamer, goblet, plate w/rabbit center, $3^{1}/_{2}''$d. flat sauce, spoonholder, covered sugar bowl, and wine. The goblet is entirely new and not part of the original set.

Items made	Clear	Clear/ Frosted
Bowl, master berry, round	65.00	85.00
Butter dish, covered	100.00	125.00
Celery vase	65.00	90.00
Compote, covered, high standard	125.00	155.00
Creamer	65.00	90.00
Pickle dish, flat, leaf shaped	35.00	45.00
Pitcher, water, $^{1}/_{2}$ gallon	175.00	225.00
Plate, "Rabbit Head" center	55.00	65.00
Sauce dish, round, flat, "Rabbit Head" center	25.00	35.00
Spoonholder	65.00	85.00
Sugar bowl, covered	90.00	125.00
Tumbler	40.00	55.00

CABBAGE ROSE

Master salt; water tumbler; covered high standard compote; egg cup; wine.

OMN: Central's No. 140, Rose.

Non-flint. Central Glass Co. (pattern line No. 140), Wheeling, WV. ca. 1870.

Designed and patented by John Oesterling (design patent No. 4,263) July 26, 1870 and originally named the "Rose" pattern, Cabbage Rose is illustrated in the ca. 1876-1881 Central Glass Co. catalog.

Original color production: Clear. Covered pieces have a rose bud finial.

Reproductions: The Mosser Glass Co., Inc., Cambridge, OH. reproduced both the goblet and spoonholder from new molds during the early 1960s in amber, amethyst, blue, clear and green. Heavier in weight than the originals, new pieces lack fine detail of design.

References: Brn-SD (P. 51), Bros-TS (P. 30), Eige-CGM WV (P. 15), Jef-WG (P. 85), Kam-3 (P. 40), Kam-7 (PP. 68-69), Lee-EAPG (Pl. 122, No. 4), Mil-1 (Pl. 52), Mtz-1 (PP. 54-55), Oliv-AAG (P. 60), Pet-GPP (PP. 137-138), Rev-APG (P. 110), Uni-1 9(P. 199), Wlkr-PGA (Fig. 8, Nos. 7, 16, 18, 27).

Items made	Clear	Items made	Clear
Basket, handled, 12″h	100.00	Cake stand, high standard	
Bottle, bitters, 6¼″h	100.00	9″d	35.00
Bowl, flat		9½″d	35.00
Oval, open, 6″l	30.00	10″d	45.00
Round		11″d	55.00
Covered		12″d	60.00
6″d	55.00	12½″d	65.00
7″d	60.00	Celery vase, pedestaled	50.00
7½″d	65.00	Champagne	50.00
Open		Compote	
5″d	25.00	Covered, high standard	
6″d	25.00	Deep bowl	
7″d	30.00	6″d	75.00
7½″d	30.00	6½″d	75.00
Butter dish, covered, flat	25.00	7″d	80.00
Cake plate, square, flat	65.00	7½″d	80.00

Items made	Clear	Items made	Clear
8"d	90.00	Open, high standard	
8½"d	90.00	6½"d	50.00
9"d	100.00	7½"d	65.00
11"d	125.00	8½"d	75.00
Regular bowl		9½"d	85.00
8"d	90.00	Cordial	55.00
9"d	100.00	Creamer, applied handle, 5½"h	60.00
10"d	110.00	Egg cup, single, plain or handled	60.00
Shallow bowl		Goblet (2 styles)	45.00
6"d	75.00	Mug	60.00
7"d	80.00	Pickle dish	35.00
8"d	90.00	Pitcher	
Low standard		Milk, 1 quart	125.00
Deep bowl		Water	
7"d	80.00	½ gallon	150.00
8"d	90.00	3 pint	175.00
9"d	100.00	Relish dish, flat, tapered at one end,	
Regular bowl		8½"l, rose filled horn of plenty center	35.00
8"d	90.00	Salt, master, open, footed, beaded rim	10.00
9"d	100.00	Sauce dish, round, flat, 4"d	10.00
10"d	125.00	Spoonholder	40.00
Shallow bowl		Sugar bowl, covered	40.00
6"d	75.00	Tumbler, water, flat	40.00
7"d	80.00	Wine	45.00
8"d	90.00		

CABLE

High standard open compote; whiskey tumbler.

AKA: Atlantic Cable, Cable Cord.

Flint. The Boston & Sandwich Glass Co., Sandwich, MA. ca. 1850.

Original color production: Clear. Rare in clear with amber stain, jade green, opalescent, opaque green, blue, white, translucent turquoise-blue, or any other color is very rare.

Reproductions: None.

Champagne; creamer; goblet.

References: Bros-TS (P. 9), Brn-SD (P. 53), Chip-ROS (P. 85), Drep-ABC OG (P. 153), Grow-GAG (P. 172, Fig. 44-"4"), Lee-EAPG (Pl. 36, No. 4), Lee-VG (Pl. 4), Lee-SG (Plts. 210, 216), Lind-HG (P. 150), Mar-ARG (P. 253), McCn-PGP (P. 375), McKrn-AG (Plts. 205, 207), Mil-1 (Pl. 37), Mtz-1 (PP. 130-131), Oliv-AAG (P. 52), Spil-AEPG (P. 273), Uni-2 (P. 28), Wlkr-PGA (Fig. 8, Nos. 15, 18, 24).

Items made	Clear
Bowl, open	
Flat, 9″d	70.00
Footed, 8″d	70.00
Butter dish, covered, flat	100.00
Cake stand, high standard, 9″d	90.00
Celery vase	75.00
Champagne	250.00
Compote, open	
High standard	
5½″d., jelly	65.00
10″d	200.00
Low standard	
7″d	50.00
9″d	55.00
11″d, 5¾″h	75.00
Creamer, applied handle	155.00
Decanter	
1 Pint	155.00
1 Quart, ground stopper	155.00
Egg cup, footed, covered	225.00
Goblet	75.00

Items made	Clear
Honey dish, flat, round	15.00
Lamp, original burner	
All glass, 8¾″h	135.00
Brass standard, marble base, 8¾″h	100.00
Mug, applied handle	75.00
Pitcher, water, ½ gallon, applied handle (R)	500.00
Plate, round, 6″d	75.00
Salt	
Individual, flat	35.00
Master, covered, 3⅓″h	45.00
Sauce dish, flat, round	20.00
Spoonholder	40.00
Sugar bowl, covered	175.00
Syrup pitcher, applied handle, original top	225.00
Tumbler	
Water, footed	175.00
Whiskey, flat	175.00
Wine	175.00

Creamer; plate; covered butter dish; flat sauce dish.

OMN: U.S. Glass No. 15,059, Beaded Grape [Lee, Millard]. AKA: Beaded Grape and Vine, Grape and Vine.

Non-flint. The United States Glass Co., Pittsburgh, PA. ca. 1899. Attributed by Canadian researchers to the Burlington Glass Works, Hamilton, Ontario, Canada and the Sydenham Glass Co., Wallaceburg, Ontario, Canada ca. 1910.

Original color production: Clear, emerald green (with or without gilt). Most pieces are square in form with beaded rims. Water pitchers may be either round or square.

Reproductions: California has been reproduced from the early 1960s by a number of companies including the Westmorland Glass Co., Grapeville, PA. who reproduced the line extensively in milk white. The following items have been reproduced from new molds in amber, amethyst, blue, clear, green and milk white throughout the 1960s and 1970s: 8¼″ square plate, 4″ flat square sauce, tumbler, wine, square covered high standard compote, and goblet.

Reproductions in emerald green lack the vibrant depth of color of old pieces. Amber copies are too harsh and orangey. All new items lack the clarity and depth of the originals, and have poor design quality.

References: Bat-GPG (P. 133), Enos-MPG (Chart-1), Hart/Cobb-SS (P. 15), Hea-1 (P. 14), Hea-3 (P. 87), Hea-5 (P. 39, Nos. 82-84), Hea-6 (P. 19), Kam-4 (P. 94), Hea-TPS (P. 101), Kam/Wod Vol.11 (P. 77), Lee-EAPG (Pl. 63, No. 1), McCn-PGP (P. 173), Mil-1 (Pl. 79), Mtz-1 (P. 83), Mtz-2 (P. 76), Mur-CO (P. 15), Oliv-AAG (P. 67), Pet-Sal (P. 132), Pyne-PG (P. 146), Rev-APG (P. 310), Spil-AEPG (P. 325), Spnc-ECG (P. 43), Stev-ECG (PP. 68-69, Uni-1 (P. 215), Uni-2 (P. 230), Uni-TCG (PP. 65, 220), Uni/Wor-CHPGT (P. 45), Wlkr-PGA (Fig. 8, Nos. 14, 18, 21, 46).

Items made	Clear	Emerald Green
Bowl, flat		
Round		
Covered, 8″d	40.00	55.00

Items made	Clear	Emerald Green
Open, 8″d	25.00	30.00
Square		
Covered		
7″	40.00	55.00
8″	40.00	55.00
9″	45.00	65.00
Open		
5$\frac{1}{2}$″	20.00	30.00
6″	20.00	30.00
7″	30.00	40.00
7$\frac{1}{2}$″	35.00	45.00
8″	35.00	45.00
9″	40.00	50.00
Butter dish, covered, flat, flanged base	65.00	100.00
Cake stand, high standard, 9″ sq.	65.00	85.00
Cake plate, footed, sq.	65.00	85.00
Celery		
Tray, oblong	30.00	45.00
Vase, 5$\frac{1}{2}$″h	45.00	65.00
Compote, square, high standard		
Covered		
4″, jelly compote	55.00	75.00
7″	65.00	95.00
8″	65.00	95.00
9″	85.00	110.00
Open		
4″, jelly compote	25.00	40.00
5″	35.00	50.00
6″	35.00	50.00
7″	40.00	55.00
8″	40.00	55.00
9″	45.00	60.00
Cordial	60.00	80.00
Creamer	40.00	50.00
Cruet, original swirled stopper	65.00	110.00
Dish, open		
Olive, handled	20.00	35.00
Flat		
Rectangular, shallow		
6″ x 8$\frac{1}{4}$″	20.00	25.00
7″ x 10$\frac{1}{4}$″	20.00	25.00
7″ x 4$\frac{1}{2}$″	20.00	25.00
Square		
5$\frac{1}{4}$″	20.00	25.00
6$\frac{1}{4}$″	20.00	25.00
7$\frac{1}{2}$″	25.00	35.00
8$\frac{1}{4}$″	25.00	35.00
9$\frac{1}{4}$″	25.00	35.00
Footed		
Square, 6″h, 7$\frac{1}{2}$″sq.	25.00	40.00
Preserve, rectangular, flat	25.00	40.00
Goblet	35.00	50.00
Honey dish, square, flat, open, 3$\frac{1}{2}$″.	10.00	20.00
Jug, water, squatty	75.00	90.00
Olive dish, flat, square, single tab handle	20.00	35.00
Pickle dish, rectangular	20.00	30.00
Pitcher		
Tankard, round, water, $\frac{1}{2}$ gallon	85.00	125.00

Items made	Clear	Emerald Green
Square		
Water, ½ gallon	85.00	125.00
Milk, square, 1 quart	75.00	90.00
Plate, square		
Bread, 10¼" x 7¼"	25.00	45.00
Dinner		
8¼"	25.00	40.00
8½"	25.00	40.00
Platter, oblong (R), 10¼" x 7¼"	55.00	85.00
Preserve dish, flat, oblong	20.00	35.00
Salt shaker (tall), original lid	20.00	35.00
Sauce dish, flat, square, plain or handled, beaded rim		
3½"sq	15.00	20.00
4"sq	15.00	20.00
4½"sq	15.00	20.00
Spoonholder	30.00	45.00
Sugar bowl, covered		
Flat base	45.00	55.00
Low footed (originally called "The Australian Sugar")	65.00	90.00
Sugar shaker, original top	75.00	90.00
Toothpick holder, 2½"h	35.00	65.00
Tray, bread, rectangular	40.00	65.00
Tumbler, water, flat, round	25.00	40.00
Vase, 6"h	25.00	40.00
Wine	35.00	65.00

CANADIAN

Creamer; covered butter dish; covered sugar bowl; spoonholder.

Non-flint. Manufacturer unknown. Shards have been found at the site of the Burlington Glass Works, Hamilton, Ontario, Canada.

Original color production: Clear. Unlike the Cape Cod pattern that depicts a water scene, the main design element of Canadian consists of large, arched vertical panels of rural scenes against a lightly stippled background with ivy and berry sprays. The stems of goblets are smooth, with covered pieces sporting conventional finials. Handles are pressed.

Reproductions: A flower vase has been made from a new mold in milk white that "resembles" the Canadian pattern, although the design elements are completely different when compared to the original.

References: Hlms-BCA (P. 278), Kam-1 (PP. 39-40), Kam-8 (PP. 68-69), Kam/Wod Vol.1 (P. 118), Lee-EAPG (Pl. 112, No. 3), McCn-PGP (Pl. 262), Mil-1 (Pl. 35), Mtz-1 (PP. 110-111), Spnc-ECG (PP. 102-103), Stev-ECG (PP., 240-241), Stu-BP (P. 118), Uni-2 (P. 137), Uni-TCG (PP. 73-75), Uni/Wor-CHPGT (PP. 64-65).

Items made	Clear	Items made	Clear
Bowl		7"d	35.00
Covered, flat, tab-handled, 6"d	75.00	8"d	40.00
Open, footed, no handles, 7"d., 4½"h	35.00	Creamer, 6"h	55.00
Butter dish, covered, 6"h	85.00	Goblet, 6¼"h	65.00
Cake stand, high standard, 9¼"sq	95.00	Jam jar, covered, 6½"h	110.00
Celery vase	75.00	Mug, small	40.00
Compote		Pitcher	
Covered		Milk, 1 quart	95.00
High standard		Water, ½ gallon	110.00
6"d	75.00	Plate, tab handled	
7"d	85.00	Bread	55.00
8"d	125.00	Dinner	
10"d	125.00	6"d	30.00
Low standard		8"d	35.00
6"d	55.00	9½"d	45.00
7"d	55.00	10"d	45.00
8"d	65.00	12"d	55.00
Open		Sauce dish, round	
High standard		Flat, 4"d	15.00
6"d	35.00	Footed, 4"d	20.00
7"d	45.00	Spoonholder, 5¾"h	45.00
8"d	50.00	Sugar bowl, covered, 8"h	95.00
Low standard		Wine, 4⅛"h	45.00
6"d	30.00		

Oval bowl; goblet; creamer.

OMN: Hobnail, McKee's. AKA: Cane Insert, Cane Seat, Hobnailed Diamond and Star.

Non-flint. Attributed to Gillinder & Sons, Philadelphia, PA. McKee Glass Co., Pittsburgh, PA. ca. 1885. Illustrated in the McKee Glass Co. catalog of 1894 as "Hobnail".

Original color production: Amber, apple green, blue, clear, vaseline. The main pattern element of Cane consists of well defined crisscross weaving with clear hexagonal buttons resembling the seat of a caned chair.

Reproductions: None.

References: Drep-ABC OG (P. 153), Kam/Wod Vol.1 (P. 124), Kam-3 (PP. 39-40), Kam-6 (Pl. 5), Lee-EAPG (Pl. 132, No. 2), McCn-PGP (Pl. 34), Mil-1 (Pl. 122), Mtz-1 (PP. 158-159), Pet-Sal (P. 156), Rev-APG (P. 238), Stev-ECG (P. 67), Uni-1 (P. 263), Uni/Wor-CHPGT (P. 71), Wlkr-PGA (Fig. 8, Nos. 51, 57, 58).

Items made	Amber	Green	Blue	Clear	Vas
Bowl, open					
Oval, 9½"	15.00	—	—	—	—
Round					
Berry, master	25.00	35.00	40.00	20.00	35.00
Finger	20.00	30.00	35.00	15.00	30.00
Waste	35.00	30.00	35.00	20.00	30.00
Butter dish, covered, flat	45.00	30.00	75.00	40.00	60.00
Celery vase	35.00	50.00	40.00	30.00	40.00
Compote, open, low standard, 5¾"d	25.00	30.00	35.00	25.00	35.00
Cordial	—	—	—	25.00	—
Creamer	35.00	40.00	50.00	25.00	30.00
Goblet	25.00	60.00	45.00	20.00	40.00
Honey dish, flat	—	—	—	15.00	—
Match holder, kettle shape	15.00	—	35.00	30.00	35.00
Pickle dish	25.00	20.00	25.00	15.00	20.00
Pitcher					
Milk, 1 quart	60.00	55.00	65.00	40.00	55.00
Water, ½ gallon	60.00	55.00	65.00	40.00	55.00
Plate, toddy, 4½"d	20.00	25.00	30.00	10.00	15.00

Items made	Amber	Green	Blue	Clear	Vas
Relish tray	25.00	20.00	25.00	15.00	20.00
Salt shaker, original top	35.00	35.00	40.00	15.00	45.00
Sauce dish, round					
Flat, 4½"d	—	10.00	—	5.00	—
Footed, 4½"d	—	10.00	—	5.00	—
Slipper	30.00	—	25.00	15.00	30.00
Spoonholder	40.00	35.00	30.00	20.00	30.00
Sugar bowl, covered	55.00	50.00	55.00	45.00	55.00
Tray, water	35.00	35.00	45.00	30.00	40.00
Tumbler, water, flat	25.00	30.00	35.00	20.00	25.00
Wine	35.00	50.00	55.00	25.00	40.00

CANE HORSESHOE

Creamer; relish tray; wine; mug.

OMN: U.S. Glass No. 15,118, Paragon.

Non-flint. The United States Glass Co. (pattern line No. 15,118), Pittsburgh, PA. ca. 1909 at Factory "F" (Ripley & Co., Pittsburgh, PA.). Illustrated in the ca. 1909 United States Glass Co. Factory "D" No. 111 catalog.

Original color production: Clear (with or without gilt). Clear with amber stain or any other color is scarce.

Reproductions: None.

References: Kam-1 (P. 100), Hea-3 (PP. 76, 87), Hea-5 (PP. 151, 168), McCn-PGP (P. 253), Pet-Sal (P. 24), Uni-1 (P. 163).

Items made	Clear
Bowl, open, flat	
5"d., vegetable	15.00
8"d., master berry	15.00
Butter dish, covered, flat	25.00
Cake stand, high standard	30.00
Celery	

Items made	Clear
Tray	20.00
Vase	25.00
Compote, round	
Covered, high standard, 8"d	35.00
Open	
High standard, jelly, 4"d	20.00

Items made	Clear	Items made	Clear
Low standard	20.00	Salt shaker, original top	10.00
Creamer		Sauce dish, round	
Berry	20.00	Flat	
Individual tankard	20.00	4"d	5.00
Table size	25.00	4½"d	5.00
Cruet, original stopper	30.00	Footed	
Cup, custard, handled	5.00	4"d	5.00
Dish, olive, handled	8.00	4½"d	5.00
Goblet	20.00	Spoonholder, handled	20.00
Mug, handled, 6 ounce	10.00	Sugar bowl	
Pickle dish, boat shaped	10.00	Berry, true open, double handles	10.00
Plate, round, 7"d	10.00	Table size, covered, handled	30.00
Pitcher		Syrup pitcher, original top	35.00
Individual, tankard	15.00	Toothpick holder	20.00
Milk, 1 quart, 7⅝"h	30.00	Tumbler, water, flat	15.00
Water, ½ gallon	40.00	Wine	20.00
Relish tray	15.00		

CAPE COD

Goblet.

Non-flint. Attributed to the Boston & Sandwich Glass Co., Sandwich, MA. ca. 1870.

Original color production: Clear. Unlike the Canadian pattern that depicts a rural scene, the main design element of Cape cod consists of a large oval medallion depicting a water scene of sail boats, a light house and cove against a lightly stippled background with ivy and berry sprays.

Reproductions: None.

References: Enos-MPG (Chart-2), Kam-8 (PP. 68, 75), Lee-EAPG (Pl. 114), Lee-SG (P. 538), McCn-PGP (P. 535), Mil-1 (Pl. 176), Mtz-1 (P. 68), Stu-BP (P. 119), Uni-1 (P. 137).

Items made	Clear	Items made	Clear
Bowl, open, flat, double handles, 6"d	30.00	Compote, round	
Butter dish, covered, flat	65.00	Covered	
Celery vase, flat, smooth rim	55.00	High standard	

Items made	Clear	Items made	Clear
6"d	55.00	Water, ½ gallon	85.00
7"d	75.00	Plate, closed handles	
8"d	125.00	5"d	30.00
12"d	175.00	6"d	30.00
Low standard		8"d	35.00
6"d	50.00	10"d	45.00
7"d	70.00	Platter, open handles	45.00
8"d	85.00	Sauce dish, round	
Open, high standard, 7"d	50.00	Flat, 4"d	15.00
Creamer	45.00	Footed, 4"d	20.00
Goblet, 5½"h	40.00	Spoonholder	55.00
Marmalade jar, covered	65.00	Sugar bowl, covered	55.00
Pitcher		Wine (VR)	75.00
Milk, 1 quart	65.00		

CARDINAL

Sauce dish (footed); covered sugar bowl; sauce dish (flat).

AKA: Blue Jay, Cardinal Bird.

Non-flint. Attributed to the Ohio Flint Glass Co., Lancaster, OH. ca. 1875. Shards have been found at the site of the Burlington Glass Works, Hamilton, Ontario, Canada.

Original color production: Clear. The main pattern element of Cardinal Bird consists of embossed birds, on a clear background, posed in varying positions. The covered butter dish had originally been made plain or with a "Red Bird", "Pewit", and "Titmouse" center.

Reproductions: The Summit Art Glass Co., Mogadore/Rootstown, OH. reproduced from a new mold the goblet in blue, clear, and green as illustrated in the company's 1977 brochure.

References: Drep-ABC OG (P. 66), Enos-MPG (Chart-7), Hlms-BCA (P. 278), Kam-1 (PP. 31-32), Kam/Wod Vol.1 (P. 115), Lee-EAPG (Pl. 100, No. 1), McCn-PGP (Pl. 8), Mil-1 (P. 158), Mtz-1 (PP. 92-93), Oliv-AAG (P. 60), Uni-1 (P. 189), Uni-/Wor-CHPGT (P. 72).

Items made	Clear	Items made	Clear
Bowl, master berry, open, flat	65.00	Sauce dish, round	
Butter dish, covered, flat		Flat	
Regular	65.00	4"d	10.00
With "Redbird, Pewitt, Titmouse"		4½"d	10.00
center	125.00	5"d	15.00
Cake stand, high standard	75.00	Footed	
Creamer, 5¾"h	35.00	4"d	15.00
Goblet	35.00	4½"d	15.00
Honey dish, round, flat, 3½"d		5"d	20.00
Covered	45.00	Spoonholder	35.00
Open	20.00	Sugar bowl, covered	65.00
Pitcher, water, ½ gallon	125.00		

CAROLINA

Goblet; milk pitcher; water pitcher; wine.

OMN: U.S. Glass No. 15,083 Carolina. AKA: Inverness [Millard], Mayflower.

Non-flint. Bryce Brothers, Pittsburgh, PA. ca. 1890. Reissued by the United States Glass Co. (pattern line No. 15,083), Pittsburgh, PA. ca. 1903. Illustrated in the United States Glass Co. 1904 catalog, the Butler Brothers August, 1906, and the Charles "Broadway" Rousse, New York City, NY. July-August, 1914 general merchandise catalogs.

Original color production: Clear. Occasional souvenired items may be found in clear with purple or ruby stain.

Reproductions: None.

References: Bar-RS (Pl. 14), Bros-TS (P. 42), Hart/Cobb-SS (P. 16), Hea-5 (P. 167, Pl. B), Hea-6 (P. 48, Fig. 416), Hea-7 (P. 89), Kam-2 (PP. 28-29), Kam-6 (P. 35), McCn-PGP (Pl. 15), Migh-TPS (Pl. 3), Mil-2 (Pl. 53), Mtz-2 (PP. 130-131), Rev-APG (P. 310).

Items made	Clear	Items made	Clear
Bowl, oval, flat, open, beaded rim		5"d	10.00
(deep or shallow)		6"d	10.00

109

Items made	Clear	Items made	Clear
7"d	15.00	6"d	20.00
8"d	15.00	7"d	20.00
9"d	15.00	8"d	25.00
Butter dish, covered	50.00	Creamer, pint	
Cake stand, high standard		Tankard	20.00
9½"d	35.00	Table size	20.00
10¼"d	40.00	Cruet, original stopper	45.00
11"d	40.00	Dish, oval, open, flat	
Compote		7"	10.00
High standard		8"	10.00
Covered		9"	15.00
5"d	35.00	Goblet	30.00
6"d	35.00	Mug, handled	30.00
7"d	35.00	Pickle dish	10.00
8"d	40.00	Pitcher	
Open		Milk, 1 quart	55.00
Crimped bowl		Water	
6"d	20.00	3 pints	40.00
7"d	20.00	½ gallon	50.00
8"d	20.00	Plate, round, dinner	
9"d	25.00	7"d	10.00
Deep bowl		7½"d	10.00
5"d	15.00	Relish tray	10.00
6"d	20.00	Salt shaker, original top	15.00
7"d	20.00	Sauce dish, round	
8"d	20.00	Flat	
Saucer bowl		4"d	10.00
8"d	20.00	4½"d	10.00
9"d	25.00	Footed	
10"d	25.00	4"d	10.00
Low standard		4½"d	10.00
Covered		Spoonholder	25.00
5"d	35.00	Sugar bowl, covered	30.00
6"d	35.00	Syrup pitcher, original top	40.00
7"d	35.00	Tray, bread, handled	40.00
8"d	40.00	Tumbler, water, flat	20.00
Open		Wine	20.00
5"d	20.00		

Fish-shaped relish; creamer; h.s. covered compote; covered sugar; covered butter. All deep amethyst.

OMN: Orion. AKA: Waffle and Fine Cut.

Non-flint. Bryce Brothers, Pittsburgh, PA. ca. 1885. Reissued by the United States Glass Co., Pittsburgh, PA. after 1891 and again in 1898. Illustrated in an undated Bryce Brothers catalog.

Original color production: Amber, amethyst, blue, vaseline, clear, clear with ruby stain. Ruby stained pieces were produced after the 1891 U.S. Glass Co. merger. The main pattern element of Cathedral consists of large vertical arches filled with alternating clear and divided cubes, each arch separated by a series of clear, vertical ribs.

Reproductions: None.

References: Bar-RS (Pl. 11), Drep-ABC OG (P. 153), Enos-MPG (Chart-2), Grow-GAG (P. 233, Fig. 44-"4"), Hea-5 (P. 51, Fig. 243), Hea-7 (P. 27), Hea-OPG (PP. 26-27), Kam-1 (PP. 19-20), Kam-2 (P. 99), Kam-7 (Pl. 1), Lee-EAPG (Pl. 58, No. 1), Lind-HG (P. 213), Mil-1 (Pl. 18), Mtz-1 (PP. 158-159), Mur-MCO (P. 65), Rev-APG (PP. 87-88), Spil-AEPG (P. 308), Uni-2 (P. 139).

Items made	Amber	Amethyst	Blue	Clear	Ruby	Vas
Bowl, open, flat, round, scalloped rim						
5"d	20.00	35.00	25.00	10.00	30.00	25.00
6"d	25.00	40.00	30.00	15.00	35.00	30.00
7"d	30.00	45.00	35.00	20.00	55.00	35.00
8"d	35.00	50.00	40.00	25.00	85.00	40.00
Butter dish, covered, 7"d	60.00	110.00	60.00	50.00	125.00	65.00
Cake stand, high standard	50.00	75.00	60.00	40.00	125.00	65.00
Celery vase	35.00	60.00	40.00	30.00	95.00	40.00
Compote, covered						
High standard, 8"d., 11"h	80.00	125.00	100.00	70.00	175.00	90.00
Open						
High standard						
9½"d	50.00	85.00	65.00	40.00	85.00	—
Ruffled rim, jelly	—	—	—	25.00	50.00	—

Items made	Amber	Amethyst	Blue	Clear	Ruby	Vas
Low standard, 7"d	45.00	80.00	35.00	25.00	225.00	—
Creamer						
Flat, square	50.00	80.00	—	35.00	75.00	50.00
Tall, 6½"h	45.00	80.00	50.00	30.00	65.00	45.00
Cruet, original stopper	80.00	—	—	45.00	—	—
Dish, footed, round, scalloped rim	50.00	50.00	50.00	—	40.00	40.00
Goblet, 6"h	50.00	70.00	50.00	30.00	65.00	55.00
Lamp, oil, 12¾"h, original burner and chimney	—	—	185.00	—	—	—
Mug, pressed handle	—	—	—	20.00	30.00	—
Pitcher, water						
Bulbous, applied handle						
½ gallon	75.00	110.00	75.00	65.00	250.00	100.00
3 quart	85.00	120.00	85.00	70.00	250.00	110.00
Relish tray, fish shaped	50.00	50.00	50.00	—	40.00	40.00
Salt, boat shape	15.00	30.00	20.00	10.00	45.00	15.00
Sauce dish, round						
Flat, smooth rim, 4"d	15.00	30.00	20.00	10.00	30.00	15.00
Footed, smooth rim						
4"d	15.00	30.00	20.00	10.00	30.00	15.00
4½"d	15.00	30.00	20.00	10.00	30.00	15.00
Spoonholder	45.00	65.00	50.00	35.00	65.00	45.00
Sugar bowl, covered	70.00	100.00	60.00	50.00	100.00	60.00
Tumbler, water, flat, 3¾"h	40.00	60.00	55.00	30.00	45.00	50.00

CHAIN

Creamer; covered sugar bowl.

Non-flint. Maker unknown, ca. 1870s.

Original color production: Clear.

Reproductions: None.

References: Enos-MPG (Chart-2), Kam-1 (P. 24), Lee-EAPG (Pl. 132), Lee-VG (Pl. 76), McCn-PGP (Pl. 35), Mtz-1 (P. 133), Swn-PG (P. 65), Uni-1 (P. 102), Wlkr-PGA (Fig. 8, No. 45).

Items made	Clear	Items made	Clear
Butter dish, covered, flat	40.00	7"d	20.00
Celery vase	35.00	11"d	30.00
Compote, covered, high standard	45.00	Relish tray, oval	20.00
Creamer	25.00	Sauce dish, round	
Goblet	30.00	Flat	10.00
Pickle dish	15.00	Footed	12.00
Pitcher		Spoonholder	30.00
Milk, 1 quart	65.00	Sugar bowl, covered	35.00
Water, ½ gallon	85.00	Wine	25.00
Plate, round			

CHAIN WITH STAR

Spoonholder; h.s. true open compote; creamer; goblet.

OMN: Bryce No. 79. AKA: Chain [Millard], Frosted Chain.

Non-flint. Bryce Brothers (pattern line No. 79), Pittsburgh, PA. ca. 1882. Reissued by The United States Glass Co., Pittsburgh, PA. ca. 1890. Shards have been found at the site of The Burlington Glass Works, Hamilton, Ontario, Canada. Illustrated in the Bryce Brothers 1890 catalog, and the ca. 1891 United States Glass Co. catalog of member firms.

Original color production: Clear. The main pattern design element depicts a continuous pointed chain. Below each upper and lower point on the chain appears a clear ornament, while between each point are rays suggestive of "stars".

Reproductions: None.

References: Hea-3 (PP. 77-78), Hea-5 (P. 86), Kam-8 (PP. 12-13), Lee-VG (PP. 244, 246), Lee-EAPG (P. 572), Mil-1 (Pl. 175), Mtz-1 (P. 117), Oliv-AAG (P. 60), Rev-APG (P. 87), Spil-AEPG (P. 304), Swn-PG (P. 65), Thur-1 (P. 198), Uni-1 (P. 103), Uni/Wor-CHPGT (P. 75), Wlkr-PGA (Fig. 8, No. 36).

Items made	Clear	Items made	Clear
Bowl, open		Low footed, scalloped rim, 9½"d	30.00
Flat, shallow, 7½"d	25.00	Butter dish, covered, low foot, 6"d	35.00

Items made	Clear	Items made	Clear
Cake stand, high standard		Pitcher, water, applied handle, circular	
8¾"d	30.00	foot, 9¼"h	55.00
9½"d	35.00	Plate	
10½"d	35.00	Dinner, round	
Compote		7"d	25.00
Covered		10"d	35.00
High standard		Bread, round, tab handles, 11"d	35.00
7"d	55.00	Relish dish	10.00
9"d	55.00	Salt shaker, original top	25.00
Low standard, 9"d	45.00	Sauce dish, round	
Open		Flat, 4"d	10.00
High standard, scalloped rim	30.00	Footed, 4"d	10.00
Low standard, 7"d	35.00	Spoonholder	20.00
Creamer, 5½"h	25.00	Sugar bowl, covered	35.00
Dish, oval, open, flat, 5¾" x 7½"	20.00	Syrup pitcher, original top	85.00
Goblet	25.00	Wine	25.00
Pickle dish, oval	10.00		

CHAMPION

Flat dish; jelly compote; goblet; champagne; triangular dish.

OMN: McKee's No. 103. AKA: Fan(s) with Cross Bars [Metz], Seagirt [Millard].

Non-flint. McKee & Brothers, Jeannette, PA., McKee-Jeannette Glass Co., Jeannette, PA. National Glass Co., Pittsburgh, PA. ca. 1894 to as late as 1917. Illustrated in the McKee & Brothers 1894 catalog and the McKee Glass Co. 1917 catalog.

Original color production: Clear, clear with amber stain and clear with ruby stain (stained items being decorated by the Beaumont Glass Works, Pittsburgh, PA. who sold it as their own product). Emerald green or any other color is scarce.

Reproductions: None.

References: Hea-1 (P. 17, Figs. 47-48), Hea-3 (P. 18), Hea-6 (P. 22), Hea-7 (Figs. 448-466), Kam-1 (P. 106), McCn-PGP (Pl. 69), Mil-2 (Pl. 90), Mil-1 (Pl. 90), Mil-2 (Pl. 90), Mtz-1 (P. 228-

Toothpick holder; 5 oz. cruet (n.o.s.); goblet; hat shaped bowl; sauce dish.

229), Mur-CO (PP. 9, 69), Pet-Sal (P. 123), Pet-GPP (P. 123), Rev-APG (P. 238), Stot-McKe (PP. 209, 216, 334).

Items made	Clear	Clear/ Amber	Clear/ Ruby
Bowl, open, flat, serrated rim			
Hat shape, flat, tooled from celery vase	30.00	55.00	55.00
Round, master berry	45.00	55.00	65.00
Square, master berry	45.00	55.00	65.00
Butter dish, covered, flat	45.00	100.00	100.00
Cake stand, high standard			
7½"d	30.00	85.00	60.00
8½"d	30.00	85.00	60.00
10"d	35.00	100.00	90.00
11"d	35.00	100.00	90.00
Carafe	50.00	135.00	150.00
Castor set (3 bottles, toothpick holder with matching glass holder)	125.00	—	—
Celery vase, flat, scalloped rim	40.00	100.00	100.00
Compote, high standard			
Covered	50.00	175.00	200.00
Open, round			
Belled bowl, scalloped rim			
5"d, jelly	20.00	65.00	65.00
6"d	20.00	65.00	65.00
7"d	25.00	85.00	85.00
8"d	25.00	85.00	85.00
9"d	30.00	100.00	100.00
Deep bowl, scalloped rim			
5"d, jelly	20.00	65.00	65.00
6"d	20.00	65.00	65.00
7"d	25.00	85.00	85.00
8"d	25.00	85.00	100.00
9"d	35.00	100.00	100.00
Shallow bowl, scalloped rim, jelly, 5"d	20.00	65.00	65.00
Creamer, applied handle			
Individual	15.00	20.00	20.00
Table size	25.00	60.00	60.00
Cruet, o.s.			
4 ounce (R)	30.00	175.00	200.00
5 ounce (R)	30.00	175.00	200.00

Items made	Clear	Clear/ Amber	Clear/ Ruby
Cup, custard	10.00	25.00	25.00
Decanter, original stopper	35.00	85.00	85.00
Dish, flat			
Round, folded sides, jelly	25.00	50.00	50.00
Triangular, handled	30.00	55.00	55.00
Goblet	25.00	65.00	65.00
Ice bucket	40.00	85.00	85.00
Marmalade jar, covered	40.00	90.00	90.00
Perfume bottle, o.s.			
Bulbous, squatty, teardrop stopper	20.00	40.00	40.00
Straight, tall, teardrop stopper	20.00	40.00	40.00
Pickle dish, 8"l	15.00	25.00	25.00
Pitcher, water, tankard, applied handle, ½ gallon	70.00	150.00	175.00
Plate, round, dinner			
6"d	25.00	50.00	75.00
8"d	25.00	50.00	75.00
10"d	25.00	35.00	75.00
Punch bowl, footed, 14"d	100.00	250.00	250.00
Rose bowl	25.00	40.00	40.00
Salt, open			
Individual	35.00	10.00	35.00
Master, flat (R)	65.00	25.00	65.00
Shaker, original top	15.00	35.00	35.00
Sauce dish, flat, serrated rim			
Round	5.00	20.00	20.00
Square	5.00	20.00	20.00
Spice set, complete	125.00	250.00	250.00
Spoonholder	20.00	40.00	45.00
Sugar bowl			
Individual, true open	35.00	60.00	65.00
Table size, covered	40.00	75.00	85.00
Syrup pitcher, original top	75.00	200.00	200.00
Toothpick holder	20.00	65.00	75.00
Tray			
Water, round	45.00	—	—
Wine, round	45.00	—	—
Tumbler, water, flat	15.00	45.00	45.00
Wine	20.00	45.00	45.00

Tumbler; spoonholder (etched); tankard water pitcher; celery vase.

OMN: O'Hara's No. 82, Crown Jewels.

Non-flint. O'Hara Glass Co. (pattern line No. 82), Pittsburgh, PA. ca. 1888. Reissued by the United States Glass Co., Pittsburgh, PA. at Factory "L" (O'Hara Glass Co., Pittsburgh, PA.) after the 1891 merger. Illustrated in the ca. 1890 United States Glass Co. Factory "L" catalog.

Original color production: Clear (plain or copper wheel engraved).

Reproductions: None.

References: Hea-5 (P. 16), Kam-2 (PP. 114-115), Kam/Wod Vol.1 (P. 133), Lee-VG (Pl. 68, No. 1), Mil-1 (Pl. 163), Mtz-1 (P. 49), Mtz-2 (PP. 130-131), Pet-Sal (P. 24), Rev-APG (PP. 275-276), Spnc-EGC (P. 72), Uni-1 (P. 245), Uni-TCG (PP. 84-85), Uni/Wor-CHPGT (P. 76).

Items made	Etched	Plain
Banana stand		
High standard	100.00	85.00
Low standard	90.00	75.00
Bowl, open		
Flat, smooth-flared rim		
6"d	30.00	35.00
7"d	30.00	35.00
8"d., master berry	35.00	40.00
Finger	45.00	35.00
Fruit, high standard, scalloped rim, 7½"h., 9"d	85.00	75.00
Violet	—	40.00
Butter dish, covered, flat, 6½"d	90.00	70.00
Cake stand, high standard, 10"d	85.00	95.00
Castor set, complete	150.00	150.00
Celery vase, flat, smooth rim	35.00	40.00
Compote		
Covered		
High standard		
Round		
6"d	75.00	65.00
7"d	85.00	75.00

Items made	Etched	Plain
8"d	95.00	85.00
Square, 8"	95.00	90.00
Low standard	75.00	80.00
Open		
Round		
High standard, 9½"d	65.00	55.00
Low standard		
9½"d	55.00	45.00
10"d., fruit bowl	45.00	40.00
Square, 9"sq., 7½"h	65.00	75.00
Creamer, 5"h	65.00	55.00
Goblet	85.00	75.00
Inkwell, flat, marked "Davis automatic Inkstand, Patented May 8, 1889"	—	85.00
Pitcher, water, tankard, applied reeded handle		
½ pint	65.00	55.00
Pint	65.00	55.00
Quart	90.00	85.00
½ gallon	125.00	110.00
Salt		
Master, flat, open, 2"h., 2¾"d	—	40.00
Shaker, tall, original top	40.00	35.00
Sauce dish, flat, round		
3¼"d	18.00	15.00
4"d	18.00	15.00
Sponge dish	—	30.00
Spoonholder, flat, smooth rim	45.00	50.00
Sugar bowl, covered, 7½"h	85.00	75.00
Sugar shaker, original top	90.00	80.00
Tray, water, round, handled	65.00	55.00
Tumbler, water, flat	45.00	40.00
Wine (R)	90.00	90.00

CHERRY

Champagne; goblet.

Non-flint. Bakewell, Pears & Co., Pittsburgh, PA. ca. 1870. Designed and patented by William M. Kirchner April 5, 1870 (patent No. 3,954). Illustrated in the ca. 1875 Bakewell, Pears & Co. catalog.

Original color production: Clear, milk white.

Reproductions: Westmorland Glass Co., Grapeville, PA. reproduced the Cherry pattern in milk white (plain or enamel decorated) with the company's entwined "WG" monogram in the following items: double handled covered cookie jar, $3\frac{1}{4}$"h. creamer, $2\frac{1}{4}$"h. flat double handled sugar bowl, $5\frac{1}{2}$" high standard covered honey dish, $10\frac{1}{2}$" high standard scalloped rim true open compote, and 12"h. double handled covered compote.

The following items were reproduced in amber, amethyst, clear, green, ruby red, vaseline, milk white, blue milk glass, and cobalt blue: covered butter dish, goblet, salt dip, covered sugar bowl, toothpick holder, tumbler and water pitcher. Comparing original items with reproductions, the later design is much more pronounced and sharper to the sight than is the original which is rounded and much softer to the touch.

References: Belnp-MG (P. 106), Drep-ABC OG (P. 153), Enos-MPG (Chart-5), Fer-YMG (P. 168), Inn-EGP (P. 53), Inn-PG (PP. 353, 411), Lee-EAPG (Pl. 66, No. 2), Mil-1 (Pl. 114), Mtz-1 (PP. 90-91), Pear-CAT (PP. 6, 18, 22, 24-25), Phil-EOG (P. 188), Rev-APG (PP. 44, 49), Wlkr-PGA (Fig. 8, Nos. 7, 39, 47).

Items made	Clear	Milk White
Butter dish, covered, flat	65.00	90.00
Celery vase	40.00	70.00
Champagne	30.00	45.00
Compote		
Covered, high standard, 8"d	75.00	125.00
Open		
High standard, 8"d	40.00	50.00
Low standard, 8"d	40.00	50.00
Creamer, applied handle	45.00	85.00
Goblet	35.00	65.00
Sauce dish, round, flat	15.00	20.00
Spoonholder, pedestaled, scalloped rim	35.00	60.00
Sugar bowl, covered	50.00	75.00
Wine	30.00	40.00

Creamer.

AKA: OMN: No. 475. Cherry with Thumbprint(s), Panelled Cherry.

Non-flint. Northwood Glass Co., Martin's Ferry, OH., ca. late 1880s. Kokomo Glass Mfg. Co., Kokomo, IN., ca. 1904.

Reproductions: Some.

References: BOND-AG (P. 116), ENOS-MPG (Chart 4), Kam-4 (P. 128), Lee-EAPG (PP. 474-475), McCn-PGP (P. 321), Mil-1 (P. 132), Mtz-1 (PP. 90-91), Uni-1 (P. C235).

Items made	Clear	Clear w/ Stain
Bowl		
Covered, flat	35.00	65.00
Open, master berry, flat	15.00	30.00
Butter dish, covered, flat	45.00	90.00
Creamer, 4¾"h	35.00	65.00
Cup, pedestaled	15.00	30.00
Goblet	30.00	60.00
Mug, marked "Sweet Heart" in the base	25.00	50.00
Pitcher, water, ½ gallon	80.00	110.00
Sauce dish, round		
Flat	15.00	20.00
Footed	15.00	20.00
Spoonholder	35.00	55.00
Sugar bowl, covered	65.00	85.00
Syrup, original glass cover	70.00	135.00
Toothpick holder	25.00	45.00
Tumbler		
Lemonade	35.00	45.00
Water, flat	30.00	45.00
Wine	30.00	45.00

Sauce dish; 10½"d. "Warrior" plate; water pitcher; sauce dish.

Covered butter dish; covered sugar bowl.

Non-flint. Gillinder & Sons, Philadelphia, PA. ca. 1875.

Original color production: Clear with acid finish. Bases are either collared or footed, the latter being either stippled or frosted. Milk white or any other color is extremely rare. Items are clear and acid finished, the decorative panels alternating between gothic-styled arches filled with daisy and button and high-classical motifs. Finials are bunches of acorns and oak leaves. Earliest type bases are open-legged, replaced by thick collared bases that were less susceptible to breakage. The plate may be found with the name "Jacobus" embossed thereon. A very rare variant of Classic portrays frosted panels portraying "cupid's hunt" rather than classical figures.

Reproductions: None.

References: Bros-TS (P. 41), Enos-MPG (Chart-5), Grow-GAG (Fig. 20), Kam-4 (PP. 108-109), Lee-EAPG (Pl. 97), Lind-HG (PP. 316-317), McCn-PGP (P. 395), Mil-1 (Pl. 74), Mil-OG (Pl. 218), Oliv-AAG (P. 60), Rev-APG (P. 169), Stu-BP (PP. 105-106), Spil-AEPG (P. 279), Spil-TBV (P. 86), Swn-PG (P. 85), Uni-1 (P. 259).

Items made	Clear/Frosted	Items made	Clear/Frosted
Bowl, 7″d		Milk, 1 quart	300.00
Covered, log feet	125.00	Water	
Open, master berry	85.00	Collared base	225.00
Butter dish, covered, log feet, 5³/₄″d	200.00	Log feet	350.00
Celery vase		Plate, dinner, round, 10½″d	
Collared base	100.00	"Blaine"	185.00
Log feet	125.00	"Cleveland"	185.00
Compote, covered		"Hendricks"	175.00
Collared base		"Logan"	250.00
6½″d	150.00	"Warrior"	150.00
8½″d	175.00	Sauce dish, round	
12½″d	300.00	Collared base, 4¼″d	30.00
Log feet		Log feet, 4¼″d	40.00
6½″d	225.00	Spoonholder	
7½″d	250.00	Collared base	75.00
Open, log feet, 7³/₄″d	100.00	Log feet	95.00
Creamer, log feet	125.00	Sugar bowl, covered	
Goblet	225.00	Collared base	150.00
Marmalade jar, covered	350.00	Log feet	175.00
Pitcher		Sweetmeat jar, covered	200.00

CLASSIC MEDALLION

Footed sauce dish; spoonholder; covered sugar bowl; creamer.

AKA: Cameo [Lee].

Non-flint. Maker unknown ca. 1870s-1880s.

Original color production: Clear.

Reproductions: None.

References: Kam-1 (PP. 22-23), Lee-VG (Pl. 36, No. 1), McCn-PGP (P. 393), Mtz-1 (PP. 102-103), Uni-1 (P. 89).

Items made	Clear	Items made	Clear
Bowl, open, smooth rim, round		Open, low standard, 7"d., 3¾"h	30.00
Flat, straight sides, 8"	30.00	Creamer, 5½"h	25.00
Footed, 6¼"d	40.00	Goblet	35.00
Butter dish, covered	40.00	Pitcher, water, ½ gallon	85.00
Celery vase	35.00	Sauce dish, round, footed	15.00
Compote, round		Spoonholder	25.00
Covered, high standard	45.00	Sugar bowl, covered	40.00

CLEAR DIAGONAL BAND

Flat sauce; celery vase; pickle castor set (complete); high standard open compote.

AKA: California State.

Non-flint. Maker unknown, ca. 1880s. Shards have been found at the site of the Burlington Glass Works, Hamilton, Ontario, Canada.

Original color production: Clear. Color would be rare.

Reproductions: None.

References: Enos-MPG (Chart-2), Kam-1 (P. 44), Kam/Wod Vol.1 (P. 40), Lee-EAPG (Pl. 156, No. 2), Lind-HG (P. 114), McCn-PGP (P. 513), Mil-1 (Pl. 12), Mtz-1 (P. 172-173), Oliv-AAG (P. 63), Pet-Sal (P. 27), Rev-APG (P. 294), Stu-BP (P. 1), Uni/Wor-CHPGT (P. 77), Wlkr-PGA (Fig.8, No. 2).

Items made	Clear	Items made	Clear
Bowl, footed, covered	30.00	Cordial	25.00
Butter dish, covered	40.00	Creamer, 6"h, pressed handle	25.00
Cake stand, high standard	40.00	Dish, oval, open, flat	10.00
Celery vase, pedestaled	25.00	Goblet	20.00
Compote, high standard, round		Marmalade jar, covered	35.00
Covered	45.00	Pitcher, water, ½ gallon	40.00
Open	30.00	Plate, dinner, round, 7¼"d	15.00

Items made	Clear		Items made	Clear
Platter, inscribed "Eureka" center	40.00		Footed	10.00
Relish tray, oval	10.00		Spoonholder	20.00
Salt shaker, original top	15.00		Sugar bowl, covered	40.00
Sauce dish, round			Wine	25.00
Flat	5.00			

CLEMATIS

Spoonholder.

AKA: Fuchsia [Unitt].

Non-flint. Maker unknown, ca. 1875-1885.

Original color production: Clear.

Reproductions: None.

References: Enos-MPG (Chart-5), Kam-3 (P. 25), Kam/Wod Vol.1 (P. 170), Lee-EAPG (Pl. 75, No. 2), McCn-PGP (P. 289), Mtz-1 (PP. 54-55), Mil-1 (Pl. 31), Uni-1 (P. 203), Uni/Wor-CHPGT (P. 78).

Items made	Clear		Items made	Clear
Bowl, oval, open, flat	40.00		Pickle tray	10.00
Butter dish, covered, flat	35.00		Pitcher, water, ½ gallon	65.00
Creamer, 5½"h	35.00		Sauce dish, flat, round, 4"d	10.00
Goblet	25.00		Spoonholder	30.00
Lamp, oil, 12"h. metal base, frosted			Sugar bowl, covered	45.00
font, glass stem, original burner and				
chimney	50.00			

Custard cup; covered butter dish; covered sugar; individual creamer.

Ruffled footed sauce dish; 8½"d ruffled footed bowl.

OMN: U.S. Glass No. 15,057 Colorado. AKA: Jewel, Lacy Medallion [Kamm].

Non-flint. The United States Glass Co., Pittsburgh, PA. ca. 1899 to as late as 1920. Reviewed in the January 13, 1898 issue of the *Crockery and Glass Journal* and the August, 1906 and 1899 Butler Brothers catalogs, and illustrated in the United States Glass Co. ca. 1904 catalog.

Original color production: Blue (originally termed "Dewey Blue"), clear, green (plain or copper wheel engraved). Black, clear with ruby stain, vaseline or any other color is rare. Very similar to Lacy Medallion which has no feet, Colorado was often used by decorators as souvenir ware. Rims of bowls and sauces may be round and smooth or hand tooled into ruffles.

Reproductions: The Summit Art Glass Co., Mogadore/Rootstown, OH., reproduced, from a new mold, the toothpick holder in both clear and original colors. Reproductions lack the refined nature of the original design, "gilding" appears painted and poorly fired, while colors are are not as mellow and vibrant as the originals.

References: Bar-RS (Pl. 14), Bros-TS (PP. 42-43), Hart/Cobb-SS (P. 18), Hea-1 (P. 17), Hea-5 (P. 36, Nos. 38-40), Hea-7 (P. 92), Hea-TPS (PP. 22, 26), Kam-1 (P. 106), Kam-2 (PP. 115-116), Kam-5 (P. 78), Kam-6 (Pl. 94), McCn-PGP (Pl. 39), Mig-TPS (Pl. 3), Pet-Sal (P. 25), Pyne-PG (P. 149), Rev-APG (P. 310), Uni-2 (P. 232), Wlkr-PGA (Fig. 8, No. 57).

Items made	Blue	Clear	Green
Banana stand, footed, 7″	45.00	25.00	40.00
Bowl, open			
Round			
Flat, 6″d	35.00	20.00	30.00
Footed			
Cafe, handled			
7½″d	40.00	25.00	35.00
8½″d	60.00	45.00	55.00
Crimped rim			
5″d	35.00	20.00	30.00
6″d	45.00	30.00	40.00
7″d	55.00	35.00	50.00
8″d	55.00	35.00	50.00
Flared rim			
5″d	35.00	20.00	30.00
6″d	45.00	30.00	40.00
7″d	55.00	35.00	50.00
8″d	55.00	35.00	50.00
Smooth rim			
5″d	35.00	20.00	30.00
6″d	45.00	30.00	40.00
7″d	55.00	35.00	50.00
8″d	55.00	35.00	40.00
Violet, footed	50.00	20.00	45.00
Triangular, footed	40.00	25.00	35.00
Butter dish, covered, footed, flanged rim	225.00	65.00	125.00
Cake stand, high standard	70.00	55.00	65.00
Celery vase	65.00	35.00	45.00
Cheese dish, open, footed	65.00	35.00	45.00
Cologne bottle, original ball stopper, 4 ounce	100.00	45.00	90.00
Compote, open, high standard			
5″d	45.00	20.00	40.00
6″d	45.00	20.00	40.00
7″d	60.00	35.00	45.00
8″d	75.00	35.00	55.00
9″d	95.00	35.00	65.00
Creamer			
Individual			
Bulbous, 3⅝″h	40.00	20.00	35.00
Tankard, 3¼″h	40.00	20.00	35.00
Table size	95.00	45.00	75.00
Cup, custard, applied handle, footed			
Large	30.00	20.00	25.00
Small	30.00	20.00	25.00
Dish			
Crimped rim, 8″d	50.00	25.00	40.00
Flared edge, 8″d	50.00	25.00	40.00
Scalloped rim, handled			
4″d	35.00	20.00	30.00
5″d	35.00	20.00	30.00
Jar, cracker, covered	125.00	50.00	100.00
Mug	40.00	20.00	30.00
Olive dish	40.00	20.00	30.00

Items made	Blue	Clear	Green
Pickle dish	40.00	20.00	30.00
Pitcher, bulbous, applied handle			
Milk, 1 quart	145.00	80.00	100.00
Water, ½ gallon	400.00	125.00	200.00
Plate, round			
6"d	50.00	15.00	45.00
8"d	65.00	20.00	60.00
Salt shaker, bulbous, o.s.	65.00	30.00	50.00
Sauce dish, footed, round, 4"d			
Flared rim	35.00	15.00	20.00
Ruffled rim	35.00	15.00	20.00
Sherbert cup			
Large	30.00	20.00	25.00
Small	30.00	20.00	25.00
Spoonholder, footed	75.00	40.00	60.00
Sugar bowl			
Individual, open			
Handles	35.00	20.00	35.00
Handleless	35.00	20.00	35.00
Table size, covered	80.00	65.00	70.00
Toothpick holder	60.00	30.00	45.00
Tray			
Calling card	45.00	25.00	35.00
Jewel	45.00	25.00	35.00
Tumbler, water plain or handled	35.00	15.00	30.00
Vase, 12"h	85.00	35.00	60.00

COMET

Goblet; whiskey tumbler.

Flint. The Boston and Sandwich Glass Co., Sandwich, MA. ca. late 1840s-early 1860s.

Original color production: Clear. Sapphire blue, canary-yellow or any other color is rare. Handles are applied.

Reproductions: None.

References: Enos-MPG (Chart-1), Kam-4 (P. 13), Lee-EAPG (Pl. 49, No. 3), McKrn-AG (PP. 400-401), Mil-1 (Pl. 161), Mtz-1 (PP. 12, 13), Oliv-AAG (P. 52), Spil-AEPG (P. 260), Uni-1 (P. 43).

Items made	Clear	Items made	Clear
Butter dish, covered	200.00	Spoonholder	85.00
Compote, open, low standard	145.00	Sugar bowl, covered	175.00
Creamer, applied handle	175.00	Tumbler, flat	
Goblet, 6"h	110.00	Water	100.00
Mug, applied handle	135.00	Whiskey	100.00
Pitcher, water, applied handle, ½ gallon	550.00		

CONNECTICUT States Series

Covered marmalade jar; h.s. covered compote; h.s. true open compote; cruet o.s.

OMN: U.S. Glass No. 15,068, Connecticut.

Non-flint. The United States Glass Co., Pittsburgh, PA. (pattern line No. 15,068) ca. 1900. Illustrated in the United States Glass Co. 1898 catalog.

Original color production: Clear (plain or copper wheel engraved). Odd pieces may be found in clear with ruby stain, often souvenired. Produced in an extended table setting.

Reproductions: None.

References: Hart/Cobb-SS (P. 19), Hea-RUTPS (Fig. 1190), Hea-5 (P. 166), Hea-7 (P. 93), Kam-4 (P. 65), Kam-5 (P. 68), McCn-PGP (Pl. 61), Pet-Sal (P. 125), Rev-APG (P. 312).

Items made	Clear	Items made	Clear
Basket, handled	50.00	6"d	10.00
Biscuit jar, covered	25.00	7"d	15.00
Bottle, water	45.00	8"d	15.00
Bowl, open, smooth rim, collared base		Patterned rim	
Patterned base		6"d	15.00
5"d	10.00	8"d	15.00

Items made	Clear	Items made	Clear
Butter dish, covered	35.00	Lamp, oil, fire enamel decor, original	
Cake stand, high standard, 10″d	40.00	burner and chimney	75.00
Celery		Lemonade, handled	20.00
Tray	20.00	Marmalade jar, covered	40.00
Vase	25.00	Pickle jar, covered	25.00
Compote, round		Pitcher	
Covered		Bulbous	
High standard		3 pint	40.00
5″d	20.00	$^1/_2$ gallon	40.00
5$^1/_2$″d	20.00	Tankard	
6″d	25.00	Pint	25.00
7″d	30.00	Quart	30.00
8″d	35.00	$^1/_2$ gallon	40.00
Low standard, 7″d	30.00	Plate, cheese, covered	50.00
Open		Relish tray	10.00
High standard, saucer bowl,		Salt shaker, original top	
scalloped rim	45.00	Bulbous	10.00
6″d	20.00	Straight-sided (table size)	10.00
7$^1/_2$″d	20.00	Tall (hotel size)	10.00
8$^1/_2$″d	20.00	Sauce dish, flat, round	
9$^1/_2$″d	25.00	Belled bowl, patterned base	
Low standard, 7″d	35.00	4″d	10.00
Creamer	25.00	4$^1/_2$″d	10.00
Cruet, original stopper	25.00	Straight-sided bowl, patterned base	
Cup, handled		4″d	10.00
Custard	5.00	4$^1/_2$″d	10.00
Sherbert	5.00	Spoonholder	20.00
Dish		Sugar bowl, covered	35.00
Oblong, open, flat, 8″l	20.00	Sugar shaker, original top	35.00
Round, flat, handled		Toothpick holder	40.00
4$^1/_2$″d	15.00	Tumbler, water, flat	15.00
5″d	15.00	Vase	15.00
Goblet	20.00	Wine	35.00

CORD AND TASSEL

Wine; goblet.

129

Non-flint. The LaBelle Glass Co., Bridgeport, OH. ca. 1872. The Central Glass Co., Wheeling, WV. ca. 1879.

Original color production: Clear. Designed, patented and named by Andrew H. Baggs, July 23, 1872 (patent No. 6,002), assignor to the LaBelle Glass Co. Patented for a 3 $\frac{1}{2}$ year period, the Baggs patent expired in January, 1876 at which time the design became public domain and was reissued by the Central Glass Co. Shards have been found at the site of the Burlington Glass Works, Hamilton, Ontario, Canada.

Reproductions: None.

References: Hlms-BCA (P. 278), Lee-EAPG (Pl. 116, No. 2), McCn-PGP (Pl. 167), Mil-2 (Pl. 127), Mtz-1 (PP. 130-131), Oliv-AAG (P. 60), Pet-GPP (PP. 32-33), Rev-APG (P. 110), Uni-1 (PP. 276-277), Uni/Wor-CHPGT (P. 85).

Items made	Clear	Items made	Clear
Bottle, castor	25.00	Lamp, footed, applied finger grip	100.00
Bowl, oval, open, flat	25.00	Mug, applied handle	55.00
Butter dish, covered, flat	65.00	Mustard jar, covered	45.00
Cake stand, high standard, 9½"d	50.00	Pickle dish, oval	15.00
Celery vase	40.00	Pitcher, water, applied handle, ½	
Compote, high standard		gallon	95.00
Covered	90.00	Salt shaker, bulbous, original top	30.00
Open	35.00	Sauce dish, round, flat	10.00
Cordial	45.00	Spoonholder	25.00
Creamer	25.00	Sugar bowl, covered	55.00
Dish, oval, flat, vegetable	25.00	Syrup pitcher, original top	125.00
Egg cup, single, open	35.00	Tumbler, water, flat	45.00
Goblet	40.00	Wine	30.00

CORD DRAPERY

Tumbler; pickle dish; goblet.

OMN: Indiana Tumbler No. 350, Indiana.

Non-flint. National Glass Co. Combine ca. 1901. Indiana Tumbler & Goblet Co. (pattern line No. 350), Greentown, IN. ca. 1898. Indiana Glass Co., Dunkirk, IN. after 1907. Advertised on

January 17, 1901 as "Indiana", and illustrated in the Baltimore Bargain House catalogs No. 479 (August, 1903), No. 483 (December, 1903), and No. 496 (August 15, 1904).

Original color production: Amber, blue, clear, emerald green. Odd pieces in canary-yellow, chocolate, opaque white or any other color are rare.

Reproductions: None.

References: Bond-AG (Items 204, 205, 212, 213), Bros-TS (P. 39), Hart/Cob (P. 32), Hea-1 (P. 18, Fig. 63), Hea-3 (P. 21), Hea-6 (P. 24, Figs. 98-100), Kam-5 (Pl. 5), Kam-1 (P. 79), Kam-7 (P. 287), Meas-GG (PP. 59-61), Mil-1 (Pl. 58), Mil-OG (Pl. 241), Mtz-1 (PP. 130-131), Mur-MCO (P. 73), Pet-Sal (P. 25), Rev-APG (P. 203), Uni-1 (P. 99), Wlkr-PGA (Fig. 15, No. 92).

Items made	Amber	Blue	Clear	Emerald Green
Bowl, open				
Oval	135.00	145.00	60.00	135.00
Rectangular	135.00	145.00	60.00	135.00
Round				
Flat, 8″d., deep, beaded rim	110.00	125.00	35.00	110.00
Footed				
Fluted rim				
6¼″d	145.00	155.00	45.00	145.00
8¼″d	155.00	165.00	55.00	155.00
Plain rim				
6¼″d	125.00	135.00	45.00	125.00
8¼″d	135.00	145.00	55.00	135.00
Butter dish, covered				
4¾″d	195.00	185.00	65.00	165.00
5⅛″d	165.00	165.00	55.00	145.00
Cake stand, high standard	175.00	200.00	65.00	—
Compote, high standard, round				
Covered				
4¼″d	150.00	165.00	50.00	150.00
6½″d	—	—	65.00	—
9″d	—	—	85.00	—
Open, 8½″d	—	225.00	65.00	—
Creamer				
4¼″h	110.00	135.00	45.00	110.00
4¾″h	120.00	145.00	55.00	120.00
Cruet, original stopper	325.00	400.00	90.00	325.00
Cup, punch	—	125.00	20.00	—
Goblet	175.00	190.00	100.00	175.00
Mug	125.00	145.00	60.00	—
Pickle dish, oval, 9¼″l	85.00	100.00	35.00	90.00
Pitcher, water, ½ gallon	185.00	200.00	65.00	185.00
Salt shaker, original top	90.00	125.00	55.00	95.00
Sauce dish, round				
Flat, hand fluted rim	75.00	85.00	25.00	75.00
Footed				
3⅞″d	60.00	65.00	25.00	60.00
4⅛″d	60.00	65.00	25.00	60.00
Spoonholder	65.00	75.00	35.00	65.00
Sugar bowl, covered	115.00	125.00	45.00	120.00
Syrup pitcher, original top	300.00	350.00	90.00	300.00
Toothpick holder	500.00	500.00	80.00	—
Tray, water	175.00	185.00	75.00	175.00
Tumbler, water, flat	100.00	125.00	35.00	115.00
Wine	125.00	145.00	85.00	135.00

Individual creamer (emerald green); toothpick holder (clear).

OMN: Cordova.

Non-flint. The O'Hara Glass Co., Pittsburgh, PA. ca. 1891. Reissued by the United States Glass Co., Pittsburgh, PA. ca. 1891. Designed and patented by John G. Lyon, December 16, 1890 for the O'Hara Glass Co., the pattern was first exhibited at the Pittsburgh Glass Show of 1890. Reviewed in the February 4, 1891 issue of *China, Glass and Lamps*, the pattern is illustrated in the 1898, 1904, and 1918 United States Glass Co. catalogs.

Original color production: Clear. Odd items may be found in emerald green and clear with ruby stain although complete table services were not produced in either color. Some items were produced over a thirty five year period.

Reproductions: None.

References: Bar-RS (Pl. 14), Hea-1 (P. 18, Figs. 64-65), Hea-5 (P. 162, Plt. D), Hea-7 (P. 95), Kam-1 (P. 105), Kam-5 (P. 47), Kam-6 (Plts. 2,3), Lee-VG (Plt. 66, No. 1), McCn-PGP (P. 457), Mtz-2 (PP. 168-169), Pet-GPP (P. 114), Pet-Sal (P. 1577, Fig. "N"), Rev-APG (PP. 275-276), Wlkr-PGA (Fig. 15, Nos. 18, 59).

Items made	Clear	Items made	Clear
Bottle, cologne, original pyramidal		Straight bowl	
stopper	20.00	6"d	15.00
Bowl, flat		7"d	20.00
Covered		8"d	20.00
6"d	25.00	9"d	20.00
7"d	25.00	Berry, master, covered	30.00
8"d	30.00	Finger	15.00
9"d	30.00	Punch	85.00
Open		Butter dish, covered, flat, handled	50.00
Flared bowl		Cake stand, 10"d., high standard	70.00
6"d	20.00	Casserole, flat	
7"d	20.00	Plain rim	
8"d	20.00	6"d	30.00
9"d	25.00	7"d	30.00
		8"d	30.00

Items made	Clear	Items made	Clear
Flared rim		Inkwell, original metal top	100.00
6"d	30.00	Jar, cracker, covered	85.00
8"d	30.00	Jug, ½ pint	40.00
Catsup, covered, handled	75.00	Mug, handled	15.00
Celery vase	35.00	Mustard jar, covered	45.00
Cologne bottle, original cover, 4 ounce	25.00	Nappy, flat, handled, 6"d	10.00
Compote		Pickle jar, covered	35.00
Covered, high standard		Pitcher, tankard	
6"d	35.00	½ pint	25.00
7"d	40.00	Pint	30.00
8"d	45.00	Milk, 1 quart	30.00
Open		Water, ½ gallon	45.00
High standard		Salt	
Flared bowl		Individual, round, flat	25.00
7"d	25.00	Shaker, original top	20.00
8"d	35.00	Sauce dish, flat, round	
9"d	35.00	4"d	10.00
Straight sides		4½"d	10.00
6"d	25.00	Spoonholder	35.00
7"d	30.00	Sugar bowl, covered	
8"d	35.00	Individual	25.00
Low standard		Table size	40.00
Round, berry bowl	25.00	Syrup pitcher, original top	45.00
Square, fruit bowl	30.00	Toothpick holder	15.00
Cracker jar, covered	45.00	Tray	
Creamer		Lemonade	50.00
Individual, 3¼"h	30.00	Water	50.00
Table size	35.00	Tumbler, water, flat	15.00
Cruet, original stopper	45.00	Vase, bud	
Cup		Flared top	
Custard	15.00	7"h	10.00
Punch	15.00	8"h	10.00
Dish		9"h	15.00
Almond, square	20.00	Straight top	
Cheese	45.00	7"h	10.00
Jelly, round, handled, 5"	15.00	8"h	10.00
Olive, triangular shape	20.00	9"h	15.00

COTTAGE

Saucer (emerald green); dinner plate (amber); jelly compote (emerald green); saucer (blue).

OMN: Cottage, Adams, Bellaire's No. 456 [goblet only]. AKA: Dinner Bell, Fine Cut Band [Kamm].

Non-flint. Adams & Co., Pittsburgh, PA. ca. 1874. Reissued by the United States Glass Co., Pittsburgh, PA. at Factory "A" (Adams & Co., Pittsburgh, PA.) after 1891. Bellaire Goblet Co. ca. 1891 (goblet only). Illustrated in the Adams & Co. 1874 catalog, the Bellaire Glass Co. ca. 1889-1890 catalog (goblet only), and the United States Glass Co. catalogs of ca. 1891, 1895-1896, ca. 1898, the No. 4280 Export catalog, and the 1919 Export catalog.

Original color production: Clear. Odd items may be found in amber, blue and emerald green. Clear with ruby stain or any other color is rare.

Reproductions: Both the goblet and wine have been reproduced from new molds in amber, blue and clear. Reproductions are heavier in weight than the originals and lack the refined design features of original pieces.

References: Hea-5 (P. 51, No. 253), Kam-1 (P. 38), Kam/Wod Vol. 1 (P. 158), Lee-VG (Pl. 64, No. 4), Mil-1 (Pl. 171), Mtz-1 (Pl. 153-154), Pet-Sal (P. 157), Rev-APG (PP. 18-19), Smth-FG (P. 10), Stu-BP (P. 54), Uni-2 (P. 167), Wlkr-PGA (Fig. 8, No. 7, 39).

Items made	Clear	Items made	Clear
Banana stand, high standard	55.00	Shallow	
Bowl, open, flat		Covered, 8"d	35.00
Oval		Open, 8"d	15.00
Shallow, preserve		Butter dish	
7½"	15.00	Flat	
9½"	20.00	Flanged with flared bowl	45.00
Deep		Dinner bell lid (scarce)	125.00
7½"	15.00	Footed	45.00
9½"	20.00	Cake stand, high standard	
Round		9"d	35.00
Deep		10"d	35.00
Berry, master, 10"d	20.00	Celery vase, pedestaled, scalloped rim	35.00
Finger	25.00	Champagne	35.00
Fruit	35.00	Claret	45.00
Waste	25.00		

Items made	Clear	Items made	Clear
Compote		Goblet	25.00
Covered		Mug	20.00
High standard		Pickle dish, leaf shaped	20.00
6″d	65.00	Pitcher	
7″d	70.00	Milk	
8″d	75.00	1 pint	35.00
Low standard		1 quart	30.00
6″d	45.00	Water, ½ gallon	50.00
7″d	50.00	Plate, round	
8″d	55.00	6″d	10.00
Open		7″d	10.00
High standard		8″d	15.00
4½″d., jelly	30.00	9″d	15.00
5″d	35.00	10″d	20.00
6″d	35.00	Relish tray	15.00
7″d	40.00	Salt shaker, bulbous, original nickel top	35.00
8″d	40.00	Sauce dish, round, 4″d.	
9″d., fruit	45.00	Flat, flared rim	
10″d., fruit	55.00	4″d	10.00
Low standard		4½″d	10.00
6″d	35.00	Footed	
7″d	40.00	4″d	10.00
8″d	40.00	4½″d	10.00
Creamer, 5¼″h	20.00	Saucer, for custard cup	10.00
Cruet, applied handle, original		Spoonholder, pedestaled, scalloped rim	20.00
patterned stopper	65.00	Sugar bowl, covered	45.00
Cup, custard, handled	15.00	Syrup pitcher, original top	85.00
Dish		Tray, water, round	35.00
Berry, flat, 5″d	15.00	Tumbler, water, flat	35.00
Oval, deep, flat	20.00	Wine	30.00

CROESUS

Master berry bowl and sauce dish (both emerald green with gold).

OMN: Riverside's No. 484.

Non-flint. Riverside Glass Works (pattern line No. 484), Wellsburg, WV. ca. 1897. McKee & Brothers, Pittsburgh, PA. ca. 1901. Illustrated in the McKee/National Glass Co. 1901 catalog.

Original color production: Amethyst and green (McKee Glass Co.), clear (Riverside Glass Works).

Reproductions: Croesus has been reproduced jointly by the Guernsey Glass Co., Cambridge, OH. and the L.E. Smith Glass Co., Mt. Pleasant/Greensburg, PA. from new molds in the original shades of green and amethyst as well as crystal in the following items: creamer, covered butter dish, spoonholder, covered sugar bowl, toothpick holder, and the water tumbler. Both the Mosser Art Glass Co., Cambridge, OH. and the Summit Art Glass Co., Mogadore/Rootstown, OH. reproduced the tumbler from a new mold in clear and color.

Reissues of the toothpick holder can be identified by the "scroll" appearing at at the top: on new items the scroll does not curl all the way under as it does on the old. On new items, the gilt is painted rather than fired on.

References: Bat-GPG (PP. 196-197), Eige-CGM WV (PP. 22-23), Hea-1 (P. 19, Fig. 70), Hea-2 (P. 119), Hea-3 (P. 58), Hea-6 (P. 24, Figs. 101-104), Hea-OPG (PP. 39, 41), Hea-TPS (P. 39), Kam-4 (P. 112), Kam-6 (Pl. 92), Lecnr-SS (P. 64), Mig-TPS (Pl. 111), Mtz-1 (P. 221), Mtz-2 (PP. 144-145), Mur-CO (PP. 5, 64), Mur-MCO (P. 72), Pet-Sal (P. 26), Rev-APG (PP. 295-296).

Items made	Amethyst	Clear	Green
Bowl			
Covered			
Flat, 7″d	100.00	30.00	85.00
Footed			
7″d	135.00	30.00	110.00
8″d	150.00	35.00	135.00
Open			
Flat			
7″d	90.00	20.00	70.00
8″d	175.00	—	125.00
Footed, scalloped rim			
6¼″d	225.00	85.00	125.00
7″d	125.00	30.00	125.00
8″d	125.00	30.00	125.00
10″d	185.00	—	135.00
Butter dish, covered	200.00	100.00	185.00
Cake stand, high standard, 10″d	200.00	45.00	150.00
Celery vase	300.00	65.00	145.00
Compote high standard			
Covered			
5″d	125.00	30.00	100.00
6″d	135.00	30.00	150.00
7″d	145.00	35.00	165.00
Open			
Plain rim			
5″d	75.00	20.00	65.00
6″d	75.00	20.00	65.00
6½″d	80.00	20.00	65.00
7″d	95.00	25.00	80.00
Scalloped rim			
5″d	75.00	20.00	65.00
6″d	75.00	25.00	65.00
6½″d	80.00	20.00	65.00
7″d	95.00	25.00	80.00
Condiment set (cruet, salt/pepper, under tray) complete	250.00	200.00	200.00

Items made	Amethyst	Clear	Green
Creamer			
Individual, "berry"	125.00	60.00	75.00
Table size	165.00	65.00	75.00
Cruet, original stopper			
Large	350.00	150.00	200.00
Small	250.00	100.00	125.00
Pickle dish	75.00	35.00	65.00
Pitcher, water, applied handle, $\frac{1}{2}$ gallon	375.00	90.00	250.00
Plate, footed			
8"d	75.00	20.00	65.00
10"d	85.00	30.00	75.00
Relish tray, boat shaped	75.00	35.00	65.00
Salt shaker, original top	80.00	25.00	80.00
Sauce dish, round, 4"d			
Flat	45.00	20.00	35.00
Footed	55.00	20.00	35.00
Spoonholder	90.00	60.00	80.00
Sugar bowl, covered			
Individual (originally termed the "berry sugar")	165.00	60.00	100.00
Table size	200.00	100.00	150.00
Toothpick holder	125.00	25.00	85.00
Tray, condiment	85.00	35.00	40.00
Tumbler, water, flat	75.00	30.00	55.00

CRYSTAL WEDDING, Adam's

H.s. covered compote (etched); h.s. cake stand (plain); h.s. covered compote (plain); salt shaker (plain).

OMN. AKA: Collins [Millard], Crystal Anniversary.

Non-flint. Adams & Co., Pittsburgh, PA. ca. 1890 with continued production by the United States Glass Co., Pittsburgh, PA. ca. 1891. Designed and patented by James B. Lyon (design patent No. 8,464) July 6, 1875, Crystal Wedding is illustrated in an undated Adams & Co. catalog, reviewed in the February 12, 1891 issue of the *Crockery and Glass Journal*, and is illustrated in the United States Glass Co. ca. 1891 (domestic), 1898 (domestic), and 1919 export catalogs.

137

Original color production: Clear, clear with acid finish and clear with ruby stain (plain, banded or copper wheel engraved, engravings ranging from simple fern and berry motifs to what the United States Glass Co. termed "Fancy Engraved": Bird in Bower, Rose Sprig, and Bird and Cattail designs). Occasional items may be found in clear with amber stain, cobalt blue, and vaseline but are considered rare.

Reproductions: The Westmorland Glass Co., Grapeville, PA., throughout the early 1970s and later, reproduced the following items from new molds: 10″ high standard covered compote, 8″ high standard covered compote, 6″ low standard candy dish (plain or fire enameled). Both the goblet and high standard covered compote have been reproduced in clear and clear with light cranberry stain and blue lustre. New items show a light green tint when held to a strong light in comparison to the brilliant clarity of the originals.

References: Bar-RS (Pl. 10), Enos-MPG (Chart-3), Hea-3 (P. 83), Hea-5 (P. 47, Nos. 192-195), Hea-7 (Figs. 146-150), Hea-OPG (P. 42), Inn-PG (P. 381), Kam-3 (PP. 74-75), Kam-8 (Plt. 12), Lee-VG (P. 48, No. 2), McCn-PGP (P. 144), Mil-1 (Pl. 145), Mil-2 (Pl. 43), Mtz-1 (P. 144), Pet-GPP (PP. 111, 114), Pet-Sal (P. 126), Rev-APG (PP. 18-19), Stu-BP (P. 54), Thur-1 (P. 323), Uni-1 (P. 107).

Items made	Clear	Clear/ Frosted	Clear w/ Ruby
Banana dish, high standard (originally termed "fruit basket")	90.00	110.00	—
Bowl, square, flat			
Covered			
6″	50.00	60.00	75.00
7″	55.00	65.00	85.00
8″	60.00	70.00	85.00
Open			
Design covers lower half of bowl, scalloped rim			
6″	65.00	40.00	65.00
7″	65.00	45.00	85.00
8″	85.00	45.00	95.00
Design covers entire bowl scalloped rim, 8″	55.00	65.00	75.00
Butter dish, covered, 5¼″h., 6¼″sq	50.00	75.00	125.00
Cake plate, square	45.00	55.00	85.00
Cake stand, high standard, 10″sq	60.00	75.00	—
Celery vase, flat, scalloped rim	45.00	75.00	125.00
Claret	85.00	95.00	125.00
Compote			
Covered			
High standard			
6″sq	65.00	75.00	110.00
7″sq	65.00	75.00	110.00
8″sq	75.00	85.00	125.00
Open, scalloped rim			
High standard			
6″sq	40.00	45.00	55.00
7″sq	45.00	45.00	55.00
8″sq	50.00	55.00	65.00
Low standard			
5″sq	30.00	35.00	45.00
6″sq	40.00	45.00	55.00
7″sq	40.00	45.00	55.00
8″sq	50.00	55.00	60.00
Creamer, flat, square, applied handle	65.00	75.00	125.00
Cruet, original stopper, (R)	125.00	150.00	225.00
Dish, flat, square	30.00	35.00	55.00
Goblet, 5¾″h	45.00	55.00	65.00

Items made	Clear	Clear/ Frosted	Clear w/ Ruby
Ice tub	80.00	90.00	—
Lamp, oil, tall (several sizes), original burner and chimney	100.00	125.00	—
Nappy, flat, handled, 4³/₄"sq	20.00	25.00	35.00
Pickle dish, rectangular	25.00	30.00	40.00
Pitcher, tankard			
Round			
Milk			
1 pint	75.00	85.00	125.00
1 quart	110.00	125.00	185.00
Water, ¹/₂ gallon	135.00	155.00	200.00
Square			
Milk, 1 quart	145.00	175.00	225.00
Water, ¹/₂ gallon	175.00	200.00	250.00
Plate, cake, 10"sq	35.00	40.00	50.00
Relish tray	25.00	30.00	40.00
Salt			
Dip, individual, round	25.00	30.00	40.00
Master			
Square, design covers entire item	45.00	55.00	85.00 (R)
Square, design half way up from base	45.00	55.00	85.00 (R)
Shaker, pyramid shape, original top	65.00	65.00	85.00
Sauce dish, square			
Flat design covers entire item			
4"	15.00	20.00	25.00
4¹/₂"	15.00	20.00	25.00
Footed	20.00	—	—
Spoonholder, 4³/₄"h	35.00	40.00	65.00
Sugar bowl, covered, 7"h, square	60.00	65.00	90.00
Syrup pitcher, original top, (R)	150.00	175.00	250.00
Tumbler, water, flat, 3³/₄"h	35.00	40.00	45.00
Vase, bouquet			
Footed, twisted	25.00	—	—
Swung style	25.00	—	—
Wine	50.00	65.00	85.00

Goblet; water pitcher; milk pitcher; champagne.

OMN: Richards and Hartley No. 500. AKA: Guardian Angel, Minerva [Lee].

Non-flint. Richards & Hartley Glass Co. (pattern line No. 500), Pittsburgh, PA., ca. 1875. Reissued by the United States Glass Co., Pittsburgh, PA., ca. 1891. Illustrated in the Richards & Hartley Glass Co. 1888 catalog.

Original color production: Clear. Limited production in amber and vaseline. Most pieces are footed. Handles are pressed with thumb rests.

Reproductions: None

References: Drep-ABC OG (P. 153), Enos-MPG (Chart-7), Hea-5 (P. 118), Kam-1 (P. 28), Lee-EAPG (Pl. 70, Nos. 3-4), Luc-TG (PP. 170-171), McCn-PGP (P. 395), Mil-1 (Pl. 121), Oliv-AAG (P. 61), Stu-BP (P. 76), Uni-1 (PP. 258-259), Wlkr-PGA (Fig. 8, Nos. 17, 56).

Items made	Clear	Items made	Clear
Bowl		Creamer, 6"h	35.00
Flat, oval, open, 9"d	30.00	Cruet, pedestaled, applied handle,	
Footed, round		original maltese stopper (R)	175.00
Covered, 8"d	30.00	Goblet	65.00
Open, master berry, 8"d	30.00	Marmalade jar, covered	65.00
Butter dish, covered	50.00	Mug	
Cake stand, high standard	60.00	Large, 3½"h	40.00
Celery vase, pedestaled, smooth rim	50.00	Medium, 2½"h	35.00
Champagne	90.00	Small, 2"h	30.00
Compote		Pickle castor, complete in original	
Covered		frame with top and tongs	150.00
High standard, 8"d	100.00	Pitcher	
Low standard		Milk, 1 quart	75.00
7"d	55.00	Water, ½ gallon	85.00
9"d	75.00	Plate	
Open		Bread, 10½"d, handled	45.00
High standard, 9¼"d	45.00	Cake, 11"d	45.00
Low standard, scalloped rim, 8½"d	55.00	Dinner, 10"d	40.00
Cordial, 3½"h	80.00	Relish dish, oval (3 sizes)	15.00

Items made	Clear	Items made	Clear
Sauce dish, round		5″d	15.00
Flat	10.00	Spoonholder	35.00
Footed		Sugar bowl, covered	65.00
4″d	10.00	Wine, 3³/₄″h	85.00
4¹/₂″d	15.00		

CURRANT

Sauce dish; goblet; celery vase; honey dish (3¹/₂″d).

OMN: Currant Ware. AKA: Currant Double Row.

Non-flint. Campbell, Jones & Co., Pittsburgh, PA. ca. 1871. Shards have been found at the site of the Boston & Sandwich Glass Co., Sandwich, MA. and the Burlington Glass Works, Hamilton, Ontario, Canada. Designed and patented by Mary B. Campbell (design patent No. 4,774), April 11, 1871. Variations in standards and bases of covered items indicate more than one manufacturer.

Original color production: Clear.

Reproductions: None.

References: Hlms-BCA (P. 278), Inn-PG (P. 334), Kam-8 (P. 8), Kam/Wod Vol.1 (P. 278), Lee-EAPG (Pl. 139, No. 3), McCn-PGP (P. 152), Mil-1 (Pl. 59), Mtz-1 (PP. 88-89), Rev-APG (P. 233), Spil-AEPG (P. 285), Uni/Wor-CHPGT (P. 93), Wlkr-PGA (Fig. 8, Nos. 18, 20, 46).

Items made	Clear	Items made	Clear
Bowl, oval, open, flat		Compote, round	
5″ x 7″	15.00	Covered	
6″ x 9″	15.00	High standard	
Butter dish, covered, flat	55.00	8″d	65.00
Cake stand, high standard		9″d	135.00
9¹/₂″d., plain standard	65.00	12″d	175.00
10¹/₂″d., hexagonal standard	65.00	Low standard, 8″d	45.00
11″d	75.00	Open	
Celery vase, pedestaled, scalloped-		High standard, 6″d., scalloped rim	30.00
flared rim	50.00	Low standard, 6″d	30.00

Items made	Clear	Items made	Clear
Cordial	45.00	Relish dish, oval	15.00
Creamer, pedestaled, applied handle	45.00	Salt, master, footed, open, smooth rim	30.00
Egg cup, single, pedestaled, smooth		Sauce dish, flat (with or without cable	
rim	35.00	edge)	
Goblet, (height varies)	35.00	Flat	
Honey dish, flat (with or without cable		4″d	15.00
edge), 3½″d	15.00	4¾″d	15.00
Jam jar, covered	45.00	Footed	
Pitcher, applied handle		4″d	20.00
Milk, 1 quart	125.00	4¾″d	20.00
Water, ½ gallon	100.00	Spoonholder	25.00
Plate		Sugar bowl, covered	55.00
5″ x 7″	25.00	Tumbler, water, footed	30.00
6″ x 9″	30.00	Wine	25.00

CURRIER AND IVES

Syrup; decanter (o.s.); creamer.

Possible OMN: Eulalia.

Non-flint. Bellaire Goblet Co., Findlay, OH., ca. 1889-1898. Illustrated in the T.M. Roberts 1898 catalog.

Original color production: Clear (complete table setting). Rare pieces may be found in amber, blue, cobalt blue, and vaseline, but complete table settings in color were not produced. Clear with ruby stain, milk white or any other color is very rare. Currier and Ives is quite similar to the Daisy and Button pattern but with convex plain buttons.

Reproductions: None.

References: Bar-RS (Pl. 8), Cod-OS (Pl. 42), Drep-ABC OG (P. 237), Drep-FR (PP. 206-207), Meas/Smth-FG (PP. 56, 63), Fer-YMG (P. 22), Hea-3 (P. 22), Hea-6 (P. 22, Fig. 84), Hea-7 (PP. 98, 112), Hrtng-P&P (P. 17), Kam-3 (P. 117), Lee-EAPG (Pl. 110), Lee-VG (Pl. 86), Lind-HG (P. 165), Mrsh-SRG (P. 26), McCn-PGP (Pl. 94), Mil-1 (Pl. 128), Mtz-1 (P. 158-159), Oliv-AAG (P. 61), Pet-Sal (P. 26), Smth-FG (PP. 10, 51, 96), Stu-BP (P. 135), Thur-1 (PP. 248-249), Uni-1 (p. 269), War-MGA (Pl. 13), Wlkr-PGA (Fig. 8, No. 43).

Oval relish dish; water tray; cup.

Items made	Clear	Items made	Clear
Bowl, oval, flat, canoe shaped, 10"l	30.00	Bread, handled	25.00
Butter dish, covered, rectangular	50.00	Dinner	
Celery vase	35.00	7"d	15.00
Compote, high standard, round		10"d	20.00
Covered, 7½"d	95.00	Relish dish	
Open, scalloped rim, 7½"d	50.00	Boat shape, 6"l	20.00
Cordial	45.00	Oval	20.00
Creamer, 6¼"h	30.00	Salt	
Cup/Saucer	35.00	Master, open	40.00
Decanter, original stopper, 12"h	60.00	Shaker, tall, original top	30.00
Goblet		Sauce dish	
Knob stem	30.00	Flat, round	10.00
Plain stem	25.00	Oval	10.00
Lamp, oil, high standard, 9½"h,		Spoonholder	35.00
original chimney and burner	75.00	Sugar bowl, covered	45.00
Mug	25.00	Syrup pitcher, original top	65.00
Pickle dish	25.00	Tumbler, water, flat	40.00
Pitcher		Tray, water, round, "Balky Mule"	
Milk, 1 quart	65.00	center	
Water, ½ gallon	75.00	9½"d	35.00
Plate		12¼"d	40.00
		Wine, 3¼"h	25.00

CURTAIN

Creamer; high standard open deep compote; high standard open shallow compote.

OMN: Sultan.

Non-flint. Bryce Brothers, Pittsburgh, PA., ca. late 1870s.

Original color production: Clear.

Reproductions: None.

References: Drep-ABC OG (P. 195), Kam-3 (PP. 60-61), Lee-EAPG (Pl. 85), McCn-PGP (P. 521), Mil-1 (Pl. 173), Mtz-1 (P. 130-131), Oliv-AAG (P. 61), Pet-Sal (P. 26), Rev-APG (PP. 87, 90), Uni-1 (PP. 260-261).

Items made	Clear	Items made	Clear
Bowl		Celery	
Finger	30.00	Boat	25.00
Round		Tray	30.00
Collared base		Vase	
Covered		Plain rim	30.00
5″d	20.00	Scalloped rim	30.00
6″d	30.00	Compote, high standard	
7″d	40.00	Covered	
8″d	45.00	6″d	25.00
Open		7″d	35.00
5″d	20.00	8″d	45.00
6″d	20.00	10″d	55.00
7″d	25.00	Open, deep or shallow	
8″d	30.00	6″d	40.00
Flat, open		7″d	45.00
7½″d	20.00	8″d	55.00
8″d	20.00	10″d	50.00
Butter dish, covered	55.00	Creamer	25.00
Cake stand, high standard		Cruet, original stopper	45.00
8″d	40.00	Goblet	30.00
9″d	40.00	Mug, large	25.00
9½″d	45.00	Mustard pot	40.00
10″d	45.00	Pickle dish	15.00
Castor set (salt, pepper, mustard)	100.00		

Items made	Clear	Items made	Clear
Pitcher		4½"d	10.00
Milk, 1 quart	45.00	4¾"d	10.00
Water, ½ gallon	75.00	Flat	
Plate, square		4½"d	12.00
Dinner		4¾"d	12.00
7"	20.00	Spoonholder	25.00
8"	20.00	Sugar bowl, covered	35.00
Bread	20.00	Tray, water, round	35.00
Salt shaker, original top	25.00	Tumbler, water, flat	20.00
Sauce dish, round			
Collared base			

CURTAIN TIE BACK

Water pitcher.

Non-flint. Maker unknown, ca. 1860s.

Original color production: Clear. Originally produced in either flat or footed form.

Reproductions: None. Handles are pressed.

References: Bat-GPG (PP. 214-215), Kam-3 (PP. 118-119), Lind-HG (PP. 215, 250), McCn-PGP (P. 383), Mil-1 (Pl. 35), Mtz-1 (PP. 130-131), Pet-Sal (P. 26), Spil-AEPG (P. 308), Stu-BP (P. 138), Uni-1 (P. 261).

Items made	Clear	Items made	Clear
Bowl, square, open, flat		Pickle dish	10.00
7"	15.00	Pitcher, water, ½ gallon	45.00
7½"	15.00	Plate, bread	10.00
Butter dish, covered	40.00	Relish tray	15.00
Celery		Salt shaker, tall, original top	10.00
Tray	25.00	Sauce dish, round	
Vase	35.00	Flat	10.00
Compote, covered, high standard,		Footed	10.00
round	40.00	Spoonholder	30.00
Creamer	25.00	Sugar bowl, covered	30.00
Goblet		Tray, water, round	30.00
Design on base	30.00	Tumbler, water, flat	15.00
Plain base	25.00	Wine	20.00

Master salt; individual covered sugar; helmet shaped pitcher; covered honey dish; cruet (o.s.).

OMN: Ethol. AKA: Cat's Eye and Block.

Non-flint. Bryce, Higbee and Co., Pittsburgh, PA., ca. 1889. The Westmorland Specialty Glass Co., Grapeville, PA., ca. 1896. Illustrated in the 1899 Butler Brothers catalog.

Original color production: Clear. Camphor or any other color is rare. Similar to Broken Column, the main design element of Cut Log consists of finely marked notches in the so-called "log" ends. Handles may be either applied or pressed with the matching "cut log" motif.

Reproductions: None.

References: Brn-SD (P. 1360), Grow-GAG (P. 251, Fig. 50-"s"), Hrtng-P&P (P. 26), Kam-1 (P. 118), Kam-8 (P. 61), Lee-VG (Pl. 53, No. 4), McCn-PGP (P. 459), Mil-1 (Pl. 10), Mtz-1 (P. 140, 143), Oliv-AAG (P. 61), Pet-Sal (P. 26), Rev-APG (PP. 92, 172, 322), Uni-1 (P. 253), Wlkr-PGA (Fig. 8, Nos. 44, 47).

Items made	Clear	Items made	Clear
Banana stand (R)	90.00	5"d., 4³/₄"h., jelly	45.00
Biscuit jar, covered	95.00	7¹/₄"d	85.00
Bowl, flat		7¹/₂"d	85.00
Oblong		8"d., 8"h	85.00
Relish, 2¹/₄"h., 5"w., 8"l	25.00	12¹/₂"d	90.00
Vegetable, 1¹/₂"h., 3¹/₂"d., 9¹/₄"l	25.00	Open, high standard	
Round		Flared rim	
1¹/₂"h., 4¹/₄"d	25.00	6"d., 4¹/₂"h	45.00
1³/₄"h., 2¹/₂"d	30.00	7¹/₂"d	50.00
2¹/₈"h., 8"d	35.00	8"d	55.00
Butter dish, covered, 7"d	65.00	8¹/₂"d	60.00
Cake stand, high standard		Scalloped rim	
9¹/₄"d	45.00	6¹/₈"d	45.00
10¹/₂"d	55.00	10³/₄"d	65.00
Celery		Smooth rim, 5¹/₄"d	45.00
Tray	25.00	Low standard	
Vase, 6"h	40.00	Flared	
Compote		Scalloped rim	
Covered, high standard		9³/₄"d	65.00

Items made	Clear	Items made	Clear
10"d	85.00	Tankard, applied handle, 12¼"h	85.00
Smooth rim		Relish tray	25.00
5¾"d	30.00	Salt	
8¼"d	30.00	Individual, flat, round	35.00
Round bowl, plain rim, 5¼"d	30.00	Master, flat, round, 2"h., 3"d (R)	85.00
Creamer		Shaker, 2¼"h., original top	60.00
Individual, 3"h	15.00	Sauce, round	
Table size, 5½"h	40.00	Flat	20.00
Cruet, original patterned stopper		Footed	
3¾"h	40.00	Plain rim, 2¼"h., 4¼"d	25.00
4"h	40.00	Scalloped rim, 2¼"h., 4½"d	25.00
5"h	45.00	Spoonholder, 4½"h., flat, scalloped rim	35.00
Goblet, 6"h	45.00	Sugar bowl, covered	
Marmalade jar, covered	85.00	Individual, 3¼"h	30.00
Honey dish, covered, flat, 7"sq	90.00	Table size, 5⅛"h	55.00
Mug, handled, 3¼"h	20.00	Tumbler	
Mustard jar, notched lid	50.00	Water, flat, 3¼"h	50.00
Olive dish, handled, 5"d	20.00	Juice, flat, 3½"h	45.00
Pitcher		Vase, flat (various heights)	45.00
Helmet shape, design on handle,		Wine, 4"h	25.00
8¾"h	85.00		

DAHLIA

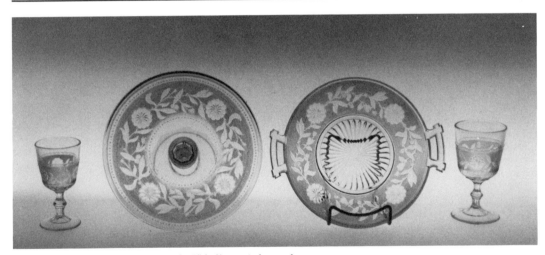

Wine; high standard cake stand; 9"d dinner plate; champagne.

AKA: Stippled Dahlia.

Non-flint. Portland Glass Co., Portland, ME. ca. 1865. Canton Glass Co., Canton, OH. ca. 1880. Shards have been found at the site of the Diamond Flint Glass Co., Ltd. (Dominion Glass Co., Ltd., de Lorimier Avenue, Montreal, Quebec, Canada), and the Burlington Glass Works, Hamilton, Ontario, Canada.

Original color production: Amber, apple green, blue, clear, and vaseline. The main pattern design element consists of clear embossed dahlia flowers and foliage against a stippled background. Handles are usually applied. Finials are in the shape of flat, stylized dahlias.

147

Reproductions: None.

References: Drep-FR (P. 199), Enos-MPG (Chart-2), Hlms-BCA (P. 278), Kam-1 (PP. 73-74), Kam/Wod-Vol.1 (P. 199), Lee-EAPG (PP. 402-404), McCn-PGP (Pl. 132), Mil-1 (Pl. 18), Mtz-1 (PP. 64-65), Oliv-AAG (P. 61), Pap-GAG (P. 197), Rev-APG (P. 106), Stu-BP (P. 26), Swn-PG (PP. 63-64), Uni-1 (P. 149), Uni-TCG (P. 93), Uni/Wor-CHPGT (P. 94), Wlkr-PGA (Fig. 8, No. 36).

Items made	Amber	Green	Blue	Clear	Vas
Bowl, oval, flat, open, 6"x 8¾"	30.00	25.00	25.00	25.00	30.00
Butter dish, covered	55.00	50.00	50.00	45.00	55.00
Cake stand, high standard					
9½"d	70.00	50.00	50.00	25.00	70.00
10"d	70.00	50.00	50.00	25.00	70.00
Champagne, 5"h	80.00	65.00	45.00	30.00	60.00
Compote, high standard, round					
Covered, 7"d	100.00	85.00	45.00	30.00	60.00
Open, 8"d	60.00	45.00	45.00	30.00	60.00
Cordial, 4½"h	55.00	50.00	50.00	35.00	55.00
Creamer	40.00	35.00	35.00	25.00	40.00
Egg cup					
Double	80.00	65.00	65.00	50.00	80.00
Single	55.00	40.00	40.00	25.00	55.00
Goblet, 5¾"h	65.00	55.00	55.00	35.00	65.00
Mug, handled					
Large	55.00	55.00	55.00	35.00	55.00
Small	50.00	45.00	40.00	30.00	50.00
Pickle dish	35.00	30.00	30.00	20.00	35.00
Pitcher					
Milk, 1 quart	70.00	55.00	55.00	40.00	70.00
Water, ½ gallon	110.00	100.00	100.00	85.00	100.00
Plate, round					
Bread, 7"d	45.00	40.00	40.00	20.00	45.00
Dinner, 9"d., handled	35.00	45.00	40.00	15.00	50.00
Platter, oval, 11"l					
Fan handles	50.00	45.00	45.00	30.00	50.00
Grape handles	50.00	45.00	45.00	30.00	50.00
Relish					
Dish, 9½"l	20.00	20.00	20.00	15.00	20.00
Jar (small handled mug), original notched patterned handle with "pickle" finial (R)	100.00	125.00	125.00	75.00	125.00
Salt, individual, footed	35.00	30.00	30.00	5.00	35.00
Sauce dish, round, scalloped					
Flat, 4"d	15.00	10.00	10.00	10.00	15.00
Footed, 4"d	20.00	15.00	15.00	10.00	15.00
Spoonholder	50.00	45.00	50.00	35.00	50.00
Sugar bowl, covered	75.00	60.00	60.00	40.00	75.00
Syrup pitcher, original top	125.00	—	—	75.00	—
Wine, 4¹⁄₁₆"h	65.00	50.00	55.00	35.00	65.00

Yacht pickle tray; covered butter; creamer; tooth pick holder.

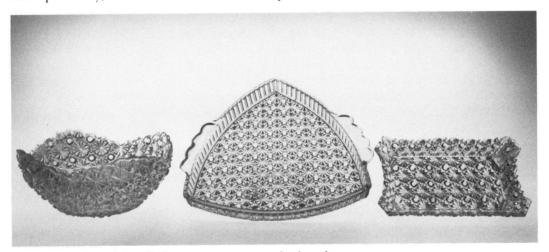

Bowl; triangular tab handled water tray; rectangular bread tray.

OMN: Doyle's No. 300 (Daisy & Button), Bryce's Daisy & Button, Fashion. Hobb's No. 101, Duncan's Octagon Rosette.

Non-flint. Bryce Brothers, Pittsburgh, PA. (reissued by the United States Glass Co.). Doyle & Co., (pattern line No. 300) Pittsburgh, PA., ca. 1880s (reissued by the United States Glass Co. Hobbs, Brockunier & Co. (pattern line No. 101), Wheeling, WV. ca. 1885 (reissued by the United States Glass Co.). Attributed by both Kamm and Lee to the Boston & Sandwich Glass Co., Sandwich, MA. ca. 1880s. Reviewed in the May 1, 1884, November 19, 1885, and February, 1886 issues of the *Pottery and Glassware Reporter*, and illustrated in the A.J. Beatty & Sons ca. 1885-1889 and 1890-1891, the Hobbs, Brockunier & Co. ca. 1875-1888, and United States Glass Co. ca. 1898 catalogs.

Original color production: Amberina, amber, blue, clear, apple green, and vaseline. Amberina, a color fading from deep ruby to amber, was developed in 1883 by Joseph Locke for the New England Glass Works, East Cambridge, MA. Produced by numerous companies, the treatment of finials, handles, stems, and bases varies considerably.

Variants: Daisy & Button (George Duncan & Sons, Pittsburgh, PA. ca. 1885), Daisy & Button with Almond Band (Clio. Challinor, Taylor & Co. ca. 1885). Daisy & Button with Amber Stripe(s) (OMN: Adam's No. 86, Adams & Co., Pittsburgh, PA. ca. 1886 and reissued by the United States Glass Co. ca. 1891). Daisy & Button Band (OMN: O'Hara's No. 650. O'Hara Glass Co., Pittsburgh, PA. ca. 1885. Reissued by the United States Glass Co. ca. 1891). Daisy & Button with Clear Lily (Indiana Glass Co., Dunkirk, IN. ca. 1910). Daisy & Button with Clear Stripe (Dalzell, Gillmore & Leighton, Findlay, OH. ca. 1888). Daisy & Button with Cross Bar (OMN: No. 99, Richards & Hartley Glass Co., Pittsburgh, PA. ca. 1885 reissued by the United States Glass Co. ca. 1891). Daisy & Button Crossbar, Daisy & Button-Double Panel, Daisy & Button-Double Pillars, Daisy & Button with Fine Cut Panels, Daisy & Button with Flat Stem, Daisy & Button-Octagon (George Duncan & Sons, Pittsburgh, PA. ca. 1890). Daisy & Button-Oval Medallion, Daisy & Button with Oval Panels (OMN: Richards & Hartley No. 900, Richards & Hartley Glass Co., Pittsburgh, PA. ca.1887, reissued by the United States Glass Co.), Daisy & Button-Panelled [Millard] (McKee Brothers, Pittsburgh, PA. ca. 1885), Daisy & Button Petticoat (Dalzell, Gillmore & Leighton, Findlay, OH. ca. 1888), Daisy & Button with Petticoat Band, Daisy & Button with Pointed Panels, Daisy & Button with Prisms, Daisy & Button with Red Dots, Daisy & Button with Rimmed Panel, Daisy & Button Scalloped (OMN: Challinor No. 3030, Challinor, Taylor & Co., Pittsburgh, PA. ca. 1885, reissued by the United States Glass Co.), Daisy & Button-Scalloped Band (OMN: Gillinder No. 413, Gillinder & Sons, Philadelphia, PA. ca. 1880s, reissued by the United States Glass Co. ca. 1891), Daisy & Button with Scroll Panel, Daisy & Button-Single Panel, Daisy & Button-Square, Daisy & Button with Thin Bars (Gillinder & Sons, Philadelphia, PA. ca. 1885, reissued by the United States Glass Co. ca. 1891), Daisy & Button with Thumbprint (OMN: Adams No. 86, Adams & Co., Pittsburgh, PA. ca. ca. 1886, reissued by the United States Glass Co. ca. 1891), Daisy & Button with Thumbprint Panels, Daisy & Button with V Ornament (OMN: A.J. Beatty No. 555, A.J. Beatty & Sons ca. 1886, reissued by the United States Glass Co. ca. 1891-1892).

Reproductions: Reproduced from the early 1930s, Daisy and Button has been reissued in original and new colors for more than fifty years. In general, reproductions are thicker and heavier than original items. New items display a cloudy, muddy appearance that is too slick and brilliant. Original items are lighter and more mellow. Although lacking the crisp impression of the original, new items are rougher to the touch. Reproduced by numerous concerns, perhaps the most prolific producer of both original and new forms is the L.G. Wright Glass Co., New Martinsville, WV. (distributed by Jennings Red Barn, New Martinsville, WV., and Carl Forslund, Grand Rapids, MI.). As early as 1970 the Wright catalog supplement illustrated the castor set complete with silver plate holder and tongs in amber, amberina, and cobalt blue. In 1971 the Wright catalogs illustrated the following items: basket with applied handle (green satin), 4-footed bowl (pink and amber satin), 5″ oval footed open bowl (vaseline), castor complete in silver plate frame with cover (vaseline, vaseline satin), 4″d high standard covered compote (amber satin), 4″d. low standard covered compote (green satin), goblet (amber satin, vaseline), 10″d plate with plain rim (vaseline), rose bowl with deep fluted rim (blue satin), wine (vaseline). By 1974 the L.G. Wright master catalog illustrated the following items: handled basket (amber, amethyst, blue, green, vaseline), 4 toed candleholder (amber, amethyst, blue, green, pink, vaseline), 4 toed 10″d open bowl (amber, amberina, amethyst, blue, green, pink), 8-sided flat open bowl (amber, amethyst, blue, green), oval 4 toed open bowl (amber, amberina, amethyst, blue, green, pink, vaseline), covered oval butter dish (amber, blue, pink), bell shaped covered candy dish (amber, blue, green, vaseline), 1½″l. canoe (amber, blue), covered cow standard 6″d. compote (amber, amberina, amethyst, blue, cobalt, pink, green), creamer with square handles (amber, blue, pink), 6 ounce cruet (amber, amethyst, blue, clear), fan ash tray (amber, amethyst, blue, green), goblet (amber, blue), gypsy kettle (amber, clear, vaseline), kitten slipper (blue milk glass, custard), 10″d scalloped plate (amber, blue, pink, vaseline), 6″ square plate (amber, amberina, blue, clear, green, pink, vaseline, ruby red), 8″d scalloped rim shallow plate (amber, blue, pink), flat crimped rose bowl (amber, blue, cobalt, blue-green), round deep salt dip (amber, amethyst, blue, green), triangular salt dip (amber, amethyst, blue, green, ruby red), tall salt shaker (amber, amethyst, blue, green), footed square sauce dish termed the "sherbert" (amber, blue, pink), small sleigh without candle well (amber, blue, pink, ruby red), large sleigh without candle well (amber, blue, pink, ruby red), small sleigh with candle well (amber, blue, pink, ruby red), small medium slipper (amber, amethyst, blue, blue milk glass, green, ruby red), spoonholder (amber, blue, clear, cobalt blue, vaseline), true open sugar bowl with square handles (amber, blue, pink), round toothpick holder (amber, amethyst, blue-green, ruby red), triangular toothpick holder (amber, amethyst, blue-green, ruby red), and the wine (amber, amberina, blue, clear, green, pink, and vaseline).

The Degenhart Glass Co., Cambridge, OH. issued the following sizes of the toothpick holder, each signed with a "D" in a diamond: $2\frac{1}{2}$″h. (pink opalescent), $2\frac{1}{4}$″h. (blue), and $3\frac{1}{2}$″h. (blue). Degenhart also reproduced the the round, flat $1\frac{3}{4}$″d. salt in blue ca. 1970s. The Imperial Glass Co., Bellaire, OH., ca. 1950s reproduced the whisk broom pickle dish in clear and original color. The Fenton Art Glass Co., Williamstown, WV., ca. 1930s reproduced the Duncan Cornucopia vase and the individual hat shaped salt in clear and all original colors.

References: Bred-EDG (P. 89), Eige-CGM WV (PP. 7, 9), Hea-1 (P. 20), Hea-3 (P. 66). Hea-5 (P. 80), Hea-6 (PP. 54, 60), Hea-7 (P. 100), Hea-OS (Fig. 594), Hrtng-P&P (P. 20), Kam-6 (P. 45), Kam-7 (P. 112), Kam-8 (P. 13), Lee-EAPG (Pl. 169), McCn-EPG (Pl. 83), Mtz-1 (PP. 224-225), Mtz-2 (PP. 220-221), Pet-Sal (P. 26), Rev-APG (P. 139), Thur-1 (P. 297), Uni-1 (P. 31).

Items made	Amber	Blue	Clear	Green	Vas
Ale glass, stemmed					
4 ounce	25.00	30.00	20.00	35.00	40.00
$4\frac{1}{2}$ ounce	25.00	30.00	20.00	35.00	40.00
5 ounce	25.00	30.00	20.00	35.00	40.00
Basket, (candy dish), applied handle, flat	35.00	40.00	25.00	45.00	45.00
Bottle					
Bar, original faceted stopper	55.00	65.00	35.00	70.00	75.00
Caster					
Mustard	20.00	25.00	15.00	25.00	25.00
Pepper	20.00	25.00	15.00	25.00	25.00
Vinegar	20.00	25.00	15.00	25.00	25.00
Cologne, original faceted stopper	40.00	45.00	30.00	55.00	55.00
Bowl					
Covered, flat, round, tab handles, faceted knob finial, 8″d	65.00	85.00	45.00	85.00	85.00
Open					
Collared base, oval, scalloped rim, 9″ x 12″ x 6″ (R)	90.00	125.00	75.00	140.00	140.00
Flat					
Octagonal, scalloped rim, 10″d., 5″h. (R)	90.00	125.00	75.00	140.00	140.00
Round					
Deep					
Finger bowl, smooth rim	30.00	35.00	20.00	50.00	45.00
Flared scalloped rim, 6″d	30.00	35.00	20.00	50.00	45.00
Ice bowl, smooth rim with drainer	—	—	50.00	—	85.00
Point and scallop rim 8″d	35.00	40.00	25.00	55.00	50.00
Scalloped rim					
9″d	35.00	40.00	25.00	55.00	50.00
$9\frac{1}{2}$″d	35.00	40.00	25.00	55.00	50.00

Items made	Amber	Blue	Clear	Green	Vas
10"d	40.00	45.00	30.00	60.00	55.00
Shallow bowl					
5½"d	30.00	35.00	20.00	50.00	45.00
7"d	30.00	35.00	20.00	50.00	45.00
9"d ("crown bowl" with four tab handles	65.00	75.00	45.00	85.00	75.00
Square, scalloped rim					
Flared sides, 5"	30.00	35.00	20.00	50.00	45.00
Straight sides					
5"	30.00	35.00	20.00	50.00	45.00
6½"	30.00	35.00	20.00	50.00	45.00
8½"	35.00	40.00	25.00	55.00	50.00
Triangular, scalloped rim	40.00	45.00	25.00	45.00	65.00
Butter dish, covered, flat					
Quarter pound	65.00	65.00	45.00	80.00	85.00
Table size					
Round	75.00	75.00	55.00	90.00	95.00
Square	100.00	110.00	65.00	120.00	125.00
Butter pat					
Clover cut	10.00	15.00	8.00	20.00	20.00
Round, smooth rim	30.00	35.00	25.00	35.00	40.00
Square	10.00	15.00	8.00	20.00	20.00
Canoe					
4"	10.00	15.00	10.00	25.00	25.00
8½"	25.00	30.00	25.00	30.00	35.00
12"	30.00	30.00	25.00	35.00	40.00
14"	35.00	35.00	25.00	40.00	40.00
Castor set					
4 bottle, with original glass holder	115.00	120.00	110.00	135.00	150.00
5 bottle, original metal holder	125.00	125.00	100.00	125.00	125.00
Celery					
Tray, yacht shape	25.00	30.00	25.00	30.00	35.00
Vase					
Hat shape	50.00	55.00	40.00	65.00	60.00
Tall, square, flat, tab handled rim	35.00	40.00	30.00	45.00	55.00
Cheese dish, matching underplate	100.00	125.00	75.00	125.00	135.00
Compote, high standard					
Covered, 6"d	75.00	95.00	45.00	85.00	110.00
Open, 8"d	35.00	45.00	30.00	55.00	65.00
Creamer					
Table size, bulbous, collared base, 6"h	35.00	40.00	25.00	45.00	50.00
Individual					
Barrel shape, hand tooled flared scalloped rim, applied handle (made from toothpick)	25.00	30.00	15.00	35.00	40.00
Round, pinched spout, applied handle (made from punch cup)	25.00	30.00	15.00	35.00	40.00
Tankard, flat, applied handle, 5⅛"h	35.00	40.00	25.00	45.00	50.00
Cruet, flat, applied handle, original faceted stopper					
Bulbous base	125.00	145.00	55.00	—	145.00
Tall, straight-sided	110.00	125.00	45.00	—	135.00
Cup, punch, applied ring handle	10.00	15.00	8.00	15.00	15.00
Dish, open, flat					
Oval, 10"l	35.00	40.00	25.00	55.00	50.00
Rectangular, shallow (cranberry)	35.00	40.00	25.00	55.00	50.00
Egg cup, pedestaled, single	25.00	30.00	15.00	35.00	35.00
Goblet					
Barrel shaped bowl	35.00	40.00	25.00	50.00	45.00

152

Items made	Amber	Blue	Clear	Green	Vas
Straight-sided bowl	35.00	40.00	25.00	50.00	45.00
Ink well, chair shape	40.00	45.00	30.00	50.00	45.00
Lamp, oil, high standard, all glass, patterned font, plain standard, original burner	150.00	200.00	125.00	200.00	200.00
Match safe, flat, two compartment	25.00	30.00	20.00	35.00	35.00
Pickle					
Castor, complete with original silver plate frame	125.00	150.00	85.00	125.00	150.00
Dish					
Fish shape	30.00	35.00	25.00	40.00	40.00
Yacht shape	30.00	35.00	25.00	40.00	40.00
Jar, original matching lid, no finial	55.00	65.00	45.00	65.00	65.00
Whisk broom tray					
6³/₈″ x 4″	25.00	30.00	15.00	35.00	35.00
7¹/₂″ x 5″	25.00	30.00	15.00	35.00	35.00
Pitcher					
Bulbous					
Milk, 1 quart, applied air twist handle, 8″h	175.00	—	135.00	—	—
Water, applied reeded handle, ¹/₂ gallon	125.00	150.00	100.00	125.00	150.00
Tankard					
Milk, 1 quart, applied handle	75.00	90.00	50.00	85.00	90.00
Water, applied handle, ¹/₂ gallon	100.00	125.00	65.00	125.00	125.00
Plate					
Leaf shape, 5″	20.00	25.00	15.00	30.00	25.00
Round					
Scalloped rim					
6″d. (sugar under plate)	15.00	20.00	10.00	25.00	30.00
7″d. (butter under plate)	15.00	20.00	10.00	25.00	30.00
7¹/₂″d. (cheese underplate)	15.00	20.00	10.00	25.00	30.00
10″d. (dinner plate)	25.00	30.00	20.00	35.00	40.00
Plain rim					
6″d	15.00	20.00	10.00	25.00	30.00
7″d	15.00	20.00	10.00	25.00	30.00
7¹/₂″d	15.00	20.00	10.00	25.00	30.00
10″d	25.00	30.00	20.00	35.00	40.00
Square, 7″	25.00	30.00	15.00	35.00	35.00
Platter					
Oval, double handled, 13″l	35.00	40.00	25.00	45.00	50.00
Rectangular, four applied feet	35.00	40.00	25.00	45.00	50.00
Punch bowl, footed on standard	125.00	150.00	85.00	145.00	150.00
Salt					
Individual					
Band master's hat, 2″h	45.00	55.00	35.00	60.00	60.00
Hat, brimmed	25.00	35.00	15.00	40.00	40.00
Rectangular, flat	25.00	25.00	10.00	25.00	25.00
Triangular	25.00	25.00	10.00	25.00	25.00
Tub, tab handle					
1³/₄″d	20.00	20.00	10.00	20.00	20.00
2″d	20.00	20.00	10.00	20.00	20.00
Master					
Canoe, 5″l	20.00	25.00	15.00	30.00	30.00
Hat, brimmed	30.00	40.00	20.00	45.00	45.00
Shoe, open, low heel, 4¹/₂″l	35.00	45.00	25.00	65.00	65.00
Yacht	20.00	25.00	15.00	30.00	30.00
Shaker, original top					
Flat					
Bulbous	30.00	35.00	20.00	45.00	40.00

Items made	Amber	Blue	Clear	Green	Vas
Slender	30.00	35.00	20.00	45.00	40.00
Straight sided	25.00	30.00	15.00	40.00	35.00
Tapered	25.00	30.00	15.00	40.00	35.00
Footed, tall	25.00	30.00	15.00	40.00	35.00
Sauce dish, flat					
Basket, handled	25.00	30.00	15.00	35.00	35.00
Octagonal	20.00	22.00	10.00	22.00	22.00
Round, 4½"d.					
Flared rim	15.00	20.00	10.00	20.00	20.00
Four folded edges	15.00	20.00	10.00	20.00	20.00
Point and scallop rim	15.00	20.00	10.00	20.00	20.00
Smooth scalloped rim	15.00	20.00	10.00	20.00	20.00
Square					
4 pointed scallops rim	15.00	20.00	10.00	20.00	20.00
Point and scallop rim					
4"	15.00	20.00	10.00	20.00	20.00
4½"	15.00	20.00	10.00	20.00	20.00
Triangular	20.00	22.00	10.00	22.00	22.00
Shade, gas, 4" fitter opening					
Crimped	45.00	55.00	30.00	65.00	65.00
Round	45.00	55.00	30.00	65.00	65.00
Shoe					
Baby bootie, 4¼"l., 2¼"h., marked "PATd Oct 16, 86"	45.00	50.00	40.00	50.00	55.00
Boot	40.00	45.00	35.00	45.00	50.00
Sietz bath tub (R)	55.00	60.00	50.00	60.00	65.00
Slipper					
Flat, 11½"l	35.00	40.00	30.00	50.00	50.00
High heel					
Clear toe (Duncan version, marked "PATD OCT. 19/86")					
4⅛"l	45.00	55.00	40.00	50.00	55.00
5"l	45.00	55.00	40.00	50.00	55.00
With bow	40.00	45.00	35.00	45.00	45.00
Low heel, patterned toe (Bryce version, marked "PATD OCT 19 1886")	45.00	55.00	40.00	50.00	55.00
Spoonholder, flat					
Hat shape	40.00	45.00	30.00	55.00	50.00
Point and scallop rim	40.00	45.00	35.00	55.00	55.00
Sugar bowl					
Table size, covered					
Round					
Small	40.00	50.00	30.00	50.00	50.00
Tall, faceted knob finial, tab handles	45.00	55.00	35.00	55.00	55.00
Square, footed	55.00	65.00	45.00	65.00	65.00
Syrup, original top, pressed handle					
Table size	135.00	155.00	100.00	—	155.00
10 ounce	135.00	155.00	100.00	—	155.00
Toothpick holder					
Barrel, metal band around rim	25.00	35.00	20.00	40.00	35.00
Bulbous, flat, scalloped rim	25.00	35.00	20.00	40.00	35.00
Cat on a pillow	45.00	55.00	30.00	65.00	65.00
Coal scuttle	30.00	35.00	20.00	40.00	40.00
Hat					
Fan brim	35.00	40.00	20.00	40.00	40.00
Plain rim, 2½"h	35.00	40.00	20.00	40.00	40.00
Kettle	30.00	35.00	20.00	40.00	40.00
Match box, 4 footed	35.00	45.00	25.00	55.00	55.00
Round					

Items made	Amber	Blue	Clear	Green	Vas
Collared base	25.00	35.00	20.00	40.00	35.00
Flat	25.00	35.00	20.00	40.00	35.00
Pedestaled, smooth rim, patterned base	40.00	50.00	30.00	50.00	50.00
Three legged	30.00	35.00	20.00	35.00	35.00
Square, flat, smooth rim	20.00	25.00	15.00	25.00	25.00
Tray					
Dust pan	35.00	40.00	25.00	45.00	45.00
Heart shape, with "Lily" in center	25.00	30.00	15.00	35.00	35.00
Ice cream, rectangular, shallow	45.00	50.00	35.00	55.00	55.00
Water					
Clover leaf	85.00	110.00	65.00	125.00	125.00
Oblong with cut corners	75.00	100.00	55.00	115.00	115.00
Round	65.00	75.00	35.00	85.00	85.00
Triangular, tab handled	75.00	100.00	55.00	115.00	115.00
Tumbler, flat					
Water					
Pattern on base only	15.00	20.00	10.00	20.00	20.00
Pattern lower half	20.00	30.00	15.00	35.00	35.00
Pattern lower three quarters	20.00	30.00	15.00	35.00	35.00
Pattern to rim	20.00	30.00	15.00	35.00	35.00
Whiskey, pattern on lower half, $2^3/_4$"h	15.00	20.00	10.00	20.00	20.00
Umbrella, with original handle					
Footed	80.00	90.00	60.00	90.00	90.00
Plain, 4"h	80.00	90.00	60.00	90.00	90.00
Wall pocket					
Canoe	75.00	85.00	55.00	85.00	85.00
Vase	75.00	85.00	55.00	85.00	85.00
Wine	20.00	25.00	10.00	30.00	40.00

DAISY AND BUTTON WITH CROSSBARS

Salt shaker; footed covered butter dish; cruet (n.o.s.).

OMN: Richards & Hartley No. 99, Mikado. AKA: Daisy and Thumbprint Crossbar, Daisy and Button with Crossbar and Thumbprint Band, Daisy with Crossbar.

Non-flint. Richards & Hartley Glass Co. (pattern line 99). Tarentum, PA. ca. 1885. Reissued by the United States Glass Co., Pittsburgh, PA. after the United States Glass Co. merger of 1891. Shards have been found at the site of the Burlington Glass Works, Hamilton, Ontario, Canada.

Original color production: Amber (dark), amber (light), blue, canary-yellow, clear. Less seldom found copper wheel engraved.

Reproductions: None.

References: Bat-GPG (PP. 65-67), Hea-3 (P. 72), Hea-5 (P. 39, Nos. 88-95), Hea-6 (P. 25, Figs. 110-113), Kam-3 (P. 53), Kam/Wod-Vol.1 (P. 189), Lee-EAPG (Pl. 167), Luc-TG (PP. 198-204), Mil-1 (Pl. 129), Mil-2 (Pl. 62), Mtz-1 (PP. 22-223), Mur-MCO (P. 67), Oliv-AAG (P. 62), Pet-Sal (P. 26), Rev-APG (PP. 286-288), Spil-AEPG (P. 305), Spil-TBV (PP. 196, 242), Stev-ECG (P. 216), Thu-1 (P. 323), Uni-1 (PP. 206-207), Uni-TCG (PP. 96-97), Uni/Wor-CHPGT (P. 100, Wlkr-PGA (Fig. 8, Nos. 3, 41, 43, 56).

Items made	Amber	Blue	Clear	Canary-Yellow
Bottle, ketchup	90.00	110.00	35.00	90.00
Bowl				
Finger, open, flat	35.00	40.00	30.00	35.00
Oval, open, flat				
6″d	25.00	30.00	20.00	25.00
8″d	25.00	30.00	20.00	25.00
9″d	30.00	35.00	25.00	30.00
Waste	35.00	40.00	30.00	35.00
Butter dish, covered				
Flat, flanged rim	55.00	55.00	40.00	55.00
Footed, flanged rim	55.00	55.00	40.00	55.00
Celery vase, 7⅜″h	35.00	40.00	25.00	35.00
Compote, round				
Covered				
High standard				
7″d	55.00	65.00	45.00	55.00
8″d	55.00	65.00	45.00	55.00
Low standard				
7″d	35.00	35.00	25.00	35.00
8″d	35.00	35.00	25.00	35.00
Open				
High standard				
7″d	40.00	45.00	25.00	40.00
8″d	50.00	50.00	30.00	45.00
Low collared base				
7″d	30.00	35.00	25.00	30.00
8″d	30.00	35.00	25.00	30.00
Cordial	30.00	35.00	25.00	30.00
Creamer				
Individual	25.00	30.00	15.00	25.00
Table size	40.00	45.00	35.00	40.00
Cruet, original faceted stopped, 9¾″h	75.00	100.00	35.00	65.00
Dish, preserve, open				
7″d	30.00	30.00	25.00	30.00
8″d	30.00	35.00	25.00	30.00
9″d	35.00	40.00	25.00	35.00
Goblet	40.00	40.00	25.00	40.00
Jar, pickle, covered	30.00	45.00	25.00	35.00
Lamp, oil (4 sizes) original burner and chimney	125.00	145.00	90.00	125.00

Items made	Amber	Blue	Clear	Canary-Yellow
Mug, pressed handle				
Large, 3"h	15.00	20.00	10.00	15.00
Small	15.00	20.00	10.00	15.00
Pickle dish, oblong	20.00	20.00	10.00	20.00
Pitcher				
Milk, 1 quart	50.00	60.00	35.00	50.00
Water, 1/2 gallon	65.00	85.00	45.00	65.00
Plate, bread, round	30.00	45.00	25.00	35.00
Salt shaker, original top	20.00	25.00	15.00	20.00
Sauce dish, round, 4"d				
Flat	15.00	15.00	10.00	15.00
Footed	15.00	15.00	10.00	15.00
Spoonholder, footed	30.00	35.00	25.00	30.00
Sugar bowl, covered				
Individual	25.00	35.00	10.00	25.00
Table size	50.00	60.00	25.00	55.00
Syrup pitcher, original top	150.00	150.00	65.00	150.00
Toothpick holder	40.00	40.00	30.00	35.00
Tumbler, water, flat	30.00	35.00	20.00	30.00
Tray, water, round	40.00	45.00	35.00	40.00
Wine	30.00	30.00	25.00	30.00

DAISY AND BUTTON WITH NARCISSUS

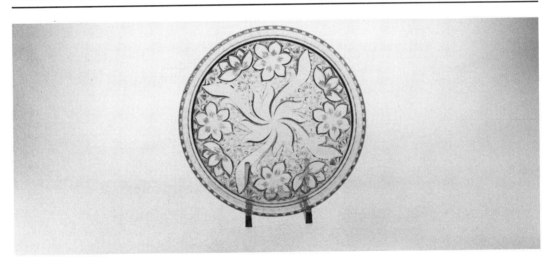

Water tray, 10"d.

OMN: Indiana Glass No. 124. AKA: Daisy and Buttton with Clear Lily.

Non-flint. Indiana Glass Co., Dunkirk, IN. ca. 1910 into the 1920s. Advertised in the Sears, Roebuck and Co. catalogs as late as 1925-1926.

Original color production: Clear, clear with cranberry stain.

Reproductions: Daisy and Button with Narcissus has been reproduced from new molds in amber, dark blue, clear, green and yellow in various sizes of flat oval bowls, vases and the wine. Reproductions are heavier in weight than the originals and lack the lustre of old glass, the design not as sharply molded and often looking "muddy".

References: Bat-GPG (PP. 185, 187), Bond-AG (PP. 81-82), Kam-4 (P. 139), Lee-VG (Pl. 34, No. 1), McCn-PGP (P. 293), Mil-1 (Pl. 152), Mtz-1 (P. 66-67), Uni-1 (PP. 206-207).

Items made	Clear	Clear w/Stain
Bowl, open		
Oval footed, 6″ x 9¼″	40.00	—
Round, flat		
7¼″d	25.00	—
8¼″d	30.00	—
Butter dish, covered	50.00	—
Celery		
Tray, oval	25.00	—
Vase	20.00	—
Compote, open		
High standard		
Fruit, large	50.00	—
Jelly, 5″d	40.00	—
Low standard	35.00	—
Creamer	25.00	—
Cup		
Punch	10.00	15.00
Sherbert	10.00	15.00
Decanter, 1 quart, original stopper	40.00	60.00
Goblet	25.00	35.00
Pickle tray, oblong, 9″	25.00	—
Pitcher		
Milk, 1 quart	50.00	75.00
Water, ½ gallon, 8½″h	50.00	75.00
Relish dish, oval	15.00	—
Salt shaker, original top	15.00	—
Sauce dish, round, deep		
Flat		
4″d	10.00	15.00
4¾″d	10.00	15.00
Footed		
4″d	10.00	15.00
4¾″d	10.00	15.00
Spoonholder	30.00	—
Sugar bowl, covered	40.00	45.00
Tray		
Water, plain edge, 10″d	30.00	40.00
Wine, serrated rim, 10″d	30.00	40.00
Tumbler, water, flat (2 sizes)	15.00	20.00
Wine	15.00	20.00

DAISY AND BUTTON WITH THUMBPRINT PANEL

Flat sauce dish; water tumbler; h.s. covered compote; goblet.

OMN: Adams No. 86. AKA: Daisy and Button with Amber Stripes, Daisy and Button with Thumbprint [Metz], Daisy and Button Thumbprint.

Non-flint. Adams & Co. (pattern line No. 86), Pittsburgh, PA. ca. 1886, reissued by the United States Glass Co., Pittsburgh, PA. ca. 1891.

Original color production: Clear, clear with amber, blue and pink stain. Solid colors of amber, blue and vaseline. Clear with ruby stain, solid green or any other color is rare.

Reproductions: Champagne, goblet, wine (clear w/colored stain, solid amber and blue). Reproductions are heavier than the originals, with a dull design.

References: Hart-AG (P. 84), Hea-3 (P. 22), Hea-5 (P. 70), Kam-3 (P. 73), Lee-EAPG (P. 594, Plts. 167-169), McCn-EPG (Pl. 83), Mil-1 (PLt. 11), Mtz-1 (P. 222), Rev-APG (P. 19), Wlkr-PGA (Fig. 8, No. 3).

Items made	Clear	Clear w/Stain	Solid Amber	Blue	Vas
Bowl					
Heart shape, 7″	25.00	45.00	30.00	35.00	30.00
Oval, 9″l	25.00	45.00	30.00	35.00	30.00
Round					
Covered					
6″d	25.00	45.00	35.00	40.00	35.00
7″d	30.00	50.00	40.00	45.00	40.00
8″d	35.00	55.00	45.00	50.00	45.00
Open					
5″d	10.00	25.00	15.00	20.00	15.00
6″d	10.00	25.00	15.00	20.00	15.00
7″d	15.00	30.00	20.00	25.00	20.00
8″d	20.00	35.00	25.00	30.00	25.00
Square, open	15.00	30.00	20.00	25.00	20.00
Waste	15.00	35.00	25.00	30.00	25.00
Butter dish, covered	40.00	75.00	55.00	65.00	55.00
Butter pat, square	10.00	20.00	15.00	15.00	15.00
Cake stand, high standard	40.00	75.00	55.00	65.00	55.00

Items made	Clear	Clear w/Stain	Solid Amber	Blue	Vas
Celery vase, 10"h	30.00	75.00	55.00	65.00	55.00
Champagne	20.00	45.00	30.00	35.00	30.00
Claret	20.00	45.00	30.00	35.00	30.00
Compote					
Covered					
High standard					
6"d	45.00	85.00	65.00	75.00	65.00
7"d	55.00	95.00	75.00	85.00	75.00
8"d	65.00	110.00	85.00	95.00	85.00
Low standard					
6"d	45.00	85.00	65.00	75.00	65.00
7"d	55.00	95.00	75.00	85.00	75.00
8"d	65.00	110.00	85.00	95.00	85.00
Open					
High standard					
6"d	20.00	45.00	30.00	35.00	30.00
7"d	25.00	50.00	35.00	40.00	35.00
8"d	30.00	55.00	40.00	45.00	40.00
Low standard					
5"d	15.00	40.00	25.00	30.00	25.00
6"d	20.00	45.00	30.00	35.00	30.00
7"d	25.00	50.00	35.00	40.00	35.00
8"d	30.00	55.00	40.00	45.00	40.00
11"d	40.00	65.00	50.00	55.00	50.00
Creamer, 5¼"h., applied handle	25.00	55.00	35.00	40.00	35.00
Cruet, original stopper	50.00	150.00	150.00	150.00	150.00
Goblet	25.00	45.00	35.00	40.00	35.00
Lamp, oil, pedestaled base, applied finger grip, with original burner and chimney	125.00	200.00	150.00	175.00	150.00
Mug	20.00	40.00	30.00	35.00	30.00
Pickle dish	20.00	40.00	30.00	35.00	30.00
Pitcher, water, ½ gallon, applied handle	80.00	175.00	125.00	135.00	125.00
Plate, bread, oval	30.00	55.00	40.00	45.00	40.00
Salt					
Master, flat, open	15.00	40.00	30.00	35.00	30.00
Shaker, original top	20.00	85.00	30.00	35.00	30.00
Sauce dish, square, 4½"					
Flat	15.00	25.00	20.00	20.00	20.00
Footed	15.00	25.00	22.00	22.00	22.00
Spoonholder	25.00	55.00	35.00	40.00	35.00
Sugar bowl, covered	35.00	65.00	45.00	50.00	45.00
Syrup, original top	55.00	200.00	150.00	175.00	150.00
Tray, water, oblong, double handled	35.00	60.00	45.00	50.00	45.00
Tumbler, flat, water	15.00	40.00	30.00	35.00	30.00
Wine	25.00	45.00	30.00	35.00	30.00

DAISY AND BUTTON WITH V ORNAMENT

Mug (vaseline); tumbler (amber); oil lamp (clear font, enameled milk glass standard); celery vase (sapphire blue); finger bowl (vaseline).

OMN: Beatty's No. 555, 558, Vandyke. AKA: Daisy with V Ornament.

Non-flint A.J. Beatty & Co., Steubenville, OH. ca. 1886-1887. Reissued by the United States Glass Co., Pittsburgh, PA. ca. 1892. Federal Glass Co., Columbus, OH. ca. 1914. Illustrated in the A.J. Beatty & Co. ca. 1890-1891 catalog as "Vandyke", and the United States Glass Co. 1895-1896 catalog.

Original color production: Amber, blue, vaseline, clear. Pieces are most often found plain, although copper wheel engraved items are illustrated in the United States Glass Co. ca. 1895-1896 catalog. Double numbers in the original catalog illustrations designate items with or without "patterned bottoms".

Reproductions: None.

References: Bat-GPG (PP. 67-69), Hea-1 (P. 20), Kam-5 (P. 112), Lee-EAPG (Pl. 168), Mtz-1 (P.223), Oliv-AAG (P. 62), Pet-Sal (P. 158), Rev-APG (PP.55, 57), Stev-ECG (P. 216), Uni/Wor-CHPGT (P. 105), Wlkr-PGA (Fig. 8, Nos. 19, 28).

Items made	Amber	Blue	Clear	Vas
Bowl, octagonal				
Berry, master, deep, flared rim				
5½"d	25.00	45.00	25.00	55.00
8½"d	25.00	45.00	25.00	55.00
10"d	40.00	45.00	25.00	55.00
Finger, bulbous, flat				
Belled bowl, smooth rim (originally termed "Style A")	25.00	45.00	25.00	55.00
Smooth rim (originally termed "Style B")	25.00	45.00	25.00	55.00
4-scalloped smooth rim (originally termed "Style C")	25.00	45.00	25.00	55.00
6-scalloped smooth rim (originally termed "Style D")	25.00	45.00	25.00	55.00
Butter dish, covered, flat	85.00	80.00	65.00	90.00
Celery vase				
Crimped rim, 4-scalloped	50.00	55.00	30.00	55.00
Flared rim	50.00	55.00	30.00	55.00
Straight-sided, 7⅜"h	50.00	55.00	30.00	55.00

Items made	Amber	Blue	Clear	Vas
Creamer	30.00	50.00	50.00	30.00
Dish, oblong, open, deep	25.00	30.00	45.00	40.00
Goblet, Daisy And Button variant without "V Ornament"	20.00	30.00	20.00	35.00
Match holder	30.00	40.00	35.00	25.00
Mug (4 sizes)				
No. 2 (largest)	20.00	30.00	20.00	35.00
No. 3	20.00	30.00	20.00	35.00
No. 4	15.00	25.00	15.00	30.00
No. 5 (smallest)	15.00	25.00	15.00	30.00
Pickle castor, complete with original silver plate holder and tongs	120.00	120.00	100.00	85.00
Pickle jar, covered with no finial	60.00	85.00	55.00	45.00
Pitcher, applied handle				
Milk, 1 quart	50.00	75.00	45.00	30.00
Water, ½ gallon	65.00	90.00	60.00	45.00
Plate (design does not contain "V Ornament")				
Round, scalloped rim				
6"d	25.00	25.00	35.00	15.00
7"d	25.00	25.00	35.00	15.00
Round, scalloped edge, deep rim				
6"d	25.00	25.00	35.00	20.00
7"d	25.00	25.00	35.00	20.00
8"d	30.00	40.00	35.00	25.00
9"d	30.00	40.00	35.00	25.00
Sauce dish, flat				
Round, shallow bowl, 4"d	15.00	15.00	10.00	15.00
Straight-sided, 5"d	15.00	15.00	10.00	15.00
Pointed scalloped rim, octagonal, 4"d	15.00	15.00	10.00	15.00
Shade, gas, 4"d, fitter opening	60.00	85.00	55.00	45.00
Sherbert cup, handled	15.00	20.00	15.00	10.00
Spoonholder, flat, scalloped rim	40.00	35.00	35.00	45.00
Sugar bowl, covered, flat	60.00	50.00	75.00	40.00
Toothpick holder	30.00	40.00	35.00	25.00
Tray, water, canoe shape	55.00	65.00	55.00	35.00
Tumbler, water, flat				
7½ ounce	25.00	20.00	35.00	15.00
9 ounce	25.00	20.00	35.00	15.00
Wine	30.00	35.00	25.00	20.00

(Numbers indicate engraving design numbers).

Milk pitcher (76); cake basket (76); tankard water pitcher (80).

Creamer (76); milk pitcher (80); covered sugar (76); Cruet (n.o.s.) (76); salt shaker (76).

(OMN). AKA: Baby Thumbprint, Thumbprint Band, Thumbprint Band-Clear [Millard], Thumbprint Band-Red Top [Millard].

Non-flint. Ripley & Co., Pittsburgh, PA. ca. 1885. Reissued by the United States Glass Co., Pittsburgh, PA. ca. 1898. Illustrated in the ca. 1895 and 1898 United States Glass Co. catalogs, and the Montgomery Ward 1901 (No. 69), catalog.

Original color production: Clear, clear with ruby stain. Plain or copper wheel engraved often used for souvenir ware). Cobalt blue or any other color is rare.

The Dakota pattern was originally produced in two distinct forms: a "hotel set" characterized by ruffled edges and flat bases, and a "household set" characterized by plain edges and pedestaled, circular bases. Both versions were produced in complete table sets either plain or copper-wheel engraved with such known engravings as No. 76 (Fern & Berry), No. 79 (Fish), No. 80 (Fern, Butterfly & Bird), and No. 157 (Oak Leaf). Additional copper wheel engravings include Fern without Berry, Vintage Grape, Swan, Peacock, Bird and Insect, Bird and Flowers, Ivy and Berry, Stag, Spider and Insect in Web, Buzzard, and Crane Catching Fish.

Reproductions: None.

References: Bar-RS (Pl. 13), Drep-ABC OG (P. 253), Hart/Cobb-SS (P. 20), Hea-2 (P. 73), Hea-5 (P. 120, Plts. A-B), Hea-7 (Figs. 238-245), Inn-PG (PP. 383-387), Kam-1 (P. 194), Kam-6 (Pl. 6), Lee-VG (Pl. 67, No.1), McCn-PGP (Pl. 15), Mil-1 (Pl. 151), Mil-2 (Pl. 37), Mtz-1 (PP. 144-145), Oliv-AAG (P. 63), Pet-Sal (P. 158), Phil-EOG (P. 189), Rev-APG (PP. 293-294), Spil-AEPG (P. 310), Spil-TBV (Figs. 1209-1210), Uni-1 (P. 77), Wlkr-PGA (Fig. 8, No. 43).

Items made	Clear/ Etched	Clear/ Plain	Ruby Stained
Basket, cake, metal bail, 10″d			
Flat	200.00	150.00	175.00
Footed (4 clear applied ball feet)	225.00	175.00	200.00
Bottle, o.s.			
Cologne (VR)	85.00	65.00	—
Pepper sauce (VR), original top	75.00	70.00	—
Bowl, round, open, flat			
Master berry, flared rim	45.00	35.00	65.00
Waste, smooth rim	65.00	50.00	75.00
Butter dish, covered			
Hotel	75.00	65.00	125.00
Table	75.00	65.00	125.00
Cake cover, high dome (VR)			
8″d	300.00	200.00	—
9″d	325.00	225.00	—
10″d	350.00	250.00	—
15″d	375.00	275.00	—
Cake stand, high standard			
8″d	45.00	35.00	—
9″d	50.00	35.00	—
9½″d	60.00	45.00	—
10″d	65.00	45.00	—
10½″d	65.00	50.00	—
Celery			
Tray	45.00	30.00	—
Vase			
Hotel	45.00	30.00	—
Table	45.00	30.00	—
Compote, high standard			
Covered			
5″d	60.00	50.00	—
6″d	80.00	60.00	—
7″d	85.00	60.00	—
8″d	90.00	60.00	—
9″d	95.00	65.00	—
10″d	110.00	75.00	—
12″d	125.00	85.00	—
Open			
5″d	30.00	35.00	—
6″d	35.00	40.00	—
7″d	35.00	40.00	—
8″d	40.00	45.00	—
9″d	40.00	45.00	—
10″d	45.00	40.00	—
Low standard, 7″d	55.00	40.00	—

Items made	Clear/Etched	Clear/Plain	Ruby Stained
Creamer			
Hotel	55.00	35.00	65.00
Table	55.00	35.00	65.00
Cruet, original patterned stopper	125.00	100.00	—
Cruet set (originally termed "salad castor") with nickel plated handles			
(2 cruets, 2 salt shakers, undertray)	450.00	300.00	—
Cruet undertray (R)	85.00	75.00	—
Dish, oblong, open, flat			
8″	40.00	35.00	50.00
9″	50.00	40.00	55.00
10″	60.00	45.00	65.00
Goblet (height varies)	35.00	25.00	75.00
Honey dish, flat or footed, round	20.00	25.00	30.00
Mug, applied handle	45.00	55.00	65.00
Pitcher, applied handle, flat (height varies)			
Jug			
Milk			
1 pint	110.00	90.00	175.00
1 quart	110.00	90.00	—
Water, ½ gallon	95.00	75.00	110.00
Tankard			
Milk			
1 pint	85.00	65.00	175.00
1 Quart	85.00	65.00	—
Water, ½ gallon	125.00	95.00	200.00
Plate, round, 10″d	85.00	75.00	—
Relish tray, flat	40.00	35.00	—
Salt shaker, tall, original top	65.00	45.00	85.00
Sauce dish, round			
Flat			
4″d	20.00	15.00	25.00
5″d	20.00	15.00	25.00
Footed			
4″d	22.00	15.00	30.00
5″d	25.00	15.00	30.00
Spoonholder			
Hotel	65.00	55.00	85.00
Table size	30.00	25.00	65.00
Sugar bowl, covered			
Hotel	65.00	55.00	85.00
Table size	65.00	55.00	85.00
Tray, water, round, pie crust rim			
Hotel	100.00	75.00	—
Table size, 13″d	100.00	75.00	—
Wine, 10½″d	95.00	85.00	—
Tumbler, water, flat	45.00	35.00	45.00
Wine	40.00	20.00	55.00

Goblet.

Non-flint. Maker unknown, ca. 1880s.

Original color production: Clear.

Reproductions: None.

References: Kam-3 (P. 4), McCn-PGP (P. 173), Mtz-1 (P. 216), Thur-1 (P. 298).

Items made	Clear	Items made	Clear
Bowl, open, round, flat	10.00	Creamer, 6⅝"h	25.00
Butter dish, covered	25.00	Goblet	25.00
Compote, high standard		Pitcher, water, ½ gallon	35.00
Covered		Sauce dish, round, footed	12.00
5⅛"d	45.00	Spoonholder	20.00
8½"d	35.00	Sugar bowl, covered	35.00
Open, jelly	20.00	Tumbler, water, flat	15.00

Creamer; goblet (both etched).

High standard covered compote (plain).

AKA: Frosted Dog.

Non-flint. American manufacturer unknown. Shards have been found at the site of the Burlington Glass Works, Hamilton, Ontario, Canada.

Original color production: Clear or clear and acid finished with or without etched design. Handles are applied and finials are full figured, well designed frosted dogs. When etched, items display scenes of a deer hunt.

Reproductions: None.

References: Hlms-BCA (P. 278), Kam-1 (P. 51), Kam/Wod Vol.1 (P. 195), Lee-EAPG (Pl. 101, No. 1), Mil-2 (Pl. 38), Mtz-1 (P. 99), Mtz-2 (PP. 92-93), Uni-1 (PP. 170-171), Uni-TCG (PP. 102-103), Uni/Wor-CHPGT (P. 79).

Items made	Clear	Clear/ Etched
Butter dish, covered	55.00	165.00
Celery vase, pedestaled	30.00	90.00
Champagne	20.00	85.00
Cheese dish, covered, flat	45.00	145.00
Compote		
Covered		
High standard		
7"d	45.00	135.00
8¼"d	55.00	165.00
Low standard, 7¾"d	35.00	100.00
Open, high standard	25.00	65.00
Cordial	25.00	90.00
Creamer, 7"h	30.00	75.00
Goblet		
Bulbous bowl	25.00	85.00
"U"-shaped bowl	25.00	85.00
Marmalade jar, covered	30.00	125.00

Items made	Clear	Clear/Etched
Mug, handled	20.00	45.00
Pitcher, water, tankard, applied handle, 10"h	55.00	125.00
Sauce dish, round		
Flat	10.00	20.00
Footed	15.00	20.00
Spoonholder, 5"h	25.00	20.00
Sugar bowl, covered, 9"h., 4½"d	75.00	65.00
Wine	20.00	125.00
		75.00

DEER AND PINETREE

Cake stand (on side); water pitcher; water tray.

OMN: McKee's Band Diamond. AKA: Deer and Doe.

Non-flint. McKee & Brothers, Pittsburgh, PA. ca. 1886.

Original color production: Amber, apple green, blue, canary-yellow, clear. Odd pieces in color may be found with or without gilt.

Reproductions: First reproduced in 1938, the L.G. Wright Glass Co., New Martinsville, PA. (distributed by Jennings Red Barn, New Martinsville, WV. and Carl Forslund, Grand Rapids, MI.) reproduced the goblet in clear, from a new mold, as illustrated in the company's 1970 catalog supplement. The old goblet has a highly refined element of design with a vine climbing the pine tree which does not appear on the new. The old goblet has a well defined row of connected diamonds running across the rim of the bowl. The new goblet displays dots simulating diamonds. Underneath the landscape on the old goblet appears much more grass and shrubs with a much larger, more defined tree than on the new. On the old goblet the deer's ear is easily seen but is missing on the new.

References: Grow-WCG (P. 228, Fig. 42-"13"), Kam-4 (PP. 31-32), Lee-EAPG (Pl. 119, No. 1), Mtz-1 (P. 96), Mil-1 (Pl. 119), Stu-BP (P.46), Oliv-AAG (P. 63), Uni-1 (PP. 256-257), Uni-2 (P. 221), Wlkr-PGA (Fig. 8, No. 45).

Items made	Amber	Blue	Clear	Green
Bowl, waste, open, flat	—	—	55.00	—
Butter dish, covered, flat	100.00	110.00	85.00	125.00
Cake stand, high standard	—	—	85.00	—
Celery vase	—	—	85.00	—
Compote, oblong, high standard				
Covered				
7"sq	—	—	75.00	—
8"sq	—	—	85.00	—
9"sq	—	—	95.00	—
Open				
7"sq	—	—	30.00	—
8"sq	—	—	30.00	—
9"sq	—	—	35.00	—
Creamer, 5½"h	95.00	85.00	65.00	90.00
Dish, oblong, open, flat, shallow bowl				
5½" x 7¼"	—	—	25.00	—
5½" x 8"	—	—	30.00	—
5¾" x 9"	—	—	35.00	—
Goblet	—	—	45.00	—
Jar, marmalade, covered	—	—	125.00	—
Mug				
Large	45.00	50.00	40.00	45.00
Small	40.00	50.00	40.00	45.00
Pickle dish, oblong, deep bowl	—	—	—	30.00
Pitcher				
Milk, 1 quart	—	—	125.00	—
Water, ½ gallon	125.00	125.00	125.00	—
Plate, bread, oblong	—	80.00	55.00	65.00
Platter, oblong	90.00	100.00	75.00	100.00
Sauce dish, oblong				
Flat	—	—	20.00	—
Footed (2 sizes)	—	—	20.00	—
Spoonholder	—	—	65.00	80.00
Sugar bowl, covered	—	—	85.00	95.00
Tray, water, 11" x 15"	125.00	125.00	100.00	—

Spoonholder; creamer; covered sugar bowl; covered butter dish. All cranberry flashed with gilt.

OMN: Diamond's No. 206 New Century, U.S. Glass No. 15,065 (Delaware) AKA: American Beauty, Four Petal Flower.

Non-flint. United States Glass Co. (pattern line No. 15,065), Pittsburgh, PA. introduced in 1899 with production continued to 1909. Diamond Glass Co., Montreal, Quebec, Canada. ca. 1902. Illustrated in the United States Glass Co. 1900 catalog as "American Beauty", the No. 111 1904 Factory "D" catalog, and the Diamond Glass Co. (Canada) catalog as No. 206-"New Century".

Original color production: Clear, clear with rose stain and gilt, emerald green with gilt. Amethyst with gilt (VR), clear with ruby stain and gilt (VR), milk white with blue stain (S), opaque white (R), opaque ivory (R). Any other color would be very rare. The main design element of Delaware consists of long, slender leaves with four-petal flowers against a finely stippled background. Handles are pressed, and finials are broad, wide leaves.

Reproductions: None.

References: Bat-GPG (PP. 133-134), Boyd-GC (P. 16), Hart/Cobb-SS (P. 22), Hea-1 (P. 19), Hea-4 (P. 54), Hea-5 (PP. 34, 45), Hea-6 (PP. 25, 95), Hea-OPG (PP. 46-47), Hlms-BCA (P. 281), Kam-1 (P. 103), McCn-PGP (P. 307), Migh-TPS (Pl. 3), Mtz-1 (PP. 86-87), Mur-MCO (P. 75), Pet-Sal (P. 27), Rev-APG (P. 312), Stev-ECG (P. 103), Uni/Wor-CHPGT (P. 167), Wlkr-PGA (Fig. 8, No. 49).

Items made	Clear	Green w/Gold	Rose w/Gold
Banana bowl, flat, open	50.00	55.00	65.00
Basket, bride's, original silver plate holder, compote	75.00	125.00	165.00
Bowl, round			
Berry, master			
Scalloped-flared rim, 9"d	30.00	35.00	50.00
Smooth rim, 8"d	30.00	35.00	50.00
Finger	20.00	35.00	45.00
Fruit			
Oval, pointed ends, 11½"l	25.00	45.00	55.00

Items made	Clear	Green w/Gold	Rose w/Gold
Round			
8"d	25.00	45.00	55.00
11"d	35.00	50.00	60.00
Butter dish, covered	60.00	125.00	145.00
Celery vase, flat, smooth rim	75.00	90.00	95.00
Claret jug	75.00	125.00	155.00
Compote	55.00	85.00	110.00
Creamer			
Individual	45.00	60.00	70.00
Table size	45.00	60.00	75.00
Cruet, original patterned stopper	90.00	150.00	175.00
Cup, custard	15.00	40.00	40.00
Pin tray	30.00	55.00	55.00
Pitcher, tankard, water	50.00	150.00	175.00
Pomade box, covered, jeweled lid	100.00	200.00	300.00
Puff box, covered, jeweled lid	100.00	175.00	300.00
Salt shaker, tall, original top (VR)	75.00	125.00	150.00
Sauce dish			
Flat			
Boat shape, 5"	15.00	35.00	30.00
Round, 4"d	15.00	25.00	20.00
Shade			
Electric, straight sided	85.00	—	—
Gas, bulbous, flared rim, 4" fitter opening	85.00	—	—
Spoonholder	45.00	60.00	55.00
Sugar bowl, covered			
Individual	35.00	50.00	60.00
Table size	65.00	85.00	55.00
Toothpick holder	45.00	100.00	125.00
Tumbler, water, flat	20.00	45.00	50.00
Vase			
6"h	25.00	45.00	75.00
8"h	25.00	45.00	75.00
9½"h	40.00	80.00	90.00

DEWDROP AND RAINDROP

Wine; sherbert cup.

OMN: Kokomo No. 50, Federal's No. 50. AKA: Dew With Raindrop [Millard], Dewdrop And Rain.

Non-flint. Kokomo Glass Co. (pattern line No. 50), Kokomo, IN., ca. 1901. Federal Glass Co. (pattern line No. 50), Columbus, OH., ca. 1913-1914. Indiana Glass Co., Dunkirk, IN., ca. 1902.

Original color production: Clear. Clear with ruby stain is very rare. Items produced by the Federal Glass Co. lack the tiny dewdrops on the stems of items.

Reproductions: The clear wine was first reproduced from a new mold in the early 1930s. Through the years, the following items have been reissued from new molds: cordial (amber, blue, and clear with light ruby top), sherbert cup (clear), goblet (clear), and the wine (clear). New items are heavier and do not have the fine dewdrop motif of the originals.

References: Bar-RS (Pl. 9), Bros-TS (P. 33), Brn-SD (P. 136), Drep-ABC OG (P. 161), Hea-7 (P. 103), Kam-4 (P. 113), Kam-5 (P. 124), Lee-EAPG (Pl. 69, No. 2), Mil-1 (Pl. 78), Mtz-1 (P. 188-189), Oliv-AAG (P. 64), Pet-Sal (P. 158), Rev-APG (P. 224), Uni-1 (P. 123).

Items made	Clear	Items made	Clear
Bowl, open, flat, master berry, 8″d	40.00	Sauce dish, round, flat	
Butter dish, covered	65.00	4″d	15.00
Cordial, plain stem	25.00	4½″d	15.00
Creamer	35.00	Sherbert cup	10.00
Goblet, dewdrop stem	30.00	Spoonholder	25.00
Mug	35.00	Sugar bowl, covered	35.00
Pitcher, water, ½ gallon	65.00	Tumbler, water, flat	35.00
Salt shaker, original top	20.00	Wine, plain stem	20.00

High standard cake stand; handled plate.

OMN: Greensburg Glass No. 67.

Non-flint. Brilliant Glass Works, Brilliant, OH., ca. 1888. Greensburg Glass Co., Greensburg, PA., ca. 1889. Illustrated in an undated Greensburg Glass Co. catalog.

Original color production: Clear, the main design element consisting of clear points resembling inverted "icicles" against a finely stippled background. Handles are pressed. Finials are flat and circular. Rims are smooth. Stems may be either solid or hexagonal (with or without knobs).

Reproductions: None.

References: Kam-3 (P. 13), Kam-8 (P. 163), Lee-EAPG (Pl. 87), Lee-VG (Pl. 36, No. 3), McCn-PGP (P. 337), Mil-1 (P. 130), Mtz-1 (PP. 180-181), Stu-BP (P. 6), Uni-1 (P. 123).

Items made	Clear	Items made	Clear
Butter dish	40.00	Pitcher, water, ¹/₂ gallon, pressed	
Cake stand, high standard, 10¹/₂"d	40.00	handle	35.00
Compote		Plate, round	
Covered, high standard	60.00	Dinner, 12"d., handled	25.00
Open		Bread	25.00
High standard		Platter, bread, handled, vine border, 9"	
7"d	25.00	x 11³/₄"	25.00
8"d	25.00	Sauce dish, round	
Low standard	25.00	Flat, 4¹/₂"d	10.00
Creamer, 6¹/₄"h	30.00	Footed, 4¹/₂"d	15.00
Goblet	25.00	Spoonholder	25.00
Pickle dish	25.00	Sugar bowl, covered	40.00
		Wine	35.00

High standard covered compote; bread plate; covered sugar bowl.

AKA: Dewdrop And Star [Kamm], Dewdrop with Small Star, Star and Dewdrop.

Non-flint. Campbell, Jones & Co., Pittsburgh, PA. ca. 1877. Designed and patented by Jenkins Jones (design patent Nos. 10,096, 10,296, and 10,297), July 17, 1877.

Original color production: Clear.

Reproductions: The following items have been reproduced from new molds in both clear and colors: 7"d round plate, 7 1/4"d round plate, 7 1/2"d. round plate, footed master open salt, and the footed round sauce. New goblets are not original to the pattern.

References: Brn-SD (P. 55), Gor-CC (P. 102), Inn-PG (Figs. 374-375), Kam-3 (PP. 67-68), Kam-7 (P. 71), Lee-EAPG (Pl. 73), McCn-PGP (P. 507), Mil-1 (Pl. 15), Mtz-1 (P. 119), Mtz-2 (PP. 104-105), Oliv-AAG (P. 64), Rev-APG (PP. 98, 101-102), Spil-AEPG (P. 275), Uni-2 (P. 289), Wlkr-PGA (Fig. 15, Nos. 68, 69).

Items made	Clear	Items made	Clear
Bowl, open		Open	
Flat		Flat, star base, 6"d	10.00
6"d	8.00	Footed, star base, 7"d	15.00
7"d	10.00	Goblet	20.00
Footed, 9"d	20.00	Honey dish, covered, with underplate	75.00
Butter dish, covered, star in base,		Lamp, all glass, patented "Aug. 29,	
domed lid	50.00	1876", footed with finger grip	85.00
Cake stand, high standard (2 sizes)	40.00	Pickle dish, oval	15.00
Celery vase, star in base	40.00	Pitcher, water, applied handle	125.00
Cheese dish, covered	100.00	Plate	
Compote		Dinner	
Covered		4 1/2"d	10.00
High standard	75.00	5"d	10.00
Low standard	75.00	5 1/4"d	10.00
Open, high standard	45.00	5 1/2"d	10.00
Cordial	35.00	6"d	15.00
Creamer, applied handle, 4 3/4"h	35.00	6 1/4"d	15.00
Dish		6 1/2"d	15.00
Covered, flat, open (2 styles)	35.00	7"d	15.00

Items made	Clear	Items made	Clear
7¼"d	15.00	5"d	10.00
7½"d	15.00	5¼"d	10.00
7¾"d	15.00	5½"d	15.00
8¼"d	20.00	6"d	15.00
9"d	20.00	Footed	
Bread, "Sheaf of Wheat" center	35.00	3½"d	10.00
Salt, master, footed, open, scalloped,		4"d	10.00
1½"h., 3⅛"d	20.00	4½"d	15.00
Sauce dish, round		Spoonholder	35.00
Flat		Sugar bowl, covered	50.00
4"d	10.00		

DEWEY

Creamer (table size); serpentine tray; mug.

OMN: Flower Flange.

Non-flint. Indiana Tumbler & Goblet Co. Dunkirk, IN. ca. 1898, with continued production by the United States Glass Co., Pittsburgh, PA. until 1904. Illustrated in the September 15, 1898 issue of *China, Glass and Lamps* and the Butler Brothers 1900 catalog.

Original color production: Amber, blue (scarce), vaseline, clear, emerald green, chocolate, Nile green, opaque white (hard to find), dull yellow-green. Not all pieces are found in all colors. Named by the Indiana Tumbler & Goblet Co. to commemorate Admiral Dewey's Spanish-American War victories.

Reproductions: The Imperial Glass Corp., Bellaire, OH., reproduced the large covered butter dish (termed the "No. 972 Box and Cover") in deep amber, clear, olive green, milk white, purple-carnival, and purple slag, sometimes marked on the base with the company's "I.G." insignia. New colors are clouded and muddy in comparison to the originals.

References: Boyd-GC (Nos. 150-151), Bros-TS (P. 34), Fer-YMG (PP. 77, 149), Hea-6 (P. 26, Figs. 118-120), Herr-GG (P. 15, Figs. 92-110), Kam-1 (PP. 84-85), Kam-2 (PP. 84-85), Kam-5 (PP. 124-125), Lind-HG (Fig. 399), Lip-GG (PP. 28-29), Mrsh-SRG (PP. 245, 359), Meas-GG (PP. 56-67), Mil-OG (Pl. 1240), Mtz-1 (P. 221), Mtz-2 (P. 106), Mur-CO (PP. 5, 12), Mur-MCO

(P. 71), Pet-Sal (P. 27), Rev-APG (PP. 201, 203), Spil-AEPG (P. 327), Wlkr-PGA (Fig. 8, No. 43).

Items made	Amber	Chocolate	Clear	Green	Vas
Bowl, master berry, open, footed, 8"d	80.00	225.00	60.00	80.00	95.00
Butter dish, covered					
Quarter pounder, 4"d	65.00	200.00	45.00	65.00	75.00
Table size, 5"d	95.00	350.00	65.00	95.00	110.00
Creamer					
Individual, 4"h, covered	45.00	85.00	25.00	45.00	55.00
Table size, 5"d	65.00	275.00	35.00	65.00	75.00
Cruet, original stopper	125.00	950.00	85.00	150.00	175.00
Mug, handled	55.00	350.00	45.00	55.00	75.00
Parfait	65.00	140.00	45.00	65.00	75.00
Pitcher, water, ½ gallon, 9½"h	120.00	—	75.00	100.00	135.00
Plate, round, footed, 7½"d	45.00	—	35.00	55.00	65.00
Salt shaker, original top	55.00	400.00	35.00	55.00	65.00
Sauce dish, round, flat	35.00	65.00	20.00	35.00	40.00
Spoonholder, 5"h	45.00	165.00	35.00	45.00	60.00
Sugar bowl, covered					
Individual, 2¼"d	55.00	100.00	35.00	55.00	65.00
Individual, 2½"d	55.00	100.00	35.00	55.00	65.00
Table size, 4"d	85.00	350.00	55.00	85.00	95.00
Tray, serpentine shape					
Large	55.00	—	35.00	55.00	65.00
Small	45.00	400.00	25.00	45.00	55.00
Tumbler, water, flat	55.00	—	45.00	55.00	65.00

DIAGONAL BAND

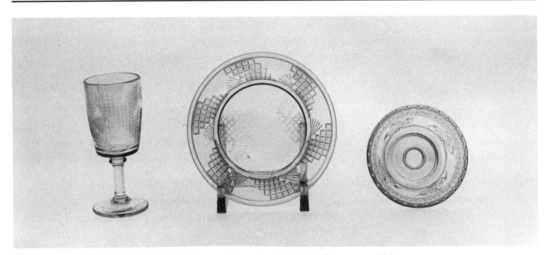

Champagne; 6"d. dinner plate (Diagonal Band with Fan); flat sauce dish.

AKA: Diagonal Block And Fan.

Non-flint. American maker unknown, ca. 1875-1885 period. Shards have been found at the site of the Burlington Glass Works, Hamilton, Ontario, Canada.

Original color production: Amber, apple green, clear.

Reproductions: None.

References: Hlms-BCA (P. 278), Kam-7 (P. 8), Kam/Wod-Vol.1 (P. 40), Lee-EAPG (Pl. 140, No. 4), McCn-PGP (P. 311), Mil-2 (Pl. 71), Mtz-1 (PP. 172-173), Oliv-AAG (P. 63), Uni-2 (PP. 292-293), Uni/Wor-CHPGT (P. 108), Wlkr-PGA (Fig. 8, Nos. 4, 20).

Items made	Amber	Apple Green	Clear
Butter dish, covered	60.00	80.00	35.00
Cake stand, high standard	40.00	55.00	30.00
Castor insert	45.00	50.00	30.00
Celery vase	45.00	50.00	25.00
Champagne	—	—	25.00
Compote, high standard			
Covered			
7"d	65.00	80.00	55.00
7¼"d	65.00	80.00	55.00
Open 7½"d	45.00	50.00	20.00
Creamer	40.00	50.00	20.00
Goblet	30.00	45.00	25.00
Pickle dish, oval, 6⅞"l	15.00	15.00	10.00
Pitcher			
Milk, 1 quart	65.00	85.00	45.00
Water, ½ gallon	65.00	85.00	45.00
Plate, round			
Dinner, 6"d	—	—	10.00
Bread	30.00	35.00	25.00
Plate, oblong	25.00	45.00	30.00
Sauce dish, round			
Flat	—	—	5.00
Footed	—	15.00	10.00
Spoonholder	25.00	40.00	20.00
Sugar bowl, covered	40.00	50.00	30.00
Wine	35.00	45.00	20.00

DIAMOND POINT

Claret; covered sugar bowl; champagne; whiskey tumbler (applied handle).

OMN: Sharp Diamond. AKA: Diamond Point with Ribs, Pineapple, Sawtooth, Stepped Diamond Point.

Flint, non-flint. The Boston & Sandwich Glass Co., Sandwich, MA. New England Glass Co., East Cambridge, MA. ca. 1860s. Other factories throughout the century. Illustrated in the 1868 New England Glass Co. catalog.

Original color production: Clear. Amethyst, blue, canary-yellow, green opal, colored opaque, opaque white, clambroth, translucent jade green or any other color is very rare.

Reproductions: None.

References: Bat-GPG (PP. 42-43), Cod-OS (Pl. 19), Drep-ABC OG (P. 177), Hea-OS (P. 135, No. 2546), Kam-4 (PP. 134-135), Lee-EAPG (Pl. 42), McKrn-AG (Pl. 209), Mil-1 (Plt. 123), Mil-2 (Pl. 64), Mtz-1 (P. 34), Mtz-2 (P. 46), Oliv-AAG (P. 53), Rev-APG (P. 252), Spil-AEPG (P. 253), Spil-TBV (PP. 20, 293), Uni-1 (P. 130), Uni-2 (P. 142), Wat-CG (P. 153), Wlkr-PGA (Fig. 8, Nos. 14, 24, 25).

Items made	Flint	Non-flint
Ale glass, knob stem, 6¼"h	85.00	—
Bottle		
Castor	25.00	10.00
Pepper, original Brittania screw top	25.00	10.00
Vinegar	25.00	10.00
Bowl, flat		
Covered		
5"d	65.00	20.00
7"d	65.00	20.00
8"d	75.00	25.00
Open		
5"d	40.00	15.00
6"d	40.00	15.00
7"d	45.00	20.00
8"d	45.00	20.00
Butter dish, covered	95.00	50.00
Cake stand, high standard		
9"d	140.00	55.00
10"d	150.00	55.00
11"d	160.00	65.00
12"d	170.00	65.00
14"d	185.00	—
Candlesticks, 6½"h., pair	145.00	—
Carafe, with tumble up	150.00	—
Celery vase	75.00	35.00
Champagne, knob stem, clear base	75.00	35.00
Claret	65.00	—
Compote		
Covered		
High standard, saucer bowl		
6"d	125.00	60.00
7"d	125.00	60.00
8"d	125.00	60.00
Low standard, saucer bowl		
6"d	75.00	40.00
7"d	85.00	45.00
8"d	85.00	50.00
Open		
High standard		
Deep bowl		
6"d	40.00	25.00
7"d	40.00	25.00
8"d	40.00	25.00

Items made	Flint	Non-flint
9″d	45.00	30.00
10″d	45.00	30.00
10½″d	50.00	—
Saucer bowl		
6″d	40.00	25.00
7″d	40.00	25.00
8″d	40.00	25.00
Low standard, deep bowl		
6″d	40.00	25.00
7″d	40.00	25.00
7½″d	40.00	25.00
8″d	45.00	30.00
9″d	45.00	30.00
10″d	50.00	35.00
Cordial, knob stem, plain base	125.00	40.00
Creamer, applied handle, footed	100.00	—
Cruet, original stopper	125.00	55.00
Decanter		
Bar lip		
1 pint	150.00	—
1 quart	150.00	—
Patterned stopper		
1 pint	100.00	—
1 quart	100.00	—
Dish, open, oval, flat		
7″	30.00	—
8″	30.00	—
9″	35.00	—
10″	35.00	—
Egg cup, single, pedestaled	40.00	20.00
Goblet, knob stem		
Gentleman's (large)	45.00	30.00
Lady's (small)	45.00	30.00
Honey dish, round, flat, 3½″d., 10 point star base	15.00	—
Jug		
½ pint	80.00	—
Pint	80.00	—
Quart	175.00	—
Three Pint	200.00	—
Lamp, oil, tall, original burner and chimney	250.00	—
Mug, applied handle	125.00	—
Mustard jar, Brittania cover	25.00	—
Pitcher, applied handle		
Milk		
½ pint	125.00	—
1 pint	125.00	—
1 quart	250.00	—
3 pint	275.00	—
Water, ½ gallon	250.00	—
Plate, round		
3″d	25.00	—
5½″d., star center	35.00	—
6″d	35.00	—
7″d	45.00	—
8″d	50.00	—
Salt dip		
Individual, 1⅜″d	15.00	10.00
Master, covered, pedestaled	65.00	35.00
Sauce, round, flat, smooth rim, 4″d	15.00	—

Items made	Flint	Non-flint
Spillholder	45.00	—
Spoonholder	45.00	25.00
Sugar bowl, covered		
Flat, octagonal base	65.00	40.00
Footed	65.00	40.00
Syrup pitcher, original top	175.00	75.00
Tumbler		
$1/_2$ pint	45.00	—
Gill	45.00	—
Bar	65.00	35.00
Jelly	45.00	—
Lemonade	55.00	—
Water	65.00	35.00
Whiskey, applied handle	125.00	—
Wine, knob stem, plain base	75.00	35.00

DIAMOND QUILTED

Goblet (vaseline); clover leaf water tray (amethyst); celery vase (vaseline); footed sauce dish (vaseline).

AKA: Quilted Diamond.

Non-flint. Maker unknown ca. 1880.

Original color production: Amethyst (pale), amber, blue (light), vaseline, clear.

Reproductions: The goblet, master salt and tumbler have been reproduced from new molds in both the original colors of amethyst, amber, blue, canary-yellow and clear and in the new colors of green and ruby red. Unlike the mellow colors of original items, new items are too harsh in appearance, often not resembling the pattern.

References: Drep-ABC OG (P. 153), Grow-WCG (Fig. 18), Hea-OS (P. 42, No. 423), Lee-EAPG (Pl. 140, No. 1), Mil-1 (P. 151), Mtz-1 (P. 140), Pet-Sal (P. 158).

Items made	Amethyst	Amber	Blue	Clear	Vas
Bowl, open, flat					
Oval	35.00	30.00	35.00	20.00	35.00

Items made	Amethyst	Amber	Blue	Clear	Vas
Round					
6″d	35.00	30.00	35.00	20.00	35.00
7″d	35.00	20.00	35.00	10.00	25.00
Butter dish, covered, footed	100.00	100.00	100.00	50.00	75.00
Celery vase, pedestaled, scalloped	65.00	60.00	50.00	35.00	40.00
Champagne 6¼″h	35.00	35.00	35.00	20.00	35.00
Compote, round					
Covered					
High standard, 8″d	140.00	125.00	125.00	40.00	90.00
Low standard	—	—	—	15.00	30.00
Open					
High standard, 8″d	80.00	65.00	65.00	40.00	65.00
Low standard	80.00	65.00	65.00	40.00	65.00
Cordial	70.00	65.00	65.00	35.00	65.00
Creamer	45.00	40.00	70.00	25.00	55.00
Goblet					
Regular stem	35.00	40.00	40.00	35.00	35.00
Short stem	35.00	40.00	40.00	30.00	35.00
Mug	—	30.00	40.00	—	—
Pitcher, water, ½ gallon	75.00	85.00	80.00	50.00	75.00
Salt, flat, rectangular, open					
Individual	25.00	20.00	20.00	10.00	20.00
Master	40.00	35.00	40.00	20.00	35.00
Sauce dish, round					
Flat, design in base	10.00	10.00	15.00	8.00	20.00
Footed	15.00	15.00	15.00	10.00	20.00
Spoonholder, footed	35.00	40.00	40.00	30.00	50.00
Sugar bowl, covered, footed	50.00	75.00	55.00	40.00	60.00
Tray, water					
Clover leaf shape	55.00	70.00	70.00	30.00	65.00
Round	55.00	70.00	70.00	30.00	65.00
Tumbler, water, flat	45.00	40.00	40.00	25.00	30.00
Vase, 9″h	—	—	—	50.00	—
Wine	25.00	50.00	45.00	20.00	30.00

DIAMOND AND SUNBURST

Champagne; goblet.

OMN: Bryce No. 77. AKA: Diamond Sunburst [Millard], Plain Sunburst.

Non-flint. Bryce Brothers, Pittsburgh, PA. ca. 1882. Shards have been found at the site of the Burlington Glass Works, Hamilton, Ontario, Canada. Designed and patented by John Bryce (design No. 7,948) December 22, 1874 for Bryce Brothers.

Original color production: Clear.

Reproductions: None.

References: Hea-5 (P. 86), Hlms-BCA (P. 278), Kam-1 (P. 12), Kam/Wod Vol.1 (P. 219), Lee-EAPG (Pl. 78), Lee-VG (Pl. 33), McCn-PGP (Pl. 88), Mil-1 (Pl. 176), Mtz-1 (P. 192), Pet-GPP (P. 56), Rev-APG (P. 87), Uni-1 (P. 278-279), Uni/Wor-CHPGT (P. 111).

Items made	Clear	Items made	Clear
Butter dish, covered	40.00	Goblet	25.00
Butter pat, flat	10.00	Pickle dish	10.00
Cake stand, high standard	35.00	Pitcher, water, ½ gallon	50.00
Celery vase	25.00	Relish dish	10.00
Champagne	25.00	Salt, master, open, footed	15.00
Compote, covered		Sauce dish, flat, round	8.00
High standard, 8¼"d	50.00	Spoonholder	15.00
Low standard, 8¼"d	30.00	Sugar bowl, covered	25.00
Creamer, 6½"h	35.00	Syrup pitcher, original top	45.00
Cup plate	25.00	Tumbler, star base center	25.00
Decanter, original stopper	45.00	Wine	30.00
Egg cup, single, pedestaled	25.00		

DIAMOND THUMBPRINT

Low standard open compote 6"d; high standard open compote decanter; tumbler.

AKA: Diamond And Concave.

Flint. Attributed to the Boston and Sandwich Glass Co., Sandwich, MA. ca. 1850, and the Union Glass Co., Somerville, OH. ca. 1850s.

Original color production: Clear. Opaque white, light green, sapphire blue, canary-yellow, clambroth, amethyst, amber, milk white or any other color is rare. The main pattern element of Diamond Thumbprint consists of a large diamond-shaped block with a large thumbprint center. Of heavy, brilliant flint, handled items are beautifully crimped while footed pieces may have either concentric circles or elaborate diamond thumbprints in the bases. Produced by several factories, the stems of footed pieces may be either bulbous or low footed. Cruder pieces are pontil marked (ca. 1840-1845), more refined items are of a later date.

Reproductions: The Sandwich Museum, Sandwich, MA. authorized the Viking Glass Co. to reissue the following items, from new molds, in amber, amethyst, blue, clear, ruby, and vaseline: covered butter dish, creamer, 6½"h. goblet, spoonholder, covered sugar bowl and water tumbler, each item permanently embossed with the museum's "S.M." insignia.

References: Bat-GPG (PP. 9-10), Drep-ABC OG (P. 165), Enos-MPG (Chart-4), Grow-WCG (P. 218, Fig 41-"1"), Lee-EAPG (Pl. 3, NO. 4), McKrn-AG (Plts. 205-206, 208), Mtz-1 (P. 10, No. 36), Mtz-2 (P. 3), Oliv-AAG (P. 53), Rev-APG (P. 238), Spil-AEPG (P. 256), Tas-AG (P. 74), Uni-1 (PP. 258-259), Wlkr-PGA (Fig. 8, Nos. 1, 27, 44, 52).

Items made	Clear	Items made	Clear
Ale glass, knob stem, 6¼"h	90.00	Open	
Bottle		Plain rim	
Bitters, applied lip, original pewter		5"d	65.00
pourer	450.00	6"d	65.00
Castor	30.00	7"d	75.00
Bowl, flat		8"d	75.00
Covered		Scalloped rim	
6"d	150.00	5"d	65.00
7"d	150.00	6"d	65.00
8"d	175.00	7"d	65.00

183

Items made	Clear	Items made	Clear
8″d	75.00	Decanter	
Waste, flat, open	90.00	Applied bar lip	
Butter dish, covered	200.00	1 pint	175.00
Cake stand, high standard (R)		1 quart	175.00
9″d	300.00	Original stopper	
10″d	350.00	1 pint	225.00
11″d	400.00	1 quart	225.00
12″d	400.00+	Dish, open, oval, flat	
Candlestick, $6\frac{1}{2}$″h	150.00	7″	65.00
Celery vase, pedestaled, scalloped rim	185.00	8″	65.00
Champagne, knob stem		9″	75.00
Large	250.00	10″	85.00
Small	250.00	Egg cup, footed, single	85.00
Compote		Finger bowl	100.00
Covered		Glass, jelly	90.00
High standard		Goblet, knob stem (R)	300.00
6″d	225.00	Honey dish, round, $3\frac{1}{2}$″d	
7″d	250.00	Plain center	25.00
8″d	275.00	Ten point star center	25.00
Low standard		Jar, sweetmeat, covered	250.00
6″d	200.00	Jug	
7″d	225.00	$\frac{1}{2}$ pint	225.00
8″d	250.00	1 pint	225.00
Open, scalloped rim		3 pint	400.00
High standard		Wine with attachment for hanging	
5″d	65.00	glasses (VR)	2500.00
6″d	65.00	Mug, applied handle	200.00
7″d	75.00	Pitcher, applied handle	
8″d	75.00	Milk, 1 quart	450.00
9″d	85.00	Water, $\frac{1}{2}$ gallon	550.00
10″d	90.00	Sauce dish, flat, round	25.00
Low standard		Spoonholder, $6\frac{1}{4}$″h, flat	85.00
5″d	65.00	Sugar bowl, covered	
6″d	65.00	Concentric rings in base	150.00
7″d	75.00	Scalloped foot	150.00
8″d	75.00	Tumbler	
9″d	85.00	Bar	125.00
10″d	90.00	Water, flat	85.00
Cordial, knob stem		Whiskey	
Large	300.00	Applied handle	300.00
Small	250.00	Non-handled	125.00
Creamer, footed, applied handle	225.00	Wine (R)	250.00
Cruet (VR), original stopper	400.00		

DOUBLE DAISY

Water pitcher (clear w/ruby stain).

AKA: Rosette Band [Millard].

Non-flint. Original manufacturer unknown, ca. 1893.

Original color production: Clear, clear with ruby stain. Handles are applied and finials are in the shape of flat, stylized "daisies".

Reproductions: None.

References: Kam-7 (P. 23), McCn-PGP (Pl. 136), Mtz-1 (P. 124), Mil-2 (Pl. 24), Uni-1 (P. 303).

Items made	Clear	Clear w/Ruby
Butter dish, covered, flat daisy finial	40.00	100.00
Compote, high standard, round		
Covered, flat daisy finial	85.00	225.00
Open	45.00	90.00
Celery vase	35.00	85.00
Cracker jar, covered	90.00	225.00
Creamer, tankard, 5½"h., applied handle	30.00	65.00
Goblet	35.00	65.00
Pitcher, water, tankard, applied handle	85.00	185.00
Plate		
8"d	35.00	—
10"d	35.00	—
Relish tray	20.00	40.00
Salt, master, open, 4 stump legs (R)	20.00	45.00
Sauce dish, square, 4 applied stump legs	15.00	30.00
Spoonholder	20.00	50.00
Sugar bowl, covered, flat	35.00	85.00
Syrup, original top	85.00	225.00
Tumbler, water, flat	20.00	45.00
Wine	30.00	55.00

DRAPERY

Egg cup; creamer; spoonholder.

OMN: Doyle's No. 30, Lace.

Non-flint. Doyle & Co., Pittsburgh, PA. ca. 1870. Reissued by the United States Glass Co., Pittsburgh, PA. after 1891. Shards have been found at the site of the Boston and Sandwich Glass Co., Sandwich, MA. Designed and patented by Thomas Bakewell Atterbury, February 22, 1870 (design patent No. 3,854), assignor to William Doyle (patent illustrated in the Jeremiah Quinlan of New York catalog). Patent specifications describe the pattern as " . . . a drapery or curtain which is formed by dots or beads on the outside edge of the curtain, and the inside being composed of frosting, the same being had with suitable tassels . . . " Pieces with finely stippled backgrounds have applied handles, while those with coarsely stippled backgrounds have pressed handles. Finials are in the shape of "pine cones".

Original color production: Clear.

Reproductions: None.

References: Bat-GPG (PP. 121, 123), Kam-5 (P. 19), Kam-7 (P. 144), Lee-EAPG (Pl. 108, No. 3), Mil-1 (Pl. 133), Mtz-1 (P. 180), Oliv-AAG (P. 63), Pet-GPP (PP. 5-7), Rev-APG (P. 132), Uni-1 (P. 261), Wlkr-PGA (Fig. 15, No. 71).

Items made	Clear	Items made	Clear
Butter dish, covered	45.00	Goblet	35.00
Compote		Pitcher, water, 1/2 gallon, applied	
Covered, high standard, 7"d	65.00	handle	65.00
Open, low standard, 7"d	55.00	Plate, round, 6"d	35.00
Creamer, 5³/₄"h		Sauce dish, round, flat, 4"d	15.00
Applied handle	30.00	Spoonholder	35.00
Pressed handle	25.00	Sugar bowl, covered	35.00
Dish, oval, flat	30.00	Tumbler, water, flat	30.00
Egg cup, footed	25.00		

DUNCAN BLOCK

Covered sugar; spoonholder; creamer; covered butter.

OMN: Duncan's Nos. 308, 309 (collared base variant). AKA: Block [Lee], Waffle Variant [Kamm].

Non-flint. George Duncan & Sons (pattern lines No. 308, 309), Pittsburgh, PA., ca. 1887, with continued production by the United States Glass Co., Pittsburgh, PA. at Factory "D" (George Duncan & Sons, Pittsburgh, PA.) and Factory "P" (Doyle & Co., Pittsburgh, PA.) ca. 1891 through 1904. Illustrated in the ca. 1891 and 1904 United States Glass Co. catalogs.

Original color production: Clear. Occasional pieces may be found in clear with ruby stain (plain or copper wheel engraved). Duncan Block is similar to Late Block and Bellaire's No. 552 Ware as illustrated in the ca. 1891 Bellaire Glass Co. catalog.

Reproductions: None.

References: Bred-EDG (PP. 98-101), Hea-5 (PP. 100-101), Hea-6 (P. 33), Kam-1 (P. 118), Kam-5 (Pl. 31), Krs-YD (PP. 30-32), Lee-VG (P. 117, Pl. 41), McCnPGP (Pl. 222), Rev-APG (PP. 148-149), Uni-1 (P. 161).

Items made	Clear	Items made	Clear
Basket, flat		8"d	25.00
7"	50.00	9"d	25.00
9"	50.00	Plain rim	
Bottle		7"d	10.00
Catsup	45.00	8"d	10.00
Cologne, cut or pressed stopper		9"d	15.00
1 ounce	30.00	Butter dish, covered	
2 ounce	30.00	Collared base	40.00
4 ounce	35.00	Flat, flanged rim	45.00
6 ounce	35.00	Carafe	50.00
8 ounce	35.00	Celery	
16 ounce	40.00	Boat, flat, 4 turned up sides	25.00
Water, with tumble up	35.00	Tray, flat	25.00
Bowl, open, round, flat		Vase	
Finger	12.00	Flat, scalloped rim	35.00
Salad		Footed, scalloped rim	35.00
Crimped rim		Cheese dish, covered	45.00
7"d	25.00		

Items made	Clear	Items made	Clear
Creamer		Plate	
Individual, 3″h	15.00	7″d	10.00
Table size		8″d	10.00
Collared base	25.00	Puff box, covered	
Flat	25.00	Squat	35.00
Cruet, cut or pressed stopper		Tall	35.00
Round		Salt	
1 ounce	25.00	Dip	
2 ounce	25.00	Individual, cut	12.00
4 ounce	30.00	Master, pressed	15.00
6 ounce	30.00	Shaker (4 styles), original top	15.00
Square		Sauce dish, round	
1 ounce	25.00	Flat	
2 ounce	25.00	4″d	10.00
4 ounce	25.00	4½″d	10.00
6 ounce	25.00	5″d	10.00
Cup		Footed	
Custard	8.00	4″d	12.00
Sherbert	8.00	4½″d	12.00
Dish, open, oval, flat		5″d	15.00
Deep		Spoonholder	
7″l	15.00	Collared base	25.00
8″l	15.00	Flat base	25.00
9″l	20.00	Sugar bowl, covered	
10″l	20.00	Collared base	35.00
11″l	20.00	Flat base	35.00
Shallow		Sugar shaker, original top	40.00
7″l	15.00	Syrup pitcher, original plated top	40.00
8″l	15.00	Tray	
9″l	20.00	Rectangular, ice cream, with or	
Egg cup, footed, single	15.00	without handles	
Gas globe, 4″ fitter ring		Deep	25.00
4-sided ruffle	35.00	Shallow	25.00
Round	35.00	Round	
Mustard jar, original silver plate top	40.00	7″d	25.00
Pickle boat, 4 turned up sides	20.00	8″d	25.00
Pitcher		Tumbler	
Bulbous, ½ gallon	60.00	Water	15.00
Tankard		Champagne	15.00
Milk, 1 quart	35.00	Wine	15.00
Water, ½ gallon	45.00		

Creamer; covered sugar bowl; goblet.

AKA: Bean, Stippled Oval.

Non-flint. Maker unknown, ca. 1880s.

Original color production: Clear. Amber, blue or any other color is rare.

Reproductions: None.

References: Drep-ABC OG (P. 245), Drep-FR (P. 197), Enos-MPG (Chart-2), Kam-3 (Pl. 71), Lee-VG (Plt. 67, No. 4), Mil-1 (Pl. 141), Mtz-1 (P. 180), Oliv-AAG (P. 65), Pet-Sal (P. 129), Stu-BP (P. 55), Uni-1 (P. 143), Uni-2 (P. 143).

Items made	Clear	Items made	Clear
Butter dish, covered	45.00	Relish tray	10.00
Cake stand, high standard	40.00	Salt shaker, original top	35.00
Compote, covered, high standard, jelly	35.00	Sauce dish, flat, round	10.00
Creamer, 4½"h	30.00	Spoonholder, smooth rim	15.00
Dish, flat, swan center	40.00	Sugar bowl, covered	35.00
Goblet	40.00	Tray	
Marmalade jar, covered	45.00	Bread, octagonal	30.00
Pitcher		Water, round	40.00
Milk, 1 quart	40.00	Tumbler, water, flat	30.00
Water, ½ gallon	45.00	Wine	35.00
Platter, rectangular, flat, deep (several)	30.00		

Covered sugar bowl; bread tray; creamer; spoonholder.

AKA: Parthenon.

Non-flint. Attributed to the Boston & Sandwich Glass Co., Sandwich, MA. ca. 1870.

Original color production: Clear, the main design element being the Parthenon, pyramids, and palm trees. The existence of numerous variations in design (such as the round plate) indicate more than one manufacturer.

Reproductions: Salt Lake Temple bread platter in clear.

References: Drep-ABC OG (P. 99), Kam-1 (P. 31), Lee-EAPG (Plts. 111, 118), Lind-HG (P. 507), Mil-1 (Pl. 82), Mtz-1 (PP. 110-111), Mtz-2 (PP. 182, 189, 200, 201), Oliv-AAG (P. 65), Stu-BP (P. 120), Uni-1 (PP. 997, 139), Uni-2 (P. 96), Wlkr-PGA (Fig. 8, No. 46).

Items made	Clear	Items made	Clear
Bowl, open, round, flat		Plate	
8″d	45.00	Closed handles	
8½″d	50.00	6″d	50.00
Butter dish, covered	85.00	8″d	55.00
Butter mold, pyramid shape (VR)	150.00	10″d	65.00
Celery vase	75.00	Pyramid handles (R), 12″d	85.00
Compote		Platter	
Covered		"Cleopatra" center, 8½″ x 13″	40.00
High standard, sphinx base		"Salt Lake Temple" center, 8½″ x	
7″d	250.00	13″	300.00
8″d	150.00	Relish tray	20.00
Low standard		Sauce dish	
7″d	65.00	Flat	10.00
8″d	75.00	4″d	10.00
Open, high standard, 5″d	50.00	4½″d	10.00
Creamer, 6″h	50.00	Footed	
Goblet, "Ruins of Parthenon"	45.00	4″d	15.00
Honey dish, flat, round, 3½″d	15.00	4½″d	15.00
Pickle, oblong, 4½″l	20.00	Spoonholder	40.00
Pitcher, water, ½ gallon	185.00	Sugar bowl, covered	75.00

EMPRESS

Covered sugar bowl; creamer; tumbler. All emerald w/gilt.

OMN: Riverside No. 492. AKA: Double Arch [Kamm].

Non-flint. Riverside Glass Works (pattern line No. 492), Wellsburgh, WV., ca. 1898.

Original color production: Clear, emerald green (plain or gilt). Amethyst or any other color is rare.

Reproductions: None.

References: Eige-CGM WV (P. 22), Hea-1 (P. 22, Fig. 103), Hea-3 (P. 23), Hea-6 (P. 26, Fig. 128), Hea-OPG (PP. 66, 68), Kam-7 (P. 59), Lecnr-SS (P. 64), McCn-PGP (PP. 361, 381), Migh-TPS (Pl. 20), Mur-CO (P. 11), Mur-MCO (P. 73), Pet-GPP (PP. 65,67), Pet-Sal (P. 160), Revi-APG (P. 296).

Items made	Clear	Emerald Green
Bowl, master berry, open, flat, 8½"d	25.00	45.00
Butter dish, covered	50.00	100.00
Celery vase	50.00	85.00
Compote, open, high standard, 6"d	35.00	100.00
Creamer		
Individual	20.00	40.00
Table size, 5¼"h	35.00	75.00
Cruet, original stopper	50.00	225.00
Lamp, oil, original burner and chimney		
Finger (2 sizes)	55.00	145.00
Stand (3 sizes)	75.00	—
Pitcher, water, applied handle, ½ gallon	65.00	150.00
Salt shaker, original top	35.00	55.00
Sauce dish, round, 4½"d	15.00	25.00
Spoonholder	30.00	45.00
Sugar bowl, covered	45.00	125.00
Sugar shaker, original top	55.00	125.00
Syrup pitcher, original Britannia top	60.00	250.00+
Toothpick holder	55.00	225.00
Tumbler, water, flat	30.00	55.00

ESTHER, Riverside's

Individual creamer; 5″d. h.s. jelly compote; tumbler. All emerald green w/gold.

OMN: Esther Ware. AKA: Tooth And Claw [Millard].

Non-flint. Riverside Glass Works, Wellsburgh, WV. ca. 1896 to as late as 1900.

Advertised as "Esther Ware" in *China, Glass and Lamps* in the Spring of 1896. Decorated by Beaumont Glass Company, Martin's Ferry, OH.

Original color production: Clear, emerald green (with or without gilt), clear with amber stain, clear with ruby stain, clear with enameled flowers. Often souvenired.

Reproductions: None.

References: Bar-RS (Pl. 12), Eige-CGM WV (PP. 22-23), Hea-1 (P. 22, Figs. 104-105), Hea-TPS (Fig. 239), Hea-3 (P. 55), Hea-6 (P. 26), Hea-7 (Figs. 772-774), Hea-OPG (PP. 71-72), Hea-TPS (PP. 28, 53), Kam-1 (P. 109), Kam-5 (PP. 54-55), Kam/Wod-Vol.1 (P. 231), Lee-VG (Pl. 40, No. 4), Migh-TPS (Pl. 20), Mil-1 (Pl. 114), Mil-2 (Pl. 114), Mtz-1 (PP. 220-221), Mur-CO (P. 15), Mur-MCO (P. 73), Pet-Sal (P. 28), Rev-APG (PP. 62, 296), Uni-1 (P. 159), Uni-TCG (P. 107), Uni/Wor-CHPGT (P. 118).

Items made	Clear	Clear/ Amber	Clear/ Ruby	Green
Bowl, master berry, open, footed, scalloped rim	35.00	50.00	60.00	70.00
Butter dish, covered, flanged, 5¾″h x 7¾″d	65.00	100.00	150.00	165.00
Cake stand, high standard 10½″d	60.00	85.00	95.00	110.00
Castor set, 4 bottles	85.00	—	—	—
Celery				
Tray	25.00	40.00	45.00	55.00
Vase	40.00	65.00	75.00	85.00
Cheese dish, covered	85.00	125.00	125.00	135.00
Compote, high standard				
Covered, 5″d., jelly	50.00	75.00	85.00	100.00
Open, scalloped rim				
5″d., jelly	25.00	40.00	45.00	55.00
6″d., straight bowl	25.00	40.00	45.00	55.00
8″d., flared bowl	30.00	45.00	50.00	60.00
Cracker jar, covered	85.00	175.00	200.00	225.00

Items made	Clear	Clear/ Amber	Clear/ Ruby	Green
Creamer				
Individual, 3¹/₈″h	45.00	55.00	65.00	75.00
Table size	45.00	65.00	75.00	85.00
Cruet, original stopper	45.00	250.00	275.00	300.00
Goblet, 6″h	40.00	65.00	75.00	90.00
Jam jar, covered	45.00	65.00	75.00	90.00
Lamp, oil, original burner and chimney	125.00	—	—	—
Pickle dish	15.00	25.00	25.00	30.00
Pitcher, water, bulbous, applied handle	65.00	200.00	250.00	300.00
Plate, round, 10″d	25.00	60.00	60.00	75.00
Relish tray				
Oblong	15.00	25.00	25.00	30.00
Oval	15.00	25.00	25.00	30.00
Salt shaker, original top	25.00	40.00	45.00	55.00
Sauce dish, round, cupped, 4″d	10.00	20.00	20.00	25.00
Spoonholder	35.00	50.00	60.00	65.00
Sugar bowl, covered	55.00	75.00	100.00	125.00
Syrup pitcher, original top (R)	65.00	175.00	175.00	225.00
Toothpick holder	45.00	75.00	100.00	125.00
Tumbler, water, flat	25.00	45.00	55.00	65.00
Vase	20.00	35.00	45.00	55.00
Wine	35.00	45.00	45.00	55.00

EUGENIE

Champagne; goblet.

Flint. McKee Brothers, Pittsburgh, PA. ca. 1859. Illustrated in the McKee Brothers catalogs of 1859-1860 and 1868.

Original color production: Clear. Unlike patterns of the late 1850s and early 1860s, the main design elements of Eugenie exhibit some foreign influence. Heavy, brilliant flint, the main pattern element consists of a row of connected ovals with a band of shield-like ornaments above and elongated petals below radiating from the base. Unlike conventional pieces, finials on covered items resemble standing flower forms, the most unusual being a "dolphin" with its tail extended overhead. Handles are applied.

Reproductions: None.

References: Enos-MPG (Chart-11), Inn/Spil-McKe (PP. 25-27), Lee-EAPG (P. 61), Lee-VG (Pl. 96), Mil-1 (Pl. 125), Oliv-AAG (P. 53), Rev-APG (PP. 231, 233), Stot-McKe (P. 38), Wlkr-PGA (Fig. 8, No. 14).

Items made	Clear	Items made	Clear
Bottle		8"d	145.00
Castor	25.00	Low standard	
Mustard	25.00	7"d	90.00
Pepper	25.00	8"d	110.00
Vinegar	25.00	Cordial	90.00
Bowl, covered, flat		Creamer	175.00
7"d	55.00	Egg cup, single, pedestaled	30.00
9"d	65.00	Goblet	65.00
Celery vase	90.00	Lamp, whale oil, all glass	150.00
Champagne	85.00	Sugar bowl, covered, dolphin finial	
Compote, covered		(VR)	200.00+
High Standard		Tumbler, water, footed, 4³/₄"h	40.00
7"d	125.00	Wine	35.00

EUREKA, McKee's

Wine; goblet; egg cup.

OMN: Eureka, McKee's.

Flint. McKee & Brothers, Pittsburgh, PA. ca. 1866. Illustrated in the McKee & Brothers Catalog of 1868, the Eureka pattern was designed and patented by Charles Ballinger (design No. 2,323) May 22, 1866 for McKee Brothers.

Original color production: Clear. Of heavy, brilliant flint, Eureka is a simple pattern, the main design element consisting of vertical arched panels with indented centers emanating from the bases of items against a solid background. Finials are tall and non-conventional, resembling a closed flower "bud".

References: Hea-6 (P. 75), Inn/Spil-McKe (PP. 123-125), Kam-3 (P. 17), Lee-EAPG (P. 69, Pl. 6), Mil-1 (Pl. 147), Mtz-1 (PP. 20, 232), Oliv-AAG (P. 53), Pet-GPP (PP. 34-36), Rev-APG (PP.

231-232), Stu-BP (P. 39), Stot-McKe (PP. 39, 71), Uni-2 (PP. 62-63), Wlkr-PGA (Fig. 15, No. 91).

Items made	Clear	Items made	Clear
Bowl		Low standard	
Round, covered, 6"d	25.00	6"d	40.00
Open, oval		7"d	50.00
7"	30.00	8"d	50.00
8"	40.00	Cordial	40.00
Butter dish, covered	65.00	Creamer, footed, applied handle, 6"h	45.00
Champagne	85.00	Dish, oval, shallow bowl	
Compote		6"	35.00
Covered		7"	40.00
High standard		8"	50.00
6"d	70.00	9"	60.00
7"d	80.00	Egg cup, single, footed	25.00
8"d	90.00	Goblet	35.00
Low standard		Pitcher, water, applied handle, 1/2	
6"d	65.00	gallon	125.00
7"d	70.00	Salt, master, open, footed, scalloped	
8"d	75.00	rim	30.00
Open		Sauce dish, flat, round, 4"d	10.00
High standard		Spoonholder	40.00
6"d	70.00	Sugar bowl, covered	50.00
7"d	80.00	Tumbler, water, footed	25.00
8"d	90.00	Wine	30.00

EUREKA, National's

Toothpick holder (clear with ruby stain).

OMN: Eureka, National's.

Non-flint. National Glass Co. at McKee Brothers Factory, Jeannette, PA. ca. 1901-1904. Reviewed in the *Crockery and Glass Journal* in 1901.

Original color production: Clear, clear with ruby stain.

Reproductions: None.

References: Bar-RS (Pl. 8), Hea-1 (P. 22, Fig. 106), Hea-6 (P. 26), Hea-7 (Figs. 490-494), Kam-5 (Pl. 5), McCn-PGP (P. 203), Meas-GG (P. 34), Migh-TPS (Pl. 233), Pet-Sal (P. 160), Rev-APG (P. 249), Stot-McKe (PP. 340-342), Wlkr-PGA (Fig. 15, No. 92).

Items made	Clear	Clear w/Ruby
Bottle, cologne, original faceted stopper	35.00	85.00
Bowl Round, open, flat		
Straight-sided, scalloped rim, 8″d	25.00	65.00
Rose, 5″	30.00	80.00
Triangular, 8″d., scalloped-crimped rim	30.00	65.00
Butter dish		
Covered, flat	35.00	100.00
Open, flat, flanged rim	35.00	—
Cake stand, high standard, 11″d	40.00	175.00
Celery vase	30.00	75.00
Compote, high standard, open		
Belled bowl, 9″d	50.00	175.00
Round bowl, 4½″d., jelly	25.00	65.00
Square, 4½″	20.00	55.00
Shallow bowl, 10″d	35.00	125.00
Straight-sided, deep bowl	35.00	125.00
Creamer	25.00	45.00
Cruet, 8 ounce, original diamond faceted stopper	30.00	225.00
Pickle dish, oblong, handled	20.00	45.00
Pitcher, tankard, water, applied handle, 7¾″h	65.00	175.00
Relish dish, oblong, scalloped-serrated rim	15.00	30.00
Salt		
Individual, round	10.00	35.00
Master (R)	15.00	15.00
Shaker		
Bulbous, original top	10.00	35.00
Tall, original top	10.00	35.00
Sauce dish, flat		
Round		
4″d	10.00	20.00
4½″d	10.00	20.00
Square		
4″	10.00	20.00
4½″	10.00	20.00
Spoonholder	25.00	55.00
Sugar bowl, covered, flat	35.00	75.00
Syrup pitcher, original top, squatty	65.00	225.00
Toothpick holder, 2½″h	25.00	65.00
Tumbler, water, flat	15.00	40.00
Vase, 9″h	15.00	40.00

EXCELSIOR

Various footed tumblers; egg cup.

OMN: Excelsior. AKA: Barrel Excelsior, Flare Top Excelsior, Giant Excelsior.

Flint. McKee Brothers, Pittsburgh, PA. ca. 1859-1860. Ihmsen & Co., Pittsburgh, PA. ca. 1851. Shards have been found at the site of the Boston & Sandwich Glass Co., Sandwich, MA. Illustrated in the McKee Brothers catalogs of 1859-1860, 1864, and 1868.

Original color productions: Clear. The main design element of Excelsior is much more fussy than its contemporaries, Ashburton and Argus. Geometric in form and of heavy, brilliant flint, large disconnected circles above loops separate what appears to be a "maltese-like cross" ornament. Handles are beautifully applied while standards may vary somewhat.

Reproductions: None.

References: Bat-GPG (PP. 59, 61), Drep-ABC OG (P. 153), Enos-MPG (Chart-5), Grow-WCG (P. 237, Fig. 45-"4"), Inn-EGP (PP. 53-54), Inn-PG (PP. 343-344), Inn/Spil-McKe (PP. 16-18), Kam-3 (PP. 32-33), Kam-5 (PP. 20, 29), Lee-EAPG (P. 20, Pl. 7), Mag-FIEF (P. 4, Fig. 3), McKrn-AG (Plts. 206, 208), Mil-1 (Pl. 19), Mtz-1 (PP. 16, 232), Mtz-2 (PP. 192-193), Oliv-AAG (P. 53), Rev-APG (PP. 231, 233, 238), Spil-AEPG (P. 244), Stot-McKe (PP. 34, 40), Uni-2 (P. 63), Wlkr-PGA (Fig. 8, No. 1).

Items made	Clear	Items made	Clear
Ale glass	50.00	Champagne	60.00
Bottle		Claret	45.00
Bar	40.00	Compote	
Bitters	50.00	Covered, low standard	45.00
Medicine	75.00	Open, high standard, 10"d.,	
Water, with tumble up	125.00	scalloped rim	125.00
Bowl, round, flat		Cordial	85.00
Covered	125.00	Creamer	
Open, 10"d	40.00	Table size, full-pressed, 6½"h	40.00
Butter dish, covered	100.00	Made from tumbler mold	65.00
Candlesticks		Decanter, heavy bar lip	
9½"h., each	125.00	1 pint	85.00
8¼"h., each	150.00	1 quart	85.00
Celery vase, knob stem, scalloped rim	75.00	Small, footed	85.00

Items made	Clear	Items made	Clear
Dish, open, oval, flat	40.00	Spillholder	75.00
Egg cup		Spoonholder	65.00
Double, open	65.00	Sugar bowl, covered, double-knob	
Single		finial	85.00
Covered	80.00	Syrup pitcher, applied handle, original	
Open, knob stem, 4¾"h	40.00	tip top	125.00
Glass, jelly (R)	55.00	Tumbler	
Goblet (2 styles)	55.00	Flat	
Lamp, hand, whale oil with Maltese		⅓ quart	50.00
Cross, original burner	95.00	½ pint, ship tumbler	50.00
Mug	35.00	Footed	
Pickle jar, covered	45.00	⅓ gill	50.00
Pitcher		⅓ pint	50.00
Milk		⅓ quart	60.00
1 pint	250.00	Water (height varies)	45.00
1 quart	250.00	Whiskey	65.00
Water, ½ gallon	350.00	Vase (height varies)	80.00
Salt, master, open, footed	30.00	Wine (height varies)	55.00

EYEWINKER

High standard cake stand.

AKA: Cannon Ball, Crystal Ball, Winking Eye.

Non-flint. Attributed to Dalzell, Gilmore & Leighton Glass Co., Findlay, OH. ca. 1889.

Original color production: Clear.

Reproductions: The goblet in Eyewinker has been reproduced from a new mold in both clear and colors not original to the pattern from the early 1960s. In 1967 the L.G. Wright Glass Co., New Martinsville, WV. (distributed by Jennings Red Barn, New Martinsville, WV. and Carl Forslund, Grand Rapids, MI.) catalog illustrates the covered marmalade jar in clear. By 1970, the L.G. Wright catalog supplement lists the following reissues in clear and color: compote (open, high standard, 7½"d.), honey dish (covered, flat), pitcher (water), tumbler (water), and wine, and in 1971, the company issued the following items in ruby satin: compote (covered, high standard, 4"d), and 6"h. legged vase.

Master berry bowl; round sauce dish.

The L.G. Wright Glass Company's 1974 master catalog illustrates the following reissues in amber, blue, clear, green, ruby and vaseline: covered butter dish, 4″d. high standard covered compote, 6″d. high standard covered compote, 5″d. low standard covered compote, 7½″d. high standard true open compote, creamer, 10 ounce 6¼″h. goblet, 5½″d. covered honey dish, covered marmalade jar, quart milk pitcher, 4½″d. plate (termed the "ashtray"), flat salt dip, 4″d. flat round sauce dish, 3 ½″h. sherbert, covered sugar bowl, toothpick holder, 6″h. 3-legged vase, 3-legged 8″h. vase, and 4 ounce wine.

The Sturbridge Yankee Workshop, Sturbridge, MA. reissued the 6″h. goblet in clear, made from the original mold, most likely through the Imperial Glass Co.

References: Meas/Smth-FG (PP. 20, 66), FG (P. 113), Hea-OS (Pl. 61, No. 893), Hea-TPS (P. 40), Kam-5 (P. 76), McCn-PGP (P. 35), Mtz-1 (P. 210), Pet-Sal (P. 28), Stu-BP (P. 55), Thu-1 (P. 249), Uni-1 (PP. 54-55), Uni-2 (P. 221).

Items made	Clear	Items made	Clear
Banana dish, flat, upturned sides, 7¼″	85.00	8½″d	80.00
Bowl, flat		9″d	85.00
Open		9½″d	90.00
Master berry, 9″d	50.00	10″d	95.00
Vegetable bowl, 6½″d	25.00	10½″d	100.00
Covered, 9″d	65.00	11″d	110.00
Butter dish, covered	75.00	11½″d	115.00
Cake stand, high standard		12″d	125.00
8″d	65.00	12½″d	125.00
9½″d	70.00	Open	
10″d	75.00	4″d	30.00
Celery vase	55.00	4½″d	45.00
Compote, round, high standard		5″d	50.00
Covered		5½″d	55.00
4″d	30.00	6″d	60.00
4½″d	45.00	6½″d	60.00
5″d	45.00	7″d	65.00
5½″d	50.00	7½″d	65.00
6″d	55.00	8″d	65.00
6½″d	60.00	8½″d	70.00
7″d	60.00	9″d	70.00
7½″d	70.00	9½″d	75.00
8″d	75.00	10″d	75.00

Items made	Clear	Items made	Clear
10½"d	80.00	5"	35.00
11"d	85.00	7"	35.00
11½"d	90.00	8½"	45.00
12"d	100.00	9"	65.00
12½"d	110.00	10"	75.00
Creamer, 5½"h	45.00	Salt shaker, original top	35.00
Cruet, original stopper	65.00	Sauce dish, flat	
Honey dish, flat, square	40.00	Round (2 sizes)	15.00
Lamp, kerosene (3 types) original		Square (2 sizes)	15.00
burner and chimney	175.00	Spoonholder	35.00
Pitcher		Sugar bowl, covered	65.00
Milk, 1 quart	80.00	Syrup pitcher, original pewter lid	125.00
Water, ½ gallon	95.00	Tumbler, water, flat	35.00
Plate, square, upturned rim			

FANCY LOOP

Triangular sauce dish; goblet; cruet (n.o.s.); relish tray.

Goblet; cracker jar; flat round sauce dish.

OMN: Heisey's No. 1205 & 1205½.

Non-flint. A.H. Heisey Co. (pattern line No. 1205 & 1205$^1/_2$), Newark, OH. ca. 1897. Illustrated in the 1897 A.H. Heisey & Co. catalog.

Original color production: Clear, emerald green (plain or w/gilt). Clear w/ruby stain or other colors scarce. Produced before introduction of Heisey "H in-a-diamond" trademark.

Reproductions: None.

References: Batty-GPG (PP. 94-95), Hea-1 (P. 22, Fig. 108), Hea-2 (P. 119), Hea-7 (P. 115), Hea-TPS (PP. 24, 28, 50), Kam-2 (P. 97), Kam-7 (Pl. 31), McCn-PGP (P. 257), Mig-TPS (Pl. 21), Pet-Sal (P. 33), Rev-APG (P. 176), Sears/97 (P. 685), Vogel-Heis/96 (P. 257)

Items made	Clear	Items made	Clear
Bon bon dish, tri-cornered	25.00	Punch bowl, flat, scalloped rim	125.00
Bowl, flat, open	25.00	Punch cup	15.00
Butter dish, covered		Salt	
Individual	45.00	Dip	
Table size	65.00	Individual	15.00
Celery		Master	35.00
Tray	25.00	Shaker, original top	35.00
Vase	35.00	Sauce dish, flat	
Champagne	45.00	Round	15.00
Claret	45.00	Triangular	15.00
Cracker jar, covered		Sherry	40.00
Large	100.00	Spoonholder	30.00
Medium	90.00	Sugar bowl, covered	
Creamer		Hotel	55.00
Hotel	35.00	Individual (true open)	35.00
Individual	25.00	Table size	55.00
Table size	35.00	Toothpick holder	65.00
Cruet, original stopper	85.00	Tumbler, flat	
Goblet	35.00	Bar	30.00
Jelly dish, handled, 3-cornered	25.00	Water	30.00
Pitcher, tankard, water, $^1/_2$ gallon	90.00	Vase, cylindrical, tall	25.00

FAN WITH DIAMOND

Wine; spoonholder; water pitcher; flat covered butter dish.

OMN: McKee's No. 3, Shell.

Non-flint. McKee & Brothers, Pittsburgh, PA. ca. 1880. Illustrated in the McKee Glass Co. 1880 catalog.

Original color production: Clear. Handles are applied.

Reproductions: None.

References: Enos-MPG (Charts 2,3), Kam-3 (PP. 18-19), Lee-EAPG (Pl. 76), McCn-PGP (P. 199), Mil-1 (Pl. 64), Mtz-1 (PP. 154-155), Rev-APG (P. 241), Spil-AEPG (P. 278), Spil-TBV (P. 234), Stot-McKe (PP. 67-73), Uni-1 (P. 213).

Items made	Clear	Items made	Clear
Butter dish, covered		Goblet	25.00
4⅛″d	35.00	Pitcher, water, bulbous, applied	
6⅛″d	40.00	handle, ½ gallon	55.00
Compote, covered		Sauce dish, round, flat, 4″d	10.00
High standard	55.00	Spoonholder, pedestaled, scalloped rim	20.00
Low standard	45.00	Sugar bowl, covered	35.00
Cordial	40.00	Syrup, applied handle, original pewter	
Creamer, applied handle, 5½″h	35.00	top	80.00
Dish, oval, flat, deep, 9″ x 6¾″	20.00	Wine	35.00
Egg cup, pedestaled	35.00		

FEATHER

Spoonholder (smooth rim); creamer (smooth rim); covered butter (flanged base); covered sugar; spoonholder (scalloped rim); wine.

OMN: Cambridge Glass No. 669, McKee's Doric. AKA: Cambridge Feather, Feather And Quill, Fine Cut And Feather, Indiana Feather, Indiana Swirl, Prince's Feather, Swirl, Swirl(s) And Feather(s).

Non-flint. Beatty-Brady Glass Co., Dunkirk, IN. ca. 1903. Cambridge Glass Co., Cambridge, OH. ca. 1902-1903. McKee Glass Co., Pittsburgh, PA. ca. 1896-1901. Illustrated in the McKee & Brothers 1901 catalog, the Cambridge Glass Co. 1903 catalog, the Montgomery Ward's catalogs from 1896 through 1901, and the Baltimore Bargain House August 15, 1904 catalog.

Original color production: Clear, clear with amber stain, emerald green, chocolate (water pitcher only). Feather was later reissued with variations and quality differences: a) glossy,

202

brilliant finish, and b) poor quality finish with little luster. One variation has a more distinct swirl, while bases may be either rayed or have a medallion.

Reproductions: The wine has been reproduced from a new mold in clear with pink stain from the early 1950s.

References: Camb-Rep (P. 93), Grow-WCG (Fig. 21), Hea-1 (P. 22, Figs. 109-110), Hea-6 (P. 27, Fig. 137), Herr-GG (P. 33), Hart/Cob (P. 32), Kam-1 (P. 73), Kam-6 (Pl. 6), Lee-VG (Pl. 57, No. 3), Meas-GG (P. 83), Migh-TPS (Pl. 21), Mil-1 (Pl. 30), Mtz-1 (PP. 140-141), Mur-MCO (P. 67), Oliv-AAG (P. 66), Pet-Sal (P. 28), Rev-APG (P. 238), Sears-97 (PP. 685-686), Spil-AEPG (P. 337), Stu-BP (P. 21), Swn-PG (P. 49), Uni-1 (P. 99).

Items made	Clear	Green	Amber Stain
Banana dish			
Flat	75.00	175.00	—
Footed	100.00	175.00	—
Bowl, flat, open			
Oval			
8½″	25.00	65.00	—
9¼″, vegetable, smooth rim	20.00	75.00	—
Round			
Scalloped rim, 8″d	25.00	85.00	100.00
6″d	20.00	65.00	—
7″d	25.00	75.00	—
Square, scalloped rim, 8″	45.00	—	—
Butter dish, covered, flat			
Flanged rim, 8⅛″d	55.00	125.00	175.00
Plain rim, 8⅛″d	55.00	125.00	175.00
Cake plate, round, flat, grooved base, blown lid	125.00	—	—
Cake stand, high standard			
8″d	40.00	125.00	150.00
9½″d	50.00	150.00	175.00
11″d	85.00	—	—
Celery vase, flat, scalloped rim	35.00	85.00	125.00
Champagne	85.00	150.00	—
Cheese dish, grooved base, blown domed lid	145.00	—	—
Compote			
Covered			
High standard			
Deep bowl			
6″d	90.00	150.00	200.00
7″d	90.00	150.00	200.00
8″d	125.00	225.00	275.00
8¼″d	125.00	225.00	275.00
Shallow bowl			
7″d	90.00	150.00	200.00
8″d	90.00	150.00	200.00
9″d	125.00	225.00	275.00
10″d	125.00	225.00	275.00
Low standard, deep bowl			
6″d	90.00	150.00	200.00
7″d	90.00	150.00	200.00
8″d	125.00	175.00	225.00
8½″d	125.00	225.00	225.00
Open, low standard			
4¼″d., jelly	20.00	90.00	125.00
6″d	20.00	90.00	125.00
7″d	25.00	90.00	125.00

Items made	Clear	Green	Amber Stain
8"d	30.00	100.00	135.00
8¼"d	95.00	100.00	135.00
Cordial	125.00	150.00	150.00(R)
Creamer, 4⅝"h	45.00	80.00	90.00
Cruet, original faceted stopper	40.00	250.00+	350.00+
Dish, round, open, flat			
7"d	40.00	65.00	75.00
8"d	40.00	65.00	75.00
9"d	40.00	65.00	75.00
Goblet	55.00	150.00	250.00
Honey dish, flat, plain rim	15.00	25.00	—
Marmalade jar, covered	100.00	150.00	—
Pitcher			
Milk, 1 quart, 7½"h	50.00	175.00	225.00
Water, ½ gallon	55.00	250.00	300.00
Plate, 10"d., scalloped border	45.00	65.00	85.00
Relish tray, flat	15.00	40.00	65.00
Salt shaker, original top			
Tall	55.00	85.00	100.00
Squatty	55.00	85.00	100.00
Sauce dish			
Flat			
Round			
Plain rim			
4"d	15.00	25.00	—
4½"d	15.00	25.00	—
Scalloped rim			
4"d	15.00	25.00	—
4½"d	15.00	25.00	—
Square, scalloped rim			
4"d	25.00	35.00	—
4½"d	25.00	35.00	—
Footed, round			
Scalloped rim			
4"	15.00	25.00	—
4½"	15.00	25.00	—
Smooth rim			
4"	15.00	25.00	—
4½"	15.00	25.00	—
Spoonholder, scalloped or smooth rim	25.00	65.00	90.00
Sugar bowl, covered (2 styles)	45.00	95.00	125.00
Syrup pitcher, original lid	125.00	250.00	300.00
Toothpick holder, scalloped rim	90.00	125.00	225.00
Tumbler, water, flat	55.00	85.00	—
Wine			
Cut feathers	20.00	—	—
Scalloped feathers	40.00	90.00	—

Jelly compote; celery vase; h.s. covered compote; bread tray.

OMN: U.S. Glass No. 15043. AKA: Huckle, Rosette Medallion.

Non-flint. The United States Glass Co. (pattern line No. 15043), Pittsburgh, PA. ca. mid 1895. Illustrated in the United States Glass Co. catalogs of 1898 and 1904, and the Butler Brothers catalog of 1899.

Original color production: Clear, emerald green.

Reproductions: None.

References: Hea-5 (P. 13), Kam-2 (P. 42), Kam-6 (Pl. 4), Kam/Wod-Vol.1 (P. 271), Lee-VG (Pl. 64, No. 3), Lind-HG (P. 336), McCn-PGP (Pl. 126), Mtz-2 (PP. 174-175), Mil-2 (Pl. 77), Pet-Sal (P. 28), Rev-APG (P. 309), Stu-BP (P. 42), Uni-1 (P. 311), Uni/Wor-CHPGT (P. 121), Wlkr-PGA (Fig. 8, Nos. 16, 20).

Items made	Clear	Emerald Green
Bowl, flat, round		
Covered		
5"d	25.00	35.00
6"d	25.00	35.00
7"d	30.00	40.00
8"d	30.00	45.00
Open		
5"d	10.00	15.00
6"d	10.00	15.00
7"d	15.00	20.00
8"d	15.00	20.00
Butter dish, covered, flat		
Flanged rim	35.00	45.00
Plain rim	35.00	45.00
Cake stand, high standard		
8"d	15.00	25.00
9"d	20.00	30.00
10"d	25.00	35.00
11"d	30.00	40.00

Items made	Clear	Emerald Green
Celery vase	20.00	30.00
Compote, round		
Covered		
High standard		
5″d	35.00	45.00
6″d	35.00	45.00
7″d	40.00	50.00
8″d	45.00	60.00
Low standard		
5″d	35.00	45.00
6″d	35.00	45.00
7″d	40.00	50.00
8″d	45.00	60.00
Open		
High standard		
Deep bowl		
5″d	15.00	20.00
6″d	15.00	20.00
7″d	20.00	25.00
8″d	20.00	25.00
Saucer bowl		
7″d	20.00	25.00
8″d	20.00	25.00
9″d	25.00	30.00
10″d	25.00	35.00
Low standard	25.00	30.00
Creamer, 5″h	25.00	30.00
Dish, open, oblong, flat		
7″	10.00	15.00
8″	10.00	15.00
9″	10.00	15.00
Egg cup	25.00	35.00
Mug, pressed handle	15.00	20.00
Pickle dish, flat, oblong	10.00	15.00
Pitcher		
Milk, 1 quart	40.00	65.00
Water, ½ gallon	40.00	60.00
Plate		
Rectangular, "McKinley Gold Standard 1896" (R)	250.00	—
Round, 7″d	15.00	25.00
Platter, bread, rectangular	15.00	30.00
Relish tray	15.00	20.00
Salt shaker, original top	15.00	25.00
Sauce dish, flat, round		
4″d	8.00	15.00
4½″d	8.00	15.00
Spoonholder	20.00	30.00
Sugar bowl, covered	20.00	40.00
Tray, water, round, 11½″d	25.00	40.00
Tumbler, flat, water	10.00	20.00
Wine	30.00	45.00

Creamer; 10″d. water tray; covered butter dish.

Non-flint. Maker unknown. Illustrated in the 1894 Montgomery Ward catalog as "Frosted Glass Water Set".

Reproductions: None.

References: Enos-MPG (Chart-2), Kam-1 (P. 950), Kam-6 (Pl. 5), Lee-EAPG (Pl. 166), McCn-PGP (P. 337), Mtz-1 (PP. 134-235), Stu-BP (P. 19), Swn-PG (P. 81), Wlkr-PGA (Fig. 80 Nos. 45, 54).

Items made	Clear
Bowl, open, flat	
Finger or waste	25.00
Rectangular	
7″ x 4½″	25.00
9″	30.00
Round	
7″d	20.00
8″d	20.00
10″d	25.00
Butter dish, covered, flanged rim	55.00
Cake stand, high standard	
9″d	40.00
10″d	40.00
Compote, high standard	
Covered	80.00
Open	65.00
Creamer, 4½″h	35.00
Dish, open, flat, oblong (2 sizes)	20.00

Items made	Clear
Mug	35.00
Pickle	
Castor, complete in silver plate	
frame	110.00
Dish, 9″ x 5½″ in silver plate frame	40.00
Jar, covered	65.00
Pitcher, water, ½ gallon	40.00
Plate, plain rim	
7″d	30.00
8″d	30.00
8¼″d	30.00
9″d	35.00
Relish tray, 4½″ x 7¼″	20.00
Sauce dish, flat, round, 4½″d	8.00
Spoonholder	35.00
Sugar bowl, covered	45.00
Tray, water, round	30.00

FINE CUT

Wine; dinner plate; finger bowl.

OMN: Bryce No. 720. AKA: Finecut, Flower In Square.

Non-flint. Bryce Brothers (pattern line No. 720), Pittsburgh, PA. ca. 1885. Reissued by the United States Glass Co., Pittsburgh, PA. ca. 1891.

Original color production: Amber, blue, vaseline, clear.

Reproductions: None.

References: Belnp-MG (P. 21), Hea-5 (P. 41, Nos. 116-119), Kam-6 (PP. 21-22), Kam-8 (P. 21), Lee-EAPG (Pl. 138), Mil-1 (Pl. 110), Mtz-1 (PP. 160-161), Oliv-AAG (P. 65), Rev-APG (P. 87), Uni-1 (P. 262-263).

Items made	Amber	Blue	Clear	Vas
Bowl, open				
Flat, 8¼"d	15.00	20.00	10.00	15.00
Footed, finger	15.00	20.00	10.00	15.00
Butter dish, covered	50.00	60.00	25.00	50.00
Cake stand, high standard	—	—	30.00	—
Celery				
Tray	—	45.00	—	—
Vase, silver plated holder	—	—	—	125.00
Compote, covered, high standard	65.00	75.00	45.00	75.00
Creamer	35.00	30.00	20.00	75.00
Dish, oblong, deep, open, vegetable	20.00	25.00	15.00	20.00
Goblet	45.00	55.00	20.00	40.00
Pitcher, water, ½ gallon	95.00	95.00	95.00	85.00
Plate, round				
6"d	—	20.00	8.00	—
6¼"d	—	20.00	8.00	—
7"d	25.00	40.00	15.00	10.00
7¼"d	25.00	40.00	15.00	10.00
10"d	30.00	50.00	20.00	45.00
10¼"d	30.00	50.00	20.00	45.00
Relish tray	35.00	40.00	15.00	35.00
Sauce dish, round, flat	15.00	15.00	10.00	15.00

Items made	Amber	Blue	Clear	Vas
Spoonholder	30.00	45.00	15.00	40.00
Sugar bowl, covered	45.00	55.00	35.00	45.00
Tray, water, round	50.00	55.00	25.00	50.00
Tumbler, water, flat	30.00	30.00	20.00	25.00
Wine	35.00	35.00	25.00	30.00

FINECUT AND BLOCK

Cordial; egg cup; goblet (gentleman's); lady's goblet; spoonholder.

OMN: King's No. 25.

Non-flint. King, Son & Co., Pittsburgh, PA. ca. 1890. Attributed to the Portland Glass Co., Portland, ME., and the Model Flint Glass Co., Findlay, OH. Illustrated in the ca. 1890-1891 King Glass Co. catalog.

Original color production: Clear, clear with amber, blue, and pink stained blocks, and the solid colors of amber, blue and canary-yellow. Two styles were made in toilet wares and lamps.

Reproductions: The Fenton Art Glass Co. reissued numerous items including the wine in clear and colors from new molds. Reproductions are heavier in weight and lack the clarity of fine old glass.

References: Drep-ABC OG (P. 241), Hea-5 (P. 52, No. 267), Hea-OS (P. 42, No. 450), Kam-1 (P. 42), Lee-EAPG (Pl. 161), Mil-1 (Pl. 29), Mtz-1 (PP. 160, 232), Oliv-AAG (P. 65), Rev-APG (P. 216), Uni-1 (P. 295).

Items made	Clear	Solid Colors	Amber Block	Blue Block	Pink Block
Bottle					
Cologne	65.00	75.00	95.00	95.00	95.00
Perfume (5 sizes)	65.00	75.00	95.00	95.00	95.00
Bowl, flat, open					
Finger, round, scalloped rim	20.00	40.00	55.00	55.00	55.00

Items made	Clear	Solid Colors	Amber Block	Blue Block	Pink Block
Round					
Handled					
6"d	20.00	30.00	35.00	35.00	35.00
7"d	20.00	30.00	35.00	35.00	35.00
8"d	20.00	35.00	35.00	35.00	35.00
9"d	25.00	40.00	40.00	40.00	40.00
10"d	30.00	40.00	55.00	55.00	55.00
No handle					
6"d	20.00	30.00	35.00	35.00	35.00
7"d	20.00	30.00	35.00	35.00	35.00
8"d	20.00	35.00	35.00	35.00	35.00
Orange, flat, deep, large point and scallop rim with matching 12"d. under tray					
8"d	30.00	65.00	75.00	75.00	75.00
10"d	40.00	85.00	85.00	85.00	85.00
Butter dish, covered					
Individual	30.00	—	—	—	—
Table size					
Flat	65.00	—	—	—	—
Footed	75.00	95.00	125.00	125.00	125.00
Cake stand, high standard, scalloped, galleried rim					
8"d	35.00	—	—	—	—
9"d	35.00	—	—	—	—
10"d	40.00	—	—	—	—
11"d	40.00	—	—	—	—
12"d	45.00	—	—	—	—
Celery tray, slightly turned sides	30.00	45.00	50.00	45.00	60.00
Champagne					
Round bowl	25.00	—	50.00	50.00	50.00
Saucer bowl	25.00	—	50.00	50.00	50.00
Claret, round bowl	30.00	—	45.00	45.00	45.00
Cologne bottle, original matching patterned stopper					
Bulbous base, long slender neck	25.00	—	—	—	—
Tall, hexagonal shape					
2 ounce	25.00	—	—	—	—
4 ounce	25.00	—	—	—	—
6 ounce	30.00	—	—	—	—
8 ounce	30.00	—	—	—	—
10 ounce	35.00	—	—	—	—
Compote					
High standard, open, jelly	15.00	50.00	75.00	75.00	75.00
Low standard					
Covered	35.00	—	—	—	—
Open, 8½"d	30.00	—	45.00	40.00	45.00
Cordial	45.00	65.00	75.00	65.00	75.00
Creamer	45.00	65.00	75.00	65.00	75.00
Cup, custard	15.00	25.00	35.00	30.00	35.00
Dish, round, flat, tab handled, scalloped rim					
6"	15.00	25.00	35.00	30.00	35.00
7"	15.00	25.00	35.00	30.00	35.00
8"	20.00	30.00	40.00	35.00	40.00
9"	20.00	30.00	40.00	35.00	40.00
10"	25.00	35.00	45.00	40.00	45.00
Egg cup	20.00	25.00	45.00	35.00	45.00

Items made	Clear	Solid Colors	Amber Block	Blue Block	Pink Block
Goblet					
Large (gentleman's)	35.00	65.00	65.00	65.00	60.00
Small (lady's)	35.00	65.00	65.00	65.00	60.00
Lamp, oil, handled	85.00	—	—	—	—
Mug	20.00	30.00	40.00	35.00	40.00
Pickle jar, covered	40.00	—	—	—	—
Pitcher					
Milk, 3 pints	40.00	50.00	65.00	65.00	65.00
Water, ½ gallon	45.00	85.00	95.00	95.00	125.00
Plate, round, deep scalloped rim					
5¾"d	10.00	—	—	—	—
6"d	10.00	—	—	—	—
7"d	10.00	—	—	—	—
12"d	12.00	—	—	—	—
Relish tray, rectangular	10.00	—	65.00	50.00	55.00
Salt					
Dip, flat, scalloped rim					
Individual	10.00	20.00	20.00	20.00	20.00
Master	20.00	30.00	35.00	35.00	35.00
Shaker, flat, tall, original top	10.00	20.00	20.00	15.00	—
Sauce dish, round					
Flat, handled					
4"d	10.00	15.00	15.00	10.00	—
5"d	10.00	15.00	15.00	10.00	—
Footed					
4"d	10.00	15.00	15.00	15.00	15.00
5"d	10.00	15.00	15.00	15.00	15.00
Soap dish, rectangular, bracketed for hanging	35.00	—	—	—	—
Soap slab, flat, rectangular	35.00	—	—	—	—
Spice barrel, covered novelty in the shape of a barrel on four wagon-type wheels	85.00	—	—	—	—
Spoonholder	30.00	20.00	55.00	65.00	50.00
Sugar bowl, covered	45.00	—	125.00	135.00	125.00
Tray					
Ice cream	65.00	—	—	—	—
Orange bowl underplate	65.00	—	—	—	—
Water	60.00	—	—	—	—
Tumbler, water, flat	20.00	50.00	50.00	45.00	45.00
Wine	30.00	—	45.00	45.00	45.00

Plate 6¼″; relish tray; milk pitcher; creamer.

OMN: No. 260, Russian. AKA: Button And Oval Medallion, Nailhead And Panel.

Non-flint. Bryce Brothers, Pittsburgh, PA. Richards & Hartley Glass Co., Pittsburgh, PA. ca. 1889. Reissued by the United States Glass Co. (pattern line No. 260), at Factory "B" (Bryce Brothers, Pittsburgh, PA.) after the 1891 merger. Illustrated in an undated Richards & Hartley Flint Glass Co. catalog as "Russian", and the ca. 1891 United States Glass Co. catalog.

Original color production: Amber, blue, vaseline, clear. Pieces often came in silver plated frames or holders.

Reproductions: None.

References: Hea-5 (PP. 49, 80), Kam-5 (P. 32, Pl. 19), Kam-7 (P. 82), Lee-EAPG (Pl. 61), Mil-1 (Pl. 89), Oliv-AAG (P. 65), Rev-APG (P. 312), Uni-2 (P. 156).

Items made	Amber	Blue	Clear	Vas
Bowl, flat, open				
Round				
Master berry, 7″d	25.00	35.00	15.00	25.00
Waste	30.00	35.00	20.00	35.00
Oval, 8″d	55.00	—	18.00	30.00
Butter dish, covered, square	45.00	75.00	40.00	60.00
Cake stand, high standard, 10″d	50.00	55.00	30.00	50.00
Compote, high standard				
Covered	125.00	135.00	50.00	130.00
Open	65.00	60.00	35.00	60.00
Cordial	30.00	35.00	20.00	35.00
Creamer	35.00	50.00	25.00	40.00
Cup	15.00	20.00	10.00	18.00
Dish, open, oblong, deep vegetable				
7″	30.00	35.00	20.00	35.00
8″	30.00	35.00	20.00	35.00
9″	30.00	35.00	20.00	35.00
Goblet	40.00	50.00	20.00	35.00
Pickle dish, flat	15.00	20.00	10.00	15.00

Items made	Amber	Blue	Clear	Vas
Pitcher				
Milk, 1 quart	65.00	—	—	50.00
Water, ½ gallon	85.00	65.00	50.00	45.00
Plate				
Dinner, round				
6¼″d	25.00	30.00	15.00	25.00
7¼″d	25.00	30.00	15.00	25.00
Platter, oblong, 7¼″	30.00	50.00	25.00	30.00
Relish tray	20.00	30.00	15.00	15.00
Sauce dish, square, footed	15.00	25.00	10.00	15.00
Spoonholder	35.00	45.00	20.00	30.00
Sugar bowl, covered	35.00	40.00	30.00	30.00
Tray				
Bread	50.00	45.00	30.00	—
Water, round	60.00	55.00	50.00	60.00
Tumbler, water, flat	25.00	30.00	20.00	40.00
Wine	30.00	35.00	20.00	35.00

FINE RIB

Egg cup; decanter w/bar lip; goblet.

OMN: New England Glass Co.'s Reeded. AKA: Fine Rib to Top, Reeded.

Flint, non-flint. New England Glass Co., East Cambridge, MA. ca. 1860s. McKee & Brothers Glass Co., Pittsburgh, PA. ca. 1868-1869. Later reissued in non-flint. Shards have been found at the site of the Boston & Sandwich Glass Co., Sandwich, MA. Illustrated in the 1868 New England Glass Co. catalog.

Original color production: Clear. Opaque white, translucent white, translucent blue or any other color is rare. Colored pieces in non-flint are of much later date. Of good quality flint, the main pattern design of Fine Rib consists of vertical fine ribbing, lacking both flower and vine motifs as evidenced in Bellflower, Ribbed Grape, and Ribbed Ivy. Produced by numerous concerns, handles, shapes and stems may vary.

Reproductions: None.

References: Brn-SD (P. 53), Drep-ABC OG (P. 177), Cod-OS (P. 20), McCn-PGP (447), Lee-EAPG (Pl. 27), Mag-FIEF (P. 4, Fig. 4), McKrn-AG (P. 404), Mil-1 (Pl. 75), Mtz-1 (PP. 38-39), Spil-AEPG (P. 262), Stot-McKe (P. 40), Uni-1 (PP. 70-71), Wat-CG (P. 95), Wat-NEGCO Co. (P. 154), Wlkr-PGA (Fig. 8, No. 24).

Items made	Clear	Items made	Clear
Ale glass	50.00	10″d	45.00
Bottle		Saucer bowl	
Bitters	50.00	6″d	30.00
Water with matching tumble up	125.00	7″d	30.00
Bowl, flat		8″d	35.00
Covered		Cordial	45.00
5½″d	50.00	Creamer, applied handle	125.00
6″d	50.00	Cup, custard, footed	35.00
7″d	65.00	Decanter	
Open		With bar lip	
5″d	30.00	Pint	75.00
5½″d	30.00	Quart	75.00
6″d	35.00	With original stopper	
7″d	35.00	Pint	75.00
8″d	35.00	Quart	75.00
Butter dish, covered	75.00	Dish, flat	
Castor set, complete	200.00	Covered	
Celery vase	50.00	5½″d	45.00
Champagne, 5¼″h	65.00	6″d	45.00
Compote, round		7″d	55.00
Covered		Open	
High standard		Oval	
Deep bowl		7″l	20.00
6″d	65.00	8″l	20.00
7″d	75.00	9″l	20.00
Saucer bowl		10″l	25.00
6″d	65.00	Round, shallow bowl	
7″d	75.00	5½″d	20.00
Low standard		6″d	25.00
Deep bowl		7″d	25.00
6″d	65.00	8″d	25.00
7″d	75.00	Egg cup, pedestaled	
Saucer bowl		Double	45.00
6″d	65.00	Single	40.00
7″d	75.00	Goblet	
Open		Plain band around top of bowl	60.00
High standard		Ribbed to top of bowl	60.00
Deep bowl		Honey dish, flat, round, 3½″d	15.00
6″d	30.00	Jelly glass	40.00
7″d	30.00	Lamp, applied handle (2 sizes)	150.00
8″d	35.00	Lemonade glass	65.00
9″d	35.00	Mug, applied handle	45.00
10″d	45.00	Pitcher, water, applied handle	300.00
Saucer bowl		Plate, round	
6″d	30.00	6″d	20.00
7″d	30.00	7″d	20.00
8″d	35.00	Salt	
Low standard		Dip, individual, open	35.00
Deep bowl		Master	
6″d	30.00	Covered, footed	85.00
7″d	30.00	Open	
8″d	35.00	Oval, flat	60.00
9″d	35.00	Round, footed	40.00

Items made	Clear	Items made	Clear
Sauce dish, round, flat, 4″d	15.00	Bar, ½ pint	85.00
Spoonholder, pedestaled, scalloped rim		Gill	60.00
Tall	65.00	Taper, ½ pint	60.00
Short	65.00	Whiskey, applied handle	75.00
Sugar bowl, covered	75.00	Wine	50.00
Tumbler			

FISHSCALE

Salt shaker; celery vase; water pitcher; spoonholder.

OMN: Coral.

Non-flint. Bryce Brothers, Pittsburgh, PA. ca. 1888. Reissued by the United States Glass Co., Pittsburgh, PA. ca. 1891-1898. Attributed to the Burlington Glass Works, Hamilton, Ontario, Canada. Illustrated in the ca. 1891 and 1894 United States Glass Co. catalog of member firms.

Original color production: Clear. Erroneously reported to have been produced in clear with ruby stain. Handles are pressed. Most items, such as bowls, compotes, and sauces, are round with square corners.

Reproductions: None.

References: Enos-MPG (Chart-5), Hea-5 (P. 79, Plts. C-D), Hea-7 (PP. 94-95, erroneously thought to be ruby stained), Kam-1 (P. 58), Kam-7 (Pl. 1), Kam/Wod-Vol.1 (P. 249), Lee-EAPG (Pl. 120, 156), McCn-PGP (P. 469), Mil-1 (Pl. 87), Mtz-1 (PP. 140-141), Oliv-AAG (P. 66), Pet-Sal (P. 127), Rev-APG (PP. 87-87), Spil-AEPG (P. 304), Stev-ECG (PP. 56-57), Stu-BP (P. 56), Uni-1 (PP. 58-59), Uni-TCG (P. 110), Uni/Wor-CHPGT (P. 122), Wlkr-PGA (Fig. 8, Nos. 39, 45).

Items made	Clear	Items made	Clear
Ash tray, Daisy And Button slipper		Bowl, flat	
attached to a Fishscale rectangular		Covered, round	
tray	65.00	6″	40.00

Items made	Clear	Items made	Clear
7″	45.00	7″d	25.00
8″	45.00	8″d	30.00
9½″	55.00	9″d	30.00
Open		10″d	35.00
Round, saucer bowl		Creamer	30.00
4½″, jelly	15.00	Goblet	30.00
6″	15.00	Lamp, finger, flat, applied handle	75.00
7″	20.00	Mug, 3⅞″h	40.00
8″	20.00	Pickle scoop, tapered at one end	15.00
10″d	30.00	Pitcher	
Waste	25.00	Milk, 1 quart	35.00
Butter dish, covered, 6″d	45.00	Water, ½ gallon	55.00
Cake stand, high standard		Plate, square, rounded corners	
9″d	30.00	7″	25.00
10″d	30.00	8″	30.00
10½″d	35.00	9″	35.00
11″d	35.00	10″	35.00
Celery vase, pedestaled, scalloped rim	30.00	Relish dish, pointed at one end	15.00
Compote, high standard		Salt shaker, original top (R)	65.00
Covered		Sauce dish, round	
4½″d., jelly	35.00	Flat, 4″d	5.00
6″d	50.00	Footed, 4″d	10.00
7″d	75.00	Spoonholder	25.00
8″d	85.00	Sugar bowl, covered	55.00
9″d	95.00	Syrup pitcher, original top	100.00
10″d	120.00	Tray	
Open, saucer bowl		Condiment, rectangular	35.00
4½″d., jelly	20.00	Water, round	35.00
6″d	20.00	Tumbler, water, flat, ½ pint (R)	85.00

FLAMINGO HABITAT

Champagne; goblet.

Non-flint. Maker unknown ca. 1870s.

Original color production: Clear with acid etched design. Handles are applied.

Reproductions: None.

References: Mtz-2 (PP. 92-93), Mil-1 (P. 61), Uni-1 (P. 169).

Items made	Clear	Items made	Clear
Bowl, oval, open, flat, 10"d	40.00	5"d	35.00
Butter dish, covered	65.00	6"d	40.00
Celery vase, pedestaled, scalloped rim	45.00	6½"d	40.00
Champagne	35.00	Creamer	50.00
Cheese dish, blown, folded rim, domed		Goblet	
lid	100.00	Design covers lower half of bowl	40.00
Compote, high standard		Design covers ¾ of bowl	40.00
Covered		Sauce dish, footed, round	15.00
4½"d, jelly	75.00	Spoonholder, pedestaled.	25.00
6½"d	95.00	Sugar bowl, covered	50.00
Open		Tumbler, water, flat	20.00
4½"d, jelly	35.00	Wine	45.00

FLAT DIAMOND

Spoonholder; apothecary jar (o.s.); goblet; covered marmalade jar.

OMN: Pillar. AKA: Lippman.

Non-flint. Richards & Hartley Glass Co., Tarentum, PA. ca. 1880s. Reissued by the United States Glass Co., Pittsburgh, PA. after the 1891 merger. Shards have been found at the site of the Burlington Glass Works, Hamilton, Ontario, Canada.

Original color production: Clear.

Reproductions: None.

References: Bat-GPG (PP. 56, 59), Hlms-BCA (P. 278), Lee-VG (Pl. 32, No. 4), Luc-TG (P. 267), Mtz-1 (PP. 198-199), Rev-APG (P. 287), Uni-1 (P. 121), Uni/Wor-CHPGT (P. 124), Wlkr-PGA (Fig. 8, No. 45).

Items made	Clear	Items made	Clear
Apothecary jar, o.s.	25.00	Pitcher, water, ½ gallon	45.00
Butter dish, covered	45.00	Marmalade jar, covered	30.00
Celery vase	35.00	Sauce dish, round	
Creamer	30.00	Flat	8.00
Goblet	25.00	Footed	8.00

Items made	Clear	Items made	Clear
Spoonholder, pedestaled, scalloped rim, 5½"h	25.00	Tumbler, water, flat	40.00
Sugar bowl, covered	45.00	Wine	25.00

FLEUR-DE-LIS

Flat banana dish; high standard cake stand; handled olive dish.

OMN: Fleur-de-Lis. AKA: Arched Fleur-de-Lis [Peterson], Fleur-de-Lis-Ingaglio [Batty], Late Fleur-de-Lis [Brothers].

Non-flint. Bryce, Higbee & Co., Homestead, PA. ca. 1898 to 1907. Advertised throughout the Butler Brothers Catalogs of 1905, 1906, and 1907, and illustrated in the 1904 United States Glass Co. catalog.

Original color production: Clear, clear with ruby stain (ruby stained items most likely decorated by the Oriental Glass Co., Pittsburgh, PA.).

Reproductions: None.

References; Bar-RS (Pl. 70), Beatty (P. 173), Hea-RUTPS TPS (Fig. 1136), Hea-7 (Figs. 907-910), Kam-5 (P. 145), Pet-GPP (P. 223), Pet-Sal (P. 223, Pl. 161-"D"), PGP-1 (P. 5), PGP-2 (P. 12), Rev-APG (P. 92), Stev-ECG (PP. 145-147), Stev-GIC (PP. 126-127).

Items made	Clear	Clear w/Ruby
Banana stand		
Flat, folded sides	35.00	125.00
High standard	40.00	135.00
Bowl, oval, open, flat, 9"	18.00	40.00
Butter dish, covered, footed, flanged base	40.00	135.00
Cake stand, high standard	40.00	70.00
Compote, round, covered, high standard, jelly	18.00	40.00
Creamer	30.00	75.00
Dish, open, flat, shallow, 7"d	12.00	25.00
Mug, handled, 3¼"h	15.00	40.00

Items made	Clear	Clear w/Ruby
Olive dish, handled	15.00	20.00
Pitcher, water, applied handle, $\frac{1}{2}$ gallon, $8\frac{1}{4}$"h	125.00	300.00
Plate, square, 7"	15.00	45.00
Relish tray, 8"l	15.00	25.00
Salt shaker, original top	15.00	40.00
Sauce dish, round, flat	10.00	20.00
Spoonholder, double handled	20.00	65.00
Sugar bowl, covered, double handled	35.00	100.00
Toothpick holder	35.00	250.00
Tumbler, water, flat, $3\frac{3}{4}$"h	15.00	45.00
Vase, 10"h	35.00	75.00
Wine	25.00	55.00

FLEUR-DE-LIS AND DRAPE

Creamer; spoonholder.

Covered butter dish; spoonholder.

OMN: U.S. Glass No. 15009. AKA: Fleur-de-Lis And Tassel.

Non-flint. Adams & Co., Pittsburgh, PA. ca. 1888. Reissued by the United States Glass Co., (pattern line no. 15,009) Pittsburgh, PA. at Factory "A" (Adams & Co., Pittsburgh, PA.) ca. 1898-1907. Illustrated in the United States Glass Co. 1895-1896 and 1898 catalogs.

Original color production: Clear, emerald green, milk white.

Reproductions: Throughout the mid 1980s, the wine was reproduced from a new mold in amethyst, blue, orange, and yellow opalescent colors which are not original to the set.

References: Hea-3 (P. 82), Hea-5 (PP. 18, 61), Kam-3 (P. 50), Lee-VG (Pl. 59, No. 40), McCn-PGP (P. 381), Mil-2 (Pl. 14), Mtz-1 (PP. 138-139), Mtz-2 (Pl. 14), Pet-Sal (P. 29), Rev-APG (PP. 18-19), Stu-BP (P. 27), Thu-1 (P. 321), Uni-2 (P. 41).

Items made	Clear	Emerald Green
Bottle, water	50.00	125.00
Bowl, open, flat, smooth rim		
Finger or waste	30.00	40.00
Berry		
6"d	10.00	20.00
8"d	15.00	30.00
Butter dish, covered		
Flat	45.00	55.00
Footed, flanged rim	45.00	65.00
Cake stand, high standard		
9"d	35.00	55.00
10"d	40.00	60.00
Celery		
Tray, oval	25.00	40.00
Vase	25.00	40.00
Claret	35.00	50.00
Compote		
Covered		
High standard		
5"d	30.00	40.00
6"d	35.00	40.00
7"d	35.00	40.00
8"d	45.00	50.00
Low standard		
5"d	30.00	40.00
6"d	35.00	45.00
8"d	45.00	60.00
Open		
High standard		
5"d	20.00	30.00
6"d	20.00	30.00
7"d	30.00	35.00
8"d	35.00	40.00
Low standard		
5"d	20.00	30.00
6"d	20.00	30.00
7"d	25.00	35.00
8"d	30.00	40.00
Cordial	25.00	45.00
Creamer, 5⅜"h	25.00	45.00
Cruet, original stopper	45.00	85.00
Custard cup	20.00	30.00
Dish, oblong, flat, open, 8"	15.00	20.00
Goblet	35.00	45.00

Items made	Clear	Emerald Green
Honey dish		
Covered, square, ribbed lid	40.00	55.00
Round		
Flat, 3½"d	10.00	15.00
Footed, 3½"d	10.00	15.00
Lamp, oil, tall, complete with original burner and chimney	125.00	175.00
Mustard, covered, handled	35.00	50.00
Pickle dish, boat shaped	15.00	20.00
Pitcher		
Milk, 1 quart	40.00	60.00
Water, ½ gallon	50.00	65.00
Plate, round		
6"d	10.00	25.00
7"d	20.00	35.00
8"d	20.00	35.00
9"d	20.00	35.00
10"d	25.00	40.00
Relish tray, oval	20.00	30.00
Salt shaker, original top	15.00	35.00
Sauce dish, round		
Flat		
4"d	8.00	15.00
4½"d	8.00	15.00
Footed		
4"d	8.00	15.00
4½"d	8.00	15.00
Saucer, underplate to custard cup	10.00	15.00
Spoonholder	25.00	40.00
Sugar bowl, covered	30.00	55.00
Sugar shaker, original top	40.00	85.00
Syrup pitcher, original top	50.00	125.00
Tray, water, round, 11½"d	25.00	50.00
Tumbler, water, flat	20.00	30.00
Wine	25.00	45.00

Creamer; 9¼" plate; cruet (o.s.).

OMN: United States Glass No. 15,056, Florida. AKA: Emerald Green Herringbone (in emerald green only) [Kamm], Panelled Herringbone [Millard] (in clear only), Prism and Herringbone [Millard].

Non-flint. The United States Glass Co. (pattern line No. 15,056), Pittsburgh, PA. at Factory "B" (Bryce Bros., Pittsburgh, PA.) ca. 1898. Illustrated in the United States Glass Co. 1904 catalog, the Baltimore Bargain House general merchandise catalog No. 496 August 15, 1904, and the Charles "Broadway" Rousse July-August, 1914 general merchandise catalog.

Original color production: Clear, emerald green.

Reproductions: The 5¾"h. goblet has been reproduced from a new mold as early as the 1960s in amber, amethyst, blue, green, and ruby red. New emerald green goblets are not as deep in color as the original while the glass is thinner and lighter in weight.

References: Grow-WCG (P. 213, Fig. 39-"8"), Hart/Cob (P. 24), Hart-AG (P. 63), Hea-5 (P. 38, Nos. 68-74), Hea-6 (P. 29), Kam-1 (P. 46), Kam-6 (Pl. 93), Kam/Wod-Vol.1 (P. 308), Lee-EAPG (Pl. 164), McCn-PGP (P. 545), Mil-1 (Pl. 87), Mtz-1 (PP. 176-177), Oliv-AAG (P. 65), Pet-Sal (P. 28), Rev-APG (P. 312), Uni-1 (P. 93), Wlkr-PGA (Fig. 15, No. 1).

Items made	Clear	Emerald Green
Bowl, round, flat		
Covered, 4"d	25.00	40.00
Open		
7¾"d.	20.00	25.00
9"d	20.00	25.00
Butter dish, covered	40.00	55.00
Cake stand, high standard	30.00	40.00
Celery vase	30.00	35.00
Compote, square, high standard		
Covered, 6½"d	30.00	45.00
Open, 6½"d	25.00	40.00
Cordial	25.00	55.00
Creamer	30.00	45.00
Cruet, original stopper	40.00	95.00

Items made	Clear	Emerald Green
Goblet	25.00	40.00
Mustard pot, covered, attached underplate	25.00	45.00
Pickle dish, oval	25.00	45.00
Pitcher, water, ½ gallon	50.00	75.00
Plate, square		
7¼"	10.00	20.00
9¼"	15.00	20.00
Relish tray		
Oval	15.00	20.00
Square		
6"	10.00	15.00
8½"	10.00	15.00
Salt shaker, original top	25.00	50.00
Sauce dish, round, square top		
Handled	8.00	10.00
Handleless	8.00	10.00
Spoonholder	20.00	35.00
Sugar bowl, covered	30.00	50.00
Syrup pitcher, original top	65.00	175.00
Tumbler, water, flat	20.00	30.00
Wine	25.00	50.00

FLOWER BAND

Goblet; spoonholder; creamer.

AKA: Bird Finial, Frosted Flower Band.

Non-flint. Maker unknown ca. 1870s.

Original color production: Clear, clear with frosted band. Finials are entwined love birds. A variant of the pattern is known as "Fruit Band" when the flowers of the design are replaced by fruit in the wide pattern band. Both forms are trimmed with the oak leaf and acorn motif.

Reproductions: The Fenton Art Glass Co., Williamstown, WV., reproduced the 6¼"h. goblet in amber, cobalt and sapphire blue, and pastel colors from a new mold.

References: Enos-MPG (Chart-4), Kam-4 (PP. 47-48), Kam/Wod-Vol.1 (P. 49), Lee-EAPG (Plts. 107, 109), McCn-PGP (Pl. 149) Mil-1 (Pl. 74), Mtz-1 (PP. 64-65), Mtz-2 (PP. 66-67), Uni-1 (P. 205), Uni-2 (P. 222), Uni/Wor-CHPGT (P. 128).

Items made	Clear	Clear/ Frosted
Butter dish, covered, flat, love bird finial	100.00	145.00
Celery vase, 2 handles	55.00	75.00
Compote, covered		
High standard, round, 8"d	135.00	175.00
Collared base		
Oval	125.00	145.00
Round	125.00	145.00
Creamer, 6"h	65.00	90.00
Goblet	60.00	85.00
Pitcher		
Milk, 1 quart	65.00	110.00
Water, $\frac{1}{2}$ gallon	85.00	125.00
Sauce dish, round		
Flat	10.00	20.00
Footed	10.00	20.00
Spoonholder, handled	45.00	65.00
Sugar bowl, covered, handled	95.00	125.00

FLOWER POT

Spoonholder; covered sugar bowl; covered butter dish; flat sauce dish.

AKA: Flower Plant, Potted Plant.

Non-flint. Maker unknown, ca. late 1870s, early 1880s.

Original color production: Clear. Amber, vaseline or any other color is rare. The main design element of Flower Pot is a clear, high embossed stylized urn in which a single flower and leaves rest against a finely stippled background.

Reproductions: None.

References: Enos-MPG (Chart-5), Kam-1 (P. 87), Kam-3 (P. 58), Lee-EAPG (Plts. 133, 136), Lind-HG (P. 216), Mtz-1 (P. 61), Mtz-2 (P. 60), Pet-Sal (P. 29), Stu-BP (P. 28), McCn-PGP (P. 268).

Items made	Clear	Items made	Clear
Butter dish, covered, 4 footed	55.00	Water, $\frac{1}{2}$ gallon	55.00
Cake stand, high stand, $10\frac{1}{2}''$ d	50.00	Salt shaker, original top	20.00
Compote, high		Sauce dish	
Covered, 7"d	50.00	Flat, oblong, handled	15.00
Open, $7\frac{1}{4}''$d	20.00	Footed, square, double handled	15.00
Creamer	35.00	Spoonholder, double handled	30.00
Goblet	35.00	Sugar bowl, covered, double handled	40.00
Pitcher		Tray, bread, oblong, "We Trust In	
Milk, 1 quart, 7"h	40.00	God" center	50.00

FLUTE

Bar tumbler ($3\frac{1}{4}''$h cobalt blue); footed tumbler ($4\frac{3}{4}''$h clear w/engraved amber stained panels); champagne (clear); flip ($5\frac{1}{4}''$h. clear); water tumbler ($4\frac{1}{4}''$h clear); whiskey tumbler ($3\frac{1}{4}''$h clear).

OMN: Flute.

Flint, non-flint. Bakewell, Pears & Co., Pittsburgh, PA. ca. 1868. McKee & Brothers, Pittsburgh, PA. ca. 1859-1864. Illustrated in the ca. 1872 Adams & Co. catalog, the 1875 Bakewell, Pears & Co. catalog, and the McKee & Brothers catalogs of 1859-1860, 1864, and 1880.

Original color production: Clear. Odd pieces in amethyst, clear with amber stain (plain or copper wheel engraved) cobalt blue, deep green, or any other color are scarce. A simple pattern consisting of vertically connected flat, arched panels, more than fifteen variants of Flute were produced in flint and non-flint from the 1850s through the 1890s including Beaded Flute, Bessimer Flute, and New England Flute. Originally, manufacturers and wholesalers designated items by the number of flutes on an article: six flute, eight-flute, and ten-flute. Produced by numerous concerns for over a forty year period, a wide range of variations may be found in the treatment of finials, stems, handles, and bases.

Reproductions: None.

References: Lee-EAPG (Plts. 1,3), Mtz-1 (PP. 40-41), Oliv-AAG (P. 54), Rev-APG (PP. 87, 238), Stot-McKe (P. 84), Uni-1 (P.19).

Items made	Clear	Items made	Clear
Ale glass		Mug	
6-flute	25.00	8-flute, applied handle, pony	75.00
10-flute	50.00	10-flute, beer	75.00
Bottle, bitters		Pitcher, water, $\frac{1}{2}$ gallon	35.00
6-flute	75.00	Sauce dish, round, flat	15.00
8-flute	75.00	Sugar bowl, covered	50.00
Butter dish, covered, low standard	60.00	Syrup pitcher, applied handle, original	
Candlestick, 6-flute, no socket, 4"h	45.00	top	85.00
Champagne, 6-flute, 5$\frac{1}{2}$"h	25.00	Tumbler	
Claret	45.00	6-flute	
Compote, open, low standard		$\frac{1}{5}$ pint	20.00
8$\frac{1}{2}$"d	40.00	$\frac{1}{3}$ pint	20.00
9$\frac{1}{2}$"d	45.00	$\frac{1}{2}$ pint, (termed the jelly glass)	25.00
Creamer	45.00	8-flute	
Decanter, with bar lip, 1 quart	100.00	$\frac{1}{3}$ pint	20.00
Egg cup, footed		$\frac{1}{2}$ pint	20.00
Double	30.00	Toy, applied handle	20.00
Single	30.00	9-flute	
Glass		$\frac{1}{4}$ pint	20.00
Ale, 10-flute	30.00	$\frac{1}{2}$ pint	20.00
Jelly	30.00	Bar, 3$\frac{1}{4}$"h	20.00
Pony ale, 10-flute	30.00	Flip, 5$\frac{1}{4}$"h	20.00
Punch		Jelly, 10-flute	25.00
8-flute	25.00	Toy, $\frac{1}{2}$ gill	25.00
10-flute	25.00	Water, 4$\frac{1}{4}$"h	20.00
Goblet, 6-flute	35.00	Whiskey, applied handle, 3"h	30.00
Honey dish, round, flat	15.00	Wine, 6-flute	25.00
Lamp, original burner and chimney	125.00		

FLYING STORK

Low footed open bowl; high standard covered compote; goblet.

Non-flint. Maker unknown. Attributed by McCain to the Whitall-Tatum Glass Co., Millville, NJ. ca. late 1870s, early 1880s. Most likely Ihmsen Glass Co., Ltd., Millville, NY.

Original color production: Clear, the main pattern design consisting of a large stork-like bird in flight. Impressions are usually of the "oatmeal-type" on a clear background.

Reproductions: None.

References: McCn-PGP (Pl. 9), Mil-2 (Pl. 117), Mtz-2 (P. 86), Uni-1 (P. 190), Wlkr-PGA (P. 368).

Items made	Clear	Items made	Clear
Bowl, low circular foot, shallow bowl	30.00	Marmalade jar, covered	50.00
Butter dish, covered	50.00	Pitcher, water, 1/2 gallon	55.00
Celery vase	35.00	Sauce dish, round, footed	10.00
Compote, covered, high standard	65.00	Spoonholder	30.00
Creamer	30.00	Sugar bowl, covered	45.00
Goblet	65.00		

FRANCESWARE (HOBNAIL/SWIRL)

Francesware Hobnail: creamer; covered sugar bowl (frosted w/amber stained rims). Francesware Swirl: spoonholder; covered butter dish (frosted w/amber stain).

Francesware Hobnail: OMN: Francesware.
Francesware Swirl: OMN: Hobb's No. 326. AKA: Hobb's Blown Swirl.

Non-flint. Francesware Hobnail: Hobbs, Brockunier & Co., Wheeling, WV. ca. 1880. Francesware Swirl: Hobb's Brockunier & Co. (pattern line No. 326), Wheeling, WV. ca. 1888-1890. Both illustrated in two undated (ca. 1888-1891) Hobbs, Brockunier & Co. catalogs.

Original color production: Hobnail. Clear, clear/frosted, clear/frosted with amber stain. The Hobnail version of Francesware is a pressed ware with applied handles, most items being round. **Swirl.** Clear, clear and acid finished with amber stained rims. The Swirl version of Francesware is a blown ware with applied handles, most items being oval.

Reproductions: None.

References: Hea-2 (P. 1A), Hea-3 (P. 28, Fig. 151), Hea-6 (P. 25, Fig. 117), Mur-MCO (PP. 37, 49).

Items made	Clear	Clear/ Frosted	Clear/ Frosted/ Amber
HOBNAIL			
Basket, bride's in original silver plate holder	110.00	135.00	150.00
Bottle, barber	65.00	90.00	125.00
Bowl, open			
Oval			
7″	50.00	75.00	75.00
8″	50.00	75.00	75.00
9″	60.00	85.00	85.00
Round			
7$\frac{1}{2}$″d	50.00	75.00	75.00
8″d	50.00	75.00	75.00
Waste or finger, 4″d	40.00	50.00	50.00
Square			
7$\frac{1}{2}$″	50.00	75.00	75.00
8″	50.00	75.00	75.00
Butter dish, covered, flat			
Flanged rim	45.00	65.00	75.00
Plain rim	80.00	110.00	110.00
Celery vase, flat	35.00	55.00	65.00
Creamer, flat, applied handle	25.00	40.00	55.00
Cruet, original faceted stopper	35.00	100.00	250.00
Pitcher, bulbous, applied handle			
Lemonade	100.00	165.00	185.00
Milk, 8$\frac{1}{2}$″h	90.00	150.00	150.00
Water			
Miniature water	65.00	85.00	200.00
Table size	100.00	165.00	185.00
Salt shaker, original top	35.00	50.00	65.00
Sauce dish, ruffled rim			
Round, flat			
4″d	15.00	20.00	30.00
4$\frac{1}{2}$″d	15.00	20.00	30.00
Square, flat			
4″	15.00	20.00	30.00
4$\frac{1}{2}$″	15.00	20.00	30.00
Spoonholder, flat, ...	45.00	45.00	55.00
Sugar bowl, covered, flat	60.00	65.00	85.00
Syrup, applied handle, original top	65.00	150.00	350.00
Toothpick holder	35.00	80.00	90.00
Tray, water			
Leaf shaped, 12″	85.00	125.00	125.00
Oval	75.00	125.00	150.00
Rectangular, rounded edges, 9$\frac{1}{2}$″ x 14″	35.00	45.00	65.00
SWIRL			
Bowl, open, flat, round			
Berry, master			85.00
Finger			35.00
Butter dish, covered, matching underplate			125.00
Castor set, complete with salt/pepper shakers, oil and vinegar cruets with original silver plate			
holder			600.00
Celery			
Tray, oval			65.00

Vase	85.00
Creamer, flat, applied handle	55.00
Cruet, original faceted stopper	225.00
Cruet set (two cruets, salt/pepper, undertray)	600.00
Lamp, oil, miniature, complete with matching shade, burner and chimney	400.00
Mustard jar, covered	85.00
Pickle dish, oval	35.00
Pitcher, water, ovid, applied handle, flat, ½ gallon	150.00
Plate, round, 5"d	30.00
Salt shaker, original top	55.00
Sauce dish, flat, oval	
Deep, slightly pinched sides	22.00
Shallow bowl	22.00
Shade, gas	
Bulbous, scalloped rim	90.00
Tall, scalloped rim	90.00
Spoonholder, flat	45.00
Sugar bowl, covered, flat, faceted knob-stem	85.00
Sugar shaker, original top	150.00
Syrup pitcher, applied handle, original top	250.00
Toothpick holder, ruffled rim	145.00
Tumbler, flat, water, smooth rim	40.00

FROSTED CHICKEN

Salt shaker; h.s. covered compote (copper wheel engraved); covered compote (plain); pepper shaker.

AKA: Chicken, Chick.

Non-flint. Maker unknown, ca. late 1870s, early 1880s.

Original color production: Clear (plain or copper wheel engraved). The main design element of Frosted Chicken consists of large, clear concave panels, separated by clear vertical convex panels. Finials are frosted chicks emerging from an egg shell. A difficult pattern to recognize without the finial, identifying characteristics are pressed handles, and solid columnar standards with clear glass knobs at the top and bottom.

Reproductions: None.

References: Lee-VG (P. 20), McCn-PGP (Pl. 7), Mtz-2 (P. 84), Pet-Sal (P. 24), Uni-2 (PP. 97, 175).

Items made	Clear	Items made	Clear
Butter dish, covered, handles, chick finial	125.00	Marmalade jar, covered, double handled, chick finial (R)	200.00
Bowl, covered, low standard, chick finial	150.00	Salt shaker, double handled, original top	30.00
Celery vase, double handled	45.00	Sauce dish, footed, round, double handled	15.00
Compote, covered, high standard, round, chick finial	175.00	Spoonholder, double handled	30.00
Creamer	35.00	Sugar bowl, covered, double handled, chick finial	150.00
Goblet	40.00		

FROSTED CIRCLE

Tumbler; h.s. open compote; salt shaker; covered sugar bowl; pepper shaker; creamer; cruet (o.s.).

OMN: U.S. Glass No. 15,007, Horn of Plenty. AKA: Clear Circle (without acid finish).

Non-flint. Bryce Brothers, Pittsburgh, PA. ca. 1876 to 1885. Reissued by the United States Glass Co. (pattern line No. 15,007), Pittsburgh, PA. after the 1891 merger. Illustrated in the United States Glass Co. 1898 catalog as "Horn of Plenty", the United States Glass Co. 1904 catalog, and in the 1899 Butlers Brothers catalog as "Diamond" pattern.

Original color production: Clear, clear with acid finished circles. The pattern is termed "Clear Circle" when not frosted. Both versions were produced in a complete line of tablewares. Handles on water pitchers may be applied.

Reproductions: The goblet in clear with frosted circles was reproduced from a new mold from the early 1960s. Unlike the original, the new goblet has oval shaped circles that appear to be ground down and flat.

References: Enos-MPG (Chart-1), Hea-5 (PP. 13, 18), Kam-4 (PP. 19-20), Kam-6 (Pl. 85), Lee-EAPG (Plts. 76, 96, 131), Lee-VG (Pl. 83), McCn-EPG (Pl. 40), Mil-1 (P. 94), Mtz-1 (P. 138), Oliv-AAG (P. 76), Pet-Sal (P. 124), Rev-APG (PP. 263-264), Uni-1 (P. 43).

Items made	Clear	Clear/ Frosted
Bowl, flat		
Covered		
5"d	25.00	35.00
6"d	25.00	35.00
7"d	30.00	40.00
8"d	30.00	40.00
9"d	35.00	45.00
Open		
5"d	10.00	15.00
6"d	10.00	15.00
7"d	10.00	15.00
8"d	15.00	20.00
9"d	15.00	20.00
Butter dish		
Covered, 5"d	55.00	65.00
Open	45.00	55.00
Cake stand, high standard		
8"d	30.00	35.00
9"d	30.00	35.00
9½"d	40.00	50.00
10"d	40.00	50.00
Celery vase	30.00	35.00
Champagne	40.00	65.00
Compote, high standard		
Covered		
5"d	35.00	45.00
6"d	35.00	45.00
7"d	40.00	55.00
8"d	45.00	65.00
Open		
5"d	15.00	20.00
6"d	20.00	25.00
7"d	25.00	30.00
8"d	30.00	35.00
Creamer, footed, pressed handle	25.00	35.00
Cruet, original patterned stopper, pressed handle	45.00	65.00
Cup, custard	15.00	20.00
Pickle		
Dish, oblong, flat	10.00	20.00
Jar, covered	35.00	50.00
Plate, round, 7"d, smooth rim	20.00	35.00
Salt shaker, tall, flat, original top	25.00	35.00
Saucer, underplate for custard cup	10.00	15.00
Spoonholder, footed, scalloped rim	20.00	30.00
Sugar bowl, covered	35.00	50.00
Sugar shaker, tall, original top	35.00	45.00
Syrup pitcher, pressed handle, original top	55.00	90.00
Tumbler, water, flat	25.00	35.00
Wine	30.00	40.00

Creamer (plain); covered sugar (plain); h.s. covered compote (plain); covered butter (plain); spoonholder (etched).

AKA: Frosted Hawk, Old Abe.

Non-flint. Attributed by Kamm to the Crystal Glass Co., Bridgeport, OH ca. 1883.

Original color production: Clear, clear with acid finish (plain or copper wheel engraved). Finials are well sculptured frosted American bald eagles. Handles are pressed and items are footed.

Reproductions: None.

References: Enos-MPG (Chart-2), Gor-CC (PP. 115-117), Hea-Fen (PP. 51, 55), Kam-5 (PP. 22-23), Kam-6 (P. 62), Lee-EAPG (Pl. 99), Mrsh-SRG (PP. 298-299), McCn-PGP (P. 405), Mtz-1 (PP. 94-95), Pet-Sal (P. 29), Rev-APG (P. 132), Spil-AEPG (P. 283).

Items made	Clear/ Frosted	Items made	Clear/ Frosted
Bowl, collared base, covered, 6¼"d	175.00	Pitcher, water, ½ gallon	100.00
Butter dish, covered, frosted eagle		Salt	
finial		Dip	
Handled, double-ring 8"d	225.00	Individual	25.00
No handles, 8"d	175.00	Master	50.00
Celery vase	65.00	Shaker, original top	30.00
Compote, covered, high standard,		Spoonholder, double handled	35.00
frosted eagle finial	225.00	Sugar bowl, covered, frosted eagle	
Creamer, 6"h., pressed handle	40.00	finial	150.00

FROSTED LEAF

Covered sugar bowl.

Flint. Attributed to the Portland Glass Co., Portland, ME. ca. 1873-1874. The Boston & Sandwich Glass Co., Sandwich, MA. ca. 1860.

Original color production: Clear/frosted (frosting being machine ground rather than acid finished). Amethyst or any other color is very rare. The main pattern design element consists of a single vine of "ground" leaves on a clear horizontal band. Beneath, are vertical clear columns.

Reproductions: The Smithsonian Institution, Washington, D.C. ca. 1978 authorized the Imperial Glass Co., Bellaire, OH., to reissue from new molds the following items in clear and frosted lead crystal: covered butter dish, creamer, spoonholder, covered sugar bowl, and wine, each item being embossed with the Smithsonian's "S.I." monogram.

References: Lee-EAPG (Pl. 94), Lee-SG (P. 536), McCn-PGP (P. 431), McKrn-AG (Pl. 209), Mil-1 (Pl. 114), Mtz-1 (PP. 26-27), Mtz-2 (PP. 118-119), Oliv-AAG (P. 54), Spil-AEPG (P. 265), Swn-PG/49 (PP. 73-74), Uni-1 (P. 211), Wlkr-PGA (Fig. 8, Nos. 24, 27, 46).

Items made	Clear	Items made	Clear
Butter dish, covered	150.00	Brass stem, marble base, matching shade	500.00
Celery vase, scalloped edge, plain base	145.00	Brass stem, milk white base	350.00
Champagne	175.00	Pitcher, water, applied handle, ½ gallon	450.00
Compote, high standard		Salt	
Covered	250.00	Individual	50.00
Open	150.00	Master, footed	125.00
Cordial	150.00	Sauce dish, round, star in base	
Creamer	400.00	Flat, 4"d	25.00
Decanter		Spoonholder	145.00
Pint, cut shoulders, matching patterned stopper	275.00	Sugar bowl, covered	175.00
Quart, matching patterned stopper	275.00	Tumbler	
Egg cup, single	100.00	Flat	125.00
Goblet		Footed	175.00
Gentleman's	150.00	Wine	125.00
Lady's	175.00		
Lamp, oil, original burner			

FROSTED RIBBON

Creamer; spoonholder; celery vase; milk pitcher; covered butter dish.

OMN: Duncan's No. 150. AKA: Ribbon [Lee].

Non-flint. George Duncan & Sons (pattern line No. 150), Pittsburgh, PA. ca. 1878-1886. Reissued by the United States Glass Co. after the merger of 1891. Illustrated in the undated George Duncan & Sons catalog, and reviewed in the February 7, 1878 issue of the *Crockery and Glass Journal.*

Original color production: Clear (plain or copper wheel engraved, designs running horizontally around items), clear/frosted (plain or copper wheel engraved, designs appearing on alternating clear panels). Popular engravings include Nos. 84, 91, 92, 94, 95, 281, 291, 500, and 501). The Duncan version of Frosted Ribbon is distinguished from others by the thumbprints appearing on the knob of stemmed items. Handles are pressed.

Reproductions: None.

References: Bred-EDG (PP. 47-49), Hea-5 (P. 102), Lee-EAPG (Pl. 69), Lee-VG (Pl. 64), McCn-PGP (P. 371), Mil-1 (Pl. 37), Mtz-1 (PP. 170-171), Oliv-AAG (P. 76), Rev-APG (P. 149), Uni-1 (Pl. 119).

Items made	Clear/ Frosted	Items made	Clear/ Frosted
Bottle, bitters	45.00	6"d	35.00
Butter dish, covered, 6"d, footed	55.00	7"d	35.00
Celery vase, pedestaled, scalloped rim	35.00	8"d	65.00
Champagne	55.00	9"d	85.00
Claret	65.00	10"d	95.00
Compote		Open	
Covered		High standard	
High standard		Deep bowl	
6"d	35.00	5"d	20.00
7"d	35.00	6"d	20.00
8"d	65.00	7"d	25.00
9"d	95.00	8"d	25.00
10"d	95.00	9"d	35.00
Low standard, deep bowl		10"d	35.00

Items made	Clear/Frosted	Items made	Clear/Frosted
Saucer bowl		Goblet	25.00
5"d	20.00	Pickle jar, covered	85.00
6"d	20.00	Pitcher	
7"d	25.00	Milk, 1 quart	75.00
8"d	25.00	Water, ½ gallon	65.00
9"d	35.00	Salt	
10"d	35.00	Master, footed, open, scalloped rim	15.00
Low standard		Shaker, flat, original top	15.00
5"d	20.00	Sauce dish, round, flared bowl	
6"d	20.00	Flat	
7"d	25.00	Flared, scalloped	
8"d	25.00	4"d	10.00
9"d	35.00	4½"d	10.00
10"d	35.00	Straight-sided bowl, scalloped rim,	
Cordial	50.00	4"d	10.00
Creamer	45.00	Footed, scalloped rim	
Cup, custard	10.00	4"d	15.00
Decanter, 1 quart, original faceted		4½"d	15.00
stopper	85.00	Sherry	35.00
Dish, octagonal, flat, open		Spoonholder	35.00
7"l	15.00	Sugar bowl, covered	50.00
8"l	15.00	Tumbler, water, flat	25.00
9"l	15.00	Wine	65.00
Egg cup, footed	15.00		

FROSTED STORK

Goblet; creamer.

AKA: Flamingo, Frosted Crane.

Non-flint. The Crystal Glass Co., Bridgeport, OH. ca. 1880. Shards have been found at the site of the Burlington Glass Works, Hamilton, Ontario, Canada.

Original color production: Clear, clear with acid finish. Covered items have well sculptured "stork" finials. Handles are pressed.

Reproductions: The A.A. Importing Co., Inc., St. Louis, MO. and Carson/San Francisco, CA., reproduced from new molds the goblet and $11^{3}/_{4}$"l. bread tray in clear with acid finish and color as illustrated in the company's 1976 bicentennial No. 33 Spring-Summer catalog.

References: Hlms-BCA (P. 278), Kam-4 (P. 62), Kam-5 (PP. 22-23), Kam-6 (P. 62), Lee-EAPG (Pl. 100), McCn-PGP (Pl. 19), Mil-1 (P. 61), Mtz-1 (PP. 94-95), Rev-APG (P. 132), Spil-AEPG (P. 283), Uni-1 (P. 189), Uni/Wor-CHGT (P. 130).

Items made	Clear/ Frosted	Items made	Clear/ Frosted
Bowl, open, flat		Pickle jar, covered	125.00
Round		Pitcher, water, ½ gallon	150.00
Berry		Plate, round, handled, 9"d	40.00
8"d	45.00	Platter	
9"d	45.00	Oval, 11½" x 8"	
Finger	50.00	One-O-One border	50.00
Ice, for water set	50.00	Scenic border	65.00
Oval, flat	40.00	Relish tray	20.00
Butter dish, covered	85.00	Sauce dish, round, flat	20.00
Creamer	45.00	Spoonholder	45.00
Dish, oval, open, deep, 9" x 6"	30.00	Sugar bowl, covered	95.00
Goblet	65.00	Water tray, round	100.00
Marmalade jar, covered	125.00		

GALLOWAY

Covered butter (clear w/blush); cracker jar (orig. lid); tankard water pitcher (clear w/blush); olive dish.

OMN: U.S. Glass No. 15,086, Mirror. Jefferson's No. 15,601. AKA: Mirror Plate, U.S. Mirror, Virginia, Woodrow.

Non-flint. The United States Glass Co. (pattern line No. 15,086), Pittsburgh, PA. ca. 1904 through 1919. Jefferson Glass Co. (pattern line No. 15,601), Toronto, Canada between 1900 and 1925. Illustrated in the Butler Brothers catalog of August, 1906, and the United States Glass Co. catalogs No. 111 (Factory "D" ca. 1904), 1907 (as "Mirror"), 1909 domestic catalog as "Mirror Plate" and the 1915 and 1918 export catalogs.

Footed sherbert; syrup; h.s. open compote; cruet (o.s.); water tumbler.

Original color production: Clear, clear with rose blush. Clear with ruby stain or any other color is rare. Galloway was produced in two versions: a) the table set which is straight- sided and b) the "hotel set" which is squatty and originally called the "Mirror Set". Handles may be applied or pressed.

Reproductions: The $2^1/_2$"h. toothpick holder, issued from a new mold in amber, blue, clear, green and other colors (most likely by the Summit Art Glass Co., Mogadore/Rootstown, OH.), has been available for many years from Trans-World Trading Co., Robinson, IL.

References: Bros-TS (P. 44), Hea-1 (P. 43, Fig. 313), Hea-3 (P. 88), Hea-5 (P. 154, Plts. A-B), Hea-6 (P. 45, Fig. 380), Hea-7 (P. 152), Hrtng-P&P (P. 95), Kam-2 (P. 89), Kam-3 (P. 89), Migh-TPS (Pl. 3), Mil-1 (Pl. 218), Mtz-1 (PP. 218-219), Spil-AEPG (P. 316), Stev-ECG (PP. 247, 256), Stot-McKe (P. 18), Uni-1 (P. 243), Uni-2 (P. 316), Uni-TCG (PP. 180-181).

Items made	Clear	Clear w/Rose
Basket, applied handle, made from a celery vase	75.00	125.00
Bottle, water	40.00	85.00
Bowl, flat		
Open		
Belled, round		
5½"d	20.00	35.00
6½"d	20.00	35.00
7½"d	25.00	45.00
8½"d	30.00	55.00
10"d	35.00	65.00
Oblong		
8"	35.00	50.00
8½"	35.00	50.00
Rectangular		
6"	25.00	40.00
9"	30.00	45.00
Round		
5½"d	20.00	30.00
6½"d	20.00	30.00
7½"d	25.00	45.00
8½"d	30.00	55.00
9½"d	35.00	50.00
11"d	45.00	65.00
Waste	40.00	65.00

Items made	Clear	Clear w/Rose
Butter dish, covered		
Hotel size	65.00	125.00
Quarter Pound	45.00	90.00
Table size	65.00	125.00
Cake stand, high standard		
8½″d	65.00	90.00
9″d	65.00	90.00
10″d	65.00	100.00
Celery vase, flat, scalloped	55.00	75.00
Champagne	55.00	185.00
Compote, high standard		
Covered		
6″d	90.00	125.00
7″d	110.00	145.00
8″d	125.00	165.00
Open, deep bowl		
5½″d	25.00	40.00
6½″d	30.00	45.00
7½″d	30.00	45.00
8″d	40.00	55.00
8½″d	40.00	55.00
9″d	45.00	65.00
10″d	55.00	75.00
10¼″d	55.00	75.00
Cracker jar, covered, original Brittania or patterned lid (R)	150.00	225.00
Creamer		
Hotel size	30.00	50.00
Individual	15.00	35.00
Table size, tankard shape, 4½″h	30.00	50.00
Cruet, original stopper, 5 ounce	45.00	125.00
Custard cup	10.00	15.00
Dish, flat, open		
Oblong		
8″	25.00	45.00
9″	30.00	50.00
10″	35.00	55.00
11″	45.00	65.00
Oval		
Crimped rim		
6½″	20.00	35.00
8½″	25.00	45.00
Ledged rim, 5¼″	20.00	35.00
Plain rim		
5¼″	20.00	35.00
8½″	25.00	45.00
9½″	30.00	50.00
10″	35.00	55.00
Round		
Belled bowl		
6½″d	20.00	35.00
7½″d	20.00	35.00
8½″d	25.00	45.00
10″d	35.00	55.00
Flared bowl		
8½″d	25.00	45.00
9½″d	30.00	50.00
10″d	35.00	55.00
11″d	45.00	65.00

Items made	Clear	Clear w/Rose
Egg cup, single	40.00	60.00
Goblet, 6″h (straight or flared bowl)	75.00	95.00
Jelly, flat, handled, 5″	20.00	35.00
Lemonade, tall, handled	35.00	45.00
Mug, handled	30.00	50.00
Olive dish, round		
Handled, 5¼″	25.00	45.00
No handle, 5¼″	25.00	45.00
Tri-cornered, 5¾″	25.00	45.00
Pickle		
Castor, complete in original silver plate holder	125.00	200.00
Dish, 2½″ h. x 8½″l., crimped rim	25.00	45.00
Jar, true open	35.00	55.00
Pitcher		
Ice jug, 2 quart, applied handle	75.00	140.00
Milk, 1 quart	55.00	80.00
Tankard		
Large	75.00	125.00
Medium	65.00	110.00
Small	55.00	100.00
Water		
Child's miniature, 4⅛″h	30.00	45.00
½ gallon with ice lip	65.00	125.00
Plate, round		
4″d	30.00	40.00
5″d	35.00	45.00
6″d	35.00	45.00
8″d	40.00	55.00
Punch bowl, footed, 15″d	175.00	250.00
Punch bowl underplate	100.00	150.00
Relish tray	20.00	30.00
Rose bowl	25.00	65.00
Salt		
Dip		
Individual, oblong, flat	25.00	40.00
Master		
Oblong, flat	35.00	65.00
Round, flat	35.00	65.00
Shaker, original nickel or Brittania top		
Squatty, bulbous base	20.00	40.00
Tall, bulbous, original top	20.00	40.00
Sauce dish, round, flat		
Flared, belled rim		
4″d	10.00	22.00
4½″d	10.00	22.00
Straight-sided		
4″d	10.00	22.00
4½″d	10.00	22.00
Sherbert, footed, 3¼″h., 4¼″d	20.00	30.00
Spoonholder		
Hotel size, 4″h	30.00	65.00
Table size, 4″h	30.00	65.00
Sugar bowl, covered		
Hotel size, 7¼″h	55.00	85.00
Individual, oval, open, flat, scalloped rim	25.00	35.00
Table size, 7¼″h	55.00	85.00
Sugar shaker, original top	40.00	100.00

Items made	Clear	Clear w/Rose
Syrup pitcher, original silver plate, nickel or Brittania top		
7 ounce	65.00	135.00
10 ounce, 5½"h	65.00	165.00
Toothpick holder	25.00	85.00
Tray, water		
8½"d	75.00	110.00
10"d	85.00	125.00
Tumbler, pressed or ground base		
Child's miniature	10.00	20.00
Hotel	30.00	45.00
Water, table size, 4"h	30.00	45.00
Vase		
Bulbous base, tapered center with flared rim, 8"h	25.00	50.00
Cylindrical shape, pulled rim, 11"h	25.00	50.00
Straight		
5½"h	25.00	50.00
18"h	25.00	50.00
Wine	40.00	65.00

GARDEN OF EDEN

Creamer; high standard open compote; spoonholder.

AKA: Fish, Lotus, Lotus and Serpent [Metz], Lotus with Serpent, Turtle.

Non-flint. Maker unknown, ca. late 1870s, early 1880s.

Original color production: Clear. Items in Garden of Eden may be found with or without serpent. Handles are pressed.

Reproductions: None.

References: Bat-GAG (PP. 167, 169), Kam-3 (P. 58), Kam-7 (P. 12), Lee-VG (Pl. 73-A), Lind-HG (P. 222), McCn-PGP (Pl. 6), Mil-1 (Pl. 114), Mil-2 (Pl. 8), Mtz-1 (P. 76), Mtz-2 (P. 124), Stu-BP (P. 140), Swn-PG (PP. 80, 82), Uni-1 (P. 270), Wlkr-PGA (Fig. 8, Nos. 1, 38).

Items made	Clear	Items made	Clear
Butter dish, covered	65.00	Pitcher, water, $^{1}/_{2}$ gallon	90.00
Cake stand, high standard	55.00	Plate	
Compote, open, high standard, shallow		Oval, bread, handled, "Give Us This	
bowl, scalloped rim, 9"d	45.00	Day Our Daily Bread" center	40.00
Creamer		Round, 6"d., handled	20.00
Individual, $3^{1}/_{2}$"h	25.00	Relish dish, oval, flat	
Table size, 5"h	40.00	Handles	20.00
Egg cup, single	30.00	No handles	20.00
Goblet		Salt, master, open, footed	35.00
Plain stem	40.00	Sauce dish, round	
Serpent stem	85.00	Flat	10.00
Honey dish	10.00	Footed	15.00
Mug	35.00	Spoonholder	35.00
Pickle dish, oval	25.00	Sugar bowl, covered	65.00

GARFIELD DRAPE

Goblet (lady's); goblet (gentleman's); covered sugar bowl; covered butter; creamer.

AKA: Canadian Drape.

Non-flint. Attributed by Lee to Adams & Co., Pittsburgh, PA., and by Canadian researchers to Canadian manufacturer.

Original color production: Clear. Supposedly issued shortly after the death of President Garfield, September 19, 1881. The Canadian version has a longer and wider "drape" than American made items.

Reproductions: None.

References: Drep-ABC OG (P. 161), Enos-MPG (Chart-4), Hlms-BCA (P. 278), Kam-1 (P. 24), Kam/Wod-Vol.1 (P. 283), Kyes-Antiques 1938 (PP. 240, 167), Lee-EAPG (Pl. 98), Lind-HG (P. 310), Mrsh-SRG (P. 315), McCn-PGP (P. 345), Mil-1 (Pl. 133), Mtz-1(PP. 114-115), Mtz-2 (PP. 182-183), Oliv-AAG (P. 66), Spnc-ECG (P. 89), Spil-AEPG (P. 302), Spil-TBV (P. 88), Stev-ECG (P. 222), Stu-BP (P. 125), Uni-1 (P. 277), Uni-TCG (PP. 76-77), Uni/Wor-CHPGT (PP. 66-67), Wlkr-PGA (Fig. 8, No. 54).

Items made	Clear	Items made	Clear
Bowl, flat, open	25.00	Pickle dish, oval	20.00
Butter dish, covered, footed	60.00	Pitcher, bulbous, applied handle	
Cake stand, high standard, 9½"d	75.00	Milk, 1 quart	75.00
Celery vase, pedestaled, 8½"h	40.00	Water, 7"h., ½ gallon	100.00
Compote		Plate, bread, 11"d	
Covered		"Memorial portrait of Garfield"	65.00
High standard, 8"d	100.00	"We Mourn Our Nation's Loss"	
Low standard, 6"d	65.00	portrait	75.00
Open, high standard, 8½"d	40.00	"Star" center	35.00
Creamer		Relish tray, oval	15.00
Applied handle, 5½"h	45.00	Sauce dish, round	
Pressed handle, 5½"h	35.00	Flat, 3½"d	10.00
Goblet		Footed, 3½"d	12.00
Gentleman's	40.00	Spoonholder	30.00
Lady's (R)	55.00	Sugar bowl, covered	65.00
Honey dish, round, flat	15.00	Tumbler, water	
Lamp, oil, original burner and		Flat	35.00
chimney	90.00	Footed	45.00

GEORGIA States Series

High standard open compote 6"d (shallow bowl); cruet (n.o.s.)

OMN: U.S. Glass No. 15,076. AKA: Peacock Eye, Peacock Feather(s) [Lee].

Non-flint. Richards & Hartley Glass Co., Pittsburgh, PA. Reissued by the United States Glass Co. (pattern line No. 15,076) at Factory "E" (Richards & Hartley Glass Co., Pittsburgh, PA.) from 1902 to 1910. Advertised in 1902 as part of the "States Series", Georgia is illustrated in the United States Glass Co. ca. 1904 catalog, and the Baltimore Bargain House August 15, 1904 catalog No. 496.

Original color production: Clear. Blue or any other color is rare. Handles are pressed.

Reproductions: None.

References: Bros-TS (P. 28), Enos-MPG (Chart-6), Grow-WCG (Fig. 19), Hart/Cobb-SS (P.25), Hea-5 (PP. 13, 18), Kam-1 (PP. 77-78), Lee-EAPG (Pl. 106), McCn-PGP (P. 545), Mtz-1

(P. 220), Pet-Sal (P. 35), Pyne-PG (P. 156), Rev-APG (P. 314), Spil-AEPG (P. 321), Spil-TBV (PP. 57, 194), Thu-1 (P. 282).

Items made	Clear	Items made	Clear
Bowl, flat, open, round		6"d	25.00
5"d	20.00	7"d	30.00
6"d	20.00	8"d	35.00
7"d	20.00	9"d	45.00
8"d	25.00	10"d	50.00
Butter dish, covered		Creamer, $4^{1}/_{4}$"h	35.00
Quarter Pound	45.00	Cruet, original stopper, $8^{1}/_{4}$"h	55.00
Table size	55.00	Decanter, 14 ounce	55.00
Cake stand, high standard		Lamp, oil, original burner and	
$8^{1}/_{2}$"d	35.00	chimney	
9"d	35.00	Chamber, pedestaled, 7"h	150.00
10"d	45.00	Flat, ring handle, $5^{3}/_{4}$"h	65.00
11"d	45.00	Mug	35.00
Condiment set, salt/pepper with		Pickle dish	15.00
original glass stand	75.00	Pitcher, water, $^{1}/_{2}$ gallon	75.00
Celery		Plate, $5^{1}/_{4}$"d	15.00
Tray, boat shaped	35.00	Preserve dish, 8"l	10.00
Vase	35.00	Relish tray	10.00
Compote		Salt shaker, original top	35.00
Covered, high standard		Sauce dish, round, flat	
5"d., jelly	45.00	4"d	10.00
6"d	50.00	$4^{1}/_{2}$"d	10.00
7"d	55.00	Spoonholder	30.00
8"d	65.00	Sugar bowl, covered	45.00
Open, low standard		Syrup pitcher, original top, $6^{3}/_{4}$"h	65.00
Deep bowl, sweetmeat, 5"d	20.00	Tumbler, water, flat	25.00
Shallow bowl			
5"d., jelly	20.00		

Wine; water tray; wine tray; water pitcher.

OMN: Bellaire's No. 151, U.S. Glass No. 157. AKA: Bulls Eye and Spearhead [Metz & Millard], Bulls Eye Variation [Lee], Concave Circle, Excelsior.

Non-flint. Bellaire Goblet Co. (pattern line No. 151), Bellaire, OH. ca. 1889. Model Flint Glass Co. ca. 1891. Reissued by the United States Glass Co., Pittsburgh, PA. after 1891.

Original color production: Clear.

Reproductions: None.

References: Bond-AG (P. 18), Bros-TS (P. 45), Hea-5 (P. 18), Kam-2 (P. 101), Lee-VG (P. 139), McCn-PGP (P. 71), Mil-1 (Pl. 5), Mil-2 (Pl. 149), Mtz-1 (P. 208), Rev-APG (P. 71), Smth-FG (P. 52), Spil-AEPG (P. 322), Uni-1 (P. 105).

Items made	Clear:	Items made	Clear:
Bottle		Wine	50.00
Brandy, original patterned stopper		Goblet	35.00
12 ounce	55.00	Lamp, night, "Remmington", tall	
16 ounce	55.00	domed shade	125.00
22 ounce	55.00	Pitcher, pressed handle	
Perfume, original patterned stopper	25.00	Claret, 7"h	65.00
Bowl, open, flat, 8"d	25.00	Water, ½ gallon	75.00
Butter dish, covered	45.00	Relish tray	15.00
Cake stand, high standard	30.00	Sauce dish, round, flat, 4"d	8.00
Cheese dish, covered	45.00	Spoonholder, scalloped rim	30.00
Compote, high standard		Sugar bowl, covered, flat	60.00
Covered	75.00	Syrup, original nickel top	
Open		Large	65.00
Flared rim	40.00	Small	65.00
Scalloped-pointed rim	40.00	Tray, round	
Condiment set, cruet, salt/pepper		Water	45.00
shakers, mustard	85.00	Wine	35.00
Creamer, 4¾"h	30.00	Tumbler, water, flat	30.00
Cruet, original patterned stopper	45.00	Vase	
Decanter, original matching stopper		7"h	35.00
Claret	50.00	8"h	35.00

Items made	Clear:	Items made	Clear:
9"h	35.00	Wine	30.00

GONTERMAN

Low standard covered compote; water pitcher; celery vase.

OMN: Duncan No. 95.

Non-flint. George Duncan's Sons (pattern line No. 95), Pittsburgh, PA. ca. 1887-1890. Reviewed in the *Pottery and Glassware Reporter*, July 21, 1887.

Original color production: Acid finished body with amber stain. The main pattern design element of Gonterman consists of alternating clear and beaded panels with a horizontal band of ovals above. Most items are pedestaled with covered items having matching patterned finials. Handles are applied.

Reproductions: None.

References: Bred-EDG (PP. 96, 162), Mtz-1 (PP. 184-185), Mil-1 (Pl. 71), Uni-2 (P. 123).

Items made	Acid Finished w/Amber	Items made	Acid Finished w/Amber
Bowl		8"d	125.00
Covered, high standard		Open	
7"d	90.00	5"d	60.00
8"d	90.00	7"d	70.00
Open, low standard (fruit)		8"d	80.00
7"d	80.00	Creamer	110.00
8"d	80.00	Goblet (VR)	350.00+
Butter dish, covered	125.00	Honey, round, 3½"d	
Cake stand, high standard, 10"d	100.00	Flat	20.00
Celery vase, pedestaled, smooth rim	90.00	Footed	20.00
Compote, round, high standard		Pitcher	
Covered		Milk, 1 quart	135.00
5"d	100.00	Water, ½ gallon	200.00
7"d	110.00	Salt shaker, original top	65.00

Items made	Acid Finished w/Amber	Items made	Acid Finished w/Amber
Sauce dish, round		4″d	20.00
Flat		4½″d	20.00
4″d	20.00	Spoonholder	65.00
4½″d	20.00	Sugar bowl, covered	100.00
Footed			

GOOD LUCK

Spoonholder; 7″d. plate; doughnut stand; creamer; master salt.

AKA: Horseshoe, Prayer Mat, Prayer Rug.

Non-flint. Adams & Co., Pittsburgh, PA. ca. 1881. Possibly other factories. Designed by Samuel G. Vogeley.

Original color production: Clear. Finials and handles are in the shape of horseshoes. Handles on pitchers are pressed.

Reproductions: The Good Luck 10″ x 14″ platter has been reproduced in clear from a new mold from the early 1960s.

References: Bros-TS (P. 31), Grow-WCG (P. 213, Fig. 39-"7"), Kam-1 (P. 66), Kam/Wod-Vol.1 (P. 307), Lee-EAPG (Pl. 112), Mtz-1 (PP. 114-115), Mtz-2 (PP. 194-195), Mil-1 (Pl. 54), Inn-PG (P. 88), Oliv-AAG (P. 66), Rev-APG (P. 20), Uni-1 (PP. 138-139), Uni-TCG (PP. 112-113), Uni/Wor-CHPGT (P. 134), Swn-PG (P. 31), Stu-BP (P. 60), Wlkr-PGA (Fig. 8, No. 3).

Items made	Clear	Items made	Clear
Bowl, flat, oval		8″	200.00
Open		Round, flat, finger, open	85.00
5″ x 8″	40.00	Butter dish, covered	
5¾″ x 9¼″	45.00	Collared lid	85.00
6½″ x 10¼″	50.00	Plain lid	85.00
Covered		Cake plate	40.00
7″	150.00	Cake stand, high standard	

Items made	Clear	Items made	Clear
8"d	75.00	Water, ½ gallon	110.00
9"d	75.00	Plate	
10"d	85.00	Bread	
Celery		Double horseshoe handles,	
Dip, horseshoe shape, flat	75.00	14" x 10"	65.00
Vase		Single horseshoe handles	45.00
Knob stem	40.00	Dinner	
Plain stem	35.00	7"d	45.00
Cheese dish, covered, woman churning		7¼"d	45.00
in center	275.00	8¼"d	55.00
Compote, covered		10¼"d	60.00
High standard		Platter, oval, small	45.00
7½"d	65.00	Relish tray, 5" x 7"	15.00
8"d	75.00	Salt	
11"d	85.00	Individual, horseshoe shape, flat	20.00
Low standard		Master	
7½"d	45.00	Horseshoe shape, flat	90.00
8"d	45.00	Round, design from base to rim	
Creamer, 6½"h	35.00	(R)	125.00
Dish, oblong, flat		Sauce, round	
Covered, 8½", horseshoe finial	175.00	Flat	
Open, 6" x 9" x 2", vegetable	65.00	3¾"d	15.00
Doughnut stand, high standard	75.00	4"d	15.00
Goblet		4¼"d	15.00
Knob stem	35.00	Footed	
Plain stem	35.00	3¾"d	20.00
Marmalade jar, covered	125.00	4"d	20.00
Pickle dish	15.00	4¼"d	20.00
Pickle jar, covered	90.00	Spoonholder	35.00
Pitcher		Sugar bowl, covered	75.00
Milk, 1 quart	85.00	Wine (R)	200.00

GOOSEBERRY

Spoonholder; creamer; covered sugar (all milk white).

Non-flint. Manufacturer unknown. Shards have been found at the site of the Boston & Sandwich Glass Co., Sandwich, MA. and the Burlington Glass Works, Hamilton, Ontario, Canada.

Original color production: Clear, milk white, the main pattern design element being well-designed gooseberries and leaves against a solid background. Variations in bases indicate more than one source of manufacture.

Reproductions: The goblet and wine were first reproduced in the early 1960s in both clear and milk white.

References: Belnp-MG (P. 84), Drep-ABC OG (P. 153), Fer-YMG (PP. 38, 55), Kam-4 (PP. 66-67), Lee-EAPG (Pl. 166), McCn-PGP (Pl. 157), Mil-1 (Pl. 132), Mtz-1 (PP. 88-89), Uni/Wor-

Goblet; mug (applied handle). Both clear.

CHPGT (P. 135), Uni-1 (PP. 230-231), Uni/Wod-Vol.1 (P. 280), Wlkr-PGA (Fig. 8, Nos. 27, 28).

Items made	Clear	Milk White
Bowl, flat, open, master berry	25.00	45.00
Butter dish, covered	50.00	60.00
Cake stand, high standard	55.00	—
Compote, covered, high standard		
6"d	45.00	65.00
7"d	55.00	75.00
8"d	65.00	85.00
Creamer, 5"h	30.00	50.00
Goblet	35.00	45.00
Honey dish, covered	35.00	40.00
Lemonade glass, applied handle	35.00	—
Mug, applied handle	30.00	40.00
Pitcher, water, applied handle, ½ gallon	85.00	100.00
Sauce dish, round, flat	10.00	15.00
Spoonholder	25.00	30.00
Sugar bowl, covered	45.00	55.00
Syrup pitcher, original top	75.00	100.00
Tumbler, water, flat	35.00	40.00

Goblet; flat open bowl; covered sugar bowl; wine.

AKA: Cathedral [Lee].

Flint. Maker unknown. Attributed to the Union Glass Co., Somerville, MA. Shards have been found at the site of the Boston & Sandwich Glass Co., Sandwich, MA. ca. 1860.

Original color production: Clear. Handles are applied. Finials are conventional knobs.

Reproductions: None.

References: Bat-GPG (PP. 17, 20), Enos-MPG (Chart-5), Lee-EAPG (Pl. 58), Lind-HG (P. 213), McKrn-AG (Pl. 208), Mil-1 (Pl. 125), Oliv-AAG (P. 54), Uni-1 (P. 80).

Items made	Clear
Bowl, flat, open, scalloped rim	
7"d	70.00
8"d	70.00
Butter dish, covered	85.00
Castor set, complete	100.00
Celery vase	85.00
Champagne (R)	125.00
Compote	
Covered	
High standard	
7"d	110.00
8"d	125.00
Low standard, 8"d	100.00
Open	
High standard, 8"d	80.00
Low standard	

Items made	Clear
7"d	65.00
8"d	65.00
Cordial	100.00
Creamer	75.00
Egg cup	50.00
Goblet	
Plain base	55.00
Rayed base	65.00
Pickle dish, oval, 4¾" x 7"	20.00
Plate (R)	125.00
Salt, master, footed, open	60.00
Sauce dish, round, flat, 4"d	20.00
Spoonholder, pedestaled, scalloped rim	40.00
Sugar bowl, covered	85.00
Tumbler, water, flat	95.00
Wine	95.00

Covered butter dish (clear with ruby stain).

(OMN). AKA: Spearpoint Band [Kamm].

Non-flint. McKee-Jeannette Glass Company, Jeannette, PA. ca. 1904.

Original color production: Clear, clear with ruby stain, and a horizontal frosted band and gilt. Handles are applied and finials are pyramid shaped.

Reproductions: None.

References: Hea-1 (P. 41), Hea-7 (P. 43, Nos. 436-447), Kam-7 (P. 31), Stot-McKe (PP. 330, 343, 345).

Items made	Clear	Clear w/Color
Bowl		
Fruit, flat, open	45.00	100.00
Master berry, flat, open, scalloped rim	45.00	100.00
Vegetable, oblong, flat, scalloped rim	25.00	45.00
Butter dish, covered, flat, pyramid shaped finial	40.00	85.00
Celery vase, flat, scalloped rim	35.00	85.00
Compote, open, jelly, high standard, scalloped rim	15.00	55.00
Cordial.	20.00	35.00
Creamer, 4¼"h	25.00	45.00
Egg cup, footed.	15.00	35.00
Pitcher, water, ½ gallon	65.00	100.00
Relish tray.	15.00	25.00
Salt shaker, flat, tall, original top	15.00	35.00
Sauce dish, flat, round.	15.00	30.00
Spoonholder, flat, scalloped rim	15.00	45.00
Sugar bowl, covered	35.00	65.00
Toothpick holder, flat, scalloped rim	35.00	85.00
Tumbler, water, flat	20.00	30.00
Wine	15.00	30.00

Spoonholder; h.s. cake stand; flat covered butter.

OMN: New Grand. AKA: Diamond Medallion, Fine Cut and Diamond, Fine Cut Medallion.

Non-flint. Bryce, Higbee & Co., Pittsburgh, PA. ca. 1885. Attributed to the Diamond Glass Co., Ltd., Montreal, Quebec, Canada. Illustrated in the Bryce, Higbee & Co. catalog of 1885 as "Grand", and the National Merchandise Co. 1885 catalog.

Original color production: Clear. Clear with ruby stain or any other color is very rare.

Reproductions: None.

References: Kam-1 (P. 23), Kam-8 (Plts. 20-21), Kam-6 (Pl. 3), Kam/Wod-Vol.1 (P. 278), Lee-VG (Pl. 31, No. 2), McCn-PGP (P. 163), Mil-1 (Pl. 32), Mil-2 (Pl. 108), Mtz-2 (PP. 138-139), Pet-Sal (P. 127), Rev-APG (P. 92), Spnc-ECG (P. 95), Uni-1 9 (P. 315), Uni-TCG (P. 106), Uni/Wor-CHPGT (P. 112), Wlkr-APG (Fig. 8, No. 37).

Items made	Clear	Items made	Clear
Bowl		6"d	60.00
Covered		7"d	65.00
Flat, 6"d	30.00	7½"d	75.00
Low footed, 6"d	30.00	8"d	75.00
Open, low footed		Low standard	
6"d	20.00	6"d	60.00
7"d	20.00	7"d	65.00
Waste, collared base	30.00	8"d	75.00
Butter dish, covered		Open	
Flat, 5½"h., 6¼"d	35.00	High standard	
Footed, 6¼"d	45.00	6"d	25.00
Cake stand, high standard		7"d	25.00
8"d	30.00	8"d	30.00
8½"d	30.00	9"d	35.00
10"d	35.00	Low standard	
Celery vase, pedestaled	25.00	6"d	25.00
Compote		7"d	30.00
Covered		8"d	35.00
High standard		Cordial, 2"h	50.00
5½"d	60.00	Creamer, 5"h	25.00

Items made	Clear	Items made	Clear
Decanter, original stopper	85.00	Relish dish, oval, 7½″	10.00
Dish, oval, flat, open		Salt shaker, original top	25.00
7″	15.00	Sauce dish, round, 4″d	
9″	15.00	Flat, plain rim	10.00
Goblet		Footed, scalloped rim	10.00
Plain stem	25.00	Sherbert	15.00
Ring stem	25.00	Spoonholder	20.00
Mug	25.00	Sugar bowl, covered	
Pitcher, water, ½ gallon, applied		Plain rim	35.00
handle	40.00	Scalloped rim	35.00
Plate, scalloped rim		Syrup pitcher, original top	85.00
10″d	25.00	Tray, water, round	25.00
11″d	25.00	Wine	25.00

GRAPE AND FESTOON

Plate; goblet; celery vase; goblet w/shield variant; spoonholder.

OMN: Doyle's No. 25, Wreath.

Non-flint. The Boston & Sandwich Glass Co., Sandwich, MA. ca. 1880s. Doyle & Co., Pittsburgh, PA. Reissued by the United States Glass Co., Pittsburgh, PA. ca. 1891.

Original color production: Clear. Grape and Festoon appears in four variants: a) clear leaf, b) stippled leaf, c) veined leaf, and d) stippled grape. Finials on covered pieces are in the shape of acorns. Produced in several variants (Grape and Festoon-Stippled Leaf, Grape and Festoon-Clear Leaf, Grape and Festoon with American Shield), such items are not original to the pattern.

Reproductions: None.

References: Kam-1 (P. 10), Kam-7 (P. 114), Lee-EAPG (Pl. 63), McCn-PGP (P. 315), Mil-1 (Plts. 48, 51), Mil-2 (Pl. 56), Mtz-1 (PP. 78-79), Rev-APG (PP. 138, 314), Swn-PG (P. 70), Uni-1 (P. 224), Uni-2 (P. 83), Wlkr-PGA (Fig. 8, Nos. 18, 24, 38).

Items made	Clear	Items made	Clear
Bowl, flat, open, 6"d	25.00	Pickle tray, oval	10.00
Butter dish, covered	50.00	Pitcher, applied handle	
Celery vase	40.00	Milk, 1 quart	65.00
Compote, covered		Water, ½ gallon	85.00
High standard, 8"d	100.00	Plate, 6"d	25.00
Low standard	85.00	Relish tray, oval	10.00
Cordial	50.00	Salt, master, footed, open	20.00
Creamer, applied handles (2 styles) ...	45.00	Sauce dish, round, flat, 4"d	10.00
Egg cup, pedestaled (2 styles)	20.00	Spoonholder	35.00
Goblet	35.00	Sugar bowl, covered	50.00
Lamp, oil, 7½"h., complete with		Wine	45.00
original burner and chimney	65.00		

GRAPE BAND

Wine; pickle dish; goblet; master salt.

AKA: Ashburton with Grape Band, Early Grape Band, Grape Vine.

Flint. Bryce, Walker & Co., Pittsburgh, PA. ca. 1869. Non-flint by other factories. Designed and patented by John Bryce, October 19, 1869 for Bryce, Walker & Company (design patent No. 3,716).

Original color production: Clear, the main pattern design element consisting of a horizontal vine of grapes and leaves against a clear background. Handles are applied. Finials are grape bunches.

References: Belnp-MG (P. 85), Brn-SD (P. 53), Fer-YMG (P. 39), Kam-1 (P. 8), Lee-EAPG (Pl. 64), McCn-PGP (P. 319), Mil-1 (Pl. 51), Mil-OG (Pl. 263), Mtz-1 (PP. 82-83), Pet-GPP (PP. 54-55), Rev-APG (P. 81), Thur-1 (P. 95), Uni-1 (P. 244), Uni-2 (P. 84), Wlkr-PGA (Fig. 8, Nos. 7, 24, 34).

Items made	Flint	Non-flint
Butter dish, covered	75.00	50.00
Compote		
Covered		
High standard	—	50.00
Low standard	—	40.00
Open, high standard	—	25.00
Cordial	65.00	—
Creamer, applied handle	—	50.00
Egg cup, single, footed	—	20.00
Goblet	40.00	25.00
Pickle dish, scoop shape	—	15.00
Pitcher, water, ½ gallon	—	85.00
Plate, round, 6″d	—	20.00
Salt, master, footed, open	—	20.00
Spoonholder	—	30.00
Sugar bowl, covered	—	45.00
Tumbler, water, flat	35.00	20.00
Wine	35.00	25.00

GRASSHOPPER

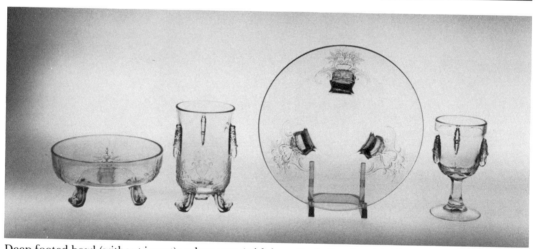

Deep footed bowl (without insect); celery vase (with insect); shallow bowl (without insect); goblet (with insect—reproduction).

AKA: Locust, Long Spear.

Non-flint. Maker unknown., ca. late 1870s—early 1880s.

Original color production: Clear. Amber, blue, vaseline or any other color is rare. Originally produced either flat or footed, Grasshopper can be found in three distinct variants: a) with insect, b) without insect, and c) with long spear.

Reproductions: The goblet in clear and color produced from a new mold is not original to the set.

References: Kam-1 (P. 89), Lee-VG (Pl. 38, No. 3), Mtz-1 (PP. 94-95), Mtz-2 (PP. 82-83), Spil-AEPG (P. 297), Kam-8 (P. 57), McCn-PGP (P. 21).

Items made	Amber	Clear
Bowl,		
Covered, low	55.00	35.00
Open, footed		
Deep	—	25.00
Shallow, flared rim	—	35.00
Butter dish, covered, 6¼″d	85.00	65.00
Celery vase	90.00	80.00
Compote, high standard, covered		
7″d	—	65.00
8½″d	—	75.00
Creamer, 5½″h	65.00	45.00
Marmalade jar, covered	—	125.00
Pickle dish	—	20.00
Pitcher, water, ½ gallon	125.00	75.00
Plate, footed, round		
8½″d	—	25.00
9″d	—	25.00
10½″d	—	25.00
Salt		
Shaker, original top (R)	—	35.00
Dip, individual	—	40.00
Sauce dish, round		
Flat	—	10.00
Footed	—	15.00
Spoonholder	75.00	65.00
Sugar bowl, covered		
Flat	70.00	50.00
Footed	80.00	65.00

HAIRPIN

Champagne; celery vase; goblet; handled whiskey tumbler.

AKA: Early Loop, Hairpin Plain, Hairpin with Rayed Base, Sandwich Loop.

Flint. The Boston & Sandwich Glass Co., Sandwich, MA. ca. 1850.

Original color production: Clear, milk white. Handles are applied, finials are in the shape of acorns.

Reproductions: None.

References: Belnp-MG (P. 136), Brn-SD (PP. 48-49), Cod-OS (Pl. 15), Drep-ABC OG (Pl. 150), Fer-YMG (P. 57), Kam-1 (P. 6), Lee-EAPG (P. 26), Lee-VG (P. 84, Pl. 31), Mil-1 (Pl. 3), Mil-2 (P. 45), Uni-1 (P. 25).

Items made	Clear	Milk White
Butter dish, covered	45.00	100.00
Celery vase	40.00	90.00
Champagne	50.00	125.00
Compote, high standard		
Covered		
Large	90.00	200.00
Small, jelly	75.00	175.00
Open	50.00	90.00
Creamer	45.00	100.00
Egg cup, pedestaled	30.00	65.00
Goblet, plain stem		
Plain base	40.00	85.00
Rayed base	40.00	85.00
Salt, master, covered, footed	85.00	175.00
Sauce dish, round, flat	15.00	20.00
Spoonholder	40.00	85.00
Sugar bowl, covered	95.00	200.00
Tumbler	30.00	65.00
Whiskey, handled, flat	50.00	125.00
Wine	35.00	90.00

HALEY'S COMET

Tankard water pitcher; wine.

OMN: Etruria. AKA: Halley's Comet.

Non-flint. Model Flint Glass Co., Findlay, OH. ca. 1891. The National Glass Co., Pittsburgh, PA. ca. 1891 through 1902.

Original color production: Clear (plain or copper wheel engraved). Clear with ruby stain or any other color is rare.

Reproductions: None.

References: Bar-RS (Pl. 14), Bond-AG (PP. 50-51), Meas/Smth-FG (P. 121), Hea-7 (P. 112), Herr-GG (Fig. 331), Mil-1 (Pl. 164), Mtz-1 (P. 208), Smth-FG (P. 86), Uni-1 (P. 63).

Items made	Clear	Items made	Clear
		8"d	30.00
Bowl		Creamer	35.00
Open, flat		Cruet, original stopper	35.00
7"d	25.00	Cup, punch	15.00
8"d	25.00	Dish, candy	20.00
Covered, 3-legged, 4"d	30.00	Goblet	40.00
Butter dish, covered	80.00	Pitcher	
Cake stand, high standard	75.00	Milk, 1 quart	65.00
Celery vase	45.00	Water, $\frac{1}{2}$ gallon	85.00
Compote, high standard		Relish tray	25.00
Covered		Salt shaker, original top	25.00
6"d	50.00	Sauce dish, round, 4"d	10.00
7"d	60.00	Spoonholder	35.00
8"d	65.00	Sugar bowl, covered	65.00
10"d	75.00	Tray, water, round, 8"d	55.00
Open		Tumbler, water, flat	25.00
6"d	25.00	Wine	30.00
7"d	30.00		

HAMILTON

Spoonholder; creamer; flat covered butter dish; footed egg cup.

OMN: Cape Cod's No. 64. AKA: Cape Cod.

Flint. Cape Cod Glass Co., Sandwich, MA. ca. 1860s. Shards have been found at the site of the Boston & Sandwich Glass Co., Sandwich, MA.

Original color production: Clear. Deep blue or any other color is rare. Identical to Hamilton with Leaf with the replacement of a cross-hatched diamond motif instead of a horizontal molded vine of leaves ground to produce a frosted finish. Handles are applied and crimped. Bases are patterned. Finials are pseudo acorn shapes similar to those found on common Bellflower examples.

Reproductions: None.

References: Bat-GPG (PP. 17, 19), Brn-SD (P. 55), Bros-TS (P. 837), Cod-OS (P. 21), Drep-ABC OG (P. 169), Enos-MPG (Chart-4), Lee-EAPG (Pl. 56), McCn-PGP (P. 98), McKrn-AG (Plts. 207, 208), Mil-1 (Pl. 117), Mtz-1 (P. 26), Pap-GAG (P. 191), Spil-AEPG (P. 271), Uni-1 (P. 314).

Items made	Clear	Items made	Clear
Butter dish, covered, flat	85.00	Pitcher, water, applied handle, ½ gallon	200.00
Castor set, original pewter standard, 4 bottles	175.00	Sauce dish, round, flat	
Celery vase, pedestaled, scalloped rim	60.00	Plain rim	
Compote		4"d	10.00
Covered, high standard, 6"d	65.00	4⁷⁄₈"d	10.00
Open		Scalloped rim	
High standard, Hamilton bowl, Bellflower base	90.00	4"d	10.00
Low standard, scalloped rim	45.00	5"d	10.00
Creamer		Spoonholder, pedestaled	
Applied handle	55.00	Plain rim	35.00
Pressed handle	40.00	Scalloped rim	35.00
Decanter, original patterned stopper	145.00	Sugar bowl, covered, pedestaled	65.00
Egg cup, single, footed, 3½"h	40.00	Syrup, applied handle, original top ...	225.00
Goblet	45.00	Tumbler	
Hat, made from tumbler mold	125.00	Water, flat	85.00
Honey dish	15.00	Whiskey, flat, applied handle (R) ...	110.00
Master, salt, footed, smooth rim, open	35.00	Wine	85.00

HAMILTON WITH LEAF

Handled whiskey; goblet.

AKA: Hamilton with Vine.

Wine; water tumbler.

Flint. Cape Cod Glass Co., Sandwich, MA. ca. 1860s.

Original color production: Clear, clear with "machine ground" leaf. Identical to Hamilton with the replacement of a horizontal molded vine of leaves, instead of cross-hatched diamond blocks, ground to produce a frosted finish against a clear background. Handles are applied and crimped. Finials are pseudo acorn shapes similar to those found on common Bellflower examples.

Reproductions: None.

References: Brn-SD (P. 55), Cod-OS (Pl. 21), Kam-4 (P. 18), Lee-EAPG (P. 177), Lee-SG (P. 537), Lee-VG (P. 18), McCn-PGP (Pl. 196), McKrn-AG (Pl. 208), Mil-1 (Pl. 147), Mtz-1 (P. 26), Mtz-2 (PP. 48-49), Oliv-AAG (P. 54), Uni-2 (PP. 90-91), Wlkr-PGA (Fig. 15, No. 114).

Items made	Clear	Clear/ Frosted
Butter dish, covered, flat	85.00	110.00
Celery vase	50.00	65.00
Compote		
Covered, high standard	100.00	150.00
Open		
High standard	40.00	60.00
Low standard	40.00	60.00
Creamer		
Applied handle	60.00	75.00
Pressed handle	55.00	70.00
Egg cup, single, pedestaled	45.00	65.00
Goblet	50.00	65.00
Hat (made from tumbler mold)	120.00	150.00+
Honey dish, flat, round	15.00	20.00
Lamp, oil, stand, original burner and chimney	125.00	150.00
Salt, master, footed, open	45.00	55.00
Sauce dish, flat, round, 4″	10.00	20.00
Spoonholder	45.00	65.00
Sugar bowl, covered	65.00	90.00
Tumbler, flat,		
Bar	65.00	85.00
Water	85.00	100.00
Whiskey, applied handle	90.00	125.00
Wine	75.00	95.00

Creamer; celery vase; goblet; wine; cordial.

OMN: O'Hara No. 90. AKA: Pennsylvania, O'Hara's. Pennsylvania Hand.

Non-flint. O'Hara Glass Company (pattern line No. 90), Pittsburgh, PA. ca. 1880.

Original color production: Clear. Finials on covered pieces are a clinched hand holding a bar, the main pattern design element being alternating horizontal clear and diamond point filled panels. Most items are footed.

Reproductions: None.

References: Drep-ABC OG (P. 142), Enos-MPG (Chart-4), Hart/Cobb-SS (59), Lee-EAPG (Pl. 107, No. 4), McCn-PGP (P. 375), Mil-1 (Pl. 120), Mtz-1 (P. 162), Mtz-2 (P. 194), Pet-Sal (P. 132), Rev-APG (P. 271), Uni-1 (P. 125), Wlkr-PGA (Fig. 8, No. 27).

Items made	Clear	Items made	Clear
Bowl, flat, open, round		8"d	30.00
7"d	30.00	9"d	30.00
8"d	30.00	10"d	35.00
9"d	30.00	Goblet	50.00
10"d	35.00	Honey dish, round, flat	10.00
Butter dish, covered	75.00	Marmalade jar, covered	65.00
Cake stand, high standard	40.00	Mug, handled	40.00
Celery vase	40.00	Pickle tray	20.00
Compote		Pitcher, water, ½ gallon, pressed	
Covered, high standard		handle	75.00
7"d.	85.00	Platter	35.00
8"d.	95.00	Sauce dish, round	
Open		Flat, 4"d	10.00
High standard, 7¾"d	45.00	Footed, 4"d	15.00
Low standard, 9"d	25.00	Spoonholder	30.00
Cordial, 3½"h	75.00	Sugar bowl, covered	75.00
Creamer, pressed handle	45.00	Syrup pitcher, original top	135.00
Dish, oval, flat, open		Tray, water,	55.00
7"d	30.00	Wine	55.00

High standard cake stand; covered sugar bowl.

Creamer; celery vase.

OMN. AKA: Block with Stars, Blockhouse, Hanover Star.

Non-flint. Richards & Hartley Glass Co., Tarentum, PA. ca. 1888. Reissued by the United States Glass Co., Pittsburgh, PA. after 1891.

Original color production: Amber, blue, vaseline, clear.

Reproductions: None.

References: Hea-5 (P. 40, No. 104), Kam-1 (P. 113), Lee-EAPG (Pl. 54, No. 40), Lee-VG (P. 170), Luc-TG (PP. 208-211), McCn-PGP (P. 485), Mil-1 (Pl. 133), Mtz-1 (P. 156), Mtz-2 (P. 156),Rev-APG (PP. 286-287), Spil-AEPG (P. 307), Uni-1 (PP. 104-105), Wlkr-PGA (Fig. 155, No. 114).

Items made	Clear	Amber	Blue
Bowl, open, flat, round			
7″d	20.00	30.00	35.00
8″d	20.00	30.00	35.00
10″d	20.00	35.00	40.00
Butter dish, covered	40.00	75.00	90.00
Cake stand, high standard, 10″d	40.00	65.00	85.00
Celery vase	25.00	40.00	60.00
Cheese dish, covered, 10″d	50.00	95.00	125.00
Compote			
Covered, high standard	45.00	90.00	125.00
Open			
High standard			
7″d	40.00	50.00	65.00
8″d	40.00	50.00	65.00
Low standard			
7″d	40.00	50.00	65.00
8″d	40.00	50.00	65.00
Creamer, pressed handle	30.00	45.00	60.00
Cruet, original stopper	20.00	—	—
Goblet	25.00	55.00	65.00
Mug, pressed handle			
Large	20.00	45.00	45.00
Small	15.00	40.00	40.00
Pitcher, pressed handle			
Milk, 1 quart	50.00	85.00	100.00
Water, ½ gallon	50.00	85.00	100.00
Plate, round			
4″d	20.00	25.00	30.00
6″d	20.00	30.00	35.00
10″d	25.00	40.00	55.00
Platter	30.00	55.00	65.00
Puff box, original glass lid	10.00	—	—
Sauce dish, round, footed	10.00	15.00	20.00
Spoonholder	25.00	35.00	40.00
Sugar bowl, covered	45.00	55.00	65.00
Tumbler, water, flat	25.00	30.00	40.00
Wine	25.00	45.00	55.00

Spillholder.

Whale oil lamp.

OMN: Harp. AKA: Lyre.

Flint. Bryce Brothers, Pittsburgh, PA. ca. 1859-1860. Possibly the Boston & Sandwich Glass Co., Sandwich, MA. at an earlier date. Illustrated in the McKee Brothers 1859 catalog, variants of the Harp pattern have an additional "oval" alternating with the "Harp" design in the panels.

Original color production: Clear. Canary-yellow or any other color is very rare.

Reproductions: None.

References: Bat-GPG (PP. 7, 9), Brn-SD (P. 53), Cod-OS (Pl. 24), Drep-ABC OG (P. 153), Enos-MPG (Chart-6), Grow-WCG (P. 75, No. 7-"2"), Inn/Spil-McKe (PP. 18, 22), Lee-EAPG (Pl. 13), Lee-SG (P. 537), Lee-VG (Pl. 26, No. 1), McCn-PGP (P. 383), Mc-Krn-AG (P. 400),

Mtz-1 (P. 14), Mil-1 (Pl. 37), Rev-APG (PP. 80, 238), Spil-AEPG (P. 444), Uni-1 (P. 259), Wlkr-PGA (Fig. 8, Nos. 24, 34)

Items made	Clear	Items made	Clear
Bowl, covered, flat, 6½"d	150.00	Lamp, oil	
Butter dish, covered	150.00	Handled, double wick with snuffers	125.00
Compote, covered, low standard, 6"d		Stand	200.00
(termed sweetmeat)	200.00	Salt, master, open, footed, 3⅓"h	75.00
Goblet (R)		Sauce, flat, round	20.00
Flared bowl	1000.00	Spillholder	85.00
Straight bowl	1000.00	Spoonholder, hexagonal	95.00
Honey dish, flat, round	20.00	Sweetmeat jar, covered	200.00

HARTLEY

Celery vase; water pitcher; milk pitcher.

OMN: Hartley. AKA: Daisy and Button with Oval Panels, Panelled Diamond Cut and Fan, U.S. Glass No. 900.

Non-flint. Richards & Hartley Glass Co., Tarentum, PA. ca. 1887. Reissued by the United States Glass Co., (pattern line No. 900), Pittsburgh, PA. ca. 1891.

Original color production: Amber, blue, vaseline, clear (plain or copper wheel engraved with such etchings as No. 86 "Fern & Berry".

Reproductions: None.

References: Grow-WCG (Fig. 18), Hea-5 (P. 110, Plts. A-C), Kam-1 (PP. 69-70), Lee-VG (Pl. 42, No. 3), Luc-TG (PP. 254-256), McCn-PGP (P. 149), Mtz-1 (P. 222), Mtz-2 (PP. 136-137), Rev-APG (P. 228), Stu-BP (P. 58), Uni-1 (P. 156), Wlkr-PGA (Fig. 8, Nos. 15, 38).

Items made	Amber	Blue	Canary	Clear
Bowl, open, round				
Flat				
6"d	25.00	30.00	30.00	15.00
7"d	25.00	30.00	30.00	15.00

Items made	Amber	Blue	Canary	Clear
8″d	30.00	40.00	40.00	20.00
9″d	30.00	40.00	40.00	20.00
Footed, 7″d	30.00	40.00	40.00	20.00
Bread plate, tri-lobed	30.00	40.00	40.00	20.00
Butter dish, covered	55.00	65.00	65.00	45.00
Cake stand, high standard, 10″d	45.00	55.00	55.00	40.00
Celery vase	35.00	45.00	45.00	30.00
Compote				
Covered				
High standard				
7″d	55.00	75.00	75.00	40.00
8″d	65.00	85.00	85.00	50.00
Low standard, 7¾″d	55.00	75.00	75.00	40.00
Open, high standard				
7″d	35.00	45.00	45.00	25.00
8″d	35.00	45.00	45.00	25.00
Creamer	35.00	40.00	40.00	30.00
Dish, center piece, flat	45.00	50.00	50.00	25.00
Goblet	40.00	45.00	45.00	30.00
Pitcher, pressed handle				
Milk, 1 quart	85.00	95.00	95.00	85.00
Water, ½ gallon	95.00	100.00	100.00	95.00
Plate, dinner	45.00	50.00	50.00	35.00
Relish tray	20.00	20.00	20.00	15.00
Sauce dish, flat, round, 4″d	15.00	20.00	20.00	10.00
Spoonholder	35.00	35.00	35.00	25.00
Sugar bowl, covered	45.00	55.00	55.00	35.00
Tumbler	35.00	35.00	35.00	20.00
Wine	45.00	45.00	45.00	30.00

HARVARD YARD

Salt shaker.

OMN: Harvard. AKA: Tarentum's Harvard.

Non-flint. Tarentum Glass Co., Tarentum, PA. ca. 1896.

Original color production: Clear (plain or with gilt). Emerald green, pink, clear with ruby stain or any other color is scarce.

Reproductions: None.

References: Bat-GPG (PP. 98-99), Hea-4 (P. 54), Hea-7 (P. 125), Hea-6 (P. 95), Hea-OS (P. 135, No. 2538), Kam-6 (P. 38), Luc-TG (PP. 300-306), Mil-2 (Pl. 89), Mtz-2 (P. 1040), Pet-GPP (PP. 187-188), Pet-Sal (P. 162-"S"), Rev-APG (P. 238), Wlkr-PGA (Fig 8, Nos. 2, 57).

Items made	Clear	Items made	Clear
Bowl, round (various sizes)	20.00	Salt	
Butter dish, covered	30.00	Dip, individual, 1¾"d	15.00
Cake stand, high standard	30.00	Shaker, original top	15.00
Condiment set (complete)	45.00	Sauce dish, flat, round	5.00
Cordial	25.00	Spoonholder	20.00
Creamer	15.00	Sugar bowl, covered	25.00
Egg cup, single, footed	15.00	Toothpick holder	15.00
Goblet	25.00	Tray, oval, flat	35.00
Jug	45.00	Tumbler, water, flat	20.00
Pitcher, water, ½ gallon	40.00	Wine	15.00
Plate, round, 10"d	15.00		

HEART WITH THUMBPRINT

Cruet; celery vase; h.s. true open compote; covered butter dish.

OMN: Tarentum's Hartford. AKA: Bulls Eye in Heart, Columbia, Columbian, Heart and Thumbprint.

Non-flint. Tarentum Glass Company, Tarentum, PA. ca. 1898 to 1906. Illustrated in the Baltimore Bargain House August, 1903 (catalog No. 479), December, 1903 (catalog No. 483), and August 15, 1904 (catalog No. 496).

Original color production: Clear, clear with ruby stain, emerald green (plain or with gilt). Nile green, cobalt blue, custard or any other color is experimental and rare. The main design element consists of clear hearts with bulls eye centers, the heart with bulls eye motif being carried to finials and the stems of footed pieces. Handles are applied.

Reproductions: None.

References: Byd-GC (P. 26), Enos-MPG (Chart-3), Hea-4 (PP. 56, 66), Hea-7 (P. 125), Kam-2 (P. 102), Kam-5 (P. 42), Kam-6 (Pl. 51), Lee-VG (Pl. 23). Luc-TG (P. 320), Mil-1 (Pl. 63), Mtz-1 (P. 214), Oliv-AAG (P. 66), Pet-GPP (P. 188), Pet-Sal (P. 30), Rev-APG (P. 286), Spil-AEPG (P. 334), Spil-TBV (P. 222), Stu-BP (P. 23), Uni-1 (P. 54), Wlkr-PGA (Fig. 8, No. 41).

Items made	Clear	Clear w/Ruby	Green
Banana boat, flat with turned up sides			
Large	85.00	125.00	—
Small	75.00	110.00	—
Bottle			
Barber	100.00	—	—
Cologne	100.00	—	—
Bowl, open, flat, scalloped rim			
Round			
6″d	35.00	65.00	95.00
9″d	40.00	75.00	100.00
Square			
7″	35.00	85.00	100.00
9½″	40.00	95.00	125.00
10″	40.00	95.00	125.00
Finger	45.00	65.00	85.00
Butter dish, covered, 8″d, flanged base	85.00	135.00	175.00
Cake stand, high standard, 9″d	125.00	185.00	—
Carafe	100.00	150.00	—
Card tray, flat, up-turned sides	20.00	40.00	55.00
Celery vase, flat, scalloped rim	65.00	90.00	—
Compote, open, high standard, scalloped rim			
7½″d	125.00	175.00	—
8½″d	145.00	195.00	—
Cordial, 3″h	125.00	150.00	175.00
Creamer			
Individual	20.00	35.00	45.00
Table size	65.00	90.00	125.00
Cruet, patterned or faceted stopper	85.00	—	—
Goblet, bulbous, 3 hearts with thumbprint stem	55.00	110.00	125.00
Hair receiver, original metal lid	65.00	85.00	100.00
Ice bucket, scalloped rim	65.00	—	—
Lamp, oil, original burner and chimney			
Finger	65.00	—	135.00
Stand, 8″h	50.00	—	175.00
Mustard pot, original silver plate cover	90.00	—	110.00
Pitcher, water, bulbous, applied handle	200.00	—	—
Plate, round			
6″d	25.00	35.00	45.00
10″d	55.00	75.00	90.00
Powder jar, original silver plate cover	65.00	—	—
Punch cup	20.00	35.00	40.00
Rose bowl			
Large	85.00	95.00	—
Small	65.00	75.00	—
Sauce dish, round, ruffled rim (many)	15.00	30.00	35.00
Spoonholder	55.00	75.00	90.00
Sugar bowl			
Individual, true open with handles	25.00	35.00	35.00
Table size, covered	85.00	—	125.00
Syrup, with original attached lid			
Large	85.00	—	—
Small	65.00	—	—

Items made	Clear	Clear w/Ruby	Green
Tray, condiment, 8¼" x 4¼"	35.00	55.00	65.00
Tumbler, water, flat	45.00	65.00	85.00
Vase			
6"h	35.00	55.00	65.00
10"h	65.00	85.00	100.00
Wine	45.00	125.00	150.00

HEAVY GOTHIC

Covered butter and 5½" h.s. open compote (both clear); sugar shaker (clear w/ruby stain).

Spoonholder; covered sugar bowl; creamer. All clear.

OMN: U.S. Glass No. 15,014. AKA: Whitton.

Non-flint. The Columbia Glass Co., Findlay, OH. ca. 1890. The United States Glass Co. (pattern line no. 15,014), Pittsburgh, PA. ca. 1891 to as late as 1899. Illustrated in the Butler Brothers 1899 catalog, and the United States Glass Co. 1892-1893, 1898, and 1904 catalogs.

Original color production: Clear, clear with ruby stain. Green or any other color is rare. Pieces are flat with pressed handles.

Reproductions: None.

References: Bar-RS (Pl. 10), Hea-5 (P. 131, Pl. B), Hea-7 (Figs. 88-89), Kam-2 (P. 109), Meas/Smth-FG (PP. 34-36), Mil-2 (Pl. 133), Mtz-2 (P. 144), Pet-Sal (P. 132), Rev-APG (PP. 125-127), Smth-FG (PP. 73, 106), Uni-1 (P. 105), Wlkr-PGA (Fig. 15, No. 120).

Items made	Clear	Clear w/Ruby
Bowl, flat		
Covered, round		
5"d	30.00	65.00
6"d	30.00	65.00
7"d	40.00	75.00
8"d	40.00	75.00
Open		
Belled		
5½"d	15.00	25.00
6½"d	15.00	25.00
7½"d	20.00	35.00
9"d	20.00	35.00
Flared		
5½"d..	15.00	25.00
6½"d	15.00	25.00
7½"d	20.00	35.00
8½"d	20.00	35.00
10"d	30.00	45.00
Butter dish, covered, flat, 5¼"d, flanged base	40.00	125.00
Cake stand, high standard		
9"d	30.00	100.00
10"d	30.00	100.00
Celery vase	25.00	125.00
Claret	35.00	65.00
Compote, high standard, round		
Covered		
5"d	30.00	90.00
6"d	35.00	90.00
7"d	35.00	110.00
8"d	45.00	125.00
Open		
Belled bowl		
5½"d	15.00	40.00
6½"d	20.00	40.00
7½"d	25.00	50.00
8½"d	25.00	50.00
9"d	25.00	60.00
Flared bowl		
5½"d	15.00	35.00
6½"d	20.00	45.00
7½"d	25.00	55.00
8½"d	25.00	55.00
Creamer, 4¼"h	25.00	50.00
Dish, oblong, flat, open		
7"l	10.00	20.00
8"l	10.00	20.00
9"l	15.00	25.00
Goblet, 6¼"h	25.00	50.00
Honey dish, covered, low footed, with underplate (with or without notched lid)		

Items made	Clear	Clear w/Ruby
4"d	45.00	90.00
5"d	45.00	90.00
Lamp, oil, stand, original burner and chimney	90.00	—
Pickle jar, covered	50.00	125.00
Pitcher, water, ½ gallon	45.00	250.00
Salt shaker, tall, original top	15.00	45.00
Sauce dish		
Flat, scalloped rim		
Belled bowl		
4"d	8.00	15.00
4½"d	10.00	20.00
5"d	10.00	20.00
Scalloped bowl		
4"d	8.00	15.00
4½"d	10.00	20.00
5"d	10.00	20.00
Footed		
4"d	10.00	20.00
4½"d	10.00	20.00
5"d	10.00	20.00
Spoonholder	20.00	55.00
Sugar bowl, covered		
Breakfast size	25.00	45.00
Table size	35.00	65.00
Sugar shaker, original top	40.00	200.00
Syrup pitcher, original top	50.00	175.00
Tumbler, water, flat	20.00	35.00
Wine	15.00	35.00

HENRIETTA

Tumbler; individual creamer.

OMN: Columbia Glass, No. 14. AKA: Big Block, Diamond Block, Hexagon Block.

Non-flint. The Columbia Glass Co., Findlay, OH. (pattern line No. 14) ca. 1889. Reissued by the United States Glass Co., Pittsburgh, PA. at Factory "J" (Columbia Glass Co., Findlay, OH.) ca. 1891-1892. Illustrated in the United States Glass Co. ca. 1891 Factory "J" (Columbia Glass Co., Findlay, OH.) catalog.

Original color production: Clear (plain or copper wheel engraved). Clear with ruby stain, emerald green or any other color is rare. The lamp was introduced into the Henrietta line in July, 1890. Often confused with Hexagon Block and Big Block, Henrietta has clear hexagonal buttons.

Reproductions: None.

References: Bar-RS (Pl. 12), Hea-OPG (PP. 80-81), Hea-3 (P. 70), Hea-5 (P. 128), Hea-6 (P. 90), Kam-1 (P. 110), Kam-5 (P. 124), Lee-VG (Pl. 70, No. 4), McCn-PGP (P. 223), Meas/Smth-FG (PP. 31-32), Mtz-1 (P. 210), Pet-Sal (P. 163), Rev-APG (PP. 20, 125, 314), Smth-FG (PP. 4, 54), Wlkr-PGA (Fig. 15, No. 124).

Items made	Clear	Items made	Clear
Bowl, open		Jar, covered, tall, marked "Confection"	35.00
Rectangular, 5″ x 8″	20.00	Lamp, oil	50.00
Rose	20.00	Mustard jar, original nickel plate top	35.00
Round, deep		Pickle jar, covered	45.00
7″d	20.00	Pitcher, water, applied handle	
8″d	20.00	Bulbous, $\frac{1}{2}$ gallon	45.00
9″d	22.00	Tankard	45.00
Butter dish, covered, $5\frac{1}{2}$″h	30.00	Plate, bread, oval	18.00
Cake stand, high standard, 10″d	40.00	Salt	
Castor set, complete with 2 bottles	50.00	Dip	
Celery		Individual	10.00
Tray, 8″l	20.00	Master, round, open	15.00
Vase	20.00	Shaker, original top	
Compote, open, high standard,		Hotel size	25.00
scalloped rim	25.00	Table size	15.00
Cracker jar, covered	35.00	Sauce dish, flat, round, $4\frac{1}{2}$″d	10.00
Creamer		Saucer	12.00
Individual	15.00	Shade, electric lamp	30.00
Table size	20.00	Spoonholder	20.00
Cruet, original stopper	25.00	Sugar bowl, covered, handled	30.00
Cup, custard, footed, handled	10.00	Sugar shaker, original nickel plate top	35.00
Dish, open		Syrup pitcher, original top	40.00
Bone, oval.	15.00	Tumbler, water, $3\frac{7}{8}$″h., $\frac{1}{2}$ pint	20.00
Bon bon	15.00	Vase	
Oblong		5″h	25.00
7″	12.00	7″h	25.00
8″	12.00	9″h	30.00
Olive, shallow	15.00		

HEXAGON BLOCK

Goblet (clear); tankard water pitcher (clear/ruby, etched); tumbler (clear/ruby, etched).

OMN: Hobb's No. 335. AKA: Henrietta [Barret].

Non-flint. Hobbs, Brockunier & Co. (pattern line No. 335), Wheeling, WV. ca. 1889. Reissued by the United States Glass Co., Pittsburgh, PA. after the 1891 merger. Reviewed in the February 4, 1891 issue of *China, Glass and Lamps,* and illustrated in the undated United States Glass Co. Factory "H" catalog.

Original color production: Clear, clear with amber or ruby stain. Plain or etched (originally termed "Gold Etching"), conventional etchings being Fern and Berry (engraving No. 364), and Bird and Flower. Most items have scalloped, circular feet; handles are applied. Rims are either plain or point and scalloped.

Reproductions: None.

References: Bar-RS (Pl. 12), Hea-3 (PP. 26, 70), Hea-5 (P. 126), Hea-OPG (P. 81), Pet-Sal (P. 30-"T"), Rev-APG (P. 193).

Items made	Clear	Clear with Amber/ Ruby
Bowl, round, open, flat		
Berry or vegetable		
Deep bowl, point and scallop rim		
7"d	20.00	35.00
8"d	20.00	35.00
9"d	25.00	40.00
Shallow bowl, design covers entire surface, large scalloped rim without points		
7"d	20.00	35.00
8"d	20.00	35.00
9"d	25.00	45.00
Finger, round, point and scallop rim	20.00	40.00
Butter dish, covered, flat, flanged base	35.00	125.00
Celery vase, footed	25.00	75.00
Compote		
Covered, high standard, smooth rim		

Items made	Clear	Clear with Amber/ Ruby
Deep bowl, smooth rim		
7"d	45.00	90.00
8"d	55.00	110.00
Saucer bowl, scalloped rim		
8"d	45.00	90.00
9"d	55.00	110.00
Open, high standard, point and scallop rim		
Deep bowl		
7"d	25.00	45.00
8"d	30.00	55.00
Saucer bowl		
8"d	30.00	55.00
9"d	35.00	65.00
Creamer, applied handle, footed	25.00	65.00
Cup, custard, footed, applied handle	15.00	25.00
Goblet	25.00	45.00
Pickle jar, covered, footed, smooth rim	40.00	85.00
Pitcher, footed, applied handle		
Milk, 1 quart	75.00	135.00
Water		
Bulbous, 1/2 gallon	65.00	145.00
Tankard, 3 pint	65.00	135.00
Salt shaker, footed, original top	15.00	35.00
Sauce dish, flat, round, point and scallop rim		
4"d	10.00	20.00
4 1/2"d	10.00	20.00
Spoonholder, footed, smooth rim	20.00	45.00
Sugar bowl, covered, footed	30.00	95.00
Syrup pitcher, original top attached to pressed handle	45.00	250.00
Tumbler, flat, water	15.00	35.00

HIDALGO

Flat sauce dish; cruet (o.s.); water pitcher; syrup.

OMN: Adams No. 5. AKA: Frosted Waffle, Waffle-Red Top.

Non-flint. Adams & Co. (pattern line No. 5), Pittsburgh, PA. ca. 1880. Reissued by the United States Glass Co., Pittsburgh, PA. ca. 1891. Illustrated in the ca. 1891 United States Glass Co. catalog.

Original color production: Clear with machine ground panels (plain or copper wheel engraved). Clear with amber stain, clear with ruby stain or any other color is rare. The main pattern design of Hidalgo is a plain waffle-like design against a clear ground. Handles are applied.

Reproductions: None.

References: Bar-RS (Pl. 14), Hart-AG (P. 89), Hea-3 (P. 83), Hea-5 (PP. 68-69), Hea-7 (P. 129), Kam-3 (P. 56), Lee-VG (Plts. 49, 74), McCn-PGP (Pl. 220), Mil-1 (Pl.176), Mtz-1 (P. 168), Oliv-AAG (P. 66), Pet-Sal (P. 31), Rev-APG (P. 20).

Items made	Clear/Frosted Panel	Items made	Clear/Frosted Panel
Bowl, open, square		Creamer	40.00
Berry, master, 10"sq	20.00	Cruet, original bulbous stopper	65.00
Finger or waste	25.00	Cup & saucer, the set	35.00
Butter dish, covered	50.00	Goblet	30.00
Celery vase, flat	20.00	Pickle dish, boat shaped	10.00
Compote		Pitcher	
Covered		Milk, 1 quart	45.00
High standard		Water, ½ gallon, applied rope	
6"d	55.00	handle	40.00
7½"d	65.00	Plate, bread, cupped edges, 10"sq	60.00
10"d	75.00	Salt	
Low standard		Master, square	25.00
6"	55.00	Shaker, original top	25.00
7½"	65.00	Sauce dish, flat, square with tab handle	10.00
Open		Spoonholder, flat	25.00
High standard		Sugar bowl, covered, flat	40.00
6"d	40.00	Sugar shaker, original top	45.00
7½"d	45.00	Syrup pitcher, original top	65.00
10"d	55.00	Tray, water	55.00
11"d	60.00	Tumbler, water, flat	25.00

Creamer; goblet; champagne.

AKA: Banded Diamond Point, Diamond Point with Panels [Lee].

Flint. The Boston & Sandwich Glass Co., Sandwich, MA. ca. late 1850s.

Original color production: Clear, the main pattern design element being fine diamond point below clear, horizontal panels. Handles are applied.

Reproductions: None.

References: Lee-EAPG (Plt. 153, No. 11), Mil-1 (Pl. 7), Mtz-1 (PP. 28-29), Rev-APG (PP. 261-262), Uni-1 (P. 131), Uni-2 (P. 53), Lee-VG (P. 54, Plt. 20).

Items made	Clear	Items made	Clear
Butter dish, covered	85.00	Spoonholder	35.00
Celery vase	65.00	Sugar bowl, covered	75.00
Champagne	65.00	Sweetmeat, covered, high standard	85.00
Creamer	75.00	Tumbler	
Egg cup, single, footed	35.00	Flat, water	45.00
Goblet	65.00	Footed, whiskey	55.00
Salt, master, open, footed	35.00	Wine	65.00

HOBBS' BLOCK

Goblet, spoonholder, creamer (all clear); goblet (frosted/amber).

OMN: Hobb's, Brockunier and Co. No. 330. AKA: Divided Squares [Metz].

Non-flint. Hobbs, Brockunier & Co. (pattern line No. 330), Wheeling, WV. ca. 1888. Reissued by the United States Glass Co., Pittsburgh, PA. ca. 1891. Illustrated in the Hobbs, Brockunier and Co. 1891 catalog.

Original color production: Clear, clear with amber stain, clear with acid finish, clear with acid finish and amber stain. Opaque blue, opaque white or any other color is scarce. Most pieces are oval in shape. Finials are faceted and handles are applied. Pattern may be "starred" or plain.

Reproductions: Several.

References: Hea-GC Vol. 3 (P. 57, Fig. 80), Hea-3 (P. 55), Hea-5 (P. 19), Hea-6 (P. 30, Fig. 172), Kam-3 (PP. 95-96), McCn-PGP (P. 487), Mtz-2 (PP. 148-149), Pet-Sal (P. 23), Rev-APG (P. 183), Uni-2 (P. 159).

Items made	Clear	Clear/ Amber	Frosted/ Amber
Bottle, water	45.00	65.00	85.00
Bowl, flat, scalloped rim, open			
Finger, round, flat, scalloped rim	25.00	35.00	45.00
Oval			
7"d	25.00	35.00	45.00
8"d	25.00	35.00	45.00
9"d	30.00	40.00	45.00
10"d	30.00	40.00	45.00
Butter dish, covered, flat	35.00	55.00	75.00
Celery tray, boat shape, flat	25.00	45.00	65.00
Creamer, oval, flat, applied handle	25.00	35.00	45.00
Cruet, bulbous, original stopper	50.00	100.00	155.00
Goblet	35.00	100.00	125.00
Pitcher, tankard, water, applied handle, ½ gallon	40.00	85.00	125.00
Salt shaker, tall, original top	20.00	30.00	35.00
Sauce dish, flat, oval, scalloped rim, 4½"	10.00	15.00	20.00
Spoonholder, flat	25.00	30.00	35.00

Items made	Clear	Clear/Amber	Frosted/Amber
Sugar bowl, covered, flat	35.00	45.00	55.00
Syrup pitcher, original top	55.00	100.00	175.00
Tumbler, water, flat	15.00	20.00	30.00

HOLLY

Water tumbler; covered bowl; water pitcher; covered butter dish.

Non-flint, ca. 1860s to early 1870s. Shards have been found at the site of the Boston & Sandwich Glass Co., Sandwich, MA.

Original color production: Clear, the main pattern design element being sprays of holly and berries against a clear background. Finials are well defined acorns. Handles are applied. Opal or any other color is very rare.

Reproductions: None.

References: Kam-8 (P. 5), Kam/Wod-Vol.1 (P. 316), Lee-EAPG (Pl. 116), Lee-SG (P. 538), McCn-PGP (P. 433), Mil-1 (Pl. 83), Mtz-1 (PP. 74-75), Mtz-2 (PP. 192-193), Uni-2 (P. 75), Wlkr-PGA (Fig. 15, No. 130).

Items made	Clear	Items made	Clear
Bowl, covered, round		Salt	
Flat	125.00	Individual	45.00
Low standard, 8″d	150.00	Footed, round, open	50.00
Butter dish, covered, flat	150.00	Sauce dish, flat, round, 4″d	20.00
Cake stand, high standard, 11″d	125.00	Spoonholder, pedestaled, scalloped rim	65.00
Celery vase, pedestaled, scalloped rim	65.00	Sugar bowl, covered	
Compote, covered		Flat	125.00
High standard, 8″d	165.00	Pedestaled	125.00
Low standard, 8½″d	165.00	Syrup pitcher (R), original top	150.00
Creamer, footed, applied handle	125.00	Tumbler, water	
Egg cup, single, footed, smooth rim	65.00	Flat	125.00
Goblet	100.00	Footed	125.00
Pickle dish, oval	30.00	Wine	125.00
Pitcher, water, bulbous, circular foot	185.00		

HONEYCOMB

Footed tumbler; goblet (etched); celery vase; water pitcher; spoonholder (frosted/etched).

OMN: Bellaire No. 40. Cape Cod No. 96 [Cape Cod Glass Co.]. Central No. 136. Cincinnati [McKee Glass Co.]. Doyle's No. 500. New York, Cincinnati [J.B. Lyon & Co.]. New York, Vernon [New England Glass Co.]. New York, Cincinnati Honeycomb [United States Glass Co.]. O'Hara No. 3. AKA: Midget New York, Honeycomb External, Thousand Faces.

Flint, non-flint. Bakewell, Pears & Co., Pittsburgh, PA. ca. 1875. Bellaire Goblet Co., Bellaire, OH. ca. 1889-1890. Doyle & Co., (pattern line No. 500), Pittsburgh, PA. ca. 1880s. Boston Silver & Glass Co. ca. 1869, East Cambridge, MA. Gillinder & Sons, Philadelphia, PA. ca. 1865. Grierson & Co., Pittsburgh, PA. ca. 1875. J.B. Lyon & Co., Pittsburgh, PA. McKee Brothers (stemmed items only), Pittsburgh, PA. ca. 1880. New England Glass Co., East Cambridge, MA. O'Hara Glass Co., Pittsburgh, PA. United States Glass Co., Pittsburgh, PA. (Doyle's pattern line No. 500) ca. 1891. Illustrated in the catalogs of Adams & Co. ca. 1872. Bakewell, Pears & Co. ca. 1875. Bellaire Glass Co. ca. 1889-1890. Central Glass Co. ca. 1876-1881. King, Son & Co. ca. 1875. Grierson & Co. ca. 1875. The United States Glass Co. ca. 1891.

Original color production: Clear (plain or copper wheel engraved). Amber, apple green, blue, emerald green, opaque white, opaque green, pink, firey opalescent or any other color is exceedingly rare in flint. Produced by numerous concerns, Honeycomb was produced in two major variants: [New England Glass Co.]: New York (plain upper $\frac{1}{3}$ of bowl covered with the design. Vernon (all over design). Cincinnati (all over design). Variants of Honeycomb include Four-Row Honeycomb, Honeycomb with Diamond, Looped Band Honeycomb Band, Honeycomb Band, Honeycomb with Pillar, and Stretched Honeycomb.

Reproductions: None in flint.

References: Grow-WCG (Fig. 26), Hea-1 (P. 21), Hea-5 (P. 52), Hea-OS (P. 41, No. 0404), Inn-EGP (PP. 341-342, Plt. 363), Kam-6 (P. 13), Lee-EAPG (Plt. 60, No. 3), McKrn-AG (Pl. 205, No. 7), Mtz-1 (P. 45), Mtz-2 (P. 34), Oliv-AAG (P. 68), Pet-GPP (PP. 110-111), Rev-APG (PP. 76-77), Spil-AEPG (P. 252), Spil-TBV (P. 24), Stev-ECG (P. 183), Swn-PG (P. 13), Uni/Wor-CHPGT (P. 143), Uni-1 (PP. 41, 51), Wat-PG (Fig. 4), Wlkr-PGA (Fig. 15, No. 229).

Items made	Flint	Non-flint
Ale		
New York		
Large (No. 1)	50.00	—
Medium	50.00	—
Pony	50.00	—
Small (No. 2)	50.00	—
8″h., knob stem	50.00	25.00
Bottle		
Barber	45.00	25.00
Bitter (New York)	45.00	—
Castor	45.00	—
Catsup (New York)	25.00	—
Pepper or saloon (New York)	30.00	—
Water (New York) with tumble up	65.00	—
Bowl		
Covered, round		
Collared base, Brittania or Tin lid		
6″d	55.00	—
7″d	65.00	—
8″d	75.00	—
9″d	85.00	—
Flat, original glass lid		
5½″d	55.00	—
6″d.	55.00	—
7″d	65.00	—
8″d	75.00	—
Open, flat		
Oval, 7¼″, dated "May 11, 1869"	90.00	—
Round		
Collared base		
Deep bowl		
6″d	35.00	—
7″d	40.00	—
8″d	45.00	—
9″d	50.00	—
Saucer bowl		
7″d	40.00	—
8″d	45.00	—
9″d	50.00	—
10″d	50.00	—
Flat, deep bowl		
5″d	30.00	—
6″d	35.00	—
7″d	40.00	—
8″d	45.00	—
Finger, round, deep bowl	55.00	25.00
Butter dish, covered, 6¼″d	65.00	45.00
Butter pat	35.00	20.00
Cake stand, high standard, 11¼″d	85.00	45.00
Candlestick		
No. 2 size	150.00	—
No. 3 size	150.00	—
Celery vase, pedestaled		
Scalloped rim	45.00	25.00
Smooth rim	45.00	25.00
Champagne	45.00	35.00
Claret	35.00	—
Compote, round		
Covered		

Items made	Flint	Non-flint
High standard		
Deep bowl		
6"d	90.00	45.00
7"d	90.00	45.00
8"d	110.00	55.00
9"d	110.00	55.00
10"d	125.00	65.00
Saucer bowl		
6"d	90.00	—
7"d	90.00	—
8"d	110.00	—
Low standard, saucer bowl		
6"d	65.00	—
7"d	65.00	—
8"d	75.00	—
Open		
High standard		
Deep bowl		
6"d	35.00	25.00
7"d	35.00	25.00
8"d	40.00	30.00
9"d	40.00	30.00
10"d	45.00	35.00
Saucer bowl		
6"d	35.00	25.00
7"d	35.00	25.00
8"d	40.00	30.00
Low standard		
Deep bowl		
6"d	35.00	25.00
7"d	35.00	25.00
8"d	40.00	30.00
9"d	40.00	30.00
10"d	45.00	35.00
Saucer bowl		
6"d	35.00	25.00
7"d	35.00	25.00
8"d	40.00	30.00
Cordial		
3"h. (R)	65.00	—
3½"h., knob stem	35.00	30.00
Creamer, applied or pressed handle	55.00	20.00
Cup		
Custard, footed, applied handle	65.00	—
Punch	—	15.00
Decanter		
Bar lip		
Pint	55.00	—
Quart	75.00	—
Original honeycomb stopper		
Pint	85.00	65.00
Quart	110.00	85.00
Dish, flat		
Oval, open		
7"	20.00	10.00
8"	20.00	10.00
9"	25.00	15.00
10"	25.00	15.00
Round, covered		

Items made	Flint	Non-flint
5½"d	45.00	30.00
6"	55.00	30.00
7"	65.00	40.00
8"	75.00	40.00
Egg cup, single, footed		
Flared	20.00	15.00
Straight-sided	20.00	20.00
Goblet	25.00	15.00
Honey dish, round, flat		
3"d	10.00	15.00
3½"d	15.00	20.00
Lamp, oil, original burner and chimney		
All glass	—	90.00
Glass font, marble base	—	110.00
Mug		
½ pint	25.00	15.00
Beer	25.00	15.00
Lemonade, footed, applied handle	35.00	—
Pony	30.00	—
Pickle jar, covered	90.00	65.00
Pitcher, applied or pressed handle		
Milk, 1 quart	85.00	65.00
Water, bulbous, ½ gallon		
Dated handle, "Pat. 1865"	125.00	—
Plain handle, ½ gallon	100.00	65.00
3 pint	110.00	65.00
Plate, round		
6"d	—	20.00
7"d	—	25.00
Pomade jar, covered	50.00	20.00
Relish dish	30.00	20.00
Salt		
Dip		
Individual		
Oblong	15.00	10.00
Round	15.00	10.00
Master, footed		
Covered	65.00	—
Open, round, flat	25.00	15.00
Salt shaker, original top	—	35.00
Sauce dish, flat, round, 4"d	10.00	5.00
Spillholder	35.00	20.00
Spoonholder, scalloped, pedestaled	35.00	25.00
Sugar bowl, covered, pedestaled	75.00	45.00
Syrup, original top		
½ pint	200.00	—
1 pint	235.00	100.00
3 pint	250.00	—
Quart	275.00	—
Tumbler		
½ pint	45.00	—
⅓ pint	45.00	—
Gill	45.00	—
Bar	35.00	—
Lemonade	55.00	—
Water		
Flat	40.00	—
Footed	45.00	—
Whiskey, applied handle	125.00	—

Items made	Flint	Non-flint
Twine holder		
No. 1	125.00+	—
No. 2	125.00+	—
Vase		
7½"h	45.00	—
10½"h	75.00	—
Wine	35.00	15.00

HORN OF PLENTY

Wine; goblet; champagne.

Creamer; handled whiskey tumbler.

OMN: Comet. AKA: Peacock Tail.

Flint, non-flint. Bryce, McKee & Co., Pittsburgh, PA. ca. 1850s. McKee & Brothers, Pittsburgh, PA. ca. 1850-1860. Shards have been found at the site of the Boston & Sandwich

Glass Co., Sandwich, MA. ca. 1860s-1870s. Illustrated in an undated McKee & Brothers catalog as "Comet" and the 1859-1860, 1864 & 1868 catalogs.

Original color production: Clear. Canary-yellow, milk white, brilliant blue, amber, clear edge in color, amethyst, or any other in flint is rare. Handles are applied.

Reproductions: Reissued by the L.G. Wright Glass Co., New Martinsville, WV. (distributed by Jennings Red Barn, New Martinsville, WV. and Carl Forslund, Grand Rapids, MI.), and the Fostoria Glass Co., Fostoria, OH., the Horn of Plenty goblet and tumbler were first reproduced ca. 1938 in both clear and milk white from new molds. Each has been continually reproduced to the present time by numerous concerns, the Fostoria Glass Co., Fostoria, OH. marking goblets with the company's name in script embossed under the foot. Both a look alike hat and creamer (produced from the tumbler mold and not original to the set), were produced ca. 1938-1940. The tall stand oil lamp with metal connector has been reissued in amethyst, amber, blue, clear and milk white. Look-alikes, issued in non-flint, are smaller in proportion and lighter in weight than the originals and lack the distinct clarity of design.

References: Bat-GPG (PP. 25, 27), Drep-ABC OG (PP. 213, 217), Enos-MPG (Chart-5), Grow-WCG (P. 79, Fig. 42-"10"), Inn/Spil-McKe (PP. 16, 18, 23, 55), Kam-4 (P. 52), Lee-EAPG (P. 143, Plts. 47-48), Lee-VG (Plts. 1, 3), Lee-SG (P. 513), Lind-HG (P. 518), Mag-FIEF (P. 11, Fig. 10), McKrn-AG (PP. 400, 404), Mil-1 (Pl. 118), Mil-2 (P. 156), Mtz-1 (P. 12), Mtz-2 (PP. 190-191), Nortn-PG (P. 111), Oliv-AAG (P. 54), Rev-APG (PP. 237-238), Schwtz-AG (P. 120), Spil-AEPG (PP. 258-260), Spil-TBV (PP. 56, 146-147), Stot-McKe Gls (P. 42), Uni-1 (P. 43), Uni-2 (P. 220), Wlkr-PGA (Fig. 8, Nos. 18, 23, 25).

Items made	Clear	Items made	Clear
Bottle		6¼"d	110.00
Pepper sauce, original pewter top	200.00	7"d	125.00
Medicine, applied lip		7¼"d	125.00
4¼"h	150.00	8"d	145.00
6"h	150.00	8¼"d	145.00
7⅛"h	175.00	9"d	155.00
8⅜"h	175.00	9¼"d	155.00
10⅜"h	200.00	10"d	175.00
Bowl, open, round		10¼"d	175.00
Flat		Low standard	
7⅛"d	85.00	6"d	85.00
8½"d	95.00	6¼"d	85.00
Footed, 8½"d	110.00	7"d	90.00
Butter dish, covered, flat		7¼"d	90.00
Acorn finial	125.00	8"d	95.00
Washington head finial (R)	450.00	8¼"d	95.00
Conventional finial, 6"d	125.00	9"d	100.00
Butter pat, flat	25.00	9¼"d	100.00
Cake stand, high standard	450.00	10"d	110.00
Celery vase, pedestaled, scalloped rim	175.00	10¼"d	110.00
Champagne, 5¼"h	150.00	Oval, high standard, open, scalloped	
Claret, 4⅞"h	175.00	rim, patterned base, 6⁶/₁₆"h., 10"l.,	
Compote		7¹/₁₆"w	250.00
Round		Cordial	125.00
Covered		Creamer	
High standard		Applied handle	
6"d	225.00	Bulbous, 5½"h	225.00
6¼"d	225.00	Tall, straight-sided, 6⁹/₁₆"h	225.00
Open		Pressed handle, 7"	175.00
High standard		Decanter, original stopper	
6"d	110.00	Pint	150.00

Items made	Clear	Items made	Clear
Quart	100.00	Milk, 1 quart (R)	650.00
Half gallon	175.00	Plate, round, scalloped rim	
Dish, flat		6"d	100.00
Oblong, covered, 6½" x 4"	250.00	6½"d	100.00
Oval, open		Relish tray, 7"l x 5"w	45.00
7"	55.00	Salt, master, oval, flat, scalloped rim	
8"	65.00	open, 1¼"h., 2⅜"w	75.00
8½"	65.00	Sauce dish, flat, round, scalloped edge,	
9"	75.00	rounded corner	
10"	85.00	5"d	25.00
11½"	95.00	5¼"d	25.00
Egg cup, pedestaled		6"d	25.00
Flared rim	45.00	Shot glass, 3"h	100.00
Straight-sided	45.00	Spillholder	65.00
Goblet, knob stem	75.00	Spoonholder	45.00
Honey dish, round, plain scalloped		Sugar bowl, covered	125.00
rim, 3¼"d	20.00	Tumbler, flat	
Lamp		Bar	85.00
All glass, hexagonal stem	175.00	Water	85.00
Glass font, brass stem, marble base	150.00	Whiskey	
Mug, small, applied handle, 3"h. (R)	200.00	Applied handle	125.00
Pickle dish, oval, 7" x 5"	45.00	Handleless	100.00
Pitcher, applied handle		Wine	125.00
Water, ½ gallon	550.00		

HORSESHOE STEM

Creamer; h.s. covered compote; celery vase; goblet (frosted bowl); goblet.

Non-flint. O'Hara Glass Co., Ltd., Pittsburgh, PA. ca. 1880. Design and patent attributed by Revi to Joseph Anderson, O'Hara Glass Co. superintendent, July 6, 1880.

Original color production: Clear, clear with acid finish (plain or copper wheel engraved). Horseshoe Stem is an exceedingly plain pattern, the major design element being "horseshoe shaped" stems and finials. Bases are flat and either plain or rayed, plain domed bases being less common. Handles are pressed, suggestive of half horseshoes.

Reproductions: None.

References: Mil-2 (Pl. 166), Mtz-1 (P. 114), Pet-GPP (P. 85), Rev-APG (PP. 271, 274, 276), Uni-1 (P. 316).

Items made	Clear or Clear/ Frosted	Items made	Clear or Clear/ Frosted
Cake stand, high standard, 8″d	65.00	Milk, 1 quart	90.00
Celery vase, smooth rim	40.00	Water, ½ gallon	110.00
Compote, covered, low standard	90.00	Sauce dish, round, footed	15.00
Creamer	65.00	Spoonholder	35.00
Goblet	75.00	Sugar bowl, covered	70.00
Pitcher		Tumbler	55.00

HUBER

Champagne; cordial.

OMN: Cape Cod No. 22, Central's No. 139. AKA: Flaring Huber, Straight Huber.

Flint, non-flint. New England Glass Co., Cambridge, MA. ca. 1860. McKee & Brothers, Pittsburgh, PA. ca. 1860s. Bakewell-Pears, Cape Cod Glass Co., George A. Duncan & Sons, Richards & Hartley, King Son & Co., J.B. Lyon & Co., the United States Glass Co., possibly others. Illustrated in the 1868 New England Glass Co. catalog.

Original color production: Clear (plain or copper wheel engraved). Unlike Flute, Huber's simple pattern consists of vertical, slightly convex arched panels. Produced by numerous concerns for many years, variations appear in the treatment of finials, standards and bases.

Reproductions: None.

References: Drep-ABC OG (P. 173), Enos-MPG (Chart-6), Inn-PG (PP. 306-308), Inn/Spil-McKe (PP. 174, 178), Kam-4 (P. 56), Krs-EDG (P. 206), Lee-EAPG (P. 49, Pl. 11), Luc-TG (PP. 183-184), Mil-1 (Plts. 21, 38), Mtz-1 (P. 34), Oliv-AAG (P. 66), Pap-GAG (P. 188), Pear CAT (P. 6), Pet-GPP (P. 113), Pyne-PG (PP. 18-20), Rev-APG (P. 252), Stot-McKe (PP. 70, 72), Uni-1 (P. 16), Wat-CG (P. 93), Wlkr-PGA (Fig. 8, No. 54).

Items made	Clear	Items made	Clear
Ale glass	25.00	8″d	40.00
Bottle, bitters	40.00	Low standard	
Bowl, flat		Covered	
Covered, round		Shallow bowl	
Medium (originally termed the "preserve")		6″d	55.00
		7″d	65.00
6″d	35.00	8″d	65.00
7″d	40.00	Open	
Shallow		Deep bowl, scalloped rim	
6″d	35.00	6″d	35.00
7″d	40.00	7″d	40.00
8″d	45.00	8″d	45.00
Open		9″d	50.00
Oval, medium bowl, smooth rim		10″d	55.00
6″	20.00	Shallow bowl, smooth rim	
7″	20.00	6″d	30.00
8″	20.00	7″d	35.00
9″	25.00	8″d	40.00
10″	25.00	Cordial	
Round		Hotel, barrel shaped bowl	35.00
Medium bowl, smooth rim (originally termed the "preserve")		Table size, straight-sided bowl	30.00
		Creamer, footed, pressed handle	50.00
		Custard cup, footed, applied handle	50.00
6″d	20.00	Decanter, bar	
7″d	20.00	Applied heavy bar lip	
Shallow bowl, smooth rim		Pint	45.00
6″d	20.00	Quart	55.00
7″d	20.00	Original patterned stopper	
8″d	20.00	Pint	55.00
Celery vase, footed, smooth rim	35.00	Quart	65.00
Champagne		Egg cup, single, footed	30.00
Hotel, barrel shaped bowl	30.00	Glass, jelly, long slender bowl, short foot	20.00
Table size, straight-sided bowl	25.00		
Compote		Goblet	
High standard		Gentleman's, straight-sided bowl, thick stem	20.00
Covered			
Medium bowl (originally termed the "preserve")		Hotel, barrel shaped bowl	20.00
		Lady's, straight-sided bowl, thin stem	20.00
6″d	55.00	Honey dish, round, flat, 3½″d	15.00
7″d	65.00	Jug	
Shallow bowl		Quart	45.00
6″d	55.00	3 pint	65.00
7″d	65.00	Mug, pressed handle	
8″d	65.00	Beer	
Open		1½ pint	30.00
Deep bowl, scalloped rim		Tall beer	35.00
6″d	35.00	Pony	
7″d	40.00	Large, pressed handle	30.00
8″d	45.00	Small, applied handle	25.00
9″d	50.00	Pitcher, tall, applied handle, low circular foot	
10″d	55.00		
Medium bowl, smooth rim (originally termed the "preserve")		Quart	95.00
		3 pints	125.00
		Plate, round, smooth rim	
6″d	30.00	6″d	15.00
7″d	35.00	7″d	20.00
Shallow bowl, smooth rim		Salt, master	
6″d	30.00	Individual	15.00
7″d	35.00	Footed, open, smooth rim	15.00

Items made	Clear
Sauce dish, round, flat, 4"d., smooth rim	15.00
Spoonholder, smooth rim	
Large	25.00
Small	25.00
Sugar bowl, covered, footed	55.00
Tumbler	
Gill	20.00
Lemonade (small pony beer mug without handle)	20.00

Items made	Clear
½ pint	
Short	20.00
Tall	20.00
Taper	
Bar	20.00
Short	20.00
Tall	20.00
Wine	
Hotel, barrel shaped bowl	20.00
Table size, straight sided bowl	15.00

HUMMINGBIRD

Creamer (clear); spoonholder (blue); water pitcher (blue); celery vase (amber); goblet (canary).

AKA: Bird and Fern, Fern and Bird, Flying Robin, Hummingbird and Fern, Thunder Bird.

Non-flint. Maker unknown. ca. 1880s.

Original color production: Amber, blue, canary-yellow, clear.

Reproductions: None.

References: Kam-4 (P. 25), Lee-VG (Pl. 35, No. 1), Mil-1 (Pl. 101), Mil-OG (Pl. 146), Mtz-1 (P. 92), Uni-1 (PP. 186-187).

Items made	Amber	Blue	Canary	Clear
Bowl, waste, 5¼"d	—	—	—	35.00
Butter dish, covered, flat	110.00	110.00	85.00	65.00
Celery vase	95.00	95.00	75.00	50.00
Compote, open, high standard	95.00	95.00	75.00	50.00
Creamer, footed, 5½"h	75.00	75.00	65.00	45.00
Goblet	55.00	65.00	75.00	50.00
Pitcher				
Milk, 1 quart	65.00	95.00	85.00	55.00
Water, ½ gallon	125.00	150.00	100.00	90.00
Sauce dish, round				

Items made	Amber	Blue	Canary	Clear
Flat	20.00	25.00	25.00	15.00
Footed	25.00	30.00	30.00	20.00
Spoonholder	40.00	75.00	65.00	35.00
Sugar bowl, covered	100.00	100.00	100.00	65.00
Tray, water, round	150.00	125.00	125.00	65.00
Tumbler, water, flat	75.00	75.00	75.00	45.00
Wine	—	—	—	55.00

ICICLE

Creamer; covered sugar bowl; covered butter dish; spoonholder.

AKA: Single Icicle.

Flint. Bakewell, Pears and Co., Pittsburgh, PA. ca. 1874. Designed and patented by Washington Beck (design patent No. 7,755) September 15, 1874. Illustrated in the Bakewell, Pears & Co. ca. 1878 catalog.

Original color production: Clear, milk white. Any other color would be very rare. The main pattern design element consists of clear, vertical prisms suggestive of "icicles" against a clear background. Feet are low and circular and handles are applied.

Reproductions: None.

References: Inn-PG (P. 348), Lee-EAPG (P. 48, Plts. 19-20), Oliv-AAG (P. 69), Pet-GPP (PP. 40-41), Rev-APG (PP. 45, 50), Thu-1 (P. 91), Wlkr-PGA (Fig. 15, No. 134).

Items made	Clear	Milk White
Butter dish, covered		
Flat, plain rim	65.00	100.00
Footed, flanged rim	85.00	125.00
Compote		
Covered, high standard		
6"d	75.00	150.00
8"d	100.00	175.00
Open		
High standard		

Items made	Clear	Milk White
6"d	40.00	65.00
8"d	60.00	85.00
Low standard		
6"d	35.00	50.00
8"d	50.00	75.00
Creamer, footed, applied handle	85.00	125.00
Dish, open, oval, flat		
7"	20.00	35.00
8"	20.00	35.00
9"	20.00	40.00
Goblet	60.00	85.00
Honey dish, flat, round, 3½"d (originally termed the "individual butter")	20.00	35.00
Lamp, 9"h., complete with original burner	100.00	185.00
Pickle scoop, tapered at one end	20.00	25.00
Pitcher, water, ½ gallon, applied handle	200.00	400.00
Salt, master, open	20.00	35.00
Sauce dish, flat, round, 4"d	15.00	20.00
Spoonholder, footed, scalloped rim	35.00	60.00
Sugar bowl, covered	80.00	100.00

ILLINOIS States Series

Cruet (n.o.s.); tankard water pitcher (emerald green w/silver plate rim); water tumbler.

OMN: U.S. Glass No. 15,052. AKA: Clarissa, Star of the East [Batty].

Non-flint. The United States Glass Co. (pattern line No. 15,052), Pittsburgh, PA. at Factory "G" (Gillinder & Sons, Greensburg, PA.) and "P" (Doyle & Co., Pittsburgh, PA.) ca. 1897. Illustrated in the United States Glass Co. 1898 and 1904 catalogs, and the August 8, 1906 Butler Brothers catalog.

Original color production: Clear. Clear with ruby stain, emerald green or any other color is scarce. Produced in both a hotel and table set. Most forms are square in shape. Handles are either applied or pressed.

Reproductions: The L.E. Smith Glass Co., Mt. Pleasant/Greensburg, PA. reproduced from new molds the covered butter dish in both clear and colors. New items appear "blurred" and dull, lacking the crisp impression and clarity of the original metal.

References: Bat-GPG (PP. 215-218), Hart/Cobb-SS/Cob (P. 30), Hea-5 (P. 40, No. 102), Hea-7 (P. 132), Hea-OS (P. 37, No. 298), Hea-TPS (PP. 75, 84), McCn-PGP (P. 259), Migh-TPS (Pl. 3), Pet-Sal (P. 163-"U"), Pyne-PG (P. 141), Thu-1 (P. 285), Uni-1 (P. 234), Uni-2 (P. 234), Wlkr-PGA (Fig. 8, Nos. 14, 57).

Items made	Clear	Items made	Clear
Basket, applied handle, 11½"h	100.00	Pickle	
Bon bon dish, high standard, open		Dish, rectangular, flat, 7¼"l	20.00
5"d	30.00	Jar, matching cover, square	55.00
8"d	40.00	Tray, rectangular, 7½"l	25.00
Bottle, oil	25.00	Pitcher	
Bowl, flat, open		Bulbous, applied handle	
Round		1 pint	45.00
5"	20.00	1½ pint	55.00
8"	25.00	½ gallon	65.00
Square, scalloped rim	20.00	Water, pressed handle	
6"	25.00	Squatty, ½ gallon	75.00
8"	30.00	Tankard, ½ gallon, with or	
9"	35.00	without silver plate rim	85.00
Finger, round, scalloped rim		Plate	
(originally termed the open hotel		Round, 7"d	25.00
sugar bowl)	25.00	Square, 7"	25.00
Butter dish, covered, flat, high domed		Puff box, covered, matching patterned	
lid, flat square base	45.00	glass lid	45.00
Butter pat, individual, square	25.00	Relish tray, 8½" x 3"	15.00
Cake stand, high standard, square		Salt, square	
5" (termed the "almond dish")	45.00	Individual	15.00
7" (termed the footed "bon bon")	45.00	Master	20.00
11"	65.00	Shaker, original silver or pewter top	
Candlesticks, pair, 9¼"h	100.00	Tall, no neck	35.00
Celery		Squatty, with neck	35.00
Tray, rectangular, scalloped rim, 11"l	40.00	Sauce dish, square, flat, scalloped rim	
Vase, flat, scalloped rim	30.00	4"	15.00
Cheese dish, covered, flat	50.00	4½"	15.00
Compote, open, high standard, square,		Spoonholder	
scalloped rim		Hotel size	35.00
5" sq	55.00	Table size	35.00
9" sq	110.00	Strawholder, matching patterned cover	175.00
Creamer		Sugar bowl	
Large (table size)	40.00	Hotel size, true open	45.00
Medium	25.00	Individual	30.00
Small (individual)	30.00	Medium, true open	45.00
Cruet, original matching patterned		Table size, covered	55.00
stopper	65.00	Sugar shaker, original pewter or silver	
Dish		plate top	75.00
Ice cream, rectangular, flat,		Syrup pitcher, original pewter top	95.00
scalloped rim, 5"	35.00	Toothpick holder	35.00
Olive	15.00	Tray	
Jug, water, squatty, square, pressed		Ice cream, rectangular, flat,	
handle	50.00	scalloped rim, 12"l	40.00
Lamp, banquet, matching shade (2		Spoon, oblong, 8½"l	35.00
sizes)	750.00	Tumbler, water, flat	25.00
Marmalade jar, covered	135.00	Vase, 6"h	35.00
Olive dish, oblong, scalloped rim	20.00		

Flat handled jelly dish.

OMN: U.S. Glass No. 15,029, Indiana. AKA: Doric, Prison Window(s) [Peterson].

Non-flint. The United States Glass Co. (pattern line No. 15,029), Pittsburgh, PA. at Factory "U", Gas City, IN. ca. 1897. Illustrated in the United States Glass Co. 1897 and 1904 catalogs.

Original color production: Clear. Clear with ruby stain is very rare.

Reproductions: None.

References: Hart/Cobb-SS/Cob (P. 31), Hea-5 (PP. 13, 19), Kam-4 (P. 105), Lee-VG (P. 113, Plt. 39), McCn-PGP (P. 549).

Items made	Clear	Items made	Clear
Bottle		Oval, flat, open	
Catsup	65.00	7″	15.00
Perfume	60.00	8″	15.00
Water	50.00	9″	15.00
Bowl		Round, ice cream, flat, open,	
Finger	20.00	handled	
Round, flat, scalloped rim		5″d	15.00
5″d	15.00	6″d	15.00
6″d	15.00	Jelly dish, flat, open, handled, 4½″d	15.00
7″d	15.00	Pitcher, water, tankard, ½ gallon	65.00
8″d	20.00	Salt shaker, original top	20.00
9″d	20.00	Sauce dish, flat	
Butter dish, covered	45.00	4″d	15.00
Celery		4½″d	15.00
Tray	25.00	Spoonholder	35.00
Vase	30.00	Sugar bowl, covered	45.00
Compote, open, high standard, jelly	30.00	Syrup pitcher, original top	45.00
Creamer	35.00	Tray, oblong, flat	50.00
Cruet with matching undertray	40.00	Tub, ice cream	75.00
Dish		Tumbler, water, flat	35.00

INVERTED FERN

Sauce dish; egg cup; spoonholder; covered sugar; creamer; tumbler.

Flint. Maker unknown ca. 1860s. Shards have been found at the site of the Boston & Sandwich Glass Co., Sandwich, MA.

Original color production: Clear. Somewhat similar to Ribbed Palm, the main design element of Inverted Fern is a finely ribbed body upon which clear fern-like ornaments stand and hang in high relief. While the bases of goblets and egg cups may be clear or rayed, finials are pseudo shaped acorns. The "width" of the ribbing in the pattern indicates several factories were involved in the production of Inverted Fern.

Reproductions: The goblet has been reissued in clear and colored non-flint glass from the early 1960s.

References: Brn-SD (P. 53), Cod-OS (P. 24), Drep-ABC OG (P. 149), Lee-EAPG (Pl. 36, No. 3), Lee-SG (P. 537), McCn-PGP (P. 417), McKrn-AG (P. 405), Mil-1 (Pl. 66), Mtz-1 (PP. 30-310, Oliv-AAG (P. 57), Rev-APG (P. 304), Spil-AEPG (P. 262), Uni-1 (P. 71), Uni-2 (PP. 76-77), Wat-AGG (Pl. 20), Wlkr-PGA (Fig. 8, Nos. 7, 15).

Items made	Clear	Items made	Clear
Bowl, footed, open, smooth rim	40.00	Plain base, plain clear band at top of	
Butter dish, covered, flat	95.00	bowl	40.00
Champagne	125.00	Rayed base	40.00
Compote, open, high standard, 8"d ...	55.00	Honey dish, flat, round, 3½"d	15.00
Creamer, applied handle	125.00	Pitcher, water, applied handle,	
Dish, honey, flat, round, 1"h., 3½"d	10.00	½ gallon	250.00+
Egg cup, single, footed		Plate, round, 6"d	100.00
Plain base	30.00	Salt, master, footed, open	35.00
Rayed base		Sauce dish, flat, round, 4"d	10.00
Coarse ribbing	40.00	Spoonholder, pedestaled, scalloped rim	65.00
Fine ribbing	40.00	Sugar bowl, covered	75.00
Goblet		Tumbler, water, flat	95.00
		Wine	65.00

INVERTED STRAWBERRY

Goblet.

OMN: Cambridge No. 2,870, Strawberry. AKA: Late Strawberry Variant [Brothers].

Non-flint. Cambridge Glass Co. (pattern line No. 2,870), Cambridge, OH. ca. 1912-1918.

Original color production: Clear. Items made be found in clear with ruby stain that are most likely souvenired. Advertised in the 1915 Butler Brothers catalog.

Reproductions: The Guernsey Glass Co., Cambridge, OH. issued the following look-alike items, from new molds, in amethyst, carnival colors, clear, and emerald green with gold: cruet, pitcher (water), plate, toothpick holder, and tumbler.

References: Bar-RS (Pl. 14), Ben-CG (Plts. 52-53), Hrtng-P&P (P. 49), Hea-6 (P. 31, Fig. 191), McCn-PGP (P. 327), Mil-2 (P. 48), Mtz-1 (P. 89), Mtz-2 (PP. 64-65), Uni-2 (PP. 86-87), Wlkr-PGA (P. 11).

Items made	Clear:	Items made	Clear:
Basket, applied handle	65.00	Goblet	25.00
Bowl, round, flat		Mug	20.00
Master berry, 9″d	25.00	Pitcher, water, ½ gallon	45.00
Rose	30.00	Plate, 10″d	25.00
Butter dish, covered	65.00	Relish tray, 7″l	10.00
Celery tray, flat, handled	30.00	Salt dip, individual	20.00
Compote, open, high standard, 5″d ...	40.00	Sauce dish, flat, round, 4″d	15.00
Creamer	25.00	Sugar bowl, covered	45.00
Cruet, original stopper	40.00	Toothpick holder	25.00
Cup, punch	10.00	Tumbler, water, flat	25.00

Custard cup; wine; tankard water pitcher; goblet; toothpick holder.

OMN: U.S. Glass No. 15,069, Iowa. AKA: Panelled Zipper.

Non-flint. The United States Glass Co. (pattern line No. 15,069), Pittsburgh, PA. at Factory "G" (Gillinder & Sons, Greensburg, PA.) and "P" (Doyle & Co., Pittsburgh, PA.) ca. 1900. Illustrated in the United States Glass Co. ca. 1904 catalog.

Original color production: Clear (plain or with gilt). Clear with rose blush, clear with ruby stain, amber, blue, canary, green or any other color is rare.

Reproductions: None.

References: Hart/Cobb-SS (P. 33), Hea-1 (P. 28, Figs. 164-165), Hea-3 (P. 82), Hea-5 (PP. 173, 180), Hea-6 (P. 31, Fig. 194), Lecnr-SS (P. 68), McCn-PGP (P. 38), Mil-2 (Pl. 139), Mtz-1 (PP. 198-199), Pet-GPP (PP. 126-128), Pet-Sal (P. 164), Uni-1 (P. 165).

Items made	Clear	Items made	Clear
Bottle, water	35.00	Salt shaker, with original top	
Bowl, open, flat, master berry	10.00	Large	25.00
Butter dish, covered	40.00	Small	25.00
Cake stand, high standard	35.00	Sauce dish, flat, round, 4½"d	5.00
Compote, high standard, covered, 8"d	40.00	Spoonholder	30.00
Creamer	30.00	Sugar bowl, covered	35.00
Cruet, original patterned stopper	30.00	Toothpick holder	25.00
Cup, custard, handled	15.00	Tumbler, water, flat	25.00
Goblet	30.00	Vase	
Jug, corn liquor, original stopper	60.00	6"h	15.00
Lamp, oil	125.00	8"h	20.00
Olive tray, round, open, handled	15.00	10"h	25.00
Pitcher, water, tankard, ½ gallon	50.00	Wine	35.00
Plate, bread, with motto in center	50.00		

Creamer; 7"d plate; 8"d. high standard cake stand.

Tumbler; high standard covered compote; syrup.

OMN: Forest. AKA: Forest Ware, Ivy in Snow-Red Leaves [Millard].

Non-flint. Co-Operative Flint Glass Co., Beaver Falls, PA. ca. 1898.

Original color production: Clear, the main pattern design element being clear ivy branches with buds against a finely stippled background. Finials are clear and double knobbed. Clear with ruby, amber stain, milk white, or any other color is rare.

Reproductions: The Phoenix Glass Co., Monaco, PA. first reissued Ivy in Snow in clear between 1937 and 1942 as their Forestware line in the following items: covered butter dish, high standard cake stand, celery vase, creamer, goblet, water pitcher, and covered sugar bowl. These items, as well as the covered compote, round plate, sauce dish, and spoonholder, were still being reissued as late as the early 1960s and possibly later. John E. Kemple Glass Works, East Palestine, OH., also reissued many forms in the early 1940s. Most reproductions in Ivy in Snow are in new milk white.

References: Bar-RS (Pl. 10), Belnp-MG (P. 270), Cod-OS (P. 21), Drep-ABC OG (P. 161), Enos-MPG (Chart-2), Hea-7 (PP. 118-119), Inn-PG (P. 381), Kam-3 (P. 97), Kam-5 (PP. 116-117), Kam-6 (P. 23), Lee-EAPG (Pl. 119, No. 4), McCn-PGP (P. 425), Mil-1 (Pl. 146), Mil-OG (Pl. 92), Mtz-1 (P. 68), Rev-APG (PP. 129, 279), Stu-BP (P. 39), Uni-1 (PP. 215, 181), Wlkr-PGA (Fig. 8, Nos. 49, 56).

Items made	Clear	Clear w/Ruby
Bowl, flat		
Covered	40.00	—
Open		
Berry, master		
7"d	20.00	—
8"d., 5½"h	30.00	—
Finger	25.00	—
Butter dish, covered, flat	55.00	—
Cake stand, high standard, 8"sq	55.00	—
Celery vase, pedestaled, scalloped rim	25.00	125.00
Champagne	35.00	55.00
Compote, high standard		
Covered		
6"d	45.00	75.00
8"d	55.00	—
Open, jelly	35.00	55.00
Cordial	35.00	—
Creamer		
Table size, squatty	30.00	75.00
Tankard	35.00	135.00
Cup/saucer	30.00	—
Goblet, 5¾"h	35.00	65.00
Marmalade jar, covered	35.00	—
Mug	25.00	45.00
Pitcher, flat		
Milk, 1 quart	85.00	200.00
Water, ½ gallon	55.00	250.00
Plate		
Cake		
Round	30.00	65.00
Square	30.00	65.00
Dinner		
6"d	20.00	—
7"d	25.00	—
10"d	30.00	
Relish tray	20.00	30.00
Sauce dish, round, flat, 4"d	15.00	20.00
Spoonholder	35.00	65.00
Sugar bowl, covered	50.00	100.00
Syrup pitcher, original top	75.00	300.00
Tumbler, water, flat, 3½"h	25.00	55.00
Wine, 4"h	30.00	85.00

Wine; cake stand; h.s. covered compote; water pitcher; 6"d. plate.

Master salt; wine; creamer; oval bowl.

OMN: Imperial, U.S. Glass No. 4,778. Original patent name: Imperial. AKA: Maltese.

Non-flint. Bryce, McKee & Co., Pittsburgh, PA. Reissued by the United States Glass Co., Pittsburgh, PA. ca. 1891. The Diamond Glass Co., Canada ca. 1902. Designed and patented by John Bryce (patent No. 9,335) June 13, 1876 as "Imperial." Illustrated in the ca. 1891, 1904, and 1907 United States Glass Co. catalogs and the 1902 Diamond Flint Glass Co. catalog as "Imperial." Jacob's Ladder appeared in U.S. advertisements throughout the 1880s and 1890s as "Maltese". A much earlier variant in Flint may be found, primarily in the form of bowls and honey dishes.

Original color production: Clear. Amber, blue, canary-yellow, muddy green, pink or any other color is very rare. Handles are pressed on creamers and applied on water pitchers. Finials are in the shape of a maltese cross.

Reproductions: None.

References: Brn-SD (P. 51), Grow-WCG (P. 92, Fig. 11-"11"), Hea-3 (PP. 77-78), Hea-5 (P. 33, No. 4C), Hea-6 (P. 32, Fig. 202), Hlms-BCA (P. 278), Inn-PG (P. 359), Grow-GAG (P. 92, Fig. 7-"10"), Kam-1 (P. 20), Kam/Wod-Vol.2 (P. 346), Lee-EAPG (Pl. 50, No. 3), Lind-HG (P. 227), Mil-1 (Pl. 74), Mtz-1 (PP. 140-141), Oliv-AAG (P. 69), Rev-APG (PP. 83, 88), Spil-TBV (P. 147), Stu-BP (P. 60), Swn-PG (P. 50), Uni-1 (PP. 267, 269), Uni-TCG (PP. 116-117), Uni/Wor-CHPGT (P. 145), Wlkr-PGA (Fig. 8, No. 36).

Items made	Clear
Bottle	
Cologne, Maltese cross finial, footed	85.00
Castor	15.00
Bowl, flat	
Covered, round, 6″d	35.00
Open	
Oval	
5½″ x 7¾″	15.00
6″ x 8¾″	25.00
6¾″ x 9¾″	25.00
7½″ x 10¾″	25.00
Round, master berry, 9″d	25.00
Butter dish, covered, flat, flanged rim, 5¼″h., 6½″d	75.00
Cake stand, high standard	
8″d	50.00
9″d	50.00
11″d	75.00
12″d	75.00
Castor set, original holder	
4 bottles	100.00
5 bottles	100.00
Celery vase, pedestaled, scalloped rim, 9″h	40.00
Compote	
Covered, round, maltese cross finial	
High standard	
6″d	60.00
6½″d	60.00
7″d	70.00
7½″d	70.00
8″d	80.00
8½″d	80.00
9″d	90.00
9½″d	100.00
Open	
Round, high standard, scalloped rim	
7″d	30.00
7½″d	30.00
8″d	35.00
8½″d	35.00
9″d	40.00

Items made	Clear
9½″d	40.00
10″d	40.00
10½″d	45.00
12″d	55.00
Oblong, dolphin stem, smooth rim (R)	300.00
Creamer, pedestaled, 6¼″h	35.00
Cruet, footed, original maltese stopper	85.00
Dish, oval, open, flat	
7″	20.00
8″	20.00
9″	25.00
10″	25.00
Goblet, knob stem	65.00
Honey dish, round, flat, 3½″d	10.00
Marmalade jar, covered	85.00
Mug, large, applied handle	85.00
Pickle tray, double handles	10.00
Pitcher, water, bulbous, applied handle, ½ gallon	175.00
Plate, round, 6″d	30.00
Platter, bread, oblong	40.00
Relish dish, oval, 9½″ x 5½″	15.00
Salt, master, footed, open	25.00
Sauce dish, round	
Flat	
4″d	10.00
4½″d	10.00
5″d	10.00
Footed	
4″d	10.00
4½″d	10.00
5″d	10.00
Spoonholder, pedestaled, scalloped rim, 6″h	35.00
Sugar bowl, covered, maltese cross finial	85.00
Syrup pitcher	
Plain conventional lid	100.00
Knight's head finial	135.00
Tumbler, bar, flat, ½ pint (R)	85.00
Wine	35.00

JAPANESE

Fan-shaped plate; creamer; water pitcher; covered sugar; spoonholder.

(OMN). AKA: Bird in Ring, Butterfly and Fan (Duncan), Grace, Japanese Fan [Lee].

Non-flint. George Duncan & Sons, Pittsburgh, PA. ca. 1880. Reviewed in the *American Pottery and Glassware Reporter* on July 15, 1880, and November 11, 1880.

Original color production: Clear. Japanese is often mistaken for Richard's & Hartley's Grace pattern which has splayed feet rather than stems. Although no two items of Japanese carry the same design element, the most notable characteristic of the pattern is a panel of "zig-zag" ornamentation that appears varyingly on each item. Unlike the flat, round finials of the "Grace" pattern, finials on Japanese are of square shape upon which rests a half sphere, while footed items are always stemmed with circular bases. Handles are pressed.

Reproductions: None.

References: Bred-EDG (P. 56), Kam-2 (P. 16), Kam-7 (PP. 76-77), Lee-VG (P. 86, Pl. 32), McCn-PGP (P. 399), Mil-1 (Pl. 140), Mtz-1 (P. 106), Spil-AEPG (P. 297), Stu-BP (P. 57), Uni-1 (P. 205), Wlkr-PGA (Fig. 8, Nos. 17, 28).

Items made	Clear	Items made	Clear
Bowl, flat, round	20.00	Goblet	35.00
Butter dish, covered		Pickle jar, covered	65.00
Flat, flanged rim	45.00	Pitcher, water, ½ gallon	65.00
Footed, low standard	55.00	Plate, oriental fan shape	15.00
Celery vase, footed, scalloped rim	35.00	Sauce dish, round, smooth rim, 4"d	
Compote, high standard		Flat	10.00
Covered	75.00	Footed	12.00
Open	40.00	Spoonholder, scalloped rim	25.00
Creamer, footed, bamboo-like handle	30.00	Sugar bowl, covered	45.00

Cake stand; h.s. covered compote; bulbous water pitcher (3 pint).

High standard open compote; bulbous water pitcher (½ gallon); cake stand.

AKA: Belt Buckle, Eleanor, Late Buckle.

Non-flint. Bryce Brothers, Pittsburgh, PA. ca. 1880. Reissued by the United States Glass Co., Pittsburgh, PA. at Factory "B" (Bryce Brothers, Pittsburgh, PA.) after the 1891 merger. Illustrated in the ca. 1891 United States Glass Company catalog of member firms.

Original color production: Clear. Blue or any other color is rare. Handles are applied.

Reproductions: none.

References: Brn-SD (P. 55), Chip-ROS (P. 141), Cod-OS (P. 22), Hea-5 (P. 19), Kam-2 (P. 13), Lee-EAPG (P. 557, Pl. 72), McCn-PGP (P. 109), Mil-1 (Pl. 109), Rev-APG (P. 88), Uni-1 (P. 153), Wlkr-PGA (Fig. 8, Nos. 37, 43).

Items made	Clear	Items made	Clear
Bowl, open, round, flat		Oval, deep bowl, scalloped rim	
5"d	15.00	7"	15.00
6"d	15.00	8"	15.00
Butter dish, flat, covered	35.00	9"	20.00
Cake stand, high standard		10"	20.00
8"d	25.00	Round, smooth rim	
9"d	25.00	7"d	15.00
11"d	30.00	8"d	15.00
12"d	30.00	9"d	20.00
Cologne bottle, footed, bulbous,		10"d	20.00
original stopper	65.00	Goblet	25.00
Compote, high standard		Pickle dish, handled	15.00
Covered		Pitcher	
6"d. (originally called the		3 pint	55.00
sweetmeat)	35.00	½ gallon	65.00
7"d	45.00	Salt, master, footed, open, scalloped	
8"d	55.00	rim	15.00
9"d	65.00	Sauce dish, round	
Open, scalloped rim		Flat	
7"d	15.00	4"d	8.00
8"d	20.00	4½"d	8.00
10"d	25.00	Footed	
12"d	30.00	4"d	10.00
Creamer, 6"h	25.00	4½"d	10.00
Cruet, applied handle (made from		Spoonholder	20.00
cologne bottle) (R)	90.00	Sugar bowl, covered, footed	35.00
Dish, open, flat		Wine	25.00

JERSEY SWIRL

Goblet; high standard cake stand; dresser tray.

OMN: *Windsor Swirl. AKA: Swirl, Swirl and Diamonds, Windsor.*

Non-flint. The Windsor Glass Co., Pittsburgh, PA. ca. 1887.

Original color production: Amber, blue, canary-yellow, clear.

301

Reproductions: The Jersey Swirl goblet has been reproduced in clear and cornflower blue from new molds as early as the 1960s. By 1971, the L.G. Wright Glass Co., New Martinsville, WV. (distributed by Jennings Red Barn, New Martinsville, WV. and Carl Forslund, Grand Rapids, MI.), issued the wine in yellow and yellow opalescent and the goblet in yellow, yellow opalescent, and green satin. In 1974, the following items were listed in the L.G. Wright master catalog in amber, blue, clear, green, ruby, amethyst, canary-yellow and vaseline opalescent: 4"d. covered compote with collared base, high standard 6½"d. ruffled rim compote, 11 ounce goblet, footed master salt, 5"d. footed flared sauce, and the 3½ ounce wine. All forms were reissued from new molds, the 2¼"d. collared salt dip being totally different from the original in shape, dimension, and color.

References: Drep-ABC OG (P. 157), Drep-FR (PP. 207, 209), Hea-2 (P. 91, Fig. 599), Kam-3 (P. 49), Kam-6 (P. 112), Lee-EAPG (Pl. 69, No. 3), McCn-PGP (P. 525), Mil-1 (Plts. 18, 28), Pet-Sal (P. 174), Stu-BP (P. 17), Uni-1 (PP. 135-136), Uni-2 (P. 216), Wlkr-PGA (Fig. 15, No. 220).

Items made	Amber	Blue	Canary	Clear
Bowl, open, round, flat, 9¼"d	55.00	55.00	45.00	35.00
Butter dish, covered	55.00	55.00	50.00	40.00
Cake stand, high standard, 9"d	75.00	70.00	45.00	30.00
Candlestick	50.00	50.00	45.00	40.00
Compote, high standard				
Covered, 8"d	50.00	50.00	45.00	35.00
Open, scalloped rim, 8"d	35.00	35.00	30.00	20.00
Creamer, 6¼"h	45.00	45.00	40.00	30.00
Cruet, original stopper	—	—	—	35.00
Cup	15.00	20.00	15.00	10.00
Dresser tray, fan shaped	45.00	45.00	40.00	35.00
Goblet	40.00	40.00	35.00	30.00
Marmalade jar, covered	—	—	—	50.00
Pickle castor, complete in original frame	—	—	—	125.00
Pitcher, water, ½ gallon	50.00	50.00	45.00	35.00
Plate, round				
6"d	25.00	25.00	20.00	15.00
8"d	25.00	25.00	20.00	15.00
10"d	35.00	35.00	30.00	25.00
12"d	40.00	40.00	35.00	25.00
Salt				
Individual	20.00	20.00	15.00	15.00
Master, open	35.00	35.00	30.00	15.00
Sauce dish, round, collared base, 4½"d	20.00	20.00	15.00	10.00
Spoonholder	3.00	30.00	25.00	20.00
Sugar bowl, covered	40.00	40.00	35.00	30.00
Syrup pitcher, original top	75.00	75.00	75.00	35.00
Tumbler, water, flat	30.00	30.00	25.00	20.00
Wine	50.00	50.00	40.00	15.00

Salt shaker; h.s. cake stand; bulbous water pitcher; goblet; water tumbler. All clear/frosted with blue/amber stain.

OMN: Imperial (Co-Operative Flint Glass). AKA: Late Moon and Star [Unitt], Moon and Star Variant, Moon and Star Variation, Moon and Star with Waffle Stem.

Non-flint. Co-Operative Flint Glass Co., Beaver Falls, PA. ca. 1896.

Original color production: Clear, clear/acid finish, clear with blue and yellow stain (clear or acid finished "moons"). Similar in design to Moon and Star pattern, the main pattern design element of Jeweled Moon and Stars consists of a horizontal row of star-like circles. Directly beneath appears a second row of clear circles with a third row of star-like circles at the base. Stems are pineapple shapes consisting of knobs of fine diamond point. Handles are applied.

Reproductions: The Phoenix Glass Co., Monaca, PA. ca. 1937, and John E. Kemple Glass Works, East Palestine, OH. and Kenova, WV., ca. 1950s reproduced the following items in undecorated clear, pearl white, and emerald green: low footed open bowl, h.s. open compote, goblet, and wine. Reproductions are heavier than the originals.

References: Chip-ROS (P. 95), Hea-3 (P. 48, Fig. 351), Hea-7 (P. 241), Kam-1 (P. 131), Lee-VG (Pl. 28, No. 3), McCn-PGP (P. 301), Mil-1 (Pl. 62), Mil-2 (Pl. 62), Mtz-2 (PP. 210-211), Pet-Sal (P. 34), Uni-1 (P. 305).

Items made	Clear	Clear/ Frosted	Clear/ Color Stain
Bottle, water, 5 pint	50.00	55.00	65.00
Bowl			
Covered, round, flat			
6"d	30.00	35.00	55.00
7"d	35.00	40.00	65.00
Open, flat			
Flared scalloped rim			
6"d	20.00	25.00	30.00
7"d	20.00	25.00	30.00
Straight sided, scalloped rim			
6"d	20.00	25.00	30.00

Items made	Clear	Clear/ Frosted	Clear/ Color Stain
7"d	20.00	25.00	30.00
8"d	25.00	30.00	35.00
Bread plate, 6"d	30.00	35.00	45.00
Butter dish, covered, collared base	45.00	55.00	90.00
Cake stand, high standard			
9"d	40.00	50.00	65.00
10"d	45.00	55.00	75.00
Celery			
Tray	25.00	30.00	40.00
Vase	25.00	30.00	45.00
Compote, high standard			
Covered			
6"d	50.00	65.00	85.00
7"d	60.00	75.00	100.00
9"d	75.00	90.00	125.00
Open, scalloped rim			
6"d	30.00	35.00	65.00
7"d	35.00	40.00	65.00
Creamer	35.00	40.00	65.00
Cruet, 6 ounces, original over- sized stopper	40.00	50.00	125.00
Egg cup, single	35.00	40.00	50.00
Goblet, $\frac{1}{2}$ pint	40.00	40.00	95.00
Pitcher, water, applied handle circular foot, bulbous, $\frac{1}{2}$ gallon	65.00	75.00	125.00
Plate, round, 6"d	25.00	30.00	45.00
Relish dish, oval	30.00	35.00	45.00
Sauce dish, flat, round	15.00	15.00	20.00
Salt shaker, bulbous, original nickel plate top	30.00	35.00	55.00
Spoonholder	35.00	40.00	55.00
Sugar bowl, covered	50.00	60.00	85.00
Syrup pitcher, glass lip, original nickel plate lid	75.00	95.00	225.00
Tray, water, round	50.00	60.00	85.00
Tumbler, water, flat, $\frac{1}{3}$ pint	25.00	30.00	45.00
Wine	40.00	50.00	90.00

Spoon rack.

Covered compote; creamer (with Barnum-head handle).

Non-flint. Attributed to the Aetna Glass & Manufacturing Co., Bellaire, OH., and the Canton Glass Co., Canton, OH. ca. 1884.

Original color production: Clear, clear with acid finish. Amber, blue or any other color is very rare. The Jumbo spoon rack base is dated "Patented Sept. 23, 1884." Designed and patented by David Baker in 1884, the Jumbo patent was assigned to the Canton Glass Co. Canton made items are adorned with "Barnum Head" handles. The 3 bottle castor set, goblet and elephant toothpick holder commonly associated with the Jumbo pattern are not original to the set. Any item in Jumbo is rare.

Reproductions: None.

References: Inn-PG (P. 359), Kam-5 (P. 14), Lee-EAPG (P. 116, Pl. 94), Lind-HG (P. 520), Mtz-1 (P. 95), Mtz-2 (P. 190), Rev-APG (PP. 103-104), Spil-AEPG (P. 295), Spil-TBV (P. 296).

Items made	Clear/Frosted	Items made	Clear/Frosted
Butter dish, covered		12"d	800.00
Oblong, 4-footed with attached		Creamer, Barnum-head design at base	
spoon rack	400.00	of handle	225.00
Round, Barnum-head handles	300.00	Pitcher, water, ½ gallon, Barnum-head	
Compote, covered, high standard,		handle	550.00
elephant finial		Sauce dish, round, flat	50.00
7"d	400.00	Spoon rack (VR) 11½"h	350.00
8"d	500.00	Spoonholder, Barnum-head handles	100.00
10"d	700.00	Sugar bowl, covered, elephant finial	400.00

Toothpick holder; water pitcher; mug; water tumbler.

OMN: U.S. Glass No. 15,072, Kansas. Kokomo No. 8. AKA: Jewel and Dewdrop, Jewel with Dewdrop [Lee], Jewel with Dewdrops.

Non-flint. The United States Glass Co. (pattern line No. 15,072) , Pittsburgh, PA. ca. 1901. Kokomo Glass Manufacturing Co., Kokomo, IN. ca. 1903. Federal Glass Co., Columbus, OH. ca. 1914. Illustrated in the United States Glass Co. ca. 1904 and 1907 catalogs as "Kansas".

Original color production: Clear, the main pattern design element consisting of alternating clear and stippled vertical panels, the latter containing one oval and two round clear ornaments. Handles are pressed. Items in clear with pink or gold stained jewels may be found although a complete table setting was not produced in this fashion.

Reproductions: None.

References: Grow-WCG (P. 173, Fig. 26-"3"), Hart/Cobb-SS/Cobb-SS (P. 35), Hea-TPS (P. 74), Hea-5 (PP. 13, 19), Kam-1 (P. 78), Lee-EAPG (Pl. 75), McCn-PGP (P. 341), Migh-TPS (Pl. 3), Mil-1 (Pl. 47), Mtz-2 (PP. 106-107), Oliv-AAG (P. 64), Pet-Sal (P. 164), Pyne-PG (P. 153), Rev-APG (P. 314), Stu-BP (P. 9), Uni-1 (P. 155), Uni-2 (P. 235), Wlkr-PGA (Fig. 8, No. 45).

Items made	Clear	Items made	Clear
Banana stand, flat	50.00	9"d	50.00
Bowl, flat, open		10"d	65.00
Oval, 7"	25.00	Low standard	
Round, deep, scalloped rim		8"d	50.00
6"d	25.00	9"d	50.00
6½"d	25.00	10"d	65.00
7"d	30.00	Celery vase, flat, scalloped rim	40.00
7½"d	30.00	Compote	
Butter dish, covered		Covered, high standard	
Flanged, attached underplate	65.00	Beading on base of pedestal	
Round, without underplate	55.00	7"d	65.00
With notched lid (R)	75.00	8"d	75.00
Cake stand, scalloped rim		No beading on base of pedestal	
High standard		5"d	
8"d	50.00	Solid lid	40.00

Items made	Clear	Items made	Clear
Notched lid	55.00	Cup, handled	15.00
6"d.		Dish, oval, preserve, 8½" x 6¼" x 2½"	
Solid lid	40.00	deep	15.00
Notched lid	55.00	Goblet	50.00
Open		Mug, large	45.00
High standard		Pickle dish, oblong, scalloped rim	15.00
Beading on base of pedestal		Pitcher, pressed handle, flat	
6"d	30.00	Milk, 1 quart	50.00
7"d	35.00	Water, ½ gallon	55.00
8"d	40.00	Plate, oval	
No beading on base of pedestal,		Bread, "Give Us This Day Our Daily	
5"d	25.00	Bread" center, oval	60.00
Low standard		Cake	45.00
Deep bowl, scalloped rim		Relish tray, oval, 8½"l	20.00
5"d., jelly	25.00	Salt shaker, original top	40.00
6"d	30.00	Sauce dish, round, flat, scalloped rim,	
6½"d	30.00	deep, 4"d	15.00
7"d	35.00	Spoonholder, flat, scalloped rim	35.00
8"d	35.00	Sugar bowl, covered, flat	50.00
Saucer bowl, scalloped rim		Syrup, original top	125.00
7½"d	35.00	Toothpick holder	45.00
8½"d	40.00	Tumbler, flat	
9½"d	45.00	Water	40.00
Cordial	40.00	Whiskey	30.00
Creamer, pressed handle, scalloped		Wine	45.00
rim	40.00		

KENTUCKY States Series

Custard cup; water tumbler; goblet; footed sauce dish.

OMN: U.S. Glass No. 15,051, Kentucky.

Non-flint. The United States Glass Co. (pattern line No. 15,051), Pittsburgh, PA. ca. 1897. Illustrated in the United States Glass Co. 1898 and 1904 catalogs.

Original color production: Clear, emerald green. Clear with amber stain, clear with ruby stain, cobalt blue, or any other color is rare. Retooled from the older United States Glass Co.

"Millard" line (pattern line No. 15,016), the only distinguishable difference between Millard and Kentucky is the latter's use of small diamond point in the clear panels.

Reproductions: None.

References: Brn-SD (P. 135), Hart/Cobb-SS/Cob (P. 36), Hea-1 (P. 28, Fig. 161), Hea-5 (P. 43, No. 143), Hea-7 (P. 136), Kam-4 (P. 68), Lee-VG (Pl. 39, No. 4), McCn-PGP (P. 205), Migh-TPS (Pl. 3), Pet-Sal (P. 31).

Items made	Clear	Items made	Clear
Bowl, flat, round, open		Oblong, flat	
7"d	20.00	7"	15.00
8"d	20.00	8"	15.00
Butter dish, covered, flat	50.00	9"	20.00
Cake stand, high standard		10"	20.00
9½"d	40.00	Square, flat, open, 5"	15.00
10½"d	45.00	Goblet	20.00
Celery		Olive dish, flat, handled	25.00
Tray		Pitcher, water, ½ gallon	50.00
Large	30.00	Plate, square	
Small	30.00	7"	15.00
Vase	35.00	9"	15.00
Compote, high standard		10"	20.00
Covered		Salt shaker, original top	10.00
5"d	35.00	Sauce dish, square	
6"d	45.00	Flat	
7"d	55.00	4"	8.00
8"d	65.00	4½"	8.00
Open		Footed	
5"d	20.00	4"	8.00
6"d	20.00	4½"	8.00
7"d	25.00	Spoonholder	35.00
8"d	25.00	Sugar bowl, covered	30.00
Creamer	25.00	Syrup pitcher, original top	65.00
Cruet, original stopper	45.00	Toothpick holder	35.00
Cup, custard	10.00	Tumbler, water, flat	20.00
Dish		Wine	25.00

Water tumbler (cobalt blue); water tumbler (clear/frosted); cruet (o.s., clear); custard cup (cobalt blue).

OMN: King's 500. AKA: Bone Stem, King's Comet (lamps only), Parrot, Swirl and Thumbprint.

Non-flint. King Glass Co., Pittsburgh, PA. ca. 1891. Designed and patented by William C. King (patent design No. 20,505), February 3, 1891. Reissued by the United States Glass Co., Pittsburgh, PA. at Factory "K" (King Glass Co., Pittsburgh, PA.) ca. 1891-1898. Reviewed in the January 14, 1891 issue of *China, Glass and Lamps* and illustrated in the King Glass Co. ca. 1890-1891 and United States Glass Co. Factory "K" ca. 1891-1895 catalogs.

Original color production: Clear, clear with acid finish (plain or copper wheel engraved, No. 299 engraving being the most common), cobalt blue (with or without gilt). Clear with ruby stain, green, or any other color is rare. Most forms are squat and bulbous in shape and handles are applied, either solid or reeded. Salt shakers were produced with opposite motifs.

Reproductions: None.

References: Hea-3 (P. 29), Hea-5 (P. 37, No. 52), Hea-6 (P. 22, Fig. 208), Hea-7 (P. 137), Kam-5 (PP. 71-72), Kam-8 (PP. 72-73), McCn-PGP (P. 523), Mtz-2 (P. 116), Pet-GPP (P. 98), Pet-Sal (P. 164-"N"), Revi-APG (P. 214), Spil-TBV (Fig. 1251), Spil-AEPG (P. 322), Thu-1 (P. 314), Uni-1 (P. 316), Wlkr-PGA (Fig. 8, No. 5).

Items made	Clear	Cobalt
Bowl, round, open, flat		
5"d	8.00	10.00
7"d	10.00	30.00
8"d	10.00	35.00
9"d	15.00	45.00
Finger, low circular, foot, smooth rim	15.00	35.00
Rose	20.00	45.00
Butter dish, covered, flanged base	50.00	125.00
Cake stand, high standard	40.00	100.00
Castor set, complete		
2 bottle	65.00	175.00
3 bottle	75.00	200.00
4 bottle	85.00	225.00
Celery vase, low circular foot, scalloped rim	20.00	65.00

Items made	Clear	Cobalt
Cologne bottle, original pressed faceted stopper		
1 ounce	35.00	75.00
2 ounce	35.00	75.00
4 ounce	40.00	85.00
6 ounce	45.00	95.00
8 ounce	45.00	95.00
Compote, high standard, round		
Covered		
Deep bowl		
8″	50.00	75.00
9″	50.00	85.00
Open	35.00	—
Deep bowl, smooth rim		
8″	25.00	40.00
9″	25.00	40.00
Saucer bowl, smooth rim		
9″	25.00	40.00
10″	35.00	55.00
Cracker jar, original patterned lid, low circular foot (R)	85.00	125.00
Creamer, bulbous, applied handle		
Individual, flat	20.00	35.00
Table size, low circular foot	30.00	50.00
Cruet, original swirled stopper		
4 ounce	45.00	200.00
8 ounce	45.00	225.00
Cup, custard	15.00	15.00
Dish		
Round, applied finger handle (termed "olive dish")	10.00	20.00
Square, flat		
Covered		
7″	35.00	55.00
8″	35.00	55.00
Open		
7″	15.00	20.00
8″	15.00	20.00
Goblet, design on stem only	45.00	85.00
Lamp, oil, complete with original burner and chimney		
Hand	55.00	—
Stand	65.00	—
Pitcher, applied handle		
Bulbous		
3 pint	50.00	200.00
½ gallon	75.00	200.00
Jug (straight-sided)		
3 pint	50.00	200.00
½ gallon	75.00	200.00
Relish tray	20.00	30.00
Salt shaker, original top (VR)		
Bulbous, squatty	25.00	55.00
Tall, straight-sided	25.00	55.00
Sauce dish, round, flat, smooth rim, 4″d	15.00	20.00
Saucer, design in base only, 4½″d	10.00	20.00
Spoonholder, scalloped rim, low circular foot	30.00	65.00
Sugar bowl, covered, handled		
Individual	20.00	40.00
Table size	45.00	75.00
Tray, water, round, tab handles	45.00	95.00
Syrup pitcher, original top	45.00	225.00
Tumbler, water, flat	20.00	45.00

Items made	Clear	Cobalt
Whiskey jug (VR), 8½"h, original locking top or ground glass stopper	100.00	—
Wine, design on stem only	35.00	65.00

KING'S CROWN

Footed punch bowl.

Toothpick holder(clear w/amber stain); goblet (clear/green eyes); milk pitcher (clear w/ruby stain); tumbler (clear w/ruby stain, engraved); wine (engraved).

OMN: X.L.C.R., Excelsior. AKA: Blue Thumbprint, Ruby Thumbprint (when ruby stained) [Millard], Ruby Thumbprint-Clear [Millard].

Non-flint. Adams & Co., Pittsburgh, PA. ca. 1880. Reissued by the United States Glass Co., Pittsburgh, PA. at Factory "A" (Adams & Co., Pittsburgh, PA.) ca. 1891 through the early 1900s. Reviewed in the January 28 and May 6, 1891 issues of *China, Glass and Lamps*, and illustrated in the ca. 1891, 1898, and 1904 United States Glass Co. catalogs, and the Charles "Broadway" Rousse July-August, 1914 general merchandise catalog.

Original color production: Clear, clear with with ruby stain, clear stained with amethyst, gold, green, or yellow. Known as Ruby Thumbprint when stained with ruby. Plain or copper wheel engraved with Fern & Berry, Bird, or Floral sprays. Also souvenired. Copper wheel engravings can be highly refined or crudely souvenired. Catalog designation of "Fancy Engraved" include: Daisy Bouquet, Bird in Marsh, and Bird in Bough.

Reproductions: Glasscrafts & Ceramics, Inc., Yonkers, NY. advertised a look-alike goblet in clear, produced from a new mold, as early as September, 1954. L.G. Wright Glass Co., New Martinsville, WV. (distributed by Jennings Red Barn, New Martinsville, WV. and Carl Forslund, Grand Rapids, MI.) reproductions appeared as early as 1967 in clear with pale ruby and amber stain, and solid colors of ruby red and green including: champagne, goblet, wine, footed sauce, 5"d. high standard covered compote, cordial, individual sugar bowl, individual creamer, footed sherbert (not original to the set), flat sauce, 8"d plate, cup and saucer, high standard cake stand, lemonade tumbler (not original to the set), small tumbler (not original to the set), and tall oil lamps: King's Crown base and daisy and button font, and King's Crown base with milk white beaded font. New items are thicker and heavier than the old, and are stained in a light cranberry rather than ruby red.

References: Bar-RS (Plts. 1-2), Hea-1 (P. 62), Hea-5 (P. 48, Nos. 196-203), Hea-7 (PP. 113-114), Hea-3 (P. 90), Inn-PG (P. 369), Kam-1 (P. 104), Kam-5 (PP. 82, 114), Kam-6 (Pl. 20), Lee-EAPG (Pl. 162, No. 4), Mil-1 (Pl. 46), Mil-2 (P. 92), Mtz-1 (PP. 144-146), Rev-APG (P. 18), Uni-1 (PP. 78-79), Uni-2 (P. 135), Pet-Sal (P. 31), Thu-1 (PP. 320-321), Wlkr-PGA (Fig. 8, No. 57).

Items made	Clear	Clear w/Ruby
Banana dish, high standard, folded sides, 10" (made from a cake stand)	125.00	175.00
Bowl		
Open		
Flat		
Belled bowl, round		
5"d	15.00	25.00
6"d	20.00	35.00
7"d	25.00	45.00
8"d	35.00	65.00
9"d	35.00	65.00
Boat shape, serrated rim, round		
8"l	35.00	90.00
9½"l	35.00	90.00
Flared bowl, serrated rim, round		
6¾"d	20.00	35.00
8½"d	35.00	65.00
Straight-sided bowl, serrated rim		
5"d	15.00	25.00
6"d	20.00	35.00
7"d	25.00	45.00
8½"d	35.00	65.00
9½"d	35.00	65.00
11"d	40.00	75.00
Collared base		
Flared, serrated rim		
6"d	20.00	35.00
7"d	25.00	45.00
8"d	35.00	65.00
8½"d	35.00	65.00
9½"d	35.00	65.00
11"d	40.00	75.00

Items made	Clear	Clear w/Ruby
Plain rim, round		
5"d	15.00	25.00
6"d	20.00	35.00
7"d	25.00	45.00
8"d	35.00	65.00
9"d	35.00	65.00
Footed, orange, extra large, h.s., serrated rim	55.00	95.00
Covered, collared base		
5"d	35.00	55.00
6"d	35.00	55.00
7"d	45.00	65.00
8"d	55.00	75.00
9"d	65.00	85.00
Butter dish, covered, $5^3/_4$"h., $7^1/_2$"d	65.00	125.00
Cake stand, high standard, serrated rim, crown or knob finial		
9"d	90.00	150.00
10"d	90.00	150.00
Castor set, 4 bottles, original stoppers and frame	185.00	300.00
Celery vase, serrated rim, $6^1/_2$"h	45.00	85.00
Champagne	25.00	35.00
Cheese dish, covered, flat, 7"d	100.00	225.00
Claret	35.00	55.00
Compote, round		
Covered, high standard		
5"d	65.00	125.00
6"d	85.00	140.00
7"d	85.00	140.00
8"d	100.00	175.00
$8^1/_2$"d	100.00	175.00
9"d	125.00	200.00
12"d	150.00	250.00
Open		
Belled bowl, serrated rim		
5"d	30.00	45.00
6"d	30.00	45.00
7"d	40.00	65.00
8"d	45.00	75.00
9"d	50.00	85.00
10"d	55.00	100.00
Flared bowl, serrated rim		
$5^1/_2$"d	30.00	45.00
$6^1/_2$"d	30.00	45.00
$7^1/_2$"d	40.00	65.00
$8^1/_4$"d	45.00	75.00
9"d	50.00	85.00
$9^1/_2$"d	50.00	85.00
10"d	55.00	100.00
$11^1/_2$"d	65.00	125.00
Creamer, applied handle		
Individual		
Squatty, 3"h	25.00	35.00
Tankard, $3^1/_4$"h	25.00	35.00
Table size, bulbous, $4^7/_8$"h	50.00	65.00
Cup/saucer set	50.00	65.00
Custard cup	15.00	25.00
Dish		
Desert, square, 8"	30.00	45.00
Olive, round, handled	25.00	45.00

Items made	Clear	Clear w/Ruby
Preserve, oval		
6″l	20.00	35.00
10″l	35.00	50.00
Fruit basket, high standard	125.00	175.00
Goblet	30.00	45.00
Honey dish, covered, tab handles, 8″ sq	100.00	225.00
Lamp, oil, stand, complete with original burner and chimney	125.00	—
Marmalade jar, covered, 5″h	85.00	185.00
Mustard jar, covered, original notched lid, 4″h	40.00	75.00
Pickle		
Castor, complete in original silver plate frame	125.00	250.00
Jar, covered	85.00	185.00
Tray, oval, serrated rim, 6¼″ x 5¼″	20.00	40.00
Pitcher, applied handle		
Bulbous, serrated rim		
Milk, 1 quart, 6½″h	65.00	95.00
Water, ½ gallon, 8″h	95.00	225.00
Tankard, smooth rim		
Milk		
7″h	75.00	95.00
8⅜″h	75.00	95.00
Water, 11¼″h	110.00	200.00
Plate, round, 7″d	25.00	45.00
Punch bowl, flat, serrated rim, 9″h., 12″d	150.00	300.00
Salt		
Individual		
Rectangular	15.00	35.00
Square	15.00	35.00
Master		
Rectangular, 2¼″l., 1¾″h	35.00	65.00
Square	30.00	65.00
Shaker, bulbous, 3⅛″h., original top	30.00	40.00
Sauce dish, flat		
Boat shape, serrated rim		
4″l	20.00	22.00
5¼″l	20.00	22.00
Round, serrated rim		
Belled		
4″d	15.00	20.00
4½″d	15.00	20.00
Flared, 5″d	20.00	22.00
Straight-sided		
4″d	15.00	20.00
4½″d	15.00	20.00
Spoonholder, flat, bulbous, serrated rim, 4¼″h	40.00	55.00
Sugar bowl		
Individual, open, 2½″h	25.00	45.00
Table size, covered, 6¾″h	55.00	95.00
Toothpick holder, serrated rim, 2¾″h	25.00	45.00
Tumbler, water, flat, 3¾″h	25.00	35.00
Wine, 4⅜″h	25.00	40.00

Salt shaker; tumbler; champagne; water pitcher (clear/frosted w/amber stain); oval dish (clear).

OMN: Dalzell No. 75 & 75D, Amberette. AKA: English Hobnail Cross, Frosted Amberette, Klondyke.

Non-flint. Dalzell, Gilmore & Leighton Glass Co., Brilliant, OH. ca. 1898. Illustrated in the Dalzell, Gilmore & Leighton Glass Co. ad in the January 12, 1898 issue of *China, Glass and Lamps*, the January, 1898 issue of *Illustrated Glass and Pottery World*, and the Butler Brothers 1899 catalog.

Original color production: Clear, clear with acid finish, clear with acid finish and amber stain. Allegedly made in clear with acid finish and lilac stain. Items offered in plain crystal were known as "75D." Most forms are square in form. Handles are pressed.

Reproductions: The look-alike covered sugar bowl from a new mold appeared in the mid 1980s in solid amber.

References: Bar-RS (Pl. 8), Bat-GPG (PP. 221, 222), Hea-1 (P. 28), Hea-6 (Plts. C-D), Hea-7 (Figs. 185-188), Kam-2 (P. 100), Kam-5 (P. 21, Pl. 15), Kam-7 (Pl. 96), Luc-TG (PP. 230-234), McCn-PGP (Pl. 226), Mil-1 (Pl. 142), Mtz-2 (PP. 114-115), Mur-MCO (PP. 60-61), Pet-Sal (P. 31), Rev-APG (P. 286), Smth-FG (P. 20), Uni-1 (P. 80).

Items made	Clear	Clear/ Amber	Clear/ Frosted/ Amber
Bowl, open, square, flat, berry or fruit			
7"	35.00	125.00	175.00
8"	40.00	125.00	200.00
9"	45.00	150.00	225.00
11"	50.00	175.00	250.00
Butter dish, covered	150.00	250.00	350.00
Cake stand, high standard, 8"sq	200.00	350.00	500.00
Celery			
Tray, oblong	45.00	150.00	225.00
Champagne (VR)	110.00	400.00	550.00
Condiment set (cruet, salt/pepper shaker, under tray)	350.00	1000.00	1000.00
Creamer	55.00	125.00	250.00
Cruet, original stopper	150.00	350.00	550.00

Items made	Clear	Clear/ Amber	Clear/ Frosted/ Amber
Cup, custard	30.00	100.00	125.00
Dish, oval, flat, shallow	35.00	110.00	150.00
Goblet	90.00	250.00	450.00
Pitcher, water, ½ gallon			
Round, tankard, applied handle	175.00	375.00	650.00
Square	200.00	350.00	550.00
Relish tray, boat shape, 9" x 4"	35.00	100.00	150.00
Salt shaker, original top			
Squatty	45.00	75.00	100.00
Tall	55.00	85.00	100.00
Sauce dish, square			
Flat	25.00	55.00	75.00
Footed	35.00	65.00	85.00
Spoonholder	50.00	150.00	200.00
Sugar bowl, covered, 6¾"h	65.00	150.00	250.00
Syrup pitcher, original pewter lid (VR)	200.00	450.00	650.00
Toothpick holder	150.00	300.00	400.00
Tray, flat, 5½"sq	40.00	175.00	200.00
Tumbler, water, flat	35.00	100.00	125.00
Vase, trumpet shape			
7"h	35.00	175.00	250.00
8"h	35.00	175.00	250.00
9"h	35.00	175.00	250.00
10"h	40.00	200.00	275.00
Wine (VR)	200.00	400.00 +	500.00 +

KOKOMO

High standard open compote; tankard water pitcher; goblet; syrup.

OMN: Richards & Hartley No. 190. AKA: Bar and Diamond [Lee], Jenkins No. 623, R&H Swirl Band [Millard].

Non-flint. Richards & Hartley Glass Co. (pattern line No. 190), Tarentum, PA. ca. 1885. Reissued by the United States Glass Co., Pittsburgh, PA. ca. 1891. Kokomo Glass Co., Kokomo, IN. ca. 1901. Illustrated in the ca. 1888 Richards & Hartley Glass Co. catalog.

Original color production: Clear, clear with ruby stain (plain or copper wheel engraved). Handles on water pitchers are applied. Rimmed pieces may be either pressed or hand crimped.

Reproductions: None.

References: Bar-RS (Pl. 8), Hea-1 (P. 28, Fig. 163), Hea-3 (P. 73), Hea-5 (P. 116), Hea-7 (Figs. 185-188), Hea-CG-Vol.3 (P. 59, Figs. 84-85), Kam-3 (P. 84), Kam-7 (Pl. 15), Lee-VG (P. 195), Luc-TG (PP. 230-234), Mil-1 (P. 142), Migh-TPS (Pl. 4), Mtz-1 (PP. 212-213), Oliv-AAG (P. 69), Pet-Sal (P. 21), Rev-APG (P. 286), Smth-FG (P. 20), Uni-1 (P. 112).

Items made	Clear	Clear w/Ruby
Bowl, open, round		
Flat		
Berry		
6"d	20.00	—
7"d	25.00	—
8"d	30.00	—
Finger	25.00	35.00
Footed, 8½"d	20.00	—
Butter dish, covered		
Flat	35.00	—
Footed	40.00	—
Cake stand, high standard	45.00	165.00
Celery vase	15.00	45.00
Compote		
Covered, high standard		
5"d	25.00	—
6"d	30.00	—
7"d	35.00	—
8"d	40.00	—
Open		
High standard		
5"d	20.00	—
6"d	25.00	—
7"d	30.00	—
8"d	35.00	—
Low standard		
5"d	20.00	—
6"d	25.00	—
7"d	30.00	—
7½"d	30.00	—
8"d	35.00	—
Condiment set, oval tray, cruet, salt & pepper shakers	80.00	200.00
Creamer, applied handle	30.00	50.00
Decanter, original stopper, 9¾"h	55.00	150.00
Dish, oblong, open, flat		
7"	15.00	—
8"	15.00	—
9"	20.00	—
10"	25.00	—
Goblet	25.00	45.00
Jug, wine, 32 ounces	45.00	100.00
Lamp, oil, low footed, handled, original burner	50.00	85.00

Items made	Clear	Clear w/Ruby
Pickle dish, oval	15.00	35.00
Pitcher		
Bulbous		
Milk, 1 quart	45.00	110.00
Water, ¹/₂ gallon	55.00	125.00
Tankard		
Milk water, tankard		
¹/₂ pint	30.00	110.00
Quart	40.00	125.00
Water		
¹/₂ gallon	55.00	90.00
Salt		
Master, footed, open	20.00	45.00
Shaker, original top	20.00	35.00
Sauce dish		
Flat		
4″d	5.00	10.00
5″d	5.00	10.00
Footed		
4″d	5.00	10.00
5″d	5.00	10.00
Spoonholder	25.00	45.00
Sugar bowl, covered	45.00	65.00
Sugar shaker, original lid	35.00	90.00
Syrup pitcher, original top, pressed handle	45.00	135.00
Tray		
Bread, oblong, with rim	30.00	50.00
Water, round	35.00	90.00
Tumbler, water, flat, 3¹/₂″h	20.00	35.00
Wine, 3³/₄″h	20.00	35.00

LEAF AND DART

Covered master salt; syrup; creamer; goblet (double leaf variant); wine.

OMN: Pride. AKA: Double Leaf and Dart.

Non-flint. Richards and Hartley Flint Glass Co., Pittsburgh, PA. ca. 1875. Reissued by the United States Glass Co., Pittsburgh, PA. ca. 1891. Shards have been found at the site of the Boston and Sandwich Glass Co., Sandwich, MA., and the Burlington Glass Works, Hamilton, Ontario, Canada.

Original color production: Clear. Handles are applied.

Reproductions: None.

References: Bat-GPG (PP. 31-33), Brn-SD (PP. 32-33), Cod-OS (P. 19). Grow-WCG (P. 228, Fig. 42-"12"), Hlms-BCA (P. 278), Kam-1 (P. 111), Kam/Wod-Vol.2 (P. 372), Lee-EAPG (Pl. 149, No. 1), Luc-TG (PP. 178-179), Mil-1 (Pl. 42), Mtz-1 (PP. 178-179), Oliv-AAG (P. 69), Rev-APG (P. 288), Stev-ECG (Fig. 246), Thu-1 (P. 198), Uni-1 (P. 198), Uni-TCG (PP. 188-199), Uni/Wor-CHPGT (P. 152), Wlkr-PGA (Fig. 8, Nos. 18, 37, 46).

Items made	Clear	Items made	Clear
Bowl, footed, open, 8¼"d	25.00	Honey dish, round, flat	5.00
Butter dish, covered, flanged base,		Lamp, finger, flat	75.00
7"d., 5"h	85.00	Pitcher, bulbous, applied handle	
Butter pat	20.00	Milk, 1 quart	75.00
Celery vase, pedestaled, scalloped rim	40.00	Water, ½ gallon	85.00
Compote		Relish tray	15.00
Covered, low standard	65.00	Salt, master, covered, footed	65.00
Open, high standard	35.00	Sauce dish, flat, round, 4"d	7.00
Creamer, pedestaled, applied handle,		Spoonholder, footed, 5½"h	35.00
6"h	40.00	Sugar bowl, covered, 7½"h	45.00
Cruet, pedestaled, applied handle	100.00	Syrup	125.00
Egg cup, single, pedestaled	20.00	Tumbler, footed, water	25.00
Goblet	35.00	Wine	35.00

LEAF AND FLOWER

Syrup; salt shaker; celery vase; pepper shaker; tumbler; spoonholder.

OMN: Hobbs No. 339.

Non-flint. Hobbs, Brockunier and Co. (pattern line No. 339), Wheeling, WV. ca. 1890 with continued production by the United States Glass Co., Pittsburgh, PA. ca. 1891.

Original color production: Clear (plain or acid finished), clear with amber stain (plain or acid finished), original decoration numbers being No. 25 and No. 30. Clear with ruby stain is very rare. Most forms are round with scallop and point rims. Handles on pitchers are applied. Originally, lemonade sets were comprised of six tumblers and a tankard pitcher on a flat metal tray. Water sets consisted of two tumblers, a tankard pitcher and finger bowl (most likely used to hold "additional ice") on a metal tray.

Reproductions: None.

References: Eige-CGM WV (P. 6), Lee-VG (Plts. 50, 75), Mtz-1 (P. 76), Pet-Sal (P. 164), Rev-APG (P. 193), Hea-3 (PP. 30, 69), Hea-5 (PP. 42, 126), McCn-PGP (P. 307).

Items made	Clear Stained	Clear Frosted/ Stained
Bowl, round, flat		
Berry, scalloped		
Deep bowl		
5"d	25.00	35.00
7"d	25.00	35.00
8"d	30.00	40.00
Shallow bowl, saucer shape		
7"d	25.00	35.00
8"d	30.00	40.00
9"d	35.00	45.00
Finger, round, scalloped rim	25.00	35.00
Butter dish, covered, flat, flanged base	55.00	85.00
Celery		
Basket shape, flat, scalloped, pressed rope handle	35.00	65.00
Vase, flat, scalloped	35.00	75.00
Condiment set, leaf-shaped under tray complete with salt/pepper shakers, mustard and oil bottle	125.00	150.00
Creamer, flat, applied handle, scalloped rim, low circular foot	30.00	45.00
Pitcher, water, tankard, applied handle, low circular foot	65.00	90.00
Salt shaker, original top	20.00	35.00
Sauce dish, round, flat, 4"d	15.00	20.00
Spoonholder, flat, squatty, scalloped	25.00	40.00
Sugar bowl, covered, flat	35.00	65.00
Syrup pitcher, original top	125.00	250.00
Tumbler, water, flat	20.00	35.00

Spoonholder; relish tray; goblet; flat sauce dish.

OMN: New Martinsville No. 711. AKA: Tobin.

Non-flint. New Martinsville Glass Manufacturing Co. (pattern line No. 711), New Martinsville, WV. ca. 1909-1915. Illustrated in the Butler Brothers 1910 and 1916 catalogs and the ca. 1916 New Martinsville Glass Co. catalog.

Original color production: Clear. Clear with ruby stain, iridescent carnival orange or any other color is rare. The main pattern element of Leaf and Star consists of stylized "C" scrolls separated by vertical prisms forming a seven-point star between each set of "C" scrolls. Handles are pressed and notched, while finials are pseudo-melon shapes. Items may be flat, low footed, or on low circular bases.

Reproductions: None.

References: Hea-1 (P. 28, Fig. 167), Hea-7 (P. 50, Fig. 590), Hea-TPS (P. 97), Kam-2 (P. 36), Kam-6 (P. 17), McCn-PGP (P. 439), Mil-2 (Pl. 136), Milr-MG-1 (PP. 17, 23), Milr-NMG (PP. 17, 23), Mtz-1 (PP. 218-219), Pet-GPP (PP. 130-132), Pet-Sal (P. 24), Uni-1 (PP. 156-157), Uni-2 (P. 143).

Items made	Clear	Items made	Clear
Banana dish, low standard, 8½"	40.00	Creamer, 4½"h	25.00
Bowl, open, footed		Cruet, 5 ounce, flat base, original	
Berry, master, round, deep		faceted stopper	35.00
Flared rim, 7"d	20.00	Custard cup	10.00
Scalloped rim, 8"d	20.00	Dish	
Fruit, crimped rim, 10"d	20.00	Flat	
Nut, 4"d., footed		Bon bon, turned up sides, 5"	15.00
Crimped rim, 4½"d	15.00	Ice cream 6"d	15.00
Cupped rim, 4"d	15.00	Footed, candy, folded sides, 6½"h	15.00
Flared rim, 4½"d	15.00	Dresser jar, original metal lid	20.00
Butter dish, covered, flat, flanged base	35.00	Goblet	20.00
Celery		Hair receiver, original metal top.	15.00
Tray, 11"l	20.00	Humidor, 5"h., 4"d., original silver	
Vase	25.00	plate top	45.00
Compote, jelly, open, high standard	15.00	Pitcher	

Items made	Clear	Items made	Clear
Water, ½ gallon		4½″d	10.00
Ice lip, 8½″h	50.00	Footed, flared rim	
Plain lip	50.00	4″d	15.00
Plate, round		4½″d	15.00
6″d	10.00	Spoonholder	25.00
8″d	10.00	Sugar bowl, covered	30.00
Relish tray	15.00	Toothpick holder	15.00
Salt shaker, original nickel plate top	10.00	Tumbler, water, flat	15.00
Sauce dish, round		Vase, tulip, 8¼″h	15.00
Flat, crimped rim		Wine	20.00
4″d	10.00		

LEVERNE

Wine; bulbous water pitcher.

OMN: Bryce Brothers No. 80. AKA: Star in Honeycomb.

Non-flint. Bryce Brothers (pattern line No. 80), Pittsburgh, PA. ca. late 1880s. Reissued by the United States Glass Co., Pittsburgh, PA. ca. 1891 at Factory "B" (Bryce Brothers, Pittsburgh, PA.). Shards have been found at the site of the Burlington Glass Works, Hamilton, Ontario, Canada. Illustrated in the late 1880s Bryce Brothers/United States Glass Co. catalog.

Original color production: Clear. Odd pieces may be found in amber and apple green.

Reproductions: None.

References: Bat-GPG (PP. 71-72), Drep-FR (P. 215), Hea-5 (P. 82), Hlms-BCA (P. 278), Kam-2 (PP. 122-123), Kam-8 (P. 62), Kam/Wod-Vol.2 (P. 538), Lee-VG (Pl. 77), McCn-PGP (Pl. 249), Mil-1 (Pl. 168), Mtz-1 (PP. 118-119), Rev-APG (P. 90), Spil-AEPG (P. 303), Uni-1 (PP. 132-133), Uni/Wor-CHPGT (P. 163), Wlkr-PGA (Fig. 8, Nos. 37, 45).

Items made	Clear	Items made	Clear
Bowl		Butter dish, covered	40.00
Oval, open, flat. 2″h., 6¼″d	20.00	Cake stand, high standard	35.00
Round, master	20.00	Celery vase	35.00

Items made	Clear	Items made	Clear
Compote, round		Relish dish, oval, $7^1/_4$"l x $5^1/_4$"w	15.00
Covered, high standard, $8^1/_2$"d.,		Sauce dish, round	
$2^1/_2$"h	45.00	Flat	10.00
Open, high standard, $8^1/_2$"d	35.00	Footed, $4^1/_4$"d	10.00
Creamer	35.00	Spoonholder	30.00
Goblet	30.00	Sugar bowl, covered	35.00
Pickle tray	15.00	Tumbler, water, flat	20.00
Pitcher, water, applied handle, $^1/_2$		Wine	20.00
gallon, bulbous	45.00		

LIBERTY BELL

Creamer; covered sugar bowl; spoonholder; covered butter dish.

OMN: Liberty Bell. AKA: Gillinder's Centennial.

Non-flint. Gillinder & Co., Pittsburgh, PA. ca. 1876.

Original color production: Clear. Milk white or any other color is very rare. Designed and patented by James C. Gillinder (design patent No. 8,663) September 28, 1875 (with a seven year patent), Liberty Bell was manufactured and sold at the Gillinder factory built at the Philadelphia Exhibition of 1876. Such items as the snake handled mugs and liberty bell-shaped salt shakers were produced as "Centennial" souveniers and are not original to the set. Handles are reeded and applied.

Reproductions: The American Historical Replica Co., Grand Rapids, MI. issued the following look-alike items from new molds in the Liberty Bell pattern all marked "1776-1976 Declaration of Independence" in clear: 7 ounce goblet, 10 ounce goblet, signers platter (13" x $9^1/_2$" inscribed "Two Hundred Years Ago 1776-1976 Declaration of Independence", freedom platter (oval, handled, $12^1/_2$" x 9" inscribed "Give Us This Day Our Daily Bread" and "Liberty And Freedom 1776-1976", and the John Hancock platter (oval, handled, 13" x $9^1/_2$", inscribed "Two Hundred Years Ago 1776-1976 Declaration of Independence" with John Hancock's signature in $1^1/_2$"h. letters).

References: Belnp-MG (P. 59), Fer-YMG (PP. 117-118), Gor-CC (PP. 77, 97, 110-113), Hrtng-P&P (P. 57), Hea-TPS (PP. 78, 88), Inn-PG (P. 432), Kam-1 (PP. 25-26), Lee-EAPG (Pl.

58, No. 2), Lind-HG (PP. 42-43), McCn-PGP (P. 531), Mil-1 (Pl. 29), Mtz-1 (P. 112), Oliv-AAG (P. 70), Pet-GPP (PP. 106-108), Rev-APG (P. 167), Spil-AEPG (PP. 288-289), Spil-TBV (P. 277), Stu-BP (P. 96), Uni-1 (P. 275), Wlkr-PGA (Fig. 8, No. 7).

Items made	Clear	Items made	Clear
Bowl, master berry, footed, open, 8″d	100.00	Pitcher, water, applied reeded handle	650.00
Butter dish, covered, table size, flat ...	100.00	Plate, round, handled	
Celery vase, pedestaled, scalloped rim	85.00	6″d, dated	75.00
Compote, open, collared base, round		8″d	75.00
6″d	75.00	10″d	85.00
6³⁄₄″d	75.00	Platter	
8″d	85.00	"100 Years Ago, John Hancock" with	
Creamer, footed, table size		twig handles, 13³⁄₈″l	85.00
Applied clear handle, 7¹⁄₄″h	100.00	"Signer's Border", 13″l	65.00
Applied reeded handle	100.00	"Thirteen States", 13″l	65.00
Goblet	45.00	Relish tray, oval	45.00
Miniatures		Salt	
Butter dish, covered	150.00	Dip, individual, oval, flat, 1″h., 2¹⁄₄″l	35.00
Creamer, pressed handle	75.00	Shaker, shaped like the Liberty Bell,	
Mug, pressed handle, 2″h., embossed		original top (not original to the set)	
"1776-1876" between two liberty		Embossed "1776-1876" on bottom	95.00
bells	200.00	Plain bottom	80.00
Spoonholder (R)	200.00	Sauce dish, round	
Sugar bowl, covered	150.00	Flat, handled, 4¹⁄₂″d	20.00
Mug, Liberty bell shape, footed, snake		Footed, 4¹⁄₂″d	25.00
shaped handle, impressed on base		Spoonholder, pedestaled, scalloped	
"Manufactured at the Centennial		rim, table size, 6¹⁄₄″h	45.00
Exhibition by Gillinder And Sons"		Sugar bowl, covered, pedestaled, table	
(not original to the set)	450.00	size	100.00
Pickle dish, flat	45.00		

LILY OF THE VALLEY

Bulbous milk pitcher; spoonholder.

Goblet

AKA: Lily of the Valley on Legs (footed pieces only).

Non-flint. The Boston & Sandwich Glass Co., Sandwich, MA. ca. 1870s. King, Son and Co., Pittsburgh, PA. ca. 1870s. Shards have been found at the site of the Burlington Glass Co., Hamilton, Ontario, Canada.

Original color production: Clear. Produced in two variations: a) items with hexagonal stems, with applied handles, and b) 3-legged items with pressed handles. To date, only the four piece table set and covered master salt have been noted in the 3-legged version.

Reproductions: None.

References: Cod-OS (Pl. 19), Enos-MPG (Chart-1), Hlms-BCA (P. 278), Kam-4 (PP. 4-5), Kam/Wod-Vol.2 (P. 373), Lee-EAPG (Pl. 126, No. 2), McCn-PGP, (Pl. 139), Mil-1 (Pl. 43), Mtz-1 (PP. 58-59), Oliv-AAG (P. 70), Uni-1 (PP. 196-197), Uni/Wor-CHPGT (PP. 154-155), Uni-TCG (PP. 120-121), Wlkr-PGA (Fig. 8, Nos. 24, 27).

Items made	Clear	Items made	Clear
Bowl, master berry, open, flat	45.00	Honey dish, round, flat, 3½"d	10.00
Butter dish, covered		Pickle scoop, 8"l., tapered at one end	20.00
Flat	65.00	Pitcher, bulbous, applied handle,	
3-legged	85.00	circular foot	
Cake stand, high standard	65.00	Milk, 1 quart	100.00
Celery		Water, ½ gallon, 8½"h	125.00
Tray	40.00	Relish dish, oval, tapered	20.00
Vase, pedestaled, scalloped rim, 8"h	45.00	Salt, master	
Compote, high standard		Covered, 3-legged	125.00
Covered 8½"d	90.00	Open, footed, smooth rim	40.00
Open 8½"d	50.00	Sauce dish, flat, round, cable edge, 4"d	10.00
Cordial (R)	85.00	Spoonholder	
Creamer		Pedestaled, scalloped rim	30.00
Pedestaled, applied handle	65.00	3-legged	25.00
3-legged, pressed handle	55.00	Sugar bowl, covered	
Cruet, pedestaled, applied handle,		Pedestaled	65.00
original stopper	125.00	3-legged	85.00
Dish, vegetable, oval, flat (3 nested		Tumbler, water (R)	
sizes) each	30.00	Flat	85.00
Egg cup, single, footed	30.00	Footed	65.00
Goblet (height varies)	55.00	Wine (R)	175.00

Low standard open compote; syrup pitcher.

Covered butter dish; goblet; egg cup.

AKA: Oval and Lincoln Drape.

Flint, non-flint. The Boston & Sandwich Glass Co., Sandwich, MA. ca. 1865-1880.

Original color production: Clear. Cobalt blue, opaque white, green or any other color is very rare. Produced with or without the "tassel ornament". Handles are applied.

Reproductions: None.

References: Brn-SD (P. 51), Cod-OS (Pl. 21), Enos-MPG (Chart-4), Inn-PG (P. 177), Lee-EAPG (Pl. 46, No. 4), Lind-HG (P. 292), McKrn-AG (PP. 400, 405), Mil-1 (Pl. 118), Mtz-1 (P. 12), Oliv-AAG (P. 56), Pap-GAG (P. 191), Phil-EOG (P. 188), Schwtz-AG (P. 120), Spil-AEPG (P. 272), Uni-1 (P. 277), Wlkr-PGA (Fig. 8, Nos. 24, 47).

Items made	Clear	Items made	Clear
Butter dish, covered, flat	100.00	Lamp, oil	
Celery vase, pedestaled, scalloped rim	90.00	All glass	
Compote		Miniature, with original matching	
Covered, high standard		shade, burner and chimney	100.00
7½"d	125.00	Stand lamp	150.00
8½"d	150.00	Marble base	125.00
Open, low standard		Pitcher, water, applied handle (R)	450.00
6"d	65.00	Plate, round, 6"d	85.00
7½"d	65.00	Salt, master, footed, open	25.00
Creamer, applied handle	125.00	Spoonholder, pedestaled, scalloped rim	75.00
Decanter	300.00	Sugar bowl, covered	175.00
Egg cup, single, footed	50.00	Syrup pitcher, applied handle, original	
Goblet		top	175.00
Gentleman's (large), 6"h	125.00	Tumbler, flat	125.00
Lady's (small)	165.00	Wine (R)	150.00
Honey dish, flat, round	20.00		

LION

Egg cup; goblet; 9"h. syrup; 6½"h. syrup; wine; master salt.

AKA: Frosted Lion.

Non-flint. Gillinder & Sons, Philadelphia, PA. ca. 1877.

Original color production: Clear with acid finish (plain or copper wheel engraved). Unlike the "Lion Head" pattern, items in Frosted Lion have collared bases with complete lion finials (Lion and Tree Trunk or Rampant Lion figures). Interchangeable items between Lion Head and Frosted Lion are stemmed items such as the celery vase, goblet and wine. Produced in a complete table setting in clear with acid finish, all-clear pieces are unusual. Items not original to the set are the Lion tumbler (produced at a much later date) and the reclining lion paperweight marked "Centennial, 1876" (produced to commemorate the Centennial as a souvenir item).

Spoonholder (etched); bulbous water pitcher; celery vase (etched); oval compote.

Reproductions: Reproduced from the early 1930s by numerous concerns including the Imperial Glass Co., Bellaire, OH., the Summit Art Glass Co., Mogadore/Rootstown, OH., and the Westmorland Glass Co., Grapeville, PA., early reproductions have a chalk-like finish that is rough to the touch, while the lion's mouth appears to sag downward. In the early 1960s, the Imperial Glass Co., Bellaire, OH. issued the amber Lion compote with the entwined "I.G." insignia on the base and "Patented August 6th, 1889" inside the lid. By 1984, the Summit Art Glass Co. issued a look-alike $2^7/_8''$d. round dish with circular foot in clear, blue, green and light cobalt blue, often mistaken for a master salt. To date, the following items have been reissued from new molds: 4"d. sauce dish (clear/frosted), $10^1/_2''$d. handled bread plate (amber, blue, canary-yellow), covered butter dish (clear/frosted), celery vase (clear/frosted), oval high standard covered compote (clear/frosted), covered sugar bowl (clear/frosted), egg cup (clear/frosted), goblet (clear/frosted), medium oval bowl (clear/frosted), water pitcher (clear/frosted), and spoonholder (clear/frosted).

References: Chip-ROS (P. 81), Drep-ABC OG (P. 145), Enos-MPG (Charts 1, 5), Gor-CC (P. 123), Grow-GAG (P. 149, Fig. 22-"4"), Hrtng-P&P (P. 58), Kam-1 (P. 43), Kam-5 (P. 40), Lee-AF (Plts. 72-75), Lee-EAPG (Plts. 90-93), Lee-VG (Plts. 2, 8), Lind-HG (P. 518), McKrn-AG (Plts. 209, 211), Mil-1 (Pl. 149), Mor-OG (Fig. 3), Mtz-1 (P. 96), Mtz-2 (P. 192), Nortn-PG (PP. 49-57), Oliv-AAG (P. 76), Rev-APG (P. 171), Shu-LPG (Plts. 1-33), Spil-AEPG (P. 283), Stu-BP (P. 84), Uni-1 (P. 90).

Items made	Clear/ Frosted	Items made	Clear/ Frosted
Butter dish, covered, preying lion finial	125.00	8"d	150.00
Celery vase, pedestaled, scalloped rim	85.00	Three lion face stem, rampant lion finial	
Cheese dish, covered, rampant lion finial	400.00	6"d	150.00
Cologne bottle, original stopper (VR)	350.00+	7"d	175.00
Compote, covered		8"d	200.00
Oval, collared base, preying lion finial		9"d	225.00
$6^7/_8''$	100.00	Cordial, 3 lion face stem, $4^3/_4''$h (R)	300.00+
$7^3/_4''$	125.00	Egg cup, collared base	85.00
$8^3/_4''$	145.00	Marmalade jar, preying lion finial	85.00
Round, collared base, rampant lion finial		Pitcher, applied handle, base matches collared items, bulbous	
7"d	150.00	Milk, 1 quart	275.00
		Water, $^1/_2$ gallon	450.00

Items made	Clear/Frosted	Items made	Clear/Frosted
Platter, 13″l., oval, reclining lion handles	75.00	Sugar bowl, covered, collared base, preying lion finial	100.00
Goblet, 3 lion face stem	75.00	Syrup, applied handle, original top	
Salt, master, rectangular, collared base	250.00	6½″h., lid dated "July 16, '72— C&W"	350.00
Sauce dish, collared base, smooth rim		7⅜″h., lid dated "July 16, '72"	350.00
4″d	25.00	9″h., lid not dated	400.00
4½″d	25.00		
Spoonholder, collared base, scalloped rim	65.00		

LION AND BABOON

Covered sugar bowl; celery vase; covered butter dish; spoonholder.

Non-flint. Maker unknown, ca. late 1870s, early 1880s.

Original color production: Clear. A simple pattern composed of slightly convex vertical clear panels, the most outstanding characteristics of Lion and Baboon are the baboon-like feet that rest upon clear circular bases and lion-heads that form both finials and the tops of handles. Any piece in Lion and Baboon is rare.

Reproductions: None.

References: Kam-3 (P. 57), Mtz-1 (P. 96), Mtz-2 (P. 84), Righ-IC (P. 341).

Items made	Clear	Items made	Clear
Butter dish, covered, flanged rim	125.00	Water, ½ gallon (VR)	175.00
Celery vase	65.00	Milk, 1 quart (VR)	150.00
Creamer	55.00	Spoonholder	45.00
Pitcher, pressed handle		Sugar bowl, covered	110.00

LION AND CABLE

Goblet; spoonholder; bread plate; covered sugar bowl; salt shaker.

OMN: Richards and Hartley No. 525, Proud Lion. AKA: Tiny Lion.

Non-flint. Richards & Hartley Glass Co. (pattern line No. 525), Tarentum, PA. ca. 1880s.

Original color production: Clear, clear with acid finish (plain or copper wheel engraved). Unlike Lion and Lion Head, footed items in Lion & Cable have cable edges, handled items having tiny reclining lion forms. Finials are also tiny reclining lions.

Reproductions: None

References: Kam-2, Mtz-2 (P. 82).

Items made	Clear	Items made	Clear
Butter dish, covered, reclining lion finial	50.00	Marmalade jar, reclining lion finial, handled	55.00
Celery vase, handled	40.00	Pitcher	
Compote, covered, reclining lion finial		Milk, 1 quart, tiny lion on handle	45.00
High standard		Water, ½ gallon, tiny lion on handle	55.00
7″d	55.00	Plate, bread (similar handles as on butter), "Proud Lion" center	40.00
8″d	65.00		
9″d	75.00	Salt shaker, no lions on handles, original top	25.00
Low standard		Sauce dish (similar handles as on butter)	15.00
7″d	55.00		
8″d	65.00	Spoonholder	25.00
9″d	75.00	Sugar bowl, covered, reclining lion finial	40.00
Creamer, pressed handle	30.00		
Goblet (previously unlisted)	45.00		

Creamer and covered sugar (both etched); covered compote, covered butter, sauce dish (all plain).

Non-flint. Possibly Gillinder & Sons, Philadelphia, PA. ca. 1877.

Original color production: Clear with acid finish. Lion Head differs from Gillinder's "Lion" in that bases in Lion Head are plain with a cable edge, the finials of covered pieces being lion heads with or without thumbprints. Although collected by lion collectors, the frosted lion head paperweight is not original to the pattern.

Reproductions: A look-alike master salt not original to the set has been issued in clear with acid finish in the mid 1980s with lion heads around the base.

References: Chip-ROS (P. 81), Drep-ABC OG (P. 145), Enos-MPG (Charts 1,5), Hrtng-P&P (P. 58), Kam-1 (P. 43), Kam-5 (P. 50), Lee-AF (Plts. 72-75), Lee-EAPG (Plts. 90-93), Lee-VG (Plts. 2, 8), Lind-HG (P. 518), McKrn-AG (Plts. 209, 211), Mil-1 (Pl. 149), Mor-OG (Fig. 3), Mtz-1 (P. 96), Mtz-2 (P. 192), Nortn-PG (PP. 49-57), Rev-APG (P. 171), Shu-LPG (Plts. 1-33), Spil-AEPG (P. 283), Stu-BP (P. 84), Uni-1 (P. 90).

Items made	Clear/ Frosted
Butter dish, covered	
Lion head finial	65.00
Lion head with thumbprint finial	65.00
Child miniature items	
Butter dish, covered, lion head finial	175.00
Creamer	100.00
Cup/saucer set	90.00
Spoonholder	90.00
Sugar bowl, covered	150.00
Creamer, plain cable base (no lion)	25.00
Compote, covered, high standard	
Plain cable edged base, 7″d., low lion head finial without thumbprints	86.00
Three-Lion-Face standard	
Lion Head finial	
6″d	75.00
7″d	80.00

Items made	Clear/ Frosted
8″d	85.00
9″d	90.00
Lion Head finial with thumbprints	
6″d	75.00
7″d	80.00
8″d	85.00
9″d	90.00
Marmalade jar, covered, lion head finial	85.00
Sauce dish, footed, plain cable base	
4″d	20.00
4½″d	20.00
5″d	20.00
Spoonholder, plain cable base (no lions)	30.00
Sugar bowl, covered, plain cable base, lion head finial with thumbprints	45.00

Footed covered butter (etched/crown finial); celery vase; covered sugar (lion finial); covered sugar (crown finial); flat butter (lion finial).

Non-flint. Maker unknown, ca. late 1880s.

Original color production: Clear. Produced in two distinct finial styles: a) crown shape, and b) a reclining lion. Differences in standards include more than one source of manufacturer.

Reproductions: None.

References: None.

Items made	Clear	Items made	Clear
Butter dish, covered		Creamer (no lion)	25.00
Crown finial	40.00	Pitcher, water, $\frac{1}{2}$ gallon	55.00
Reclining lion finial	40.00	Spoonholder (no lion)	25.00
Celery vase (no lion).	30.00	Sugar bowl, covered	
Compote, covered, high standard,		Crown finial	35.00
8¼"d., tiny reclining lion on scalloped		Reclining lion finial	35.00
finial	50.00		

High standard open compote.

Goblet.

OMN: Heisey No. 160. AKA: Stippled Beaded Shield [Millard].

Non-flint. A.H. Heisey Co., Inc. (pattern line No. 160), Newark, OH. ca. 1896. Illustrated in an undated (ca. 1897) A.H. Heisey catalog.

Original color production: Clear. Clear with ruby stain (plain or with gilt). Clear pieces were purchased by the Oriental Glass Co., Pittsburgh, PA., decorated, and sold as their own product. Green, milk white, vaseline or any other color is very rare. The main pattern design element of Locket on Chain consists of large beaded oval medallions suspended from what resembles a beaded looped chain. Separating each medallion vertically and continuing the beading at the base is a more solid ornamental band.

Reproductions: None.

References: Brn-H (P. 28), Hea-1 (P. 52), Hea-3 (P. 56, Fig. 437), Hea-6 (P. 34, Fig. 225), Hea-7 (P. 143), Hea-TPS (PP. 27, 52), Kam-2 (P. 57), Kam-8 (Pl. 88), McCn-PGP (P. 90), Mil-2 (Pl. 118), Pet-Sal (Pl. 33), Rev-APG (P. 177), Uni-2 (P. 119), Vog-H 1896-1905 (P. 101).

Items made	Clear	Clear w/Ruby
Bowl, open, flat, master berry, 8"d	85.00	125.00
Butter dish, covered	100.00	250.00
Cake stand, high standard	125.00	—
Celery vase	90.00	165.00
Compote, high standard		
Covered, 8"d	175.00	—
Open, 8"d	125.00	—
Creamer, 4⅝"h, 1 pint	85.00	150.00
Cruet, original stopper (VR)	150.00	1500.00
Goblet	85.00	—
Pickle tray	45.00	85.00
Pitcher, water, ½ gallon	185.00	—
Plate, 8"d	65.00	—
Salt shaker, original top	65.00	125.00
Sauce dish, flat, round, 4"d	35.00	50.00

Items made	Clear	Clear w/Ruby
Spoonholder	75.00	140.00
Sugar bowl, covered	15.00	250.00
Syrup pitcher, original top (VR)	150.00	1500.00
Toothpick holder (VR)	300.00	1200.00
Tumbler, water, flat	80.00	150.00
Wine	75.00	250.00

LOG CABIN

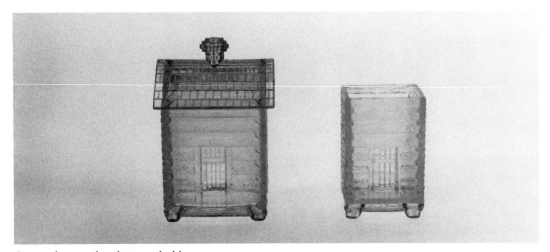

Covered sugar bowl; spoonholder.

OMN: Central's No. 748.

Non-flint. The Central Glass Co. (pattern line No. 748), Wheeling, WV. ca. 1875.

Original color production: Clear, the main pattern design element consisting of clear stippled logs. Similar to each other in form and design, pieces are square shaped and rest on four stubby log feet, while the standards of compotes are in the form of tree trunks. Handles are pressed. To date, neither a goblet nor a tumbler have surfaced. Amber, blue, vaseline or any other color is very rare.

Reproductions: The following items have been reproduced from the mid–1980s in clear, cobalt blue and chocolate: covered sugar bowl, 5″h. creamer, and spoonholder.

References: Drep-ABC OG (P. 145), Eige-CGM WV (P. 17), Enos-MPG (Chart-2), Kam-6 (PP. 59-60), Lee-EAPG (Pl. 106, No. 2), Lind-HG (P. 198), McCn-PGP (P. 497), Mtz-1 (P. 6), Rev-APG (PP. 111, 115), Wlkr-PGA (Fig. 15, No. 43).

Items made	Clear	Items made	Clear
Bowl, covered		10½″d	350.00
8″ x 5¼″ x 3⅝″	225.00	Creamer, 5″h	125.00
8¾″l., 8⅜″w., 8¾″h.	225.00	Marmalade jar, covered	300.00
Butter dish, covered	350.00	Pitcher, water, ½ gallon, 8¼″h	350.00
Compote, covered, high standard		Sauce dish, flat, rectangular, smooth	
4¾″d., 8¾″h	275.00	flat rim	85.00

334

Items made	Clear	Items made	Clear
Spoonholder, smooth flat rim	125.00	Sugar bowl, covered (R)	350.00

LOOP

Wine; l.s. open compote; h.s. open compote; covered sugar; covered butter.

OMN: Central's No. 145, O'Hara No. 9. Portland Petal. AKA: McKee's O'Hara pattern, Seneca Loop.

Flint, non-flint. Central Glass Co. (pattern line No. 145), Wheeling, WV. ca. 1870. Challinor, Taylor & Co., Pittsburgh, PA. ca. 1875. Doyle and Co., Pittsburgh, PA. ca. 1875. James B. Lyon and Co., Pittsburgh, PA. ca. 1860s. McKee Brothers, Pittsburgh, PA. ca. 1875. O'Hara Glass Co. (pattern line No. 9), Pittsburgh, PA. ca. 1860s. Portland Glass Co., Portland, ME. Boston & Sandwich Glass Co., Sandwich, MA. (firey opalescent items). Reissued by the United States Glass Co., Pittsburgh, PA. ca. 1891. Shards have been found at the site of the Burlington Glass Works, Hamilton, Ontario, Canada. Illustrated in the 1875-1890 O'Hara Glass Co. catalog and the 1891 United States Glass Co. catalog.

Original color production: Clear. Amethyst, amber, blue, green or any other color is rare. As numerous factories produced a loop pattern, differences in bases, finials, handles, and stems are commonplace.

Reproductions: None.

References: Chip-ROS (P. 79), Enos-MPG (Charts, 1,3), Hlms-BCA (P. 278), Inn-PG (PP. 306-309), Kam-3 (PP. 30-31), Kam-4 (P. 16), Lee-EAPG (P. 638), Le/Ros-CP (No. 270), Lee-SG (Pl. 192), Mag-FIEF (P. 15, Fig. 13), McKrn-AG (Pl. 197, Nos. 1, 3), Mil-1 (Pl. 13), Mtz-1 (PP. 38-39), Pet-GPP (P. 113), Rev-APG (P. 116), Spil-AEPG (PP. 220, 222), Stot-McKe (PP. 70-73), Uni-1 (P. 21), Uni/Wod-CHPGT (P. 198).

Items made	Flint	Non-flint
Bottle		
Bitters	45.00	—
Water	65.00	—
Bowl, covered, flat, 9″d	80.00	25.00
Butter dish, covered, flat		

Items made	Flint	Non-flint
"Old Style", scalloped rim	60.00	40.00
"New Style", smooth rim	60.00	40.00
Cake stand, high standard	100.00	—
Celery vase, pedestaled, scalloped rim	65.00	20.00
Champagne	45.00	20.00
Compote, high standard, round		
Covered		
7½"d., 8½"h	135.00	85.00
9½"d	150.00	85.00
Open		
Deep bowl		
7"d	75.00	—
9"d	100.00	35.00
10"d	125.00	40.00
Shallow bowl, 7"d	75.00	—
Cordial, 2¾"h	40.00	20.00
Creamer, footed, applied handle (designated as "Old and New" style)	75.00	35.00
Decanter		
"Old Style", short neck		
Bar lip, quart	75.00	—
Patterned stopper		
Pint	65.00	—
Quart	90.00	—
"New Style", patterned stopper		
Pint	65.00	—
Quart	90.00	—
Egg cup, single	25.00	15.00
Goblet		
Gentleman's	20.00	15.00
Lady's	20.00	15.00
Lamp, oil, 9¾"h, original burner and chimney	225.00	100.00
Pitcher		
3 pint, milk	150.00	85.00
½ gallon, water	175.00	65.00
Plate, round	40.00	25.00
Salt, master, footed, open	25.00	15.00
Spoonholder, 5½"h	35.00	20.00
Sugar bowl, covered		
"Old Style", scalloped rim	75.00	30.00
"New Style", smooth rim	75.00	30.00
Syrup pitcher, applied handle, original top	100.00	—
Tumbler, water		
Flat	40.00	20.00
Footed	25.00	15.00
Vase		
9¾"h	40.00	20.00
10¾"h	40.00	20.00
11¾"h	40.00	20.00
Wine	30.00	10.00

Footed tumbler; goblet; flat sauce dish.

Spoonholder; goblet; footed tumbler.

Non-flint. Richards & Hartley Glass Co., Tarentum, PA. ca. 1888. Portland Glass Co., Portland, ME. ca. 1869. Shards have been found at the site of the Boston & Sandwich Glass Co., Sandwich, MA. Designed and patented by Annie W. Henderson (design patent No. 3,515).

Original color production: Clear, the main pattern design element standing in high relief against a heavily stippled background. Handles are applied and crimped at the base. Stems are hexagonal in shape.

Reproductions: None.

References: Brn-SD (P. 55, No. 336), Cod-OS (Pl. 24), Enos-MPG (Chart-7), Hart-AG (P. 87), Kam-8 (PP. 4-5), Lee-EAPG (Pl. 149, No. 3), Luc-TG (P. 177), Mil-1 (Pl. 42), Mtz-1 (PP. 178-179), Oliv-AAG (P. 69), Rev-APG (P. 285), Uni-1 (P. 179), Wlkr-PGA (Fig 15, No. 150).

Items made	Clear	Items made	Clear
Bowl, oval, flat, 9″	25.00	Lamp, oil, complete with original	
Butter dish, covered	45.00	burner and chimney	85.00
Cake stand, high standard, 10″d	40.00	Pickle tray	15.00
Celery vase, pedestaled, scalloped rim	35.00	Pitcher, water, bulbous, applied handle	85.00
Compote, covered, round		Plate, 6″d. (R)	40.00
High standard, 8″d	85.00	Relish tray	15.00
Low standard, 8″d	65.00	Salt, master, footed, covered	65.00
Cordial	45.00	Sauce dish, round	
Creamer, pedestaled, applied handle,		Flat, 4″d	8.00
6¼″h	35.00	Footed, 4″d	8.00
Cruet, pedestaled, applied handle,		Spoonholder, pedestaled, scalloped rim	30.00
original stopper	90.00	Sugar bowl, covered, pedestaled	55.00
Cup plate	30.00	Tumbler, water	
Egg cup, single, footed	25.00	Flat	30.00
Goblet	30.00	Footed	40.00
		Wine	35.00

LOOP AND DART, ROUND ORNAMENT

Relish tray; h.s. covered compote; honey dish.

AKA: Portland Loop and Jewel.

Flint, non-flint. The Portland Glass Co., Portland, ME., ca. 1869. Shards have been found at the site of the Boston & Sandwich Glass Co., Sandwich, MA.

Original color production: Clear. Designed and patented by W.O. Davis, May 11, 1869 (design patent No. 3,494).

References: Bat-GPG (P. 31, No. 29), Cod-OS (Pl. 24), Kam-3 (PP. 3, 121), Lee-EAPG (Pl. 149, No. 2), Lee/Rose (P. 501, No. 891), Mtz-1 (P. 178), Mil-1 (Pl. 42), Mtz-2 (P. 194), Oliv-AAG (P. 69), Rev-APG (P. 2820), Spil-AEPG (P. 269), Swn-PG (PP. 54-58), Tass-AG (P. 77), Uni-1 (P. 179), Wlkr-PGA (Fig. 15, No. 151).

Items made	Clear	Items made	Clear
Bowl, oval, flat, 9″d	20.00	Pickle dish, oval (2 sizes)	15.00
Butter dish, covered, flat	45.00	Pitcher, water, bulbous, applied	
Celery vase, pedestaled, scalloped rim	30.00	handle, ½ gallon	90.00
Champagne	85.00	Plate, round, 6″d	30.00
Compote, round		Relish tray, oval	15.00
Covered, 8″d		Salt, master, footed, open	15.00
High standard	85.00	Sauce dish, flat, round	
Low standard	85.00	3¾″d., star base	5.00
Open, 8″d		4″d., loop and dart in base	5.00
High standard	45.00	Spoonholder, pedestaled, scalloped rim	25.00
Low standard	45.00	Sugar bowl, covered	
Creamer, pedestaled, applied handled	35.00	Cover fits inside of base	40.00
Cup plate, 3″d	25.00	Cover fits over outside of base	40.00
Egg cup, single, footed, smooth rim	20.00	Tumbler	
Honey dish, round, flat	5.00	Footed	40.00
Goblet	25.00	Flat	40.00
Lamp, oil	75.00	Wine	35.00

LOOP AND DART WITH DIAMOND ORNAMENT

Goblet; wine.

Flint, non-flint. Shards have been found at the site of the Boston & Sandwich Glass Co., Sandwich, MA.

Original color production: Clear. Handles are applied, stems are hexagonal.

Reproductions: None.

References: Chip-ROS (P. 85), Kam-1 (P. 11), Mil-1 (Pl. 42), Mtz-1 (P. 178), Oliv-AAG (P. 69), Uni/Wor-CHPGT (P. 152), Uni-1 (P. 151).

Items made	Clear	Items made	Clear
Bowl, open, oval, 9″l	20.00	Low standard	55.00
Butter dish, covered, flat	65.00	Open	
Celery vase, pedestaled	35.00	High standard	35.00
Compote, round		Low standard	25.00
Covered		Cordial	50.00
High standard	65.00	Creamer, pedestaled, applied handle	40.00

339

Open sugar bowl (lid missing); egg cup.

Items made	Clear
Egg cup, single, pedestaled, smooth rim	25.00
Goblet	30.00
Pitcher, water, bulbous, applied handle, ½ gallon	125.00
Plate, round, 6"d	35.00
Relish tray, oval	15.00

Items made	Clear
Salt, master, footed, covered	85.00
Sauce dish, round, flat	8.00
Spoonholder	35.00
Sugar bowl, covered	45.00
Tumbler, water, footed	25.00
Wine	35.00

LOOP AND JEWEL

Sauce dish 4"d.; covered butter; berry sugar bowl; sauce 4½"d.

AKA: Jewel and Festoon, Queen's Necklace [Kamm], Venus.

Non-flint. Indiana Glass Co., Dunkirk, IN. ca. 1903. National Glass Co., Dunkirk, IN. ca. 1905 until 1915. Illustrated in the Baltimore Bargain House August 15, 1904 catalog No. 496.

Original color production: Clear. Milk white or any other color is rare. Compote lids may be plain or designed. Handles are pressed.

Reproductions: None.

References: Bond-AG (P. 69), Drep-ABC OG (P. 141), Hea-OPG (PP. 87-88), Kam-1 (PP. 66-67), Lee-VG (Pl. 28, No. 4), Lee-VG (Plts. 27-28), McCn-PGP (P. 345), Mil-2 (Pl. 1340), Mtz-1 (P. 192), Pet-Sal (P. 33).

Items made	Clear	Items made	Clear
Bowl, open, flat, round		Shaker, original top	15.00
6"d	15.00	Sauce dish	
7"d	20.00	Flat	
8"d	20.00	4"d	5.00
Butter dish, covered, flat	55.00	4½"d	5.00
Compote, open, high standard, 6½"d	20.00	Footed	
Creamer, 4½"h	25.00	4"d	7.00
Cup, sherbert	15.00	4½"d	7.00
Dish, flat, 5" square	15.00	Spoonholder, beaded rim	20.00
Goblet	20.00	Sugar bowl	
Pickle dish, rectangular, 8½"l x 4½"w	15.00	Berry, true open, three handled	20.00
Pitcher, water, ½ gallon	45.00	Individual, true open, three handled	20.00
Plate, 5½"sq	15.00	Table size, covered	40.00
Relish tray, rectangular, 8"l	15.00	Syrup pitcher, original top	55.00
Salt		Vase, 8¾"h., original top	40.00
Master, footed, open	20.00	Wine	30.00

LOOP WITH DEWDROP(S)

Tumbler; creamer; covered sugar bowl; goblet; wine.

OMN: U.S. Glass No. 15,028.

Non-flint. The United States Glass Co. (pattern line No. 15,028), Pittsburgh, PA. ca. 1892. Illustrated in the ca. 1895, 1895-1896, and 1898 United States Glass Co. catalogs.

Original color production: Clear. Handles are pressed.

Reproductions: None.

References: Hea-5 (PP. 13, 20), Kam-1 (P. 72), Kam-6 (P. 29), Lee-EAPG (Pl. 79), McCn-PGP (P. 341), Mil-1 (Pl. 89), Mtz-1 (Pl. 188), Pet-Sal (P. 33), Rev-APG (PP. 309, 314), Uni-1 (P. 312), Wlkr-PGA (Fig. 8, Nos. 45).

Items made	Clear	Items made	Clear
Bowl, round, open, flat, deep		8"d	25.00
5"d	10.00	Condiment set under tray, handled	15.00
6"d	10.00	Creamer	20.00
7"d	10.00	Cup	10.00
8"d	15.00	Cruet, original stopper	45.00
9"d	15.00	Dish, open, oval, flat	
Butter dish, covered, flat		7"	10.00
No handles	35.00	8"	10.00
Tab handles	40.00	9"	15.00
Cake stand, high standard		Goblet	25.00
9"d	30.00	Pickle dish, oval, handled	15.00
10"d	35.00	Pitcher, water, ½ gallon	40.00
Celery vase, smooth rim	30.00	Plate, bread, handled	25.00
Compote, high standard, round		Salt shaker, original top	25.00
Covered		Sauce dish, round	
5"d	25.00	Flat, 4"d	10.00
6"d	25.00	Footed, 4"d	10.00
7"d	30.00	Saucer	10.00
8"d	35.00	Spoonholder, smooth rim	15.00
Open		Sugar bowl, covered, footed	35.00
4½"d	15.00	Syrup pitcher, original top	50.00
5"d	15.00	Tumbler, water, flat	15.00
6"d	20.00	Wine	30.00
7"d	20.00		

LORRAINE

Creamer; condiment set; covered sugar bowl; spoonholder.

OMN: Fostoria No. 301, Lorraine. AKA: Flat Diamond.

Non-flint. Fostoria Glass Co. (pattern line No. 301), Fostoria, OH. ca. 1893.

Original color production: Clear, clear with ruby stain. Shapes are square, with square pointed finials.

References: Bar-RS (Pl. 14), Hea-3 (P. 24), Kam-3 (PP. 94, 147), Kam-5 (P. 82), Mtz-2 (P. 132), Pet-Sal (P. 28), Rev-APG (P. 157), Wlkr-PGA (Fig. 15, No. 99).

Items made	Clear	Clear w/Ruby
Bowl, open, flat, straight-sided, master berry, scalloped rim	25.00	40.00
Creamer	25.00	45.00
Condiment set (tab handled undertray, salt & pepper shakers with original tops, covered mustard)	75.00	125.00
Cruet, original faceted stopper	35.00	165.00
Pitcher, water, ½ gallon	50.00	125.00
Salt shaker, tall, flat, original top	20.00	35.00
Spoonholder, flat, smooth rim	20.00	35.00
Sugar bowl, covered, flat	35.00	65.00
Syrup pitcher, original top	45.00	150.00
Tumbler, flat, water	15.00	35.00

LOUISIANA

Goblet; covered sugar bowl; h.s. 5″ jelly compote; salt shaker.

OMN: U.S. Glass No. 15,053, Louisiana. AKA: Granby, Sharp Oval and Diamond.

Non-flint. Bryce Brothers, Pittsburgh, PA. ca. 1870s. Reissued by the United States Glass Co. (pattern line No. 15,053), Pittsburgh, PA. at Factory "B" (Bryce Brothers, Pittsburgh, PA.) ca. 1898. Illustrated in the United States Glass Co. 1898, and 1904 catalogs.

Original color production: Clear, clear with acid finish.

Reproductions: None.

References: Bros-TS (P. 44), Hart/Cobb-SS (P. 37), Hrtng-P&P (P. 61), Hea-5 (P. 164, Pl. A), Kam-1 (P. 59), Kam-6 (Pl. 93), McCn-PGP (P. 231), Mil-1 (Pl. 92), Pet-Sal (P. 33), Rev-APG (P. 314), Uni-1 (P. 313), Wlkr-PGA (Fig. 8, No. 54).

Items made	Clear	Items made	Clear
Bowl, flat, round		8"d	25.00
Covered		Flared bowl, 6"d	15.00
6"d.	25.00	Saucer bowl	
7"d	30.00	8"d	25.00
8"d	35.00	10"d	30.00
Open		Creamer	35.00
Round		Dish, flat, handled	
6"d	15.00	Covered, 6"d	25.00
7"d	20.00	Open, 6"d	15.00
8"d	20.00	Goblet	30.00
Square		Match holder, attached saucer base	30.00
6"	20.00	Mug, handled	25.00
7"	20.00	Mustard, covered with matching	
8"	25.00	patterned underplate	40.00
9"	25.00	Pickle dish, boat shaped	15.00
Butter dish, covered, flat, flanged base	70.00	Pitcher, pressed handle	
Cake stand, high standard		Milk	55.00
7"d	45.00	Water, ½ gallon	65.00
9"d	50.00	Relish tray	15.00
10"d	55.00	Salt shaker, original top	25.00
Celery vase	30.00	Sauce dish, flat	
Compote, high standard, round		Round	
Covered		4"d	10.00
6"d	40.00	4½"	10.00
7"d	45.00	Square	
8"d	50.00	4"	10.00
Open		4½"	10.00
Deep bowl		Spoonholder	25.00
5½"d., jelly	15.00	Sugar bowl, covered	45.00
6"d	15.00	Tumbler, water, flat	25.00
7"d	20.00	Wine	40.00

MAGNET AND GRAPE, Frosted Leaf

Champagne; goblet; covered sugar bowl; goblet w/ American shield variant; wine.

Flint, non-flint. The Boston & Sandwich Glass Co., Sandwich, MA. ca. 1860.

Original color production: Clear with frosted leaf, frosting being machine ground. Handles are applied. Items in Magnet and Grape with an American shield are not original to the set.

Reproductions: The Metropolitan Museum of Art, New York City, NY. authorized the Imperial Glass Co., Bellaire, OH., to reissue, from new molds, items in Magnet and Grape, faithfully following both design and quality of glass. Produced from a fine grade of lead crystal, each item is marked with the Museum's "M.M.A." monogram. In 1971, the museum catalog listed both the creamer and covered sugar bowl in clear. In 1972, both the 10 ounce 7"h. creamer with clear applied handle and $8^3/_4$"h. covered sugar bowl were issued for the first time in "sapphire blue" while the $6^1/_2$"h. goblet and $3^1/_2$"h. water tumbler appeared in clear. By 1980-81, the museum catalog listed the $6^1/_4$"h. ale glass in clear and in 1985 all items were still available through the museum's stores and catalog.

Earlier reproductions of the goblet, issued during the 1960s in non-flint crystal, appear pale green when held to a bright light, with grape and design elements completely different from the original.

References: Bat-GPG (PP. 15, 17), Brn-SD (P. 51), Kam-1 (PP. 7-8), Lee-EAPG (Plts. 62-63), McCn-PGP (P. 317), McKrn-AG (P. 206), Mil-1 (Plts. 13, 98), Mil-2 (Pl. 30), Mtz-1 (P. 78), Mtz-2 (P. 190), Oliv-AAG (P. 56), Pap-GAG (P. 192), Schwtz-AG (P. 120), Spil-AEPG (P. 265), Swn-PG (P. 75), Uni-1 (P. 228), Wlkr-PGA (Fig. 8, Nos. 8, 20, 46).

Items made	Clear w/Frosted Leaf	Items made	Clear w/Frosted Leaf
Butter dish, covered	185.00	Milk, 1 quart	300.00
Celery vase	175.00	Water, $^1/_2$ gallon	350.00
Champagne	125.00	Relish dish, oval	40.00
Compote, round		Salt, master, footed, open	65.00
Covered, high standard, $7^1/_2$"d	125.00	Sauce dish, flat, round, smooth rim,	
Open		4"d	25.00
High standard, $7^1/_2$"	90.00	Spoonholder	100.00
Low standard	90.00	Sugar bowl, covered	150.00
Cordial	100.00	Syrup pitcher, original top	250.00
Creamer, applied handle, $6^1/_2$"h	175.00	Tumbler, flat	
Decanter, original patterned stopper		Water	125.00
Pint	150.00	Whiskey	140.00
Quart	200.00	Wine	125.00
Goblet		Wine jug, dated spicket (VR)	
Low stem	75.00	With inscription	2500.00
Regular stem, $6^5/_8$"h	75.00	Without inscription	2500.00
Pitcher, applied handle			

Syrup; 8"d h.s. open compote; 5"d h.s. covered compote. All emerald green.

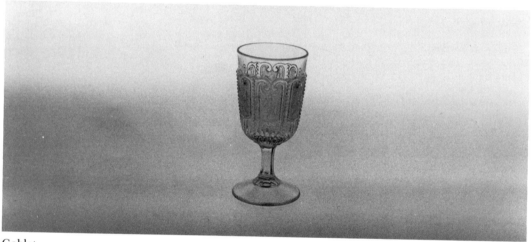

Goblet.

OMN: U.S. Glass No. 15,066. AKA: Panelled Flower [Stuart], Panelled Stippled Flower, Stippled Panelled Flower, Stippled Primrose [Stuart].

Non-flint. The United States Glass Co. (pattern line No. 15,066), Pittsburgh, PA. ca. 1899.

Original color production: Clear (plain or with fire enameled flowers in green, pink and white), emerald green.

Reproductions: None.

References: Hart/Cobb-SS (P. 38), Hea-5 (P. 36, No. 47), Kam-4 (PP. 86-87), Lee-EAPG (Pl. 77, No. 2), Lee-VG (Pl. 52, No. 10), McCn-PGP (P. 555), Mtz-1 (PP. 66-67), Pet-Sal (P. 33), Rev-APG (P. 314), Stu-BP (P. 31).

Items made	Clear	Emerald Green
Bowl, flat		
Covered, flared, 8"d, round	45.00	—
Open		
Flared, 8"d	25.00	40.00
Oval, 8"l x 6"w	25.00	—
Round		
6"d	20.00	30.00
7"d	25.00	35.00
8"d	30.00	40.00
Butter dish, covered, flanged	50.00	—
Cake stand, high standard		
8"d	35.00	55.00
9"d	40.00	55.00
10"d	45.00	65.00
11"d	45.00	65.00
Celery vase	30.00	—
Compote		
Open		
High standard		
Flared bowl		
8"d	30.00	55.00
9"d	35.00	65.00
10"d	40.00	65.00
Round bowl, deep		
5"d	20.00	40.00
6"d	20.00	40.00
7"d	25.00	45.00
8"d	30.00	55.00
Low standard		
8"d	30.00	55.00
9"d	35.00	55.00
Covered, high standard, jelly, 5"d	50.00	65.00
Creamer	30.00	50.00
Cruet, original stopper	65.00	—
Goblet (VR)	90.00	—
Mug, handled	30.00	—
Pickle tray, 8"l (2 styles)	15.00	30.00
Pitcher		
Milk, 1 quart	55.00	85.00
Water, ½ gallon	50.00	125.00
Plate		
Bread, oval, 10" x 7¾"	30.00	55.00
Dinner, 10"d	35.00	—
Preserve dish, 8"l	25.00	35.00
Relish tray	15.00	30.00
Salt shaker, original top	20.00	—
Sauce dish, flat, 4"d, round	15.00	—
Spoonholder	25.00	40.00
Sugar bowl, covered	45.00	75.00
Syrup pitcher, original top	65.00	225.00
Toothpick holder	100.00	—
Tumbler, water, flat	20.00	45.00
Wine	40.00	65.00

MANHATTAN

Relish tray; goblet; master berry (clear w/ruby stain); oval dish; tumbler.

OMN: U.S. Glass No. 15,078, New York.

Non-flint. The United States Glass Co. (pattern line No. 15,078), Pittsburgh, PA; at Factory "G" and "P" ca. 1902. Reviewed in the February 20, 1902 issue of the *Crockery and Glass Journal* and advertised in the Butler Brothers catalog of 1912, Manhattan is illustrated in the United States Glass Co. 1904 domestic and ca. 1919 export catalogs.

Original color production: Clear, clear with rose stain. Clear with blue, green, or any other color is scarce. Decorated by the Oriental Glass Co., Pittsburgh, PA.

Reproductions: Both the Anchor Hocking Glass Co. and the Tiffin Glass Co., Tiffin, OH. issued look-alikes of the Manhattan pattern from the early 1950s.

References: Hart/Cobb-SS (P. 53), Hrtng-P&P (P. 62), Hea-3 (P. 88), Hea-5 (P. 52, Fig. 260), Hea-7 (P. 148), Hea-TPS (PP. 31, 73), Kam-6 (P. 44), Lechn-SS (P. 68), McCn-PGP (P. 567), Migh-TPS (Pl. 22), Mtz-2 (P. 146), Pet-Sal (P. 166), Pyne-PG (P. 136), Rev-APG (P. 316), Uni-1 (PP. 108-109), Uni-2 (P. 236), Wlkr-PGA (Fig. 8, No. 28).

Items made	Clear	Clear/ Rose
Basket	80.00	125.00
Biscuit jar, covered	60.00	85.00
Bottle, water	40.00	85.00
Bowl, open, flat, round		
Berry		
6"d	15.00	35.00
7"d	20.00	45.00
8"d	20.00	55.00
8¼"d	25.00	65.00
8½"d	25.00	65.00
Fruit or vegetable		
9½"d	30.00	75.00
10"d	30.00	85.00
11"d	35.00	95.00
12½"d	40.00	95.00

Items made	Clear	Clear/Rose
Violet	25.00	50.00
Cake stand, high standard		
8"d	35.00	85.00
9"d	35.00	85.00
10"d	45.00	10.00
Celery vase	35.00	85.00
Cheese dish, covered, 8³⁄₈"d	45.00	125.00
Compote, high standard, round		
Covered, 9¹⁄₂"d	45.00	125.00
Open		
Flared-scalloped rim, 9¹⁄₂"d.	45.00	65.00
Straight sided bowl.	45.00	65.00
Cracker jar, covered	65.00	150.00
Creamer		
Individual, 2¹⁄₄"h	20.00	35.00
Table size	30.00	55.00
Cruet, original stopper		
Bulbous	65.00	175.00
Tapered	50.00	175.00
Cup, custard	10.00	20.00
Dish		
Jelly		
Round, flat, handled	10.00	20.00
Triangular, handled	15.00	25.00
Marmalade, silver plate underplate and lid	35.00	55.00
Oval, scalloped rim	15.00	25.00
Preserve, 7¹⁄₂"l	15.00	25.00
Goblet	25.00	—
Ice bucket	50.00	85.00
Olive tray	20.00	35.00
Pickle		
Castor, complete in original silver plate frame	100.00	150.00
Dish, flat, pointed ends	15.00	30.00
Jar, original covered lid	45.00	85.00
Pitcher, applied handle		
Bulbous, water, ¹⁄₂ gallon	60.00	90.00
Tankard		
Milk	45.00	65.00
Water, ¹⁄₂ gallon	60.00	90.00
Plate, scalloped rim		
5"d	10.00	—
6"d	10.00	30.00
8"d	15.00	30.00
9¹⁄₂"d	15.00	—
10³⁄₄"d	20.00	—
11"d	20.00	—
12"d	25.00	—
Punch bowl		
Flat	125.00	300.00
Footed, two piece	150.00	350.00
Relish tray, 6"l	10.00	25.00
Salt shaker, original top		
Cafe, large bulbous base	10.00	25.00
Table size, tapered, slender neck	20.00	35.00
Shade		
Electric		
Belled shape	30.00	—
Cupped shape	30.00	—

Items made	Clear	Clear/ Rose
Gas		
Belled shape	30.00	—
Straight-sided	30.00	—
Sauce dish, round		
Flat		
4½"d	10.00	20.00
5"d	10.00	20.00
Footed		
4½"d	15.00	—
5"d	15.00	—
Spoonholder	20.00	40.00
Straw jar, covered	65.00	—
Sugar bowl, covered		
Individual	15.00	40.00
Table size	40.00	65.00
Syrup pitcher, original top	50.00	250.00
Toothpick holder	30.00	125.00
Tray, trinket, flat, folded sides, 5"	35.00	55.00
Tumbler		
Iced tea	35.00	35.00
Water, flat	20.00	35.00
Vase, scalloped rim, twist stem		
6"h	20.00	—
8"h	20.00	—
Wine	20.00	—

MAPLE LEAF

Sauce dish; 10"d. diamond center plate; covered bowl.

AKA: Leaf [Stuart], Maple Leaf on Trunk.

Non-flint. Maker unknown, ca. 1885.

Original colors: Amber, blue, canary-yellow, clear, frosted. Most pieces are oval in shape with "log" feet. Finials are clusters of grapes and leaves.

Reproductions: During the early 1970s, the L.G. Wright Glass Co. reproduced from new molds the following items in amber, amethyst, blue, clear, dark blue, and ruby: covered butter dish, creamer, compote (high standard), cake stand (high standard), goblet, spoonholder, sugar bowl (covered), toothpick holder, 6″ tray, 12″ tray, tumbler, and pitcher (water).

References: Kam-4 (PP. 143-144), Keyes (*Antiques,* Nov. 1938, PP. 240-245), Lee-EAPG (Pl. 143), Lee-VG (Pl. 73-"A"), McCn-PGP (P. 413), Mtz-1 (PP. 72-73), Spil-AEPG (P. 301), Stu-BP (P. 48), Uni-1 (P. 222), Uni-2 (P. 217), Wlkr-PGA (Fig. 8, Nos. 47, 56).

Items made	Amber	Blue	Canary	Clear	Frosted
Bowl, covered, 4 legged					
5½″.	45.00	55.00	55.00	25.00	35.00
11″l	65.00	85.00	75.00	45.00	55.00
Butter dish, oval, footed	80.00	90.00	85.00	55.00	65.00
Cake stand, high standard 11″d	65.00	85.00	75.00	45.00	55.00
Celery vase	55.00	70.00	60.00	35.00	40.00
Compote, covered, footed, round 9″d	75.00	95.00	85.00	55.00	65.00
Creamer, 4 footed, pressed handle	60.00	70.00	50.00	35.00	45.00
Cup plate	40.00	45.00	40.00	20.00	25.00
Dish					
Oval, 4 footed					
Covered					
With grape handles	55.00	65.00	65.00	35.00	45.00
Without handles	45.00	55.00	55.00	25.00	35.00
Open	40.00	45.00	45.00	25.00	30.00
Square, 10″, concave sides	55.00	65.00	65.00	35.00	45.00
Goblet	85.00	100.00	90.00	55.00	65.00
Pitcher, footed					
Milk, 1 quart	85.00	95.00	95.00	65.00	75.00
Water, ½ gallon	85.00	100.00	100.00	65.00	75.00
Plate					
10″d., "Diamond" center with maple leaf border	45.00	65.00	55.00	30.00	40.00
10½″d., "U.S. Grant" center inscribed "Let Us Have Peace" and "Born April 27 1882 Died July 23 1885", with maple leaf border	65.00	85.00	75.00	45.00	55.00
Platter, oval, "Diamond" center, 10½″l	45.00	55.00	55.00	35.00	40.00
Sauce dish, leaf shaped, 3-legged					
5″	15.00	20.00	20.00	10.00	15.00
6″	15.00	20.00	20.00	10.00	15.00
Spoonholder, footed, scalloped rim	60.00	75.00	65.00	35.00	45.00
Sugar bowl, covered, footed	65.00	75.00	75.00	45.00	55.00
Tray					
Oblong, 10″ x 13¼″l	45.00	55.00	55.00	35.00	40.00
Oval, leaf rim, 13¼″l	45.00	55.00	55.00	35.00	40.00
Tumbler, flat	45.00	55.00	55.00	30.00	35.00

Cordial; small cocktail; saucer champagne; large cocktail; egg cup; ice water.

Pomade jar; finger bowl; water bottle; syrup; puff jar.

OMN: Duncan No. 42, Empire. AKA: Panelled English Hobnail with Prisms [Millard], Siamese Necklace [Batty].

Non-flint. George Duncan's Sons & Co., Washington, PA. ca. 1899, continued production by Duncan & Miller Glass Co. (pattern line No. 42, after the name change) ca. 1898 to as late as 1920.

Original color production: Clear, clear with ruby stain (plain or gilt). Dark amber, sapphire blue, clear with amber stain, clear with frosting, or any other color is rare. Produced in two versions: a) plain rim, and b) ring-and-thumbprint rim. The bases of tankards may be either flat or low and circular. Handles are applied or pressed.

Reproductions: Punch cup.

References: Bar-RS (Pl. 9), Bat-GPG (PP. 202-203), Bons-BDG (PP. 68-69), Hrtng-P&P (P. 19), Hea-1 (P. 47), Hea-1000 TPS (Fig. 220), Hea-2 (P. 119), Hea-OPG (PP. 63-64), Hea-OS

(P. 135, No. 2534), Kam-5 (P. 70), Kam-7 (P. 33), Krs-EDG (PP. 132-133), McCn-PGP (P. 171), Migh-TPS (Pl. 4), Mil-1 (Pl. 111), Mtz-2 (PP. 164-165), Pet-Sal (P. 27-"B"), Rev-APG (P. 149).

Items made	Clear	Clear w/Ruby
Banana boat, flat, folded sides, 8″l., 5″w	45.00	125.00
Bon bon dish, silver plated foot, scalloped rim, 7″l., 4¾″w	40.00	65.00
Bottle		
Bitters, bulbous, slender neck, 6¼″h	75.00	—
Water, 8¾″h	65.00	125.00
Bowl, open		
Round		
Flat		
Berry, master, 8″d	18.00	—
Deep, flat, scalloped		
8½″d., 3½″h	20.00	65.00
9″d., 3¾″h	20.00	75.00
9½″d, 9¾″h	25.00	75.00
10″d., 3¾″h	25.00	85.00
Finger	20.00	—
Fruit, shallow, scalloped, low footed, 3″h, 10″d	25.00	85.00
Rose, 3½″h., 4″d	25.00	50.00
Footed		
8″d., 4¾″h	25.00	—
8¼″d., 4¼″h	25.00	—
Square, open, flat, scalloped rim		
6″ x 2¾″h	25.00	—
7¾″	25.00	—
Butter dish, covered, flat.	45.00	150.00
Butter pat, 3½″d., scalloped rim	10.00	
Cake stand, high standard		
9½″d., turned down scalloped rim	55.00	—
10″d., turned up scalloped rim	65.00	—
11¾″d., turned up scalloped rim	65.00	—
Celery tray, flat, scalloped rim, 5¾″h	45.00	
Champagne		
Cupped bowl	30.00	—
Saucer bowl	30.00	—
Claret	35.00	—
Cocktail		
Large	25.00	—
Small	25.00	—
Compote, high standard, round		
Covered	55.00	165.00
Open		
Deep bowl, scalloped rim		
7¾″d, 7″h	30.00	55.00
8″d., 7″h	30.00	65.00
9¼″d., 8″h	40.00	—
9¾″d., 7¼″h	40.00	—
Shallow bowl, scalloped rim, 6″d., 5″h	30.00	—
Cordial	35.00	55.00
Cracker jar, covered, flat, 8″h	75.00	175.00
Creamer		
Individual		
Barrel shape, 3″h	20.00	55.00
Oval shape, 2¼″h	20.00	55.00
Table size, 4⅜″h	35.00	65.00
Cruet, original patterned stopper, 5″h	45.00	165.00

Items made	Clear	Clear w/Ruby
Egg cup, single	20.00	—
Epergne, silver plate foot, complete with center lily	150.00	—
Goblet	35.00	65.00
Lamp shade for electric light	35.00	65.00
Miniatures		
Butter dish, covered, 4¼"h	125.00	—
Creamer, 2⅞"h	40.00	85.00
Honey jug, child's miniature, 2½"h	35.00	90.00
Rose bowl, 2"h., 2½"d	25.00	50.00
Spoonholder, 2¾"h	40.00	90.00
Sugar bowl, covered	125.00	—
Mustard jar, flat, covered, 3¼"h., notched lid	35.00	—
Nappy, flat, handled, scalloped rim		
Round		
5"d	15.00	30.00
6¼"d	15.00	30.00
Triangular		
5"	15.00	30.00
6¼"	15.00	30.00
Olive dish, flat, turned up sides, scalloped rim, 5"l., 3"w	15.00	40.00
Pickle dish, flat		
Round	20.00	30.00
Square	20.00	35.00
Pickle jar, covered	40.00	—
Pitcher		
Milk, bulbous, applied handle, 1 quart	50.00	200.00
Water, ½ gallon		
Bulbous, Ring and Thumbprint rim, applied handle, 8¼"h.	100.00	200.00
Straight sided, applied handle		
Plain rim, 7¾"h	100.00	200.00
Silver plate rim, 11"h	100.00	—
Tankard		
Ring and Thumbprint rim, pressed handle, 9¼"h	100.00	200.00
Smooth rim, applied handle, 9¼"h	100.00	200.00
Plate, round		
5"d	5.00	—
6"d	10.00	—
6½"d	10.00	—
7"d	15.00	—
7¾"d	15.00	—
8"d	15.00	—
Pomade jar, original sterling lid, flat, 1¾"h	35.00	—
Puff jar, covered, round, flat, 4¾"d	35.00	—
Punch bowl, 2 piece, round, flat, scalloped rim		
12¼"d	50.00	—
14"d	65.00	—
Punch cup, 2"h	10.00	—
Relish tray	10.00	—
Salt		
Dip		
Individual		
Oval, flat, 1¾"d., 2¼"l., 1"h	5.00	25.00
Round, flat, 1¾"d., 1¼"h	5.00	25.00
Master		
Oval	25.00	65.00
Round, flat, scalloped rim, 2½"d	25.00	65.00
Shaker, salt, original top		
Bulbous, tall neck, 2¾"h	25.00	45.00

Items made	Clear	Clear w/Ruby
Pyramid shape, 2½"h	25.00	45.00
Tall, straight-sided, 2¼"h	25.00	55.00
Sandwich tray, silver plate foot and handle, 11½"d	35.00	—
Sauce dish		
Round		
Collared base, scalloped-flared rim shallow, 5¾"d	10.00	20.00
Flat		
3¾"d	10.00	20.00
4¾"d	10.00	20.00
5½"d	10.00	20.00
Square, flat, shallow, scalloped rim, 4"	10.00	20.00
Saucer, round, 5½"d	5.00	25.00
Shade, gas		
Bullet shape, tall, 9"h., 3¼" fitter opening	25.00	85.00
Straight-sided, flared-scalloped rim, 2¼"d fitter	25.00	85.00
Sherry		
Flared bowl	20.00	—
Straight bowl	20.00	—
Spoonholder, 4"h	25.00	65.00
Sugar bowl, covered, table size, flat, 6½"h	35.00	100.00
Syrup pitcher, original top	65.00	—
Toothpick holder	45.00	100.00
Tumbler		
Bar	25.00	40.00
Champagne	20.00	45.00
Ice Water	30.00	40.00
Water	30.00	40.00
Vase		
Bulbous, 9¾"h., 5"d base, 3½"d. top, scalloped rim	20.00	—
Trumpet shape, circular footed, scalloped rim		
6½"h	20.00	—
8"h	20.00	—
10"h	25.00	—
Wine	30.00	65.00
Wine jug, bulbous, slender neck, 9¼"h	75.00	125.00

Water tumbler; milk pitcher; flat banana dish.

OMN: U.S. Glass No. 15,049. AKA: Inverted Loop(s) and Fan(s) [Millard], Loop and Diamond, Loop(s) and Fan(s).

Non-flint. Bryce Brothers, Pittsburgh, PA. Reissued by the United States Glass Co. (pattern line No. 15,049), Pittsburgh, PA. at Factory "B" (Bryce Brothers, Pittsburgh, PA.) ca. 1897 to as late as 1899. Illustrated in the Butler Brothers 1899 catalog as "Astor" pattern, and the United States Glass Co. 1904 catalog.

Original color production: Clear, clear with ruby stain. Handles are pressed.

Reproductions: None.

References: Bar-RS (Pl. 14), Bros-TS (P. 42), Enos-MPG (Chart-7), Hart/Cob-SS (P. 39), Hea-5 (PP. 20, 148), Hea-7 (P. 149), Kam-1 (P. 60), Lee-EAPG (Pl. 153, No. 15), Lee-VG (Pl. 37, No. 2), McCn-PGP (P. 195), Mil-1 (Pl. 139), Mtz-1 (P. 155), Pet-Sal (P. 33), Rev-APG (P. 316), Stu-BP (P. 63), Uni-1 (P. 265), Uni-2 (PP. 58-59), Wlkr-PGA (Fig. 8, No. 54).

Items made	Clear	Clear/Ruby
Banana dish, flat with turned in sides	30.00	85.00
Bowl, open, flat, round		
6"d	15.00	35.00
7"d	15.00	—
8"d	20.00	—
Butter dish, covered, flat, flanged base	65.00	100.00
Cake stand, high standard		
8"d	35.00	—
9"d	40.00	—
10"d	45.00	—
Celery		
Tray	20.00	35.00
Vase	25.00	65.00
Compote, high standard		
Covered, round		
6"d	45.00	—
7"d	55.00	—

Items made	Clear	Clear/ Ruby
8″d	65.00	—
Open		
Deep bowl		
5″d., jelly	15.00	45.00
6″d	20.00	55.00
7″d	25.00	—
8″d	30.00	—
Flared rim, sweetmeat, 7″d	35.00	—
Saucer bowl		
7″d	25.00	—
8″d	30.00	—
10″d	40.00	—
Creamer, 4½″h	30.00	55.00
Cup, custard	20.00	—
Dish, preserve, round, shallow, 8″	15.00	—
Goblet	30.00	55.00
Honey dish, flat, round, 3″d	15.00	—
Jelly dish	15.00	25.00
Olive dish, handled	10.00	—
Pickle dish, oval, flat, handled	20.00	35.00
Pitcher		
Milk, 1 quart	40.00	135.00
Water, ½ gallon	50.00	175.00
Plate		
Bread	25.00	—
Dinner, 7″d	25.00	—
Relish tray, oval	20.00	—
Salt shaker, original top	30.00	55.00
Sauce dish, flat, round, 4″d	15.00	25.00
Spoonholder	30.00	55.00
Sugar bowl, covered	45.00	65.00
Toothpick holder (R)	65.00	150.00
Tumbler, water, flat	25.00	50.00
Wine	40.00	65.00

Finger bowl (amber); covered jar (clear); covered bowl (etched); waste bowl (etched).

Spoonholder; creamer; covered sugar bowl; covered butter dish. All etched.

OMN: Mascotte. AKA: Dominion [Stevens], Etched Fern and Waffle [Kramm], Minor Block.

Non-flint. Ripley & Co., Pittsburgh, PA. ca. 1874. Reissued by the United States Glass Co., Pittsburgh, PA. at Factory "F" (Ripley & Co., Pittsburgh, PA.) ca. 1891. Illustrated in the United States Glass Co. 1904 catalog. Patented May 20, 1873, although only the covered jar can be found marked with the patent date embossed under the base. Also attributed to Canadian manufacture.

Original color production: Clear (plain or copper wheel engraved with engraving No. 75: Fern Spray). Amber, milk white or any other color is very rare. Goblets may be found with long or short stems and straight or flared bowls.

Reproductions: None.

References: Hea-5 (P. 123, Pl. B), Hea-7 (P. 149), Hea-OS (P. 136, No. 2582), Kam-1 (PP. 17-18), Kam-6 (P. 44), Lee-VG (Pl. 42, No. 4), McCn-PGP (P. 221), Mil-2 (P. 132), Mtz-1 (PP. 150-

151), Oliv-AAG (P. 70), Pet-GPP (P. 172), Pet-Sal (P. 33), Rev-APG (PP. 293-294), Stev-ECG (Fig. 197), Uni-1 (P. 265), Wlkr-PGA (Fig. 15, No. 229).

Items made	Clear	Etched
Banana stand, high standard	25.00	35.00
Bowl, flat, round		
Covered		
5"d	30.00	35.00
6"d	30.00	35.00
7"d	30.00	35.00
8"d	45.00	50.00
9"d	45.00	50.00
Open		
Flared bowl		
5"d	20.00	25.00
6"d	20.00	25.00
7"d	20.00	25.00
8"d	25.00	30.00
9"d.	25.00	30.00
Straight-sided bowl		
5"d	15.00	20.00
6"d	15.00	20.00
7"d	20.00	25.00
8"d	25.00	30.00
9"d	30.00	35.00
Finger, round bowl	25.00	35.00
Waste, straight-sided bowl	25.00	35.00
Butter dish, covered		
"Maude S"	100.00	100.00
Regular	50.00	65.00
Butter pat	15.00	—
Cake basket, metal handle	65.00	85.00
Cake stand, high standard		
8"d	25.00	40.00
9"d	35.00	50.00
10"d	35.00	50.00
12"d	50.00	65.00
Celery		
Tray	30.00	35.00
Vase	30.00	35.00
Cheese dish, covered	40.00	45.00
Compote, round		
Covered		
High standard		
5"d	35.00	40.00
6"d	40.00	45.00
7"d	45.00	50.00
8"d	55.00	60.00
9"d	65.00	75.00
Open		
High standard		
Flared bowl		
5"d	20.00	25.00
6"d	20.00	25.00
7"d	25.00	30.00
8"d	30.00	25.00
9"d	30.00	35.00
10"d	35.00	40.00
11"d	40.00	45.00

Items made	Clear	Etched
Straight bowl		
5″d	20.00	25.00
6″d	20.00	25.00
7″d	25.00	30.00
8″d	30.00	35.00
9″d	30.00	35.00
10″d	35.00	40.00
11″d	40.00	45.00
Low standard, straight bowl, 8″d	30.00	45.00
Creamer, 6½″h	40.00	45.00
Goblet (2 styles)	40.00	45.00
Honey dish, round, flat, 3½″d	10.00	15.00
Jar		
Bulbous, open, footed (termed the "Fish Globe")	85.00	100.00
Egyptian Jar, straight-sided, 2 ounce	40.00	45.00
Patent globe jar, covered, footed, bulbous	85.00	100.00
Pyramid, covered		
Flat base, 3 jars high	55.00	55.00
Footed		
7 jars high	110.00	125.00
9 jars high	125.00	135.00
Sample bottle, covered, footed, 15″h	55.00	65.00
Jelly, stemmed	25.00	30.00
Pitcher, water, ½ gallon	55.00	65.00
Plate, turned up sides	35.00	40.00
Platter	45.00	50.00
Salt		
Dip, individual.	25.00	—
Master	25.00	35.00
Shaker, original top	15.00	20.00
Sauce dish, round		
Flat, 4″d	10.00	12.00
Footed, 4″d	10.00	12.00
Spoonholder	30.00	35.00
Sugar bowl, covered	45.00	50.00
Tray, water, round	40.00	55.00
Tumbler, water, flat, 3¾″h	20.00	30.00
Wine	25.00	30.00

Basket; syrup; decanter (o.s.); cruet (n.o.s.), champagne; wine.

OMN: U.S. Glass No. 15,054, Massachusetts. AKA: Arched Diamond Points [Millard], Cane Variant [Kamm], Geneva [Millard], Star And Diamonds.

Non-flint. Original manufacturer unknown ca. 1880s. Reissued by the United States Glass Co. (pattern line No. 15,054), Pittsburgh, PA. at Factory "K" (King Glass Co., Pittsburgh, PA.) ca. 1898-1909. Advertised in an 1898 issue of the *Crockery and Glass Journal*, illustrated in the Lyon Brothers 1904 (No. 411) and 1906 (No. 453) general merchandise catalogs, and the United States Glass 1904, undated "Massachusetts", and 1907 catalogs.

Original color production: Clear. Odd pieces may be found in emerald green. Cobalt blue, clear with ruby stain or any other color is rare. Handles are pressed.

Reproductions: Imported by A.A. Importing Co., St. Louis, MO. and Carson/San Francisco, CA. and offered as "Star Diamonds", Massachusetts has been reproduced in both clear and color from new molds including the covered butter dish. Recent reissues lack the clarity of older items, the pattern is distorted and too heavy.

References: Hart/Cobb-SS (P. 41), Hea-RUTPS (P. 56), Hea-1 (P. 46, Fig. 340), Hea-5 (P. 144, Pl. A), Hea-7 (P. 149), Hea-OS (Fig. 3730), Kam-2 (PP. 131, 136), McCn-PGP (P. 237), Mil-1 (Pl. 131), Mil-2 (Pl. 59), Pet-Sal (P. 33-"Q"), Rev-APG (P. 314), Uni-2 (PP. 114-115), Wlkr-PGA (Fig. 15, No. 158).

Items made	Clear	Items made	Clear
Basket, small, 4½"h., applied handle	50.00	Water	35.00
Bottle		Wine, with original patterned	
Brandy	45.00	stopper	65.00
Cologne, 7½"h., original patterned		Bowl, flat, open	
stopper	35.00	Round	20.00
Liqueur		Square	
Individual, original cut stopper	65.00	Folded sides	
Bar size		6"	15.00
Bar lip	45.00	9"	20.00
With original cut stopper	55.00	Pointed sides	
With original metal shot glass lid	45.00	6"	15.00
Tabasco sauce	45.00	7"	15.00

Items made	Clear
8″	20.00
Straight-sided	
7″	15.00
9″	20.00
Butter dish, covered, flat	65.00
Candy dish, flat, oblong	
8″	20.00
9″	20.00
Celery	
Tray, rounded base, 11⁷⁄₈″ x 7¹⁄₄″	25.00
Vase, flat	30.00
Champagne, saucer bowl	35.00
Claret	35.00
Cocktail	35.00
Compote, low standard, open, cupped (very large)	35.00
Condiment set, cruet, salt shaker, mustard, matching tray	125.00
Cordial	55.00
Creamer	
Individual, 3¹⁄₄″h	15.00
Medium	20.00
Table size	25.00
Cruet, original patterned stopper	
Large	40.00
Small, 3¹⁄₂″h	55.00
Cup, custard	15.00
Decanter, original patterned stopper	
High shoulders, short neck	35.00
Sloped shoulders, long neck	35.00
Dish	
Almond, oblong, flat, 5″	20.00
Bon bon, flat, 5″	20.00
Mayonnaise, flat, handled	20.00
Olive, oblong, flat	
6″	15.00
8¹⁄₂″	20.00
Goblet	
Round bowl	40.00
Square bowl	40.00
Gravy boat, flat handled	30.00
Hot whiskey, stemmed	35.00
Lamp, oil, matching globe, original burner and chimney	
Banquet size	750.00
Table size	650.00
Mug, handled	
Large	25.00
Small	20.00
Mustard jar, covered	35.00
Pitcher, square, water, ¹⁄₂ gallon	
Squatty	75.00
Tankard	75.00
Plate	
Round	
8¹⁄₄″d, slightly cupped	30.00
8¹⁄₄″d., 2 sides turned upward	30.00

Items made	Clear
Square, 6″	30.00
Relish tray, rectangular	
Flared sides	
4¹⁄₂″ x 2³⁄₄″	10.00
4³⁄₄″ x 2³⁄₄″	10.00
4″ x 2¹⁄₄″	10.00
5¹⁄₂″ x 3¹⁄₄″	15.00
6″ x 3³⁄₄″	20.00
Rum jug	
Large	90.00
Medium	80.00
Small	60.00
Salt shaker, original top	
Large, square	25.00
Small, bulbous	25.00
Tall, round	25.00
Sauce dish, flat	
Oval, handled	15.00
Square, 4″	
Pointed sides	15.00
Straight-sided	15.00
Sherry	40.00
Spoonholder, double handled	20.00
Sugar bowl	
Covered	
Individual	20.00
Table size	40.00
Open, scalloped rim	35.00
Syrup pitcher, original top	75.00
Toothpick holder	65.00
Tray	
Orange, 9″	35.00
Pin, square, 5″ x 5″	20.00
Spoon, flat with rolled sides	20.00
Toast	25.00
Tumbler	
Juice	25.00
Lemonade or bar	
Flared rim	30.00
Straight-sided	30.00
Pony beer or seltzer	
Flared rim	25.00
Straight-sided	25.00
Shot	15.00
Water	
Round	30.00
Square	30.00
Whiskey	25.00
Vase, trumpet shape	
7″h	25.00
6¹⁄₂″h	25.00
9″h	35.00
10″h	40.00
Wine	
Round bowl	40.00
Square bowl	40.00

MEDALLION

Goblet; cake stand; sauce dish.

AKA: Hearts and Spades, Spades.

Non-flint. Maker unknown, ca. 1885-1895.

Original color production: Amber, apple green, blue, canary-yellow, clear.

Reproductions: The Medallion covered butter dish has been reproduced by the Imperial Glass Co. Bellaire, OH. Reproductions appear with the design reversed from side to side. The new design is not as crisp, less defined, and smaller in proportion. New colors are harsh and lack the mellow feeling and appearance of the old. New items are marked with the company's "I.G." monogram.

References: Drep-ABC OG (P. 149), Hea-5 (P. 41, Nos. 112-115), Kam-5 (PP. 5, 19), Lee-EAPG (Pl. 102, No. 2), Mil-1 (Pl. 35), Mtz-1 (PP. 126-127), Wlkr-PGA (Fig. 8, No. 4).

Items made	Amber	Blue	Canary	Green	Clear
Bottle, castor	65.00	55.00	55.00	45.00	35.00
Bowl, waste	30.00	45.00	30.00	45.00	20.00
Butter dish, covered	40.00	50.00	40.00	50.00	35.00
Cake stand, high standard, 9¼″d	45.00	55.00	45.00	55.00	25.00
Celery vase	30.00	40.00	30.00	40.00	20.00
Compote, high standard					
Covered	60.00	50.00	50.00	50.00	40.00
Open	30.00	30.00	40.00	40.00	20.00
Creamer, 5½″h	40.00	45.00	40.00	45.00	30.00
Egg cup, single	25.00	40.00	25.00	40.00	20.00
Goblet	35.00	45.00	35.00	45.00	25.00
Pickle dish	20.00	25.00	20.00	25.00	15.00
Pitcher, water, ½ gallon	55.00	65.00	55.00	65.00	45.00
Relish tray	20.00	25.00	20.00	25.00	15.00
Sauce dish					
Flat, 4″d	10.00	15.00	10.00	15.00	5.00
Footed, 4″d	15.00	20.00	15.00	20.00	8.00
Spoonholder	30.00	45.00	30.00	45.00	20.00
Sugar bowl, covered	45.00	55.00	45.00	55.00	30.00
Tray, water, round	55.00	65.00	55.00	75.00	35.00

Items made	Amber	Blue	Canary	Green	Clear
Tumbler, water, flat	25.00	35.00	25.00	35.00	15.00
Wine	30.00	40.00	30.00	40.00	20.00

MEDALLION SUNBURST

Mug; goblet; plate; covered sugar bowl; spoonholder; tumbler.

Non-flint. Bryce, Higbee and Co., Bridgeport, PA. ca. 1905. Profusely illustrated in the Butler Brothers 1899 catalog.

Original color production: Clear.

Reproductions: None.

References: Bat-GPG (PP. 94-95), Hea-OS (P. 135, No. 2543), Hea-TPS (P. 74), McCn-PGP (P. 245), Mil-2 (Pl. 114), Mtz-1 (PP. 228-229), Pet-Sal (P. 166), Spil-AEPG (P. 335, No. 1315), Uni-1 (P. 287), Uni-2 (PP. 138-139), Wlkr-PGA (Fig. 8, No. 6).

Items made	Clear	Items made	Clear
Banana dish		Cup, custard	15.00
Flat	20.00	Goblet	25.00
High standard	35.00	Marmalade jar, covered	40.00
Bowl, open		Mug, 3¼″h	15.00
Round, 9¼″d	30.00	Mustard jar, original notched cover ...	35.00
Square, 8¼″	30.00	Olive dish, flat, round, handled	20.00
Butter dish, covered	50.00	Pitcher, applied handle	
Butter pat	5.00	Milk, 1 quart	45.00
Cake stand, high standard		Water, ½ gallon	55.00
9¼″d	65.00	Plate	
10½″d	75.00	Round	
Celery		6½″d	20.00
Tray	20.00	7½″d	25.00
Vase	25.00	9½″d	25.00
Compote, open, high standard, 8″d ...	25.00	Square	
Creamer		7¼″	25.00
Individual	15.00	Relish tray	15.00
Table size	25.00	Salt	
Cruet, original stopper	20.00	Dip, individual, 1¼″d	10.00

Items made	Clear	Items made	Clear
Shaker, original top	10.00	Individual, handled	20.00
Sauce dish, round, flat		Table size	30.00
4"d	10.00	Toothpick holder	225.00
4½"d	10.00	Tumbler, flat, water	20.00
Spoonholder	20.00	Vase, 9½"h	30.00
Sugar bowl, covered		Wine	30.00

MELROSE

Goblet; celery vase; tankard water pitcher; tumbler; wine.

AKA: Diamond Beaded Band [Millard].

Non-flint. Greensburg Glass Co., Greensburg, PA. ca. 1889. Reissued by the Brilliant Glass Co., Brilliant, OH. ca. 1887-1888. McKee Brothers, Jeannette, PA. ca. 1901 (chocolate items only). John B. Higbee Glass Co., Bridgeville, PA. ca. 1907. New Martinsville Glass Co., New Martinsville, WV. ca. 1916, and the Dugan Glass Co. (Diamond Glassware Co., Indiana, PA.) ca. 1915.

Original color production: Clear (plain or copper wheel engraved), chocolate (McKee Brothers at Jeannette). Clear with ruby stain (plain or copper wheel engraved) or any other color is rare.

Reproductions: None.

References: Bar-RS (Pl. 8), Boyd-GC (No. 266), Hea-7 (PP. 149-150), Herr-GG (P. 32), Kam-3 (P. 128), Kam-5 (P. 47), Kam-8 (Plts. 66-67), McCn-PGP (P. 197), Meas-GG (P. 84), Mil-2 (Pl. 93), Milr-MG-1 (P. 27), Mtz-2 (PP. 134-135), Pet-Sal (P. 33), Rev-APG (P. 172), Uni-2 (P. 121), Wlkr-PGA (Fig. 8, No. 48).

Items made	Clear	Items made	Clear
Bowl, round, flat		Cake stand, high standard	30.00
Berry, master	25.00	Celery vase, 6"h., flat rim	25.00
Waste	20.00	Compote, high standard, open, round	
Butter dish, covered	45.00	6"d	40.00
Cake plate	30.00	7"d	40.00

Items made	Clear	Items made	Clear
9"d	55.00	Plate	
Creamer, tankard, 5¼"h	30.00	7"d	10.00
Goblet	20.00	8"d	10.00
Mug	15.00	Salt	
Pickle dish	15.00	Individual	5.00
Pitcher, applied handle		Shaker, original top	10.00
Bulbous		Sauce dish, flat, round	5.00
Milk, 1 quart	30.00	Spoonholder	30.00
Water, ½ gallon	45.00	Sugar bowl, covered	35.00
Tankard		Tray, water, round, 11½"d	45.00
Milk, 1 quart	35.00	Tumbler, flat, water	15.00
Water, ½ gallon	50.00	Wine	20.00

MICHIGAN States Series

Spoonholder; covered sugar; covered butter; creamer.

OMN: U.S. Glass No. 15,077, Michigan. AKA: Loop and Pillar [Millard], Loop with Pillar, Panelled Jewel.

Non-flint. The United States Glass Co. (pattern line No. 15,077), Pittsburgh, PA. at Factory "G" (Gillinder & Sons, Greensburg, PA.) ca. 1902. Illustrated in the United States Glass Co. ca. 1904 catalog, and as "Michigan" in the Sears, Roebuck & Co. 1902 No. 112 catalog.

Original color production: Clear, clear with rose, yellow or blue stain (plain or enameled). Decorated by the Oriental Glass Co., Pittsburgh, PA. Clear with ruby stain or any other color is rare. Handles may be applied.

Reproductions: Degenhart Glass Co., Cambridge, OH. reproduced the 2¾"h. toothpick holder from a new mold in non-original colors such as red, cobalt blue, green custard, several opaque colors, often signed with a "D" in a heart. The Crystal Art Glass Co., Cambridge, OH. reportedly also issued items from new molds in all colors.

References: Bar-RS (Pl. 14), Bros-TS (P.44), Drep-FR (P. 212), Grow-GPG (P. 189, Fig. 30-"2"), Hart/Cobb-SS (P. 42), Htng-P&P (P. 64), Hea-1 (P. 50), Hea-3 (P. 56, Fig. 439), Hea-5 (P. 35, Nos. 19-24), Hea-6 (P. 35, Fig. 238), Hea-7 (PP. 150-151), Hea-OPG (P. 199), Kam-1 (P. 106), Kam/Wod-Vol.2 (P. 401), McCn-PGP (P. 365), Migh-TPS (Pl. 3), Mil-2 (Pl. 44), Mil-2 (Pl.

44), Mtz-1 (PP. 194-195), Pet-Sal (P. 33), Pyne-PG (P. 135), Rev-APG (P. 316), Uni-1 (PP. 242-243), Uni-2 (P. 237), Uni-TCG (P. 123), Uni/Wor-CHPGT (P. 158), Wlkr-PGA (Fig. 8, No. 41).

Items made	Clear	Clear w/Rose
Basket, bride's, silver plate holder (complete)	65.00	125.00
Bottle, water	45.00	85.00
Bowl, flat, round		
Deep		
6"d	10.00	25.00
7"d	15.00	30.00
8½"d	20.00	40.00
Shallow		
Flared rim		
5"d	10.00	20.00
7½"d	15.00	30.00
8½"d	20.00	40.00
10"d	30.00	45.00
Straight-sided		
6"d	10.00	25.00
7"d	15.00	30.00
Crushed fruit	30.00	45.00
Finger	25.00	45.00
Butter dish, covered,		
Quarter pound	45.00	—
Table size	60.00	110.00
Candlestick (R)	75.00	—
Celery vase	35.00	85.00
Compote, high standard		
Covered, round		
Deep bowl, 5"d		
Notched lid	50.00	85.00
Plain lid	45.00	75.00
Shallow bowl, 5"d., jelly	45.00	75.00
Open		
Deep, straight-sided bowl		
6"d	25.00	40.00
7"d	30.00	55.00
8"d	35.00	65.00
Shallow, flared bowl		
7½"d	30.00	65.00
8½"d	35.00	75.00
9½"d	40.00	85.00
Creamer		
Individual, tankard, 6 ounce	30.00	45.00
Table size.	30.00	45.00
Cruet, original stopper	60.00	225.00
Cup		
Sherbert, handled	7.00	15.00
Custard, flared rim, with saucer	8.00	20.00
Dish, open, flat		
Oval		
7½"	15.00	—
9½"	15.00	—
10½"	20.00	—
12½"	20.00	—
Round, handled, jelly	35.00	—
Goblet	35.00	65.00

Items made	Clear	Clear w/Rose
Honey dish, flat	10.00	20.00
Miniatures, child's		
Butter dish, covered, 5¼"d, 3¾"h	150.00	200.00
Creamer, 2⅞"h	60.00	100.00
Nappy, handled, flat, 5¼"	60.00	—
Pitcher, water, 4"h	30.00	55.00
Spoonholder, 3"h	60.00	125.00
Stein set		
Individual stein, 2"h	10.00	—
Main stein, 2⅞"h	45.00	—
Sugar bowl, covered, 4¾"h	80.00	125.00
Tumbler, water, 2⅛"h	10.00	—
Mug, lemonade	20.00	25.00
Olive dish, flat, double handles	15.00	35.00
Pickle dish, oval, flat, double handled	10.00	20.00
Pitcher		
Milk, 1 quart, 8"h	50.00	90.00
Water		
Helmet shape, 3 pint	50.00	—
Tankard, ½ gallon, 12"h	70.00	150.00
Plate, round, 3½"d	15.00	30.00
Punch bowl, 8½"d	50.00	—
Relish tray	10.00	20.00
Salt		
Pepper, tapered body, no neck	20.00	35.00
Shaker, short fluted neck	20.00	35.00
Sauce dish, round		
Flat		
Flared rim		
4"d	10.00	20.00
4½"d	10.00	20.00
Straight-sided bowl		
4"d	10.00	20.00
4½"d	10.00	20.00
Footed		
4"d	10.00	22.00
4½"	10.00	22.00
Saucer	8.00	—
Spoonholder, table size	40.00	50.00
Sugar bowl		
Individual, open, 3½"h Inside ledge, known as the sweetmeat sugar	15.00	—
No ledge	15.00	—
Table size, covered	50.00	65.00
Syrup pitcher, original top	75.00	250.00
Toothpick holder	45.00	175.00
Tumbler, water, flat	30.00	45.00
Vase		
Bud		
8"h	25.00	35.00
12"h	25.00	35.00
13"h	25.00	—
15½"h	25.00	—
16"h	30.00	—
17"h	30.00	—
Table		
6"h	20.00	—
8"h	25.00	—
Wine	35.00	65.00

Creamer; water pitcher; 10"d Mars bread plate; spoonholder.

OMN: Minerva. AKA: Roman Medallion.

Non-flint. The Boston & Sandwich Glass Co., Sandwich, MA. ca. 1870s. Possibly other firms. Attributed to the Burlington Glass Works, Hamilton, Ontario, Canada.

Original color production: Clear. Handles are pressed.

Reproductions: None.

References: Drep-ABC OG (P. 149), Enos-MPG (Chart-2), Hlms-BCA (P. 278), Kam-1 (P. 41), Kam/Wod-Vol.2 (P. 402), Lee-EAPG (Pl. 115, No. 2), McCn-PGP (P. 395), Mil-1 (Pl. 54), Mtz-1 (PP. 108-109), Stu-BP (P. 78), Thu-1 (P. 202), Uni-1 (P. 139), Uni-TCG (PP. 126-127), Uni/Wor-CHPGT (P. 165).

Items made	Clear	Items made	Clear
Bowl, open		Open, low standard, 10"d	55.00
Rectangular, flat		Creamer, 5½"h	45.00
7"	25.00	Goblet	85.00
8"	30.00	Honey dish, flat, round, 3¾"d	10.00
9"	35.00	Marmalade jar, covered	165.00
Round, low foot, 8"d	35.00	Pickle dish, oval, "Love's Request Is	
Butter dish, covered, flat	65.00	Pickles" inscribed in base	30.00
Cake stand, high standard		Pitcher	
8"d	95.00	Milk, 1 quart, plain rim	175.00
10"d	135.00	Water, ½ gallon, scalloped rim, 9½"h	175.00
10½"d	135.00	Plate, closed handles	
11"d	135.00	Bread, oval	
Champagne	90.00	"Give Us This Day" center	70.00
Compote, round		"Mars" center	60.00
Covered		Dinner, round	
High standard		8"d	55.00
7"d	90.00	9"d	55.00
8"d	80.00	Platter, oval, 13"	75.00
Low standard		Sauce dish, round	
7"d	90.00	Flat	
8"d	80.00	4¼"d	20.00

Items made	Clear	Items made	Clear
4½"d	20.00	4½"d	20.00
Footed		Spoonholder	45.00
4¼"d	20.00	Sugar bowl, covered	85.00

MINNESOTA

Flat sauce dish; goblet; covered butter dish; creamer.

OMN: U.S. Glass No. 15,055, Minnesota. AKA: Muchness [Unitt].

Non-flint. The United States Glass Co. (pattern line No. 15,055), Pittsburgh, PA. at Factory "F" (Ripley & Co., Pittsburgh, PA.) and "G" (Gillinder & Sons, Greensburg, PA.) ca. 1898. Illustrated in the January, 1898 issue of *China, Glass and Lamps*, and in the United States Glass Co. ca. 1904 catalog.

Original color production: Clear (plain or with gilt). Clear with ruby stain, emerald green or any other color is rare.

Reproductions: None.

References: Bar-RS (Pl. 14), Hart/Cob-SS (P. 44), Hea-1 (P. 46, Fig. 341), Hea-3 (P. 33, Fig. 200), Hea-5 (PP. 141, 144, 152), Hea-TPS (PP. 20, 46), Kam-8 (PP. 51-52), McCn-PGP (P. 257), Mig-TPS (Pl. 3), Pet-GPP (PP. 125-127), Pet-Sal (P. 166), Rev-APG (P. 316), Uni-1 (PP. 162-163), Wlkr-PGA (Fig. 8, No. 2).

Items made	Clear	Items made	Clear
Banana dish, flat, turned up edges	65.00	6"l	20.00
Basket, applied handle	65.00	7"l	25.00
Biscuit jar, covered	55.00	8"l	25.00
Bottle, water	35.00	Round, flat, flared rim	
Bowl, open		6"d	15.00
Oval flat		7"d	20.00
9 ½	25.00	8"d	25.00
10"	25.00	Rose, smooth rim	35.00
Pointed ends		Square	
5"l	15.00	6"	15.00

Items made	Clear	Items made	Clear
7″	20.00	Candy, shallow, scalloped sides, pointed ends	15.00
8″	25.00	7″	15.00
Straight-sided		9″	20.00
6″d	15.00	Confection, 5″ (same shape as candy)	20.00
7″d	20.00	Olive	
8″d	25.00	5″l., straight-sided bowl	15.00
Butter dish, covered, flanged base	55.00	6″l., rounded bowl	15.00
Celery tray		Pickle, 7½″l., turned up sides with pointed ends	15.00
Oblong, 13″l	25.00	Oval, serrated scalloped rim	
Square, 10″	25.00	7″	15.00
Compote, open		8″	20.00
High standard		Rectangular	
Round		Cracker, 8″l., slightly folded sides	20.00
Deep		Preserve, 9″l., deep	20.00
Flared bowl		Goblet	30.00
7½″d	45.00	Hair receiver	30.00
8½″d	45.00	Humidor, original jeweled silver plate lid	150.00
9½″d	55.00	Match safe, flat, bulbous base, tall neck with scalloped rim	25.00
Straight-sided bowl		Mug, pressed handle	25.00
6″d	35.00	Pitcher, water, applied handle	
7″d	40.00	Bulbous	
8″d	45.00	½ gallon	90.00
Shallow bowl (originally termed "sweetmeat"), 7½″d	45.00	¾ gallon	110.00
Square		Tankard, ½ gallon	90.00
Deep		Plate	
6″	35.00	Cheese, 7″d., shallow, turned up sides, serrated rim	15.00
7″	40.00	Fruit, 8″d., serrated rim	20.00
8″	45.00	Pomade jar, original cover, flat circular base	35.00
Shallow bowl with folded sides (originally termed "fruit bowl")		Puff box, original patterned cover, flat circular base	35.00
8″	45.00	Relish tray	15.00
9″	50.00	Salt shaker, bulbous, flat, original top	25.00
10″	55.00	Sauce dish, flat, 4″	
Low standard, square		Flared	15.00
6″	25.00	Pointed ends	15.00
7″	25.00	Square	15.00
8″	30.00	Straight-sided	15.00
9″	30.00	Spoonholder, bulbous, flat circular base, scalloped rim	25.00
10″	35.00	Sugar bowl, covered, bulbous, flat circular base	40.00
Condiment set (cruet, salt/pepper, under tray)	75.00	Syrup pitcher, original top, pressed handle	55.00
Cracker jar, covered	85.00	Toothpick holder, 3-handled, flat, scalloped rim	35.00
Creamer, applied handle, flat		Tray, serrated scalloped rim	
Individual (originally termed "Jersey creamer").	20.00	Oblong	
Table size	30.00	Bread, 13″l., pointed ends	35.00
Cruet, original patterned stopper	30.00	Condiment	20.00
Crushed fruit jar, covered	85.00	Jelly, 8″l., shallow, two slightly folded sides	15.00
Cup			
Custard	15.00		
Lemonade, flat, pressed handle	15.00		
Dish, flat			
Oblong			
Almond, deep, scalloped with pointed ends	15.00		
Bon Bon, 5″, deep, two turned up sides	15.00		

Items made	Clear	Items made	Clear
Spoon tray, 9″l., folded sides with pointed ends	20.00	Mint, 6″d	15.00
		Water	45.00
Rectangular		Tumbler	
Banana, 9″l., deep folded sides ...	40.00	Juice	20.00
Orange, 10″l., slightly folded sides	40.00	Water	20.00
Round		Wine	40.00

MISSOURI States Series

Cruet (n.o.s.); high standard cake stand; creamer.

OMN: U.S. Glass No. 15,058, Missouri. AKA: Palm and Scroll, Palm Leaf and Scroll.

Non-flint. The United States Glass Co. (pattern line No. 15,058), Pittsburgh, PA. ca. 1898. Reviewed in the December 22, 1898 issue of the *Crockery and Glass Journal,* and illustrated in the ca. 1904 United States Glass Co. catalog.

Original color production: Clear, emerald green (plain or with gilt). Rare pieces may be found in amethyst, blue, and canary-yellow.

Reproductions: None.

References: Bros-TS (P. 42), Hart/Cobb-SS (P. 46), Hea-3 (P. 56, Fig. 441), Hea-5 (PP. 13, 20), Hea-6 (P. 35, Fig. 241), Kam-2 (P. 113), McCn-PGP (P. 417), Mil-2 (Pl. 51), Mtz-2 (PP. 68-69), Pet-Sal (P. 33), Pyne-PG (P. 154), Rev-APG (P. 316), Uni-1 (PP. 212-213), Uni-2 (P. 239).

Items made	Clear	Emerald Green
Bowl, open, flat, round		
6"d	15.00	35.00
7"d	15.00	35.00
8"d	20.00	40.00
Butter dish, covered	65.00	85.00
Cake stand		
High standard		
8"d	50.00	65.00
9"d	55.00	65.00
10"d	60.00	75.00
11"d	60.00	75.00
Low standard	40.00	—
Celery vase	30.00	—
Compote, high standard		
Covered		
5"d., jelly		
Notched lid	35.00	55.00
Plain lid	35.00	50.00
6"d	45.00	65.00
7"d	55.00	75.00
8"d	65.00	85.00
Open		
Deep bowl		
5"d	15.00	30.00
6"d	20.00	35.00
7"d	25.00	40.00
8"d	30.00	45.00
Saucer bowl		
8"d	30.00	45.00
9"d	35.00	50.00
10"d	40.00	55.00
Cordial	35.00	65.00
Creamer, 1 pint	25.00	40.00
Cruet, original stopper	55.00	125.00
Dish, covered, flat, 6"d	50.00	65.00
Doughnut stand, high standard, 6"d	40.00	55.00
Goblet	50.00	75.00
Mug	35.00	45.00
Olive dish	15.00	25.00
Pickle dish, rectangular	15.00	25.00
Pitcher		
Milk, 1 quart	45.00	90.00
Water, 1/2 gallon	75.00	100.00
Relish dish	15.00	25.00
Salt shaker, original top	25.00	40.00
Sauce dish, flat, round, 4"d	10.00	15.00
Spoonholder	25.00	45.00
Sugar bowl, covered	50.00	65.00
Syrup pitcher, original top	65.00	200.00
Tumbler, flat, water	20.00	40.00
Wine	35.00	55.00

Spoonholder.

Non-flint. Attributed to George Duncan & Sons, Pittsburgh, PA. ca. 1880s.

Original color production: Clear, opalescent. Clear with enamel decoration, clear with amber stain or any other color is very rare. Finials are well sculptured monkeys.

Reproductions: The A.A. Importing Co., Inc. catalog No. 33 (Bi-Centennial Spring-Summer catalog, 1976) illustrated the $4^3/_4$"h. spoonholder, reissued from a new mold, as a look alike in amber, clear and most likely other colors. Any item in Monkey is scarce.

References: Fer-YMG (P. 56), Hea-CG-Vol. 3 (P. 54, Fig. 74), Kam-4 (P. 81), Lee-EAPG (Pl. 94A), Mtz-1 (P. 96-97).

Items made	Clear	Opales-cent
Bowl		
Berry, master, open, flat	125.00	175.00
Waste	100.00	150.00
Butter dish, covered	175.00	300.00
Celery vase, flat, scalloped rim	90.00	200.00
Creamer, flat	125.00	250.00
Mug (2 styles)	85.00	150.00
Pickle jar, covered	125.00	350.00
Pitcher, water, flat, $^1/_2$ gallon	250.00	900.00
Sauce dish, flat	25.00	50.00
Spoonholder, flat, scalloped rim	90.00	125.00
Sugar bowl, covered	175.00	350.00
Tumbler, water, flat	100.00	200.00

Creamer; low footed bowl; covered butter dish; spoonholder.

OMN: Imperial, Coop's, Palace. AKA: Bull's Eye and Star, Star and Punty [Chipman].

Non-flint. Adams & Co., Pittsburgh, PA. ca. 1888. Co-Operative Flint Glass Co., Beaver Falls, PA. ca. 1896. Reissued by the United States Glass Co., Pittsburgh, PA. ca. 1890-1898. Possibly the Boston & Sandwich Glass Co., Sandwich, MA. Reviewed in the February 12, 1891 issue of the *Crockery and Glass Journal,* and illustrated in the United States Glass Co. ca. 1891 and 1898 catalogs and the ca. 1893 Pioneer Glass Co. catalog in clear with ruby stain.

Original color production: Clear, clear with acid finished "moons," clear with ruby stain (decorated by the Pioneer Glass Co., Pittsburgh, PA.). The Wilson Glass Co., Tarentum, PA. issued a similar pattern. When the firm went out of business, the molds were sold to the Co-Operative Flint Glass Co. and the pattern was renamed "Imperial". To satisfy a debt, Co-Operative sold the molds again to the Phoenix Glass Co. ca. 1937 who reissued the pattern.

Reproductions: The Moon and Star pattern has been reproduced for many years by such firms as L.G. Wright Co. (distributed by Jennings Red Barn, New Martinsville, WV. and Carl Forslund, Grand Rapids, MI.) L.E. Smith Glass Co., Mt. Pleasant, PA from both original and newly chipped molds.

Reproduced in both clear and colors from the early 1930s, the L.G. Wright 1970 catalog supplement illustrates both the covered butter dish and covered low standard 6"d. compote in clear, and in 1971 the firm's catalog illustrates the following items: covered butter dish (clear, vaseline, pink satin, vaseline satin), high standard 4"d. covered compote (clear vaseline, satin vaseline, satin ruby, satin green, satin blue), 6"d. high standard covered compote (clear vaseline, satin vaseline, satin blue), creamer with pressed handle (clear vaseline, pink satin, vaseline satin), goblet (blue satin, pink satin), salt dip (vaseline), tall salt shaker (clear vaseline, vaseline satin), spoonholder (clear vaseline, vaseline satin), covered sugar bowl (clear vaseline, vaseline satin, ruby satin, pink satin), and the toothpick holder (vaseline).

The Sturbridge Yankee Workshop, Sturbridge, MA. reissued the 6"h. goblet in both amber and ruby from the original mold, most likely by agreement with the Imperial Glass Co., Bellaire, OH.

References: Chip-ROS (P. 95), Enos-MPG (Chart-1), Hea-1 (P. 62), Hea-2 (P. 91, Fig. 617), Hea-5 (P. 51, Nos. 245-246), Hea-OS (P. 60, No. 870), Inn-EGP (P. 55), Kam-1 (P. 80), Kam-6

(Pl. 2), Kam-8 (P. 73), Lee-EAPG (Pl. 69, No. 4), McCn-PGP (P. 505), Mtz-1 (PP. 210-211), Mil-1 (Pl. 108), Oliv-AAG (P. 70), Pet-Sal (P. 166-"S"), Rev-APG (PP. 18, 20-21, 129), Spil-AEPG (P. 308), Uni-1 (P. 55), Uni-2 (P. 220).

Items made	Clear	Clear/ Frosted	Clear w/Ruby
Bottle, water	40.00	45.00	—
Bowl, flat, flared rim, round			
Covered			
6"d	35.00	40.00	60.00
7"d	35.00	40.00	60.00
8"d	40.00	45.00	65.00
10"d	45.00	50.00	75.00
Open			
6"d	25.00	30.00	50.00
7"d	25.00	30.00	50.00
8"d	30.00	35.00	60.00
10"d	35.00	40.00	60.00
Salad or fruit, 12½"d, scalloped	55.00	65.00	85.00
Waste, flat, smooth rim	45.00	45.00	65.00
Butter dish, covered	65.00	65.00	125.00
Cake stand, high standard			
9"d	45.00	55.00	—
10"d	55.00	55.00	—
Celery vase, flat, scalloped rim	35.00	40.00	—
Champagne, flared bowl	40.00	45.00	100.00
Cheese dish plate, deep center	40.00	45.00	—
Claret	45.00	55.00	—
Compote, round			
Covered			
High standard			
6"d	60.00	70.00	100.00
7"d	70.00	80.00	125.00
8"d	80.00	90.00	150.00
10"d	100.00	125.00	175.00
Collared base with star pattern			
Deep bowl, scalloped rim			
6"d	55.00	60.00	90.00
7"d	55.00	60.00	90.00
8"d	60.00	65.00	95.00
10"d	60.00	65.00	100.00
Open			
Collared base, star pattern around base			
Deep bowl, scalloped rim			
6"d.	25.00	30.00	45.00
7"d	35.00	40.00	55.00
8"d	35.00	40.00	55.00
10"d	40.00	45.00	65.00
Shallow bowl, flared, scalloped			
5½"d	25.00	30.00	45.00
7½"d	35.00	40.00	55.00
8½"d	35.00	40.00	55.00
10½"d	40.00	45.00	65.00
12½"d	50.00	60.00	75.00
High standard, scalloped rim			
7½"	40.00	45.00	65.00
8½"	45.00	50.00	75.00
10½"	50.00	60.00	85.00
12½"	60.00	65.00	95.00

Items made	Clear	Clear/ Frosted	Clear w/Ruby
Creamer, applied handle, original stopper	55.00	65.00	85.00
Dish, preserve, oblong, flat, open	20.00	25.00	40.00
Egg cup, single	35.00	40.00	60.00
Goblet	45.00	55.00	65.00
Lamp, oil, original burner.	145.00	—	—
Pickle tray, oval	20.00	20.00	35.00
Pitcher, water, bulbous, applied reeded handle	175.00	200.00	250.00
Relish tray	20.00	25.00	40.00
Salt			
Dip, individual	10.00	25.00	45.00
Shaker, original top	35.00	40.00	65.00
Sauce dish, round			
Flat			
4"d	10.00	15.00	25.00
4½"d	10.00	15.00	25.00
Footed	15.00	—	—
4"d	15.00	20.00	—
4½"d	15.00	20.00	—
Spoonholder	45.00	50.00	65.00
Sugar bowl, covered	65.00	65.00	90.00
Syrup pitcher, original top	165.00	—	—
Tray, bread			
Oblong	45.00	—	—
Rectangular	45.00	—	—
Water	65.00	—	—
Tumbler, water			
Flat	45.00	45.00	55.00
Footed	55.00	55.00	65.00
Wine	45.00	55.00	85.00

NAIL

Flat sauce dish (clear w/ruby stain); h.s. open jelly compote; water pitcher; spoonholder (clear w/ruby stain).

OMN: U.S. Glass No. 15,002. AKA: Recessed Pillar-Red Top [Millard], Recessed Pillar-Thumbprint Band [Millard].

Non-flint. Ripley and Co., Pittsburgh, PA. ca. 1892. Reissued by the United States Glass Co. (pattern line No. 15,002), Pittsburgh, PA. ca. 1892.

Original color production: Clear, clear with ruby stain (plain or copper wheel engraved). Illustrated in the April 13, 1892 issue of *China, Glass and Lamps.*

Reproductions: None.

References: Bar-RS (Pl. 14), Hea-3 (P. 56), Hea-5 (PP. 50-51), Hea-6 (P. 35, Fig. 242), Hea-7 (P. 30), Kam-2 (P. 87), Kam-6 (Plts. 5,7), McCn-PGP (P. 455), Mil-2 (Pl. 34), Mtz-2 (P. 142), Pet-Sal (P. 34), Rev-APG (PP. 293-294), Thu-1 (P. 321), Uni-1 (P. 113).

Items made	Clear	Clear w/Ruby
Bottle water	40.00	85.00
Bowl		
Berry, master, round, flat, 8"d	25.00	85.00
Finger or waste	30.00	—
Butter dish, covered, flat, flanged base	45.00	100.00
Celery vase, flat, scalloped rim	65.00	125.00
Claret	35.00	—
Compote, high standard, open		
Berry, 8"d	40.00	75.00
Jelly	20.00	40.00
Creamer, 4½"h	30.00	65.00
Cruet, original stopper	60.00	275.00
Goblet	35.00	65.00
Mustard pot, original lid (R)	50.00	85.00
Pitcher, water, ½ gallon	70.00	250.00
Salt shaker, original top	25.00	50.00
Sauce dish, round		
Flat	15.00	30.00
Footed	15.00	30.00
Spoonholder, flat	25.00	55.00
Sugar bowl, covered	35.00	95.00
Sugar shaker, original top	100.00	175.00
Syrup, original top	65.00	125.00
Tray, water, round	45.00	—
Tumbler, flat, water	20.00	40.00
Vase, 7"h	15.00	—
Wine	30.00	65.00

NAILHEAD

Wine; goblet; dinner plate; spoonholder.

OMN: Gem.

Non-flint. Bryce, Higbee & Co., Pittsburgh, PA. ca. 1885. Shards have been found at the site of the Boston & Sandwich Glass Co., Sandwich, MA. Illustrated in an undated Bryce, Higbee and Co. catalog.

Original color production: Clear. Odd pieces found in clear with ruby stain are rare.

Reproductions: None.

References: Enos-MPG (Charts 2,3), Kam-4 (PP. 41-42), Kam-8 (Plts. 45-46), Lee-EAPG (PP. 559-560), Mil-1 (Pl. 48), Mtz-1 (PP. 150-151), Pet-Sal (P. 138), Rev-APG (P. 92), Spil-AEPG (P. 278), Uni-1 (PP. 112-113), Wlkr-PGA (Fig. 8, No. 45).

Items made	Clear	Items made	Clear
Bowl, open, flat, master berry, 6″d	15.00	9½″d	30.00
Butter dish, covered	45.00	Cordial.	25.00
Cake stand, high standard		Creamer, 5¼″h	25.00
9½″d	30.00	Goblet	25.00
10½″d	35.00	Pitcher, water, ½ gallon	35.00
Celery vase	25.00	Plate	
Compote		Bread, round, deep, scalloped edge,	
Covered		star center, 9″d	20.00
High standard		Dinner, 7″sq	15.00
6″d	45.00	Sauce dish, flat, scalloped, star center,	
7″d	45.00	4″d	5.00
8″d	50.00	Spoonholder	20.00
Low standard, 7″d	50.00	Sugar bowl, covered	35.00
Open, high standard		Tumbler, water, flat	20.00
6½″d	25.00	Wine	20.00
7″d	25.00		

Handled dish; spoonholder; sauce dish.

OMN; U.S. Glass No. 15,075, Nevada.

Non-flint. The United States Glass Co. (pattern line No. 15,075), Pittsburgh, PA. ca. 1902. Illustrated in the United States Glass Co. 1904 catalog.

Original color production: Clear or clear and frosted with enamel decoration. Most forms are bulbous with "pinched" rims and low circular feet.

Reproductions: None.

References: Hart/Cobb-SS (P. 49), Hea-5 (PP. 20, 28), Hea-OS (P. 138, No. 2624), McCn-PGP (P. 407), Pyne-PG (P. 144), Uni-1 (P. 238).

Items made	Clear	Items made	Clear
Biscuit jar, covered	45.00	8"d	35.00
Bowl, round, flat		Cracker jar, covered	55.00
Covered		Creamer, footed, applied handle	30.00
6"d	35.00	Cruet, applied handle, original mellon	
7"d	40.00	stopper	35.00
8"d	45.00	Cup	
Open		Custard, applied handle	10.00
6"d	20.00	Sherbert, handleless	10.00
7"d	20.00	Dish, round, handled, flat	10.00
8"d	25.00	Jug, water, squatty, applied handle	35.00
Finger	20.00	Nappy (termed "Gainsboro"), round,	
Butter dish, covered, flanged base	50.00	footed, pointed with turned up ends,	
Cake stand, high standard, 10"d	35.00	applied single handle	20.00
Celery vase	25.00	Pickle dish, oval, 6"l	10.00
Compote, high standard, round		Pitcher, water, tankard, ½ gallon	40.00
Covered		Salt	
6"d	35.00	Individual, 2¼"d	10.00
7"d	40.00	Master	15.00
8"d	45.00	Shaker, original top	
Open		Hotel, plain bulbous base, tall	
6"d	25.00	plain neck	15.00
7"d	30.00		

Items made	Clear	Items made	Clear
Table size, patterned bulbous base, plain neck	15.00	Spoonholder, pedestaled	35.00
		Sugar bowl, covered	35.00
Sauce dish, flat, round		Syrup pitcher, pressed handle, original	
4"d	10.00	tin top	45.00
4½"d	10.00	Toothpick holder	45.00
5"d	10.00	Tumbler, water, flat	15.00

NEW ENGLAND PINEAPPLE

Champagne; covered sugar bowl; creamer; cruet (n.o.s.); footed bottle.

AKA: Loop and Jewel [Lee], Pineapple, Sawtooth.

Flint. Possibly the New England Glass Co., Cambridge, MA. ca. 1850-1870. Shards have been found at the site of the Boston & Sandwich Glass Co., Sandwich, MA.

Original color production: Clear. Any other color is rare.

Reproductions: The following items have been reissued in amber, clear and blue in non-flint from new molds ca. early 1960s: the cordial, goblet (both knob and faceted stem), and wine. Look-alikes have a smaller foot, while the glass is too thin and too light in weight. Glasscrafts & Ceramics, Inc., Yonkers, NY. advertised the look-alike goblet in clear as early as September, 1954.

References: Brn-SD (P. 53), Chip-ROS (P. 85), Cod-OS (Pl. 21), Enos-MPG (Chart-6), Grow-WCG (Fig. 26), Irw-SG (P. 54), Kam-4 (P. 54), Lee-EAPG (Pl. 53, Nos. 3-4), McKrn-AG (Plts. 207, 209), Mtz-1 (PP. 12-13), Mil-1 (Pl. 22), Oliv-AAG (P. 56), Pap-GAG (P. 189), Schwtz-AG (P. 120), Spil-AEPG (P. 2650), Spil-TBV (P. 26), Uni-1 (PP. 284-285), Uni-2 (P. 211), Wat-AG (Pl. 20), Wlkr-PGA (Fig. 8, No. 13), Wil-GNE (P. 32).

Items made	Flint	Items made	Flint
Bottle		Fruit	75.00
Castor	50.00	Butter dish, covered, flat	250.00
Oil, footed	85.00	Castor set, 4 bottles (complete in	
Bowl, open, flat, round		original pewter holder)	275.00
Berry, master, scalloped rim, 8"d ...	85.00	Champagne	175.00

Items made	Flint	Items made	Flint
Compote, round		Honey dish, flat, round, $3\frac{1}{2}''$d	
Covered, high standard		Base same as 6″d. plate	15.00
5″d	150.00	Star design in base	15.00
6″d (originally termed		Mug, applied handle	95.00
"sweetmeat")	150.00	Pickle dish	20.00
8″d	185.00	Pitcher	
Open		Milk, 1 quart	650.00+
High standard, scalloped rim		Water, applied handle, $\frac{1}{2}$ gallon.	350.00+
7″d	90.00	Plate, round, 6″d	90.00
$8\frac{1}{2}''$d	100.00	Salt	
Low standard		Dip, individual	25.00
7″d	90.00	Master, footed, open	45.00
$8\frac{1}{2}''$d	100.00	Sauce dish, round	
Cordial	175.00	Flat	15.00
Creamer, footed, applied handle		Footed	25.00
(height varies)		Spillholder	60.00
6″h	185.00	Spoonholder, footed, scalloped rim ...	50.00
7″h	185.00	Sugar bowl, covered	
Cruet, footed (2 styles), applied handle	175.00	Low footed, smooth rim, $7\frac{3}{8}''$h	125.00
Decanter, long necked with original		High foot, scalloped rim, $8\frac{1}{2}''$h	125.00
stopper, applied handle		Sweetmeat, covered, high standard	225.00
Pint	225.00	Tumbler	
Quart	225.00	Bar	110.00
Egg cup, single, footed	50.00	Water	85.00
Goblet		Whiskey, applied handle	145.00
Lady's (small)	100.00	Wine $5\frac{1}{4}''$h	150.00
Gentleman's (large)	65.00		

NEW HAMPSHIRE   States Series

Mug; tumbler; cruet (n.o.s.); creamer; relish tray.

OMN: U.S. Glass No. 15,084, New Hampshire. AKA: Bent Buckle [Kamm], Maiden's Blush, Modiste, Red Loop and Fine Cut [Millard].

Non-flint. The United States Glass Co. (pattern line No. 15,084), Pittsburgh, PA. ca. 1903. Reviewed in the March 12, 1903 issue of the *Crockery and Glass Journal,* and illustrated in the

Lyon Brothers 1905 (No. 411) and 1906 (No. 453) catalogs, and in the United States Glass Co. ca. 1904 (No. 111) catalog.

Original color production: Clear, clear with rose stain. Clear with ruby stain or any other color is rare. Handles may be either applied or pressed.

Reproductions: None.

References: Bar-RS (Pl. 14), Hart/Cobb-SS (P. 50), Hea-1 (P. 30), Hea-3 (PP. 80, 87), Hea-5 (P. 35, Fig. 246), Hea-7 (P. 159), Hea-TPS (PP. 27, 52, 101), Kam-3 (P. 97), McCn-PGP (P. 565), Mig-TPS (Pl. 3), Mil-2 (Pl. 86), Pet-Sal (P. 155), Pyne-PG (P. 143), Uni-1 (P. 163), Wlkr-PGA (Fig. 8, No. 44).

Items made	Clear	Clear w/Rose
Biscuit jar, covered, flat.	85.00	125.00
Bottle, carafe	65.00	—
Bowl, flat, open		
Round		
Flared rim		
5½"d	10.00	—
6½"d	15.00	35.00
7½"d	20.00	40.00
8½"d	20.00	45.00
Straight-sided		
6½"d	15.00	35.00
7½"d	20.00	40.00
9½"d	25.00	45.00
Square		
6½"	15.00	35.00
7½"	20.00	40.00
9½"	25.00	45.00
Butter dish, covered, flanged base	65.00	85.00
Cake stand, high standard, open, 9"d	40.00	45.00
Celery vase, flat, smooth rim	35.00	55.00
Compote, high standard		
Covered		
6"d	55.00	—
7"d	65.00	—
8"d	75.00	—
Open		
Deep bowl, flared rim		
7"d	25.00	—
8"d	30.00	—
9"d	35.00	—
Saucer bowl, 7"d	25.00	—
Creamer		
Breakfast or individual, 3¼"h	30.00	35.00
Table size	30.00	45.00
Cruet, original patterned stopper	55.00	100.00
Cup		
Custard, straight-sided bowl	10.00	15.00
Lemonade, flared bowl	10.00	15.00
Dish, olive		
Diamond shape, flat, crimped rim (originally termed the No. 2 olive), 6⅝"d	20.00	35.00
Oblong (originally termed the No. 1 olive)	20.00	35.00
Goblet	25.00	65.00
Jug, 3 pint, pressed handle	85.00	—
Mug		
Large	15.00	45.00

Items made	Clear	Clear w/Rose
Medium	15.00	45.00
Pickle dish, oval, flat, 7½"l	15.00	30.00
Pitcher		
Bulbous		
Milk, 3 pint	85.00	—
Water, ¾ gallon	95.00	—
Tankard, water, ½ gallon	85.00	125.00
Plate, round, 8"d., smooth rim	25.00	35.00
Relish tray	15.00	20.00
Salt shaker, original top		
Hotel, large, straight sided with fluted neck	25.00	40.00
Small, tapered with fluted neck	25.00	40.00
Table size, no neck	25.00	40.00
Sauce dish, flat, flared rim, 4"		
Round	8.00	15.00
Square	8.00	15.00
Spoonholder	25.00	45.00
Sugar bowl		
Covered		
Breakfast	25.00	35.00
Table size	45.00	65.00
Open, individual, double handled	15.00	35.00
Syrup, original top	75.00	—
Toothpick holder	20.00	35.00
Tumbler, water, flat	15.00	35.00
Vase		
6"h., thick stem	20.00	35.00
8"h., twist stem	25.00	40.00
9"h., narrow stem	25.00	40.00
Wine		
Flared bowl	30.00	50.00
Straight-sided bowl	30.00	50.00

NEW JERSEY States Series

Creamer; plate; salt shaker; h.s. covered butter dish; pepper shaker; low footed bowl.

OMN: U.S. Glass No. 15,070, New Jersey. AKA: Loops and Drops, Red Loop and Finecut [Millard].

Non-flint. The United States Glass Co. (pattern line No. 15,070), Pittsburgh, PA. at Factory "G" (Gillinder & Sons, Greensburg, PA.), "P" (Doyle & Co., Pittsburgh, PA.), and "D" (George Duncan & Sons, Pittsburgh, PA.) ca. 1900-1908. Reviewed in the January 10, 1901 issue of *China, Glass and Lamps,* and illustrated in the Butler Brothers 1906 Fall catalog and the United States Glass Co. 1904 and 1908 catalogs.

Original color production: Clear, clear with ruby stain (plain or gilt). Decorated by the Oriental Glass Co., Pittsburgh, PA. Handles may be either applied or pressed.

Reproductions: None.

References: Bar-RS (Pl. 11), Bros-TS (P. 43), Hart/Cobb-SS (P. 51), Hea-3 (P. 80), Hea-5 (P. 148), Hea-6 (P. 88), Hea-7 (P. 159), Hea-TPS (P. 75), McCn-PGP (P. 267), Mil-1 (Pl. 165), Mtz-2 (P. 162), Pyne-PG (P. 142), Spil-TBV (P. 52), Stu-BP (P. 63), Uni-2 (P. 244), Wlkr-PGA (Fig. 8, Nos. 18, 36).

Items made	Clear	Clear w/Ruby
Bottle, water	45.00	90.00
Bowl, open, flat, scalloped rim		
Round		
Deep bowl		
6"d	20.00	45.00
7"d	25.00	55.00
8"d	25.00	55.00
Saucer bowl		
8"d	25.00	55.00
9"d	30.00	65.00
10"d	35.00	75.00
Oval, plain or pointed ends		
6"	20.00	45.00
8"	25.00	55.00
10"	35.00	75.00
Round, low standard, open, 9"d	40.00	85.00
Butter dish, covered, flanged base		
Flat	75.00	125.00
High standard (originally termed the "sweetmeat")	90.00	—
Cake stand, high standard, 8"d	65.00	—
Celery		
Tray, rectangular	25.00	40.00
Vase, flat, scalloped rim	30.00	65.00
Compote, high standard, scalloped rim, round		
Covered		
5"d., jelly	45.00	85.00
6"d	45.00	85.00
7"d	55.00	90.00
8"d	65.00	95.00
Open		
5"d., jelly	25.00	45.00
6"d	30.00	55.00
7"d	35.00	65.00
8"d	40.00	75.00
Creamer	40.00	75.00
Cruet, original stopper	55.00	—
Dish, open, flat, scalloped rim		
6"	15.00	—
8"	20.00	—
10"	25.00	50.00
Fruit bowl, high standard, shallow bowl		

Items made	Clear	Clear w/Ruby
9½"d	45.00	85.00
10½"d	50.00	95.00
12½"d	55.00	110.00
Goblet	40.00	65.00
Olive dish, pointed ends, flared rim	15.00	—
Pickle tray, rectangular	15.00	—
Pitcher		
Milk, bulbous, 1 quart, applied handle	75.00	175.00
Water		
Bulbous, applied handle, ½ gallon	85.00	250.00
Straight-sided, pressed handle	50.00	185.00
Plate		
Flat		
Dinner, 8"d	10.00	45.00
Fruit		
9½"d	20.00	—
10½"d	25.00	—
12"d	30.00	—
Footed	10.00	85.00
Salt or pepper shaker, original top		
Bulbous	30.00	50.00
Hotel size	35.00	60.00
Sauce dish, flat, round, 4"d	15.00	30.00
Shade, gas, 4" fitter opening	35.00	85.00
Spoonholder, flat, scalloped rim	25.00	75.00
Sugar bowl, covered	65.00	110.00
Syrup pitcher, with glass lip, original top		
Straight-sided	90.00	—
Tapered sides	90.00	—
Toothpick holder	55.00	225.00
Tumbler, water, flat	25.00	45.00
Wine		
Flared bowl	40.00	55.00
Straight bowl	40.00	55.00

O'HARA'S DIAMOND

Goblet; champagne; wine.

OMN: Diamond (O'Hara) & U.S. Glass No. 15,001. AKA: Ruby Star, Sawtooth and Star [Lee].

Non-flint. O'Hara Glass Co., Pittsburgh, PA. ca. 1885. Reissued by the United States Glass Co. (pattern line No. 15,001) at Factory "L" (O'Hara Glass Co., Pittsburgh, PA.) ca. 1891-1904. Advertised in *China, Glass and Lamps* from 1891 through 1892, and illustrated in the United States Glass Co. ca. 1895 and 1898 catalogs.

Original color production: Clear, clear with ruby stain. Handles may be applied or pressed.

Reproductions: None.

References: Bar-RS (Pl. 7), Drep-ABC OG (P. 165), Hea-3 (PP. 34, 56), Hea-5 (P. 51, No. 251), Hea-6 (P. 35, Fig. 247), Hea-7 (PP. 32, 163), Hea-OS (P. 17), Kam-2 (P. 52), Kam-5 (P. 46), Kam-8 (Plts. 14-15), Lee-VG (Pl. 47, No. 1), Mtz-1 (PP. 118-119), Pet-Sal (P. 38), Rev-APG (PP. 276, 316), Uni-1 (PP. 82-83).

Items made	Clear	Clear w/Ruby
Bowl, round, flat		
Covered		
5"d	25.00	40.00
6"d	30.00	45.00
7"d	35.00	50.00
8"d	40.00	55.00
Open, scalloped rim		
5"d	10.00	25.00
6"d	10.00	25.00
7"d	15.00	30.00
8"d	20.00	40.00
Waste	15.00	20.00
Butter dish, covered, flat	45.00	125.00
Cake stand, high standard		
9"d	50.00	100.00
10"d	60.00	125.00
Celery vase, flat	30.00	95.00
Champagne	25.00	40.00

Items made	Clear	Clear w/Ruby
Claret	45.00	55.00
Compote, open, high standard, scalloped rim		
5″d	40.00	85.00
6″d	50.00	100.00
7″d	60.00	125.00
8″d	65.00	145.00
Condiment under tray	—	45.00
Creamer, 5$\frac{1}{2}$″h	20.00	55.00
Cruet, original stopper, 7″h	35.00	135.00
Cup, custard, handled, 2$\frac{3}{8}$″h	15.00	25.00
Dish, open, flat, serrated rim, round		
5″d	10.00	—
6″d	10.00	—
7″d	15.00	—
8″d	20.00	—
Goblet, 6$\frac{1}{4}$″h	25.00	65.00
Honey dish, flat, round, 3$\frac{1}{2}$″d	15.00	20.00
Lamp, oil, stand, complete with original burner and chimney	55.00	—
Pickle dish, flat	15.00	25.00
Pitcher, water, tankard, $\frac{1}{2}$ gallon	90.00	175.00
Plate, round		
7″d	20.00	—
8″d	30.00	—
10″d	40.00	—
Salt		
Master, flat, open	15.00	40.00
Shaker, original top	15.00	40.00
Sauce dish, round		
Flat, serrated rim, 4″d	10.00	—
Footed, scalloped rim		
4″d	20.00	25.00
5″d	20.00	25.00
Saucer, 5$\frac{1}{4}$″d	15.00	20.00
Spoonholder, serrated rim, 4$\frac{3}{4}$″h	20.00	60.00
Sugar bowl, covered	35.00	90.00
Syrup pitcher, original top	55.00	250.00
Tray, water, round, ruffled rim	40.00	75.00
Tumbler, water, flat, 3$\frac{7}{8}$″d	30.00	45.00
Wine	25.00	35.00

Plate 9″d.; bulbous water pitcher; plate 7″d.

AKA: Beaded 101, One Hundred and One, 1-0-1.

Non-flint. George Duncan and Sons, Pittsburgh, PA. ca. 1885. Shards have been found at the site of the Burlington Glass Works, Hamilton, Ontario, Canada.

Original color production: Clear. Odd items may be found in opaque colors of blue, pink and white. Handles may be either applied or pressed.

Reproductions: None.

References: Enos-MPG (Chart-4), Hlms-BCA (P. 278), Kam-1 (P. 71), Kam/WodVol.2 (P. 427), Lee-EAPG (Pl. 141, No. 30), Mtz-1 (PP. 188-189), Mil-1 (Pl. 82), Stev-ECG (PP. 223, 229), Stu-BP (P. 9), Uni-1 (PP. 154-155), Uni-TCG (PP. 156-157), Uni/Wor-CHPGT (P. 172), Wlkr-PGA (Fig. 8, No. 45).

Items made	Clear	Items made	Clear
Butter dish, covered	65.00	Plate	
Cake stand, high standard, 9″d	65.00	Bread, round	
Celery vase, pedestaled, scalloped rim,		One-O-One border, "Give Us This	
8⅛″h	50.00	Day Our Daily Bread" center	75.00
Compote, covered, round		Scalloped rim, 11¼″d	75.00
High standard		Dinner, round	
7″d	60.00	6″d	15.00
8″d	60.00	7″d	20.00
10″d	75.00	8″d	20.00
Low standard, 7″d	60.00	9″d	20.00
Creamer, 4½″h	40.00	Relish tray, oval	15.00
Goblet, 5⅞″h	35.00	Salt shaker, original top	15.00
Lamp, oil, complete with original		Sauce dish, round, plain rim, rayed or	
burner and chimney		star base	
Hand, flat, handled, 10″h	85.00	Flat, 4″d	10.00
Stand	100.00	Footed, 4″d	15.00
Pickle dish, oval		Spoonholder, smooth rim	25.00
Flat, tapered at one end	20.00	Sugar bowl, covered, 7″h	45.00
Collared base	20.00	Vase	25.00
Pitcher, water, bulbous, applied		Wine	65.00
handle, footed, 9½″h., ½ gallon	125.00		

Covered butter; creamer; covered sugar; goblet; egg cup.

AKA: Moss Rose.

Non-flint. Maker unknown, ca. 1870s. Shards have been found at the site of the Boston & Sandwich Glass Co., Sandwich, MA.

Original color production: Clear. Open Rose was originally produced in two styles: normal and heavy impression (heavy impressions are seen more often in the form of creamers and goblets). Handles are applied.

Reproductions: A spoonholder look-alike was issued from a new mold in the mid 1970s in amber, blue and green, which lacks the refined detail of the original.

References: Bat-GPG (PP. 54-55), Bond-AG (Pl. 21), Brn-SD (P. 51), Chip-ROS (P. 85), Cod-OS (Pl. 21), Lee-EAPG (Plt. 123, No. 3), Mil-1 (Pl. 52), Mtz-1 (PP. 54-55), Oliv-AAG (P. 71), Uni-1 (PP. 198-199), Wlkr-PGA (Fig. 8, Nos. 20, 51).

Items made	Clear	Items made	Clear
Bowl, open		6"d	25.00
Oval, flat, 9" x 6", vegetable	25.00	7"d	30.00
Round, flat, 5"d	20.00	7½"d	35.00
Butter dish, covered	55.00	8"d	40.00
Cake stand, high standard	45.00	9"d	45.00
Celery vase, pedestaled, scalloped rim	30.00	Cordial	35.00
Compote, round		Creamer	40.00
Covered, high standard		Dish, round, open, flat, 7"d	25.00
6"d	45.00	Egg cup, single	25.00
7"d	50.00	Goblet	
8"d	60.00	Lady's (small)	30.00
9"d	60.00	Gentleman's (large)	30.00
Open, low standard		Pickle dish, oval	15.00

Items made	Clear	Items made	Clear
Pitcher, bulbous, applied handle,		Sauce dish, flat, round, 4″d	10.00
Milk, 1 quart	110.00	Spoonholder, pedestaled, scalloped rim	40.00
Water, 3-pint	150.00	Sugar bowl, covered	60.00
Relish tray, oval	15.00	Tumbler, water, flat	45.00
Salt, master, footed, open, cable edge	30.00		

OREGON

Salt shaker; h.s. open compote; syrup; goblet; toothpick holder.

OMN: U.S. Glass No. 15,073, Oregon. AKA: Beaded Loop(s) [Kamm, Lee], Beaded Ovals [Hartley].

Non-flint. The United States Glass Co. (pattern line No. 15,073), Pittsburgh, PA. after the U.S. Glass merger of 1891. Illustrated in the ca. 1904 and 1907 United States Glass Co. catalogs, and the Charles "Broadway" Rousse general merchandise for July-August, 1914.

Original color production: Clear.

Reproductions: The Imperial Glass Co., Bellaire, OH., reissued from a new mold the $6^3/_4$″h. covered sugar bowl in milk white and clear iridescent carnival, and the goblet in clear.

References: Bar-RS (Pl. 8), Enos-MPG (Chart-2), Hart/Cobb-SS (P. 57), Hea-5 (PP. 21, 164), Kam-3 (P. 87), Kam-8 (P. 18), Lee-EAPG (P. 244, Pl. 76), McCn-PGP (P. 571), Mil-1 (Pl. 82), Mtz-2 (PP. 156-157), Pet-Sal (P. 22), Pyne-PG (P. 138), Rev-APG (P. 316), Spil-AEPG (P. 335), Stu-BP (P. 5), Uni-1 (P. 312), Uni-2 (P. 242), Wlkr-PGA (Fig. 8, No. 45).

Items made	Clear	Items made	Clear
Bottle, water.	35.00	8″d	15.00
Bowl, flat, round		Butter dish, covered, flat	
Covered		English	65.00
6″d	25.00	Flanged rim	65.00
7″d	25.00	Plain rim	45.00
8″d	25.00	Cake stand, high standard	
Open		6″d	35.00
6″d	15.00	8″d	45.00
7″d	15.00	9″d	50.00

Items made	Clear	Items made	Clear
10″d	55.00	12½″	35.00
Celery vase	30.00	Goblet, 6″h	35.00
Compote, round		Honey dish, flat, round, 3½″d	10.00
Covered, high standard, 5″d	45.00	Horse radish, covered, handled	50.00
Open		Mug, pressed handle	35.00
High standard		Olive dish, boat shape	15.00
Deep bowl		Pickle dish, boat shape	15.00
5″d., jelly	30.00	Pitcher	
6″d	30.00	Pint	45.00
8″d	35.00	Milk, 1 quart	45.00
9″d	40.00	Water, ½ gallon	55.00
Saucer bowl (originally termed the "fruit bowl")		Plate, bread, oval, 7½″ x 11″	35.00
		Relish tray	15.00
7¼″d	30.00	Salt	
8½″d	35.00	Master, open	15.00
10″d	40.00	Shaker, bulbous, original top	25.00
Low standard		Sauce dish, round	
5″d., jelly	25.00	Flat, 4″d	10.00
6″d	25.00	Footed, 4″d	15.00
7″d	30.00	Spoonholder	
8″d	40.00	Flat	25.00
9″d	45.00	Footed	30.00
Creamer		Sugar bowl, covered	
Flat	30.00	Flat	40.00
Footed	55.00	Footed	45.00
Cruet, original stopper	45.00	Syrup pitcher, original top	65.00
Dish, oval, flat, deep		Toothpick holder	55.00
7½″	15.00	Tumbler, water, flat	25.00
8½″	20.00	Vase	35.00
9½″	20.00	Wine	30.00
10½″	25.00		

PALMETTE

Egg cup; goblet; spoonholder; covered butter dish.

AKA: Hearts and Spades, Spades.

Non-flint. American manufacturer unknown. Shards have been found at the site of the Burlington Glass Works, Hamilton, Ontario, Canada

Original color production: Clear. Rare pieces may be found in milk white. Any other color is rare. Handles are applied. A variant of the pattern (known only in the plate) can be found in amber and blue.

Reproductions: None.

References: Belnp-NG (P. 83), Brn-SD (P. 55), Enos-MPG (Chart-4), Fer-YMG (P. 74), Hlms-BCA (P. 278), Kam-4 (PP. 20-21), Kam-7 (PP. 79-80), Kam/Wod-Vol. 1 (P. 176), Lee/Rose-CP (PP. 79-80), Lee-EAPG (Plt. 112, No. 20), McCn-PGP (P. 419), Mil-1 (P. 25), Mtz-1 (PP. 126-127), Oliv-AAG (P. 71), Pet-Sal (P. 167), Stev-ECG (PP. 214, 220), Thu-1 (P. 98), Uni-1 (P. 213), Uni-TCG (PP. 160-161), Uni/Wor-CHPGT (PP. 174-175), Wlkr-PGA (Nos. 16, 37, 41).

Items made	Clear	Items made	Clear
Bottle, castor	20.00	Egg cup, pedestaled, 4"h	45.00
Bowl, low footed, open, round		Goblet, 6"h	35.00
6"d	25.00	Honey dish, flat, round, 3¼"d	15.00
9"d	25.00	Lamp, oil, original burner	
Butter dish, covered, flat		All Glass	
Hexagonal knob-finial, 6¼"d	65.00	10"h	65.00
Handleless, 6¼"d	65.00	8½"h., 6 sided foot, No. 1 collar	65.00
Tab handles, 7⅝" handle to handle	85.00	9½"h., 6 sided foot, No. 1 collar	65.00
Butter pat (R)	35.00	Composite, No. 2 collar, patterned	
Cake plate, flat, tab handles, 9"d	35.00	font, metal with marble base	85.00
Cake stand, high standard, 10½"d	125.00	Pickle scoop, oval, flat	15.00
Castor set, 5 bottles, complete in silver		Pitcher, bulbous, applied handle	
plate holder	125.00	Water, ½ gallon, 9"h (R)	125.00
Celery		Milk, 1 quart (R)	135.00
Tray	20.00	Plate, bread, handled, 9"d	30.00
Vase, pedestaled, scalloped rim,		Relish tray	18.00
8⅜"h	45.00	Salt	
Champagne (R), 4¼"h	85.00	Master, footed, open, smooth rim,	
Compote, round		2½"h	25.00
Covered		Shaker, original top	
High standard		Bulbous, tall	55.00
7"d	65.00	Saloon (oversized salt shaker)	65.00
7¼"d	65.00	Sauce dish, round, flat	
8½"d	75.00	4"d	10.00
9¾"d	85.00	4½"d	10.00
Open		5"d	15.00
High standard, 8"d	40.00	6"d	20.00
Low standard		Spoonholder, pedestaled, scalloped	
5½"d	25.00	rim, 5"h	35.00
7"d	35.00	Sugar bowl, covered, pedestaled, 5"h	65.00
Cordial (R)	100.00	Syrup pitcher, original top, rayed base,	
Creamer, pedestaled, applied handle,		applied handle, 6¾"h	125.00
6"h	65.00	Tumbler, water	
Cruet, pedestaled, applied handle,		Flat, 4"h	65.00
original maltese cross finial (R)	135.00	footed, 5"h	35.00
Cup plate, 3⅜"d	45.00	Wine (R), 4¼"h	90.00

PANELED DAISY

Water tray; relish tray.

OMN: Brazil. AKA: Daisy and Panel, Panelled Daisy.

Non-flint. Bryce Brothers, Pittsburgh, PA. ca. 1888. Reissued by the United States Glass Co., Pittsburgh, PA. Factory "B" ca. 1891. Illustrated in the ca. 1891 United States Glass Co. catalog of member firms in thirty five pieces.

Original color production: The look-alike goblet and tumbler were first issued in the early 1960s from new molds in clear. The 1981–1982 Fenton Art Glass Co. catalog illustrates a footed toothpick holder (blue opalescent) and a votive [candle holder] (cameo opalescent, a blending of brown and tan), forms not original to the set. The Fenton January, 1982 catalog supplement illustrates the high standard covered compote in clear and the new colors of country peach, and forget-me-not blue. These are heavier and duller than the originals.

Reproductions: The look-alike goblet and tumbler were first issued in the early 1960s from new molds in clear. Reproductions are heavier and duller than originals.

References: Belnp-MG (P. 94), Drep-FR (P. 206), Enos-MPG (Chart-1), Hea-3 (P. 78), Hea-5 (P. 74), Kam-3 (P. 65), Kam-7 (Plts. 1-2), Lee-EAPG (Plt. 136, No. 4), McCn-PGP (P. 287) Mil-1 (Pl. 25), Mtz-1 (PP. 62-63), Pet-Sal (P. 34), Rev-APG (PP. 86, 88), Uni-1 (P. 141), Uni-2 (P. 215), Wlkr-PGA (Fig. 8, Nos. 27, 45).

Items made	Clear	Items made	Clear
Bottle, water	50.00	Flat	45.00
Bowl, open		Footed, flanged rim	45.00
Flared rim		Cake stand, high standard	
6"d	15.00	8"d	35.00
7"d	15.00	9"d	45.00
8"d	20.00	10"d	45.00
Shallow		11"d	55.00
7"d	15.00	Celery vase, pedestaled, scalloped rim	35.00
8"d	20.00	Compote, high standard, round	
9"d	20.00	Covered	
10"d	25.00	5"d	45.00
Waste	30.00	6"d	45.00
Butter dish, covered		7"d	50.00

Items made	Clear	Items made	Clear
8"d	55.00	10"sq	35.00
Open, scalloped rim		Round	
7"d	25.00	7"d	30.00
8"d	30.00	9"d	30.00
9"d	30.00	Relish tray	15.00
10"d	35.00	Salt shaker, tall, original top	25.00
11"d	40.00	Sauce dish, round, flared rim	
Creamer, 5½"h	35.00	Flat	
Dish, oval, open, flat		4"d	10.00
7"	15.00	4½"d	10.00
8"	15.00	Footed	
9"	18.00	4"d	10.00
10"	18.00	4½"d	10.00
Goblet	35.00	Spoonholder	25.00
Mug, large, handled	35.00	Sugar bowl, covered	45.00
Pickle scoop	15.00	Sugar shaker, original tin top	35.00
Pitcher, water, ½ gallon	55.00	Syrup pitcher, original tin top	65.00
Plate		Tray, water, round	35.00
Square		Tumbler, water, flat, ½ pint	25.00
9½"sq	35.00		

PANELED FORGET-ME-NOT

High standard open shallow compote; relish tray; high standard covered compote; bread tray.

OMN: Bryce's Regal, U.S. Glass No. 24. AKA: No. 29.

Non-flint. Bryce, Brothers, Pittsburgh, PA. ca. 1875. Reissued by the United States Glass Co. (pattern line No. 24), Pittsburgh, PA. at Factory "B" (Bryce Brothers, Pittsburgh, PA.) ca. 1891. Shards have been found at the site of the Burlington Glass Works, Hamilton, Ontario, Canada.

Original color production: Amber, blue, clear. Amethyst, green or any other color is very rare. Doyle's pattern line No. 29 closely resembles Paneled Forget-Me-Not but is not the same pattern.

Reproductions: None.

References: Enos-MPG (Chart-1), Hea-5 (P. 21), Hlms-BCA (P. 278), Kam-3 (PP. 43-44), Kam/Wod-Vol.1 (P. 263), Lee-EAPG (Pl. 79, No. 10), McCn-PGP (Pl. 138), Mil-1 (Pl.1 22), Mtz-1 (PP. 56-57), Pet-Sal (P. 167), Rev-APG (PP. 88-89), Spil-AEPG (P. 299), Spil-TBV (P. 260), Stev-ECG (P. 216, 229), Stu-BP (P. 28), Uni-1 (PP. 140-141), Uni-TCG (PP. 162-163), Uni/Wor-CHPGT (P. 177), Wlkr-PGA (Fig. 9, Nos. 36, 38, 43).

Items made	Amber	Blue	Clear
Bowl, covered, round	45.00	70.00	35.00
Butter dish, covered	45.00	60.00	30.00
Cake stand, high standard	70.00	90.00	45.00
Celery vase	45.00	70.00	35.00
Compote, high standard, round			
Covered			
7"d	90.00	110.00	65.00
8"d	80.00	100.00	65.00
8½"d	80.00	100.00	60.00
Open			
9½"d	60.00	80.00	40.00
10"d	60.00	80.00	40.00
Cordial	60.00	70.00	50.00
Creamer	45.00	60.00	35.00
Cruet, original stopper	—	—	45.00
Goblet	50.00	65.00	30.00
Jam jar, covered	65.00	85.00	40.00
Pickle tray, boat shape	25.00	35.00	15.00
Pitcher			
Milk, 1 quart	90.00	110.00	50.00
Water, ½ gallon	90.00	110.00	75.00
Relish tray, tapered at one end	55.00	55.00	35.00
Salt shaker, original top	—	—	65.00
Sauce dish, round			
Flat, 4"d	15.00	20.00	10.00
Footed, 4"d	20.00	20.00	15.00
Spoonholder	40.00	50.00	25.00
Sugar bowl, covered	60.00	80.00	40.00
Tray, bread, oval	35.00	45.00	25.00
Wine	75.00	85.00	55.00

PANELED GRAPE

Relish tray; salt shaker.

OMN: Kokomo-Jenkins No. 507. AKA: Heavy Paneled Grape, Maple.

Non-flint. The Kokomo Glass Manufacturing Co., Kokomo, IN. ca. 1904. Shards have been found at the site of the Boston & Sandwich Glass Co., Sandwich, MA.

Original color production: Clear.

Reproductions: The Paneled Grape goblet was first reissued in the 1930s in clear and colors with very little stippling on the leaves compared to the originals.

The L.G. Wright Glass Co., New Martinsville, WV. (distributed by Jennings Red Barn, New Martinsville, WV. and Carl Forslund, Grand Rapids, MI.) reproduced the following items in amber, blue, clear, green, and ruby red: 12″d crimped bowl, covered butter dish, celery vase, cordial, high standard covered compote, creamer, goblet, water pitcher, various sizes plates, flat sauce, covered sugar bowl, spoonholder and wine. The Wright 1974 master catalog illustrates the following items reproduced in amber, blue, green, ruby and amethyst: covered 4″d. high standard compote, creamer, goblet, footed sauce dish (termed the "sherbert"), the true open sugar bowl with double handles, and wine.

The Westmorland Glass Co., Grapeville, PA. reproduced the pattern in clear and milk white for L.G. Wright Glass Co. ca. 1960s (in blue) and in 1968-1970 (in canary yellow including the water pitcher, goblet, wine and high standard covered compote). The Summit Art Glass Co., Mogadore/Rootstown. OH. also reissued items from new molds in both clear and color.)

References: Boyd-GC (P. 112), Bros-TS (P. 33), Drep-ABC OG (P. 153), Hea-2 (P. 91, Figs. 609-610), Hea-OPG (PP. 113-114), Hea-TPS (PP. 76, 85), Inn-PG (P. 355), Kam-1 (P. 96), Kam-3 (P. 61), Kam-5 (P. 124), Lee-EAPG (Pl. 65, No. 1), McCn-PGP (P. 317), Mil-1 (Pl. 95), Mtz-1 (PP. 78-79), Pet-Sal (P. 162), Rev-APG (P. 224), Uni-1 (P. 87).

Items made	Clear	Items made	Clear
Ale glass, knob stem, 6¼″h	45.00	Celery vase, pedestaled, scalloped rim	35.00
Bowl, round, flat		Compote, round	
Covered, 8″d	35.00	Covered, high standard	
Open, 8″d	25.00	4″d	35.00
Butter dish, covered, flat	60.00	8″d	65.00

Items made	Clear	Items made	Clear
Open, low standard, 6½"d	25.00	Sauce dish	
Creamer, 4½"h		Flat	20.00
Plain handle	45.00	Footed	20.00
Vine handle	45.00	Spoonholder	30.00
Cup, sherbert, handled	15.00	Sugar bowl, covered	50.00
Dish, oval, flat	15.00	Syrup pitcher, original top (2 styles)	70.00
Goblet	40.00	Toothpick holder	45.00
Pitcher		Tumbler	
Milk, 1 quart	65.00	Jelly, thin top rim	35.00
Water, ½ gallon	75.00	Lemonade	35.00
Relish, oval, flat	15.00	Water	35.00
Salt shaker, original top	25.00	Wine	40.00

PANELED THISTLE

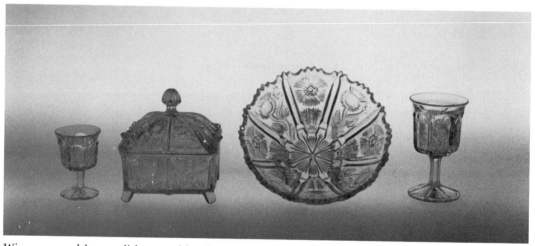

Wine; covered honey dish; round bowl; goblet.

OMN: Delta. AKA: Canadian Thistle

Non-flint. J.B. Higbee Glass Co., Bridgeville, PA. ca. 1910-1920. Issued by the Jefferson Glass Co., Toronto, Ontario, Canada. Illustrated in the Spring, 1914 issue of *Our Drummer* magazine.

Original color production: Clear. Clear with ruby stain or any other color is very rare. The Canadian version of Paneled Thistle differs slightly with an extra thistle bud on the lower part of the design. The Higbee Glass Co. trademark was a bee with the letters "H.I.G." embossed across the wings. Handles are pressed.

Reproductions: Many items were reproduced in Paneled Thistle, the first being the clear goblet ca. 1900–1910. By 1967, the L.G. Wright Glass Co., New Martinsville, WV. (distributed by Jennings Red Barn, New Martinsville, WV. and Carl Forslund, Grand Rapids, MI.) reproduced the 7½"d and 8"d plate in clear—the 1970 catalog supplement illustrated the following look-alike items in clear: 7 ½"d. deep belled flat bowl, 5½"d flat shallow bowl, goblet, 7½" square plate, 8"l. relish tray, master salt, and wine. For 1974, the L.G. Wright master catalog illustrates the following reissues of Paneled Thistle in clear: master berry bowl, covered butter, footed open bowl, h.s. 6"d. covered compote, 6"d. h.s. open compote, creamer, goblet, flat-square covered honey dish, 8"l. flat pickle dish, water pitcher, square plate, tall salt shaker, master salt, flat sauce dish, double handled spoonholder, covered small sugar, true open doubled handled sugar, sugar shaker, toothpick holder, water tumbler, and wine. By 1980, the Wright catalog supplement introduced the following reproduced in pink ice: creamer, water pitcher, double handled spoonholder, true open sugar, and water tumbler. Paneled Thistle was heavily reproduced by the Summit Art Glass Co., Mogadore/ Rootstown, OH. with a similar Bee mark, including the champagne, goblet (both barrel shaped bowl and flared rim), 7" square plate, 7" round plate, 10"d round plate, salt dip, and wine in clear. Reproductions first appeared in the early 1950s, possibly from old molds. The salt dip was recently reissued from new molds in amber, amethyst and other colors.

References: Bar-RS (Pl. 14), Brn-SD (P. 53), Enos-MPG (Chart-1), Hea-7 (P. 103), Hea-OS (P. 60), Hea-TPS (PP. 77, 86), Hlms-BCA (P. 281), Kam-1 (P. 83), Kam/Wod-Vol.2 (P. 585), Lee-EAPG (Pl. 141, No. 4) Mil-1 (Pl. 163), Mil-2 (Pl. 77), Mtz-1 (PP. 68-69), Oliv-AAG (P. 74), Pet-Sal (P. 168), Pet-GPP (P. 95), Rev-APG (P. 92), Spil-AEPG (P. 338), Stev-ECG (PP. 168-169), Stu-BP (P. 35), Uni-1 (P. 209), Uni-2 (P. 233), Uni/Wor-CHPGT (P. 70), Wlkr-PGA (Fig. 8, No. 1).

Items made	Clear	Items made	Clear
Basket, applied handle, small	50.00	Goblet	
Bowl		Flared bowl	35.00
Round, open, footed		Straight bowl	35.00
6½"d	15.00	Honey dish, 5" x 5" square, covered	75.00
7"d	15.00	Jar, covered	60.00
7½"d	20.00	Mug, handled	15.00
8"d	20.00	Pickle dish, 8¼"l	20.00
8½"d	20.00	Pitcher	
9"d	25.00	Milk, 1 quart	60.00
Rectangular, 5½"r x 7"	20.00	Water, ½ gallon	70.00
Rose, 5"	50.00	Plate	
Bread Plate	40.00	Round	
Butter dish, covered, flat, double		8¼"d	25.00
handles, 6¾"h., 5 ¾"d	60.00	9¼"d	25.00
Cake stand, high standard, 9"d	60.00	10¼"d	30.00
Celery		Square, 7¼"	40.00
Tray	20.00	Relish tray, oval	
Vase, double handled	30.00	7½"	15.00
Champagne	35.00	8¼"	20.00
Cheese dish, flat	35.00	Salt	
Compote, high standard, open, round		Dip, individual	20.00
scalloped rim		Master, footed, open	30.00
5"d., jelly	25.00	Shaker, original top	20.00
7½"d	30.00	Sauce dish	
8"d	35.00	Flat, round, flared	
9"d	35.00	3½"d	10.00
Cordial	30.00	4½"d	12.00
Creamer, 4¾"h	40.00	Footed	
Cruet, original stopper	50.00	3½"d	10.00
Cup, sherbert, handled		4½"d	15.00
Flared bowl	10.00	Spoonholder, double handles, 4½"h	25.00
Handled	10.00	Sugar bowl, covered, handled	45.00
Dish		Sweetmeat, covered, footed	45.00
Oblong	25.00	Toothpick holder	45.00
Oval, curled over edges, 7¼" x 5¼"	30.00	Tumbler, water	25.00
Square, fern, metal contained for		Vase	
plants, 7"	35.00	5"h	25.00
Doughnut stand, high standard, 6"d	25.00	9¼"h	25.00

Items made	Clear	Items made	Clear
Wine		Straight sides	30.00
Flared sides	30.00		

PAVONIA

Goblet; celery vase; water tumbler; wine.

OMN: Pavonia. AKA: Pineapple Stem [Millard].

Non-flint. Ripley & Co., Pittsburgh, PA. ca. 1885-1886. Reissued by the United States Glass Co., Pittsburgh, PA. at Factory "F" (Ripley & Co., Pittsburgh, PA.) ca. 1891 to 1898. Illustrated in the United States Glass Co. 1895 and 1898 catalogs, the 1894-1896 Montgomery Ward catalogs (Nos. 55-58), the Butler Brothers 1885 general merchandise catalog, and an undated catalog of the National Merchandise Supply Co. of Chicago, IL.

Original color production: Clear, clear with ruby stain (plain or copper wheel engraved, popular engravings being No. 106 (Oak Leaf and Acorn), No. 77 (Leaf Band), No. 119 (Wadding Bird in Marsh), No. 158 (Silhouetted Oak Leaf and Acorn), and No. 118 (Bird with Oak Leaf and Acorn). Produced in both homestyle (pedestaled) and hotel style (flat-based) sets. Handles are both applied and pressed. Stems are large and bulbous resembling "pineapples".

Reproductions: None.

References: Bar-RS (Pl. 9), Bros-TS (P. 6), Hea-5 (P. 43, No. 144), Hea-7 (Figs. 113-123), Kam-3 (P. 15), Kam-4 (P. 142), Kam-6 (Pl. 5), Lee-VG (Pl. 54, No. 2), Mil-2 (Pl. 75), Mtz-1 (PP. 146-147), Mtz-2 (Pl. 73), Oliv-AAG (P. 71), Rev-APG (P. 292-294), Uni-1 (P. 285).

Items made	Clear Plain or Etched	Clear w/Ruby
Bowl, open, flat		
Finger, blown-ruffled rim, with matching ruffled edge underplate	45.00	85.00
Round bowl, plain rim		
5"d	15.00	35.00

Items made	Clear Plain or Etched	Clear w/Ruby
6"d	15.00	35.00
7"d	20.00	45.00
8"d	20.00	45.00
Waste	25.00	55.00
Butter dish, covered		
Hotel size, ruffled base	55.00	125.00
Table size, plain base	55.00	125.00
Cake plate	20.00	—
Cake stand, high standard		
8"d	40.00	90.00
9"d	50.00	100.00
10"d	55.00	—
Celery vase, flat, smooth rim	35.00	60.00
Compote, high standard, round		
Covered		
5"d	45.00	65.00
6"d	45.00	65.00
7"d	55.00	75.00
8"d	55.00	75.00
9"d	65.00	85.00
10"d	65.00	95.00
Open		
5"d., jelly	35.00	—
6"d	35.00	75.00
7"d	40.00	80.00
8"d	40.00	80.00
9"d	45.00	90.00
10"d	45.00	90.00
Creamer		
Hotel size	35.00	75.00
Table size	35.00	75.00
Cup, custard, applied handle	15.00	20.00
Dish, flat, open, oblong		
7"	15.00	35.00
8"	20.00	45.00
9"	20.00	45.00
Goblet	35.00	50.00
Mug, handled, 4¼"h	35.00	50.00
Pickle dish		
Oblong	15.00	35.00
Square	15.00	35.00
Pitcher		
Jug		
Milk, 1 quart	50.00	—
Water, ½ gallon	65.00	125.00
Tankard, applied handle		
Lemonade	65.00	125.00
Milk, 1 quart	50.00	125.00
Water, ½ gallon, 12"h	65.00	125.00
Plate, 6½"d	15.00	—
Salt		
Dip, individual, round	15.00	40.00
Master, round	20.00	50.00
Shaker, tall, original top	25.00	35.00
Sauce dish, round		
Flat		
3"d	10.00	15.00

Items made	Clear Plain or Etched	Clear w/Ruby
3½"d	10.00	15.00
4"d	10.00	15.00
4½"d	10.00	20.00
Footed		
3"d	15.00	20.00
3½"d	15.00	20.00
4"d	15.00	20.00
4½"d	15.00	22.00
Saucer	15.00	20.00
Sherbert Cup, handleless, with underplate	15.00	35.00
Spoonholder		
Hotel size.	30.00	45.00
Table size	30.00	45.00
Sugar bowl, covered		
Hotel size	45.00	75.00
Table size	45.00	75.00
Tray		
Bread	45.00	90.00
Water	55.00	85.00
Tumbler, water, flat, 3¾"h	25.00	35.00
Wine	25.00	35.00

PENNSYLVANIA

Syrup pitcher (clear); wine (emerald green).

OMN: U.S. Glass No. 15,048 & 15,048¹/₂, Pennsylvania. AKA: Balder [Millard], Hand, Kamoni [Millard].

Non-flint. The United States Glass Co. (pattern line No. 15,048 & 15,048 ¹/₂), Pittsburgh, PA. at Factory "O" (Central Glass Co., Wheeling, WV.) and "G" (Gillinder & Sons, Greensburg, PA.) ca. 1898 through 1912. Illustrated in the 1906, 1911, and 1912 Butler Brothers catalogs, the 1898 and 1904 United States Glass Co. catalogs, and in the Sears, Roebuck & Co. 1902 catalog No. 112 as "Victoria" with "genuine solid silver tops."

Original color production: Clear. Clear with ruby stain, emerald green or any other color is rare. Handles are either applied or pressed.

Reproductions: The Pennsylvania spoonholder has been reissued as a look-alike in clear glass throughout the mid 1980s. Reproductions are heavier, with a muddy appearance.

Spoonholder; covered sugar bowl; creamer.

References: Hrtng-P&P (P. 69), Hea-1 (P. 46), Hea-3 (PP. 80, 88), Hea-5 (PP. 49-50), Hea-6 (P. 36), Hea-7 (Figs. 249-250), Hea-TPS (PP. 50, 55), Hart/Cobb-SS (P. 59), Kam-2 (P. 103), McCn-PGP (P. 2257), Mil-1 (Pl. 14), Mtz-1 (P. 229), Mur-MCO (P. 59), Pet-Sal (P. 168), Pyne-PG (P. 147), Rev-APG (P. 316).

Items made	Clear	Items made	Clear
Biscuit jar, covered	65.00	Tray, oblong, flat, scalloped	15.00
Bottle, water	45.00	Vase	40.00
Bowl, open, flat		Champagne	35.00
Round		Cheese dish, covered (same as table	
Eight-pointed bowl		size butter)	75.00
6"d	15.00	Claret	35.00
7"d	15.00	Compote, open, high standard, round,	
8"d	20.00	ruffled rim, jelly	50.00
Scalloped rim, shallow bowl		Creamer	
5"d	15.00	Child's miniature	65.00
7"d	20.00	Individual	20.00
9"d	20.00	Table size	35.00
Straight sides		Cruet, original patterned stopper	45.00
6"d	15.00	Cup, custard, applied handle (also	
7"d	15.00	termed "lemonade")	10.00
8"d	20.00	Decanter, original patterned stopper	
Square		Handled	100.00
6"	15.00	Handleless	85.00
7"	15.00	Dish, flat, round, handled, 5"d.	
8"	20.00	(originally called the "jelly dish")	15.00
Butter dish, covered		Goblet	25.00
Child's miniature	55.00	Ice tub	45.00
Hotel size, deep, straight-sided base,		Jug, handled	
low domed cover	55.00	Claret, original patterned stopper	85.00
Table size, flat, flanged base, high		Water, squatty	55.00
domed cover	45.00	Olive dish, round, flat, scalloped rim	15.00
Celery		Pickle	

Items made	Clear	Items made	Clear
Jar, covered	20.00	Straight-sided bowl	8.00
Tray, oblong, flat, scalloped rim.	20.00	Shallow, scalloped rim	8.00
Pitcher		Square, scalloped rim	8.00
Bulbous		Shot glass	10.00
Creamer, 1 ½ pint	45.00	Spoonholder	
Water, ½ gallon	65.00	Child's miniature	40.00
Tankard, water, ½ gallon	60.00	Individual	25.00
Plate, round		Table size	25.00
7″d., round, scalloped rim (originally		Sugar bowl	
termed the "cheese plate")	35.00	Child's miniature, covered	55.00
8″d	35.00	Table size	
Punch bowl, flat	175.00	Covered, flat	45.00
Salt		Open, handled	30.00
Dip, individual	20.00	Syrup pitcher, original Brittania top	
Master	30.00	Bulbous, with inside glass lip	
Shaker, original top		(originally termed the "Molasses	
Bulbous		Can")	75.00
Large, short neck	15.00	Tapered (originally termed the	
Medium, short neck	15.00	"Syrup Jug")	65.00
Small, tall neck	15.00	Toothpick holder	35.00
Straight-sided	10.00	Tumbler, flat	
Sauce dish, flat, 4″d		Juice (called the "Champagne")	10.00
Round		Water (called the "Taper Water")	25.00
Deep		Whiskey	15.00
Eight-pointed bowl	8.00	Wine	20.00

PICKET

Footed sauce dish; water pitcher; spoonholder; sauce dish.

AKA: London, Picket Fence.

Non-flint. King Glass Co., Pittsburgh, PA., ca. 1890s. Shards have been found at the site of the Burlington Glass Works, Hamilton, Ontario, Canada. Illustrated in the ca. 1890-1891 King Glass Co. catalog.

Original color production: Clear. Amber, apple green, blue or any other color is rare. Pieces are square and footed. Rims are scalloped. Handles are pressed.

Reproductions: None.

References: Chip-ROS (P. 85), Enos-MPG (Chart-4), Hea-1 (P. 35), Hea-TPS (P. 25), Kam-1 (P. 88), Lee-EAPG (Pl. 107), McCn-PGP (P. 497), Mil-1 (Pl. 175), Mtz-1 (P. 132), Rev-APG (P. 217), Uni-1 (P. 146), Wlkr-PGA (Fig. 8, No. 3).

Items made	Clear	Items made	Clear
Bowl, 4-footed, square		Creamer, 5″h	40.00
Berry, 6½″	25.00	Goblet	35.00
Finger	30.00	Jam jar, covered	65.00
Waste	30.00	Match holder	35.00
Butter dish, covered	55.00	Pickle jar, covered	50.00
Cake stand, high standard	55.00	Pitcher, water, 4-footed, ½ gallon	90.00
Celery vase	45.00	Plate, bread, oval	
Compote		5″ x 13″ "Stuart's McCormick	
Covered		Reaper" center	90.00
High standard		5″ x 13″ "Stuart's Mulberry" center	90.00
6″ sq	65.00	Small	55.00
7″ sq	75.00	Salt	
8″ sq	85.00	Dip, individual, 4-legged	10.00
Low standard, 8″ sq	85.00	Master, oblong, flat	35.00
Open		Sauce dish	
High standard		Flat, handled	15.00
7″ sq	35.00	Footed, non-handled	15.00
8″ sq	35.00	Spoonholder	45.00
10″ sq	55.00	Sugar bowl, covered	45.00
Low standard		Toothpick holder (originally termed	
6″sq	30.00	the "Match Vase")	40.00
7″sq	35.00	Tray, water, rectangular	55.00
8″sq	40.00	Wine (R).	150.00

PINEAPPLE AND FAN, Heisey's

Syrup.

OMN: Heisey's No. 1255. AKA: Pineapple with Fan.

Non-flint. A.H. Heisey and Co. (pattern line No. 1,255), Newark, OH., ca. 1897. Illustrated in the ca. 1897 Heisey Glass Co. catalog as pattern No. 1,255.

Original color production: Clear, emerald green (plain or with gilt).

Reproductions: None.

References: Boyd-GC (P. 41), Brns-HG (P. 38), Hea-1 (P. 36), Hea-2 (P. 81), Hea-3 (P. 13), Hea-4 (P. 41), Hea-6 (P. 37), Kam-2 (P. 93), McCn-PGP (P. 205), Mil-OG (P. 35), Pet-GPP (Pl. 9), Pet-Sal (P. 168), Rev-APG (P. 177), Vog-H (P. 92).

Items made	Clear	Emerald Green
Banana stand, high standard	20.00	—
Biscuit jar, covered	55.00	85.00
Bowl, open, flat		
Oval, scalloped rim, 10"d	40.00	85.00
Rose	30.00	75.00
Round, 5½"d	12.00	35.00
Butter dish, covered	50.00	175.00
Cake stand, high standard	45.00	75.00
Celery		
Tray	25.00	45.00
Vase	30.00	65.00
Compote, open, high standard, round		
5"d	30.00	—
8"d	30.00	225.00
Cracker jar, covered (4 sizes).	85.00	—
Creamer		
Hotel size	25.00	50.00
Individual, 2⅞"h	20.00	50.00
Table size	35.00	95.00
Cruet, original stopper	60.00	300.00
Cup, custard	10.00	30.00
Goblet	15.00	25.00
Mug, handled, 7 ounce, 3½"h	30.00	45.00
Pickle tray	15.00	35.00
Pitcher, water	65.00	225.00
Salt		
Dip, individual	25.00	—
Shaker, original top	25.00	65.00
Spoonholder	35.00	65.00
Sugar bowl, covered		
Individual	25.00	50.00
Table size	45.00	125.00
Syrup, original top	60.00	250.00
Toothpick holder	85.00	225.00
Tumbler, 3¾"h., 8 ½ ounce	25.00	65.00
Vase, trumpet shape, 10"h	25.00	45.00

Covered bowl; goblet; 8"d. h.s. covered compote; 6" h.s. covered compote.

OMN: Derby.

Non-flint. Bryce Brothers, Pittsburgh, PA. ca. 1882-1883. Reissued by the United States Glass Co. after the 1891 merger. Shards have been found at the site of the Burlington Glass Works, Hamilton, Ontario, Canada. Illustrated in ca. 1891 United States Glass Co. catalog of member firms.

Original color production: Clear. Odd pieces produced in amethyst, amber, blue, green, and milk white are very rare. Two types of goblets were produced; the one with extended "bars" being of American origin, the other of Canadian. Handles are pressed.

Reproductions: As early as 1896, the Westmorland Specialty Co., Grapeville, PA. issued an ale glass in Pleat and Panel which is not original to the set. During the early 1960s (and earlier), both the goblet and $7\frac{1}{2}$" square plate were reissued from new molds in clear. Reissues have faulty stippling which is faint, lacking the care and detail of the originals.

References: Enos-MPG (Charts 1, 3, 7), Hea-5 (PP. 81, 86), Kam-2 (PP. 24-25), Lee-EAPG (Plts. 105, 111), McCn-PGP (P. 373), Mil-1 (Pl. 66), Mtz-1 (P. 182), Oliv-AAG (P. 71), Pet-Sal (P. 35), Rev-APG (PP. 87-89), Stev-ECG (PP. 140-141), Stu-BP (P. 64), Thu-1 (P. 202), Uni-1 (P. 1476), Uni/Wor-CHPGT (P. 185), Wlkr-PGA (Fig. 8, No. 39).

Items made	Clear	Items made	Clear
Bowl		Celery vase, pedestaled, smooth rim,	
Vegetable, covered, low footed,		8"h	30.00
oblong, $5\frac{1}{4}$"h., 8"l., 5"w	55.00	Compote	
Waste, 3"h., $4\frac{3}{4}$"sq	55.00	Covered	
Butter dish, covered		High standard	
Low standard, tab handles, 6"sq	75.00	6" sq	65.00
Flat, no handles	60.00	7" sq	75.00
Butter pat (VR), $3\frac{1}{2}$"sq	45.00	8" sq	85.00
Cake stand, high standard		9" sq	95.00
8" sq	30.00	Low standard	
9" sq	35.00	6" sq	45.00
10" sq	45.00	7" sq	45.00
		8" sq	55.00

Items made	Clear	Items made	Clear
9″ sq	55.00	Milk, 1 quart, 7″h	85.00
Open		Water, ¹/₂ gallon, 9″h (height may	
High standard		vary)	55.00
6″ sq	20.00	Plate, square	
7″ sq	25.00	6″	15.00
8″ sq	30.00	7″	20.00
9″ sq	30.00	7¹/₂″	20.00
Low standard		8″	25.00
6″ sq	20.00	8¹/₂″	30.00
7″ sq	25.00	Platter, bread	
8″ sq	30.00	Closed handles	
9″ sq	30.00	12¹/₂″l, 8¹/₂″w	40.00
Creamer, 6¹/₂″h	35.00	13″l	40.00
Dish, serving, oblong		Open handles, 13″l	45.00
Covered		Salt	
Flat, 9″l	45.00	Master, oblong, clear panels	30.00
Footed		Shaker, original top, 3¹/₄″h	35.00
7″l	65.00	Sauce dish, square	
8″l	65.00	Flat, tab handle	
Open, flat		3¹/₂″sq	15.00
8″l	25.00	4″sq	15.00
9″l	25.00	5″sq	20.00
Goblet, 6″h (2 styles)	30.00	Footed	
Jam jar, covered, 6 ¹/₅″h	85.00	3¹/₂″sq	15.00
Lamp, oil, all glass, original burner		4″sq	20.00
Clear font, 9¹/₄″h. to top of collar ...	125.00	5″sq	20.00
Faceted font, 8″h. to top of collar	125.00	Spoonholder, footed, smooth rim,	
Frosted on alternate font facets		5¹/₂″h	25.00
7″h. to top of collar	100.00	Sugar bowl, covered, 8″h	65.00
8¹/₂″h. to top of collar	100.00	Syrup pitcher (VR), patented lid, 5¹/₂″h	350.00+
Pickle dish, 7″l	15.00	Tray, water, handled, oblong, 14¹/₂″l	45.00
Pitcher		Wine (R), 4¹/₄″h	150.00

PLUME

Square sauce dish; goblet; covered butter; covered sugar bowl; creamer.

OMN: Adams No. 30.

Non-flint. Adams & Co. (pattern line No. 30), Pittsburgh, PA. 1890. Reissued by the United States Glass Co., Pittsburgh, PA. at factory "A" (Adams & Co., Pittsburgh, PA.) ca. 1891-1898. Illustrated in the Adams & Co. 1874 catalog, and the United States Glass Co. catalogs ca. 1891 and 1898.

Original color production: Clear, clear with ruby stain (plain or copper wheel engraved). The tea set was added to the line in 1888. Handles are applied.

Reproductions: The L.G. Wright Glass Co., New Martinsville, WV. (distributed by Jennings Red Barn, New Martinsville, WV. and Carl Forslund, Grand Rapids, MI.) 1970 catalog supplement lists the goblet in clear reproduced from new molds since the early 1960s.

References: Bar-RS (Pl. 4), Hart-AG (P. 87), Hea-5 (P. 62, Plts. A-D), Hea-7 (Figs. 158-167), Inn-EPG ((P. 34), Inn-PG (P. 381), Kam-2 (P. 64), Lee-VG (Pl. 26, No. 3), McCn-PGP (P. 523), Mil-1 (Pl. 30), Mtz-1 (PP. 150-151), Oliv-AAG (P. 71), Pyne-PG (P. 381), Rev-APG (PP. 18, 21), Uni-2 (P. 91), Wlkr-PGA (Fig. 8, No. 5).

Items made	Clear	Clear w/Ruby
Bottle, bitters (vertical plume design)	85.00	125.00
Bowl		
Collared base		
Covered		
Round		
6"d	50.00	65.00
7"d	55.00	75.00
8"d	60.00	85.00
Open		
Round		
Belled bowl, plain rim		
6"d	25.00	50.00
7"d	25.00	60.00
8"d	30.00	65.00
Flared bowl		
Plain rim		
7"d	25.00	50.00
8"d	25.00	60.00
9"d	30.00	65.00
Scalloped rim		
7"d	25.00	50.00
8"d	25.00	60.00
9"d	30.00	65.00
Fruit, smooth rim		
8"d	40.00	75.00
9"d	45.00	80.00
10"d	50.00	85.00
Square, flat, open, master berry, 8"	45.00	75.00
Waste	35.00	—
Flat, open, 9"	20.00	—
Butter dish, covered, collared base, 6¾"d., 5¾"h	50.00	175.00
Cake stand, high standard		
9"d	45.00	125.00
10"d	50.00	125.00
Castor, pickle, complete in silver plate holder	150.00	250.00
Celery vase		
Horizontal plume design, 7"h	35.00	—
Vertical plume design	35.00	—

Items made	Clear	Clear w/Ruby
Compote, round		
Covered, high standard		
6″d	45.00	125.00
7″d	55.00	145.00
8″d	65.00	145.00
Open, high standard		
Belled bowl		
Scalloped rim		
7″d	45.00	70.00
8″d	50.00	85.00
9″d	55.00	100.00
Smooth rim		
6″d	40.00	60.00
7″d	45.00	70.00
8″d	50.00	80.00
Straight bowl		
Flared smooth rim		
8″d	50.00	80.00
9″d	50.00	90.00
10″d	55.00	100.00
Scalloped rim		
6″d	40.00	60.00
7″d	45.00	70.00
8″d	50.00	80.00
Creamer, applied handle, 5½″h	35.00	65.00
Goblet, 6″h	35.00	45.00
Ice tub	30.00	—
Lamp, oil, hand, original burner and chimney	85.00	—
Pickle dish, oblong	20.00	35.00
Pitcher, water		
Bulbous (termed Cider Pitcher), vertical plumes, applied handle, 8″h	65.00	200.00
Tankard, vertical plume design, ½ gallon	60.00	200.00
Sauce dish, square		
Flat, 4″	10.00	20.00
Footed, 4″	15.00	20.00
Spoonholder, serrated rim, 4⅞″h	30.00	65.00
Sugar bowl, covered	45.00	85.00
Tray, water, round	40.00	—
Tumbler, water (blown), vertical plume design	30.00	45.00

Waste bowl; goblet

AKA: Alaska, Arctic, Frosted Polar Bear, Ice Berg, North Pole, Polar Bear and Seal.

Non-flint. Attributed to the Crystal Glass Co., Bridgeport, OH. ca. 1883 based on the "C.G.C." marking on some items.

Original color production: Clear, clear with machine ground finish.

Reproductions. The Summit Art Glass Co., Mogadore/Rootstown, OH., reproduced from a new mold the goblet in clear with acid finish as illustrated in the company's 1977 sales brochure. Marked with the Summit trademark, the new goblet lacks the refined detail of the old. Any item in Polar Bear is scarce.

References: Chip-ROS (P. 96), Kam-5 (PP. 22-23), Lee-EAPG (P. 301), Lind-HG (PP. 491, 493), Mil-1 (Plts. 72-73), Mtz-1 (Plts. 96-97), Oliv-AAG (P. 77), Stu-BP (P. 117), Uni-2 (P. 94).

Items made	Clear	Clear/ Frosted
Bowl, open, round, flat		
Ice	85.00	100.00
Waste	85.00	100.00
Creamer	125.00	155.00
Goblet		
Flared rim	75.00	110.00
Straight rim	75.00	110.00
Pickle dish	50.00	65.00
Pitcher, water, ½ gallon	250.00	350.00
Plate, bread	95.00	125.00
Sauce dish, flat, round	30.00	35.00
Sugar bowl, covered	175.00	200.00
Tray, water		
Oval		
Clear iceberg	175.00	200.00
Frosted iceberg	175.00	200.00
Round	175.00	200.00

POPCORN

Goblet (clear ear); spoonholder (raised ear).   Wine; bulbous water pitcher.

Non-flint. Attributed to the Boston & Sandwich Glass Co., Sandwich, MA. ca. late 1860s.

Original color production: Clear. Produced in two versions: "raised ear of corn" and "flat ear of corn". Items have handles that are a) applied, or b) pressed in the shape of an ear of corn.

Reproductions: None.

References: Brn-SD (P. 55), Kam-8 (PP. 19-20), Lee-EAPG (Pl. 25), McCn-PGP (P. 333), Mil-1 (Pl. 73), Mtz-1 (PP. 188-189), Uni-1 (P. 97).

Items made	Clear	Items made	Clear
Butter dish, covered	65.00	With lined ear	35.00
Cake stand, high standard		Pitcher, water, bulbous, applied	
8"d	50.00	handle, ½ gallon	100.00
11"d	65.00	Sauce dish, round, flat	10.00
Cordial	75.00	Spoonholder	35.00
Creamer, 4⅞"h	30.00	Sugar bowl, covered	45.00
Goblet		Wine, with ear	65.00
With ear	50.00		

Breakfast open sugar bowl; handled basket; vase; tumbler; breakfast creamer.

OMN: U.S. Glass No. 15,121. AKA: U.S. Portland.

Non-flint. The Portland Glass Co., Portland, ME. ca. late 1870s. The United States Glass Co. (pattern line No. 15,121), Pittsburgh, PA. ca. 1910. Illustrated in United States Glass Co. undated (No. 111) and 1915 export catalogs.

Original color production: Clear. Clear with ruby stain or any other color is rare. Handles are applied and pressed.

Reproductions: The candlestick has been reissued in blue, canary-yellow and clear.

References: Hea-3 (P. 79), Hea-5 (P. 155, Pl. D), Hea-TPS (PP. 76, 86), Kam-1 (P. 107), McCn-PGP (P. 443), Migh-TPS (Pl. 23), Mil-1 (Pl. 96), Mtz-1 (PP. 196-197), Mtz-2 (P. 124), Spil-AEPG (P. 316), Swn-PG (PP. 52-53), Uni-1 (P. 36).

Items made	Clear	Items made	Clear
Basket, applied handle, made from		Cake stand, high standard, 10½"d	45.00
spoonholder	85.00	Carafe	45.00
Biscuit jar, covered	55.00	Celery, flat	
Bottle, water	40.00	Tray	15.00
Boudoir set (complete)	85.00	Vase	25.00
Bowl, round, plain rim		Compote, round	
Finger, open	25.00	Covered, high standard	
Berry, open		6"d	65.00
6"d	20.00	7"d	70.00
7"d	20.00	8"d	75.00
8"d	25.00	Open	
Covered, footed, notched lid	35.00	High standard	
Butter dish, covered	55.00	Flared bowl	
Candlestick		7"d	30.00
Cupped, 7"h	85.00	8"d	35.00
Flared, 7"h	85.00	9½"d	40.00
Regular		Straight sided bowl	
9"h	55.00	6"d	30.00
10½"h	65.00	7"d	35.00
Saucer foot	85.00	8"d	40.00

Items made	Clear	Items made	Clear
Low standard		Punch bowl, footed, 15"d	150.00
6"d	30.00	Relish tray, handled	15.00
7"d	35.00	Ring stand (R)	85.00
8"d	40.00	Salt shaker, original top	15.00
Cracker jar, covered	75.00	Sardine box, 4½"	30.00
Creamer		Sauce dish, flat	
Breakfast, oval	20.00	Oval	8.00
Table size	30.00	Round	8.00
Tankard, 6 ounce	30.00	Flared, 4"d	8.00
Cruet, original patterned or faceted cut		Straight-sided, 4"d	8.00
stopper	55.00	Square, 4"	8.00
Cup, custard, handled	15.00	Spoonholder	
Decanter, quart, handled	50.00	Large	35.00
Dish, oval, flat		Small	30.00
6"l	15.00	Sugar bowl	
7½"	15.00	Breakfast, oval, open	35.00
9"l	20.00	Table size, covered	45.00
10½"l	25.00	Sugar shaker, original Brittania or	
12½"l	25.00	nickel plate top	40.00
Goblet	35.00	Syrup pitcher, original top	
Jam jar, original silver plate cover	35.00	6 ounce	50.00
Jug, water	35.00	16 ounce	65.00
Lamp, oil, all glass, 9"h, original		Toothpick holder	20.00
burner	85.00	Tray, boudoir undertray, oval, 11"l ...	25.00
Olive dish, oval, 5½"	20.00	Tumbler, water, flat	25.00
Pickle dish, boat shape	15.00	Vase	
Pin tray	15.00	Deep	
Pitcher, water, ½ gallon		6"h	30.00
Bulbous	55.00	9"h	30.00
Tankard	55.00	Regular, 6"h	30.00
Pomade jar, original silver plate top	25.00	Wine	25.00
Puff box, original matching glass lid	30.00		

POWDER AND SHOT

Creamer; spoonholder; covered sugar bowl; goblet; covered butter dish.

AKA: Horn of Plenty [Chipman], Powderhorn and Shot.

Flint, non-flint. U.S. maker unknown. Shards have been found at the site of the Boston & Sandwich Glass Co., Sandwich, MA. and the Portland Glass Co., Portland, ME.

Original color production: Clear. Handles are applied. Finials are clear, stylized "plumes".

References: Brn-SD (P. 53), Chip-ROS (P. 85), Kam-4 (PP. 23-24), Lee-EAPG (Pl. 79, No. 3), Lee-SG (P. 8), McCn-PGP (P. 343), Mil-1 (Pl. 98), Mtz-1 (PP. 114-115), Inn-PP (PP. 51-52), Swn-PG (PP. 50-51), Uni-1 (P. 145), Wlkr-PGA (Fig 8, No. 7).

Items made	Clear
Butter dish, covered	85.00
Castor bottle, original top	45.00
Celery vase	175.00
Compote, high standard, round	
Covered	90.00
Open	65.00
Creamer, footed, applied handle	65.00
Egg cup, single, pedestaled	50.00

Items made	Clear
Goblet	60.00
Pitcher, water, 1/2 gallon, applied	
handle	150.00
Salt, master, open, footed	45.00
Sauce dish, flat, round	20.00
Spoonholder	45.00
Sugar bowl, covered	75.00

PRESSED DIAMOND

Custard cup; cruet (n.o.s.); l.s. cake stand; water tumbler; salt shaker. All amber.

OMN: Central No. 775. AKA: Block and Diamond, Zephyr.

Non-flint. The Central Glass Co. (pattern line No. 775), Wheeling, WV. ca. 1885. Reissued by the United States Glass Co., Pittsburgh, PA. at Factory "O" (Central Glass Co., Wheeling, WV.) ca. 1891.

Original color production: Amber, blue, canary, clear.

Reproductions: None.

References: Eige-CGM VW (P. 9), Grow-WCG (P. 125, Fig. 15-"5"), Hea-3 (P. 36, Fig. 233), Hea-5 (P. 22), Hea-6 (P. 37, Figs. 271-272), Hea-OS (P. 42, No. 427), Kam-8 (P. 33), Lee-VG (Pl. 70, No. 1), McCn-PGP (P. 221), Mil-2 (Pl. 13), Mtz-1 (PP. 162-163), Mur-CO (PP. 15, 65), Pet-Sal (Pl. 27), Rev-APG (P. 114).

Items made	Amber	Blue	Canary	Clear
Bowl, open, round, flat				
Berry.				
5″d	20.00	25.00	20.00	15.00
6″d	25.00	30.00	25.00	20.00
7″d	25.00	30.00	25.00	20.00
8″d	30.00	35.00	30.00	25.00
Finger	25.00	30.00	25.00	20.00
Butter dish, covered, flat	45.00	65.00	45.00	35.00
Butter pat, round	15.00	20.00	15.00	10.00
Cake stand, low standard	35.00	45.00	35.00	25.00
Celery vase	35.00	40.00	35.00	25.00
Compote, round, high standard				
Covered, 11″d	75.00	100.00	75.00	45.00
Open, 11″d	35.00	45.00	35.00	25.00
Creamer, 4³/₄″h	35.00	45.00	35.00	20.00
Cruet, pressed handle, original stopper	100.00	125.00	100.00	50.00
Cup, custard, applied handle	15.00	20.00	15.00	10.00
Goblet	45.00	70.00	45.00	35.00
Pitcher, water, flat, ½ gallon, pressed handle	70.00	90.00	70.00	55.00
Plate, round, 11″d	45.00	55.00	45.00	35.00
Salt				
Dip, individual	20.00	20.00	20.00	15.00
Shaker, tall, original top	20.00	30.00	20.00	15.00
Sauce dish, flat, round	10.00	15.00	10.00	10.00
Spoonholder, flat	30.00	40.00	30.00	25.00
Sugar bowl, covered	45.00	65.00	45.00	30.00
Tumbler, flat, water	25.00	30.00	25.00	15.00
Wine	50.00	80.00	50.00	35.00

PRESSED LEAF

Egg cup; 8″ low standard covered compote; flat oval bowl.

OMN: N.P.L. AKA: New Pressed Leaf.

Flint, non-flint. McKee Brothers, Pittsburgh, PA. ca. 1868. The Central Glass Co., Wheeling, WV. ca. 1881. Shards have been found at the site of the Boston & Sandwich Glass Co., Sandwich, MA. Illustrated in the 1868 McKee Glass Co. catalog.

Original color production: Clear. Designed and patented by H.S. McKee (design patent No. 2,825) November 5, 1867. Unlike conventional geometrical patterns of the time, the main pattern element of Pressed Leaf consists solely of long, vertical, well formed leaves. Finials are well defined acorns; handles are applied. Originally produced with either knobby hexagonal standards or low conical feet with the pattern extending from the base.

Reproductions: None.

References: Drep-ABC OG (P. 161), Enos-MPG (Chart-3), Inn/Spil-McKe (PP. 128-129), Kam-3 (PP. 20-21), Lee-EAPG (PP. 67-68), McCn-PGP (P. 415), Mil-1 (Pl. 44), Mtz-1 (P. 72), Oliv-AAG (P. 56), Rev-APG (P. 232), Stot-McKe (P. 37), Uni-1 (PP. 216-217), Wlkr-PGA (Fig. 8, Nos. 46, 49).

Items made	Clear	Items made	Clear
Bowl, oval, open, flat	20.00	6"d	35.00
Butter dish, covered	50.00	7"d	40.00
Cake stand, high standard	60.00	8"d	45.00
Champagne	45.00	Cordial	50.00
Compote		Creamer, applied handle, 5¾"h	45.00
Covered		Dish, open, oval, flat	
High standard		5"	20.00
6"d	55.00	6"	20.00
7"d	65.00	7"	25.00
8"d	75.00	8"	25.00
Low standard		9"	30.00
6"d	45.00	Egg cup, single, footed	25.00
7"d.	55.00	Goblet	30.00
8"d	60.00	Lamp, oil, handled	125.00
Open		Pitcher, water, ½ gallon	100.00
High standard		Salt, master, open, footed	35.00
6"d	35.00	Sauce dish, flat, round, 4"d	10.00
7"d	40.00	Spoonholder, footed, scalloped rim ...	25.00
8"d	45.00	Sugar bowl, covered	45.00
Low standard		Wine	40.00

Plate 7″; plate 8″; plate 6″.

OMN: Canton No. 10. AKA: Stippled Primrose.

Non-flint. The Canton Glass Co. (pattern line No. 10), Canton, OH., ca. 1885.

Original color production: Amber, blue, canary-yellow, clear, apple green (scarce). Milk white, purple slag, opaque black or any other color is rare.

Reproductions: None.

References: Bat-GPG (PP. 173, 183), Belnp-MG (Pl. 101), Drep-FR (P. 199), Enos-MPG (Chart-5), Grow-WCG (P. 134, Fig. 18-"3"), Kam-3 (P. 119), Lee-EAPG (Pl. 136, No. 30), Mil-1 (Pl. 138), Mtz-1 (PP. 54-55), Rev-APG (P. 107), Stu-BP (P. 31), Uni-2 (P. 71), Wlkr-PGA (Fig. 8, No. 41).

Items made	Amber	Canary	Blue	Green	Clear
Bowl, open, flat, round					
Berry, master	30.00	30.00	35.00	35.00	25.00
Waste	30.00	30.00	25.00	25.00	20.00
Butter dish, covered, flat	50.00	50.00	60.00	60.00	35.00
Cake stand, high standard, 10″d	50.00	50.00	65.00	65.00	45.00
Compote, covered, round					
High standard					
6″d	65.00	65.00	75.00	75.00	45.00
7½″d	70.00	70.00	80.00	80.00	50.00
8″d	75.00	75.00	85.00	85.00	55.00
9″d	85.00	85.00	95.00	95.00	65.00
Low standard					
6″d	65.00	65.00	75.00	75.00	45.00
7½″d	70.00	70.00	80.00	80.00	50.00
8″d	75.00	75.00	85.00	85.00	55.00
Cordial	40.00	40.00	45.00	45.00	30.00
Creamer	35.00	35.00	45.00	45.00	30.00
Egg cup	30.00	30.00	35.00	35.00	20.00
Goblet					
Knob stem	40.00	40.00	45.00	45.00	30.00
Plain stem	35.00	35.00	40.00	40.00	25.00

Items made	Amber	Canary	Blue	Green	Clear
Lamp, finger	—	—	—	—	200.00
Pickle dish	18.00	18.00	20.00	20.00	15.00
Pitcher					
Milk, 1 quart	45.00	45.00	55.00	55.00	35.00
Water, ½ gallon	55.00	55.00	50.00	50.00	40.00
Plate					
4½"d., toddy	15.00	15.00	20.00	20.00	10.00
6"d	30.00	30.00	35.00	35.00	20.00
7"d	30.00	30.00	35.00	35.00	20.00
8"d	30.00	30.00	35.00	35.00	20.00
9"d., handled, cake	30.00	30.00	35.00	35.00	20.00
Platter, oval, 12" x 8"	35.00	35.00	40.00	40.00	35.00
Relish tray	15.00	15.00	20.00	20.00	15.00
Sauce dish, round					
Flat					
4"d	15.00	15.00	20.00	20.00	15.00
5½"d	15.00	15.00	20.00	20.00	15.00
Footed					
4"d	20.00	20.00	25.00	25.00	15.00
5½"d	20.00	20.00	25.00	25.00	15.00
Spoonholder	25.00	25.00	30.00	30.00	20.00
Sugar bowl, covered	40.00	40.00	55.00	55.00	35.00
Tray, water	50.00	50.00	60.00	60.00	35.00
Wine	40.00	40.00	45.00	45.00	30.00

PRINCESS FEATHER

Goblet; collared covered bowl; 6"d. plate; spoonholder.

OMN: Rochelle. AKA: Lacy Medallion [Kamm], Princes' Feather.

Flint, non-flint. Bakewell, Pears & Co., Pittsburgh, PA. ca. late 1870s. The United States Glass Co., Pittsburgh, PA., ca. after 1891. Shards have been found at the site of the Boston & Sandwich Glass Co., Sandwich, MA., the Burlington Glass Works, Hamilton, Ontario, Canada, the Diamond Glass Co., Ltd. (Diamond Flint Glass Co., Ltd.), Dominion Glass Co., Ltd., de Lorimier Avenue, Montreal, Quebec, Canada. Illustrated in the 1864 and 1875 Bakewell, Pears & Co. catalogs.

Original color production: Clear. Opaque white, opaque blue or any other color is very rare. Handles are applied.

Reproductions: None.

References: Belnp-MG (P. 231), Brn-SD (P. 51), Chip-ROS (P. 42), Enos-MPG (Chart-3), Fer-YMG (P. 63), Herr-GG (P. 149), Inn-EGP (P. 53), Inn-PG (PP. 413, 415), Kam-3 (PP. 31-32), Kam/Wod-Vol.2 (P. 471), Lee-EAPG (Pl. 112, No. 1), McCn-PGP (Pl. 50), Mil-1 (Pl. 25), Mil-OG (Pl. 151), Mtz-1 (PP. 126-127), Pear-CAT (PP. 18-19, 26-28), Rev-APG (PP. 50-51), Uni-1 (PP. 266-267), Uni-TCG (P. 169), Uni/Wor-CHPGT (P. 187).

Items made	Clear	Items made	Clear
Bowl		Dish, oval, flat	
Round		Covered	35.00
Covered, collared base	65.00	Open	
Open		7″	20.00
Collared base	30.00	8″	25.00
Flat, 6″d	25.00	9″	30.00
Oval, flat, plain rim		Egg cup, single, pedestaled	40.00
6″	20.00	Goblet	35.00
7″	20.00	Honey dish, flat, round, 3″d	10.00
8″	25.00	Pitcher	
9″	30.00	Milk, 1 quart	85.00
Butter dish, covered	50.00	Water, ½ gallon	65.00
Cake plate, closed handles, 9″d	35.00	Plate, round	
Cheese dish	45.00	6″d	35.00
Celery vase, scalloped rim	40.00	7″d	35.00
Compote, covered, round		8″d	40.00
High standard		9″d	45.00
6″d	50.00	Relish tray	20.00
7″d	50.00	Salt, master, open, footed	20.00
8″d	60.00	Sauce dish, round	
Low collared base		Flat, 4″d	10.00
6″d	30.00	Footed, 4″d	15.00
7″d	30.00	Spoonholder, scalloped rim	30.00
8″d	35.00	Sugar bowl, covered, 7½″h	55.00
Creamer, applied handle, 6″h	55.00	Wine	45.00

Toothpick holder; high standard open compote; bowl.

OMN: Alexis. AKA: Late Moon and Star [Metz], Stelle, Sun and Star.

Non-flint. Dalzell, Gillmore, & Leighton, Findlay, OH. ca. late 1880s, with continued production by the National Glass Co., Pittsburgh, PA. ca. 1899. Illustrated in the Butler Brothers 1896 catalog as "Crown Jewel", the Montgomery Ward catalogs (Nos. 57 and 58) for 1896, and reviewed in the January, 1895 issue of *China, Glass and Lamps*.

Original color production: Clear. Clear with ruby stain or any other color is very rare.

Reproductions: As early as 1950, the individual creamer, goblet, individual sugar bowl, and wine were reissued in clear glass from new molds. The Fenton Art Glass Co., Williamstown, WV. in the 1950 catalog and 1951 sales brochure illustrates the following items in amber, amethyst, blue, clear, green, opalescent colors, and ruby red: 12"h. handled basket, 6" handled bon bon dish, 10½"d. flared bowl, cocktail, high standard covered compotes (various sizes), goblet, 6", 8", 12½"d. plates, 11"d. rolled-edge plate, rose bowl, flat round sauce dish, sherbert, wine, covered sugar bowl, and toothpick holder.

The L.G. Wright Glass Co., New Martinsville, WV. (distributed by Jennings Red Barn, New Martinsville, WV. and Carl Forslund, Grand Rapids, MI.) reproduced in amber, blue, green, clear and ruby the high standard 4½"d. covered compote.

References: Hea-1 (PP. 73, 82), Kam-4 (P. 92, Pl. 8), Lee-VG (Pl. 72, No. 4), Mil-1 (Pl. 141), McCn-PGP (Pl. 231), Mtz-1 (PP. 210-211), Pet-Sal (P. 35), Smth-FG (P. 97), Uni-2 (P. 167).

Items made	Clear	Items made	Clear
Banana stand, high standard	80.00	Rose	30.00
Biscuit jar, covered	145.00	Square	
Bowl		8"	20.00
Covered, round, flat, 7"d	50.00	9¼"	25.00
Open, flat		Butter dish, covered, flat	65.00
Round		Cake stand, high standard	
7"d	15.00	9½"d.	60.00
7½"d	15.00	10"d	65.00
8"d	20.00	Celery vase	45.00
10¼"d	35.00	Compote, high standard	

Items made	Clear	Items made	Clear
Covered		Mug	20.00
5"d., jelly	40.00	Pickle dish	15.00
7"d	60.00	Pitcher, water, applied handle, $\frac{1}{2}$	
8"d	60.00	gallon	
9"d	75.00	Bulbous	90.00
Open		Tankard	85.00
Scalloped rim		Plate, round	25.00
5"d	25.00	Relish dish	15.00
7"d	45.00	Sauce dish, flat	
8"d	50.00	Round	
8½"d	50.00	4"d	8.00
10"d	60.00	4½"d	8.00
Smooth rim, 5"d., jelly	25.00	Square	
Flared rim, 10"sq	65.00	4"d	8.00
Condiment tray	30.00	4½"d	8.00
Cracker jar, covered	75.00	Saucer	8.00
Creamer		Spoonholder, flat	30.00
Individual, 3"h	10.00	Salt shaker, original top	35.00
Table size	25.00	Sugar bowl, covered, flat	60.00
Cruet, original stopper	65.00	Syrup pitcher, original top	75.00
Cup	10.00	Toothpick holder	40.00
Doughnut stand, high standard	60.00	Tumbler, water, flat	25.00
Goblet	40.00	Wine	35.00

PRISCILLA, Fostoria's

Water tumbler and water pitcher (both emerald green w/gilt).

OMN: Fostoria's No. 676. AKA: Acanthus Leaf.

Non-flint. The Fostoria Glass Co., Fostoria, OH. ca. 1898.

Original color production: Clear, emerald green (with or without gilt). Limited production in custard and milk white. Illustrated in the 1900 Fostoria Glass Co. catalog.

Reproductions: None.

References: Hea-1 (P. 52), Hea-2 (PP. 36, 53), Hea-3 (PP. 36, 53), Hea-6 (P. 37, Fig. 275), Kam-5 (P. 84), Kam-7 (Pl. 100), Kam-8 (Pl. 102), McCn-PGP (P. 381), Mig-TPS (Pl. 21), Pet-Sal (P. 169), Rev-APG (P. 158), Weath-FOST (P. 19).

Items made	Clear	Emerald Green
Bottle, water	45.00	95.00
Bowl, open, flat, master berry, 8½″d, round	15.00	55.00
Butter dish, covered	65.00	95.00
Cake stand, high standard	30.00	75.00
Celery vase	35.00	85.00
Compote, high standard, round		
Covered	55.00	135.00
Open	40.00	65.00
Creamer, applied handle	35.00	75.00
Cruet, original stopper	75.00	250.00
Cup, sherbert	10.00	25.00
Egg cup, single	20.00	60.00
Goblet	25.00	85.00
Lamp, oil, original burner and chimney	100.00	175.00
Marmalade jar, covered	45.00	125.00
Pickle dish	15.00	35.00
Pitcher, water, tankard, ½ gallon, applied handle	65.00	135.00
Salt		
Cellar (2 styles)	15.00	65.00
Shaker, original top		
Large, bulbous neck	25.00	40.00
Small, bulbous base, narrow neck	25.00	40.00
Sauce dish, flat, round, 4½″d	10.00	20.00
Spoonholder	35.00	65.00
Sugar bowl, covered	45.00	95.00
Syrup pitcher, original nickel top	65.00	250.00
Toothpick holder, 4½″h	35.00	225.00
Tumbler, water, flat	25.00	40.00
Vase	25.00	45.00

PRISM WITH DIAMOND POINTS

Egg cup; champagne; goblet; tumbler.

AKA: Prism and Diamond Point(s).

Flint, non-flint. Bryce Brothers, Pittsburgh, PA. ca. 1880s. Reissued by the United States Glass Co., Pittsburgh, PA. after the 1891 merger. Shards have been found at the site of the Boston & Sandwich Glass Co., Sandwich, MA.

Original color production: Clear. Milk white or any other color is rare.

Reproductions: None.

References: Brn-SD (P. 55), Fer-YMG (P. 62), Hea-5 (P. 86), Kam-3 (P. 28), Lee-EAPG (Pl. 96), Lee-SG (P. 537), Mil-1 (Pl. 73), Mtz-1 (PP. 50-51), Thu-1 (P. 164), Uni-1 (PP. 135-136).

Items made	Clear	Items made	Clear
Bowl, open, flat	30.00	Single	35.00
Butter dish, covered	65.00	Goblet, knob stem	45.00
Celery vase	35.00	Pickle dish, flat, oval	25.00
Compote, high standard, round		Pitcher, water, ½ gallon	100.00
Covered, 6″d (originally termed the	90.00	Plate, large (later period)	25.00
sweet meat)		Salt, master, open, footed	30.00
Open, 6″d	65.00	Spoonholder	45.00
Creamer, 6½″h	75.00	Sugar bowl, covered	55.00
Egg cup		Tumbler, water, flat	45.00
Double	55.00	Wine	55.00

Covered marmalade; goblet.

Covered sugar bowl.

AKA: Cupid and Psyche.

Non-flint. Maker unknown, ca. 1870s.

Original color production: Clear. Handles are pressed.

Reproductions: None. Round plate (milk white) 7″d.

References: Drep-ABC OG (P. 153), Kam-4 (P. 3), Lee-EAPG (Pl. 75, No. 1), McCn-PGP (P. 395), Mil-1 (Pl. 121), Mtz-1 (PP. 108-109), Uni-1 (P. 259).

Items made	Clear	Items made	Clear
Butter dish, covered	75.00	Marmalade jar, covered	85.00
Celery vase	45.00	Pitcher	
Compote, covered, round		Milk, 1 quart	60.00
High standard	75.00	Water, ½ gallon	75.00
Low standard	55.00	Sauce dish, round, footed (3 sizes)	20.00
Creamer, 7″h	50.00	Sugar bowl, covered	55.00
Goblet	45.00	Wine	50.00

Plate; water bottle; ice tub (tab handles); goblet.

OMN: Duncan's No. 24. AKA: Panelled Diamond Block, Quartered Diamond.

Non-flint. George Duncan's Sons & Co., Washington, PA. ca. 1894.

Original color production: Clear, clear with ruby stain.

Reproductions: None

References: Bat-GPG (PP. 100, 103), Hea-5 (PP. 21, 46), Hea-TPS (P. 21), Kam-1 (P. 105), Kam-2 (P. 96), Kam-3 (P. 96), Kam-6 (P. 56), McCn-PGP (P. 193), Mil-2 (Pl. 146), Mtz-2 (P. 172), Pet-Sal (P. 36), Pet-GPP (P. 57), Rev-APG (PP. 149-150), Uni-2 (P. 52), Wlkr-PGA (Fig. 8, No. 54).

Items made	Clear	Clear w/Ruby
Bowl, open, flat, round		
Master berry	25.00	60.00
Orange	30.00	65.00
Bottle, water	35.00	—
Butter dish, covered	45.00	125.00
Compote, high standard, round		
Covered	50.00	—
Open	35.00	—
Creamer	30.00	65.00
Cup, custard	10.00	15.00
Goblet	35.00	—
Lamp, oil, original burner and chimney	75.00	—
Pitcher, water, ½ gallon, applied handle	45.00	150.00
Sauce dish, flat, open	8.00	15.00
Spoonholder	20.00	45.00
Sugar bowl, covered	40.00	50.00
Syrup pitcher, original top	50.00	—
Toothpick holder	35.00	100.00
Tumbler, water, flat	15.00	25.00
Vase	15.00	—
Wine	30.00	—

QUEEN

Wine and water pitcher (both blue).

High standard open compote (blue); milk pitcher (canary).

OMN: Queen. AKA: Daisy & Button with Pointed Panels, Daisy with Depressed Button [Stevens], Panelled Daisy and Button [Millard], Pointed Panel Daisy and Button [Metz], Sunk Daisy and Button.

Non-flint. McKee Glass Co., Jeannette, PA. ca. 1894. Shards have been found at the site of the Burlington Glass Works, Hamilton, Ontario, Canada.

Original color production: Amber, apple green, blue, canary-yellow, clear. Illustrated in the 1894 McKee Glass Co. catalog. Handles are pressed.

Reproductions: During the 1980s, the Boyd Glass Co., Cambridge, OH., has reissued from new molds the following items in cobalt blue and dark amber: master berry bowl, high standard cake stand, and spoonholder.

References: Kam-3 (P. 38), Kam/Wod-Vol.2 (P. 477), Hea-6 (P. 91), Lee-EAPG (Pl. 154, No. 15), McCn-PGP (P. 215), Mil-1 (Pl. 34), Mtz-1 (PP. 224-225), Rev-APG (P. 240), Spnc-ECG (P. 67), Stev-ECG (Fig. 170), Uni-TCG (PP. 94-95), Uni/Wor-CHPGT (PP. 100-101).

Items made	Amber	Apple Green	Blue	Canary	Clear
Basket	125.00	125.00	135.00	110.00	75.00
Bowl, open, flat, master berry, 8½"d, round	45.00	45.00	55.00	45.00	30.00
Butter dish, flat					
Domed lid	85.00	85.00	100.00	75.00	55.00
Tapered lid	100.00	100.00	125.00	90.00	65.00
Cake stand, high standard, 6½"d	60.00	60.00	65.00	50.00	30.00
Cheese dish, covered	100.00	100.00	125.00	90.00	65.00
Claret	65.00	75.00	75.00	65.00	45.00
Compote, high standard, round					
Covered	75.00	75.00	90.00	65.00	45.00
Open	40.00	40.00	45.00	35.00	25.00
Creamer	35.00	35.00	40.00	30.00	35.00
Dish, oval, flat, open					
7"	25.00	25.00	30.00	25.00	20.00
9"	25.00	25.00	30.00	25.00	20.00
Goblet	25.00	25.00	30.00	25.00	15.00
Pickle tray, oval (2 sizes)	15.00	20.00	20.00	15.00	10.00
Pitcher					
Milk, 1 quart	45.00	45.00	55.00	40.00	45.00
Water, ½ gallon	70.00	70.00	80.00	60.00	55.00
Platter, bread	40.00	40.00	45.00	35.00	25.00
Salt shaker, original top	25.00	25.00	30.00	25.00	15.00
Sauce dish, round					
Flat, 4"d	15.00	20.00	20.00	20.00	10.00
Footed, 4"d	15.00	20.00	20.00	20.00	10.00
Spoonholder	25.00	30.00	35.00	25.00	25.00
Sugar bowl, covered	45.00	55.00	55.00	45.00	50.00
Tumbler, water, flat	30.00	35.00	35.00	30.00	20.00
Wine	30.00	35.00	35.00	30.00	20.00

QUEEN ANNE

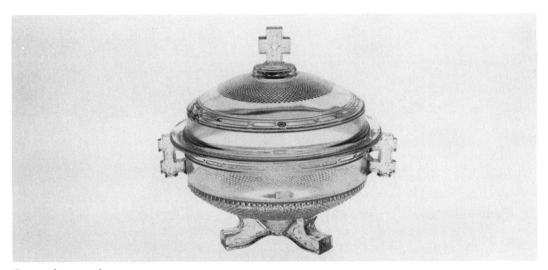

Covered casserole.

AKA: Bearded Man [Lee], Neptune, Old Man, Old Man of the Woods [Kamm], Santa Claus.

Non-flint. LaBelle Glass Co., Bridgeport, OH. ca. 1880. Designed and patented by Andrew H. Boggs (patent No. 12,006) November 2, 1880, and assigned to the LaBelle Glass Co.

Original color production: Clear (plain or copper wheel engraved). Amber or any other color is rare. Handles are pressed and square-shaped, with or without ornamental scrolls. Most forms three-legged with "the bearded man" appearing only on pitchers. Finials are maltese crosses.

Reproductions: None.

References: Bros-TS (P. 46), Hea-5 (P. 460), Kam-1 (P. 90), Kam-5 (PP. 119-120), Lee-VG (Pl. 33, No. 4), McCn-PGP (P. 399), Mtz-1 (PP. 108-109), Pet-GPP (PP. 33-34), Pet-Sal (P. 360), Rev-APG (P. 225), Wlkr-PGA (Fig. 8, No. 43).

Items made	Clear	Items made	Clear
Bowl, covered, oval, flat		Low standard, 9"d	65.00
8"	45.00	Open, high standard	45.00
9"	55.00	Creamer, 5½"h	45.00
Butter dish, covered	65.00	Egg cup, single	35.00
Casserole, covered, round		Pitcher, head under spout	
7"	65.00	Milk, 1 quart	85.00
8"	75.00	Water, ½ gallon	65.00
Celery vase, scalloped rim	35.00	Plate, bread	50.00
Compote, round		Salt shaker, footed, original top	40.00
Covered		Sauce dish, round, footed, smooth rim	15.00
High standard		Spoonholder	40.00
7"d	65.00	Sugar bowl, covered	65.00
8"d	75.00	Syrup pitcher, original top	125.00

QUESTION MARK

Covered butter dish; water pitcher; h.s. covered compote; covered sugar bowl.

OMN: Richards and Hartley No. 55. AKA: Oval Loop.

Non-flint. Richards & Hartley Glass Co. (pattern line No. 55) ca. 1888. Reissued by the United States Glass Co., Pittsburgh, PA., at Factory "F" (Ripley & Co., Pittsburgh, PA.) ca. 1892. Illustrated in the 1888 Richards & Hartley catalog.

Original color production: Clear. Clear with ruby stain or any other color is very rare.

References: Hea-5 (P. 114, Plts. A-C), Hea-7 (P. 166), Kam-4 (P. 135), Lee-VG (Pl. 44, No. 2), Luc-TG (PP. 234-236), Mil-1 (Pl. 14), Mtz-1 (PP. 208-209), Pet-Sal (P. 34), Rev-APG (PP. 286, 288).

Items made	Clear	Items made	Clear
Bowl		Low standard	
Collared, open, round		7"d	25.00
7"d	25.00	8"d	25.00
8"d	25.00	Goblet	20.00
Flat, open, oblong		Pickle jar, covered	45.00
5"	15.00	Pitcher	
6"	15.00	Bulbous	
7"	15.00	Milk, 1 quart	40.00
8"	20.00	Water, ½ gallon	45.00
9"	20.00	Tankard	
10"	24.00	Milk, 1 quart	40.00
Butter dish, covered, flat	30.00	Water, ½ gallon	45.00
Candlestick, chamber with finger loop	45.00	Salt shaker, original top	15.00
Celery vase	30.00	Sauce dish, round	
Compote, round		Collared base, 4"d	10.00
Covered, high standard		Footed, 4"d	10.00
7"d	50.00	Spoonholder	20.00
8"d	60.00	Sugar bowl, covered	25.00
Open		Sugar shaker, original top	35.00
High standard		Tray, bread	30.00
7"d	25.00	Tumbler, water, flat	15.00
8"d	25.00	Wine	20.00

RAINDROP

Creamer and water pitcher (both blue); egg cup (amber).

OMN: Dot.

Non-flint. Doyle & Co., Pittsburgh, PA. ca. 1885. Reissued by the United States Glass Co., Pittsburgh, PA. at Factory "D" (Doyle & Co., Pittsburgh, PA.) ca. 1891. Illustrated in the ca. 1885-1895 Doyle & Co. catalog and the ca. 1891 United States Glass Co. catalog.

Original color production: Amber, apple green, blue, canary-yellow, clear. Odd items may be found in milk white, opaque blue, and opaque white.

Reproductions: None.

References: Fer-YMG (P. 76), Hea-5 (P. 17), Kam-8 (PP. 47-48), Lee-EAPG (Pl. 161, No. 3), Lee-VG (Pl. 52), Mtz-1 (PP. 184-185), Rev-APG (PP. 138, 312), Uni-1 (P. 179).

Items made	Amber	Blue	Canary	Clear
Bowl, finger, round, with underplate	25.00	35.00	35.00	15.00
Butter dish, covered	45.00	55.00	45.00	35.00
Cake plate, round	40.00	50.00	40.00	30.00
Compote, round				
High standard				
Covered	55.00	65.00	55.00	45.00
Open	40.00	50.00	40.00	30.00
Low standard				
Covered	45.00	55.00	45.00	35.00
Open, 8″d	35.00	45.00	35.00	25.00
Creamer, pressed handle	35.00	45.00	35.00	20.00
Cup and saucer, set	40.00	50.00	40.00	25.00
Egg cup, double	35.00	45.00	35.00	25.00
Pickle dish, oval	25.00	35.00	25.00	20.00
Pitcher, water, ½ gallon, pressed handle	45.00	55.00	45.00	35.00
Plate				
Alphabet border	40.00	50.00	40.00	30.00
Dinner	40.00	50.00	40.00	30.00
Relish tray, oval	20.00	30.00	20.00	10.00
Sauce dish, round				
Flat	10.00	15.00	10.00	10.00
Footed	15.00	20.00	15.00	10.00
Spoonholder	40.00	50.00	40.00	30.00
Sugar bowl, covered	45.00	55.00	45.00	35.00
Syrup pitcher, original top	50.00	60.00	50.00	30.00
Tray, water, round	45.00	55.00	45.00	35.00
Tumbler, flat, water	25.00	35.00	25.00	15.00
Wine	25.00	35.00	25.00	15.00

Tumbler; goblet; covered sugar; spoonholder. All clear w/ruby stain.

OMN: Bryce No. 175, Captain Kidd [Fostoria], Central's No. 881, Central's No. 893, Doyle's No. 250, Duncan's No. 328, Eva, Fostoria No. 140, Pioneer's No. 250. AKA: Barrelled Block [Stevens], Clear Block.

Non-flint. Bryce Brothers, (pattern line No. 175), Pittsburgh, PA. (reissued by the U.S. Glass Co. ca. 1898). Central Glass Co. (pattern lines Nos. 881 and 893) Wheeling, WV. Doyle & Co., (pattern line No. 250), Pittsburgh, PA. ca. 1885 (reissued by the U.S. Glass Co. ca. 1892). Fostoria Glass Co., (pattern line No. 140), Fostoria, OH. ca. 1890. George Duncan & Sons, (pattern line No. 328), Pittsburgh, PA. (reissued by the U.S. Glass Co.). Model Flint Glass Works, Albany, IN. Pioneer Glass Works, Pittsburgh, PA. (pattern line No. 250) ca. 1890 to as late as 1907. Illustrated in the 1898 United States Glass Co. catalog.

Original color production: Clear, clear with amber stain, clear with ruby stain. Produced by many factories, numerous variations may be found in the bases, finials, and stems of items. Handles may be applied or pressed.

Reproductions: The goblet and wine in Red Block have been reproduced from new molds in clear with light amber, blue, and ruby stained blocks, iridescent amethyst, iridescent blue, and orange carnival colors.

References: Bar-RS (Pl. 3), Grow-WCG (P. 201, Fig. 18-"3"), Hea-5 (P. 22), Hea-7 (PP. 55, 184), Hlms-BCA (P. 278), Kam-1 (P. 105), Kam-2 (P. 83), Kam-5 (P. 138), Kam-7 (PP. 111-112), Kam-8 (Pl. 75), Kam/Wod-Vol.1 (PP. 58, 60), Lee-EAPG (Pl. 162, No. 3), Mil-1 (Pl. 57), Mtz-1 (PP. 164-165), Mur-MCO (P. 59), Oliv-AAG (P. 72), Pet-Sal (P. 153), Rev-APG (PP. 138-139), Smth-FG (PP. 27-28), Stev-ECG (PP. 147-148), Uni-TCG (PP. 70-71), Uni-1 (P. 165), Uni/Wor-CHPGT (PP. 51-52).

Items made	Clear	Clear w/Ruby
Banana dish, flat, folded sides	50.00	75.00
Bowl		
Round, open, flat		
6"d	30.00	60.00
8"d	40.00	75.00

Items made	Clear	Clear w/Ruby
9″d	40.00	75.00
Waste	25.00	45.00
Cake stand, high standard	30.00	75.00
Celery		
Tray	20.00	45.00
Vase, flared-scalloped rim, 6½″h	40.00	85.00
Cheese dish, covered, original underplate	65.00	125.00
Compote, covered, high standard, round	50.00	90.00
Cordial	20.00	45.00
Creamer		
Individual, 3″h	22.50	40.00
Table size	35.00	55.00
Cruet, original stopper	35.00	175.00
Decanter, original stopper, 12″h	80.00	175.00
Dish, oblong, flat, open		
8″	20.00	40.00
9″	25.00	45.00
10″	30.00	55.00
Goblet	25.00	45.00
Mug, handled	20.00	40.00
Mustard jar, covered, notched lid	25.00	55.00
Pitcher, water		
Bulbous, applied handle, 8″h	80.00	175.00
Tankard, applied handle, 8″h	80.00	175.00
Relish tray, 2″h., 5″w., 8″l	15.00	25.00
Rose bowl	35.00	75.00
Salt		
Dip, individual, 1″h., 2″d (R)	25.00	50.00
Master, open, flat (R)	30.00	60.00
Shaker, original top (R)	30.00	60.00
Sauce dish, round		
Flat		
4½″d	10.00	20.00
5″d	10.00	20.00
Footed		
4½″d	15.00	25.00
5″d	15.00	25.00
Spoonholder, scalloped rim, 4¼″h	25.00	45.00
Sugar bowl, covered, double handles, 7″h.	40.00	75.00
Syrup pitcher (2 styles), original top	50.00	125.00
Tray, water, round	45.00	90.00
Tumbler, water, flat		
Two rows of blocks	15.00	35.00
Three rows of blocks	15.00	40.00
Wine, 4″h	20.00	40.00

Master salt; spoonholder; creamer; toothpick holder (all w/platinum stain).

OMN: U.S. Glass No. 15,140, Athenia. AKA: Panelled 44.

Non-flint. The United States Glass Co. (pattern line No. 15,140), Pittsburgh, PA. ca. 1912.

Original color production: Clear. Clear with gold, clear with platinum stain. Blue or any other color is rare. Most items in Reverse 44 are signed with the United States Glass Co. "U.S.G." insignia embossed in the base. Most items are footed with double handles.

Reproductions: None.

References: Grow-WCG (P. 117, Fig. 27-"3"), Hea-5 (P. 156), Hea-TPS (P. 75), McCn-PGP (P. 297), Mil-2 (P. 150), Pet-GPP (P. 127), Pet-Sal (P. 167), Uni-1 (P. 251).

Items made	Clear	Clear w/Gold or Platinum
Basket, applied reeded handle		
6″	75.00	100.00
7″	90.00	125.00
Bon bon dish		
Flat		
Covered, 5″ d	55.00	75.00
Open, 5″ d	30.00	40.00
Footed, with or without handles, 4″	15.00	20.00
Bowl, open		
Finger bowl	25.00	35.00
Flat, round		
Flared bowl, deep		
6″d	35.00	55.00
7″d	45.00	65.00
8″d., master berry	45.00	65.00
Shallow, salad, 6″d	35.00	55.00
Straight-sided bowl, deep		
6″d	35.00	55.00
7″d	45.00	65.00
8″d	45.00	65.00

Items made	Clear	Clear w/Gold or Platinum
Footed, round		
Flared bowl		
5½"d	35.00	55.00
8½"d	45.00	65.00
Straight-sided bowl		
4½"d	20.00	25.00
7"d	40.00	60.00
Butter dish, covered	65.00	85.00
Candlestick		
4"h	45.00	65.00
7"h	55.00	75.00
Celery		
Dip	20.00	25.00
Tray	30.00	40.00
Vase, pedestaled, double handles	40.00	60.00
Compote, open, round		
High standard		
4½"	20.00	30.00
5½"	25.00	35.00
6½", flared rolled edge	35.00	45.00
Low standard		
Handled		
3"	20.00	30.00
5"	25.00	35.00
6"	35.00	45.00
Handleless		
4½"	20.00	30.00
5½"	25.00	35.00
Creamer, footed, pressed handle		
After dinner	25.00	30.00
Berry	25.00	30.00
Table size	30.00	45.00
Tankard	30.00	45.00
Cruet, original cut or ground stopper	45.00	65.00
Cup, custard		
Crimped, ground bottom	15.00	20.00
Ground bottom	15.00	20.00
Sherbert, footed, handled	15.00	20.00
Dish, open, flat		
Almond	15.00	25.00
Iced olive set	15.00	25.00
Nut, 5"d	15.00	25.00
Olive, deep bowl, 6"d	20.00	30.00
Shallow bowl, 8"d	30.00	45.00
Goblet	25.00	35.00
Pickle dish, 8"l	25.00	35.00
Pitcher		
Jug, ½ gallon, pressed handle	90.00	125.00
Tankard, footed, pressed handle	90.00	125.00
Plate, round, 5½"d	25.00	35.00
Puff box, footed		
Covered	35.00	55.00
Open	20.00	35.00
Rose bowl	40.00	65.00
Salt		
Master, footed, open, double handles	30.00	45.00
Shaker, tall, original top	25.00	35.00

Items made	Clear	Clear w/Gold or Platinum
Sauce dish, flat		
Flared bowl		
4″d	15.00	20.00
4¹/₂″d	15.00	20.00
Straight-sided bowl		
4″d	15.00	20.00
4¹/₂″d	15.00	20.00
Spoonholder, double handles	30.00	45.00
Sugar bowl		
After dinner	25.00	35.00
Basket	30.00	45.00
Berry, open	25.00	35.00
Powdered sugar with original cover	45.00	65.00
Table size, covered	45.00	65.00
Sundae		
High footed	15.00	20.00
Low footed	15.00	20.00
Syrup, original top	90.00	125.00
Toothpick holder, footed, double handles	55.00	85.00
Tumbler		
Flat, ground bottom	25.00	35.00
Iced tea, ground bottom	25.00	35.00
Lemonade, tall, handled	25.00	35.00
Vase		
11″h., handled	30.00	45.00
Table size vase	30.00	45.00
Wine	35.00	55.00

REVERSE TORPEDO

Goblet; high standard fruit basket; celery vase (etched).

OMN: Dalzell No. 490D. AKA: Bulls Eye and Diamond Point, Bulls Eye Band, Bulls Eye with Diamond Point [Dalzell], Diamonds and Bulls Eye Band [Millard], Pointed Bulls Eye [Stevens].

Non-flint. Dalzell, Gilmore & Leighton Glass Co. (pattern line No. 490D) ca. 1892. Attributed to the Burlington Glass Works, Hamilton, Ontario, Canada (Diamond Glass Co., Montreal, Canada). Illustrated in the Butler Brothers catalogs throughout 1892 and 1893, and the June 23, 1892 issue of the *Crockery and Glass Journal*.

Original color production: Clear (plain or copper wheel engraved). Edges may be plain or hand tooled. Handles are applied.

Reproductions: None.

References: Bar-RS (Pl. 13), Smth-FG (PP. 20, 60), Kam-3 (P. 100), Kam-6 (Pl. 42), Kam/Wod-Vol.1 (P. 104), Meas/Smth-FG (PP. 88-90), Mil-2 (Pl. 76), Mtz-1 (PP. 152-153), Pet-Sal (P. 156), Rev-APG (P. 134), Spnc-ECG (P. 42), Stev-ECG (P. 164), Thu-1 (P. 249), Uni-1 (P. 79), Uni-2 (P. 1050), Uni-TCG (PP. 166-167), Uni/Wor-CHPGT (P. 186), Wlkr-PGA (Fig. 15, No. 35).

Items made	Clear	Items made	Clear
Banana dish, folded sides, high standard, 9¾"	135.00	7"d	45.00
Basket		8"d	55.00
Bride's	175.00	9"d	65.00
Fruit, high standard	135.00	9½"d	65.00
Biscuit jar, covered	165.00	10"d	75.00
Bowl, open, flat, round		Creamer, tankard, flat, applied handle, 5¾"h	45.00
Fruit, 10½"d	75.00	Dish, round, flat, scalloped rim (with or without metal handle)	
Pie crust rim, 9"d	65.00		
Shallow, 8½"d	30.00	11"d	60.00
Smooth rim		11½"d	60.00
5½"d	45.00	Doughnut tray	90.00
7½"d	55.00	Goblet	85.00
Butter dish, covered, flanged rim, 5½"h., 7½"	75.00	Honey dish, square, covered	145.00
Cake stand, high standard	85.00	Jam jar, covered	85.00
Celery vase, flat, scalloped rim	55.00	Lamp, oil (several sizes)	175.00
Compote, high standard, round		Pitcher, water, tankard, applied handle	
Covered		Milk, 1 quart	90.00
4"d, jelly	65.00	Water, ½ gallon, 10¼"h	145.00
5"d	65.00	Plate	35.00
6"d	80.00	Relish dish	30.00
7"d	80.00	Salt	
8"d	90.00	Master, flat, round	35.00
9"d	100.00	Shaker, original top	40.00
9½"d	100.00	Sauce dish, flat	
10"d	125.00	Round	20.00
Open, piecrust rim		Square	20.00
4"d, jelly	35.00	Spoonholder, 4¾"h	35.00
5"d	35.00	Sugar bowl, covered, 6½"h	85.00
6"d	40.00	Syrup pitcher, original top	175.00
		Tumbler, water, flat	45.00

RIBBON CANDY

Covered sugar bowl; covered butter dish; celery vase.

OMN. U.S. Glass No. 15,010. AKA: Bryce, Double Loop, Figure Eight.

Non-flint. Bryce Brothers, Pittsburgh, PA. ca. 1885. Reissued by the United States Glass Co. (pattern line No. 15,010), Pittsburgh, PA. at Factory "B" (Bryce Brothers, Pittsburgh, PA.) ca. 1891. Illustrated in the United States Glass Co. 1898 catalog, and the 1905 Lyon Brothers general merchandise catalog.

Original color production: Clear. Green or any other color is rare. Handles are pressed.

Reproductions: None.

References: Hrtng-P&P (P. 77), Hea-5 (P. 76, Plts. A-D), Kam-1 (PP. 32-33), Kam/Wod-Vol.2 (P. 485), Lee-VG (Pl. 32, No. 3), Mil-2 (Pl. 76), Mtz-1 (PP. 154-155), Rev-APG (PP. 86, 89), Spil-AEPG (P. 275), Spil-TBV (P. 235), Uni-2 (PP. 58-59).

Items made	Clear	Items made	Clear
Bowl		Cake stand, high standard	
Oval, open, 8″	25.00	Child's miniature, 3⅛″h, 6½″d	25.00
Round		Table size	
Covered, collared base		8″d	35.00
4″d	20.00	9″d	35.00
5″d	20.00	10″d	45.00
6″d	25.00	10½″d	45.00
8″d	25.00	Celery vase, pedestaled, scalloped rim	30.00
Open		Claret	45.00
Collared base		Compote, round	
4″d	10.00	Covered	
5″d	10.00	High standard	
8″d	15.00	5″d	30.00
Flat		6″d	30.00
6″d	20.00	7″d	40.00
8″d	20.00	8″d	40.00
Butter dish, covered		Low standard	
Flat	45.00	5″d	30.00
Footed	45.00	6″d	30.00
Cake plate, 9″d	35.00	7″d	40.00

Items made	Clear	Items made	Clear
8"d	40.00	Pitcher	
Open		Milk, 1 quart	45.00
High standard		Water, ½ gallon	75.00
Straight-sided bowl		Plate, round	
5"d	15.00	Bread, 10"d	35.00
6"d	15.00	Dinner	
7"d	20.00	6"d............................	10.00
8"d	20.00	7"d............................	15.00
10"d	25.00	8"d............................	15.00
Flared bowl		9"d............................	20.00
6"d	15.00	10"d	20.00
7"d	20.00	11"d	25.00
8"d	20.00	Relish dish, oval	15.00
10"d	25.00	Salt shaker, original top	35.00
Low standard		Sauce dish, round	
5"d	10.00	Flat	
6"d	10.00	3½"d	12.00
7"d	10.00	4"d	12.00
8"d	15.00	4½"d	12.00
10"d	20.00	Footed	
Cordial	45.00	3½"d	15.00
Creamer	45.00	4"d	15.00
Cruet, original stopper	65.00	4½"d	15.00
Cup/saucer, set	40.00	Spoonholder	25.00
Goblet	55.00	Sugar bowl, covered	45.00
Honey dish, covered, square	75.00	Syrup pitcher, original top	90.00
Lamp, stand, oil, complete with		Tumbler, water, flat	35.00
original burner and chimney	85.00	Wine	50.00
Pickle dish, boat shaped	15.00		

RIBBED GRAPE

Goblet; creamer

AKA: Raisin.

Flint. Attributed to the Boston & Sandwich Glass Co., Sandwich, MA. ca. 1850.

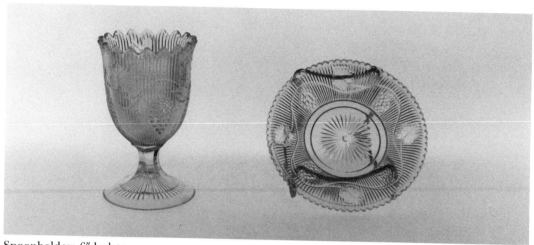

Spoonholder; 6"d plate.

Original color production: Clear. Deep blue, peacock green, milk white, opaque, sapphire blue or any other color is rare. A contemporary of Bellflower and Ribbed Ivy, Ribbed Grape is of good quality flint, the main design element being that of a clear vine on which a finely ribbed grape leaf alternates with a large cluster of clear grapes against a ribbed background. Handles are applied.

Reproductions: None.

References: Drep-ABC OG (P. 149), Lee-EAPG (Pl. 36, No. 13), McCn-PGP (P. 137), McKrn-AG (Plts. 209-210), Mil-1 9(Pl. 148), Mtz-1 (P. 30-31), Nortn-PG (P. 111), Uni-1 (P. 71), Wlkr-PGA (Fig. 8, No. 7).

Items made	Clear
Butter dish, covered	125.00
Celery vase	60.00
Compote, round	
Covered, high standard, 6"d	175.00
Open, low standard, 7¾"d	80.00
Cordial	85.00
Creamer, applied-crimped handle	150.00
Goblet	

Items made	Clear
Straight-sided, ¼" marginal band	
around rim of bowl	55.00
Straight-sided, plain bowl	55.00
Plate, 6"d, serrated rim, star center ...	45.00
Sauce dish, flat, scalloped rim	20.00
Spoonholder, pedestaled, scalloped rim	30.00
Sugar bowl, covered	100.00
Wine	60.00

Water tumbler; egg cup; champagne; goblet; handled whiskey.

Flint. Attributed to the Boston and Sandwich Glass Company, Sandwich, MA. ca. 1850.

Original color production: Clear. Similar to the Bellflower pattern, the main pattern design of Ribbed Ivy consists of 3-pointed leaves instead of conventional Bellflowers against a ribbed background. Handles are applied.

Reproductions: None.

References: Bat-GPG (PP. 21, 25), Brn-SD (P. 55), Cod-OS (Plts. 19, 21), Drep-ABC OG (P. 149), Grow-WCG (P. 91, Fig. 11-"9"), Lee-EAPG (Plts. 32, 39), Lee-SG (Pl. 214), Lee-VG (P. 390), McCn-PGP (P. 425), McKrn-AG (Pl. 213), Mil-1 (Pl. 16), Mtz-1 (P. 30), Oliv-AAG (P. 57), Spil-AEPG (P. 262), Uni-1 (PP. 70-71), Wlkr-PGA (Fig. 8, Nos. 25, 46, 52).

Items made	Clear
Bottle, castor	35.00
Bowl, flat, open, round	
6"d	15.00
8½"d., 2½"h., design in base	20.00
Butter dish, covered	100.00
Castor set, original pewter stand	225.00
Celery vase, 7¼"h	35.00
Champagne	100.00
Compote, round	
Covered, high standard, jelly	125.00
Open	
High standard, scalloped rim, 8¾"d., 7½"h	85.00
Low standard, scalloped rim, deep bowl	75.00
Cordial	125.00
Creamer, footed, crimped handle	125.00
Decanter	
½ pint (sauce bottle)	150.00
Pint	100.00
Quart	150.00
Egg cup, single, straight sides	
Clear, round stem	30.00

Items made	Clear
Plain base	30.00
Rayed base	30.00
Goblet	
Plain base	35.00
Rayed base	35.00
Hat, made from tumbler mold (R)	350.00
Honey dish, flat, round, 3½"d	15.00
Lamp, oil, Ribbed Ivy font	
Brass standard, marble base	250.00
Milk white standard	350.00
Mug, applied handle	
Large	100.00
Small	80.00
Pitcher, water, ½ gallon	150.00
Salt, master, footed	
Covered, beaded rim	125.00
Open	
Beaded rim	45.00
Scalloped rim	40.00
Sauce dish, flat, round, 4"d	15.00
Spoonholder	40.00
Sugar bowl, covered, scalloped base	85.00
Tumbler	

Items made	Clear	Items made	Clear
Bar	75.00	Applied handle	100.00
Water, straight-sided	75.00	Non-handled	75.00
Whiskey, 2¾"h		Wine	85.00

RIBBED PALM

Spoonholder; water pitcher.

OMN: McKee's Sprig. AKA: Oak Leaf.

Flint. McKee Brothers, Pittsburgh, PA. ca. 1863.

Original color production: Clear. Patented by Frederick McKee (design patent No. 1,748) April 21, 1863. Of good quality, heavy flint, the main pattern element consists of large clear, ribbed leaves embossed against a heavily ribbed background. Finials are pseudo acorns, stems of footed pieces being hexagonal with rayed bases (except for compotes). Handles are applied.

References: Brn-SD (P. 55), Cod-OS (Pl. 24), Grow-WCG (P. 175, Fig. 26-"6"), Herr-GG (P. 217), Inn-EGP (P. 53), Inn/Spil-McKe (PP. 35-36), Kam-2 (P. 65), Kam-4 (P. 55), Lee-EAPG (Plts. 37-38), McKrn-AG (Pl. 209), Mil-1 (Pl. 13), Mtz-1 (P. 30), Oliv-AAG (P. 57), Rev-APG (PP. 89, 232), Stot-McKe (P. 36), Uni-1 (P. 71).

Reproductions: The Imperial Glass Co. reproduced in clear glass, from a new mold, the goblet. Of non-flint, the look alike goblet is lighter in weight than the original.

Items made	Clear	Items made	Clear
Butter dish, covered, flat	90.00	8"d	85.00
Celery vase	65.00	10"d	95.00
Champagne	95.00	Low standard	35.00
Compote, round		Creamer, applied handle	175.00
High standard		Dish, open, flat, scalloped rim	
Covered, 6"d. (originally termed		6"d	45.00
the sweetmeat)	125.00	7"d	50.00
Open		8"d	55.00
7"d	75.00	9"d	60.00

Items made	Clear	Items made	Clear
Egg cup, pedestaled	35.00	Master salt, footed, open	35.00
Goblet	40.00	Sauce dish, round, flat, 4"d	15.00
Lamp, complete with original burner	110.00	Spoonholder, pedestaled, scalloped rim	35.00
Pitcher, flat, water, applied handle,		Sugar bowl, covered	75.00
9"h., ½ gallon	225.00	Tumbler, ½ pint	75.00
Plate, 6"d	35.00	Wine	65.00

RIBBON, Bakewell's

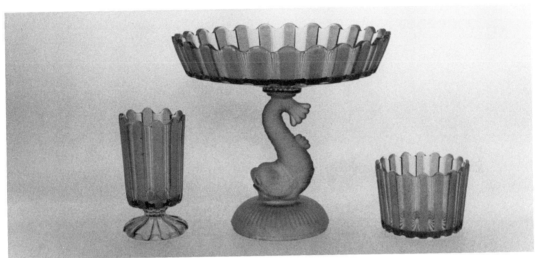

Spoonholder; dolphin standard open compote; wastebowl.

AKA: Frosted Ribbon, Rebecca at the Well, Simple Frosted Ribbon.

Non-flint. Bakewell, Pears & Co., Pittsburgh, PA. ca. 1870.

Original color production: Clear and frosted. Items are machine ground rather than acid finished. Handles are pressed. Oblong open compotes with figural standards are uncommon.

Reproductions: The L.G. Wright Glass Co., New Martinsville, WV. (distributed by Jennings Red Barn, New Martinsville, WV. and Carl Forslund, Grand Rapids, MI.) reproduced from a new mold the goblet the clear and frosted goblet as early as the 1960s. Unlike the original, the frosting on new items is rough to the touch.

References: Drep-ABC OG (P. 149), Enos-MPG (Chart-4), Inn-PG (P. 357), Lee-EAPG (Pl. 67, Nos. 1-2), McCn-PGP (P. 371), Mil-1 (Pl. 115), Mtz-1 (PP. 170-171), Mtz-2 P. 194), Oliv-AAG (P. 76), Rev-APG (P. 50), Spil-AEPG (P. 275), Uni-1 9(PP. 118-119).

Items made	Clear/ Frosted	Items made	Clear/ Frosted
Bottle, cologne, original patterned		Cake stand, high stand, 8½"d	45.00
stopper	65.00	Celery vase, pedestaled, scalloped rim	40.00
Bowl, round		Champagne	75.00
Master berry, flat, scalloped rim	55.00	Cheese dish, covered	100.00
Waste, flat, scalloped rim	45.00	Compote, round	
Butter dish, covered	75.00	Covered	

Items made	Clear/Frosted	Items made	Clear/Frosted
High standard		Straight-sided bowl	35.00
6"d	65.00	Pickle jar, covered	100.00
7"d	70.00	Pitcher	
8"d	75.00	Milk, 1 quart	65.00
Low standard, scalloped rim		Water, $\frac{1}{2}$ gallon	75.00
6"d	40.00	Plate, round	50.00
7"d	45.00	Platter, oblong, cut corners, 9" x 13"	65.00
8"d	50.00	Salt shaker, original top	40.00
Open scalloped rim		Sauce dish, round	
Dolphin standard		Flat, tab-handled	20.00
Round bowl, 10½"d	250.00	Footed, non-handled, scalloped rim	20.00
Oblong bowl, 7⅛"h., 8"l., 5¼"w	275.00	Spoonolder, footed, scalloped rim	35.00
Rebecca at the Wheel standard	300.00	Sugar bowl, covered	65.00
Creamer	30.00	Tray, water, 16¼" x 15"	125.00
Goblet		Wine (R)	175.00
Slightly bulging bowl, 6½"h	35.00		

RISING SUN

Creamer; footed bon bon; vase; goblet; champagne.

OMN: U.S. Glass No. 15,110 Sunshine. AKA: Sunrise.

Non-flint. The United States Glass Co. (pattern line No. 15,110), Pittsburgh, PA. ca. 1908.

Original color production: Clear, clear with green or rose stain. Items in clear with ruby stain and carnival colors are rare. Handles are pressed.

Reproductions: None

References: Hea-3 (P. 87), Hea-5 (P. 142, Plts. A-C), Hea-6 (P. 39, Fig. 302), Hea-7 (P. 186), Hea-OPG (P. 131), Hea-TPS (PP. 73, 82), Kam-2 (PP. 61-62), McCn-PGP (P. 257), Mig-TPS (Pl. 27), Mil-2 (Pl. 86), Uni-1 (P. 307).

Items made	Clear	Green or Rose Stain
Bon bon, footed	15.00	20.00
Bowl, open, flat, round		
Master berry		
Crimped bowl, 9½"d	15.00	25.00
Flared bowl, 8"d	10.00	20.00
Saucer bowl, 5"d	8.00	12.00
Straight-sided bowl		
8"d	10.00	20.00
9½"d	15.00	25.00
Butter dish, covered		
Hotel size	35.00	45.00
Packer's size, with inside ledge	30.00	35.00
Table size, handled	30.00	45.00
Cake stand, high standard, 10½"d	20.00	35.00
Celery vase	25.00	30.00
Champagne	15.00	20.00
Compote, round		
Covered, high standard	45.00	55.00
Open		
High standard, jelly, 4"d	20.00	25.00
Low standard, jelly, 4"d	20.00	25.00
Creamer		
Hotel size	25.00	35.00
Packers, inside ledge	25.00	35.00
Table size	25.00	35.00
Cruet, original stopper	40.00	50.00
Cup, custard, handled	10.00	15.00
Dish, open, flat		
Three-handled, jelly, 4½"d	15.00	20.00
Handleless, ruffled edge	15.00	20.00
Goblet	20.00	25.00
Pickle dish, boat shaped, 7"l	15.00	20.00
Pitcher		
Bulbous, water, ½ gallon	45.00	55.00
Tankard		
Milk, 1 quart	35.00	45.00
Water, ½ gallon	45.00	55.00
Tankard, water, ½ gallon	95.00	110.00
Relish tray	15.00	20.00
Salt shaker, original top	15.00	20.00
Sauce dish, flat, round		
Flared rim, 4"d	5.00	10.00
Straight rim, 4"d	5.00	10.00
Spoonholder, handled		
Hotel size	20.00	30.00
Packers, inside ledge	20.00	30.00
Table size, handled	20.00	30.00
Sugar bowl, covered		
Hotel size, three-handled	40.00	50.00
Packers, no handles, inside ledge	35.00	45.00
Table size, footed, two handles	35.00	40.00
Toothpick holder, three-handles	20.00	35.00
Tumbler		
Champagne.	15.00	25.00
Flared rim	15.00	25.00
Straight-sided	15.00	25.00
Whiskey	10.00	15.00

Items made	Clear	Green or Rose Stain
Vase, 7"h	15.00	25.00
Wine		
Flared bowl	25.00	35.00
Straight-sided bowl	25.00	35.00

ROANOKE

Covered butter dish; h.s. covered compote; covered sugar bowl; creamer.

(OMN). AKA: Late Sawtooth.

Non-flint. Ripley Glass Co., Pittsburgh, PA. ca. 1885. Reissued by the United States Glass Co., Pittsburgh, PA. at Factory "F" (Ripley & Co., Pittsburgh, PA.) after the merger of 1891. Illustrated in the United States Glass Co. ca. 1891, 1895 and 1898 domestic catalogs, and the 1919 export catalog.

Original color production: Clear, clear with ruby stain. Canary-yellow, emerald green or any other color is rare. Handles may be either applied or pressed.

Reproductions: None.

References: Bar-RS (Pl. 13), Bros-TS (P. 44), Drep-ABC OG (P. 249), Hea-5 (P. 122, Plts. A-B), Hea-7 (P. 187), Kam-2 (P. 99), Kam-8 (Pl. 70), Lee-VG (Pl. 46), Rev-APG (PP. 293-294), Wlkr-PGA (Fig. 15, No. 199).

Items made	Clear	Clear w/Ruby
Bowl, open, round, flat		
Deep		
Rounded sides	25.00	45.00
Straight sides	25.00	45.00
Shallow		
Pinched sides	25.00	45.00
Rounded sides	25.00	45.00

Items made	Clear	Clear w/Ruby
Rose, with chain	30.00	—
Butter dish, covered		
Flat	45.00	65.00
Footed	55.00	75.00
Cake stand, high standard, curled scalloped rim		
8"d	75.00	—
9"d	75.00	—
10"d	75.00	—
Compote, round		
Covered, high standard		
5"d	45.00	90.00
6"d	45.00	90.00
7"d	50.00	100.00
8"d	55.00	125.00
Open, scalloped rim		
Deep bowl		
5"d	25.00	40.00
6"d	30.00	45.00
7"d	35.00	60.00
8"d	40.00	75.00
Saucer bowl		
6"d	30.00	45.00
7"d	35.00	60.00
8"d	40.00	75.00
9"d	45.00	80.00
Creamer		
Flat, 3½"h	35.00	50.00
Footed	40.00	60.00
Dish, flat		
Round, covered	25.00	—
Oblong		
7"	20.00	—
8"	20.00	—
9"	20.00	—
Goblet	25.00	40.00
Pitcher, water		
Jug, ½ gallon	45.00	90.00
Tankard, applied handle, ½ gallon	45.00	90.00
Salt, flat, round		
Individual	10.00	30.00
Master	15.00	55.00
Sauce dish, round		
Flat	10.00	20.00
Footed	10.00	20.00
Spoonholder		
Flat	20.00	35.00
Footed	20.00	40.00
Sugar bowl, covered		
Flat	40.00	65.00
Footed	45.00	65.00
Tumbler, water, flat	20.00	35.00
Wine	30.00	45.00

Wine; covered sugar bowl; champagne.

AKA: Frosted Roman Key, Frosted Roman Key with Ribs, Grecian Border, Greek Key, Plain Roman Key.

Flint. The Union Glass Co., Somerville, MA. ca. 1860s. Other factories in several variants.

Original color production: Clear, clear/frosted (machine ground rather than acid finished). Handles are applied.

Reproductions: English imports of several items, including the covered sugar bowl.

References: Cod-OS (P. 21), Enos-MPG (Chart-5), Kam-3 (P. 18), Lee-EAPG (Pl. 94, No. 4), McKrn-AG (Pl. 213), Mil-1 (P. 72), Mil-2 (Pl. 150), Mtz-1 (PP. 36-37), Oliv-AAG (P. 77), Rev-APG (P. 304), Swn-PG (P. 61), Uni-1 (P. 65).

Items made	Clear	Clear/ Frosted
Bowl, open, round, flat, cable edge		
8"d	30.00	35.00
9½"d	35.00	45.00
10"d	45.00	50.00
Butter dish, covered, flat	50.00	80.00
Castor set, (bottle, shaker and covered mustard in original silver plate holder)	100.00	125.00
Celery vase, footed	40.00	80.00
Champagne	40.00	85.00
Compote, open, round, cable rim		
High standard		
8"d	40.00	60.00
9"d	50.00	80.00
10"d	60.00	90.00
Low standard		
7"d	40.00	60.00
8"d	40.00	60.00
Cordial	50.00	75.00
Creamer, footed, applied handle, 6"h	45.00	125.00
Cup, custard	15.00	30.00

Items made	Clear	Clear/ Frosted
Decanter, original matching stopper		
30-ray base		
Pint	—	165.00
Quart	—	165.00
36-ray base		
Pint	—	165.00
Quart	—	165.00
Dish, preserve, round	20.00	45.00
Egg cup, single, pedestaled	25.00	50.00
Goblet	25.00	50.00
Lamp, oil, original burner and chimney	—	150.00
Mustard jar, covered	—	45.00
Pickle dish	—	20.00
Pitcher		
Milk, 1 quart, 7"h	—	200.00
Water, ½ gallon	—	225.00
Plate, 6"d	—	35.00
Relish dish, 6¼" x 9¼" oval, cable edge	—	20.00
Salt, master, footed, open	20.00	45.00
Sauce dish, flat, round, 4"d	10.00	15.00
Spoonholder, pedestaled, scalloped rim	25.00	45.00
Sugar bowl, covered		
Hexagonal stem	45.00	90.00
Octagonal stem	45.00	90.00
Tumbler, bar		
Flat	25.00	45.00
Footed	25.00	45.00
Wine	—	85.00

ROMAN ROSETTE

Salt shaker set; bread plate; creamer.

OMN: U.S. Glass No. 15,030.

Non-flint. Bryce, Walker & Co., Pittsburgh, PA. ca. 1875-1885. Reissued by the United States Glass Co. (pattern line No. 15,030), Pittsburgh, PA. at Factory "A" (Adams & Co., Pittsburgh,

PA.) ca. 1894-1898. Attributed to the Portland Glass Co., Portland, ME. Illustrated in the ca. 1898 and 1904 United States Glass Co. catalogs and in the Baltimore Bargain House August 15, 1904 general merchandise catalog No. 496.

Original color production: Clear, clear with ruby stain. Clear with amber stain or any other color is rare. Handles are pressed.

Reproductions: The goblet has been reproduced in clear as early as the 1960s. Compared to the original, the reproduction goblet is light in weight, the foot is too thin, and the stippling too even and too light, appearing pitted rather than pebbled.

References: Bar-RS (Pl. 10), Bros-TS (P. 24), Grow-WCG (Fig. 34), Hea-5 (P. 33-4E), Hea-7 (PP. 187-188), Inn-PG (P. 381), Kam-1 (P. 34), Lee-EAPG (Pl. 157, No. 4), Lee-VG (Pl. 84), Mil-1 (P. 93), Mtz-1 (PP. 124-125), Oliv-AAG (P. 72), Pet-Sal (P. 37), Rev-APG (PP. 89, 318), Stu-BP (P. 66), Swn-PG (PP. 46-47), Uni-1 (P. 303), Wlkr-PGA (Fig. 8, Nos. 37, 54).

Items made	Clear	Clear w/Ruby
Bowl, flat, round, open, smooth rim		
5"d	10.00	—
5½"d	12.00	—
7"d	15.00	—
8"d	18.00	
8½"d	20.00	50.00
Butter dish, covered, flat, handled	55.00	125.00
Cake stand, high standard		
9"d	45.00	—
10"d	45.00	—
Caster set with original matching glass stand		
2 bottle	40.00	—
3 bottle	50.00	—
Celery vase, pedestaled, scalloped rim	30.00	95.00
Compote, round		
Covered		
High standard		
4½"d., jelly	50.00	85.00
5"d	55.00	85.00
6"d	60.00	85.00
7"d	65.00	100.00
8"d	75.00	125.00
Open, jelly, 4½"d	15.00	35.00
Condiment set		
Salt, pepper, covered mustard with matching under tray	45.00	125.00
Salt, pepper shaker with matching under tray	25.00	—
Cordial (R)	85.00	125.00
Creamer, 1 pint, 5¼"h	30.00	50.00
Egg cup	60.00	
Goblet	40.00	65.00
Honey dish, covered, square	45.00	—
Jug		
5 ounce	45.00	100.00
6 ounce	45.00	100.00
7 ounce	55.00	100.00
Mug		
Large	35.00	50.00
Small	20.00	30.00
Mustard jar, covered, notched lid	45.00	—
Pickle dish, boat shaped	20.00	45.00
Pitcher		

Items made	Clear	Clear w/Ruby
Milk, 1 quart	45.00	125.00
Water, ½ gallon	50.00	150.00
Plate		
Bread, 10″, oval	30.00	75.00
Dinner, round		
7″d	35.00	65.00
7½″d	35.00	65.00
Platter		
Oval	35.00	75.00
Round	55.00	90.00
Preserve dish, oval, flat		
7″	25.00	40.00
8″	25.00	40.00
9″	25.00	45.00
Salt		
Master, footed, open	45.00	—
Shaker, original top, 3″h	20.00	35.00
Sauce dish, round		
Flat		
4″d	15.00	20.00
4½″d	15.00	20.00
Footed		
4″d	20.00	25.00
4½″d	20.00	25.00
Sherbert, tall, stemmed	20.00	35.00
Spoonholder	25.00	45.00
Sugar bowl, covered	45.00	95.00
Syrup pitcher, original tin or nickel plate lid	65.00	125.00
Tray, underplate for salt/pepper set	20.00	35.00
Wine, 4″h	45.00	85.00

ROSE IN SNOW

Mug; goblet; water pitcher; creamer (square); creamer (round).

OMN: Bryce No. 125. AKA: Rose.

Non-flint. Bryce Brothers (square form: pattern line No. 125), Pittsburgh, PA. ca. 1880's. Ohio Glass Co. (round form), Somerville, OH. Reissued by the United States Glass Co., Pittsburgh, PA. after 1891. Both styles reissued by the Indiana Glass Co., Dunkirk, IN. [Kamm].

Original color production: Amber, blue, canary-yellow, clear. Produced in both round and square form, the main pattern design element consists of items heavily stippled with clear roses and foliage in high relief. Handles may be either applied or pressed.

Reproductions: The following items have been reproduced in amber, blue, clear and vaseline: "In Fond Remembrance" mug, 9"d plate, goblet, and pickle dish. The Imperial Glass Co., Bellaire, OH., illustrated the square covered sugar bowl (as line No. 976) in their catalogs from the 1930s through the 1970s in frosted crystal (known as Doeskin), ruby red and milk white. On Imperial reproductions the detail of leaves is completely missing or incorrect.

References: Bat-GPG (PP. 177, 180), Enos-MPG (Chart-5), Hea-5 (P. 80), Inn-PG (P. 353), Kam-4 (PP. 43-44), Lee-EAPG (Pl. 122, Nos. 1-2), Lee-VG (Pl. 8), Mtz-1 (PP. 54-55), Mil-1 (Pl. 17), Oliv-AAG (P. 72), Rev-APG (P. 90), Uni-1 (P. 199), Wlkr-PGA (Fig. 8, Nos. 12, 15, 36).

Items made	Amber	Canary	Blue	Clear
Bottle, bitters, original stopper	—	—	—	85.00
Bowl				
Covered, collared base, round	65.00	65.00	85.00	40.00
Open, flat, square				
8"	40.00	40.00	55.00	30.00
9"	40.00	40.00	55.00	30.00
Butter dish, covered				
Collared base	50.00	50.00	125.00	45.00
Flat				
Round				
No rim	50.00	50.00	125.00	45.00
Scalloped rim	50.00	50.00	125.00	45.00
Square	50.00	50.00	125.00	45.00
Cake stand, high standard, 9"d	85.00	85.00	175.00	80.00
Compote, covered, round				
High standard, 8"d	85.00	85.00	175.00	80.00
Low standard, 7"d	80.00	80.00	150.00	75.00
Creamer				
Round	60.00	60.00	150.00	50.00
Square	65.00	65.00	125.00	45.00
Dish, oval, 8½"l x 11½" x 1½"h				
Goblet	40.00	40.00	85.00	35.00
Marmalade jar, covered	70.00	70.00	135.00	60.00
Mug				
Embossed "In Fond Remembrance", pressed handle	45.00	45.00	110.00	30.00
Large, (made from tumbler)	45.00	45.00	110.00	30.00
Pickle dish, oval, plain or scalloped edge				
Double, 8½" x 7"	65.00	65.00	95.00	25.00
Single, handled	30.00	30.00	95.00	25.00
Pitcher, water, bulbous, ½ gallon, applied handle	175.00	175.00	200.00	125.00
Plate, round				
5"d	40.00	40.00	40.00	35.00
6"d	30.00	40.00	80.00	15.00
7"d	30.00	40.00	80.00	15.00
9"d	30.00	40.00	80.00	15.00
Platter, oval	—	—	125.00	15.00
Relish dish, oval	25.00	25.00	80.00	20.00

Items made	Amber	Canary	Blue	Clear
Sauce dish, round				
Flat	15.00	15.00	20.00	10.00
Footed	10.00	10.00	22.00	15.00
Spoonholder				
Round	40.00	45.00	80.00	20.00
Square	45.00	50.00	90.00	20.00
Sugar bowl, covered				
Round	65.00	75.00	125.00	40.00
Square	65.00	75.00	125.00	45.00
Sweetmeat, covered, 5³/₄"d	80.00	80.00	150.00	65.00
Toddy jar, covered, matching underplate (R)	150.00	150.00	150.00	125.00
Tumbler, water, flat	55.00	55.00	100.00	50.00

ROSE SPRIG

Sietz sauce dish; goblet; celery vase; open footed bowl.

Non-flint. Campbell, Jones and Co., Pittsburgh, PA., ca. 1886. Designed and patented by Henry Franz, May 25, 1886.

Original color production: Amber, blue, canary-yellow and clear. Produced in each color in a complete line of tableware.

Reproductions: Rose Sprig has been reproduced in the form of a new goblet and salt dip (with the patent date "1888") in the original colors of amber, blue, canary-yellow and clear ca. early 1960s. New items can be distinguished by the harsh depth of color, poor quality of design, and lack of fine detail and workmanship. New items are heavier and thicker than the old, as illustrated in the 1970 catalog supplement.

References: Belnp-MG (P. 96), Enos-MPG (Chart-5), Grow-WCG (P. 165, Fig. 24-"17"), Kam-3 (PP. 42-43), Lee-EAPG (Pl. 125, No. 1), Mtz-1 (PP. 54-55), Mtz-2 (P. 63), Mil-1 (Pl. 77), Oliv-AAG (P. 72), Pet-GPP (PP. 74-75), Pet-Sal (P. 170), Rev-APG (PP. 101-102), Uni-1 (P. 203), Wlkr-PGA (Fig. 8, Nos. 18, 49).

Items made	Amber	Canary	Blue	Clear
Biscuit jar, domed lid (R)	200.00	200.00	250.00	100.00
Bowl, open sietz shape, master berry	45.00	55.00	65.00	25.00

Items made	Amber	Canary	Blue	Clear
Cake stand, high standard, 9″d	75.00	75.00	90.00	70.00
Celery vase	50.00	50.00	60.00	40.00
Compote, round				
Covered				
High standard				
7″d	125.00	125.00	125.00	75.00
8″d	125.00	125.00	125.00	75.00
Low standard	100.00	100.00	100.00	65.00
Open				
High standard				
7″d	65.00	65.00	65.00	40.00
8″d	65.00	65.00	65.00	40.00
Low standard				
7″d	—	—	—	35.00
8″d	—	—	—	40.00
Creamer, 5¼″h., pressed handle	55.00	55.00	65.00	45.00
Dish, oblong, flat, open, 9″ x 6″	35.00	35.00	40.00	25.00
Goblet	55.00	55.00	75.00	45.00
Mug, pressed handle	55.00	55.00	55.00	40.00
Nappy, square, handled, 6″	30.00	30.00	35.00	25.00
Pickle dish, oval	30.00	30.00	35.00	25.00
Pitcher, pressed handle				
Milk, 1 quart	65.00	65.00	75.00	50.00
Water, ½ gallon	65.00	65.00	75.00	50.00
Plate, square				
6″	35.00	35.00	45.00	30.00
6½″	35.00	35.00	45.00	30.00
8″	35.00	35.00	45.00	30.00
10½″	40.00	40.00	50.00	35.00
Punch bowl, footed, scalloped rim	125.00	125.00	150.00	85.00
Relish tray, boat shape	30.00	30.00	35.00	25.00
Salt, sleigh shape, dated "1888"	65.00	75.00	85.00	45.00
Sauce dish				
Flat, Sietz bath shape	25.00	25.00	35.00	20.00
Footed	25.00	25.00	35.00	20.00
Spoonholder	40.00	40.00	45.00	25.00
Sugar bowl, covered	50.00	50.00	70.00	45.00
Tray, water	55.00	55.00	80.00	45.00
Tumbler, water, flat	40.00	40.00	45.00	30.00
Wine	55.00	65.00	75.00	50.00

ROSETTE

Goblet; tab-handled bread plate.

OMN: Magic.

Non-flint. Bryce Brothers, Pittsburgh, PA. late 1880s. Reissued by the United States Glass Co., Pittsburgh, PA. at Factory "B" (Bryce Brothers, Pittsburgh, PA.) ca. 1891. Illustrated in the ca. 1891 and 1898 United States Glass Co. catalogs.

Original color production: Clear. Handles are pressed.

Reproductions: None.

References: Grow-WCG (Fig. 20), Hea-5 (P. 79, Plt. 1-B), Kam-4 (P. 46), Kam-7 (Plts. 1-2), Lee-EAPG (Pl. 106, No. 1), Mil-1 (Pl. 77), Mtz-1 (Pl. 77), Oliv-AAG (P. 72), Pet-Sal (P. 38), Rev-APG (PP. 86, 88), Stu-BP (P. 67), Wlkr-PGA (Fig. 8, Nos. 17, 38, 39).

Items made	Clear	Items made	Clear
Bowl, round		8"d	35.00
Covered, flat, 7¼"d	30.00	9"d	35.00
Open, flat		10"d	35.00
Vegetable, smooth rim	25.00	Creamer, 5¼"h	25.00
Waste	25.00	Goblet	30.00
Butter dish, covered	35.00	Mug, pressed handle	20.00
Cake stand, high standard		Pickle tray, fish shape	10.00
7"d	25.00	Pitcher	
9"d	35.00	Milk, 1 quart	45.00
10"d	35.00	Water, ½ gallon	65.00
11"d	35.00	Plate	
Celery vase, 8"h	25.00	Bread, oval, tab handles, 9"	25.00
Compote, high standard, round		Dinner, round, 7"d	15.00
Covered		Relish tray, fish shape	15.00
6"d	40.00	Salt shaker, tall, original top	25.00
7"d	45.00	Sauce dish, flat, handled, 4"d, round	5.00
8"d	55.00	Spoonholder, beaded rim	35.00
11½"d	65.00	Sugar bowl, covered	35.00
Open, saucer bowl		Sugar shaker, original top	35.00
4½"d., jelly	15.00	Tray, water, round, 10¼"d	25.00
6"d	30.00	Tumbler, water, flat, 5"h	15.00
7"d	30.00	Wine	30.00

Round bowl; cologne bottle (o.s.); covered cracker jar; round bowl.

OMN: Tarentum's Atlanta. AKA: Diamond and Teardrop, Shining Diamonds.

Non-flint. The Tarentum Glass Co., Tarentum, PA. ca. 1894. Illustrated in the 1896 Tarentum Glass Co. catalog.

Original color production: Clear, clear with ruby stain.

Reproductions: None.

References: Bar-RS (Pl. 6), Hea-3 (P. 83), Hea-6 (P. 40), Hea-TPS (P. 28), Inn-PG (P. 381), Kam-5 (P. 78), Kam-6 (P. 31), Lee-VG (Pl. 57), Luc-TG (PP. 285-291), McCn-PGP (P. 197), Mtz-2 (P. 144), Mil-1 (Pl. 165), Pet-GPP (P. 187-188), Pet-Sal (P. 153), Rev-APG (P. 286), Stu-BP (P. 16), Wlkr-PGA (Fig. 8, Nos. 28, 44).

Items made	Clear	Clear w/Ruby
Bowl, flat, open		
Rectangular		
4½" x 7"	20.00	30.00
5¼" x 8¼"	20.00	35.00
Round, open, flat, smooth rim		
Flared bowl		
5"d	20.00	30.00
6"d	20.00	30.00
7"d	25.00	35.00
8"d	30.00	35.00
Straight bowl		
5"d	20.00	30.00
6"d	20.00	30.00
7"d	25.00	35.00
8"d	25.00	35.00

Items made	Clear	Clear w/Ruby
Square, 3¾"h., 7½"	20.00	35.00
Triangular, handled, 6"l	20.00	35.00
Bottle		
Cologne, 4 ounce, original patterned stopper	45.00	75.00
Finger	20.00	35.00
Water, 5 pint	35.00	75.00
Butter dish, covered, 6½"h	45.00	90.00
Cake stand, high standard		
9"d	40.00	75.00
9¼"d., 6¼"h	40.00	75.00
10"d	45.00	90.00
Celery vase, 6½"h	30.00	50.00
Compote, high standard, open, smooth rim, round		
6"d	20.00	40.00
7"d	25.00	50.00
Cracker jar, covered	60.00	135.00
Creamer, 5¼"h	35.00	60.00
Cruet, original patterned stopper		
5 ounce	35.00	110.00
8 ounce	45.00	125.00
Dish, round, flat, handled		
4"d	15.00	25.00
4½"d	20.00	25.00
5"d	20.00	30.00
Goblet, 6¼"h, ½ pint	25.00	40.00
Jar, candy, covered, 5¼"h	35.00	55.00
Pitcher, applied handle		
Bulbous		
Milk, 1 quart	45.00	100.00
Water, ½ gallon	60.00	125.00
Tankard, water, ½ gallon, 9½"	65.00	125.00
Plate		
Oval, bread	40.00	55.00
Round, 6"d	15.00	30.00
Salt shaker, original nickel top	15.00	35.00
Sauce dish, round		
Flat		
4"d	10.00	20.00
4½"d	10.00	20.00
Footed		
4"d	10.00	20.00
4½"d	10.00	20.00
Spoonholder, flat	30.00	45.00
Sugar bowl		
Individual, open.	20.00	35.00
Table size, covered, 7½"h	40.00	75.00
Syrup pitcher, 6"h., original nickel top	45.00	145.00
Toothpick holder	30.00	75.00
Tumbler, water, ⅓ pint, flat, 4"h	20.00	35.00
Wine, 4"h	25.00	40.00

Salt shaker (rubina); water pitcher (clear/frosted); pepper shaker (rubina).

Cruet (o.s.); toothpick holder.

OMN: Northwood's No. 287, Royal Ivy. AKA: New Jewel.

Non-flint. Northwood Glass Co. (pattern line No. 287), Ellwood City, PA. ca. 1889.

Original color production: Clear with acid finish, rubina, frosted rubina. Experimental colors of frosted rainbow cracquelle, rainbow cracquelle, clear with amber stain and clambroth, all very rare.

Reproductions: None.

References: Hea-1 (P. 39, Figs. 267-268), Hea-2 (Pl. 119), Hea-3 (P. 40, Figs. 268-272), Hea-6 (P. 40, Figs. 306-310), Kam-5 (P. 87), Migh-TPS (Pl. 11), Mtz-1 (P. 69), Mur-MCO (P. 9), Rev-APG (P. 268).

Items made	Clear/ Frosted	Clear/ Rubina	Frosted/ Rubina
Bowl, round			
Berry, master, open, flat	40.00	85.00	125.00
Finger	25.00	45.00	55.00
Butter dish, covered, flat	100.00	175.00	250.00
Creamer, applied handle	60.00	150.00	200.00
Cruet, original stopper	90.00	225.00	350.00
Lamp, miniature oil with matching shade	150.00	250.00	350.00
Marmalade jar, silver plate cover	100.00	200.00	250.00
Pickle castor, complete in original silver plate holder with tongs	100.00	200.00	350.00
Pitcher, water, ½ gallon, applied handle	100.00	175.00	275.00
Rose bowl, flat, smooth rim	55.00	75.00	85.00
Salt shaker, squatty, original top	25.00	35.00	45.00
Sauce dish, round, flat, smooth rim	20.00	30.00	35.00
Spoonholder, squatty, smooth rim	45.00	65.00	75.00
Sugar bowl, covered, flat	65.00	135.00	155.00
Sugar shaker, original top	65.00	135.00	155.00
Syrup pitcher, original top, applied handle	125.00	225.00	350.00
Toothpick holder	45.00	90.00	125.00
Tumbler, water, flat	25.00	35.00	55.00

Toothpick holder; covered butter dish; water pitcher; covered sugar.

OMN: Northwood's No. 315. AKA: Acorn.

Non-flint. Northwood Glass Co., (pattern line No. 315), Indiana, PA. ca. 1899. Advertised and illustrated in the April 22, 1889 issue of *China, Glass and Lamps*.

Original color production: Clear with acid finish, clear with rubina, frosted rubina, decorated milk. Clear with amber stain or any other color is very rare. Items are square in shape. Handles are applied.

Reproductions: None.

References: Grow-WCG (P. 131, Fig. 17-"17"), Hea-1 (P. 39, Figs. 267-268), Hea-2 (P. 119), Hea-3 (P. 40, Figs. 311-312), Hea-6 (P. 40, Figs. 273-274), Kam-5 (P. 86), Migh-TPS (Pl. 11), Mtz-1 (P. 69), Mur-MCO (P. 9), Rev-APG (P. 268).

Items made	Clear/ Frosted	Clear Rubina	Frosted Rubina
Butter dish, covered, flat	100.00	150.00	225.00
Creamer, applied handle	75.00	85.00	200.00
Cruet, applied handle, original Northwood faceted stopper	150.00	350.00	450.00
Marmalade jar, covered, flat	100.00	150.00	250.00
Pickle castor, complete in original silver plate frame	100.00	150.00	250.00
Pitcher, water, applied handle, ½ gallon	100.00	325.00	400.00
Salt shaker, original top	40.00	65.00	85.00
Sauce dish, round, flat, smooth rim	15.00	25.00	30.00
Spoonholder, flat, smooth rim	50.00	75.00	100.00
Sugar bowl, covered, flat, acorn finial	85.00	150.00	175.00
Sugar shaker, original top	75.00	135.00	165.00
Syrup pitcher, applied handle, original lid	125.00	250.00	375.00
Toothpick holder	45.00	90.00	125.00
Tumbler, water, flat	40.00	65.00	85.00

Creamer.

OMN: Fostoria's No. 450, Czar.

Non-flint. The Fostoria Glass Co. (pattern line No. 450), Fostoria, OH. ca., 1894. Illustrated in the Montgomery Ward 1896 general merchandise catalogs No. 57 and No. 58.

Original color production: Clear (plain or copper wheel engraved). Finials are finely sculptured dogs.

Reproductions: None.

References: Bat-PG (PP. 203, 207), Kam-4 (Pl. 8), Kam-5 (PP. 61, 84), McCn-PGP (P. 189), Mtz-1 (148-149), Rev-APG (P. 159).

Items made	Clear
Bowl, master berry, open, flat, round, 8″	35.00
Butter dish, covered	75.00
Cake stand, high standard	40.00
Celery vase	30.00
Compote, round	
Covered	
High standard	
7″d	50.00
8″d	60.00
Low standard, covered	50.00
Open, low standard	
6″d	25.00
7″d	30.00

Items made	Clear
8″d	35.00
Creamer	35.00
Cruet	35.00
Goblet	35.00
Jam jar, covered	55.00
Sauce dish, flat, round	10.00
Sugar bowl, covered	75.00
Pickle dish, oval, flat	30.00
Pitcher, water, ½ gallon	
Bulbous	55.00
Tankard	45.00
Salt shaker, original top	20.00
Tumbler	25.00

Spillholder.　　　　　　　　　　High standard open compote.

Flint. Attributed to the Boston & Sandwich Glass Co., Sandwich, MA. ca. 1850.

Original color production: Clear. Amethyst, jade green, opaque blue, opaque lavender, electric blue, clambroth or any other color is very rare.

Reproductions: None.

References: Drep-ABC OG (P. 161), Enos-MPG (Chart-6), Lee-EAPG (Pl. 14, No. 1), Lee-SG (P. 524), Mag-FIEF (P. 18, Fig. 15), McKrn-AG (Pl. 195), Mil-1 (P. 74), Mtz-1 (PP. 10-11), Spil-AEPG (P. 255), Uni-1 (PP. 288-289).

Items made	Clear
Butter dish, covered, flat	350.00
Champagne (VR)	350.00
Compote, open	
Dolphin standard (VR)	900.00
High standard, scalloped rim	300.00
Cordial	300.00
Creamer, applied handle	375.00
Decanter, original stopper	

Items made	Clear
Pint	125.00
Quart	125.00
Goblet (VR)	450.00 +
Lamp, whale oil	85.00
Pitcher, water, applied handle	500.00
Relish dish, oblong	65.00
Spoonholder, 5¼"h., 3¾"d	65.00
Wine (VR)	350.00 +

Goblet; 9"d. high standard covered compote; bulbous water pitcher; covered sugar bowl.

OMN: Diamond Point [Bryce], Diamond [Gillinder], Diamond [McKee], Gillinder No. 56, Cambridge Sawtooth. AKA: Crossett Sawtooth, Lumberton Sawtooth, Mitre Diamond, Pineapple [Lee], Mitre.

Flint, non-flint. New England Glass Co., East Cambridge, MA. (flint, primary producer), ca. 1865-1885. The Bryce Group (Bryce, Richards; Bryce, Walker; Bryce Brothers), Pittsburgh, PA. ca. 1854–1890s (reissued by the United States Glass Co. after the 1891 merger). James B. Lyon & Co., Pittsburgh, PA. ca. early 1860s. McKee & Brothers, Pittsburgh, PA. ca. 1859-1865. Gillinder & Sons, Philadelphia, PA. The Union Glass Co., Somerville, MA. Produced for forty years, Sawtooth is profusely illustrated in the 1868 New England Glass Co. catalog, and the 1861 James B. Lyon & Co. and 1864 McKee & Brothers catalogs.

Original color production: Clear, milk white. Deep sapphire blue, amethyst, amber, firey opalescent, medium blue, opaque blue, canary-yellow, translucent white, translucent blue, translucent jade green or any other color in flint is very rare. Produced by numerous concerns for over four decades, the treatment of bases, finials, handles, stems, and standards varies considerably.

Reproductions: The Westmorland Glass Co., Grapeville, PA. ca. 1977-1978, reissued from the original mold, the high standard covered compote in milk white. From new molds the following look-alike items were issued in milk white: flat covered butter dish, 6"d. high standard covered compote, 6½"d. covered footed dish, 9"d. covered compote; in amethyst: goblet, iced tea (not original to the set), sherbert and wine; clear: high standard covered compote; opaque pink: tumbler, goblet and wine. Westmorland reissues are often marked with the company's "W.G." monogram. By 1967 L.G. Wright Glass Co., New Martinsville, WV. (distributed by Jennings Red Barn, New Martinsville, WV. and Carl Forslund, Grand Rapids, MI.) reproduced the 6½"d., 5"h. clear covered butter dish, by 1970 the firm's catalog supplement illustrates both clear sherbert and wine. Reissuing numerous items in clear and milk white from old and new molds, perhaps the most prolific producer of Sawtooth is the Westmorland Glass Co., Grapeville, PA.

References: Bat-CPG (PP. 43-47), Belnp-MG (P. 212), Fer-YMG (P. 64), Grow-WCG (P. 93, Fig. 11-"12"), Hea-5 (P. 83, Pl. C), Hlms-BCA (P. 278), Hrtng-P&P (P. 79), Kam-1 (PP. 4-5), Kam/Wod-Vol.2 (P. 506), Lee-EAPG (Pl. 40), Mil-1 (Pl. 123), Mil-OG (Plts. 211-212), Mtz-1

(PP. 34-37), Mtz-2 (PP. 20-21), Mur-MCO (P. 67), Oliv-AAG (P. 56), Rev-APG (PP. 87, 90, 170), Spil-TBV (P. 236), Stev-ECG (Fig. 191), Stev-GIC (PP. 214, 229), Uni-2 (P. 173), Uni-TCG (P. 170), Uni/Wor-CHPGT (PP. 196-197).

Items made	Flint	Non-flint
Bottle, water with matching tumbler	55.00	—
Bowl, round		
Covered		
6″d	55.00	—
7″d	65.00	—
Open, flat		
6″d	25.00	—
7″d	25.00	—
8″d	30.00	—
9″d	35.00	—
10″d	35.00	—
Butter dish, covered, round		
Child's miniature	—	45.00
Table size	—	55.00
Cake stand, high standard, round		
9″d	85.00	45.00
10″d	85.00	55.00
11″d	95.00	65.00
12″d	110.00	—
14″d	125.00	—
Celery vase, 10″h., pedestaled, scalloped rim	60.00	30.00
Champagne, knob stem	40.00	30.00
Compote, round		
Covered		
High standard		
Deep bowl		
6″d	75.00	45.00
7″d	75.00	45.00
8″d	85.00	55.00
9″d	85.00	55.00
9½″d	85.00	55.00
10″d	110.00	—
Shallow bowl		
6″d	75.00	45.00
7″d	75.00	45.00
Low standard		
Deep bowl		
7″d	75.00	45.00
8″d	85.00	55.00
9″d	85.00	55.00
10″d	110.00	—
Shallow bowl		
6″d	75.00	45.00
7″d	75.00	45.00
Open		
High standard, flared bowl, sawtooth rim		
Deep Bowl		
6″d	35.00	30.00
7″d	35.00	30.00
8″d	45.00	35.00
9″d	45.00	35.00
10″d	50.00	40.00
Shallow bowl		
6″d	35.00	30.00

Items made	Flint	Non-flint
7"d	35.00	30.00
Low standard, deep bowl		
6"d	35.00	30.00
7"d	35.00	30.00
8"d	45.00	35.00
9"d	45.00	35.00
10"d	50.00	40.00
Cordial	85.00	25.00
Creamer		
Child's miniature, pressed handle	—	25.00
Table size		
Applied handle	75.00	40.00
Pressed handle	45.00	30.00
Cruet, original acorn stopper	85.00	45.00
Decanter, quart, original stopper	55.00	35.00
Dish, flat, open		
Oval		
5"	30.00	20.00
6"	30.00	20.00
7"	30.00	20.00
Round, preserve or fruit		
6"d	30.00	20.00
7"d	30.00	20.00
8"d	35.00	25.00
9"d	35.00	25.00
10"d	40.00	30.00
11"d	40.00	30.00
12"d	40.00	35.00
Egg cup, single, pedestaled, covered	45.00	25.00
Gas shade	—	35.00
Goblet		
Knob stem, $5^3/_4$"h	35.00	20.00
Plain stem, $5^3/_4$"h	35.00	20.00
Honey dish, flat, round	15.00	10.00
Lamp, oil (several), original burner and chimney	150.00	—
Pitcher		
Milk		
Applied handle, 1 quart	95.00	65.00
Pressed handle, 1 quart	75.00	45.00
Water		
Applied handle, $^1/_2$ gallon	125.00	—
Pressed handle, $^1/_2$ gallon	—	55.00
Plate, round, $6^1/_2$"d	45.00	30.00
Pomade jar, covered	55.00	40.00
Salt		
Master, pedestaled		
Covered	65.00	40.00
Open, sawtooth rim	25.00	20.00
Sauce dish, round, flat		
4"d	15.00	10.00
$4^1/_2$"d	15.00	10.00
5"d	15.00	10.00
Spillholder	50.00	—
Spoonholder		
Child's miniature	—	35.00
Table size		
Plain base	35.00	25.00
Rayed base	35.00	25.00
Sugar bowl, covered	50.00	35.00

Items made	Flint	Non-flint
Tray, water, round		
10"d	—	65.00
11"d	—	65.00
12"d	—	75.00
14"d	—	95.00
Tumbler, water		
Flat	45.00	25.00
Footed	45.00	25.00
Wine, 4½"h (height may vary)		
Knob stem	35.00	25.00
Plain stem	35.00	25.00

SAWTOOTHED HONEYCOMB

Toothpick holder.

OMN: Steimer's Diamond, Union's Radiant. AKA: Chickenwire [Peterson], Sawtooth Honeycomb, Serrated Block and Loop [Millard].

Non-flint. The Steimer Glass Co., Buckhannon, WV. ca. 1906, the molds acquired by the Union Stopper Co., Morgantown, WV. ca. 1906-1912. Reviewed in the January 13, 1906 issue of *China, Glass and Lamps* as "Diamond", Sawtoothed Honeycomb is illustrated in a ca. 1908 Union Stopper Co. catalog.

Original color production: Clear, clear with ruby stain (plain or gilt).

Reproductions: None.

References: Bar-RS (Pl. 10), Hea-6 (P. 85), Hea-7 (P. 182), Hea-TPS (PP. 30, 55), Kam-1 (P. 115), Mil-2 (Pl. 94), Mtz-1 (PP. 218-219), Pet-Sal (P. 156-"M").

Items made	Clear	Clear w/Ruby
Bowl, round		
Flat		
Berry, master, open, flat	20.00	45.00
Orange, 14½"d	65.00	125.00

Items made	Clear	Clear w/Ruby
Footed, orange, 14½"d, scalloped rim	125.00	75.00
Butter dish, covered, flat	40.00	100.00
Celery vase	25.00	85.00
Compote, open, high standard	35.00	50.00
Creamer, 4"h, pressed handle	25.00	55.00
Cruet, original stopper	45.00	135.00
Dish, bon bon, triangular, handled	20.00	35.00
Goblet	30.00	65.00
Pitcher, water, pressed handle		
2 pint	25.00	100.00
½ gallon	45.00	150.00
Salt shaker, original top	20.00	35.00
Sauce dish, round		
Flat		
4"d	8.00	20.00
4½"d	8.00	20.00
Footed		
4"d	10.00	22.00
4½"d	10.00	22.00
Spoonholder	30.00	45.00
Sugar bowl		
Covered	45.00	85.00
Open, double handled	30.00	40.00
Syrup pitcher, original top	50.00	185.00
Toothpick holder	25.00	150.00
Tumbler, water, flat, 3¾"h	20.00	40.00

SAXON, Adams

Cruet.

OMN: Saxon, Adam's. AKA: Saxon-Engraved [Lee]

Non-flint. Adams & Co., Pittsburgh, PA. ca. 1888. Reissued by the United States Glass Co., Pittsburgh, PA. ca. 1892. Illustrated in the ca. 1891 United States Glass Co. catalog of member firms.

Original color production: Clear (plain or copper wheel engraved). Items in clear with ruby stain (plain or copper wheel engraved, often souvenired) were most likely produced after the United States Glass Co. merger. Handles may be applied or pressed.

Reproductions: None.

References: Drep-ABC OG (P. 169), Hea-1 (P. 39, Fig. 271), Hea-3 (P. 57, Fig. 448), Hea-5 (PP. 14, 47, 60), Hea-6 (P. 41, Fig. 319), Kam-3 (P. 8), Lee-VG (Pl. 60), McCn-PGP (P. 409), Mur-MCO (P. 59), Rev-APG (PP. 21, 318).

Items made	Clear	Items made	Clear
Bowl, round		Claret	25.00
Flat		Compote, round	
Covered		Covered, high standard	
5″d	25.00	5″d	25.00
6″d	30.00	6″d	30.00
7″d	30.00	7″d	35.00
8″d	30.00	8″d	40.00
9″d	35.00	Open	
Open		High standard	
Belled bowl, scalloped rim		Belled bowl	
5″d	10.00	5″d	20.00
6″d	10.00	6″d	20.00
7″d	15.00	7″d	25.00
8″d	15.00	8″d	30.00
9″d	20.00	9″d	30.00
Flared bowl		Shallow bowl, flared-scalloped	
7½″d	20.00	rim	
9″d	20.00	6½″d	20.00
10″d	25.00	7½″d	25.00
11½″d	25.00	9″d	30.00
Footed, low standard		10″d	30.00
Covered		11½″d	35.00
5″d	25.00	Low standard, 8″d	30.00
6″d	30.00	Creamer, 7″h	25.00
7″d	30.00	Cruet, applied handle, original	
8″d	30.00	stopper.	40.00
9″d	35.00	Dish, flat, open	
Open		Oval	
Belled bowl		7″	10.00
5″d	10.00	8″	10.00
6″d	10.00	9″	15.00
7″d	15.00	Round	
8″d	15.00	7″	10.00
9″d	20.00	8″	10.00
Shallow bowl, flared-scalloped		9″	15.00
rim		Egg cup, single	20.00
6½″d	10.00	Goblet	30.00
7½″d	15.00	Mug, handled	20.00
9″d	20.00	Pickle tray, rectangular	10.00
10″d	25.00	Pitcher	
11½″d	25.00	Milk, 1 quart	35.00
Waste or finger	35.00	Water, ½ gallon	40.00
Bread platter, oval, handled, 12″	30.00	Plate, round, 6″d	35.00
Butter dish, covered, flat	35.00	Salt	
Cake stand, high standard		Individual	20.00
9″d	40.00	Master	20.00
10″d	45.00	Shaker, original top	25.00
Celery vase	25.00	Sauce dish, round	

Items made	Clear	Items made	Clear
Flat		4½″d	12.00
3″d	5.00	Spoonholder	20.00
4″d	10.00	Sugar bowl, covered	35.00
4½″d	10.00	Syrup pitcher, original top	55.00
Footed		Toothpick holder	30.00
Belled bowl		Tray, water, round	35.00
3″d	8.00	Tumbler, water, flat, ½ pint	20.00
4″d.	12.00	Wine	40.00

SCALLOPED SIX POINT(S)

Toothpick holder; goblet; bouquet vase; bouquet vase; wine; mustard pot.

OMN: Duncan's No. 30. AKA: Divided Medallion with Diamond Cut.

Non-flint. George Duncan's Sons & Co. (pattern line No. 30), Washington, PA. with continued production by Duncan & Miller Glass Co. ca. 1897 to 1912.

Original color production: Clear. Clear with ruby stain or any other color is rare. Handles may be applied or pressed.

Reproductions: None.

References: Bons-BDG (P. 109), Hea-1 (P. 39), Hea-7 (P. 190), Hea-OS (P. 37, No. 297), Hea-TPS (P. 73), Kam-5 (P. 97), Kam-7 (PP. 125-126), McCn-PGP (P. 159), Pet-Sal (P. 159), Rev-APG (P. 149), Spil-AEPG (Fig. 328), Uni-2 (P. 141), Wlkr-PGA (Fig. 15, No. 83).

Items made	Clear	Items made	Clear
Bowl, flat, open		Tray	25.00
Round, 9″d	30.00	Vase	30.00
Square, 9″	30.00	Claret	
Butter dish, covered, flat	45.00	Cupped bowl	30.00
Butter pat	10.00	Round bowl	30.00
Cake stand, high standard		Cocktail, large	30.00
Round	40.00	Compote, open, round	
Square	35.00	High standard	35.00
Celery		Low standard	30.00

Items made	Clear	Items made	Clear
Cordial.	25.00	Dip, individual, 1½″d	15.00
Cracker jar, covered	55.00	Shaker, original top	25.00
Creamer		Sherry	
Individual	10.00	Flared bowl	25.00
Table size	35.00	Straight bowl	25.00
Cruet, original stopper	30.00	Spoonholder	25.00
Cup		Sugar bowl, covered	
Custard	15.00	Individual	10.00
Sherbert	15.00	Table size	45.00
Egg cup, single	20.00	Syrup, original top	45.00
Goblet		Toothpick holder	
Cupped bowl	40.00	Conventional shape	35.00
Straight bowl	40.00	Cuspidor shape	45.00
Mustard pot, original top	15.00	Tumbler, flat	
Nappy, handled	15.00	Bar	15.00
Pickle		Champagne	20.00
Dish	20.00	Water	25.00
Jar, covered	45.00	Vase, bouquet	
Pitcher, water, applied handle		6″ h	15.00
Bulbous, ½ gallon	50.00	8″ h	20.00
Tankard, ½ gallon	50.00	Wine	
Plate, ice cream	20.00	Cupped bowl	25.00
Rose bowl	45.00	Straight bowl	25.00
Salt			

SCALLOPED TAPE

Celery vase; high standard covered compote.

AKA: Jewel Band [Lee], Jeweled Band.

Non-flint. Original maker unknown, ca. 1880s.

Original color production: Clear. Odd pieces can be found in amber, blue, canary-yellow and light green although complete table settings were not produced in these colors.

Reproductions: None.

References: Kam-2 (P. 29), Lee-VG (Pl. 30, No. 2), McCn-PGP (P. 341), Mil-1 (Pl. 24), Mtz-1 (PP. 192-193), Stu-BP (P. 3), Uni-1 (PP. 100-101), Wlkr-PGA (Fig. 8, Nos. 41, 54).

Items made	Clear	Items made	Clear
Butter dish, covered	35.00	Plate	
Cake stand, high standard	35.00	Bread, oval, "Bread Is The Staff Of	
Celery vase, pedestaled	35.00	Life" center	45.00
Compote, high standard, round		Dinner, 6"d	15.00
Covered, 8"d	55.00	Relish tray	10.00
Open, 8"d	40.00	Sauce dish, round	
Creamer, 5⅝"h, pressed handle	30.00	Flat, 4"d	5.00
Dish, covered, rectangular, flat, 8"	45.00	Footed, 4"d	10.00
Egg cup, footed	25.00	Spoonholder	35.00
Goblet	30.00	Sugar bowl, covered	35.00
Pitcher, pressed handle		Tray, 6" x 7"	25.00
Milk, 1 quart	35.00	Wine	25.00
Water, ½ gallon	50.00		

SCROLL

Egg cup.

OMN: Lilly. AKA: Stippled Scroll.

Non-flint. George Duncan & Sons, Pittsburgh, PA. ca. 1870s. Attributed to Ripley & Co.

Original color production: Clear, milk white.

Reproductions: None.

References: Kam-7 (P. 70), Lee-EAPG (Pl. 140, No. 1), Lee-VG (Pl. 22), Mtz-1 (PP. 148-149), Mil-1 (Pl. 86), Uni-2 (PP. 34-35).

Items made	Clear	Items made	Clear
Butter dish, covered	50.00	Egg cup, pedestaled	30.00
Celery vase	30.00	Goblet	35.00
Compote, round		Pitcher, water, open, footed	75.00
Covered		Salt, master, open, footed	25.00
High standard, 7"d	65.00	Spoonholder	30.00
Low standard, 7"d	45.00	Sugar bowl, covered	45.00
Open, high standard	35.00	Tumbler, footed, water	25.00
Cordial	35.00	Wine	35.00
Creamer, applied handle	40.00		

SCROLL WITH FLOWERS

Egg cup; goblet.

Non-flint. Attributed to the Central Glass Co., Wheeling, WV. ca. 1870s, and the Canton Glass Co., Canton, OH. ca. 1880's.

Original color production: Clear. Occasionally, pieces may be found in amber, apple green, and blue.

Reproductions: None.

References: Kam-1 (P. 65), Lee-EAPG (Pl. 140, No. 3), McCn-PGP (P. 275) Mil-1 (Pl. 61), Mtz-1 (PP. 58-59), Spil-AEPG (P. 300), Stu-BP (P. 33), Wlkr-PGA (Fig. 8, No. 46).

Items made	Clear	Items made	Clear
Butter dish, covered	40.00	Pitcher, water, ½ gallon	45.00
Cake plate, handled, 10½"d	25.00	Salt, master, footed, open	20.00
Compote, covered, low standard	45.00	Sauce dish, round, footed, double	
Cordial	35.00	handled	10.00
Creamer, 4½"h, pressed handle	40.00	Spoonholder	15.00
Egg cup, handled, double	20.00	Sugar bowl, covered	45.00
Goblet	25.00	Syrup pitcher, original top	75.00
Mustard pot, covered with notched lid	50.00	Wine	30.00
Pickle tray, oval, square handles	15.00		

SEASHELL

Champagne.

AKA: Boswell.

Non-flint. Original maker unknown, ca. 1870s.

Original color production: Clear, clear and frosted (plain or copper wheel engraved). Finials on covered items are well sculptued, heavily stippled "seashells."

Reproductions: None.

References: Kam-4 (P. 1), Lee-VG (Pl. 20, No.1), McCn-PGP (P. 411), Mtz-1 (PP. 142-143), Mil-2 (Pl. 66), Uni-1 (PP. 90-91).

Items made	Clear	Items made	Clear
Butter dish, covered	85.00	Pitcher, pressed handle	
Cake stand, high standard	35.00	Milk, 1 quart	55.00
Celery vase, pedestaled, scalloped rim	30.00	Water, ½ gallon	65.00
Champagne	35.00	Salt shaker, original top	15.00
Compote, covered, high standard		Sauce dish, footed, round	15.00
(several sizes), round	75.00	Spoonholder	25.00
Creamer, pressed handle	25.00	Sugar bowl, covered	65.00
Goblet	35.00	Wine	25.00

SEDAN

Wine; goblet; high standard open compote; pickle tray.

AKA: Panelled Star and Button [Kamm].

Non-flint. Original maker unknown, ca. 1870s.

Original color production: Clear. Handles are pressed.

Reproductions: None.

References: Kam-1 (P. 15), McCn-PGP (P. 87), Mil-1 (Pl. 119), Mil-2 (Pl. 119), Mtz-1 (PP. 174-175), Pet-Sal (P. 35), Uni-1 (P. 121), Wlkr-PGA (Fig. 8, No. 45).

Items made	Clear	Items made	Clear
Bowl, master berry, open, flat, round	20.00	Mug	15.00
Butter dish, covered	35.00	Pickle tray, double handled	15.00
Celery		Pitcher, water, $1/_2$ gallon	35.00
Tray	15.00	Relish tray, flat	10.00
Vase	25.00	Salt shaker, original top	20.00
Compote, round		Sauce dish, flat, round	5.00
Covered, high standard, 8½″d	35.00	Spoonholder	15.00
Open, low standard, scalloped rim	20.00	Sugar bowl, covered	35.00
Creamer	20.00	Tumbler, water, flat	20.00
Goblet	20.00	Wine	15.00

SHELL AND JEWEL

Flat sauce 4½″d; high standard cake stand; water pitcher; creamer.

OMN: Victor [Westmorland], Fostoria No. 618. AKA: Jewel and Shell, Late Nugget, Nugget.

Non-flint. Westmorland Specialty Glass Co., Grapeville, PA. ca. 1893. The Fostoria Glass Co. (pattern line No. 618), Fostoria, OH. ca. 1898. Attributed to the Sydenham Glass Co., Wallaceburg, Ontario, Canada ca. 1895 [Nugget] and the Jefferson Glass Co., Toronto, Ontario, Canada ca. 1920 [Late Nugget].

Original color production: Clear. Odd pieces can be found in amber, cobalt blue, green and carnival irridized orange and green. Manufactured in the United States and Canada, American-made items are those showing larger, more rounded "shell ornaments", while Canadian items have shorter, more "pointed" shells with a row of balls between each fan on the edges of tops. Handles are applied.

Reproductions: None.

References: Kam-1 (P. 68), Kam-6 (P. 14), Lee-VG (Pl. 73), Mtz-1 (PP. 216-217), Mtz-2 (PP. 102-103), Oliv-AAG (P. 73), Inn-PG (P. 48), Rev-APG (PP. 159, 323, 161), Stev-ECG (PP. 176-177), Swn-PG (P. 48), Uni-TCG (PP. 154-155), Uni/Wor-CHPGT (PP. 170-171), Weath-FOST (P. 9).

Items made	Clear	Items made	Clear
Banana dish, high standard, 10″ (S)	75.00	Creamer, footed, 4¼″h, pressed handle	35.00
Bowl, open, flat, round		Dish, open, oval, flat	
6″d	20.00	7″	20.00
8″d, master berry	20.00	8″	20.00
Butter dish, covered, flat		Honey dish, round, covered	25.00
Large	65.00	Jug, 3 pint	45.00
Small	65.00	Pitcher, water, ½ gallon, pressed	45.00
Cake stand, high standard, 10″d	45.00	handle	
Compote, high standard, round		Sauce dish, flat, round, 4½″d	12.00
Covered, 7″d	50.00	Spoonholder, footed, scalloped rim	30.00
Open		Sugar bowl, covered	35.00
7″d	25.00	Tray, water, round	50.00
Orange bowl	65.00	Tumbler, water, flat	20.00

Spoonholder (square); water pitcher (round); creamer (square).

OMN: Duncan No. 555. AKA: Hedlin Shell [Stevens], Shell and Spike, Shell and Tassel-Square.

Non-flint. George A. Duncan & Sons (pattern line No. 555), Pittsburgh, PA. ca. 1881. Designed and patented by Augustus H. Heisey, July 26, 1881 in two forms: frosted corner shells (patent No. 12,371) and clear corner shells (patent No. 12,372). Shards have been found at the site of the Burlington Glass Works, Hamilton, Ontario, Canada. Attributed to the Portland Glass Co., Portland, ME. although the pattern was patented 8 years after the close of the Portland Glass Works. Illustrated in the George Duncan & Sons ca. 1888 catalog, and reviewed in the *American Pottery and Glassware Reporter* for December 3, 1880 and the *Crockery and Glass Journal* for February 2, 1881, March 23, 1882, and October 21, 1884.

Original color production: Clear, (plain or copper wheel engraved). Amber, blue, canary-yellow or any other color is rare. Produced in two forms: a) square form: shell-shaped finials, scalloped rims, sometimes found with "Duncan & Sons" entwined on bases of compotes and cake stands, and b) round form: frosted dog finials and smooth rims. Handles are pressed.

Reproductions: The L.G. Wright Glass Co., New Martinsville, WV. (distributed by Jennings Red Barn, New Martinsville, WV. and Carl Forslund, Grand Rapids, MI.) reproduced, from a look-alike mold, the clear goblet as illustrated in the company's 1970 catalog supplement.

References: Bred-EDG (PP. 8, 20-21, 23), Enos-MPG (Chart-5), Grow-WCG (P. 164, Fig. 24-"15"), Inn-EGP (P. 53), Inn-PG (P. 335), Kam-3 (P. 59), Kam/Wod-Vol.2 (P. 514), Krs-EDG (PP. 120-121), Krs-YD (PP.132-133), Lee-EAPG (Pl. 157), McCn-PGP (Pl. 5), Mil-1 (Pl. 143), Mil-2 (Pl. 157), Mtz-1 (PP. 138-139), Mtz-2 (PP. 192-193), Oliv-AAG (P. 73), Pet-GPP (PP. 77-79), Pet-Sal (P. 39), Rev-APG (P. 144), Spil-AEPG (P. 295), Stev-ECG (PP. 134-137), Stu-BP (P. 69), Swn-PG (P. 23), Uni-1 (P. 271), Uni-TCG (P. 171), Uni/Wor-CHPGT (P. 199), Wlkr-PGA (Fig. 8, No. 45).

Items made	Clear

ROUND FORM: (COLLARED BASES, DOG FINIALS)

Items made	Clear
Butter dish, double handled	65.00
Celery vase, double handled, smooth rim	55.00
Creamer, pressed handle	45.00
Pitcher, water, smooth rim, pressed handle, 1/2 gallon	75.00
Spoonholder, double handled, smooth rim	45.00
Sauce dish, smooth rim, double handled, 4"d	10.00
Sugar bowl, covered, double handled	100.00

SQUARE FORM; (SHELL FINIALS, SCALLOPED RIMS)

Items made	Clear
Bowl	
Covered, collared base (R)	
6"d	110.00
7"d	125.00
8"d	145.00
Open	
Master berry	
Oblong, collared base	
Deep bowl, 12"l	65.00
Shallow, flared bowl, 12"l	65.00
Shell shape, three applied shell shaped feet, 7½"l	75.00
Butter dish, covered, footed	125.00
Butter pat, shell shaped, flat	15.00
Cake stand, high standard, square	
6"	35.00
7"	40.00
8"	50.00
9"	65.00
10"	70.00
11"	80.00
12"	95.00
Celery vase, pedestaled	65.00
Compote	
Covered, 6"	85.00
Open, high standard	
4½"	25.00
5"., jelly	25.00
6"	30.00
6½"	30.00
7"	35.00

Items made	Clear
8"	40.00
9"	45.00
10"	50.00
Creamer, footed, scalloped rim, pressed handle	55.00
Dish, rectangular, open, flat	
7"	35.00
8"	45.00
9"	55.00
10"	65.00
Goblet	
Knob stem	45.00
Plain stem	40.00
Pickle jar, covered, flat, straight-sided	150.00
Pitcher, water, 1/2 gallon collared base, scalloped rim	85.00
Plate	
Fan shape, 12", applied clear shell shaped feet	
Fruit	125.00
Tart	125.00
Round, oyster, 9½"d	225.00
Platter	
Oblong, master berry under plate	65.00
Square, bread plate, shell handles	75.00
Salt	
Individual, shell shaped	15.00
Shaker, original top (R)	100.00+
Sauce dish	
Flat, tab handled	
Shell shape, 4½"	20.00
Square	
4"	10.00
4½"	10.00
Footed, square	
3"	20.00
4"	20.00
5"	20.00
Spoonholder, footed, scalloped rim ...	45.00
Sugar bowl, covered	85.00
Tray, ice cream, rectangular, flat, tab handled	75.00
Tumbler	
Soda	
10 ounce	40.00
13 ounce	45.00
18 ounce	55.00
Table (water) 9 ounce.	40.00
Vase, footed, 7½"h., scalloped rim (S)	125.00

SHERATON

Water pitcher; 7″d. h.s. shallow compote.

OMN: Ida.

Non-flint. Bryce, Higbee & Co., Pittsburgh, PA. ca. 1885. Attributed to the Burlington Glass Works, Hamilton, Ontario, Canada.

Original color production: Amber, blue, clear. Handles are pressed.

Reproductions: None.

References: Bat-CGPG (PP. 105, 107), Drep-ABC OG (P. 197), Hlms-BCA (P. 278), Kam-3 (P. 38), Kam-8 (P. 17), Kam/Wod-Vol.2 (P. 517), Lee-VG (Pl. 55, No. 3), McCn-PGP (P. 343), Mil-1 (Pl. 127), Mtz-1 (PP. 136-137), Oliv-AAG (P. 73), Rev-APG (P. 92), Stu-BP (P. 70), Uni-1 (P. 10), Uni/Wod-CHPGT (P. 200), Uni-TCG (P. 172), Wlkr-PGA (Fig. 8, No. 20).

Items made	Amber	Blue	Clear
Bowl, master, berry, flat, open, round, 8″d	35.00	40.00	15.00
Butter dish, covered	40.00	50.00	25.00
Celery vase	30.00	35.00	25.00
Compote, round			
Covered, high standard, shallow bowl, 7″d	30.00	35.00	25.00
Open			
High standard, 7″d	40.00	45.00	30.00
Low standard, 7″d	40.00	45.00	25.00
Creamer, 5½″h	35.00	45.00	30.00
Dish, open flat			
Eight paneled sides	30.00	35.00	25.00
Round	25.00	30.00	20.00
Goblet	30.00	35.00	25.00
Pitcher			
Milk, 1 quart, 7″h	40.00	50.00	30.00
Water, ½ gallon, 9″h	45.00	55.00	35.00
Plate, bread, 9¾″ x 8″	45.00	55.00	25.00
Platter, oblong, 8 panels	40.00	45.00	35.00
Relish tray, handled	25.00	30.00	15.00
Sauce dish, round			
Flat, 3½″d.	15.00	15.00	10.00

Items made	Amber	Blue	Clear
Footed, 3½"d	15.00	15.00	10.00
Spoonholder.	25.00	30.00	15.00
Sugar bowl, covered, footed	40.00	55.00	30.00
Tumbler, water, flat	35.00	40.00	30.00
Wine	35.00	40.00	30.00

SHOSHONE

Table creamer; h.s. open compote; high standard banana stand; covered sugar bowl.

OMN: U.S. No. 15,046, Victor. AKA: Blazing Pinwheels, Floral Diamond [Kamm].

Non-flint. The United States Glass Co. (pattern line No. 15,046), Pittsburgh, PA. ca. 1895-1896. Illustrated in the United States Glass Co. catalog as "Victor" and the 1899 Butler Brothers catalog as "Progress" (emerald green).

Original color production: Clear, clear with ruby stain, clear with amber stain, emerald green. Odd pieces may be found in cobalt blue and Gainsborough olive green. Handles may be applied or pressed. Westmorland Glass Co.'s "Sterling" line is a direct copy of Shoshone.

Reproductions: None.

References: Bar-RS (Pl. 12), Hea-1 (P. 40, Fig. 287), Hea-2 (P. 119), Hea-3 (P. 57, Fig. 45), Hea-5 (PP. 23, 50), Hea-6 (P. 42, Figs. 333-334), Hea-7 (P. 209, Figs. 269-276), Hea-TPS (PP. 21, 46), Kam-4 (P. 71), McCn-PGP (P. 201), Mil-2 (Pl. 88), Mur-CO (P. 4), Pet-Sal (P. 161), Pyne-PG (P. 140), Uni-1 (P. 295), Weath-FOST (P. 9), Wlkr-PGA (Fig. 8, No. 57).

Items made	Clear	Clear/ Amber	Clear/ Ruby	Green
Banana stand, high standard, folded sided	55.00	85.00	85.00	65.00
Bowl				
Round				
Collared base, scalloped rim				
Belled bowl				
7"d	30.00	45.00	45.00	40.00
8"d	35.00	45.00	45.00	40.00

Items made	Clear	Clear/ Amber	Clear/ Ruby	Green
Straight-sided bowl				
7"d	30.00	45.00	45.00	40.00
8"d	30.00	45.00	45.00	40.00
Flat				
Flared bowl				
5"d	25.00	40.00	40.00	35.00
6"d	25.00	40.00	40.00	35.00
7"d	30.00	45.00	45.00	40.00
8"d	35.00	45.00	45.00	40.00
Straight-sided bowl				
6"d	25.00	40.00	40.00	35.00
7"d	30.00	45.00	45.00	40.00
8"d	35.00	45.00	45.00	40.00
Square, scalloped rim, 8"d., 4"h	35.00	45.00	45.00	40.00
Butter dish, covered, flat with high domed lid, flanged base.	45.00	75.00	85.00	65.00
Cake stand, high standard				
9"d	40.00	—	—	55.00
10"d	40.00	—	—	55.00
11"d	45.00	—	—	60.00
Celery vase, flat, scalloped rim	35.00	85.00	85.00	65.00
Compote				
Covered				
6"	45.00	75.00	75.00	65.00
7"	50.00	90.00	90.00	80.00
8"	50.00	90.00	90.00	80.00
Open, square, scalloped rim				
High standard, 5¼"	25.00	40.00	45.00	40.00
Low standard, 5¼"	25.00	40.00	45.00	40.00
Creamer, bulbous				
Individual	25.00	35.00	35.00	30.00
Table size, 5"h	35.00	45.00	45.00	40.00
Dish				
Jelly, flat, double handles, 5½"w	15.00	25.00	25.00	25.00
Flat, turned up sides, 6" x 6"	20.00	25.00	30.00	25.00
Oblong, 7" x 4¾" h	20.00	25.00	30.00	25.00
Rectangular, deep, 7"l	20.00	25.00	30.00	25.00
Goblet, 6½"h	30.00	55.00	65.00	—
Horse radish, covered	30.00	—	—	40.00
Ice tub, flat, straight-sided, tab handles	35.00	75.00	75.00	65.00
Olive tray, rectangular, 7¾"l	20.00	25.00	25.00	25.00
Pickle tray, oblong	20.00	25.00	25.00	25.00
Pitcher, water, applied handle, ½ gallon				
Bulbous	50.00	175.00	175.00	150.00
Tankard	50.00	175.00	175.00	150.00
Plate				
7"d	30.00	—	—	35.00
7½"d (termed "sweet meat")	30.00	—	—	35.00
Salt				
Master, round, flat, scalloped				
rim (R)	25.00	55.00	65.00	—
Shaker, tall, original top	20.00	45.00	45.00	40.00
Sauce dish, flat, round, belled, 4"d	10.00	20.00	20.00	20.00
Spoonholder, bulbous, flat	25.00	40.00	55.00	35.00
Sugar bowl, covered, flat				
Medium	35.00	55.00	65.00	55.00
Table size	40.00	65.00	75.00	65.00
Toothpick holder, 2¾"h	40.00	225.00	225.00	85.00
Tumbler, water, flat, 2¾"h	35.00	45.00	45.00	40.00

Items made	Clear	Clear/ Amber	Clear/ Ruby	Green
Wine, 4½"h	30.00	35.00	45.00	35.00

SHRINE

Salt shaker; tumbler; goblet; spoonholder; toothpick holder.

OMN: Orient [Beatty-Brady]. AKA: Jewel with Moon and Star [Kamm], Jeweled Moon and Star [McCain], Little Shrine, Moon and Star with Waffle.

Non-flint. Beatty-Brady Glass Co., Dunkirk, IN. ca. 1896. Indiana Glass Co., Dunkirk, IN. ca. 1904. Illustrated in the Baltimore Bargain House general merchandise catalogs for August, 1903 (No. 479), December, 1903 (No. 483) and August 15, 1904 (No. 496).

Original color production: Clear. Handles are pressed.

Reproductions: None.

References: Bond-AG (P. 71), Grow-WCG (P. 138, Fig. 19-"4"), Herr-GG (Figs. 277, 289), Kam-1 (P. 101), Lee-VG (Pl. 35, No. 4), McCn-PGP (P. 503), Mig-TPS (Pl. 4), Mil-1 (Pl. 11), Mtz-1 (PP. 116-117), Pet-Sal (P. 39), Uni-1 (P. 179), Wlkr-PGA (Fig. 8, No. 37).

Items made	Clear	Items made	Clear
Bowl, flat, open, round		Platter	45.00
6½"d	25.00	Relish tray	15.00
8½"d	25.00	Salt shaker, original top	
9½"d	30.00	Squatty	35.00
Butter dish, covered	50.00	Tall	35.00
Cake stand, high standard, 8½"d	45.00	Sauce dish, flat, round, 4"d	20.00
Celery vase	45.00	Spoonholder, flat, scalloped rim	35.00
Compote, open, high standard, jelly	20.00	Sugar bowl, covered	55.00
Creamer, 4½"h	40.00	Toothpick holder (R)	85.00
Goblet	65.00	Tumbler, flat	
Pickle tray	15.00	Lemonade	35.00
Pitcher, water, ½ gallon	50.00	Water	35.00

Custard cup; wine.

OMN: Indiana Tumbler No. 29. AKA: Hearts of Loch Laven [Metz], Ribbed Asterisk And Concave.

Non-flint. The Indiana Tumbler and Goblet Co. (pattern line No. 29), Greentown, IN. ca. 1896. Indiana Glass Co., Dunkirk, IN. ca. 1898.

Original color production: Clear. Odd pieces may be found in chocolate. Handles are pressed.

Reproductions: None.

References: Boyd-GC (Nos. 52, 92, 165), Bros-TS (P. 39), Herr-GG (Figs. 34-44), Kam-3 (PP. 102-103), Kam-8 (PP. 24-25), Lip-GG (P. 26), McCn-PGP (P. 509), Meas-GG (PP. 49-50), Mil-1 (Pl. 30), Mtz-1 (P. 211-212), Pet-Sal (P. 172), Rev-APG (P. 203), Uni-2 (P. 78).

Items made	Clear	Items made	Clear
Bowl, master berry, flat, open, round	25.00	Goblet (S)	60.00
Butter dish, covered	150.00	Mug	25.00
Celery vase	30.00	Pitcher, water, ¹/₂ gallon	55.00
Cordial	30.00	Salt shaker, original top	45.00
Creamer		Sauce dish, flat, round	10.00
Table size, 5¹/₂"h	30.00	Spoonholder	25.00
Tankard, 6"h	30.00	Sugar bowl, covered	40.00
Cruet, original stopper	25.00	Tumbler, water, flat	25.00
Cup, custard	10.00	Wine	20.00

Spoonholder (clear); goblet (clear w/ruby stain); creamer (clear).

AKA: Early Oregon, Richards & Hartley's Oregon.

Non-flint. Richards & Hartley Glass Co., Tarentum, PA. ca. 1890. Reissued by the United States Glass Co., Pittsburgh, PA. after the 1891 merger. Illustrated in the ca. 1891 United States Glass Co. catalog of member firms.

Original color production: Clear, clear with ruby stain. Quite similar to Richards & Hartley's No. 544 (Block and Fan). Handles are pressed.

Reproductions: None.

References: Bar-RS (Pl. 8), Bat-GPG (PP. 153-154), Hart/Cobb-SS (P. 58), Hea-5 (PP. 13, 115), Lee-VG (Pl. 44), McCn-PGP (P. 491), Mtz-1 (P. 154-155), Mil-2 (Pl. 59), Pet-Sal (P. 34), Rev-APG (PP. 286, 288), Uni-1 (PP. 252-243).

Items made	Clear	Clear w/Ruby
Bowl, flat, open		
Rectangular		
7".	20.00	—
8"	25.00	—
9"	35.00	—
Round, shallow		
5"d	15.00	—
6"d	20.00	35.00
8"d	25.00	40.00
Butter dish, covered, flat, flanged base	40.00	100.00
Cake stand, high standard	45.00	—
Celery vase	35.00	90.00
Compote, round		
Covered, high standard		
7"d	45.00	—
8"d	45.00	—
Open		
High standard		
4"d, jelly	10.00	35.00

Items made	Clear	Clear w/Ruby
7"d	25.00	—
8"d	30.00	—
Low standard, scalloped rim		
7"d	30.00	45.00
8"d	30.00	55.00
Creamer, flat	30.00	55.00
Dish		
Oblong, flat		
7"	15.00	—
8"	15.00	—
9"	20.00	—
Olive, handled	15.00	—
Goblet	35.00	50.00
Pickle tray	15.00	—
Pitcher		
Milk, bulbous, 1 quart	45.00	90.00
Water		
Bulbous, ½ gallon	55.00	125.00
Tankard, ½ gallon	55.00	125.00
Salt shaker, original top	25.00	35.00
Sauce dish, round		
Flat, 4"d	10.00	20.00
Footed, 4"d	10.00	20.00
Spoonholder, flat, scalloped rim	25.00	55.00
Sugar bowl, covered	35.00	65.00
Tray, water, round	45.00	—
Tumbler, water, flat	25.00	40.00
Wine	35.00	55.00

SMOCKING

Goblet; champagne.

AKA: *Divided Smocking, Knob Stem Smocking, Plain Smocking.*

Flint. Original maker unknown ca. 1850s. Shards have been found at the site of the Boston & Sandwich Glass Co., Sandwich, MA.

Original color production: Clear. Handles are applied.

Reproductions: None.

References: Kam-6 (P. 12), Lee-VG (Pl. 25, No. 4), Mag-FIEF (P. 2, Fig. 1), Pl. 207), McCn-PGP (Pl. 207), McKrn-AG (Pl. 207), Mil-1 (Pl. 2), Mil-2 (Pl. 6), Mtz-1 (PP. 44-45), Mtz-2 (PP. 52-53), Oliv-AAG (P. 58), Spil-AEPG (PP. 253, 256), Uni-1 (P. 58), Uni-2 (PP. 38-39), Wlkr-PGA (Fig. 8, No. 18).

Items made	Clear	Items made	Clear
Bar bottle, bar lip	100.00	Pitcher, water, ½ gallon	125.00
Bowl, open, flat, 9"d, round	75.00	Spillholder	45.00
Compote, covered, low standard, 7"d,		Spoonholder	75.00
round	90.00	Sugar bowl, covered	75.00
Creamer, applied handle, 5"h	90.00	Vase, 10"h	50.00
Egg cup, single	50.00	Tumbler	
Goblet		Water, footed	45.00
Knob stem, 6¼"h	85.00	Whiskey, flat	75.00
Straight stem, 6¼"h	85.00	Wine	45.00
Lamp, oil, 9"h, original burner and			
chimney	125.00		

SNAIL

Salt shaker; syrup; covered sugar bowl; tankard water pitcher; spoonholder; custard cup.

OMN: Duncan's No. 360 Ware. AKA: Compact [Lee], Double Snail [Kamm], Idaho, Small Comet [Millard].

Non-flint. George Duncan & Sons (pattern line No. 360), Pittsburgh, PA. ca. 1891. Reissued by the United States Glass Co., Pittsburgh, PA. at Factory "D" (George Duncan & Sons, Pittsburgh, PA.) after the 1891 merger, with production most likely continued by Factory "P" (Doyle & Co., Pittsburgh, PA.) after the Duncan plant burned. Illustrated in the 1895-1896, 1898, and 1904 United States Glass Co. catalogs and the 1885 National Merchandise Co.

catalog, trade reviews of Snail appear in *China, Glass and Lamps* for December 31, 1890, January 28, April 8, and May 20, 1891, and in the January 1, 1891 issue of *Pottery and Glass Reporter.*

Original color production: Clear, clear with ruby stain (staining being added after the U.S. Glass merger). Deep blue or any other color is rare. Plain or copper wheel engraved with No. 619 engraving [fern], the main design element consists of curves and circles suggestive of shell-like ornaments, often combined with large margins of clear glass. Finials are pointed, carrying the same design. Handles are applied. Original Duncan catalog illustrations combine both "Snail" and the so-called "Double Snail" as one pattern.

Reproductions: None.

References: Bar-RS (Pl. 5), Bros-TS (P. 44), Bred-EDG (PP. 120-123), Hea-5 (P. 48, No. 204), Hea-6 (P. 42, Fig. 335), Hea-7 (P. 194), Hea-OS (Pl. 139, No. 2656), Inn-PG (P. 381), Kam-2 (P. 69), Kam-5 (PP. 93-94), Kam-6 (Pl. 3), Kam-7 (Plts. 23-24), Krs-YD (PP. 59-61), Lee-VG (Pl. 46, No. 3), McCn-PGP (Pl. 242), Mtz-1 (P. 209), Mtz-2 (PP. 168-169), Mil-2 (Pl. 76), Pet-Sal (P. 39), Rev-APG (PP. 149-151), Uni-1 (P. 63).

Items made	Clear	Clear w/Ruby
Banana stand, high standard		
9"d	165.00	—
10"d	165.00	—
Basket, cake, flat, pewter handle		
9"d	85.00	—
10"d	95.00	—
Bowl		
Covered, circular foot, round		
7"d	65.00	—
8"d	65.00	—
Open		
Round		
Deep		
Flat		
7"d	25.00	40.00
8"d	30.00	45.00
9"d	35.00	55.00
10"d	45.00	65.00
Footed, 8"d	25.00	—
Shallow, flat, 10"d	35.00	—
Oval, flat		
7"	30.00	—
8"	30.00	45.00
9"	30.00	45.00
Finger, smooth rim	65.00	—
Rose, flat, smooth rim		
3"	40.00	—
5"	45.00	—
6"	55.00	—
7"	65.00	—
Butter dish, covered, 6"d	85.00	165.00
Cake stand, high standard		
9"d	75.00	—
10"d	85.00	—
Celery		
Tray	35.00	—
Vase, flat, scalloped rim	40.00	85.00

Items made	Clear	Clear w/Ruby
Cheese dish, covered, flat	100.00	—
Compote, high standard, round		
Covered		
6″d	50.00	—
7″d	85.00	125.00
8″d	90.00	150.00
10″d	125.00	—
Open, scalloped rim, shallow bowl		
6″d	30.00	—
7″d	35.00	—
8″d	35.00	—
9″d	45.00	—
10″d	55.00	—
Creamer		
Individual, applied handle	40.00	55.00
Table size, tankard, $5\frac{1}{4}$″h, applied handle	65.00	90.00
Cruet, original patterned stopper	100.00	300.00
Cup, custard	30.00	45.00
Goblet	85.00	125.00
Jug, Double Snail (original size designations)		
0	45.00	—
3	55.00	—
4	65.00	—
5	75.00	—
Marmalade, covered	125.00	—
Pitcher, applied handle		
Bulbous, 1 quart	125.00	175.00
Tankard		
1 pint, cream	60.00	90.00
$1\frac{1}{2}$ pint, cream	125.00	—
$\frac{1}{4}$ gallon, milk	125.00	250.00
$\frac{1}{2}$ gallon, water	125.00	250.00
Plate, round		
5″d	35.00	—
6″d	40.00	—
7″d	45.00	—
Relish dish, oval, 7″	20.00	—
Salt		
Individual, $1\frac{3}{4}$″d	25.00	40.00
Master, round, flat	55.00	95.00
Shaker, original top		
Small, bulbous	35.00	65.00
Tall, 3″h	45.00	65.00
Sauce dish, round		
Flat		
4″d	15.00	25.00
$4\frac{1}{2}$″d	15.00	25.00
Footed		
4″d	20.00	25.00
$4\frac{1}{2}$″d	20.00	25.00
Spoonholder, flat, smooth rim	35.00	65.00
Sugar bowl, covered		
Individual	55.00	—
Table size	65.00	125.00
Sugar shaker, original top, 5″h	90.00	250.00
Syrup pitcher, original top, pressed handle	125.00	250.00
Tumbler, water, flat	45.00	85.00
Vase	50.00	90.00

Footed bowl; water pitcher; flared footed bowl; goblet.

OMN: Earl. AKA: Nailhead Variant, Spirea, Square and Dot, Squared Dot.

Non-flint. Bryce, Higbee & Co., Pittsburgh, PA. ca. 1885. Illustrated in an undated Bryce, Higbee and Company catalog as "Earl."

Original color production: Amber, apple green, blue, vaseline, clear.

Reproductions: None.

References: Drep-ABC OG (P. 208), Hea-5 (P. 41, Nos. 10-11), Kam-4 (P. 34), Kam-8 (PP. 17-18), Lee-VG (Pl. 29, No. 2), Mil-1 (Pl. 177), Mtz-1 (PP. 136-137), Pet-Sal (P. 39), Rev-APG (P. 92), Stu-BP (P. 34), Uni-1 (P. 249), Wlkr-PGA (Fig. 8, No. 56).

Items made	Amber	Blue	Clear	Vas
Bowl, open, round				
Flat, master berry, open, flat, 8"d	25.00	40.00	20.00	30.00
Footed				
Deep bowl, 8"d	25.00	40.00	20.00	30.00
Shallow bowl, 8"d	25.00	40.00	20.00	30.00
Butter dish, covered	50.00	55.00	35.00	45.00
Cake stand, high standard, 11"d	45.00	50.00	40.00	45.00
Celery vase	40.00	50.00	25.00	40.00
Compote, round				
Covered				
High standard				
6"d	45.00	60.00	35.00	40.00
7"d	40.00	65.00	40.00	45.00
Low standard				
6"d	45.00	60.00	35.00	45.00
7"d	40.00	65.00	40.00	45.00
Open, high standard, 7"d	25.00	30.00	20.00	25.00
Cordial	35.00	40.00	20.00	35.00
Creamer, 5½"h, pressed handle	35.00	45.00	35.00	35.00
Dish, cereal, round	15.00	15.00	10.00	15.00
Goblet	35.00	35.00	25.00	35.00
Honey dish, round, flat	10.00	10.00	15.00	10.00

Items made	Amber	Blue	Clear	Vas
Pickle dish	15.00	15.00	15.00	10.00
Pitcher, water, 1/2 gallon, pressed handle	65.00	75.00	35.00	50.00
Platter, oval				
10 1/2″	30.00	40.00	20.00	30.00
11″	30.00	40.00	20.00	30.00
Relish tray	30.00	35.00	15.00	30.00
Salt shaker, original top	20.00	25.00	10.00	20.00
Sauce dish, round				
Flat	10.00	10.00	5.00	10.00
Footed	10.00	10.00	5.00	10.00
Spoonholder	30.00	25.00	20.00	35.00
Sugar bowl, covered	30.00	40.00	25.00	30.00
Tumbler, water, flat	25.00	35.00	20.00	30.00
Wine	30.00	35.00	20.00	30.00

SPRIG

Creamer; high standard covered compote; footed sauce dish.

OMN: Bryce's Royal. AKA: Indian Tree, Panelled Sprig.

Non-flint. Bryce, Higbee & Co., Pittsburgh, PA. ca. 1880s. Illustrated in ca. 1885 Bryce, Higbee & Co. catalog as "Royal."

Original color production: Clear. Deep blue or any other color is very rare. Handles are pressed.

Reproductions: None.

References: Kam-3 (PP. 14-15), Kam-8 (Pl. 28-29), Lee-EAPG (Pl. 78, No. 2), McCn-PGP (P. 287), Mil-1 (Pl. 126), Mtz-1 (PP. 58-59), Rev-APG (P. 92), Stu-BP (P. 34), Uni-1 (P. 220), Wlkr-PGA (Fig. 8, Nos. 20, 45).

Items made	Clear	Items made	Clear
Bowl		Creamer	30.00
Covered, flat, 6"d	45.00	Dish, oval, open, flat	
Open		7"	15.00
6"d	25.00	8"	15.00
Berry, master, scalloped rim, 10"d	40.00	9"	15.00
Butter dish, covered	65.00	Goblet	40.00
Cake stand, high standard		Pickle	
8"d	35.00	Dish, flat	15.00
9"d	40.00	Jar, covered	65.00
10"d	40.00	Pitcher, water, ½ gallon	50.00
Celery vase	40.00	Plate, bread, oval	40.00
Compote		Relish tray	12.00
Covered		Salt dip	
High standard		Individual	35.00
6"d	60.00	Master	50.00
7"d	60.00	Sauce dish, round	
8"d	65.00	Flat, 4"d	15.00
10"d	70.00	Footed, 4"d	15.00
Open		Spoonholder	25.00
Low standard		Sugar bowl, covered	50.00
6"d	45.00	Tumbler, water, flat	25.00
7"d	45.00	Wine	45.00
8"d	50.00		

SQUIRREL

Covered butter dish; standard oil lamp; flat round sauce dish.

AKA: Squirrel in Bower [Lee]

Non-flint. Original maker unknown, ca. 1880s.

Original color production: Clear. Chocolate (water pitcher only). Finials are well sculptured "squirrels." Handles are pressed.

Reproductions: None.

References: Kam-4 (P. 60), Kam-5 (P. 128), Lee-EAPG (Pl. 100, No. 4), Mil-1 (Pl. 103), Mtz-1 (PP. 94-95), Pap-GAG (P. 94), Uni-1 (PP. 182-183).

Items made	Clear	Items made	Clear
Butter dish, covered, flat	225.00	Pitcher, water, ½ gallon	200.00
Creamer	150.00	Sauce dish, round, flat	25.00
Goblet (VR)	550.00+	Spoonholder	85.00
Lamp, oil, standard	250.00	Sugar bowl, covered, flat	200.00

STAR IN BULLS EYE

Toothpick holder; low standard open compote; berry bowl; cruet (n.o.s.).

OMN: U.S. Glass No. 15,092.

Non-flint. The United States Glass Company (pattern line No. 15,092), Pittsburgh, PA. ca. 1905. Although a "berry sugar" bowl is illustrated by New Martinsville, too little is presently known to attribute manufacture to this company.

Original color production: Clear (plain or with gilt). Handles are pressed.

Reproductions: None.

References: Hea-5 (PP. 13, 23, 43), Hea-TPS (PP. 26, 52, 77), Kam-1 (P. 100), Mil-1 (Pl. 99), Mil-2 (Pl. 18), Pet-Sal (P. 173), Rev-APG (P. 318), Uni-1 (P. 164).

Items made	Clear	Items made	Clear
Bowl, open, flat, flared rim, berry, round	25.00	Dish, diamond shape	10.00
Butter dish, covered	40.00	Goblet	25.00
Cake stand, high standard	40.00	Pitcher, water, ½ gallon	45.00
Celery vase	30.00	Spoonholder	25.00
Compote, round, covered	40.00	Sugar bowl, covered	35.00
Open, low standard, scalloped, deep bowl	25.00	Toothpick holder	
		Double	35.00
		Single	30.00
Creamer	25.00	Tumbler, water	20.00
Cruet, original stopper, 4"h	30.00	Wine	15.00

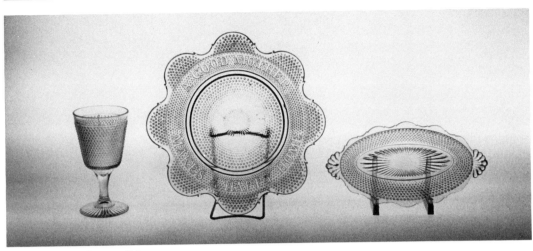

Goblet; 10"d. plate; relish tray.

OMN: Snowflake. AKA: General Grant.

Non-flint. McKee Brothers, Pittsburgh, PA. ca. 1875. Illustrated in the 1880 McKee Glass Co. catalog.

Original color production: Clear. Amber, apple green, blue, canary-yellow or any other color is rare.

Reproductions: None.

References: Kam-5 (P. 10), Lee-EAPG (Pl. 98), McCn-PGP (P. 503), Mil-1 (Pl. 38), Mtz-1 (P. 116), Mtz-2 (P. 194), Nortn-PG (P. 111), Rev-APG (P. 241), Stot-McKe (PP. 57-58), Stu-BP (P. 71), Uni-1 (P. 97), Wlkr-PGA (Fig. 8, No. 20).

Items made	Clear	Items made	Clear
Bowl, open, round		8½"d	65.00
Flat		Low standard	
7"d	15.00	7"d	50.00
8"d	15.00	8"d	55.00
9"d	20.00	8½"d	65.00
Footed, low standard		Open	
7"d	20.00	High standard	
8"d	20.00	7"d	20.00
9"d	20.00	8"d	20.00
Bread plate	40.00	8½"d	25.00
Butter dish, covered	45.00	Low standard	
Compote, round		6½"d	15.00
Covered		7"d	20.00
High standard		7½"d	20.00
7"d	50.00	8"d	20.00
8"d	55.00	8½"d	25.00

Items made	Clear	Items made	Clear
Creamer	35.00	Flat	
Goblet	35.00	3½"d	15.00
Pickle dish, oval	15.00	4"d	15.00
Pitcher, water, ½ gallon	65.00	4½"d	15.00
Plate, round		Footed	
7"d	20.00	3½"d	15.00
9"d	25.00	4"d	15.00
10"d, inscribed "A Good Mother		4½"d	15.00
Makes A Good Home"	25.00	Spoonholder	25.00
Relish tray, 9"l	10.00	Sugar bowl, covered	50.00
Sauce dish, round		Wine	45.00

STARS AND STRIPES

Wine.

OMN: Federal's No. 209 & 1903, Climax [Kokomo], Kokomo No. 209. AKA: Brilliant, Late Climax.

Non-flint. Kokomo Glass Manufacturing Co. (pattern line No. 209), Kokomo, IN. ca. 1899. The Federal Glass Co. (pattern lines No. 209 and No. 1903), Columbus, OH. ca. 1914. Illustrated in he Montgomery Ward 1899 catalog as "Brilliant."

Original color production: Clear. Odd pieces may be found in milk white. Handles are pressed.

Reproductions: None.

References: Bong-AG (P. 112), Kam-2 (P. 70), McCn-PGP (P. 171), Mig-TPS (Pl. 4), Mtz-1 (P. 198), Pet-Sal (Pl. 173).

Items made	Clear	Items made	Clear
Bowl		Creamer	15.00
Berry, master, round, open, flat	20.00	Cruet set, complete	35.00
Fruit, square, open, flat	15.00	Cup, custard	5.00
Butter dish, covered	20.00	Goblet	20.00
Celery vase	15.00	Pitcher, water, ½ gallon	40.00
Cordial	15.00	Salt shaker, original top	15.00

Items made	Clear	Items made	Clear
Sauce dish, flat		Sugar bowl, covered	20.00
Round	5.00	Tumbler, water, flat	15.00
Square	5.00	Vase	10.00
Spoonholder	15.00	Wine	20.00

STATES, THE

Individual sugar bowl; jelly dish; pickle tray; individual creamer.

OMN: U.S. Glass No. 15,093. AKA: Cane and Star Medallion [Metz].

Non-flint. The United States Glass Co. (pattern line No. 15,093), Pittsburgh, PA. ca. 1905. Illustrated in the Butler Brothers Fall, 1910 catalog.

Original color production: Clear (plain or with gilt). Odd items may be found in emerald green, although a complete table setting was not produced in this color.

Reproductions: None

References: Bat-GPG (PP. 139-140), Hart/Cobb-SS (P. 77), Hea-1 (PP. 50, 52, Fig. 384), Hea-3 (P. 80), Hea-5 (PP. 13, 23), Hea-TPS (PP. 76, 85), Kam-5 (PP. 142-143), Mtz-1 (PP. 214-215), Mil-2 (Pl. 69), Pet-Sal (P. 41), Rev-APG (P. 318), Spil-AEPG (P. 337), Uni-2 (P. 116).

Items made	Clear	Items made	Clear
Bowl, open, round, flat		Table size, round	30.00
Non-handled, 9¼"d	30.00	Cup, punch	10.00
Tri-handled, 7"d	30.00	Dish, jelly, flat	15.00
Butter dish, covered, 8¼"d	65.00	Goblet	35.00
Celery		Pickle tray, oblong	15.00
Tray	20.00	Pitcher, water, ½ gallon, pressed	
Vase	20.00	handle	45.00
Cocktail glass	25.00	Plate, round, 10"d	35.00
Compote, open, high standard, round		Punch bowl set, bowl (13"d) with 8	
7"d	35.00	cups, complete	125.00
9"d	50.00	Relish tray, diamond shape	25.00
Creamer, pressed handle		Salt shaker, original top	15.00
Individual, oval	15.00	Sauce dish, flat, tub shape, 4"d	15.00

Items made	Clear	Items made	Clear
Spoonholder	25.00	Toothpick holder, flat, rectangular	45.00
Sugar bowl		Tray, 7¼" x 5½"	20.00
Individual, open	15.00	Tumbler, water, flat	25.00
Table size, covered	40.00	Wine	30.00
Syrup pitcher, original top	65.00		

STIPPLED CHAIN

Goblet.

Non-flint. Gillinder & Sons, Philadelphia, PA. ca. 1880.

Original color production: Clear. Handles are applied.

Reproductions: None. Milk white or any other color is rare.

References: Brn-SD (P. 51), Kam-8 (P. 74), Lee-EAPG (Pl. 190), Lee-VG (Pl. 22, No. 5), Mil-1 (Pl. 98), Mtz-1 (PP. 182-183). Uni-2 (P. 36), Wlkr-PGA (Fig. 8, Nos. 24, 37).

Items made	Clear	Items made	Clear
Bowl, flat, open, round	25.00	Pitcher, water, ½ gallon	65.00
Butter dish, covered	50.00	Relish dish, flat	15.00
Cake stand, high standard	45.00	Salt, master, open, footed	15.00
Celery vase	40.00	Sauce dish, round	
Creamer	35.00	Flat, 4"d	15.00
Dish, flat, oval, open	15.00	Footed, 4"d	20.00
Egg cup, single, pedestaled	25.00	Spoonholder	25.00
Goblet	30.00	Sugar bowl, covered	40.00
Pickle tray, flat	15.00	Tumbler, water, flat	20.00

Tumbler; creamer; spoonholder; covered butter dish.

AKA: Double Loop [Lee].

Non-flint. Maker unknown, ca. 1870s.

Original color production: Clear. Handles are pressed.

Reproductions: None.

References: Enos-MPG (Chart-4), Lee-EAPG (Pl. 101), Mtz-1 (P. 178), Spil-AEPG (P. 269), Uni-2 (P. 26).

Items made	Clear	Items made	Clear
Butter dish, covered, flat	35.00	Sauce dish, round, flat	8.00
Celery vase	20.00	Spoonholder, footed, scalloped rim ...	15.00
Creamer, footed	20.00	Sugar bowl, covered	25.00
Pitcher, water, ½ gallon	35.00	Tumbler, water, flat	20.00

STIPPLED FORGET-ME-NOT

Cup; saucer.

AKA: Dot, Forget-Me-Not in Snow.

Non-flint. Findlay Flint Glass Co., Findlay, OH. ca. 1890s. Shards have been found at the site of the Model Glass Co., Findlay, OH. ca. 1891.

Original color production: Clear. Amber, blue, milk white, opal or any other color is rare.

Reproductions: None.

References: Smth-FPG (PP. 32-33), Meas/Smth-FG (PP. 133-134), Hrtng-P&P (P. 83), Kam-4 (PP. 126-127), Lee-EAPG (Pl. 128, No. 3), Lee-VG (P. 22), Kam-4 (PP. 126-127), McCn-PGP (P. 285), Mil-1 (Pl. 93), Mil-OG (Pl. 213), Mtz-1 (P. 57), Mtz-2 (PP. 62-63), Pet-Sal (P. 40), Rev-APG (P. 90), Stu-BP (P. 30), Uni-2 (P. 184), Wlkr-PGA (Fig. 8, No. 38).

Items made	Clear	Items made	Clear
Bowl, open, round, flat		6"d	25.00
Berry, master, 7"d	50.00	7"d	25.00
Waste	35.00	8"d	30.00
Butter dish, covered	50.00	Cordial	85.00
Cake stand		Creamer table size, pressed handle	35.00
9"d	35.00	Cup, handled	20.00
10"d	75.00	Dish, oblong	15.00
12"d	85.00	Goblet	45.00
Celery vase, 8"h	35.00	Lamp, oil, squatty, handled	95.00
Child's miniatures		Mug, collared base	30.00
Butter dish, covered	100.00	Pitcher, pressed handle	
Creamer	85.00	Milk, 1 quart	45.00
Mug	65.00	Water, ½ gallon	55.00
Spoonholder	90.00	Plate, round	
Sugar bowl, covered	125.00	6"d	30.00
Compote, round		7"d	
Covered, high standard		"Baby Face" center	55.00
6"d	65.00	"Star" center	35.00
7"d	65.00	8"d	30.00
8"d	85.00	9"d	
Open, low standard		Kitten center	55.00

Items made	Clear	Items made	Clear
"Star" center	55.00	Saucer	10.00
Relish dish, oval	15.00	Spoonholder, table size	35.00
Salt		Sugar bowl, covered, table size	45.00
Master		Syrup pitcher, original top	90.00
Oval, flat, open, interlaced design		Toothpick holder, hat shape	100.00
in base	35.00	Tray, water (aquatic bird and wildlife	
Round, footed. open	30.00	scene)	50.00
Sauce dish, round		Tumbler, water, flat	35.00
Flat	10.00	Wine	35.00
Footed	15.00		

STIPPLED GRAPE AND FESTOON

Goblet; creamer.

OMN: Doyle's No. 28, R&B Pattern. AKA: Clear Leaf.

Non-flint. Doyle & Co. (pattern line No. 28), Pittsburgh, PA. ca. 1870. Reissued by the United States Glass Co., Pittsburgh, PA. ca. 1890s. Shards have been found at the site of the Boston & Sandwich Glass Co., Sandwich, MA.

Original color production: Clear. Finals are well defined acorns. Handles are applied.

Reproductions: None.

References: Kam-7 (P. 114), Mtz-1 (P. 78), Mil-1 (Pl. 51), Pet-GPP (PP. 161-162), Rev-APG (PP. 140, 318), Uni-1 (P. 244), Uni-2 (P. 82).

Items made	Clear	Items made	Clear
Bowl, open, oval, flat		Tray	35.00
5″	25.00	Vase, pedestaled, scalloped rim	40.00
6″	25.00	Compote, round	
7″	25.00	Covered	
Butter dish, covered, flat		High standard	
Flanged rim	60.00	6″d	45.00
Plain rim	45.00	8″d	65.00
Celery		Low standard	

Items made	Clear	Items made	Clear
6″d	35.00	Pitcher, bulbous, applied handle	
8″d	45.00	Milk, ¼ gallon	75.00
9″d	55.00	Water, ½ gallon	100.00
Open, low standard	30.00	Plate, 6″d	35.00
Cordial.	30.00	Relish tray, oval	30.00
Creamer, pedestaled, applied handle	50.00	Sauce dish, flat, round, 4″d	10.00
Egg cup, single, pedestaled	35.00	Spoonholder, pedestaled, scalloped rim	30.00
Goblet	35.00	Sugar bowl, covered, pedestaled	65.00
Pickle tray	30.00	Wine	45.00

STIPPLED STAR

Open sugar bowl; celery vase; spoonholder.

OMN: Gillinder's Star.

Non-flint. Gillinder & Sons, Philadelphia, PA. ca. 1870. Designed and patented by William F. Gillinder, March 22, 1870 (design patent No. 3,914).

Original color production: Clear. Blue or any other color is rare. Handles are applied.

Reproductions: The L.G. Wright Glass Co., New Martinsville, WV. (distributed by Jennings Red Barn, New Martinsville, WV. and Carl Forslund, Grand Rapids, MI.) reproduced the following items, from new molds, in amber, amethyst, blue, clear, green and ruby red: round, footed 2″h salt, goblet, creamer, salt dip, covered sugar bowl, and the covered high standard covered compote.

By 1974, the L.G. Wright master catalog listed the following reissues: goblet (amber, amberina, blue, clear, ruby), individual 2⅞″d. salt (not original to the set), master salt (amber, amethyst, blue, green), and the wine (amber, blue, clear, green, ruby). Produced from new molds, reissues are heavier and coarser than the originals.

References: Bat-GPG (PP. 37-38), Gor-CC (PP. 32, 105), Hea-OS (P. 60, No. 881), Lee-EAPG (Pl. 147, No. 4), McCn-PGP (P. 503), Mil-1 (Pl. 38), Mtz-1 (PP. 116-117), Rev-APG (PP. 166-167), Uni-1 (PP. 286-287), Wlkr-PGA (Fig. 8, Nos. 7, 37, 45).

Items made	Clear	Items made	Clear
Butter dish, covered	45.00	Round	
Celery vase, pedestaled, scalloped rim	40.00	5″d	20.00
Compote, high standard		6″d	20.00
Covered, round	75.00	Egg cup, pedestaled	35.00
Open		Goblet	40.00
Deep bowl		Pickle dish	20.00
7″d	40.00	Pitcher, water, ½ gallon	90.00
8″d	45.00	Sauce dish, round	
Shallow bowl		Flat, 4″d	15.00
7″d	40.00	Footed, 4″d	20.00
8″d	45.00	Spoonholder, pedestaled, scalloped	
Creamer, pedestaled, applied handle	55.00	rim, 5½″h	30.00
Dish, open, flat		Sugar bowl, covered, pedestaled	55.00
Oval, preserve, 8″	20.00	Wine	35.00

STRAWBERRY

Goblet; water tumbler.

OMN: Strawberry. AKA: Fairfax Strawberry.

Non-flint. Bryce, Walker & Co., Pittsburgh, PA. ca. 1870. Shards have been found at the site of the Boston & Sandwich Glass Co., Sandwich, MA. and the Burlington Glass Works, Hamilton, Ontario, Canada. Designed and patented by John Bryce, February 22, 1870 (patent No. 3,855).

Original color production: Clear and milk white, the main pattern design element consisting of realistically sculptured strawberries and leaves. Finials of covered items are large strawberries. Handles are applied. Unlike the Blackberry pattern, the same molds were most likely used to produced both the clear and milk white version of Strawberry as little if any size variation exists.

Reproductions: None.

References: Belnp-MG (P. 132), Brn-SD (PP. 48-49), Cod-OS (P. 15), Enos-MPG (Chart-5), Fer-YMG (P. 151), Hlms-BCA (P. 278), Kam-5 (PP. 7-8), Kam/Wod-Vol.2 (P. 548), Lee-EAPG (Pl. 151, No. 3), McCn-PGP (Pl. 158), Mil-1 (Pl. 31), Mil-OG (Pl. 174), Mtz-1 (PP. 88-89), Pet-

GPP (PP. 55-56), Rev-APG (PP. 73, 82), Spil-AEPG (P. 286), Spil-TBV (P. 244), Uni-1 (PP. 230-231), Uni/Wor-CHPGT (P. 205), Wlkr-PGA (Fig. 15, Nos. 216-217).

Items made	Clear
Bowl, open, oval, flat, smooth rim	20.00
Butter dish, covered, flat, 7"d	65.00
Celery vase, pedestaled, scalloped rim	45.00
Compote, covered, round	
High standard, 8"d	100.00
Low standard, 9"d	85.00
Creamer, pedestaled, applied handle,	
5³/₄"h	55.00
Egg cup, single	35.00
Goblet	35.00
Honey dish, flat, round	20.00
Pickle tray, tapered at one end, 8¹/₂" x	
4³/₄"	20.00

Items made	Clear
Pitcher, water, bulbous, applied	
handle, ¹/₂ gallon	125.00
Relish tray, oval	15.00
Salt, master, open, footed	30.00
Sauce dish, flat, round	15.00
Spoonholder, pedestaled, scalloped rim	35.00
Sugar bowl, covered	45.00
Syrup pitcher, 6⁵/₈"h (original lid	
marked (Collins & Wright Jug	
Top Pat. No. 42,712) Pat May 10,	
'64	125.00
Tumbler, water, flat	40.00
Wine	40.00

STRAWBERRY AND CURRANT

Goblet.

OMN: Dalzell No. 9D. AKA: Currant and Strawberry, Multiple Fruits.

Non-flint. Dalzell, Gillmore & Leighton (pattern line No. 9D), Findlay, OH. ca. 1890s.

Original color production: Clear.

Reproductions: The first reproduction of Strawberry & Currant pattern was the clear goblet produced from a new mold ca. 1940. Unlike the original, the look alike has poor detail in the leaves and berries.

The L.G. Wright Glass Co. 1970 catalog supplement illustrates the following look-alikes in clear: high standard crimped edge open compote (not an original form), goblet, and the wine. By 1971 the company illustrated the goblet in amber satin and vaseline and by 1974 the master catalog illustrated the high standard ruffled rim compote in amber, amethyst, blue, cobalt, green, ruby and vaseline.

References: Drep-ABC OG (P. 149), Lee-EAPG (Pl. 151, No. 1), Mil-1 (Pl. 71), Mtz-1 (PP. 82-83), Uni-1 9(P. 233), Wlkr-PGA (Fig. 15, No. 66).

Items made	Clear	Items made	Clear
Butter dish, covered	50.00	Pitcher	
Celery vase	35.00	Milk, 1 quart	40.00
Cheese dish, covered	50.00	Water, ¹/₂ gallon	50.00
Compote, high standard, round		Sauce dish, footed, round	10.00
Covered	70.00	Spoonholder	30.00
Open	35.00	Sugar bowl, covered	45.00
Creamer	40.00	Syrup pitcher, original top	100.00
Goblet	35.00	Tumbler, water, flat	25.00
Mug, applied handle	35.00		

STRIGIL

Wine; cylindrical vase; table creamer; spoonholder; breakfast creamer.

AKA: Caramel Strigil, Nelly.

Non-flint. McKee Brothers, Pittsburgh, PA. ca. 1892.

Original color production: Clear. Handles are pressed.

Reproductions: None.

References: Hea-6 (P. 78), Hea-OS (P. 135, No. 2563), Herr-GG (P. 32, Fig. 253), Kam-2 (PP. 83-84), Kam-5 (P. 39), Kam-6 (Plts. 4-5), McCn-PGP (P. 463), Meas-GG (P. 85), Pet-Sal (P. 138), Rev-APG (P. 238), Stot-McKe (PP. 119, 424).

Items made	Clear	Items made	Clear
Bowl, round		Compote, open, high standard, round	25.00
Berry, master, open, flat, 8"d	20.00	Creamer	
Waste, open, flat	15.00	Breakfast, squatty, 3⁷/₈"h	15.00
Butter dish, covered	35.00	Table size, tall	25.00
Celery		Cruet, original stopper	25.00
Tray	25.00	Cup, custard	15.00
Vase	15.00	Egg cup, single	20.00

Items made	Clear	Items made	Clear
Goblet	40.00	Spoonholder	15.00
Pitcher		Sugar bowl, covered	30.00
Milk, 1 quart	30.00	Tumbler, water, flat	25.00
Water, ¹/₂ gallon	40.00	Vase, cylindrical	20.00
Salt dip, single	5.00	Wine	20.00
Sauce dish, flat, round	5.00		

SUNFLOWER

Covered butter dish; creamer.

OMN: Atterbury's Lily.

Non-flint. Atterbury & Co., Pittsburgh, PA. ca. 1872. Shards have been found at the site of the Burlington Glass Works, Hamilton, Ontario, Canada.

Original color production: Amber, clear, milk white. Odd items may be found in opaque blue and purple slag. Handles are pressed.

Reproductions: None.

References: Belnp-MG (PP. 92, 317), Fer-YMG (PP. 58, 63), Inn-PG (P. 353), Kam-1 (P.55), Kam/Wod-Vol.2 (P. 552), Lee-EAPG (Pl. 108, No. 2), Lee-VG (Pl. 93), McCn-PGP (Pl. 132), Mil-OG (Pl. 180), Mtz-1 (PP. 60-61), Pet-GPP (P. 20), Rev-APG (P. 29), Uni/Wor-CHPGT (P. 207).

Items made	Amber	Clear	Milk White
Bowl, open, round, flat	35.00	25.00	45.00
Butter dish, covered	80.00	55.00	110.00
Creamer, 4¹/₂"h	60.00	40.00	80.00
Pitcher, water, ¹/₂ gallon	75.00	60.00	45.00
Spoonholder, flat	40.00	30.00	45.00
Sugar bowl, covered	55.00	50.00	75.00

High standard open compote; bread tray ("bearded" head handles).

Spoonholder; 4"d. footed sauce.

AKA: Plain Swan, Swan with Mesh.

Non-flint. Attributed to the Canton Glass Co., Canton, OH. ca. 1882.

Original color production: Clear, amber, blue or canary-yellow. Designed and patented by David Barker (patent No. 12,887) April 18, 1882 and assigned to Charles G. Summers, Baltimore, MD. who worked for the Canton Glass Co. Finials are in the shape of finely sculptured swans. Handles are pressed.

Reproductions: Both the creamer and covered sugar bowl have been reproduced from new molds in milk white. New items are heavier than the old, and lack the refined detail of workmanship.

References: Drep-ABC OG (P. 157), Kam-1 (P. 63), Lee-EAPG (Pl. 77, No. 3), McCn-PGP (P. 31), Mil-1 (Pl. 17), Mtz-1 (PP. 104-105), Mtz-2 (P. 86), Pet-GPP (PP. 37-38), Rev-APG (PP. 104-105), Uni-2 (P. 202), Wlkr-PGA (Fig. 8, No. 16).

Items made	Amber	Blue	Canary	Clear
Butter dish, covered, swan finial	175.00	200.00	175.00	125.00
Compote, high standard, round				
Covered, swan finial	200.00	250.00	225.00	150.00
Open	145.00	175.00	145.00	100.00
Creamer, 6″h	90.00	110.00	90.00	60.00
Dish, oval, covered, flat	100.00	125.00	100.00	80.00
Goblet	100.00	135.00	100.00	85.00
Pickle jar, covered, swan finial	125.00	150.00	125.00	100.00
Pitcher, water, ½ gallon	175.00	200.00	175.00	150.00
Plate, bread, oval with "Bearded Head" handles.	—	—	—	85.00
Sauce dish				
Flat, 4″d	30.00	35.00	30.00	20.00
Footed, 4″d	30.00	35.00	30.00	20.00
Spoonholder, double handled	60.00	75.00	60.00	45.00
Sugar bowl, covered, double handled	175.00	200.00	175.00	125.00
Wine (R)	90.00	110.00	90.00	65.00

TACOMA

Toothpick holder; creamer; cruet (n.o.s.); bouquet vase; covered sugar bowl; spoonholder.

OMN: Tacoma. AKA: Model No. 907. AKA: Jewelled Diamond and Fan, Triple X.

Non-flint. Greensburg Glass Co., Greensburg, PA. ca. 1894, with continued production at the National Glass combine's Model Flint Glass Co., Albany, IN. ca. 1900 (the molds being transferred to Model by National after the closing of the Greensburg plant). Illustrated in the ca. 1901 Model Flint Glass Co. catalog as "No. 907".

Original color production: Clear, clear with ruby stain. Odd items may be found in clear with amber stain, and emerald green although complete table sets were not produced in these colors. Handles are generally applied.

Reproductions: None.

References: Bar-RS (Pl. 8), Bond-AG (PP. 25-30), Hea-1 (P. 46, Fig. 345), Hea-6 (P. 44, Fig. 357), Hea-7 (P. 200), Hea-3 (P. 57, Fig. 452), Hea-TPS (PP. 27, 46, 52), Inn-PG (P. 381), Kam-5 (P. 50), Kam-6 (P. 46), McCn-PGP (P. 193), Pet-Sal (P. 175-"A"), Rev-APG (PP. 172-173).

Items made	Clear	Clear w/Ruby
Bowl, open		
Oval, flat		
9″	25.00	65.00
10″	30.00	65.00
Round		
Berry		
7″d	25.00	45.00
8″d	25.00	55.00
Finger or waste, smooth rim	15.00	35.00
Punch		
Flat		
12″d	65.00	—
15″d	85.00	—
Pedestaled (plain or six paneled)		
12″d	80.00	—
15″d	90.00	—
Rose		
3½″	15.00	40.00
4½″	20.00	45.00
5½″	25.00	55.00
6½″	30.00	65.00
Square, flat		
7″	20.00	65.00
8″	25.00	65.00
Banana dish, flat	35.00	90.00
Butter dish, covered, flat, flanged base	45.00	125.00
Cake stand, high standard		
9″d	35.00	135.00
10″d	45.00	145.00
Carafe	30.00	165.00
Celery		
Tray	25.00	60.00
Vase	25.00	90.00
Compote, open, high standard		
Round		
Deep bowl		
7″d	45.00	175.00
8″d	45.00	175.00
Shallow bowl, 10″d	65.00	175.00
Square bowl		
7″	55.00	200.00
8″	55.00	200.00
Cracker jar, covered		
5″	50.00	—
6″	50.00	—
Creamer.	30.00	65.00
Cruet, original stopper		
Small	25.00	125.00
Large	25.00	125.00
Decanter, wine, original faceted stopper	50.00	150.00
Dish		
Oblong		
7″	15.00	—
8″	15.00	—
Round, ice cream, 5″d	15.00	—
Goblet	25.00	65.00
Pickle jar, covered	45.00	125.00

Items made	Clear	Clear w/Ruby
Pitcher, water		
Bulbous, $^1/_2$ gallon	35.00	175.00
Tankard, $^1/_2$ gallon	45.00	175.00
Plate, for finger bowl	20.00	—
Salt		
Dip		
Individual	10.00	35.00
Master	20.00	55.00
Shaker, original top		
Straight sided	15.00	35.00
Tapered	15.00	35.00
Sauce dish, flat		
Round		
4″d	10.00	20.00
4$^1/_2$″d	10.00	20.00
Square		
4″	10.00	20.00
4$^1/_2$″	10.00	20.00
Spoonholder	20.00	55.00
Sugar bowl, covered	35.00	100.00
Syrup pitcher, original top		
Squatty	45.00	200.00
Tall	45.00	200.00
Toothpick holder	25.00	200.00
Tumbler, water, flat	20.00	40.00
Vase		
Swung		
8″h	25.00	—
11″h	35.00	—
Trumpet		
8″h	25.00	—
10″h	25.00	—
Wine	20.00	45.00

High standard shallow compote; syrup.

OMN: U.S. Glass No. 15,064, Tennessee. AKA: Jewel and Crescent, Jewelled Rosette(s) [Kamm], Scrolls with Bulls Eye.

Non-flint. The United States Glass Co. (pattern line No. 15,064), Pittsburgh, PA. at Factory "K" (King Glass Co., Pittsburgh, PA.) ca. 1899.

Original color production: Clear (with or without colored jewels). Handles are pressed.

Reproductions: None.

References: Hart/Cobb-SS (P. 61), Hea-5 (P. 147), Hea-TPS (PP. 77, 86), Kam-3 (PP. 62-63), McCn-PGP (P. 113), Mig-TPS (Pl. 3), Mil-2 (Pl. 50), Pet-GPP (PP. 182-184), Pet-Sal (P. 175), Pyne-PG (P. 155), Rev-APG (P. 318), Stu-BP (P. 68), Uni-2 (P. 243).

Items made	Clear	Items made	Clear
Bowl, master berry, open, round, flat	20.00	Creamer	25.00
Butter dish, covered	40.00	Goblet	35.00
Cake stand, high standard		Mug, handled	35.00
8½"d	35.00	Pitcher	
9½"d	40.00	Milk, 1 quart	55.00
10½"d	45.00	Water, ¼ gallon	65.00
Celery vase	25.00	Plate, bread	40.00
Compote, round		Relish tray	20.00
Covered, high standard, 5"d., jelly	50.00	Salt shaker, original top (VR)	65.00
Open		Sauce dish, flat, round	15.00
High standard, flared rim, shallow		Spoonholder	35.00
bowl		Sugar bowl, covered	45.00
7"d	35.00	Syrup pitcher, original top	125.00
8"d	40.00	Toothpick holder	85.00
9"d	45.00	Tumbler, water, flat	40.00
10"d	45.00	Wine	65.00
Low standard, 7"d	35.00		

Juice tumbler; water tumbler; lemonade tumbler; champagne; claret; bar tumbler.

Relish tray.

OMN: Duncan's No. 28, Arizona. AKA: Nemesis, Tee Pee, Wigwam.

Non-flint. George Duncan's Sons & Co. (pattern line No. 28), Washington, PA. ca. 1896. Illustrated in *China, Glass and Lamps* in 1894.

Original color production: Clear. Clear with ruby stain or any other color is rare.

Reproductions: None.

References: Bat-GPG (PP. 96, 99), Hart/Cobb-SS (P. 13), Hea-3 (P. 86), Hea-OS (P. 135, No. 2539), Kam-2 (P. 78), Kam-5 (P. 94), Kam-6 (Pl. 56), McCn-PGP (P. 201), Migh-TPS (Pl. 20), Mil-1 (Pl. 23), Mil-2 (Pl. 128), Rev-APG (P. 151), Uni-2 (P. 306).

Items made	Clear	Items made	Clear
Bowl, master berry, open, round, flat	18.00	Celery vase	30.00
Butter dish, covered	40.00	Champagne	35.00
Carafe, water	40.00	Claret	25.00

Items made	Clear	Items made	Clear
Compote, open, high standard, jelly, round	20.00	Spoonholder	25.00
Creamer, 4¼"h	30.00	Sugar bowl, covered	35.00
Cup, custard	8.00	Syrup pitcher, original top	45.00
Goblet	35.00	Toothpick holder	30.00
Pitcher, water, ½ gallon	40.00	Tumbler	
Relish tray	10.00	Bar	15.00
Sauce dish, flat, round	5.00	Juice	15.00
Salt		Lemonade	15.00
Dip, individual, 1¼"d	15.00	Water	15.00
Shaker, original top	25.00	Wine	30.00

TEXAS States Series

Wine; cruet (no stopper); 9"h vase; cake stand; spoonholder.

OMN: U.S. Glass No. 15,067, Texas. AKA: Loop with Stippled Panels [Brothers, Millard].

Non-flint. United States Glass Co. (pattern line No. 15,067), Pittsburgh, PA. at Factory "K" (King Glass Co., Pittsburgh, PA.) ca. 1900. Illustrated in the 1904 and 1908 United States Glass Co. catalogs, and the Butler Brothers 1912 catalog.

Original color production: Clear, clear with rose stain (plain or with gilt). Clear with ruby stain or any other color is rare. Handles are applied or pressed.

Reproductions: Both the Crystal Art Glass Co., Cambridge, OH. and the Boyd Glass Co. Cambridge, OH., reproduced from new molds the individual creamer and open sugar bowl in a myriad of colors, including solids, opaque, and opalescent.

References: Bar-RS (Pl. 14), Bros-TS (P. 42), Hart/Cobb-SS (P. 62), Hea-1 (P. 48, Fig. 359), Hea-3 (P. 87), Hea-5 (P. 173), Hea-7 (P. 201), Hea-TPS (P. 101), Inn-PG (P. 145), Kam-2 (P. 58), Kam-8 (P. 245), Lee-VG (Pl. 27, No. 4), McCn-PGP (PP. 445, 577), Mig-TPS (Pl. 30), Mil-2 (Pl. 44), Mtz-1 (P. 212), Oliv-AAG (P. 74), Pet-Sal (P. 41), Pyne-PG (P. 145), Rev-APG (P. 318), Uni-1 (PP. 124-125), Uni-2 (P. 245), Wlkr-PGA (Fig. 8, Nos. 36, 45).

Items made	Clear	Clear w/Rose Stain
Bottle, water	85.00	150.00
Bowl, round		
Covered		
Low circular foot		
6″d	75.00	100.00
7″d	85.00	125.00
8″d	95.00	140.00
Open		
Flat, scalloped rim, 8″d	35.00	75.00
Low circular foot		
Flared		
Scalloped, rim		
7½″d	35.00	65.00
8½″d	35.00	75.00
9½″d	35.00	85.00
Smooth rim		
7½″d	35.00	65.00
8½″d	35.00	75.00
9½″d	35.00	85.00
Straight-sided bowl, scalloped rim		
6″d	25.00	55.00
7″d.	30.00	60.00
8″d	35.00	65.00
Bread tray	35.00	85.00
Butter dish, covered, flat	75.00	125.00
Cake stand, high standard, turned up gallery rim		
9″d	65.00	125.00
9½″d	65.00	125.00
10″d	75.00	135.00
10½″d	75.00	135.00
11″d	75.00	135.00
Celery		
Tray, oblong, flat, tab handles, 11½″ x 4¾″	30.00	50.00
Vase, low circular foot, scalloped rim	45.00	85.00
Compote, high standard, round		
Covered		
6″d	75.00	125.00
7″d	85.00	150.00
8″d	95.00	175.00
Open		
Smooth, flared rim		
7½″d	45.00	85.00
8½″d	55.00	100.00
9½″d	65.00	125.00
Smooth, straight rim, 5″d., jelly	45.00	75.00
Creamer, applied handle, low circular foot		
Individual, 3⅛″h	20.00	45.00
Table size	45.00	90.00
Cruet, original patterned stopper	125.00	250.00
Dish, round, open, flat, scalloped rim, 8″d (termed the "preserve")	35.00	65.00
Goblet	100.00	150.00
Horse radish, covered, notched lid (originally the individual sugar bowl)	85.00	125.00
Olive dish, oblong, flat, scalloped rim	20.00	40.00
Pickle tray, oblong, tab handles, 8½″l	65.00	85.00
Pitcher, water		
Bulbous, applied handle, ½ gallon	250.00	450.00
Straight-sided, inverted design, pressed handle, 3 pints	150.00	450.00

Items made	Clear	Clear w/Rose Stain
Plate, round, 9″d., scalloped rim	45.00	75.00
Relish tray	25.00	45.00
Salt		
Master, footed	50.00	85.00
Shaker, original top (R)		
Hotel, tall	85.00	125.00
Table size, squatty	85.00	125.00
Sauce dish, round		
Flat		
Round bowl, flared rim, 4½″d	15.00	25.00
Straight-sided bowl, 4″d.		
Scalloped rim	10.00	22.00
Smooth rim	10.00	22.00
Footed		
Round bowl, smooth rim, 4″d	15.00	30.00
Straight-sided bowl, flared rim, 5″d	15.00	30.00
Spoonholder	45.00	85.00
Sugar bowl, covered		
Individual	25.00	—
Table size	75.00	125.00
Syrup pitcher, original top	150.00	350.00
Toothpick holder	35.00	150.00
Tumbler, water, flat, inverted design	65.00	100.00
Vase		
6½″h	25.00	—
8″h	30.00	—
9″h	35.00	—
10″h	40.00	—
Wine	85.00	150.00

TEXAS BULLS EYE

Tumbler; goblet; wine.

OMN: Beatty No. 1221 (tumbler only), Bryce's Filley. AKA: Bulls Eye Variant [Lee], Notched Bulls Eye.

Non-flint. Bryce Brothers, Pittsburgh, PA. ca. 1875-1880. A.J. Beatty & Sons, Steubenville, OH. ca. 1888. Reissued by the United States Glass Co., Pittsburgh, PA. after 1891. Diamond Glass Co., Ltd., Montreal, Quebec, Canada ca. 1902. Shards have been found at the site of the Burlington Glass Works, Hamilton, Ontario, Canada. Illustrated in the 1902 Diamond Glass Co., Ltd. catalog, Montreal, Quebec, Canada, the ca. 1875-1880 Bryce Brothers catalog as "Filley", and the ca. 1891 United States Glass Co. catalog of member firms.

Original color production: Clear.

Reproductions: None.

References: Hart/Cobb-SS (P. 63), Hea-5 (P. 86), Hlms-BCA (PP. 278, 281), Kam-7 (Plts. 2, 103), Kam/Wod-Vol.1 (P. 248), Knit-EAG (Pl. 38), Lee-EAPG (Pl. 50, No. 2), Mil-1 (Pl. 156), McCn-PGP (Pl. 19), Mtz-1 (PP. 208-209), Rev-APG (P. 87), Spnc-ECG (P. 72), Stev-ECG (PP. 107, 109), Stev-ECG (Fig. 171), Thu-1 (P. 167), Uni-1 (PP. 56-57), Uni-TCG (P. 110), Uni/Wor-CHPGT (P. 123), Wlkr-PGA (Fig. 8, Nos. 1, 2, 18, 51).

Items made	Clear	Items made	Clear
Bottle, castor	65.00	Goblet	30.00
Butter dish, covered	50.00	Lamp, oil, pedestaled base, 5½"h	85.00
Castor set, complete in silver plate		Pitcher, water, ½ gallon	55.00
holder	150.00	Sauce dish, flat, round	5.00
Celery vase	35.00	Spoonholder	25.00
Champagne, 5"h	40.00	Sugar bowl, covered	45.00
Cordial	35.00	Tumbler, water, flat, 3¾"h	30.00
Creamer	35.00	Wine, 3⁹⁄₁₆"h	35.00
Egg cup, pedestaled	35.00		

THISTLE

High standard open compote; goblet.

AKA: Early Thistle, Scotch Thistle.

Non-flint. Bryce, McKee & Co., Pittsburgh, PA. ca. 1872. Shards have been found at the site of the Burlington Glass Works, Hamilton, Ontario, Canada.

Creamer; water pitcher.

Original color production: Clear. Designed and patented by John Bryce, April 2, 1872, design patent No. 5,742, the design "A Scotch thistle, consisting of the stems, leaves and flowers, so connected and repeated as to form a wreath" covering the article.

Reproductions: None.

References: Lee-EAPG (Pl. 140, No. 2), McCn-PGP (Pl. 266), Mil-1 (Pl. 132), Mtz-1 (P. 68), Oliv-AAG (P. 74), Pet-Sal (PP. 55-56), Pet-GPP (PP. 55-56), Rev-APG (PP. 82, 90), Spil-AEPG (P. 286), Stev-ECG (Figs. 236-237), Uni-1 (P. 209), Uni/Wor-CHPGT (P. 212), Wlkr-PGA (Fig. 8, Nos. 46, 58).

Items made	Clear
Bowl, master berry, round, flat, 8"d	
Covered	65.00
Open	30.00
Butter dish, covered, flat, 7"d	65.00
Cake stand, high standard	65.00
Compote	
Covered, high standard	85.00
Open	
High standard	
6"d	45.00
8"d	50.00
Low standard, 8"d	45.00
Cordial	85.00
Creamer, applied handle	65.00
Dish, oval, open, 9" x 6" x 3"	35.00
Egg cup	45.00

Items made	Clear
Goblet	55.00
Pickle dish, tapered at one end	30.00
Pitcher, applied handle	
Milk, 1 quart	125.00
Water, ½ gallon	100.00
Plate, round, 10¾"d	40.00
Relish tray, oval	25.00
Salt, master, open, footed	35.00
Sauce dish, round, flat, 4"d	15.00
Spoonholder	35.00
Sugar bowl, covered	65.00
Syrup pitcher, original top	125.00
Tumbler, water	
Flat	45.00
Footed	45.00
Wine	45.00

THOUSAND EYE

Goblet; celery vase; water pitcher; celery vase; spoonholder.

OMN: Adams No. 130, Richards & Hartley No. 103 (Daisy), AKA: Banded Thousand Eye, Three Knob.

Non-flint. Adams & Co., (pattern line No. 130), Pittsburgh, PA. ca. 1874. Richards & Hartley Glass Co. (pattern line No. 103), Pittsburgh, PA. ca. 1880. Reissued by The United States Glass Co., Pittsburgh, PA. at Factory "A" (Adams & Co., Pittsburgh, PA.) and "E" (Richards & Hartley, Tarentum, PA.) ca. 1891. Shards have been found at the site of the Burlington Glass Works, Hamilton, Ontario, Canada. Illustrated in an undated Adams & Co. catalog.

Original color production: Amber, blue, vaseline, clear, green, opalescent colors. Produced in two distinct forms: a) stems with three knobs (Adams & Co.), and b) plain stems with scalloped feet (Richards & Hartley). Handles are pressed.

Reproductions: Reissued from new molds and in the original colors of amber, blue, clear, apple green, and vaseline, and in the new colors of amberina and amethyst by numerous concerns including the Westmorland Glass Co., Grapeville, PA. The following items have been reissued from as early as 1949: cruet, goblet, mug, oil lamp (amber base, blue font and blue base, amber font), square plates (6", 7", 8½", 10", 14", 18"), toothpick holder, wine, string holder, and tumbler. On reissues, the diamond motif of the pattern is unlike the original as the original is diamond shaped while the new is round and dull to the touch. New colors are harsher and items are heavier than the originals.

Butter dish (square form); 8″d. l.f. covered bowl; footed butter dish (round form); cart master salt.

References: [Adams] Hea-3 (P. 44), Hea-5 (P. 71), Hea-6 (P. 44), Inn-EGP (P. 32), Inn-PG (P. 368), Lee-EAPG (Plts. 137, 146, 158), Lee-VG (Pl. 9), Mil-1 (Pl. 134), Mtz-1 (P. 185), Mtz-2 (P. 100), Rev-APG (P. 22), Stu-BP (P. 74), Thur-11 (P. 262). [Richards and Hartley] Brn-SD (P. 136), Drep-ABC OG (P. 157), Fer-YMG (P. 61), Hea-1 (P. 42), Hea-3 (P. 57), Hea-5 (P. 111), Hea-6 (P. 44), Hea-TPS (PP. 77, 86), Inn-EGP (PP. 32-33), Inn-PG (P. 368), Kam-1 (P. 18), Lee-EAPG (P. 503, Pl. 137), Lee-VG (P. 157), Luc-TG (P. 43), Mil-1 OG (Pl. 8), Pet-Sal (Pl. 42), Rev-APG (P. 22). [Miscellaneous references] Grow-WCG (P. 152, Fig. 23-"4"), Kam/Wod-Vol.2 (P. 574), Mig-TPS (Pl. 20), Mur-CO (P. 14), Mur-MCO (P. 71), Oliv-AAG (P. 74), Stev-ECG (P. 148), Tass-AG (P. 72), Uni/Wor-CHPGT (P. 213).

Items made	Amber	Green	Blue	Clear	Vas
ABC plate, 6″d, clock center	50.00	55.00	50.00	45.00	50.00
Bottle, cologne	25.00	45.00	35.00	20.00	45.00
Bowl					
Carriage shape	—	—	85.00	—	85.00
Round, open, flat					
5″d	35.00	—	40.00	30.00	45.00
6″d	40.00	—	45.00	35.00	50.00
7″d	45.00	—	50.00	40.00	55.00
8″d	45.00	—	50.00	40.00	55.00
Butter dish, covered					
Round					
Flat					
6¼″d	65.00	75.00	70.00	45.00	90.00
7½″d	65.00	75.00	70.00	45.00	90.00
Footed	85.00	95.00	90.00	65.00	110.00
Square, flat	85.00	95.00	90.00	65.00	110.00
Cake stand, high standard					
10″d	50.00	75.00	55.00	30.00	85.00
11″d	50.00	75.00	55.00	30.00	85.00
Celery vase					
Tall, 7″h (2 variations)	40.00	45.00	40.00	30.00	50.00
Hat shape	50.00	65.00	60.00	35.00	55.00
Christmas light	25.00	45.00	35.00	25.00	40.00
Compote, open					
Round					
High standard					
6″d	35.00	40.00	35.00	25.00	35.00
7″d	35.00	40.00	35.00	25.00	35.00

Items made	Amber	Green	Blue	Clear	Vas
8″d	40.00	50.00	45.00	35.00	45.00
9″d	45.00	55.00	50.00	40.00	50.00
10″d	55.00	65.00	60.00	45.00	60.00
Low standard, 8″d	40.00	50.00	45.00	35.00	40.00
Square					
High standard, 8″	40.00	50.00	40.00	35.00	55.00
Low standard, 8″	40.00	50.00	40.00	35.00	55.00
Cordial	35.00	50.00	40.00	25.00	55.00
Creamer, pressed handle					
4″h	30.00	40.00	35.00	25.00	35.00
6″h	35.00	75.00	55.00	35.00	70.00
Cruet					
Original stopper	40.00	60.00	50.00	35.00	60.00
Set (2 cruets on glass stand)	—	—	—	100.00	—
Dish, square, open, flat					
5″	25.00	—	40.00	30.00	45.00
6″	40.00	—	45.00	35.00	50.00
7″	40.00	—	45.00	40.00	55.00
8″	45.00	—	50.00	40.00	60.00
10″	50.00	—	55.00	45.00	65.00
Egg cup, footed	65.00	85.00	70.00	45.00	90.00
Goblet	35.00	40.00	35.00	35.00	45.00
Honey dish, covered, square					
6″ x 7¼″	85.00	85.00	90.00	75.00	90.00
Ink well	45.00	—	75.00	35.00	80.00
Jelly glass	20.00	25.00	20.00	15.00	20.00
Lamp, kerosene, original burner					
High standard					
12″h	125.00	150.00	135.00	100.00	145.00
15″h	125.00	150.00	135.00	100.00	145.00
Low standard, handled	110.00	125.00	100.00	100.00	125.00
Mug					
2″h	20.00	30.00	25.00	20.00	30.00
3″h	20.00	30.00	25.00	20.00	30.00
Pickle dish	25.00	30.00	25.00	20.00	30.00
Pitcher					
Milk, covered, 7″h	85.00	110.00	110.00	75.00	110.00
Water					
¼ gallon	70.00	85.00	80.00	55.00	80.00
½ gallon	80.00	90.00	85.00	65.00	85.00
1 gallon	90.00	100.00	95.00	85.00	95.00
Plate, square, folded corners					
6″	25.00	25.00	25.00	20.00	25.00
8″	25.00	30.00	25.00	20.00	30.00
10″d., bread	35.00	50.00	35.00	25.00	35.00
Platter					
Oblong, 8″ x 11″	40.00	45.00	40.00	35.00	45.00
Oval, 11″	75.00	80.00	55.00	40.00	75.00
Salt					
Individual	80.00	95.00	90.00	50.00	90.00
Master, cart shape, 3½″	40.00	85.00	75.00	30.00	75.00
Shaker, original top					
Banded	60.00	65.00	60.00	55.00	60.00
Plain	50.00	60.00	55.00	40.00	55.00
Sauce dish, round					
Flat, 4″d	10.00	20.00	10.00	8.00	15.00
Footed, 4″d	10.00	25.00	15.00	10.00	20.00
Spoonholder	30.00	45.00	40.00	25.00	45.00
String holder, 4″h., 4¾″h	35.00	60.00	45.00	30.00	40.00

Items made	Amber	Green	Blue	Clear	Vas
Sugar bowl, covered, 5″h	50.00	75.00	60.00	50.00	60.00
Syrup pitcher, original pewter top	80.00	100.00	80.00	55.00	85.00
Toothpick holder					
Hat shape	35.00	50.00	55.00	30.00	45.00
Regular	35.00	50.00	55.00	25.00	40.00
Thimble	55.00	—	—	—	—
Tray, water					
Oval, 14″	65.00	80.00	75.00	60.00	75.00
Round, 12½″d	65.00	70.00	65.00	55.00	60.00
Tumbler, water, flat	25.00	60.00	40.00	20.00	40.00
Wine	35.00	50.00	40.00	20.00	40.00

THREE FACE

Individual salt dip; goblet; h.s. covered compote; celery vase; h.s. covered compote.

OMN: Duncan No. 400. AKA: The Sisters, Three Sisters, Three Graces, Three Fates.

Non-flint. George Duncan and Sons (pattern line No. 400), Pittsburgh, PA. ca. 1878-1886.

Original color production: Clear, clear with acid finish. Designed and patented by John Ernest Miller, June 18, 1878 (design patent No. 10,727), Three Face finials, stems and bases are acid finished, forms being either plain or etched. George Duncan & Sons employed three forms of etching: a) copper wheel engraving, b) plate etching, and c) acid etching.

Reproductions: Reproductions of Three Face appeared as early as the 1930s. These are chalk white and coarse to the touch while the facial design lacks the fine detail of the originals. Later reproductions have better frosting which is smooth and soft to the touch. However, the nose of the new figure is not right, the hairline lacks detail, and the eyes are almost almond shaped, suggestive of an oriental influence.

Several companies reissued the Three Face pattern from new molds, one of the first items reproduced being the champagne ca. 1939-1940. The L.G. Wright Glass Co., New Martinsville, WV. (distributed by Jennings Red Barn, New Martinsville, WV. and Carl Forslund, Grand Rapids, MI.) reproduced the following items in clear with acid finish: footed sauce dish, 6″h. covered compote, 4″d. low standard covered compote,

517

sherbert (not original to the pattern), spoonholder, sugar shaker, toothpick holder, goblet, wine, covered butter dish, high standard cake stand, champagne, claret, $6\frac{1}{2}$"d. high standard covered compote, creamer, lamp, salt dip, salt shaker and covered sugar bowl. By 1970, the L. G. Wright catalog supplement illustrates the salt shaker in the satin colors of amber and blue. By 1974, the L. G. Wright master catalog lists the following reissues in clear with acid finish: 6"d. high standard covered compote, 4"d. low standard covered compote, creamer with man's face under the spout, goblet, salt dip, salt shaker, spoonholder, covered sugar bowl, sugar shaker, toothpick holder and wine.

The Metropolitan Museum of Art, New York City, NY., authorized the Imperial Glass Co., Bellaire, OH., to reproduce from new molds a series of Three Face items, each marked with the museum's "M.M.A." monogram. A.A. Importing Co., Inc., offered the $2\frac{3}{8}$"h toothpick holder in clear with acid finish. Trans-World Trading Co., Robinson, IL., (a firm that imported reproductions and featured items produced by the Summit Art Glass Co., Mogadore/Rootstown, OH.), also distributed many new items in Three Face.

References: Bat-GPG (P. 244), Bons-BDG (PP. 74-76), Bred-EDG (PP. 21, 23, 50-53), Bros-TS (P. 47), Brn-SD (P. 135), Cod-OS (P. 23), Craw-TG (Book), Drep-ABC OG (P. 145), Enos-MPG (Chart-2), Hea-5 (P. 106, Plt. C), Inn-EGP (PP. 32-33), Inn-PG (Pl. 391), Kam-3 (PP. 11-12), Krs-EDG (P. 218), Krs-YD (PP. 63-67), Lee-EAPG (Pl. 89, No. 3), Lee-VG (Pl. 7), McCn-PGP (P. 397), McKrn-AG (PP. 395, 397), Mil-1 (Pl. 149), Mrsh-SRG (P. 244), Mtz-1 (PP. 102-103), Oliv-AAG (P. 77), Pet-Sal (P. 42), Rev-APG (PP. 142-143), Spil-AEPG (P. 279), Spil-TBV (P. 279), Thu-2 (P. 300), Uni-1 (P. 9).

Items made	Clear w/ Frosting	Items made	Clear w/ Frosting
Biscuit jar, covered	500.00	9"d	125.00
Bowl, open		Low standard, smooth rim	
High standard		4"d	135.00
Beaded rim, 6"d	135.00	6"d	135.00
Smooth rim, fluted base	165.00	Open	
Low standard, plain rim, 6"d	90.00	High standard, beaded rim	
Butter dish, covered	150.00	7"d	125.00
Cake stand, high standard		8"d	150.00
9"d	140.00	9"d	175.00
10"d	155.00	Low standard, 6"d	75.00
11"d	175.00	Cordial (VR)	250.00+
Celery vase		Creamer	
Plain, rim	90.00	With face under spout	150.00
Fluted rim	90.00	Without face under spout	125.00
Champagne		Goblet	125.00
Hollow stem	250.00	Lamp, oil, complete with original	
Solid stem	125.00	burner and chimney	
Saucer bowl, solid stem	100.00	#1, pressed design on foot	200.00
Claret	100.00	#2, pressed design on foot	225.00
Compote, round		#3, pressed design on foot	250.00
Covered		#4, peg with #1 collar, plain foot	185.00
High standard		#5, peg with #1 collar, plain foot	200.00
Beaded rim		#6, peg with #1 collar, plain foot	235.00
7"d	150.00	#7, pressed design on foot.	200.00
8"d	150.00	#8, pressed design on foot	235.00
9"d	175.00	#9, pressed design on foot	250.00
10"d	175.00	Marmalade jar, covered	150.00
Plain rim, fluted base		Pitcher, applied handle	
6"d	125.00	Milk, 1 quart	250.00
7"d	125.00	Water, $\frac{1}{2}$ gallon	450.00
8"d	125.00		

Items made	Clear w/ Frosting	Items made	Clear w/ Frosting
Salt		4½"d	35.00
Dip, individual	35.00	Spoonholder	95.00
Shaker, original top	45.00	Sugar bowl, covered	125.00
Sauce dish, footed, round		Wine	200.00
4"d	35.00		

THREE PANEL

Footed sauce 4"d.; creamer; water pitcher; goblet; spoonholder.

OMN: Richards & Hartley No. 25. AKA: Button and Buckle [Stevens], Panelled Thousand Eye, Thousand Eye Three Panel.

Non-flint. The Richards & Hartley Glass Co. (pattern line No. 25), Tarentum, PA. ca. 1880s. Reissued by the United States Glass Co., Pittsburgh, PA. at Factory "E" (Richards & Hartley Glass Co., Tarentum, PA.) ca. 1891. Shards have been found at the site of the Burlington Glass Works, Hamilton, Ontario, Canada.

Original color production: Amber, blue, vaseline, clear. The major design element of Three Panel consists of three panels filled with alternating clear and designed "buttons", each panel separated from the other by two clear vertical bars. Handles are pressed.

Reproductions: As early as 1949, both the goblet and wine have been reissued from new molds in the original colors of amber, blue, canary-yellow and clear. In comparing new items with the old, the foot on new items is too light in weight, while new colors are too harsh.

References: Grow-WCG (P. 134, Fig. 18-"2"), Hea-5 (P. 113, Plts. A-B), Hea-6 (P. 44, Fig. 363), Kam-3 (P. 115), Kam/Wod-Vol. 2 (P. 587), Lee-AF (P. 175), Lee-EAPG (Pl. 159, No. 4), McCn-PGP (Pl. 27), Mil-1 (Pl. 133), Mtz-1 (PP. 158-159), Oliv-AAG (P. 75), Rev-APG (PP. 286-288), Stev-ECG (PP. 148-149), Uni-1 (PP. 264-265), Uni-2 (P. 205), Uni/Wod-CHPGT (P. 214), Uni/Wor-CHPGT (P. 214).

Items made	Amber	Blue	Clear	Vas
Bowl, open, round, low footed				
Deep				
8½"d	25.00	40.00	20.00	45.00
9½"d	25.00	40.00	20.00	45.00
10"d	40.00	50.00	35.00	45.00
Flared, 8"d	30.00	45.00	25.00	50.00
Scalloped rim				
7"d	25.00	40.00	20.00	45.00
8"d	30.00	45.00	25.00	50.00
Butter dish, covered				
Flanged cover	45.00	50.00	40.00	50.00
Regular cover	40.00	45.00	35.00	45.00
Celery vase				
Flared rim.	35.00	40.00	35.00	40.00
Ruffled rim	55.00	65.00	35.00	55.00
Plain rim	45.00	55.00	35.00	45.00
Compote, open, low standard, round flared rim, round				
7"d	35.00	55.00	25.00	40.00
8"d	35.00	55.00	25.00	40.00
9"d	35.00	55.00	25.00	40.00
10"d	40.00	60.00	30.00	45.00
Creamer	40.00	45.00	35.00	40.00
Cruet, applied handle, original stopper (R)	175.00	200.00	90.00	175.00
Goblet	40.00	45.00	30.00	40.00
Mug				
Large	35.00	45.00	25.00	35.00
Small	30.00	40.00	20.00	30.00
Pitcher				
Milk, 1 quart	85.00	100.00	65.00	100.00
Water, ½ gallon	95.00	65.00	45.00	65.00
Salt shaker, tall, original top (VR)	35.00	55.00	25.00	55.00
Sauce dish, round, footed, 4"d	20.00	20.00	10.00	20.00
Spoonholder	40.00	45.00	30.00	40.00
Sugar bowl, covered	55.00	65.00	35.00	45.00
Tumbler, water, flat	35.00	40.00	20.00	30.00

THUMBPRINT

Wine; champagne (barrel shape); h.s. open compote; footed tumbler; champagne.

AKA: Argus, Argus Thumbprint, Early Thumbprint, Giant Baby Thumbprint, Heavy Argus, Light Argus.

Flint. Bakewell, Pears & Co., Pittsburgh, PA. ca. 1850-1860. Numerous concerns including Challinor, King, McKee and Tarentum.

Original color production: Clear. Milk white or any other color is rare. Early items in Thumbprint are of heavy flint with applied handles, later issues being of non-flint, thinner, and with less thumbprints in the design. Produced by numerous concerns, the treatment of bases, finials, handles, standards and stems vary considerably.

Reproductions: The Fenton Art Glass Co., Fenton, OH. issued a thumbprint pattern in clear and colors in non-flint that is entirely unlike the original design.

References: Fer-YMG (P. 90), Grow-WCG (PP. 190-191, Figs. 31-"1" and 31-"2"), Inn-EGP (PP. 31, 41), Inn-PG (P. 339), Kam-2 (Pl. 207), Kam-7 (PP. 2-3), Lee-EAPG (Pl. 15), Lee-SG (Pl. 8), McKrn-AG (Pl. 212), Mil-1 (Pl. 154), Mil-OG (Pl. 89), Mtz-2 (P. 42), Oliv-AAG (P. 58), Pap-GAG (P. 188), Pear-CAT (P. 10), Phil-EOG (P. 187), Rev-APG (P. 48), Schwtz-AG (P. 199), Spil-AEPG (P. 250), Tass-AG (P. 72), Uni-1 (P. 46), Wlkr-PGA (Fig. 8, Nos. 18, 48, 49).

Items made	Clear	Items made	Clear
Ale glass, pony	40.00	Footed	75.00
Banana boat	150.00	Cake stand, high standard	50.00
Bottle		Celery vase, pedestaled	
Castor	35.00	Patterned base	100.00
Cologne	90.00	Plain base	85.00
Bitters	140.00	Champagne	85.00
Water, with tumble up	150.00	Claret	75.00
Bowl, round		Compote, round	
Covered, flat, 8"d	85.00	Covered	
Open		High standard	
Berry, master, flat 8"d	40.00	4"d	80.00
Punch, footed, 13½"d., 12½"h (R)	175.00	8"d	125.00
Butter dish, covered		10"d	145.00
Flat	55.00	13½"d	175.00

Items made	Clear	Items made	Clear
Low standard, 7"d	65.00	Salt, master, footed, open	45.00
Open		Sauce dish, round, flat	15.00
High standard, 6"d	65.00	Spoonholder	45.00
Low standard, scalloped flared rim	125.00	Sugar bowl, covered	65.00
Cordial	85.00	Syrup, original top	175.00
Creamer, 5³⁄₄"h	65.00	Tumbler (height of foot varies)	
Dish, jelly	25.00	Water	
Egg cup, pedestaled	40.00	Flat	40.00
Goblet	55.00	Footed	40.00
Honey dish, flat, round	10.00	Whiskey	
Mug, beer, applied handle	40.00	Flat	35.00
Pickle dish	25.00	Footed	35.00
Pitcher, water, applied handle,		Wine	
¹⁄₂ gallon	200.00+	Knob stem	75.00
Plate, round, 8"d	50.00	Plain stem	75.00
Relish dish	25.00		

TORPEDO

Tumbler (plain); spoonholder (etched); syrup (clear/ruby); goblet (etched); creamer (clear).

OMN: Thompson's No. 17. AKA: Fisheye [Unitt], Pigmy [Millard].

Non-flint. The Thompson Glass Co., Uniontown, PA. ca. 1889-1893. Illustrated in the Montgomery Ward 1894 catalog No. 55.

Original color production: Clear, clear with ruby stain (plain or copper wheel engraved). Black amethyst or any other color is very rare. Handles are applied and pressed.

References: Bar-RS (Pl. 14), Hea-OS (Pl. 135, No. 2549), Hea-3 (P. 38, Fig. 249), Hea-7 (Figs. 728-731), Kam-2 (P. 107), Kam-4 (Pl. XI), Kam-6 (Pl. 17), Kam/Wod-Vol. 2 (P. 603), McCn-PGP (P. 457), Mil-1 (Pl. 46), Mtz-1 (PP. 152-153), Rev-APG (P. 303), Thu-1 (P. 291), Uni-1 (PP. 78-79), Uni-2 (PP. 92-93), Wlkr-PGA (Fig. 8, Nos. 6, 20).

Items made	Clear	Clear w/Ruby
Banana dish, high standard, folded sides, 9¾"d	75.00	—
Bowl, round		
Covered, flat		
7"d	45.00	—
8"d	65.00	90.00
Open		
Berry, master	45.00	65.00
Finger	45.00	65.00
Rose	65.00	—
Vegetable or fruit		
Flared rim		
7"d	25.00	65.00
8"d	30.00	75.00
9"d	35.00	—
9½"d	40.00	—
Ruffled rim		
5½"d., 2½"h	20.00	—
10½"d., 2¾"h	40.00	—
Butter dish, covered		
Quarter pound, flanged base	85.00	125.00
Table size	65.00	100.00
Cake stand, high standard		
9"d	55.00	—
10"d	65.00	—
Celery vase, scalloped rim, 6¾"h	35.00	75.00
Cheese dish, covered	95.00	—
Compote, round		
Covered		
High standard		
4"d., jelly	65.00	—
6½"d., 11"h	85.00	—
13¾"d	165.00	—
Open, high standard		
4"d., flared rim, jelly	45.00	—
8½"d	50.00	—
Creamer		
Hotel size, 5¼"h	50.00	75.00
Breakfast size, tankard, 6"h	45.00	65.00
Cruet under tray	90.00	—
Cruet, applied handle, original patterned stopper	90.00	—
Cup/saucer, set	65.00	—
Decanter, original patterned stopper, 8"h	85.00	125.00
Goblet, 6¼"h	55.00	85.00
Honey dish, flat, 3½"d	15.00	—
Lamp, oil, original burner and chimney		
Finger, 3"h	75.00	—
Stand, plain base, patterned font, 8"h	75.00	—
Marmalade jar, covered	55.00	100.00
Pickle castor, complete in silver plate holder	125.00	225.00
Pitcher, tankard, applied handle		
Milk, 8½"h	75.00	150.00
Water, ½ gallon, 10½"h	85.00	175.00
Rose bowl (S)	85.00	—
Salt		
Individual, round, 1½"d	25.00	45.00
Master, round, flat	35.00	65.00
Shaker, original top		
Short	45.00	65.00

Items made	Clear	Clear w/Ruby
Tall	45.00	65.00
Sauce dish, round, smooth rim		
Flat		
3¾"d	15.00	20.00
4½"d	15.00	22.00
5½"d	15.00	25.00
Footed		
3¾"d	18.00	—
4½"d	18.00	—
5½"d	18.00	—
Spoonholder, footed, scalloped rim	35.00	55.00
Sugar bowl, covered	65.00	90.00
Syrup pitcher, original top	90.00	175.00
Tray, water		
Clover shape, 11¾"	100.00	—
Round, 10"d	85.00	—
Tumbler, water, flat	35.00	50.00
Wine	85.00	110.00

TREE OF LIFE

Covered butter dish; celery vase; fingerbowl; leaf-shaped sauce dish.

Non-flint. The Portland Glass Co., Portland, ME. ca. 1870. George Duncan & Sons, Pittsburgh, PA. ca. 1885. Hobbs, Brockunier & Co., Wheeling, WV. ca. 1888 (in limited items). The Sandwich Glass Co., Sandwich, MA. ca. 1880s. Illustrated in the ca. 1888-1891 Hobbs, Brockunier & Co. catalog.

Original color production: Clear. Amber, blue (light, dark), canary-yellow, green, cranberry, amethyst or any other color is rare. Plain or copper wheel engraved. Designed and patented by William O. Davis ca. 1867, some items are signed "Davis" on the base interwoven within the pattern or "P.G.Co" impressed on the base. Various items such as the celery vase and creamer may be found fitted in silver plate holders.

Produced by numerous glass houses, Tree of Life falls into three major categories based on the following design elements: Portland version: Items maintain a smooth rim. The main design is separated from this rim by a clear marginal band, while the design covers the bases

524

and stems of items. Stems are conical in shape. Only Portland versions are found in color. *Duncan version:* design covers the entire item with no clear marginal band; bases and stems are not patterned; items are mellon-ribbed with hand stems and ribbed bases. *Sandwich version:* design is strongly defined with well formed branches and stems; standards and bases do not carry the design although a clear marginal band does appear on rims as on Portland pieces.

Reproductions: The L.G. Wright Glass Co., New Martinsville, WV. (distributed by Jennings Red Barn, New Martinsville, WV. and Carl Forslund, Grand Rapids, MI.) 1974 master catalog illustrates the following items made from new molds in amber, blue and clear: flat crimped-flared $5^1/_2$"d. bowl; 9 ounce goblet; 3-legged 4"d round sauce, 4"h. covered sugar bowl, and the 4 ounce wine.

References: [Portland] Swn-PG 1949 (P. 43), Mtz-2 (P. 120), Kam-5 (P. 34), Rev-APG (P. 283), Bat-GPG (P. 77), Lee-VG (P. 11), Mil-1 (P. 8), Mtz-1 (P. 138), Uni-1 (P. 66). [George Duncan & Sons] Lee-VG (Pl. 11), Kam-3 (P. 7), Inn-EPG (P. 53), Mtz-1 (P. 138), McCn-PGP (P. 397), Inn-PG (P. 358), Rev-APG (P. 151), Uni-1 (P. 67), Swn-PG 1949 (P. 43), Mtz-2 (P. 1020), Hea-TPS (P. 25). [Sandwich] Lee-SG (Pl. 215), Lee-VG (Pl. 12), Mtz-2 (P. 120), Oliv-AAG (P. 75). [Miscellaneous] Grow-WCG (P. 163, Fig. 24-"14"), Wlkr-PGA (Fig. 8, Nos. 25, 55).

Items made	Clear	Items made	Clear
Bowl		Goblet	45.00
Oval, master berry, open, flat	40.00	Mug	50.00
Round, open, flat		Pitcher	
Berry, master, 8"d	40.00	Milk, 1 quart, applied handle	100.00
Finger, matching underplate	35.00	Water, $1/_2$ gallon	
Vegetable or serving, $6^1/_4$"d., 2"h	50.00	Applied handle	135.00
Butter		Pressed handle	100.00
Dish, covered	75.00	Plate, round	
Pat, round, flat, scalloped rim	25.00	Dinner or sandwich	30.00
Celery vase, plain or in original silver		Honey	30.00
plate holder	80.00	Salt, master, open, footed	35.00
Champagne	75.00	Sauce dish	
Compote, round		Leaf shape (2 sizes)	20.00
Covered, high standard, scalloped		Round, flat (several sizes)	20.00
rim	175.00	Spoonholder	40.00
Open, low standard, 10"d (often		Sugar bowl, covered	65.00
signed "Davis")	100.00	Toothpick holder, footed, scalloped	
Creamer, 6"h	65.00	rim	50.00
Dish, flat, open		Tray, water	65.00
Rectangular	40.00	Tumbler, footed	40.00
Round, fruit	55.00	Vases (several sizes)	50.00
Epergne, complete with under bowl	200.00	Wine	55.00

Water pitcher; butter dish.

AKA: Pittsburgh Tree of Life.

Non-flint. George Duncan & Sons, Pittsburgh, PA. ca. 1885.

Original color production: Clear. Handles are pressed.

Reproductions: None.

References: Hea-TPS (P. 25), Hlms-BCA (PP. 275, 278), Inn-EGP (P. 53), Inn-PG (P. 358), Kam/Wod-Vol.2 (P. 588), Lee-VG (Pl. 11), McCn-PGP (P. 397), Mtz-1 (PP. 138-139), Mtz-2 (P. 120), Rev-APG (P. 151), Spil-AEPG (P. 268), Swn-PG 1949 (P. 43), Uni-1 (P. 67), Uni/Wod-CHPGT (P. 217), Wlkr-PGA (Fig. 8, Nos. 3, 37, 45).

Items made	Clear	Items made	Clear
Bowl, flat, open		Plate, round, 6"d	35.00
Berry, master	60.00	Sauce dish	
Finger or waste bowl	45.00	Flat	20.00
Butter dish, covered	85.00	Footed	30.00
Celery vase	65.00	Spoonholder	40.00
Compote, covered, high standard	100.00	Sugar bowl, covered	75.00
Creamer	65.00	Tray, ice cream	75.00
Pitcher, water	175.00		

TRIPLE TRIANGLE

Tumbler; rectangular dish; creamer; wine.

OMN: Doyle's No. 76. AKA: Triple Triangle-Red Top, Pillar and Cut Diamond.

Non-flint. Doyle & Co. (pattern line No. 76), Pittsburgh, PA. ca. 1890. Reissued by the United States Glass Co., Pittsburgh, PA. at Factory "D" (Doyle & Co., Pittsburgh, PA.) ca. 1890-1895.

Original color production: Clear, clear with ruby stain (plain or copper wheel engraved).

Reproductions: Both the goblet and wine have been reproduced from new molds.

References: Bar-RS (Pl. 7), Bat-GAG (PP. 197-198), Grow-WCG (P. 188, Fig. 29-"11"), Hea-5 (P. 52, No. 266), Hea-7 (PP. 204-205), Kam-8 (Pl. 73), Lee-VG (Pl. 56, No. 3), Mil-1 (Pl. 165), Mtz-1 (PP. 220-221), Rev-APG (PP. 139-140), Spil-AEPG (P. 308), Uni-1 (P. 163), Uni-2 (P. 132).

Items made	Clear	Clear w/Ruby
Bowl, open, flat		
Rectangular, scalloped rim		
8"l	20.00	40.00
9"l	20.00	40.00
10"l	25.00	45.00
Round		
6"d	15.00	30.00
7"d	15.00	30.00
8"d	20.00	40.00
9"d	20.00	40.00
Butter dish, covered, handled	40.00	80.00
Celery tray, rectangular	30.00	45.00
Creamer, pressed handle	35.00	55.00
Cup, custard	10.00	25.00
Dish, rectangular, flat, scallop & point rim	15.00	30.00
Goblet, 5⅞"h	25.00	45.00
Mug	20.00	35.00
Pickle tray, boat shape	10.00	25.00
Pitcher, water, ½ gallon, 8"h, pressed handle	65.00	135.00
Plate, bread, rectangular	35.00	90.00

Items made	Clear	Clear w/Ruby
Sauce dish, flat, round, 5"d	10.00	20.00
Spoonholder, double handles	20.00	65.00
Sugar bowl, covered, handled, 6¾"h	40.00	75.00
Tumbler, water, flat	20.00	35.00
Wine	20.00	45.00

TRUNCATED CUBE

Goblet (clear and ruby stain).

Individual creamer and table size creamer (both clear and ruby stain).

OMN: Thompson's No. 77.

Non-flint. Thompson Glass Co. (pattern line No. 77), Uniontown, PA. ca. 1894. Reviewed in the January 10, 1894 issue of *China, Glass and Lamps.*

Original color production: Clear, clear with ruby stain (plain or copper wheel engraved).

Reproductions: None.

References: Bar-RS (Pl. 13), Hea-1 (P. 42, Fig. 304), Hea-3 (P. 57, Fig. 455), Hea-6 (P. 45, Fig. 372), Hea-7 (P. 205, Figs. 709-721), Kam-5 (P. 82), Kam-6 (Pl. 40), McCn-PGP (P. 457), Mil-2 (Pl. 35), Mtz-2 (PP. 142-143), Pet-Sal (P. 175-"I"), Rev-APG (P. 303), Uni-2 (P. 128).

Items made	Clear	Clear w/Ruby
Bowl, master berry, flat, open, folded-scalloped rim, 8"d, round	20.00	40.00
Butter dish, covered, flanged base, ...	50.00	90.00
Celery vase	40.00	55.00
Creamer, applied handle		
Individual, 2⅞"h	20.00	35.00
Table size	35.00	55.00
Cruet, original stopper, pressed handle	35.00	100.00
Decanter, original patterned stopper, 12"h	60.00	150.00
Goblet	30.00	50.00

Items made	Clear	Clear w/Ruby
Pitcher, applied handle		
Milk, 1 quart	50.00	110.00
Water, ½ gallon	60.00	125.00
Salt shaker, original top	15.00	30.00
Sauce dish, flat, round, serrated rim, 4″d	10.00	15.00
Spoonholder	30.00	50.00
Sugar bowl, covered		
Individual	20.00	35.00
Table size	30.00	70.00
Syrup pitcher, original top, pressed handle		
Squat, cube design on lower portion of body	40.00	100.00
Tall, cube design on upper and lower portion of body	40.00	100.00
Toothpick holder, serrated rim	30.00	45.00
Tray, water, round	20.00	40.00
Tumbler, water	20.00	35.00
Wine	35.00	40.00

TULIP WITH SAWTOOTH

Low standard open compote 6″d; celery vase; high standard open compote 8″d; decanter (bar lip); goblet.

OMN: Bryce No. 1, Tulip.

Flint, non-flint. Bryce, Richards & Company (pattern line No. 1), Pittsburgh, PA. ca. 1854. Reissued in non-flint by the United States Glass Company, Pittsburgh, PA. after the 1891 merger. Shards have been found at the site of the Burlington Glass Works, Hamilton, Ontario, Canada. Illustrated in the Bryce, Richards & Co. 1854 catalog

Original color production: Clear. Milk white, opalescent or any other color is rare.

Reproductions: Both the goblet and wine have been reproduced from new molds from the early 1960s. Reproductions are non-flint and smaller than the original.

References: Hlms-BCA (P. 278), Kam/Wod-Vol.2 (P. 598), Lee-EAPG (Pl. 53, Nos. 1-2), Mil-1 (Pl. 118), Mtz-1 (PP. 32-33), Rev-APG (PP. 80, 90), Uni-1 (P. 195), Uni/Wor-CHPGT (P. 220).

Items made	Flint	Non-flint
Bottle, bar, 1 pint	75.00	80.00
Butter dish, covered	125.00	80.00
Celery vase, 10¼"h	85.00	25.00
Champagne	75.00	35.00
Compote, round		
Covered, high standard		
6"d	90.00	—
7¼"d	90.00	—
8½"d	110.00	—
Open		
High standard		
8½"d	—	60.00
Low standard		
6"d., ruffled rim	65.00	—
8"d	65.00	—
8½"d	75.00	—
9"d	75.00	—
Creamer, applied handle	85.00	—
Cruet, original patterned stopper		
Applied handle	65.00	—
Pressed handle	—	40.00
Decanter		
Applied handle, original patterned stopper	150.00	—
Handleless, heavy bar lip	150.00	55.00
Egg cup, covered, pedestaled, 3½"h	45.00	—
Goblet, knob stem, 7"h	65.00	35.00
Honey dish, round, flat	10.00	—
Mug, applied handle	85.00	—
Pitcher, water, applied handle	250.00	—
Plate, round, 6"d	65.00	—
Pomade jar, original clear stopper, pedestaled	65.00	—
Salt, master, footed, open		
Petaled edge	25.00	15.00
Plain edge	25.00	—
Sauce dish, flat, round	15.00	10.00
Spoonholder, 6"h	35.00	25.00
Sugar bowl, covered	95.00	—
Tumbler		
Bar, flat	85.00	25.00
Water, footed	55.00	—
Wine	45.00	25.00

Tumbler; goblet; waste bowl; relish tray.

AKA: Daisy in Panel, Daisy in the Square.

Non-flint. The Richards & Hartley Glass Co., Tarentum, PA. ca. 1880s. Reissued by the United States Glass Co., Pittsburgh, PA. at Factory "B" (Bryce Bros., Pittsburgh, PA.), ca. 1891.

Original color production: Amber, apple green, blue, vaseline and clear.

Reproductions: Reproductions of both the goblet and wine appeared in the original colors of amber, apple green, blue, vaseline and clear from new molds in the early 1960s (possibly earlier). New colors are harsh and artificial when compared to the deep mellow colors of old pieces.

References: Cod-OS (Pl. 52), Hea-5 (P. 45, Nos. 177-178), Hea-OS (P. 39, No. 328), Inn-PG (P. 319), Kam-3 (PP. 45-46), Lee-EAPG (Plts. 159-160), Luc-TG (PP. 28-29), McCn-PGP (P. 483), Mil-1 (Pl. 53), Mtz-1 (PP. 158-159), Pet-Sal (P. 42), Rev-APG (PP. 287-288), Thu-1 (P. 288), Uni-2 (P. 114), Wlkr-PGA (Fig. 8, Nos. 43, 56).

Items made	Amber	Green	Blue	Clear	Vas
Bowl, oval, open, flat					
Cracker (2 sizes)	100.00	135.00	135.00	75.00	135.00
Fruit, 10″ x 8½″ x 3″	35.00	50.00	40.00	25.00	30.00
Berry, master					
5½″	35.00	40.00	40.00	20.00	25.00
8″d	35.00	40.00	40.00	15.00	25.00
Waste or finger	40.00	45.00	40.00	20.00	30.00
Butter dish, covered	50.00	55.00	55.00	30.00	40.00
Celery					
Dip	35.00	40.00	40.00	15.00	25.00
Vase	45.00	50.00	50.00	25.00	40.00
Compote, high standard, oval					
Covered 6½″d	65.00	85.00	85.00	35.00	85.00
Open	35.00	45.00	55.00	25.00	55.00
Creamer, 6″h, pressed handle	40.00	45.00	45.00	20.00	35.00

Items made	Amber	Green	Blue	Clear	Vas
Dish, open, oval					
5″	20.00	25.00	35.00	15.00	30.00
9″	25.00	30.00	40.00	20.00	35.00
10½″	30.00	35.00	45.00	25.00	40.00
Goblet	30.00	35.00	45.00	25.00	40.00
Jam jar, oval, flat, covered	75.00	95.00	110.00	45.00	110.00
Lamp, oil, original burner					
Hand	65.00	75.00	65.00	50.00	65.00
Stand	85.00	125.00	100.00	45.00	110.00
Mug (several sizes), pressed handle	30.00	35.00	40.00	20.00	30.00
Pickle dish, handled, 9″ x 4″	25.00	30.00	40.00	20.00	30.00
Pitcher, water, square, ½ gallon, pressed					
handle	60.00	60.00	65.00	35.00	50.00
Platter	30.00	30.00	30.00	25.00	30.00
Salt					
Dip, individual, oval	20.00	15.00	20.00	10.00	15.00
Master, oval, 3⅞″	20.00	25.00	20.00	10.00	10.00
Shaker, original top	40.00	45.00	40.00	25.00	30.00
Sauce dish, oval					
Flat	10.00	10.00	10.00	8.00	10.00
Footed	10.00	15.00	15.00	10.00	10.00
Spoonholder	45.00	50.00	45.00	25.00	35.00
Sugar bowl, covered	50.00	55.00	55.00	30.00	40.00
Tumbler, water, flat	35.00	40.00	35.00	15.00	40.00
Tray, water	50.00	55.00	55.00	45.00	50.00
Wine	40.00	45.00	40.00	20.00	30.00

U.S. COIN

Stand oil lamp.

OMN: United States Glass No. 15,005. AKA: American Coin, Coin (Dime), Coin (Half Dollar), Frosted Coin, Silver Age, The Silver Age.

Non-flint. The United States Glass Co. (pattern line No. 15,005), Pittsburgh, PA. at Factory "H" (Hobbs Glass Co., Wheeling, WV.) and "G" (Gillinder & Sons, Greensburg, PA.) ca. 1892, discontinued after a three–four month production by the U.S. Treasury Department because real coins dating as early as 1876 were used in the molds. The pattern was discontinued in May, 1892. Central Glass Co., ca. 1892. Hobbs, Brockunier and Co., Wheeling, WV. ca. 1892. Profusely illustrated in the ca. 1891-1892 United States Glass Co. catalog.

Original color production: Clear (plain, frosted or stained with gold or platinum). Clear with amber stain, clear with ruby stain, or any other decorative treatment is very rare.

Reproductions: The A.A. Importing Co., Inc., (St. Louis, MO. and Carson/San Francisco, CA.), 1978 No. 36 and the Spring-Summer 1981 No. 41 catalogs list the following reissues of the pattern from new molds: flat covered bowl (termed the candy jar, not original to the set), 10"w bread tray (clear with 15 frosted fifty cent coins), $2^{1}/_{4}$"h. candlestick (not original to the set), $9^{1}/_{2}$"h. high standard covered compote (clear/frosted), creamer (clear/frosted), $2^{3}/_{4}$"d. paperweights (frosted heads and tails coins in the bases), $4^{3}/_{4}$"h. spoonholder (footed, clear/frosted, not original to the set), 7"h. covered sugar bowl (clear/frosted), $2^{7}/_{8}$"h. toothpick holder (clear, clear with silver coins, clear/frosted), and the $2^{7}/_{8}$"h. water tumbler with $1.00 pieces (clear/frosted).

References: Bat-GPG (P. 57), Drep-ABC OG (P. 75), Eige-CG WV (P. 20), Enos-MPG (Chart-1), Hea-1 (P. 17), Hea-5 (PP. 13, 16), Hea-TPS (PP. 79, 89), Jef-WG (PP. 62-63), Kam-3 (P. 80), Kam-4 (P. 80), Kam-7 (Plts. 3-6), Kam-8 (Plts. 58-59), Lee-VG (Plts. 15-18), Lind-HG (PP. 82-108), Mrsh-SRG (PP. 121-123), McKrn-AG (Pl. 207), Mil-2 (Pl. 12), Mtz-1 (P. 112), Mur-MCO (PP. 60-61), Oliv-AAG (P. 77), Pap-GAG (P. 200), Pet-Sal (P. 25), Rev-APG (P. 109, 193), Schwtz-AG (P. 75), Spil-AEPG (P. 314), Thu-1 (P. 13), Uni-1 (PP. 9, 73).

Items made	Clear	Clear/ Frosted
Ale glass, footed	250.00	350.00
Bowl, round		
Covered		
6"d	225.00	275.00
7"d	250.00	325.00
8"d	270.00	375.00
Open, flat, scalloped rim		
6"d	150.00	200.00
7"d	175.00	250.00
8"d	200.00	300.00
Butter dish, covered, dollars and half dollars	300.00	500.00
Cake plate, round	175.00	250.00
Cake stand, high standard, 10"d	250.00	450.00
Celery		
Tray	200.00	—
Vase, quarters	150.00	375.00
Champagne	—	400.00
Claret	—	400.00
Compote, round		
Covered		
High standard		
6"d	350.00	550.00
7"d	350.00	500.00
8"d	—	400.00
Low standard		
6"d	350.00	500.00
Open		
High standard, scalloped rim		
6"d	175.00	250.00
7"d	200.00	300.00
8"d	225.00	325.00

Items made	Clear	Clear/Frosted
Low standard, smooth rim	200.00	300.00
Creamer, pressed handle	375.00	500.00
Cruet, original stopper, pressed handle	400.00	550.00
Epergne (R)	500.00	1200.00
Goblet		
Regular	250.00	400.00
Dimes	—	550.00
Lamp, oil, stand, original burner		
Round font	300.00	500.00
Dimes	—	550.00
Mug, beer, pressed handle	200.00	350.00
Pickle dish, oblong	200.00	—
Pitcher, pressed handle		
Milk, 1 quart	450.00	750.00
Water, dollars, ½ gallon	450.00	850.00
Plate, bread, rectangular	200.00	300.00
Salt shaker, tall, original top	100.00	150.00
Sauce dish, round		
Flat		
4″d	100.00	150.00
4½″d	100.00	150.00
Footed, smooth rim, quarters		
4″d	100.00	200.00
4½″d	100.00	200.00
Spoonholder, quarters	250.00	350.00
Sugar bowl, covered	250.00	375.00
Syrup pitcher, original dated pewter lid	—	550.00
Toothpick holder	150.00	300.00
Tray, water, rectangular	300.00	—
Waste bowl	200.00	250.00
Tumbler, water, flat	125.00	225.00
Wine	250.00	400.00

UTAH States Series

Cruet (o.s.); syrup; goblet.

OMN: U.S. Glass No. 15,080, Utah. AKA: Frost Flower [Kamm], Frosted Flower, Starlight, Twinkle Star [Metz].

Non-flint. The United States Glass Co. (pattern line No. 15,080), Pittsburgh, PA. at Factory "U" (United States Glass Co., Gas City, IN.) ca. 1901. Although an individual salt is illustrated in the 1902 Diamond Glass Co., Ltd. catalog (Montreal, Quebec, Canada), no positive proof has yet surfaced to indicate Diamond produced Utah in a complete table line.

Original color production: Clear, clear with acid finish. Handles are pressed.

Reproductions: None.

References: Hart/Cobb-SS (P. 65), Hea-5 (PP. 167, 169), Kam-4 (P. 122), Kam-6 (Pl. 59), McCn-PGP (P. 503), Mtz-2 (P. 104), Mil-1 (Pl. 38), Pet-Sal (P. 40), Pyne-PG (P. 152), Uni-1 (P. 286), Uni-2 (P. 247).

Items made	Clear	Items made	Clear
Bowl, round, flat		High standard, jelly, 6"d	15.00
Covered		Low standard, jelly, 6"d	15.00
6"d	20.00	Condiment set (salt, pepper shaker,	
7"d	20.00	original holder)	45.00
8"d	20.00	Creamer	20.00
Open		Cruet, original stopper	35.00
6"d	15.00	Goblet	25.00
7"d	15.00	Pickle tray	10.00
8"d	15.00	Pitcher, water	
Butter dish, covered		3 pints	45.00
Large	35.00	1/2 gallon	45.00
Small	35.00	Salt shaker, original top	20.00
Cake plate, 9"d	20.00	Sauce dish, round, flat, 4"d	10.00
Cake stand, high standard		Spoonholder	15.00
8"d	25.00	Sugar bowl, covered	35.00
10"d	30.00	Syrup pitcher, original nickel plate or	
Celery vase	20.00	tin top	50.00
Compote		Tumbler, water, flat	15.00
Covered, low standard, jelly, 6"d	15.00	Wine	45.00
Open			

VALENCIA WAFFLE

Salt shaker (apple green); h.s. covered compote (blue); celery vase (vaseline).

OMN: Adams No. 85. AKA: Block and Star [Kamm], Hexagonal Block [Lee].

Non-flint. Adams & Co. (pattern line No. 85), Pittsburgh, PA. ca. 1885. Reissued by the United States Glass Co., Pittsburgh, PA. at Factory "A" (Adams & Co., Pittsburgh, PA.) after 1891.

Original color production: Amber, blue, apple green, vaseline, clear.

Reproductions: None.

References: Hea-3 (PP. 44, 83), Hea-5 (PP. 24, 71), Hea-OS (P. 43, No. 452), Kam-1 (PP. 43-44), Lee-EAPG (P. 153), Lee-VG (Pl. 71, No. 2), McCn-PGP (P. 221), Mil-1 (Pl. 71), Mil-2 (P. 23), Mtz-1 (PP. 164-165), Pet-Sal (P. 42), Stu-BP (P. 75), Uni-1 (PP. 300-301).

Items made	Amber	Green	Blue	Clear	Vas
Bowl, master berry	15.00	25.00	20.00	10.00	15.00
Bread plate	30.00	35.00	30.00	25.00	35.00
Butter dish, covered	40.00	65.00	45.00	40.00	40.00
Cake stand, high standard, 10"sq	60.00	40.00	45.00	35.00	40.00
Castor set, complete in silver plate holder	60.00	75.00	65.00	50.00	60.00
Celery vase, pedestaled, smooth rim	40.00	45.00	45.00	35.00	40.00
Compote, covered, round					
High standard, 7"d	60.00	75.00	75.00	50.00	75.00
Low standard, 7"d	40.00	50.00	65.00	30.00	45.00
Creamer, 6"h, pressed handle	35.00	—	45.00	30.00	30.00
Dish, oblong, open, flat					
7"	20.00	—	25.00	10.00	20.00
8"	20.00	—	25.00	10.00	20.00
9"	20.00	—	25.00	10.00	20.00
Goblet	40.00	—	40.00	30.00	35.00
Pickle dish, oblong, flat	20.00	20.00	25.00	15.00	20.00
Pickle jar, covered	50.00	60.00	40.00	30.00	40.00
Pitcher, pressed handle					
Milk, 1 quart	40.00	50.00	45.00	35.00	40.00
Water, ½ gallon	65.00	50.00	50.00	40.00	45.00
Relish dish	20.00	20.00	25.00	15.00	20.00
Salt					
Dip	35.00	—	—	—	—
Shaker, tall, original top	20.00	30.00	35.00	15.00	35.00
Sauce dish, square, 4"					
Flat	10.00	—	15.00	15.00	10.00
Footed	10.00	—	15.00	10.00	15.00
Spoonholder, smooth rim	30.00	—	35.00	20.00	35.00
Sugar bowl, covered	40.00	—	50.00	35.00	45.00
Syrup, original top	100.00	125.00	100.00	50.00	100.00
Tray, water, 8" x 10½"	—	35.00	—	—	—
Tumbler, water, flat	25.00	—	30.00	15.00	25.00

Goblet.

OMN: Trilby. AKA: Vincent Valentine.

Non-flint. The United States Glass Co., Pittsburgh, PA. at Factory "G" (Gillinder & Sons, Pittsburgh, PA.) ca. 1891–1895. Illustrated in the ca. 1891 United States Glass Co. catalog of member firms.

Original color production: Clear. Only the water pitcher and goblet carry the woman's portrait. Handles are pressed.

Reproductions: The Degenhart Glass Co., Cambridge, OH. reproduced from new molds the toothpick holder in various colors including opalescent and clear colors, usually signed with the Co.'s "D" trademark.

References: Bar-RS (Pl. 8), Hea-5 (P. 23), Lee-EAPG (Pl. 164, No. 12), Lee-VG (Pl. 54, No. 1), McCn-PGP (P. 393), Mil-1 (Pl. 78), Mtz-1 (PP. 102-103), Uni-1(P. 259), Wlkr-PGA (Fig. 15, No. 230).

Items made	Clear	Items made	Clear
Bottle, cologne, original heart shaped stopper	85.00	Sauce dish, flat, round, scalloped rim, 4½"d	25.00
Bowl, open, flat, master berry, round	85.00	Spoonholder, scalloped rim, 3½"h	50.00
Butter dish, covered, 7½"d., 5½"h	65.00	Sugar bowl, covered, 6½"h	85.00
Creamer, 4½"h	65.00	Toothpick holder	85.00
Goblet	90.00	Tumbler, water, flat, 4¼"h	75.00
Pitcher, water, ½ gallon, 8¼"h	200.00	Wall pocket, hanging (originally a match safe)	45.00

Creamer (emerald green); celery tray (clear); covered sugar bowl (emerald green).

OMN: U.S. Glass No. 15,060 Vermont. AKA: Honeycomb with Flower Rim, Inverted Thumbprint with Daisy Band [Metz], Vermont Honeycomb.

Non-flint. The United States Glass Co. (pattern line No. 15,060), Pittsburgh, PA. ca. 1899-1903. Illustrated in the Butler Brothers catalog of 1899, and advertised in the *Pottery and Glassware Reporter* in 1889.

Original color production: Clear, green (plain or with gilt trim), decorated custard, chocolate, slag, milk white, blue). Often trimmed with enameled florals. Clear with ruby stain, clear with amber stain or any other color is rare.

Reproductions: Both the Crystal Art Glass Co., Cambridge, OH. and the Mosser Glass, Inc., Cambridge, OH. reproduced the toothpick holder in clear, dark amber, and solid colors of light blue, dark blue, blue-green, and purple. The Vermont toothpick was also reissued in chocolate. Degenhart Glass reproduced the 2½"h. toothpick holder in a myriad of colors, often marked with the company's "D" trademark. New toothpick holders are about ¼" shorter than the old.

References: Fer-YMG (P. 41), Hart/Cobb-SS (P. 66), Hea-1 (P. 43, Figs. 315-316), Hea-4 (PP. 56, 66), Hea-5 (P. 53), Hea-TPS (PP. 40, 72), Kam-2 (P. 117), Kam-6 (Pl. 19), McCn-PGP (P. 579), Mig-TPS (Pl. 11), Mil-2 (Pl. 57), Mil-OG (Pl. 94), Mtz-1 (PP. 202-203), Pet-Sal (P. 176), Rev-APG (P. 319), Uni-1 (P. 318), War-MGA (PP. 28, 46).

Items made	Clear	Green
Basket, handled	30.00	45.00
Bowl, open, round		
Berry, master	25.00	45.00
Finger or waste	25.00	45.00
Butter dish, covered	40.00	75.00
Celery tray	25.00	35.00
Compote, high standard, round		
Covered	55.00	125.00
Open	35.00	65.00
Creamer, 4¼"h, pressed handle	30.00	55.00

Items made	Clear	Green
Goblet	40.00	65.00
Pickle tray	20.00	30.00
Pitcher, water, ½ gallon, pressed handle	40.00	90.00
Salt shaker, original top	20.00	35.00
Sauce dish, round, footed	15.00	25.00
Spoonholder	25.00	75.00
Sugar bowl, covered	35.00	80.00
Toothpick holder, footed	35.00	65.00
Tray, card, handled		
Large	20.00	35.00
Medium	15.00	30.00
Small	15.00	25.00
Tumbler, water, footed	25.00	45.00
Vase	20.00	45.00

VICTORIA, Pioneer's

Salt shaker (clear/ruby); water pitcher (clear/ruby).   Celery vase (clear); wine (clear/ruby).

OMN: Victoria, Pioneer's.

Non-flint. The Pioneer Glass Co., Pittsburgh, PA. ca. 1892. Due to the transfer of molds, the marketing of Victoria may further be traced to both the Greensburg and Huntington factories who sold the pattern as their own. Designed and patented by Julius Proeger (patent design No. 21,181) November 24, 1891, and assigned to the Pioneer Glass Co., Pittsburgh, PA., Victoria was reviewed in the January 13, 1892 (Greensburg Glass Co.) and February 15, 1893 (Huntington Glass Co.) issues of *China, Glass and Lamps,* and illustrated in the Pioneer Glass Co. catalog as "Victoria".

Original color production: Clear, clear with ruby stain. Most items carry a scallop and point rim. Although known in chocolate glass, enough evidence has not yet surfaced to positively confirm the Victoria line to McKee.

Reproductions: None.

References: Bar-RS (Pl. 7), Hea-6 (P. 45, Fig. 379), Hea-7 (P. 210), Inn-PG (P. 381), Kam-3 (P. 83), Kam-8 (PP. 77-78), Meas-GG (P. 84, Fig. 188), Mtz-2 (PP. 138-139), Mur-MCO (P. 59),

Pet-GPP (PP. 164-165), Pet-Sal (PP. 164-165), Rev-APG (P. 329), Thu-1 (P. 297), Uni-2 (P. 135).

Items made	Clear	Clear w/Ruby
Banana dish, high standard, pattern on base of standard	65.00	250.00
Bowl, flat, open, smooth rim		
Berry, master, 8″d		
Round bowl	25.00	55.00
Flared bowl	25.00	55.00
Finger or waste	15.00	40.00
Orange, scalloped rim	30.00	85.00
Rose (several sizes)	20.00	50.00
Butter dish, covered, footed with flanged base	45.00	125.00
Cake plate	15.00	100.00
Cake stand, high standard		
9″d	35.00	135.00
10″d	40.00	150.00
Celery vase, scalloped rim, 6½″h	30.00	90.00
Champagne	20.00	45.00
Cheese dish, covered, flanged base with high domed lid	55.00	125.00
Cologne bottle, flat, bulbous base with slender neck, original patterned stopper	30.00	125.00
Compote, covered, high standard, 6″d, round	55.00	200.00
Cordial	30.00	55.00
Cracker jar, covered	75.00	225.00
Creamer, low circular foot, applied handle, 5″h	30.00	65.00
Cruet		
Bulbous, long slender spout, pressed handle, original patterned stopper, 7½″h	65.00	175.00
Tapered, pulled spout, applied handle, original patterned stopper	35.00	135.00
Cup, custard	10.00	20.00
Decanter, original patterned stopper	50.00	175.00
Goblet, 6″h	25.00	65.00
Jam jar, covered, attached underplate (R)	35.00	90.00
Pickle jar, covered	35.00	90.00
Pitcher		
Bulbous	65.00	145.00
Tankard, applied handle		
Milk, 1 quart,	55.00	145.00
Water, ½ gallon, 11¾″h	65.00	185.00
Salt shaker, tall, flat, original top	15.00	35.00
Sauce dish, flat, round, smooth rim, 4″d	8.00	20.00
Saucer, round	8.00	20.00
Spoonholder	25.00	65.00
Sugar bowl, covered, flat	35.00	85.00
Syrup pitcher, original top	65.00	175.00
Tray, wine, round, shallow patterned rim	25.00	55.00
Tumbler		
Lemonade, applied handle	20.00	55.00
Water, flat, 3½″h	15.00	45.00
Wine	15.00	45.00

VICTORIA, Riverside's

Water pitcher.

OMN: Riverside No. 431, Victoria. AKA: Draped Top [Metz], Draped Red Top.

Non-flint. The Riverside Glass Works, (pattern line No. 431), Wellsburg, WV. ca. 1895. Advertised in the January 16, 1895 issue of *China, Glass and Lamps.*

Original color production: Clear, clear with ruby stain. Odd pieces may be found in clear with amber stain. Handles are pressed. Rims are either smooth or treated in a scallop-and-point design. Items may be flat (such as tumblers and bowls) or set on a low, circular foot.

Reproductions: None.

References: Bar-RS (Pl. 11), Hea-1000TPS (Fig. 229), Hea-3 (P. 45, Fig. 323), Hea-6 (P. 14), Hea-7 (Figs. 755-765), Hea-TPS (PP. 27, 52), Kam-6 (P. 34), McCn-PGP (P. 163), Mtz-1 (PP. 134-135), Mil-2 (Pl. 92), Pet-Sal (P. 159-"S"), Rev-APG (P. 296).

Items made	Clear	Clear w/Ruby
Bowl, flat, open, round		
7½"d. x 3¼"h	20.00	50.00
8"d	20.00	50.00
Butter dish, covered, flat, 7¼"d., 5½"h	40.00	125.00
Cake stand, high standard	45.00	125.00
Celery vase	35.00	75.00
Compote, high standard, round		
Covered, 6"d	50.00	100.00
Open, 6"d., scalloped rim, jelly	25.00	55.00
Condiment under tray, oblong	20.00	40.00
Creamer		
Individual	20.00	60.00
Table size	25.00	80.00
Cruet, 6"h., original stopper	30.00	200.00
Goblet	30.00	75.00
Pitcher, water, scalloped rim, ½ gallon, 8"h	45.00	175.00
Salt shaker, tall, original top	15.00	40.00
Sauce dish, round, flat, 4½"d	8.00	25.00
Spoonholder, 4"h	20.00	65.00

Items made	Clear	Clear w/Ruby
Sugar bowl, covered		
Individual	25.00	65.00
Table size	35.00	90.00
Syrup pitcher, original pewter top, 6½"h	45.00	275.00
Toothpick holder, 2¾"h	35.00	200.00
Tumbler, water, flat, 3½"h	20.00	45.00

VIKING

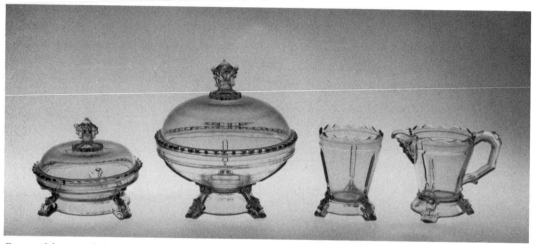

Covered butter dish; covered casserole; spoonholder; creamer.

OMN: Hobb's Centennial. AKA: Bearded Head, Bearded Prophet, Old Man of the Mountain(s).

Non-flint. Hobbs, Brockunier & Co., Wheeling, WV., ca. 1876. Designed and patented by John H. Hobbs (design patent No. 9647), November 21, 1876, the molds being made by Stephen Hipkins, with a patent taken out for 14 years.

Original color production: Clear. Items are footed with "viking head" feet and finials.

Reproductions: New goblets and tumblers, which are not original to the set, have been on the market.

References: Eige-CGM WV (P. 6), Gor-CC (PP. 122-122), Kam-1 (P. 82), Kam-7 (P. 64), Lee-VG (Pl. 33, No. 3), McCn-PGP (P. 399), Mtz-1 (PP. 6-7), Pet-GPP (PP. 198-199), Rev-APG (PP. 186-187), Spil-AEPG (P. 279), Spil-TBC (P. 243), Stu-BP (P. 75), Wlkr-PGA (Fig. 15, No. 236).

Items made	Clear	Items made	Clear
Apothecary jar, covered	45.00	High standard	
Bowl, covered, oval		7"d	75.00
8"	45.00	8"d	85.00
9"	55.00	9"d	95.00
Butter dish, covered	75.00	Low standard, 9"d	75.00
Casserole, covered, round	85.00	Open, high standard	60.00
Celery vase	45.00	Creamer, pressed handle	65.00
Compote, round		Cup, footed, applied handle	35.00
Covered		Egg cup	45.00

Items made	Clear	Items made	Clear
Marmalade jar, covered	125.00	Relish tray, oval, footed	25.00
Mug, applied handle	55.00	Salt, master, footed, open	40.00
Pickle dish, oval	40.00	Sauce dish, round, footed	15.00
Pitcher, water, ½ gallon, pressed		Spoonholder	35.00
handle	125.00	Sugar bowl, covered, footed	65.00
Platter, bread, oval	75.00		

WAFFLE

Flat sauce dish; 6"d. h.s. covered compote; covered butter; flat sauce dish.

AKA: Panelled Waffle.

Flint. Attributed to the Boston & Sandwich Glass Co., Sandwich, MA. ca. 1850s.

Original color production: Clear. Odd pieces in milk white or any other color are rare. Early items have three panels of cubes in the design whereas later items have either four panels of cubes in the design or else the entire surface is covered with cubes.

Reproductions: The goblet was first reproduced in 1938, an item which has no resemblance to the original.

References: Kam-6 (P. 18), Lee-EAPG (PP. 139-140), McCn-PGP (P. 475), Oliv-AAG (P. 58), Thu-1 (p. 79), Wlkr-PGA (Fig. 8, Nos. 20, 24, 44, 51).

Items made	Clear	Items made	Clear
Bowl, flat, open, oval, 8"	30.00	8"d	120.00
Butter dish, covered, flat	90.00	9"d	130.00
Celery vase, pedestaled, scalloped rim,		Low standard	
9"d	75.00	6"d	90.00
Champagne	100.00	7"d	100.00
Claret	100.00	8"d	120.00
Compote, round		9"d	130.00
Covered		Open, low standard	
High standard		6"d	60.00
6"d	90.00	7"d	65.00
7"d	100.00	8"d	65.00

Items made	Clear	Items made	Clear
Cordial	90.00	Pitcher, water, 9½"h., applied handle,	
Creamer, applied handle, pedestaled,		½ gallon	65.00
6¾"h	45.00	Plate, 6"d	45.00
Decanter		Relish tray, oblong, 4" x 6"., scalloped	
Pint	90.00	rim	45.00
Quart	100.00	Salt, master, footed	
Egg cup, footed	35.00	Covered	125.00
Goblet, knob stem	40.00	Open	25.00
Lamp, original burner		Sauce dish, flat, round, 4"d	15.00
All glass		Spillholder	65.00
Small, applied handle	125.00	Spoonholder	65.00
Tall, handleless	150.00	Sugar bowl, covered, pedestaled	150.00
Glass font, brass stem, marble base	125.00	Tumbler, flat	
Mug, applied handle	125.00	Water	125.00
Pickle dish, oval, tapered at one end	15.00	Whiskey	100.00
		Wine	45.00

WAFFLE AND THUMBPRINT

Tumbler; h.s. open compote; wine.

Decanter (o.s.); champagne.

OMN: Palace. AKA: Bulls Eye and Waffle, Triple Bulls Eye.

Flint. New England Glass Co., East Cambridge, MA. ca. 1868. Curling, Robertson & Co., Pittsburgh, PA. ca. 1856. Possibly other factories. Shards have been found at the site of the Boston & Sandwich Glass Co., Sandwich, MA. Illustrated in the New England Glass Co. 1869 catalog, and advertised by Curling, Robertson & Co. in 1856.

Original color production: Clear. Canary-yellow, milk white or any other color is rare. Brilliant, heavy flint, Waffle and Thumbprint is a rather fussy geometric pattern. The main pattern element consists of vertical waffle-filled panels, alternating with clear vertical panels of disconnected clear circles. Stemmed items vary, being either a) clear or fluted knobs or b) plain round standards.

Reproductions: None.

References: Bond-AG (Pl. 24), Bros-TS (P. 9), Brn-SD (P. 53), Inn-PG (PP. 304, 306), Kam-3 (PP. 29-30), Lee-EAPG (Pl. 10, No. 3), McCn-PGP (P. 477), McKrn-AG (Pl. 206), Mtz-1 (PP. 22-23), Mil-1 (Pl. 125), Mil-2 (Pl. 129), Mtz-2 (P. 14), Oliv-AAG (P. 58), Spil-AEPG (P. 260), Uni-1 (P. 159), Uni-2 (P. 20), Wat-NEG CO (P. 160), Wlkr-PGA (Fig. 8, Nos. 23, 34, 44).

Items made	Clear	Items made	Clear
Bowl, open, flat, rectangular, 5″ x 7″	30.00	Goblet	
Butter dish, covered, flat	95.00	Bulbous stem	65.00
Celery vase	100.00	Heavy stem	65.00
Champagne	85.00	Plain stem	65.00
Claret	100.00	Lamp, original burner	
Compote, round		Hand, applied handle	90.00
Covered		Stand	
High standard, sweetmeat, 6″d ...	150.00	9½″h	150.00
Low standard, 6″d	150.00	11″h. (whale oil)	175.00
Open		Pitcher, water, applied handle,	
High standard, originally termed		½ gallon	400.00
the "sweetmeat," 6″d	80.00	Salt, master, open, footed	45.00
Low standard, 6″d	80.00	Spoonholder	85.00
Cordial	100.00	Sugar bowl, covered	90.00
Creamer, applied handle	125.00	Tumbler	
Decanter, original stopper (blown or		Flip	125.00
pressed with matching pattern)		Water, footed	75.00
Pint	100.00	Whiskey, flat	65.00
Quart	100.00	Wine	65.00
Egg cup, footed	45.00		

WASHINGTON

Champagne; covered sugar bowl; decanter; celery vase; goblet.

AKA: Early Washington, Leafy Panel and Thumbprint.

Claret; egg cup.

Flint. New England Glass Co., East Cambridge, OH. ca. 1869. Illustrated in the New England Glass Co. catalog of 1869.

Original color production: Clear. Brilliant, heavy flint, the main design element of Washington consists of a clear, long vertical oval and columns of smaller clear ovals separated by long clear vertical pointed prisms. Arching above both panels and prism appear three smaller prisms connected in chain-like fashion. Handles are beautifully applied, ending in well executed volutes. Decanters were originally sold with "patent corks", a combination of cork and pewter which were cheaper to manufacture than matching glass stoppers.

Reproductions: None.

References: Drep-ABC OG (PP. 173, 270), Hrt/Cob (P. 71), Hea-OS (P. 134, No. 2504), Lee-EAPG (Pl. 10, No. 1), Migh (Pl. 3), Mil-1 (Pl. 1), Mtz-1 (PP. 18, 19), Oliv-AAG (P. 58), Revi-APG (P. 252), Uni-1 (PP. 22-23), Watk-AG (Pl. 20), Watk-CG (P. 93), Watk-NEG Co. (P.152), Wlkr-PGA (Fig. 8, No. 23).

Items made	Clear	Items made	Clear
Ale glass, flat	125.00	Claret	110.00
Bottle, bitters	85.00	Compote, round	
Bowl, flat		Covered	
Round		High standard	
Covered		Deep bowl	
5"d	85.00	6"d	125.00
6"d	85.00	7"d	125.00
7"d	110.00	8"d	140.00
8"d	125.00	9"d	160.00
Open		10"d	175.00
5"d	35.00	Shallow bowl	
6"d	35.00	6"d	125.00
7"d	40.00	7"d	125.00
8"d	55.00	8"d	140.00
Oval		Low standard, deep bowl	
7"	40.00	6"d	125.00
8"	45.00	7"d	125.00
9"	45.00	8"d	140.00
10"	55.00	9"d	160.00
Butter dish, covered	185.00	10"d	175.00
Celery vase, low pedestal, smooth rim	90.00	Open	
Champagne	125.00	High standard	

Items made	Clear		Items made	Clear
Deep bowl			Shallow bowl	
6″d	50.00		6″	35.00
7″d	50.00		7″	40.00
8″d	60.00		8″	55.00
9″d	75.00		9″	60.00
10″d	85.00		10″	65.00
Shallow bowl			Egg cup, footed	75.00
6″d	50.00		Goblet	
7″d	50.00		Large (gentleman's)	95.00
8″d	60.00		Small (lady's)	95.00
Low standard			Honey dish, round, flat, $3\frac{1}{2}$″d	30.00
Deep bowl			Lamp, original burner	145.00
6″d	50.00		Mug	
7″d	50.00		Beer	85.00
8″d	60.00		Lemonade	85.00
9″d	75.00		Pitcher, water	
10″d	85.00		$\frac{1}{2}$ gallon	300.00
Shallow bowl			3 pint	350.00
6″d	50.00		Plate, round	
7″d	50.00		6″d	60.00
8″d	60.00		7″d	65.00
Cordial	150.00		Salt	
Creamer	200.00		Dip, individual, $1\frac{7}{8}$″d	25.00
Decanter			Master	
With bar lip			Flat, round	55.00
1 pint	150.00		Footed, open	55.00
1 quart	150.00		Sauce dish, round, flat	
With original stopper			4″d	25.00
1 pint	175.00		5″d	25.00
1 quart	175.00		Spoonholder	65.00
Dish, flat, oval			Sugar bowl, covered	125.00
Covered, 10″	145.00		Syrup pitcher, applied handle, original	
Open			top	175.00
Deep			Tumbler	
6″	35.00		Jelly	65.00
7″	40.00		Water	
8″	55.00		$\frac{1}{3}$ pint	85.00
9″	60.00		$\frac{1}{2}$ pint	85.00
10″	65.00		Wine	100.00

Master salt; goblet; water pitcher; celery vase, egg cup.

AKA: Centennial [Lee]. Chain with Diamonds, Washington [Lee].

Non-flint. Gillinder & Co., Philadelphia, PA. ca. 1876. Shards have been found at the site of the Burlington Glass Works, Hamilton, Ontario, Canada.

Original color production: Clear, clear with acid finished centers (platters). Opaque, white, or any other color is rare. Handles are applied.

Reproductions: None.

References: Bat-GPG (PP. 37, 39), Cod-OS (Pl. 52), Gor-CC (PP. 22, 34, 94-95, 118-129), Hart/Cobb-SS (P. 72), Hea-OS (P. 134, No. 2528), Hlms-BCA (P. 278), Kam-2 (P. 124), Kam/Wod-Vol.2 (P. 624), Lee-EAPG (Pl. 117), Lee-VG (Pl. 51), Lind-HG (PP. 34-35), Mrsh-SRG (Pl. 51), McCn-PGP (P. 397), Mil-2 (Pl. 20), Mtz-1 (PP. 112-113), Mtz-2 (PP. 186-187), Oliv-AAG (P. 58), Rev-APG (P. 168), Stu-BP (PP. 91, 96), Uni-1 (PP. 276-277), Uni/Wor-CHPGT (P. 222), Wlkr-PGA (Fig. 8, Nos. 2, 45).

Items made	Clear	Items made	Clear
Bowl, flat, open		8″d	75.00
Oval		9″d	75.00
7″	25.00	Open	
8″	25.00	8″d	45.00
9″	25.00	9″d	45.00
Round		Creamer, applied handle	90.00
7″d	25.00	Dish, pickle, fish shape	25.00
8″d	25.00	Egg cup, footed	35.00
9″d	25.00	Goblet	45.00
Butter dish, covered	80.00	Pitcher, applied handle	
Cake stand, high standard		Milk, 1 quart	110.00
8½″d	45.00	Water, ½ gallon	125.00
10″d	65.00	Plate, 6″d (R)	75.00
Celery vase, pedestaled, scalloped rim,		Platter, oval	
7½″h	60.00	"Carpenter's Hall" center	100.00
Champagne	65.00	"Independence Hall" center	100.00
Compote, high standard, round		"Washington Head" center	100.00
Covered			

Items made	Clear	Items made	Clear
Relish tray, flat, oval, claw handles, marked "Centennial 1776-1876"	50.00	Shaker, original top	65.00
Salt		Sauce dish, flat, round	15.00
Dip, individual, 2″d	20.00	Spoonholder	35.00
Master, open, flat, oval	35.00	Sugar bowl, covered	75.00
		Syrup pitcher, original top	150.00
		Wine	35.00

WEDDING BELLS

Tumbler.

OMN: Fostoria No. 789.

Non-flint. The Fostoria Glass Co. (pattern line No. 789), Moundsville, OH. ca. 1900. Illustrated in the December 23, 1899 issue of *China, Glass and Lamps,* and illustralted in trade journal advertisements in 1900.

Original color production: Clear, clear with rose blush. Handles are applied.

Reproductions: The Fostoria Glass Co. reproduced a look-alike large covered sugar bowl in bluish-purple signed with a paper label. Ca. 1989–1990.

References: Fos-CAT (PP. 13-15), Hea-1 (P. 44), Hea-3 (P. 45, Fig. 3256), Hea-6 (P. 45, Fig. 382), Kam-4 (P. 113), Kam-5 (P. 84), Kam-6 (Pl. 91), Migh-TPS (Pl. 20), Mtz-1 (P. 173), Pet-Sal (p. 43), Rev-APG (P. 159), Weath-FOST (PP. 32, 43).

Items made	Clear	Clear w/Blush
Bowl, round		
Berry, master, flat	65.00	85.00
Finger or waste	30.00	40.00
Butter dish, covered	45.00	125.00
Celery vase	35.00	65.00
Compote, round, covered		
High standard	55.00	—
Low standard	45.00	—
Creamer, applied handle	45.00	65.00

Items made	Clear	Clear w/Blush
Cruet, original stopper	50.00	125.00
Cup, sherbert	15.00	20.00
Decanter, original stopper, 1 quart	75.00	95.00
Pitcher, water, applied handle		
Bulbous	85.00	125.00
Tankard, $^{1}\!/_{2}$ gallon	85.00	135.00
Punch bowl, flat	175.00	225.00
Relish tray, flat, triangular shaped	20.00	35.00
Salt shaker, original top	30.00	45.00
Spoonholder	40.00	65.00
Sugar bowl, covered	55.00	90.00
Syrup pitcher, original top	90.00	200.00
Toothpick holder	45.00	90.00
Tumbler, flat		
Water	20.00	40.00
Whiskey	20.00	40.00
Wine	35.00	50.00

WEDDING RING

Wine; goblet; creamer; flat sauce dish.

AKA: Double Wedding Ring.

Flint (ca. 1860s), non-flint (ca. 1870s). Original maker unknown.

Original color production: Clear.

Reproductions: The toothpick holder (originally not part of the set) was reproduced in clear and various colors. The Dalzell/Viking Glass Co., Ca. 1989–1990, has reissued the following items in flint glass in clear, pale blue, and pink: goblet, 6″d. plate, footed sherbert, covered sugar bowl and a squatty and tall toothpick holder. Items are signed with the company's label.

References: Lee-VG (Pl. 19), Mtz-1 (PP. 36-37), Thur-1 (P. 166), Uni1 (PP. 62, 222).

Items made	Clear	Items made	Clear
Butter dish, covered	100.00	Lamp, oil, finger, original burner and	
Celery vase	80.00	chimney, 5"	85.00
Champagne	90.00	Pitcher, water, ½ gallon, applied	
Cordial	85.00	handle	175.00
Creamer	85.00	Relish tray	50.00
Decanter		Sauce dish, flat, round	30.00
Applied heavy bar lip	125.00	Spoonholder	80.00
Original stopper	125.00	Sugar bowl, covered	100.00
Goblet		Syrup pitcher, applied handle, original	
Faceted knob stem	85.00	top	100.00
Plain stem	85.00	Tumbler, water, flat	85.00
		Wine	95.00

WESTWARD HO

Mug 2"h.; covered compote 5"d.; celery vase; goblet; mug 3 ½"h.

OMN: Pioneer. AKA: Tippecanoe.

Non-flint. Gillinder and Sons, Philadelphia, PA. ca. 1879.

Original color production: Clear, with acid finish. The main pattern design of Westward Ho consists of an acid-finished design in high relief consisting of bison, deer and log cabin. Covered pieces sport a crouched Indian finial. Originally produced in both plain and heavy versions, the molds to the pattern were made by Jacobus.

Reproductions: Reproduced from the 1930s from new molds, the first reproductions of Westward Ho were too white in the frosting and rough to the touch. Later reproductions gained excellent frosting although the detail of design is very poor; the hair on both the deer and the buffalo is missing where the hair on old items is distinctly visible. New pieces depict the deer's mouth open, the original being closed and resembling a straight line. Reproduced by a number of firms including Westmorland Glass Co., Grapeville, PA. and wholesaled nationally by Trans World Trading Co., Robinson, IL., and the L.G. Wright Glass Co., New Martinsville, WV. (distributed by Jennings Red Barn, New Martinsville, WV. and Carl Forslund, Grand Rapids, MI.) The following items were produced in clear, amberina, blue, green and clear with acid finish: 4"d low standard covered compote, 5"d low standard covered compote, 6″ oval covered compote, 6″d round covered compote, tumbler (not original to the set), footed sauce dish, 6″d high standard covered compote, covered butter dish, goblet, water pitcher, wine, 7½″h creamer, and the 10½″h covered sugar bowl.

The L.G. Wright Glass Co. 1970 catalog supplement illustrates the following items reissued in clear with acid finish: creamer, covered butter dish, covered sugar bowl, covered 4″d low standard covered compote, and celery vase. In the 1974 L.G. Wright Glass Co. master catalog, the following items are illustrated in clear with acid finish: covered butter dish, celery vase, 6″d round high standard covered compote, 4″d covered low standard compote, 6″ oval covered low standard compote, 6″d round low standard covered compote, creamer, goblet, footed sauce dish (termed the sherbert), covered sugar bowl, tumbler (not original to the set), and the wine.

References: Chip-ROS (P. 72), Drep-ABC OG (PP. 157, 272), Grow-WCG (Fig. 18), Hlms-BCA (P. 278), Kam-1 (P. 16), Kam/Wod-Vol. 2 (P. 634), Lee-EAPG (P. 89, Nos. 1-2), Lee-VG (Pl. 7), Lind-HG (PP. 205-206), Mrsh-SRG (P. 19), McCn-PGP (P. 397), McKrn-AG (Pl. 209), Mil-1 (Pl. 79), Mil-2 (Pl. 40), Mtz-1 (PP. 100-111), Nortn-PG (PP. 58-66), Oliv-AAG (P. 57), Pap-GAG (P. 194), Rev-APG (PP. 163, 170), Sav-GW (P. 93), Schwtz-AG (P. 121), Spil-AEPG (P. 280), Spil-TBV (P. 294), Stu-BP (P. 123), Uni-1 (PP. 94-95), Uni-2 (P. 219), Uni-TCG (PP. 178-179), Uni/Wor-CHPGT (PP. 223-224), Wat-AG (Pl. 25).

Items made	Clear/ Frosted	Items made	Clear/ Frosted
Bowl, footed, round, 5″d	125.00	Low standard, 5″d	100.00
Butter dish, covered, 8¼″d., high		Creamer, pressed handle	85.00
standard	185.00	Marmalade jar, covered	185.00
Celery vase, pedestaled, scalloped rim	125.00	Mug, pressed handle	
Compote		2″h	200.00
Oval, open, 9″	150.00	3½″h	175.00
Round		Pickle dish, oval	65.00
Covered		Pitcher, pressed handle	
High standard		Milk, 1 quart	350.00
5″d	225.00	Water, ½ gallon, 9½″h	350.00
6″d	225.00	Plate, bread, oval	100.00
9″d	250.00	Platter, oval, 9″ x 13″	100.00
Low standard		Sauce dishes, footed, round	
5″d	150.00	3½″d	25.00
6″d	150.00	4″d	25.00
8¾″d	175.00	4½″d	30.00
Open		5″d	35.00
High standard		Spoonholder, footed, scalloped rim	85.00
5″d	100.00	Sugar bowl, covered, pedestaled	175.00
8″d	125.00	Wine (R)	250.00+

Goblet.

OMN: Duquesne. AKA: Hops and Barley, Oats and Barley.

Non-flint. Bryce Bothers, Pittsburgh, PA. ca. 1880s. Reissued by the United States Glass Co., Pittsburgh, PA. at Factory "B" (Bryce Brothers, Pittsburgh, PA.) after the 1891 merger.

Original color production: Amber, blue, vaseline, clear.

Reproductions: None.

References: Enos-MPG (Chart-2), Grow-WCG (P. 147, Fig. 21-"7"), Hea-3 (P. 76), Hea-5 (PP. 41, 81), Kam-1 (PP. 41-42), Kam-5 (P. 156), Kam-7 (Plts. 1-2), Lee-EAPG (Pl. 50), McCn-PGP (P. 435), Mil-1 (Pl. 112), Mtz-1 (P. 84), Pet-Sal (P. 43), Rev-APG (PP. 87, 90), Uni-1 (P. 219), Wlkr-PGA (Fig. 8, No. 20).

Items made	Amber	Blue	Clear	Canary
Bowl, flat, round				
Covered				
6"d	30.00	35.00	20.00	30.00
7"d	30.00	35.00	20.00	30.00
8"d	35.00	40.00	25.00	35.00
Open, fruit				
6"d	20.00	25.00	10.00	25.00
7"d	20.00	25.00	10.00	25.00
8"d	25.00	30.00	15.00	25.00
Bread plate, handled	25.00	35.00	20.00	40.00
Butter dish, covered	45.00	60.00	35.00	50.00
Cake stand, high standard				
8"d	30.00	45.00	20.00	30.00
9"d	30.00	45.00	20.00	30.00
10"d	40.00	50.00	30.00	40.00
Compote, round				
Covered, high standard				
6"d				
Handled (originally termed the "sweetmeat")	45.00	55.00	40.00	45.00
Handleless	45.00	55.00	40.00	45.00
7"d	45.00	55.00	40.00	45.00

Items made	Amber	Blue	Clear	Canary
8″d	50.00	55.00	45.00	50.00
Open, high standard, shallow bowl				
6″d	30.00	40.00	30.00	35.00
7″d	35.00	45.00	30.00	35.00
8″d	40.00	50.00	35.00	40.00
10″d	45.00	55.00	40.00	45.00
Creamer, pressed handle	30.00	40.00	25.00	35.00
Dish, jelly, footed, 5″d	30.00	40.00	30.00	35.00
Goblet	35.00	45.00	25.00	40.00
Mug, large, pressed handle	30.00	40.00	20.00	35.00
Pitcher, pressed handle				
Milk, 1 quart	45.00	65.00	30.00	55.00
Water, ½ gallon	55.00	75.00	45.00	65.00
Plate				
7″d	20.00	30.00	15.00	25.00
9″d	25.00	35.00	20.00	45.00
Relish dish	20.00	30.00	15.00	25.00
Salt shaker, original top	25.00	25.00	20.00	30.00
Sauce dish, round				
Flat, handled, 4″d	12.00	15.00	10.00	15.00
Footed, 4″d	15.00	15.00	10.00	15.00
Spoonholder	30.00	40.00	25.00	30.00
Sugar bowl, covered	40.00	50.00	35.00	40.00
Syrup pitcher, original top				
½ pint	175.00	175.00	45.00	175.00
1 pint	175.00	175.00	45.00	175.00
Tumbler, water				
Flat	35.00	35.00	20.00	30.00
Footed	35.00	35.00	20.00	30.00

WILDFLOWER

Creamer; spoonholder; covered sugar bowl; covered butter dish.

OMN: Adams' No. 140.

Non-flint. Adams & Co. (pattern line No. 140), Pittsburgh, PA. ca. 1874. Reissued by the United States Glass Co., Pittsburgh, PA. at Factory "A" (Bryce Brothers, Pittsburgh, PA.) ca. 1891-1900.

Original color production: Amber, apple green, blue, vaseline, clear.

Reproductions: Wildflower has been reissued from new molds, in all original colors from early 1936 to the present by numerous factories. In 1971 the L.G. Wright Glass Co. reissued both the goblet and wine in vaseline. The L. G. Wright 1974 master catalog lists the following items in amber, blue, clear, ruby, amethyst, green, and vaseline: champagne, tall covered jar, low standard 4″d. covered compote, creamer, goblet, 10″d plate, flat rectangular salt dip, footed 4″d. round sauce dish, covered sugar bowl, tumbler and wine. Boyd Art glass, Inc. reissued the following items in opaque pink: creamer, covered sugar bowl, footed covered sauce dish, high standard covered compote, and tall covered candy jar (not original to the set), while the footed sauce has been reissued in deep black.

In the 1970s, the L. G. Wright Glass Co., New Martinsville, WV. (distributed by Jennings Red Barn, New Martinsville, WV. and Carl Forslund, Grand Rapids, MI.) reissued from a newly chipped mold a look-alike turtle master salt. Unlike the original, the look alike is $3^1/_4$″ in length, and flat, lacking the turtle base. The Crystal Art Glass Co., Cambridge, OH. also reissued the goblet from new molds and in original colors. Unlike original items in Wildflower, reissues lack the highly refined stippling that fills both the flowers and stems. Vertical stems on new items are broken and do not uniformly run around the bowl. Although old colors have been used, colors are too harsh and artificial, unlike the soft, mellow look of originals.

References: Brn-SD (P. 151), Corn-PG (P. 26), Enos-MPG (Chart-1), Grow-WCG (P. 124, Fig. 17-"3"), Hea-1 (P. 63), Hea-5 (P. 40, No. 103), Hea-OS (P. 40, No. 364), Hea-3 (P. 46, Figs. 331, 339), Inn-EGP (P. 34), Inn-PG (P. 347), Kam-1 (P. 36), Kam-5 (P. 56), Kam/Wod-Vol.2 (P. 632), Lee-EAPG (Pl. 126, Nos. 3-4), Lee-VG (Pl. 6), McCn-PGP (P. 297), Mtz-1 (PP. 62-63), Mil-1 (Pl. 53), Oliv-AAG (P. 75), Pet-Sal (P. 43), Rev-APG (PP. 18, 22), Spil-TBV (PP. 40-148), Stu-BP (P. 36), Uni-1 (PP. 193, 197), Uni-/Wor-CHPGT (P. 226).

Items made	Amber	Green	Blue	Clear	Vas
Basket, cake, oblong, metal handle	80.00	85.00	85.00	50.00	75.00
Bowl, open, flat					
Round, 6″d	25.00	35.00	35.00	20.00	25.00
Square, flat					
6″	25.00	35.00	35.00	20.00	25.00
7″	25.00	35.00	35.00	20.00	25.00
8″	25.00	35.00	35.00	20.00	25.00
9″	25.00	35.00	35.00	20.00	25.00
Waste	30.00	40.00	35.00	30.00	45.00
Butter dish, covered					
Collared base	40.00	50.00	50.00	35.00	45.00
Flat base, 8″d	35.00	45.00	45.00	30.00	40.00
Cake stand, high standard, 10½″d	50.00	80.00	70.00	45.00	50.00
Celery vase	50.00	60.00	55.00	35.00	55.00
Champagne	45.00	55.00	50.00	35.00	45.00
Compote, covered					
High standard					
Oblong, 8″	80.00	85.00	85.00	50.00	75.00
Round	80.00	85.00	85.00	50.00	75.00
Square, round flared rim	80.00	85.00	85.00	50.00	75.00
Low standard					
7″	—	—	70.00	—	—

Items made	Amber	Green	Blue	Clear	Vas
8″	—	—	70.00	—	—
Creamer, 5¹/₂″h, pressed handle	30.00	40.00	35.00	30.00	45.00
Dish, open, square, flat					
5³/₄″	15.00	25.00	25.00	10.00	15.00
6³/₄″	20.00	30.00	30.00	15.00	20.00
7″	20.00	30.00	30.00	15.00	20.00
7³/₄″	20.00	30.00	30.00	15.00	20.00
Goblet	35.00	40.00	40.00	30.00	40.00
Pitcher, water, ¹/₂ gallon, pressed handle	55.00	75.00	50.00	40.00	65.00
Plate, cake, 10″sq	30.00	30.00	45.00	25.00	30.00
Plate, oblong, 10″	40.00	45.00	40.00	30.00	30.00
Platter, scalloped rim, 8″ x 11″	—	—	45.00	—	—
Relish tray, oblong	30.00	20.00	20.00	20.00	20.00
Salt					
Master, turtle shape, 2¹/₈″h	45.00	50.00	50.00	30.00	40.00
Shaker, original top	25.00	55.00	35.00	20.00	45.00
Sauce dish					
Round					
Flat					
3¹/₂″d	10.00	15.00	15.00	10.00	10.00
4″d.	10.00	15.00	15.00	10.00	10.00
Footed					
3¹/₂″d	15.00	15.00	15.00	15.00	15.00
4″d	15.00	15.00	15.00	15.00	15.00
Square, 4¹/₂″	15.00	15.00	15.00	15.00	15.00
Spoonholder	30.00	35.00	30.00	20.00	40.00
Sugar bowl, covered, 7¹/₂″h	45.00	45.00	50.00	30.00	45.00
Syrup pitcher, original tin top, 7¹/₂″h	125.00	150.00	150.00	75.00	150.00
Tray, water, oval	50.00	60.00	60.00	40.00	55.00
Tumbler, water, flat	40.00	35.00	35.00	25.00	35.00
Wine	45.00	45.00	45.00	30.00	45.00

WILLOW OAK

Goblet (blue); cake stand and plate (both amber).

OMN: Bryce's Wreath. AKA: Acorn [Stuart], Acorn and Oak Leaf, Oak Leaf [Stuart], Stippled Daisy, Thistle and Sunflower, Willow and Oak.

Non-flint. Bryce Brothers, Pittsburgh, PA. ca. 1880. Reissued by the United States Glass Co., Pittsburgh, PA. Factory "B" (Bryce Brothers, Pittsburgh, PA.) ca. 1891.

Original color production: Amber, blue, canary-yellow, clear.

Reproductions: None.

References: Enos-MPG (Chart-6), Hea-3 (P. 215), Hea-5 (P. 42, No. 122), Kam-1 (P. 36), Kam/Wod-Vol.2 (P. 635), Lee-EAPG (Pl. 159, No. 2), McCn-PGP (P. 2285), Mil-1 (Pl. 53), Mtz-1 (PP. 62-63), Oliv-AAG (P. 75), Pet-Sal (P. 43), Rev-APG (P. 90), Spil-AEPG (P. 300), Stu-BP (P. 50), Uni-1 (P. 141), Wlkr-PGA (Fig. 8, Nos. 16, 55).

Items made	Amber	Blue	Canary	Clear
Bowl, flat, round				
Berry, master				
7"d	25.00	40.00	45.00	20.00
8"d	25.00	40.00	45.00	20.00
Finger or waste	35.00	40.00	50.00	30.00
Bread plate, closed handles, 9"d	40.00	50.00	60.00	35.00
Butter dish, covered, flanged	55.00	65.00	80.00	40.00
Cake stand, low standard				
8½"d	60.00	65.00	70.00	45.00
9"d	60.00	65.00	70.00	45.00
Celery vase	45.00	60.00	70.00	45.00
Compote, high standard				
Covered				
6"d	30.00	40.00	50.00	25.00
7½"d	50.00	65.00	80.00	40.00
9"d	55.00	60.00	85.00	50.00
Open, 7"d	30.00	40.00	50.00	25.00
Creamer, 5½"h, pressed handle	40.00	50.00	60.00	35.00
Goblet	40.00	50.00	60.00	35.00
Mug, large, pressed handle	35.00	45.00	55.00	30.00
Pitcher, pressed handle				
Milk, 1 quart	50.00	60.00	70.00	40.00
Water, ½ gallon	55.00	65.00	75.00	45.00
Plate, round, tab handles				
7"d	35.00	45.00	55.00	30.00
9"d	35.00	45.00	55.00	30.00
11"d	40.00	45.00	55.00	30.00
Salt shaker, original top	25.00	40.00	50.00	20.00
Sauce dish				
Flat, square, handled, 4"	15.00	20.00	20.00	10.00
Footed, round, 4"d	20.00	25.00	25.00	15.00
Spoonholder	35.00	40.00	50.00	30.00
Sugar bowl, covered	65.00	70.00	75.00	40.00
Tray, water, 10½"d	35.00	50.00	60.00	30.00
Tumbler, water, flat	30.00	35.00	40.00	25.00

Low footed covered compote.

Goblet; egg cup.

Non-flint. Maker unknown, ca. late 1870s.

Original color production: Clear.

Reproductions: None.

References: Cod-OS (Pl. 24), Kam-5 (PP. 4-5), Lee-EAPG (Pl. 139, No. 40), McCn-PGP (P. 295), Mil-1 (Pl. 25), Mtz-1 (PP. 62-63), Uni-1 (P. 202-203), Wlkr-PGA (Fig. 8, Nos. 4, 15, 24).

Items made	Clear	Items made	Clear
Bowl, master berry, flat, open, oval, 8″	30.00	8″d	35.00
Butter dish, covered, flat	50.00	Creamer, applied handle, pedestaled	45.00
Celery vase, pedestaled, scalloped rim	50.00	Egg cup, footed, pedestaled	35.00
Compote, round		Goblet	40.00
Covered		Pickle dish, oval, tapered at one end	15.00
High standard		Pitcher, water, applied handle,	
7″d	65.00	½ gallon	65.00
8″d	75.00	Salt, master, footed, open	25.00
Low standard		Sauce dish, flat, round	15.00
7″d	35.00	Spoonholder, pedestaled, scalloped rim	30.00
8″d	40.00	Sugar bowl, covered, pedestaled	65.00
Open, low standard		Tumbler, flat, water	45.00
7″d	35.00	Wine	45.00

Syrup pitcher; sugar shaker.

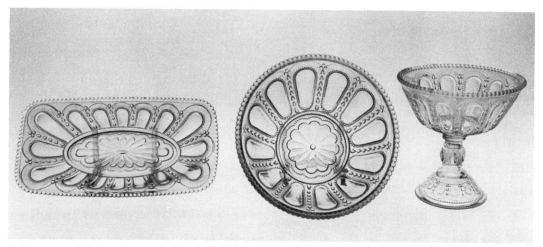

Celery tray; 8″d. bowl; 6″d high standard open compote.

OMN: U.S. Glass No. 15,079, Wisconsin. AKA: Beaded Dewdrop [Lee, Metz, Millard], Prism [Kamm].

Non-flint. The United States Glass Co. (pattern line No. 15,079), Pittsburgh, PA. at Factory "U", (Gas City, IN.) ca. 1903. Illustrated in the United States Glass Co. 1904 domestic and 1919 export catalogs, the Montgomery Ward & Co. 1908 catalog No. 76, the August 15, 1904 Baltimore Bargain House general merchandise catalog No. 496 and the 1905 Lion Brothers catalog.

Original color production: Clear. Characteristic of the pattern is the beading found on rims of items.

Reproductions: None.

References: Bros-TS (P. 25), Brn-SD (P. 53), Hea-5 (Pl. 167, Pl. "A"), Hart/Cobb-SS (P. 73), Kam-5 (P. 42), Kam-7 (P. 46), Lee-EAPG (Pl. 57), Lind-HG (P. 182), McCn-PGP (P. 583),

Migh-TPS (Pl. 3), Mil-1 (Pl. 119), Mtz-1 (PP. 188-189), Pet-Sal (P. 154), Pyne-PG (PP. 150-151), Rev-APG (P. 319), Uni-1 (P. 155), Uni-2 (P. 250).

Items made	Clear	Items made	Clear
Banana stand	75.00	Cup, custard	10.00
Bon bon dish, covered, single handle	25.00	Dish, flat	
Bottle, oil, with or without handle	25.00	Covered	
Bowl, flat		Oval, 6″, handled	50.00
Covered, oval, handled, 6″	35.00	Round	
Open		6″d	50.00
Oblong, preserve, 8″l	25.00	7″d	60.00
Oval, double handles, 5½″	20.00	8″d	65.00
Round, straight sided		Open	
6″d	25.00	Mustard	25.00
7″d	30.00	Olive, handled, 5½″d	35.00
8″d	30.00	Preserve	
Butter dish, flat		6″d	25.00
Table size, covered, flanged rim	50.00	7″d	25.00
¼ pound, flanged base	40.00	8″d	30.00
Double handled		Goblet	50.00
Covered	45.00	Jelly dish, 5″d., footed, round	
Open	35.00	Covered	65.00
Cake stand, high standard		Open	40.00
6½″d	45.00	Marmalade jar, straight sided, original	
8½″d	45.00	patterned cover	125.00
9½″d	55.00	Mug, large, pressed handle	35.00
11½″d	55.00	Mustard jar, bulbous, covered, low	
Celery		circular foot	40.00
Tray, rectangular	45.00	Pickle	
Vase, pedestaled, flat, beaded rim ..	45.00	Dish, rectangular	20.00
Compote, round		Jar, covered	100.00
Covered, high standard		Pitcher, footed, pressed handle	
5″d., jelly	55.00	Milk, 1 quart	60.00
6″d	55.00	Water	
7″d	60.00	3 pints	75.00
8″d	65.00	½ gallon	75.00
Open		Plate, square	
High standard		5″ (confection)	25.00
Deep bowl, beaded rim		6¾″	25.00
6″d	30.00	7″., scooped center	30.00
7″d	30.00	Preserve dish, flat, rectangular, deep	
8″d	35.00	6″l	25.00
Saucer bowl, beaded rim		8″l	30.00
8½″d	35.00	Relish tray, handled	20.00
9½″d	40.00	Salt shaker, original top	
10½″d	35.00	Bulbous	35.00
Low standard, cone shaped bowl		Tapered	35.00
5″d	30.00	Sauce dish, flat, round, 4″d, flat	
7″d	35.00	beaded rim	10.00
Condiment set, complete		Saucer, round, beaded rim, 5″d	15.00
Salt, pepper, individual sugar bowl,		Sherbert cup	10.00
individual creamer	100.00	Spoonholder	35.00
Salt, pepper, covered horse radish.	100.00	Sugar bowl, Hotel, bulbous, low	
Creamer, pressed handle		circular foot	
Individual	35.00	Covered	55.00
Table size	50.00	Without lid	55.00
Cruet, applied handle, original melon		Individual	30.00
stopper	110.00	Table size, tall, oval, footed	55.00
Cup/saucer, set	50.00	Sugar shaker, original top	95.00

Items made	Clear	Items made	Clear
Syrup pitcher, original lid	125.00	Vase, cylindrical, beaded rim, 6"h	35.00
Toothpick holder	85.00	Wine	85.00
Tumbler, water, flat	45.00		

WOODEN PAIL

Toothpick or match holder; creamer; spoonholder; covered butter dish (all blue).

AKA: Bucket Set, Oaken Bucket.

Non-flint. Bryce, Higbee & Company, Pittsburgh, PA. ca. 1880s, reissued by the United States Glass Company, Pittsburgh, PA. ca. 1891.

Original color production: Amber, amethyst, blue, canary-yellow, clear. Unlike most conventional patterns of the time, the main design element of Wooden Pail consists of "wooden planks" held firmly in place by what resembles metal straps, reminiscent of the old fashioned wooden barrel. Both the creamer and water pitcher display an addition in the design resembling the swagged metal handle found on the candy container.

Reproductions: None.

References: Hea-5 (PP. 25, 36), Hrtng-P&P (P. 102), Kam-1 (P. 55), Lee-VG (Pl. 67), McCn-PGP (P. 497), Mtz-1 (P. 128), Rev-APG (PP. 87-88).

Items made	Amber	Amethyst	Blue	Canary	Clear
Butter dish, covered, flat, tab-handled	95.00	225.00	110.00	95.00	65.00
Miniatures					
Butter dish covered	—	—	—	—	65.00
Creamer	—	—	—	—	40.00
Spoonholder	—	—	—	—	35.00
Sugar bowl, covered	—	—	—	—	45.00
Creamer, collared base, pressed handle	60.00	125.00	75.00	60.00	40.00
Pitcher, water, 1/2 gallon, pressed handle	95.00	225.00	110.00	95.00	65.00
Spoonholder, collared base	50.00	100.00	60.00	50.00	35.00
Sugar bowl, covered, collared base	65.00	150.00	75.00	65.00	45.00
Toothpick or matcher holder (3 sizes)	35.00	85.00	40.00	35.00	25.00

Items made	Amber	Amethyst	Blue	Canary	Clear
Tumbler	30.00	65.00	35.00	30.00	20.00

WYOMING

Relish tray; individual creamer; water pitcher; covered sugar.

OMN: U.S. Glass No. 15,081, Wyoming. AKA: Enigma, Bulls Eye.

Non-flint. The United States Glass Co. (pattern line No. 15,081), Pittsburgh, PA. at Factory "U" (United States Glass Co., Gas City, IN.) and "E" (Richards & Hartley Glass Co., Tarentum, PA.) ca. 1903. Illustrated in the 1905 Lyon Brothers catalog and the 1904 and 1907 United States Glass Co. catalogs.

Original color production: Clear.

Reproductions: None.

References: Bros-TS (P. 28), Hart/Cobb-SS (P. 74), Hea-5 (PP. 13, 25), Kam-2 (PP. 49-50), McCn-PGP (P. 585), Mil-1 (P. 140), Mtz-2 (PP. 102-103), Pet-Sal (P. 43), Pyne-PG (P. 151), Rev-APG (P. 319), Uni-2 (P. 251).

Items made	Clear	Items made	Clear
Bowl, open, round, flat, scalloped rim		Open, scalloped rim	
6"d	15.00	Deep bowl	
7"d	15.00	6"d	30.00
8"d	20.00	7"d	35.00
Butter dish, covered, flat, flanged base,		8"d	35.00
9"d	50.00	Saucer bowl	
Cake stand, high standard		7"d	35.00
9"d	40.00	8"d	35.00
10"d	45.00	9"d	40.00
11"d	50.00	10"d	40.00
Compote, round		Creamer, pressed handle	
Covered, high standard		Covered, individual, tankard	35.00
6"d	50.00	Open	
7"d	55.00	Individual, tankard	30.00
8"d	65.00	Table size	35.00

Items made	Clear	Items made	Clear
Dish, preserve, oval, 8″l	20.00	Salt shaker, original top	
Goblet	55.00	Bulbous	35.00
Mug, pressed handle	40.00	Straight-sided	35.00
Pickle dish, flat, oval, double handles	20.00	Sauce dish, flat, round, 4″d	10.00
Pitcher, pressed handle		Spoonholder, pedestaled	30.00
Milk, 1 quart	65.00	Sugar bowl, covered	45.00
Water, 3 pint	75.00	Syrup pitcher, original nickel or tin top	90.00
Plate, cake	55.00	Tumbler, water, flat	40.00
Relish tray	15.00	Wine	85.00

XRAY

Carafe (emerald green w/gold).

OMN: X ray

Non-flint. The Riverside Glass Works, Wellsburg, WV. ca. 1896 to 1898. Illustrated in *China, Glass and Lamps, 1896.*

Original color production: Clear and emerald green, (plain, with gilt, or enameled decorated). Amethyst, canary-yellow, or any other color is rare. Decorated by the Beaumont Glass Company, Martins Ferry, OH.

Reproductions: None.

References: Eige-CGM WV (PP. 22-23), Hea-1 (P. 45, Figs. 332-333), Hea-3 (P. 46, Fig. 36), Hea-6 (PP. 46-47), Hea-7 (P. 17), Kam-5 (P. 136), Lecnr-SS (P. 64), Migh-TPS (Pl. 21), Mur-CO (P. 6), Pet-GPP (PP. 204-205), Rev-APG (P. 296).

Items made	Amethyst	Clear	Emerald Green
Bowl, master berry, 8″d., beaded rim, round	55.00	25.00	45.00
Butter dish, covered, flanged rim	90.00	40.00	75.00
Celery vase	65.00	25.00	50.00
Compote			
Covered, high standard	85.00	40.00	65.00
Open, high standard, jelly, 6″d., beaded-scalloped rim	50.00	25.00	40.00

Items made	Amethyst	Clear	Emerald Green
Creamer, applied handle			
Individual	45.00	15.00	30.00
Breakfast	45.00	15.00	30.00
Table size	65.00	30.00	50.00
Cruet, original stopper	175.00	50.00	125.00
Cruet under tray	40.00	20.00	30.00
Pitcher, water, applied handle, $^1/_2$ gallon	125.00	40.00	75.00
Plate, bread	60.00	30.00	50.00
Salt shaker, original top	35.00	15.00	25.00
Sauce dish, round, flat, $4^1/_2$"d., $1^1/_2$"h	20.00	8.00	15.00
Spoonholder	50.00	25.00	40.00
Sugar bowl			
Individual, open	40.00	15.00	30.00
Table size, covered	75.00	35.00	50.00
Syrup pitcher, original top	125.00	275.00	350.00
Toothpick holder	15.00	30.00	65.00
Tray, undertray for cruet set, clover shape	40.00	60.00	80.00
Tumbler, water, flat	35.00	10.00	25.00

YALE

Creamer; covered sugar bowl; spoonholder; flat sauce dish.

OMN: Yale. AKA: Ball and Fan, Crow-foot, Turkey Track.

Non-flint. McKee & Brothers, Pittsburgh, PA. ca. 1887.

Original color production: Clear. Designed and patented by Julius Proeger, August 30, 1887 (patent design No. 17,675), and illustrated in the McKee & Brothers 1894 catalog.

Reproductions: None.

References: Bat-GPG (PP. 162-163), Kam-3 (P. 126), Lee-VG (Pl. 19, No. 3), Mtz-2 (PP. 132-133), Mil-1 (Pl. 68), Pet-GPP (PP. 163-164), Pet-Sal (P. 126), Rev-APG (PP. 234, 239, 242), Stot-McKe (P. 35), Uni-1 (P. 265), Wlkr-PGA (Fig. 15, No. 61).

Items made	Clear	Items made	Clear
Bowl, master berry, flat, open, 10½"d	20.00	Pitcher, water, ½ gallon, pressed	
Butter dish, covered	45.00	handle	55.00
Cake stand, high standard	50.00	Relish dish, oval	10.00
Celery vase	30.00	Salt shaker, original top	30.00
Compote, round		Sauce dish	
Covered, high standard	50.00	Flat, round	10.00
Open, scalloped rim		Footed	12.00
High standard	25.00	Spoonholder	25.00
Low standard	25.00	Sugar bowl, covered	35.00
Creamer, 6"h, pressed handle	35.00	Syrup pitcher, original top	85.00
Goblet	35.00	Tumbler, water, flat	20.00

ZIPPER

Water pitcher (amber); cruet (stopper missing).

AKA: Cobb, Late Sawtooth.

Non-flint. Richards & Hartley Glass Co., Tarentum, PA. ca. 1888.

Original color production: Clear. Amber or any other color is rare.

Reproductions: None.

References: Kam-2 (PP. 19, 132), Lee-VG (Pl. 36, No. 2), Luc-TG (PP. 190-192), McCn-PGP (P. 461), Mil-1 (Pl. 105), Mtz-1 (PP. 170-171), Rev-APG (P. 286), Spil-AEPG (P. 311).

Items made	Clear	Items made	Clear
Bowl, open, flat, 7"d, round	15.00	Creamer, pressed handle	
Butter dish, covered	40.00	High foot	35.00
Celery vase	25.00	Low foot	30.00
Cheese dish, covered	55.00	Cruet, original stopper	45.00
Compote, round		Dish, oblong, 9⅜" x 6"	20.00
Covered		Goblet	20.00
High standard, 8"d	45.00	Jam jar, covered	40.00
Low standard, 8"d	40.00	Pitcher, pressed handle	
Open, high standard	30.00	Milk, 1 quart	35.00

Items made	Clear		Items made	Clear
Water, ½ gallon	40.00		Footed	8.00
Relish tray, 10″l	15.00		Spoonholder	25.00
Salt dip, individual	5.00		Sugar bowl, covered	35.00
Sauce dish, round			Tumbler, flat, water	20.00
Flat	5.00			

ZIPPERED BLOCK

Tumbler; water pitcher; creamer (clear w/ruby stain).

OMN: Duncan & Sons No. 90. AKA: Cryptic [Millard], Iowa [Hartley], Nova Scotia Ribbon and Star.

Non-flint. George Duncan & Sons (pattern line No. 90), Pittsburgh, PA. ca. 1887. Reissued by the United States Glass Co. at Factory 'D" (George Duncan & Sons, Pittsburgh, PA.) ca. 1891. Shards have been found at the site of the Trenton Glass Works, Trenton-New Glasgow, Nova Scotia, and the Nova Scotia Glass Co. and Lamont Glass Co., Canada. Illustrated in the George Duncan and Sons 1887 catalog as No. 90, Zippered Block was designed and patented by John E. Miller, March 15, 1887.

Original color production: Clear, clear with ruby stain (after Duncan's joining the U.S. Glass Co. combine), clear and frosted (with or without cut stars). Plain or engraved, popular engravings being No. 562 and No. 563.

Reproductions: None.

References: Bar-RS (Pl. 13), Bred-EDG (PP. 21, 94-95), Hart/Cobb-SS (P. 33), Hea-5 (P. 102, Pl. 8), Hea-7 (Figs. 286-294), Kam-3 (P. 131), Krs-YD (PP. 71-72), McCn-PGP (P. 491), Mil-2 (Pl. 123), Mtz-2 (PP. 162-163), Rev-APG (PP. 148-149), Stev-GIC (P. 225), Thu-1 (P. 324), Uni-1 (P. 80), Uni-TCG (PP. 146-147), Wlkr-PGA (Fig. 15, No. 730).

Items made	Clear	Clear w/Ruby
Bowl		
Oblong, open		
Shallow, serrated rim		
6″	25.00	40.00

Items made	Clear	Clear w/Ruby
7″	25.00	40.00
8″	30.00	45.00
Oval		
Deep bowl, serrated rim		
7″	25.00	40.00
8″	30.00	45.00
9″	35.00	50.00
10″	40.00	65.00
Shallow bowl		
4½″	10.00	25.00
5½″	10.00	25.00
6½″	15.00	30.00
7½″	20.00	35.00
8½″	20.00	35.00
9½″	25.00	40.00
10½″	30.00	45.00
11½″	35.00	50.00
Round		
Collared base		
Covered		
6″d	40.00	55.00
7″d	45.00	65.00
8″d	55.00	75.00
Open		
6″d	20.00	35.00
7″d	25.00	40.00
8″d (orange bowl)	30.00	45.00
Flat, open, scalloped rim		
5″d, ice cream dish	15.00	20.00
7″d	15.00	25.00
8″d	20.00	30.00
9″d	25.00	40.00
Waste or finger bowl	25.00	40.00
Butter dish, covered	75.00	150.00
Cake stand, high standard, 10″d	45.00	100.00
Celery vase, flat	40.00	100.00
Compote, high standard, round		
Covered		
7″d	45.00	110.00
8″d	50.00	125.00
Open, scalloped rim		
7″d	45.00	80.00
8″d	50.00	90.00
Creamer, applied handle	45.00	65.00
Goblet	40.00	65.00
Lamp, oil, original burner and chimney		
No. 90, #1 collar (smallest)	70.00	—
No. 91, #1 collar	85.00	—
No. 92, #1 or #2 collar	100.00	—
No. 93, #2 collar	120.00	—
No. 94, #3 collar (largest)	145.00	—
Pickle		
Jar, covered	40.00	65.00
Tray, oblong	25.00	40.00
Pitcher, applied handle		
Milk, 1 quart	100.00	165.00
Water, ½ gallon	125.00	185.00

Items made	Clear	Clear w/Ruby
Plate		
Bread, 8″	25.00	45.00
Cheese, 7″	25.00	—
Dinner, 8″	25.00	—
Ice cream, 7″	25.00	40.00
Salt shaker, tall, flat, original top	50.00	45.00
Sauce dish		
Flat		
4″d.	15.00	25.00
4½″d	15.00	25.00
Footed, round		
4″d	15.00	25.00
4½″d	15.00	25.00
Spoonholder	30.00	80.00
Sugar bowl, covered		
Hotel size	60.00	100.00
Table size	60.00	100.00
Tumbler, water, flat	30.00	40.00

KEY TO REFERENCES

Key	Author	Title
Arch-IG	Archer, Margaret & Douglas	Imperial Glass
Bar-RS	Barret, Richard Carter	Popular American Ruby-Stained Glass
Barb-STTTGB	Barbour, Harriot Buxton	Sandwich: The Town that Glass Built
Barl-GSG	Barlow, Raymond E. et al.	A Guide to Sandwich Glass
Bat-GPG	Batty, Bob H.	A Complete Guide to Pressed Glass
Belnp-MG	Belknap, E. McCamly	Milk Glass
Ben-CG	Bennett, Harold & Judy	The Cambridge Glass Book
Bick-TG	Bickenhauser, Fred	Tiffin Glassmasters
Bond-AG	Bond, Marcelle	The Beauty of Albany Glass
Bons-BDG	Bones, Frances	The Book of Duncan Glass
Boul-TPS	Boultinghouse, Mark	Art & Colored Glass Toothpick Holders
Boyd-GC	Boyd, Ralph & Louise	Greentown in Color
Bred-EDG	Bredehoft, Neila et al.	Early Duncan Glassware
Brn-SD	Brown, Clark W.	Salt Dishes
Brns-HG	Burns, Mary Louise	Heisey's Glassware of Distinction
Bros-TS	Brothers, J. Stanley, Jr.	Thumbnail Sketches
Camb-REP	Reprint	1903 Cambridge Glass Co. (catalog)
Chip-ROS	Chipman, Frank W.	The Romance of Old Sandwich Glass
Cod-OS	Coddington, Mr. & Mrs. A.E.	Old Salts
Corn-PG	Spillman, Jane Shadel	Pressed Glass 1825-1925 Exhibition
Dar-GAPG	Darr, Patrick T.	Guide to Art and Pattern Glass
Dool-OSG	Dooley, William Germain	Old Sandwich Glass
Doub-PGC	Doubles, M. Ray	Pattern Glass Checklist
Drep-ABC OG	Drepperd, Carl W.	The ABC's of Old Glass
Drep-FR	Drepperd, Carl W.	First Reader for Antique Collectors

Key	Author	Title
Ed-CG	Edwards, Bill	Millersburg The Queen of Carnival
Eige-CGM WV	Eige, Eason	Century of Glass Making in WV.
Enos-MPG	Enos, Earl	Eno's Manual of Old Pattern Glass
Faust-LG	Fauster, Carl U.	Libbery Glass Since 1818
Fer-YMG	Ferson, Regis F. & Mary F.	Yesterday's Milk Glass Today
Flor-DGP	Florence, Gene	Degenhart Glass & Paperweights
Fos-CAT	Reprint	1901 Fostoria Glass Co. (catalog)
Fre-NLOL	Freeman, Dr. Larry	New Light on Old Lamps
Gaup-SS	Gaupp, Polly & Charles	A Sandwich Sampler
Gor-CC	Gores, Stan	1876 Centennial Collectibles
Grov-AGN	Grover, Ray & Lee	Art Glass Nouveau
Grow-WCG	Grow, Lawrence	Warner Guide to Pressed Glass
Ham-CC	Hammond, Dorothy	Confusing Collectibles
Ham-MCC	Hammond, Dorothy	More Confusing Collectibles
Hart-OAG	Hartley, Julia Magee	Old American Glass
Hart/Cobb-SS	Hartley, Julie and Cobb, Mary The States Series	
Hay-GTTA	Haynes, E. Barrington	Glass Through the Ages
Hea-1	Heacock, William	Toothpick Holders from A to Z
Hea-2	Heacock, William	Opalescent Glass from A to Z
Hea-3	Heacock, William	Syrups, Sugar Shakers & Cruets
Hea-5	Heacock, William	U.S. Glass from A to Z
Hea-6	Heacock, William	Oil Cruets from A to Z
Hea-7	Heacock, William	Ruby-Stained Glass from A to Z
Hea-1000TPS	Heacock, William	1000 Tooth Pick Holders
Hea-FEN	Heacock, William	Fenton Glass— The First 25 Years
Hea-GC	Heacock, William	Glass Collector, Vols. 1-3
Hea-OPG	Heacock, William	Old Pattern Glass
Hea-OS	Heacock, William et al.	5000 Open Salts
Hea-RUTPS	Heacock, William	Rare & Unlisted Toothpick Holders
Herr-GG	Herrick, Ruth, M.D.	Greentown Glass
Hlms-BCA	Holmes, Janet	Book of Canadian Antiques
House-CVPG	House, Caurtman G.	Comparative Values of Pattern Glass
Hrtng-P&P	Hartung, Marion T. et al.	Patterns & Pinafores
Inn/Spil-McKe	Innes, Lowell and Spillman J.	McKee Victorian Glass— Five Catalogs
Inn-EGP	Innes, Lowell	Early Glass of Pittsburgh District
Inn-PG	Innes, Lowell	Pittsburgh Glass, 1797-1891
Irw-SG	Irwin, Frederick T.	Story of Sandwich Glass
Jar-RG	Jarves, Deming	Reminiscences of Glass-making
Jef-WG	Jefferson, Josephine	Wheeling Glass
Jones-HTH	Jones, Nancy & David	Heisey Toothpick Holders
Kam-1	Kamm, Minnie Watson	Two Hundred Pattern Glass Pitchers

Key	Author	Title
Kam-2	Kamm, Minnie Watson	A Second Two Hundred Glass Pitchers
Kam-3	Kamm, Minnie Watson	A Third Two Hundred Glass Pitchers
Kam-4	Kamm, Minnie Watson	A Fourth Pitcher Book
Kam-5	Kamm, Minnie Watson	A Fifth Pitcher Book
Kam-6	Kamm, Minnie Watson	A Sixth Pitcher Book
Kam-7	Kamm, Minnie Watson	A Seventh Pitcher Book
Kam-8	Kamm, Minnie Watson	An Eighth Pitcher Book
Kam/Wod-EAG	Kamm, Minnie Watson et al.	Encyclopedia of Pattern Glass
King-GC	King, Thomas B.	Glass in Canada
Knit-EAG	Knittle, Rhea Mansfield	Early American Glass
Krs-EDG	Krause, Gail	Encyclopedia of Duncan Glass
Krs-YD	Krause, Gail	Years of Duncan
Lee/Rose-CP	Lee, Ruth Webb et al.	American Glass Cup Plates
Leclr-CGD	Lechler, Doris et al.	Children's Glass Dishes
Lecnr-SS	Lechner, Mildred & Ralph	The World of Salt Shakers
Lee-EAPG	Lee, Ruth Webb	Early American Pressed Glass
Lee-F&R	Lee, Ruth Webb	Fakes & Reproductions
Lee-SG	Lee, Ruth Webb	Sandwich Glass
Lee-VG	Lee, Ruth Webb	Victorian Glass Specialties
Lewis-OG	Lewis, J. Sidney	Old Glass and How To Collect It
Lind-HG	Lindsey, Bessie M.	American Historical Glass
Lip-GG	Lippert, Catherine Beth	Greentown Glass
Log-KAG	Logan, Harlan	How Much Do You Know About Glass
Luc-TG	Lucas, Robert I.	Tarentum Pattern Glass
Mag-FIEF	Magee, Arthur K.	Find & Identify Early Flint Glass
Mar-ARG	Marsh, Tracy H.	American Story Recorded in Glass
McCln-AG	McClinton, Catherine M.	American Glass
McCn-EPG	McCain, Mollie Helen	Encyclopedia of Pattern Glass
McCn-PGP	McCain, Mollie Helen	Pattern Glass Primer
McKrn-AG	McKearin, George & Helen	American Glass
McQd-GEAG	McQuade, Arthur J.	Guide to Early American Glass
Meas-GG	Measell, James	Greentown Glass
Meas-GRG	Measell, Brenda & James	Guide to Reproductions of Greentown
Meas/Smth-FG	Measell, James et al.	Findlay Glass
Mig-TPS	Mighell, Florence	Collectors Boon on Toothpick Holders
Mil-1	Millard, S.T., M.D.	Goblets
Mil-2	Millard, S.T., M.D.	Goblets 2
Mil-OP	Millard, S.T., M.D.	Opaque Glass
Milr-MG-1	Miller, Everett R. & Addie	New Martinsville Glass Story
Milr-NMG	Miller, Everett R. & Addie	New Martinsville Glass Story— 2
Mor-OG	Moore, Mrs. N. Hudson	Old Glass— European & American
Mry-HF	Murray, Melvin L.	History of Fostoria

Key	Author	Title
Mtz-1	Metz, Alice Hulett	Early American Pattern Glass
Mtz-2	Metz, Alice Hulett	Much More Early American Patern Glass
Mur-CO	Murray, Mr. & Mrs. Dean L.	Cruets Only
Mur-MCO	Murray, Dean L.	More Cruets Only
Neale-SD	Neale, L.W. & D.B.	Pressed Glass Salt Dishes
Nortn-PG	R.W. Norton Art Gallery	Pressed Glass Exhibition
Oliv-AAG	Oliver, Elizabeth	American Antique Glass
Pap-GAG	Papert, Emma	Guide to American Glass
Pear-CAT	Pears, Thomas C. III	Bakewell, Pears & Co. (glass catalog)
Pet-TG	Peterson, Arthur G.	4000 Trademarks on Glass
Pet-GPP	Peterson, Arthur G. Ph.D.	Glass Patents & Patterns
Pet-Sal	Peterson, Arthur G. Ph.D.	Glass Salt Shakers
Pet-GSS	Peterson, Arthur G. Ph.D.	333 Glass Salt Shakers
Phil-EOG	Philips, Phoebe	Encyclopedia of Glass
Pier-CG	Pierce, Edith Chown	Canadian Glass
Pull-GS	Pullin, Anne Geffken	Glass Signatures
Pyne-PG	Reprint	Pennsylvania Glassware 1870-1904
Rev-APG	Revi, Albert Christian	American Pressed Glass
Righ-IC	Righter, Miriam	Iowa City Glass
Rob-R.A.	Robertson, R.A.	Chats on Old Glass
Rose-SAPG	Rose, James H.	The Story of American Pressed Glass
Rotbrg-GMC	Rottenberg, Barbara Land	Glass Manufacturing in Canada
Sav-GW	Savage, George	Glass of the World
Schwtz-AG	Schwartz, Marvin D.	Guide to Antique American Glass
Sco-RG	Scoville, Warren C.	Revolution in Glassmaking
SGM	Sandwich Glass Museum Co.	Sandwich Glass Museum Collection
Shu-LPG	Shuman, Susan & John A.	Lion Pattern Glass
Smth-FG	Smith, Don E.	Findlay Pattern Glass
Smth-OS	Smith, Allan B. & Helen B.	Open Salts
Spil-AEPG	Spillman, Jane	American & European Pressed Glass
Spil-TBV	Spillman, Jane	Tableware, Bowls & Vases
Spnc-ECG	Spence, Hilda & Kelvin	A Guide to Early Canadian Glass
Stev-ECG	Stevens, Gerald	Early Canadian Glass
Stev-GIC	Stevens, Gerald	Glass in Canada
Stot-McKe	Stout, Sandra McPhee	Complete Book of McKee Glass
Stow-DJBD	Stow, Charles Messer	The Deming Jarves Book of Designs
Stu-BP	Stuart, Anna, Maude	Bread Plates & Platters
Swn-PG	Swan, Frank H.	Portland Glass Company
Tas-AG	Van Tassel, Valentine	American Glass
Thu-1	Thuro, Catherine M.V.	Oil Lamps— The Kerosene Era
Thu-2	Thuro, Catherine M.V.	Oil Lamps II
Uni-1	Unitt, Doris & Peter	American & Canadian Goblets

Key	Author	Title
Uni-2	Unitt, Doris & Peter	American & Canadian Goblets, Vol. 2
Uni-TCG	Unitt, Doris & Peter	Treasury of Canadian Glass
Uni/Wor-CHPGT	Unit/Wood	Canadian Handbook of Pressed Glass
Vog-H	Vogel, Clarence W.	Heisey's First Ten Years
War-MGA	Warman, Edwin G.	Milk Glass Addenda
Wat-AGG	Watkins, Laura Woodside	American Glass & Glassmaking
Wat-CG	Watkins, Laura Woodside	Cambridge Glass 1818-1888
Wat-NEGCO	Watkins, Laura Woodside	New England Glass Co.
Weath-FOST	Weatherman, Hazel Marie	Fostoria, Its First Fifty Years
Web-CG	Webber, Norman W.	Collecting Glass
Weeks-DGW	Weeks, J.D.	Directory of Glass Works of the U.S.
Wetz-CGCO	Wetz, Jon and Jacqueline	The Co-operative Glass Company
Wilms-SG	Williams, Lenore Wheeler	Sandwich Glass
Wilsn-GNE	Wilson, Kenneth M.	Glass in New England
Wlkr-CAMB	Welker, Mary, Lyle & Son	Cambridge Ohio Glass in Color
Wlkr-PGA	Welker, John & Elizabeth	Pressed Glass in America

BIBLIOGRAPHY

Books

Anon, "Early Glassmaking in East Cambridge, Mass.," *Old Time New England*, XIX, January, 1929, pp. 113-122.

Antique Canadian Glass from the John McBown Collection. March 3–May 2, 1976. The Saskatoon Gallery and Conservatory Corporation presents at the Mendel Art Gallery, Canada.

Antique Research Publications *Reprint Butler Brothers. Fall 1910 Catalog.* Chattanooga, TN: Self Published, 1968.

Antique Research Publications *Reprint Butler Brothers. 1905* catalog. Chattanooga, TN: Author, 1968.

Archer, Margaret and Douglas. *Imperial Glass.* Paducah, KY: Collector Books, 1978.

Ball State University, Muncie, Indiana Art Gallery. *Indiana Pressed Glass from the Gas-Boom Era (Exhibition) October 2–November 27, 1977.* Art Gallery, Ball State University, Muncie, IN: Ball State University, 1977.

Barbour, Harriot Buxtton. *Sandwich: The Town That Glass Built.* Boston: Houghton Mifflin Company, 1st Edition, 1948.

Barlow, Raymond E. and Kaiser, Joan E. *A Guide to Sandwich Glass: Vases, Colognes and Stoppers.* Windham, NH: Barlow-Kaiser Publishing Company, Inc., 1987.

Barret, Richard Carter. *Popular American Ruby-Stained Glass.* Manchester, VT: Forward's Color Productions, Inc., 1968.

———. *A Collectors Handbook of Blown and Pressed American Glass.* Manchester, VT: Forward's Color Productions, Inc., 1971.

Batty, Bob H. *A Complete Guide to Pressed Glass.* Gretna, LA: Pelican Publishing Co., Inc., 1978.

Belknap, E. McCamly. *Milk Glass.* New York: Crown Publishers, 1949 (Fifth Printing).

Bennett, Harold and Judy. *The Cambridge Glass Book.* Des Moines, IA: Wallace-Homestead Co., 1970.

Bickenheuser, Fred. *Tiffin Glassmasters.* 2 Volumes. Marietta, OH: Antique Publications, 1979, 1981.

Bond, Marcelle. *The Beauty of Albany Glass (1893–1902).* Berne, IN: Publishers Printing House, 1972.

Bones, Frances. *The Book of Duncan Glass.* Des Moines, IA: Wallace-Homestead Book Co., 1973.

Boultinghouse, Mark. *Art and Colored Glass Toothpick Holders*. Reynolds, IL: Self Published, 1966.

Boyd, Ralph and Louise, & Andrews, Diane. *Greentown*. Des Moines, IA: Wallace-Homestead Book Co., 1972.

———. *Greentown in Color*. Converse, IN: Self Published, 1972.

Bredehoft, Neila M. & Fogg, Georga A. & Maloney, Francis C. *Early Duncan Glassware. Geo. Duncan & Sons 1874–1892*. Saint Louisville, OH: Authors, 1987.

Borthers, J. Stanley, Jr. *Thumbnail Sketches*. Kalamazoo, MI: Author, 1940.

Brown, Clark W. *Salt Dishes*. Leon, IA: Mid-America Book Company, 1968.

———. *A Supplement to Salt Dishes*. Leon, IA: Prairie Winds Press, 1970.

Burns, Mary Louise. *Heisey's Glassware of Distinction*. Mesa, AZ: Triangle Books, 1974.

Cambridge Glass Company 1903 Catalog of Pressed and Blown Glass Ware. Reprint. 1976.

Chipman, Frank W. *The Romance of Old Sandwich Glass*. Sandwich, MA: Sandwich Publishing Company, Inc., 1932. (Second Printing 1938).

Coddington, Mr. & Mrs. A.E. *Old Salts*. Indianapolis, IN: Authors, 1940.

Corning Glass Center Glass from the Corning Museum of Glass—A Guide to the Collections. Corning, NY: The Corning Museum of Glass, 1956.

Corning Glass Works. The Corning Glass Center, Corning, NY: Author, 1958.

Darr, Patrick T. *A Guide to Art and Pattern Glass*. Springfield, MA: Pilgrim House Publishing Co. ca. 1960.

DiBartolomeo, Robert E. *American Glass from the Pages of Antiques II Pressed and Cut*. Princeton, The Pyne Press, 1974.

Dooley, William Germain. *Old Sandwich Glass*. Pasadena, CA: Esto Publishing Company, (No Date Given).

Doubles, M. Ray. *Pattern Glass Checklist*. Richmond, VA: Self Published, 1959.

Drepperd, Carl W. *First Reader for Antique Collectors*. Garden City, NY: Doubleday & Company, Inc., 1948.

———. *ABC's of Old Glass*. Garden City, NY: Doubleday & Company, Inc., 1949.

Edwards, Bill. *Millersburg the Queen of Carnival Glass*. Paducah, KY: Collector Books, 1975.

Eige, Eason. *A Century of Glassmaking in West Virginia*. Huntington, WV. Huntington Galleries, 1980.

Enos, Earl. *Eno's Manual of Old Pattern Glass*. St. Louis: Author, 1936.

Fauster, Carl U. *Libbey Glass Since 1818*. Toledo, OH: Len Beach Press, 1979.

Ferson, Regis F. & Mary F. *Yesterday's Milk Glass Today*. Greensburg, PA: Chas. H. Henry Printing Co., 1981.

Florence, Gene. *Degenhart Glass & Paperweights*. Cambridge, OH: Degenhart Paperweight and Glass Museum, Inc., 1982.

Fostoria Glass Company 1901 Catalog. Reprint. Paducah, KY: Collectors Books, 1970.

Freeman, Dr. Larry. *New Light on Old Lamps*. Watkins Glen, NY: American Life Foundation, Reprint 1984.

Gaupp, Polly & Charles. *A Sandwich Sampler*. East Sandwich, MA: The House of the Clipper Ship, 1970.

Grow, Lawrence. *The Warner Collectors Guide to Pressed Glass*. New York: The Main Street Press, 1982.

Hammond, Dorothy. *Confusing Collectibles: A Guide to the Identification of Contemporary Objects*. Revised Edition. Des Moines, IA: Wallace-Homestead Book Co., 1979.

———. *More Confusing Collectibles.* Wichita, KS: C.B.P. Publishing Company, 1972.

Hartley, Julia Magee. *Old American Glass: The Mills Collection of the Texas Christian University.* Fort Worth, TX: The Texas Cjhristian University Press, 1975.

Hartley, Julia Magee and Cobb, Mary Magee. *The State's Series Early American Pattern Glass.* Lubbock, TX: Authors, 1976.

Hartung, Marion T. *Northwood Pattern Glass in Color.* Emporia, KS: Self Published, 1969.

Hartung, Marion T. and Hinshaw, Ione E. *Patterns and Pinafores. Pressed Glass Toy Dishes.* Des Moines, IA: Wallace-Homestead Book Co., 1971.

———. *Patterns and Pinafores. Pressed Glass Toy Dishes Book II.* Des Moines, IA: Wallace-Homestead Co., 1978.

Haynes, E. Barrington. *Glass Through the Ages.* Baltimore, MD: Pengiun Books, 1969.

Heacock, William. *Collecting Glass—Vol. 1.* Marietta, OH: Antique Publications, 1984.

———. *Collecting Glass—Vol. 2.* Marietta, OH: Antique Publications, 1985.

———. *Collecting Glass—Vol. 3.* Marietta, OH: Antique Publications, Inc. 1986.

Heacock, William. *Encyclopedia of Victorian Colored Pattern Glass Book I—Toothpick Holders for A to Z.* Jonesville, MI: Antique Publications, 1974.

———. *Encyclopedia of Victorian Colored Pattern Glass Book II—Opalescent Glass for A to Z.* Jonesville, MI: Antique Publications, 1976.

———. *Encyclopedia of Victorian Colored Pattern Glass Book III—Syrups, Sugar Shakers & Cruets.* Jonesville, MI: Antique Publications, Inc., 1981.

———. *Encyclopedia of Victorian Colored Pattern Glass Book 6—Oil Cruets. from A to Z.* Marietta, OH: Antique Publications, Inc., 1981.

———. *Encyclopedia of Victorian Colored Pattern Glass Book 7—Ruby-Stained Glass for A to Z.* Marietta, OH: Antique Publications,Inc.

———. *1000 Toothpick Holders—A Collector's Guide.* Marietta, OH: Antique Publications, 1977.

———. *Fenton Glass—the First Twenty-five Years.* Marietta, OH: O-Val Advertising Corp., 1978.

———. *Fenton Glass—the Second Twenty-five Years.* Marietta, OH: Oval Advertising Corp., 1980.

———. *Old Pattern Glass According to Heacock.* Marietta, OH: Antique Publications, 1981.

———. *Rare and Unlisted Toothpick Holders.* Marietta, OH: Antique Publications, 1984.

Heacock, William and Bickenheuser, Fred. *Encyclopedia of Victorian Colored Pattern Glass Book 5—U.S. Glass for A to Z.* Marietta, OH: Antique Publications, 1978.

Heacock, William and Johnson, Patricia. *5,000 Open Salts A Collector's Guide.* Marietta, OH: Richardson Printing Corporation, 1982.

Herrick, Ruth, MD. *Greentown Glass: The Indiana Tumbler and Goblet Company and Allied Manufacturers.* Grand Rapids, MI: Author, 1959.

Holmes, Janet. *Glass and the Glass Industry. The Book of Canadian Antiques.* Edited by Donald B. Webster. Toronto: McGraw-Hill Ryerson, 1974.

———. *Patterns in Light.* The John and Mary Yaremko Glass Collection. October 31, 1987–January 3, 1988. The Royal Ontario Museum, Toronto, Canada. Ontario: Royal Ontario Museum. 1987.

House, Caurtman G. *Comparative Values of Patterned Glass. A Check List with Prices Covering More Than Six Thousand Forms in the Two Hundred Most Popular Patterns of American Pressed Glass.* Medina, NY: Self Published, 1936.

The Imperial Glass Corporation. *The Story of Hand-Made Glass.* Bellaire, OH: Author, 1941.

Innes, Lowell. *Early Glass of the Pittsburgh District 1797–1890*. Pittsburgh, PA: Carnegie Museum, 1949.

———. *Pittsburgh Glass 1797–1891. A History and Guide for Collectors*. Boston, MA: Houghton Mifflin Company, 1976.

Innmes, Lowell and Spillman, Jane. *McKee Victorian Glass—Five Complete Glass Catalogs from 1859/60 to 1871*. New York: Dover Publications, Inc., 1981.

Irwin, Frederick T. *The Story of Sandwich Glass*. Manchester, NH: Granite State Press, 1926.

Jarves, Deming. *Reminiscences of Glassmaking*. Great Neck, NY: Beatrice C. Weinstock, reprinted in 1968.

Jefferson, Josephine. *Wheeling Glass*. Mount Vernon, OH: The Guide Publishing Company, 1947.

Jones, Martha York. "The Portland Glass Works," *The Magazine Antiques*, August, 1933.

Jones, Nancy and David. *Heisey Toothpick Holders*. Newark, OH: Heisey Collectors of America, Inc., 1982.

Kamm, Minnie Watson. *Two Hundred Pattern Glass Pitchers*. Detroit: Motschall Company, 1939.

———. *A Second Two Hundred Pattern Glass Pitchers*. Grosse Pointe Farms, MI: Author, 1940.

———. *A Third Two Hundred Pattern Glass Pitchers*. Grosse Pointe Farms, MI: Author, 1943, 1946.

———. *A Fourth Pitcher Book*. Grosse Pointe Farms, MI: Author, 1950.

———. *A Fifth Pitcher Book*. Grosse Pointe Farms, MI: Author, 1948.

———. *A Sixth Pithcer Book*. Grosse Pointe Farms, MI: Author, 1949.

———. *A Seventh Pitcher Book*. Grosse Pointe Farms, MI: Author, 1953.

———. *An Eighth Pitcher Book*. Grosse Pointe Farms, MI: Author, 1954.

Kamm, Minnie W. and Wood, Serry. *The Kamm-Wood Encyclopedia of Antique Pattern Glass*. Watkins Glen, NY: Century House, 1961. 2 Volumes.

Keyes, Homer Eaton. "The Cupid and Psyche Pattern," *The Magazine Antiques*, October, 1933.

King, Thomas B. *Glass in Canada*. Erin, Ontario: The Moston Mills Press, 1987.

Knittle, Rhea Mansfield. *Early American Glass*. Garden City, NY: Garden City Publishing Company, Inc., Reprint Edition 1948.

Krause, Gail. *A Pictorial History of Duncan & Miller Glass*. Washington, PA: Author, 1976.

———. *The Encyclopedia of Duncan Glass*. Hicksville, NY: Exposition Press, 1976.

Lechler, Doris & O'Neill, Virginia. *Children's Glass Dishes*. Nashville, TN: Nelson Publishers, 1976.

Lechler, Dorris Anderson. *Children's Glass Dishes, China, and Furniture. Volume 1*. Paducah, KY: Collector Books, 1983.

———. *Children's Glass Dishes, China, and Furniture. Volume 2*. Paducah, KY: Collector Books, 1986.

Lechner, Mildred & Ralph. *The World of Salt Shakers*. Paducah, KY: Collector Books, 1976.

Lee, Ruth Webb. *Early American Pressed Glass*. Enlarged and Revised. Northboro, MA: Author, 1931, 1933.

———. "The Duncan Trio," *The Magazine Antiques*, April, 1933.

———. "Pittsburgh Versus Sandwich," *The Magazine Antiques*, January, 1934.

———. "Pittsburgh Versus Sandwich," *The Magazine Antiques*, August, 1933.

———. "The Tree of Life and its Sundry Fruits," *The Magazine Antiques*, October, 1934.

————. *Victorian Glass Specialties of the Nineteenth Century*. Wellsley Hills, MA: Lee Publications, 1944.

————. *Sandwich Glass*. Wellesley Hills, MA: Lee Publications, 1947.

————. *Price Guide to Pattern Glass*. New York: M. Barrows & Company, 1949.

————. *Current Values of Antique Glass*. Northboro, MA: Author, 1963.

————. *The Revised Price Guide to Pattern Glass*. New York: M. Barrows & Company, Inc., 1953.

————. *Antique Fakes and Reproductions*. Northborough, MA: Author, 1950.

Lee, Ruth Webb & Rose, James H. *American Glass Cup Plates*. Wellesley Hills, MA: Lee Publications, 1948.

Lewis, J. Sidney. *Old Glass and How to Collect It*. London: T Werner Lourie, Ltd. (No. Date Given).

Lindsey, Bessie M. *American Historical Glass*. Rutland, VT: Charles E. Tuttle Co., 1967.

————. *Lore of Our Land Pictured in Glass, Volume I*. Forsyth, IL: The Author, printed by Wagoner Printing Company, Galesburg, IL, 1950.

————. *Lore of Our Land Pictured in Glass, Volume II*. Forsyth, IL: The Author, printed by Wagoner Printing Company, Galesburg, IL, 1951.

Lippert, Catherine Beth. *Greentown Glass. Indianapolis Museum of Art*. October 1–November 9, 1975. Indianapolis, IN: Indianapolis Museum of Art, 1975.

Logan, Harlan. *How Much Do You Know About Glass*. New York: Dodd, Mead & Company, 1951.

Lucas, Robert I. *Tarentum Pattern Glass*. Tarentum, PA: Self Published, 1981.

McCain, Mollie Helen. *Pattern Glass Primer*. Leon, IA: Lamplighter Books, 1979.

————. *The Collector's Encyclopedia of Pattern Glass*. Paducah KY: Collector Books, 1982.

McClonton, Katharine Morrison. *American Glass*. New York: The World Publishing Company, 1950.

McKearin, George S. & Helen. *American Glass*. New York: Crown Publishers, 7th Printing, 1946.

McQuade. *Illustrated Guide to Early American Glass*. Portland, MA: Portland Lithography Company. First Printing, July, 1969.

MacLaren, George. Chief Curator of History. *Nova Scotia Glass*. Halifax, N.S.: Nova Scotia Museum, 1968.

Magee, Arthur K. *How to Find and Identify Early Flint Pattern Glass*. Denver, CO: Egan Printing Co., 1964.

Marsh, Tracy H. *The American Story Recorded in Glass*. Paynesville, MN: Author, 1962, printed by Lund Press, Inc., Minneapolis, MN.

Measell, Brenda & James. *A Guide to Reproductions of Greentown Glass*. Author, 1974.

Measell, James & Smith, Don E. *Findlay Glass Tableware Manufacturers, 1886–1902*. Marietta, OH: Antique Publications, Inc., 1986.

Measell, James. *Greentown Glass: The Indiana Tumbler & Goblet Company*. Grand Rapids, MI: Grand Rapids Public Museum, 1979. Metz, Alice Hulett. *Early American Pattern Glass*. Chicago, IL: Author, 1958.

————. *Much More Early American Pattern Glass*. Chicago, IL: Author, 1965.

Mighell, Florence. *A Collectors Book on Toothpick Holders*. Des Moines, IA: Wallace-Homestead Book Co., 1973.

Millard, S.T., MD. *Goblets*. Topeka, KS: The Central Press, 1939.

————. *Goblets II*. Holton, KS: Gossip Printers and Publishers, Second Edition, 1940.

———. *Opaque Glass.* Topeka, KS: Central Press, 1953.

Miller, Everett R. & Addie R. *The New Martinsville Glass Story.* Marietta, OH: Richardson Publishing Co., 1972.

———. *The New Martinsville Glass Story—Book II 1920–1950.* Manchester, MI: Rymack Printing Co., 1975.

Moore, Mrs. N. Hudson. *Old Glass, European and American. New York: Tudor Publishing Company, 1924.*

Mordock, John B. *American and Canadian Early Etched Goblets.* Fort Lauderdale, FL: Self Published, 1985.

Murray, Mr. & Mrs. Dean L. *Cruets Only.* Phoenix, AZ: Killgore Graphics, Inc., 1969.

Murray, Dean L. *More Cruets Only.* Phoenix, AZ: Killgore Graphics, Inc., 1973.

Murray, Melvin L. *History of Fostoria Ohio Glass, 1887–1920.* Fostoria, OH: Author, 1972.

The New England Glass Company 1818–1888. The Toledo Museum of Art, 1963.

Northend, Mary Harrod. *American Glass.* New York: Tudor Publishing Company, Reprinted 1924.

The R. W. Norton Art Gallery. *American Silver and Pressed Glass—Exhibition of American Silver and Pressed Glass.* Shreveport, LA: Mid-South Press, 1967.

Oliver, Elizabeth. *American Antique Glass.* New York: Golden Press, 1977.

Papert, Emma. *The Illustrated Guide to American Glass.* New York: Hawthorn Books, Inc., 1972.

Pears, Thomas C. III. *Bakewell, Pears & Co. Glass Catalog,* Pittsburgh, PA: Author, 1977.

Peterson, Arthur G., Ph.D. *Glass Salt Shakers: 1000 Patterns.* Des Moines, IA: Wallace-Homestead Co., 1970.

———. *Glass Patents and Patterns.* DeBary, FL: self Published, 1973.

———. *333 Glass Salt Shakers.* Tacoma Park, MD: Washington College Press, 1965.

———. *400 Trademarks on Glass.* Tacoma Park, MD: Washington College Press, 1968.

Phillips, Phoebe. *The Encyclopedia of Glass.* New York: Crown Publishers, Inc. 1981.

Pierce, Edith Chown. *Canadian Glass, A Footnote to History.* Toronto: Privately Published, 1954.

Pullin, Anne Geffken. *Glass Signatures, Trade Marks and Trade Names.* Lombard, IL: Wallace-Homestead Book Company, 1986.

Pyne Press, *Pennsylvania Glassware 1870–1904.* New York: Charles Scribner's Sons, 1972.

Revi, Albert Christian. *American Pressed Glass and Figure Bottles.* NY: Thomas Nelson & Sons, 1964. (Third Printing 1970).

Righter, Miriam. *Iowa City Glass.* Des Moines, IA: Wallace-Homestead Book Co., 1966.

Robertson, R. A. *Chats on Old Glass.* New York, NY: Dover Publications, Inc., 1969. Revised and enlarged by Kenneth M. Wilson.

Robinson, Nelle B. "Among the Latest Things in Glass," *The Magazine Antiques,* August, 1933.

Rose, James H. *The Story of American Pressed Glass of the Lacy Period, 1825–1850.* Corning, NY: The Corning Museum of Glass, Corning Glass Center, 1954.

Rottenberg, Barbara Land and Tomlin, Judith, *Glass Manufacturing in Canada: A Survey of Pressed Glass Patterns.* Ottawa, Canada: Division de l'Homme, 1982 (History Division, National Museum of Man, Ottawa, Canada).

Royal Ontario Museum. *The Edith Chown Pierce & Gerald Stevens Collection of Early Canadian Glass.* Royal Ontario Museum, Canada, 1957.

Sandwich Glass Museum. *The Sandwich Glass Museum Collection.* Sandwich, MA: Sandwich Glass Museum, 1969.

Savage, George. *Glass of the World.* New York: Gallahad Books, 1975.

Schwartz, Marvin D. *American Glass from the Pages of Antiques*. Princeton: The Pyne Press, 1974.

———. *Collector's Guide to Antique American Glass*. Garden City, NY: Doubleday & Company, Inc., 1969.

Scoville, Warren C. *Revolution in Glassmaking Entrepreneurship and Technological Change in the American Industry, 1880–1920*. Cambridge: Harvard University Press, 1948.

Shuman, Susan W. & John A. III. *Lion Pattern Glass*. Boston, MA: Granden Press, 1977.

Smith, Allan B. & Helen B. *One Thousand Individual Open Salts*. Litchfield, ME: The Country House, 1972.

———. *650 More Individual Open Salts*. Litchfield, ME: The Country House, 1973.

———. *The Third Book of Individual Open Salts*. Litchfield, ME: The Country House, 1976.

———. *Individual Open Salts Illustrated; 1977 Annual*. Litchfiedl, MA: The Country House (No Date Given).

Smith, Don E. *Findlay Pattern Glass*. Findlay, OH: Self Published, 1970.

Spence, Hilda & Kelvin. *A Guide to Early Canadian Glass*. Ontario: Don Mills, Longmans Canada Limited, 1966.

Spillman, Jane Shadel. *American and European Pressed Glassed in the Corning Museum of Glass*. Corning, NY: Corning Museum of Glass, 1981.

———. *The Corning Museum of Glass. Pressed Glass 1925–1925*. Exhibition April 29–November 1, 1983. Corning, N.Y: The Corning Museum. 1983.

———. *Glass Bottles, Lamps & Other Objects*. New York, NY: Alfred A. Knopf, 1982.

———. *Glass Tableware, Bowls & Vases*. New York, NY: Alfred A. Knopf, Inc., 1982.

———. *Glassmaking America's First Industry*. Corning, NY: The Corning Museum of Glass, 1976.

———. *Pressed glass 1825–1925*. The Corning Museum of Glass. Corning, NY: 1983.

———. "Pressed-Glass Designs in the United States and Europe," *The Magazine Antiques*, July, 1983, pp. 130–139.

Stevens, Gerald. *Canadian Glass c. 1825;'en1925*. Toronto: The Ryerson Press, 1967.

———. *Glass in Canada The First One Hundred Years*. Agincourt, Ontario, Canada: Methuen Publications, 1982.

Stout, Sandra McPhee. *The Complete Book of McKee Glass*. North Kansas City, MO: Trojan Press, Inc., 1972.

Stuart, Anna Maude. *Bread Plates and Platters*. Hillsborough, CA: Author, 1965.

Swan, Frank H. *Portland Glass*. Des Moines, IA: Wallace-Homestead Book Company, 1949. Revised and enlarged by Marion Dana.

———. *Portland Glass Company*. Providence, RI. The Roger Williams Press, 1939.

Thuro, Catherine M.V. *Oil Lamps—The Kerosene Era in North America*. Des Moines, IA: Wallace-Homestead Book Co., 1976.

———. *Oil Lamps II; Glass Kerosene Lamps*. Paducah, KY and Des Moines, IA: Collector Books and Wallace-Homestead Book Co., 1983.

Unitt, Doris & Peter. *American and Canadian Goblets*. Peterborough, Ontario, Canada: Clock House, 1970. (Third Edition 1977).

———. *American and Canadian Goblets, Volume Two*. Peterborough, Ontario, Canada: Clock House, 1974.

Van Tassel, Valentine. *American Glass*. New York: M. Barrows and Company, Inc., 1950.

Vogel, Clarence W. *Heisey's First Ten Years—1896–1905*. Galion, OH: Author, 1969.

Warman, Edwin G. *Milk Glass Addenda*. Uniontown, PA: E.G. Warman Publishing Co., 1959.

Watkins, Laura Woodside. *Cambridge Glass 1818–1888 The Story of The New England Glass Company.* Boston: Marshall Jones Company, 1930.

———. *American Glass and Glassmaking.* New York: Chanticleer Press, 1950.

Waugh, Sidney. *The Art of Glass Making.* New York: Dodd, Mead, 1937.

Weatherman, Hazel Marie. *Fostoria Its First Fifty Years.* Springfield, MO: Self Published, 1972.

Webber, Norma. W. *Collecting Glass.* New York, NY: Arco Publishing Company, Inc., 1973.

Weeks, J. D. *Directory of the Glass Works of the United States,* Washington, DC, 1880.

Welker, John W. & Elizabeth F. *Pressed Glass in America Encyclopedia of the First Hundred Years 1825–1925.* Ivyland, PA: Antique Acres Press, 1985.

Welker, Mary, Lyle & Lynn. *Cambridge Ohio Glass in Color.* New Concord, OH: Self Published, 1969.

White, Harry Hall, "New Views of Glass," *The Magazine Antiques,* January, 1934.

Williams, Lenore Wheeler. *Sandwich Glass.* Bridgeport, CT: The Park City Eng. Co., 1922.

Wilson, Kenneth M. *New England Glass and Glassmaking.* An Old Stourbridge Village Book. New York: Thomas Y. Crowell Co., 1972.

———. *New England Glass & Glassmaking.* New York, NY: Thos. Y. Crowell Co., 1972.

General Merchandise Catalogs

Butler Brothers

1885 catalog
1894 catalog
1896 catalog
1899 catalog
1900 catalog
1904 catalog
1905 No. 536 catalog
1906 catalog
1907 catalog
1910 catalog
1911 catalog
1912 catalog
1915 catalog

Crockery, Glass & Pottery Review

February, 1898
June, 1898

China, Glass & Lamps

April 22, 1889
December 31, 1890
January 14, 1891
January 28, 1891
February 4, 1891
April 8, 1891
May 20, 1891
April 13, 1892

Spring, 1896
January 2, 1898
January 12, 1898
September 15, 1898
December 23, 1899
January 10, 1901
January 13, 1906

Crockery and Glass Journal

February 7, 1878
February 7, 1889
August 1, 1889
September 5, 1889
January 10, 1890
May 13, 1890
February 12, 1891
June 23, 1892
January 14, 1893
January 10, 1894
January 13, 1898
December 22, 1898
February 20, 1902
March 12, 1903

Illustrated Glass and Pottery World, January, 1898

London Tea Company, Boston, MA. Illustrated premium list with cash prices for premiums of the London Tea Company. 33ed. Boston: London Tea Co., [1897]. 1897. (Catalogue no. 53).

Lyon Brothers, Chicago, IL. Crockery and Glassware. Catalog of Our New Lines. [1905]. (Catalog No. 411). [1] p. : ill.

Lyon Brothers, Chicago, Ill., Chicago, IL. Spring and Summer Catalog, 1906. Chicago : The Firm, 1903. Glassware ; pp. 290–315. 1. Manufacturers—Sales catalogs. 2. department stores—Sales catalogs. 3. Glassware—Sales catalogs. I. Title

Montgomery Ward

1884 catalog
1894 catalog
1895 catalog
1896 catalog
1898 catalog
1899 catalog
1900 catalog
1901 catalog
1905 catalog

National Merchandise Catalog, 1885.

Pottery and Glassware Reporter:

May 1, 1884
November 19, 1885
February 1, 1886
July 21, 1887
February 27, 1890
January 1, 1891
July 1, 1914

Charles "Broadway' Rousse General Merchandise Catalog, New York City, NY.

August, 1903 (Catalog No. 479)
December, 1903 (Catalog No. 483)
August, 1904 (Catalog No. 496)

Sears, Roebuck & Co., Chicago, IL. General Merchandise Catalog

1897 catalog
1902 catalog

T.M. Roberts, Minneapolis, MN. Wholesale Catalog [c. 1898].

Original Glass Catalogs

The following list of original catalogs and catalog pages has been compiled by and is printed here in its original form with the permission of The Corning Museum of Glass, Corning, NY. Due to the nature of attributing these materials, dates recorded are those established by the museum and not the authors.

Adams & Co., Pittsburgh, PA. Catalogue and price list of glassware, manufactured by Adams & Co. [1871-1872]. 13 leaves of ill., [4] leaves; Cover title. Includes mugs, tumblers, goblets, salts, cruets, pitchers, bowls, nappies.

Adams & Co., Pittsburgh, PA. 1874 catalogue.

Adams & Co., Pittsburgh, PA. 1875-1885 catalogue.

Bakewell, Pears & Company, Pittsburgh, PA. 1864 catalogue.

Bakewell, Pears & Co., Pittsburgh, PA. Bakewell, Pears & Co. glass catalogue 1875. [Reprint, 1977]. 6 p., 49 leaves of plates. Foreword by Thomas C. Pears, III, and introduction by Lowell Innes. Illustrated Rochelle, Icicle, Cherry, Prism, Bohemia, Thistle, Saxon, Argus, Reed, Etruscan, Arabesque, Victoria and other patterns.

Beatty, A.J., & Sons, Steubenville, OH. Illustrated catalogue of fine pressed and blown glassware; principal office & factory at Steubenville, OH. [between 1885-1889]. [5], 75 p. : ill. Cover title. Ware consists chiefly of tumblers, and ware for bar and tap rooms. United States Glass Co. invoice pasted in front. Lacks p. 10; p. 11 mutilated.

Beatty, A.J., & Sons, Tiffin, OH. Illustrated catalogue of fine pressed and blown glassware; principal office & factory at Tiffin, OH. [between 1890-1891]. [7], 37 leaves: ill. Cover title.

Beatty, A.J., & Sons, Tiffin, OH. Illustrated catalogue of fine pressed and blown glassware; principal office & factory at Tiffin, OH. [between 1890-1891]. 9 pp. : chiefly ill. Ware consists chiefly of tumblers, including engraved tumblers.

Bellaire Goblet Co., Findlay, OH. Supplement to Bellaire Goblet Company's catalogue. 1890. [5] leaves : chiefly ill. Cover rubber-stamped: U.S. Glass Co., Factory M.

Bellaire Goblet Co., Findlay, OH. Supplement to Bellaire Goblet Company's catalogue. 1891. [6] leaves : chiefly ill. Cover title. Cover rubber-stamped U.S. Glass Co., Factory M.

Bellaire Goblet Co., Findlay, OH. Supplement to catalogue [of] Bellaire Goblet Company. 1891. [6] leaves : chiefly ill. Cover title. Cover rubber-stamped U.S. Glass Co., Factory M.

Bellaire Goblet Co., Findlay, OH. The Bellaire Goblet Co., Findlay, OH, United States, manufacture goblets and tableware. 1889-1890. 33 leaves : chiefly ill. Cover rubber-stamped: U.S. Glass Co., Factory M. Includes pressed and engraved goblets, lamps, glass novelties. Engraving patterns, p. 32-33. p. 25 mutilated; p. 27 missing.

Bryce Brothers, Pittsburgh, PA. ca. 1890 catalogue.

Bryce Brothers, Pittsburgh, PA. ca. 1894 catalogue.

Bryce, Richards & Company, Pittsburgh, PA. 1854 catalogue.

Cambridge Glass Co., Cambridge, OH. Catalogue of table glassware, lamps, barware and novelties manufactured by the Cambridge Glass Co. 1st edition. Cambridge, OH.: H. Bennett, 1903. [Reprint, 1976]. 106 p. : chiefly ill. Cover title: 1903 catalogue of pressed and blown glassware manufactured by the Cambridge Glass Co., Cambridge, OH. — Reprint of the 1903 edition published by the Cambridge Glass Co., Cambridge, OH. — Toys, paperweights, fish globes, birdbaths, seed cups, photographer's supplies, novelties, caddies, candy jars.

Central Glass Co., Wheeling, WV. Illustrated catalogue of Central Glass Company flint glassware. [between 1876-1881]. 41 p. : entirely ill. Cover title. Inside front cover in a contemporary hand: "Samples for San Francisco Shipped Aug. 24th, 1881." Handwritten checked list inside back cover.

Central Glass Co., Wheeling, WV. Illustrated catalogue: flint glassware [between 1888-1891]. 107, [3] p. : chiefly ill. (some col.). Cover title.

Diamond Flint Glass Company, Canada. 1902 catalogue.

Doyle & Company, Pittsburgh, PA. 1885-1895 catalogue.

Duncan, Geo., and Sons, Pittsburgh, PA. Illustrated catalogue [ca. 1877] [34] p. : entirely ill. Alleged to be copy formerly belonging to Ruth Webb Lee. Illustration of factory at end, dated 1884 is reproduced in Lee's "Victorian Glass".

Duncan, Geo., and Sons, Pittsburgh, PA. No. 360 Ware. [1890?]. [10] p. : chiefly ill.

Duncan, Geo., and Sons, Pittsburgh, PA. [Sales catalogue]. [1888?]. 79 p. : chiefly ill. "No. 90 pattern patented," p. 58-62. Patented March 15, 1887. Includes handwritten letter annotations [price codes?], comments and cancellations. Lacks p. 30-41, 44-53.

Fostoria Glass Co., Moundsville, WV. Catalogue no. 1: general table glassware. 1904. 95 p. : chiefly ill. (Catalogue no. 1: table glassware and novelties). Cover title: Table and bar glassware. Includes vases, punch bowls, cups, colognes, pitchers, drinking vessels, cruets, toothpicks, salts, inks, jugs, lamp fonts, etc.

Fostoria Glass Co., Moundsville, WV. Catalogue no. 1: general table glassware. 1905. 82 p. : entirely ill. (Catalogue no. 1: table glassware and novelties) Lacks covers. Includes named and numbered patterns, cruets, salts, toothpicks, vases, spooners, shakers, goblets, tumblers, pitchers, inks, paperweights, colognes, etc.

Fostoria Glass Co., Moundsville, WV. Catalogue no. 1: general table glassware. 1906. 93 p. : chiefly ill. (Catalogue no. 1: table glassware and novelties). Includes celeries, cruets, shakers, salts, toothpicks, drinking vessels, pitchers, jugs, vases, spooners, lamps and lamp fonts, colognes, etc.

Fostoria Glass Co., Moundsville, WV. Catalogue no. 1: general table glassware. 1907. 95 p. : chiefly ill. (Catalogue no. 1: table glassware and novelties). Cover title: Special bar goods. Includes named and numbered patterns.

Fostoria Glass Co., Moundsville, WV. Catalogue no. 1: general table glassware. 1909. Chiefly ill. (Catalogue no. 1: table glassware and novelties). Includes named and numbered patterns, table glass, lamps, novelties.

Greensburg Glass Company, Greensburg, PA. Undated catalogue.

Grierson & Co., Pittsburgh, PA. [Sales brochure]. [ca. 1875]. [2] p. : entirely ill. New York pattern, p. 2.

Heisey, A. H. & Company, Newark, OH. 1897 catalogue.

Hobbs Glass Co., Wheeling, WV. Catalogue. [between 1888-1891]. [60] p. (various pagings) : ill. Running title on some pages is "Hobbs, Brockunier & Co., Wheeling, WV." Includes bottles, barware, lampshades, hand and stand lamps.

Hobbs Glass Co., Wheeling, WV. [Sales catalogue of assorted pages]. [1888-1891]. [87] p. : ill. (some col.). Collected pages of Hobbs Glass Co., Hobbs, Brockunier & Co. and the U.S. Glass Co., Factory H.

Hobbs, Brockunier & Co., Wheeling, WV. [Sales catalogue pages]. [1875-1888]. [47] p. (various pagings) : entirely ill. (most col.). Apparently a collection of pages from 5 different catalogues issued over a period of years. Many of the patterns were patented in 1888; firm name was used until 1888.

King Glass Co., Pittsburgh, PA. Illustrated catalogue. [between 1890-1891]. 163 p. : entirely ill. Includes tumblers, vases, jugs, bottles, inks, salts, toothpicks, toys, jars, dishes, etc.

King, Son & Co., Pittsburgh, PA. [Catalogue]. [1897-]. [Reprint, 1972]. Includes: Pennsylvania glassware, 1870-1904.

King, Son & Co., Pittsburgh, PA. Illustrated catalogue: crystal glassware. Cascade Glass Works/King, Son & Co., manufacturers of crystal glassware . . . [1875 or 1876]. 26, [1] p. : chiefly ill. Date established from presence of Centennial pattern (patented 1875).

Lyon, Jas. B., & Co., Pittsburgh, PA. [Sales catalogue]. [between 1862-1874]. 16 leaves of ill. Dated from: Innes, Lowell, "Pittsburgh Glass . . . " Illustrated Cincinnati in both "old mould" and plain. Includes tumblers, barware, and tableware.

M'Kee & Brothers, Pittsburgh, PA. Prices of glassware manufactured by M'Kee and Brother, successors to F & J M'Kee. [1859-1860]. 16 p. : [23] plates. Research establishes date to be after spring 1859 and before spring 1860.

M'Kee & Brothers, [Pittsburgh, PA]. Illustrated catalogue of glassware, manufactured by M'Kee & Brothers. 1871. 24 p. : entirely ill. Includes table glass, lamps, lanterns, toys, barware, show globes.

M'Kee & Brothers, Pittsburgh, PA. Prices of glassware. [ca. 1863]. 16 p. Probably late 1863 or early 1864. Catalogue dated July 1864 has prices about $1/3$ higher. Old-fashioned items such as solar and camphene lamps included, but not in the July 1864 edition.

M'Kee & Brothers, Pittsburgh, PA. Prices of glassware manufactured by M'Kee & Brothers. 1864. [32], 16 p. : ill. Cover title. 16-page section following the illustrations is price list dated July 1, 1864.

M'Kee & Brothers, Pittsburgh, PA. Prices of glassware manufactured by M'Kee & Brothers. 1868. 16, 32 p. : ill. Cover title. Price list, first 16 pages.

McKee/National Glass Co., Jeannette, PA. 1901 catalog.

Model Flint Glass Co., Findlay, OH. ca. 1901 catalog.

New England Glass Co., Boston, MA. [Pages from a sales catalogue of the New England Glass Co.]. ca. 1868. 24 p. : ill.

New England Glass Works, Cambridge, MA.: [1884 price list of the New England Glass Works and Joseph Locke's Amberina sketch books]. 1884. (Reprint, 1970). [14] p. : ill. Reprinted by the Antique & Historic Glass Foundation, Toledo, OH., 1970.

New Martinsville Glass Co., New Martinsville, WV. ca. 1916 catalogue.

O'Hara Glass Co., Pittsburgh, PA. [Sales catalogue of pressed glass]. [between 1875-1890]. 4 p. : chiefly ill. Probably early date. "Old style" and "New style" table decanters illustrated.

Pioneer Glass Co., Pittsburgh, PA. ca. 1893 catalogue.

Richards & Hartley Glass Co., Pittsburgh, PA. ca. 1893 catalogue.

Union Stopper Co., Morgantown, WV. Union Stopper Co., manufacturers of high grade pressed tableware & glass specialties. [between 1907-1918] 2 p. leaves, 37 p. : chiefly ill.

United States Glass Co., Pittsburgh, PA. (Catalogue of named sets of pressed ware). 1904.

United States Glass Co., Pittsburgh, PA. (Collected sales catalogues and catalogue pages of the United States Glass Co. and of companies merged to form it in 1891). Possibly contains catalogues and/or catalogue pages from predecessors of the United States Glass Company. Only dated catalogue page bears date 1895-1896.

United States Glass Co., Pittsburgh, PA. (Collected sales catalogues and catalogue pages of the United States Glass Co. and of companies merged to form it in 1891). Includes: Factory A or Adams & Co.; Factory B or Bryce Bros.; Factory C or Challinor, Taylor & Co., Ltd.; Factory D or George Duncan & Sons; Factory E or Richards & Hartley Glass Co.; Factory F or Ripley & Co.; Factory G, Factory K, and Factory P or Doyle & Co.

United States Glass Co., Pittsburgh, PA. (Collected sales catalogues and catalogue pages of the United States Glass Co. and of companies merged to form it in 1891). Contents: contains catalogues and catalogue pages from Factory A, Factory B, Factory D, Factory F, Factory G, Factory J, Factory L, and Factory U. Only dated catalogues bear date July, 1886.

United States Glass Co., Pittsburgh, PA. (Export catalogue of the United States Glass Co., largest manufacturers of pressed and blown glassware. 1919).

United States Glass Co., Pittsburgh, PA. (Illustrated catalogue. 1898). Includes: cologne bottles, glass novelties and toys, bottles, candlesticks, lamps and chandeliers.

United States Glass Co., Pittsburgh, PA. (Illustrated catalogue. 1904). Includes: novelties, toys, colognes, show jars, inks, paperweights and lamps.

United States Glass Co., Pittsburgh, PA. Massachusetts pattern. (ca. 1898).

United States Glass Co., Pittsburgh, PA. (Sales catalogue). Between 1908-1919. (Some of the items appear in the catalogues dated 1904 and 1919). This catalogue is probably from the 1908-1910 period.

United States Glass Co., Pittsburgh, PA. (Sales catalogue, probably of the United States Glass Co., Factory L formally O'Hara Glass Co.) 1890. Includes Crown Jewel pattern, Scroll pattern, No. 750 pattern, and Cordova pattern.

United States Glass Co., Factory D, Pittsburgh, PA. (Catalogue No. 111). (1904?). Includes: gold, emerald and ruby decorated table glass and lamps; also, souvenir assortment.

United States Glass Co., Factory K, Pittsburgh, PA. (Sales catalogue). Between 1891-1895. Fragments of catlogue(s) found in conjunction with the King Glass Co. catalogue.

United States Glass Co., Factory O, Pittsburgh, PA. Pattern 15,005 (1891 or 1892). All illustrations of Pattern 15,005 depict U.S. coins dated 1891 and 1892.

A.A. Importing Co., Inc., St Louis, MO. and Carson/San Francisco, CA. Bi-Centennial Spring-Summer Catalog No. 33. 1976.

A.A. Importing Co., Inc., St. Louis, MO. and Carson/San Francisco, CA. Catalog No. 36, 1978.

A.A. Importing Co., Inc., St. Louis, MO. and Carson/San Francisco, CA. Catalog No. 41, Spring-Summer, 1981.

American Historical Replica Company, Grand Rapids, MI.: Sales Brochure. 1975-1976.

Fenton Art Glass Co., Williamstown, WV. January, 1982 Catalog Supplement.

Guernsey Glass Company, Inc., Cambridge, OH. Catalog to the Trade. 1979.

Imperial Glass Corp., Bellaire, OH. Catalog to the Trade. 1977.

Imperial Glass Corp., Bellaire, OH. Catalog to the Trade. "Imperial Glass by Lenox". 1978.

Imperial Glass Corp., Bellaire, OH. "Exclusive Reproductions of Early American Glass from the Metropolitan Museum of Art." Undated.

Imperial Glass Corp., Bellaire, OH, "House of Americana Glassware," ca. 1958.

Imperial Glass Corp., Bellaire, OH. "Imperial Glass, 1930's–1970's."

Imperial Glass Corp., Bellaire, OH. "Imperial Glass by Lenox," 1980.

Imperial Glass Corp., Bellaire, OH. "Imperial Glass: An American Handcrafted Tradition," 1983.

Imperial Glass Corp., Bellaire, OH. "Imperial Hand Crafted Glass by Lenox." (Between 1973 and 1980).

Imperial Glass Corp., Bellaire, OH. "Imperial's Vintage Milk Glass: Handmade in Olden Manner," Ca. 1953-55.

Imperial Glass Corp., Bellaire, OH. Supplement 1 to Catalog No. 62, 1962.

Imperial Glass Corp., Bellaire, OH. "Milk Glass." 1956–58.

Jeannette Glass Co., Jeannette, PA. 1966 Catalog.

Jeannette Corp., Jeannette, PA. Catalog to the Trade. 1978.

Jenning's Red Barn, New Martinsville, WV. Undated illustrated Sales Catalog.

Kanawha Glass, Dunbar, WV. 1974 Catalog.

Kanawha Glass, Dunbar WV. 1976 Catalog No. 76.

Kanawha Glass, Dunbar, WV. 1978 Catalog No. 78.

Mosser Glass, Inc., Cambridge, OH. Catalog to the Trade. 1979.

Smith, L.E. Glass Co., Mount Pleasant, PA. "Handcrafted Milk Glass: the Finest Collection of Authentic Antique Reproductions." ca. 1954.

Smith, L.E. Glass Co., Mount Pleasant, PA. Catalog to the Trade. 1967-1968.

Smith, L.E. Glass Co., Mount Pleasant, PA. January 1, 1982 Illustrated Price List.

Smith, L.E. Glass Co., Mount Pleasant, PA. 1982 Illustrated Catalog for the Antique Trade.

Summit Art Glass Co., Akron, OH. Sales Brochure. 1977.

Tiara Exclusives, Dunkirk, IN. 1981 Illustrated Catalog.

Tiara Exclusives, Dunkirk, IN. 1980 Tenth Anniversary Catalog.

Viking Glass Co., New Martinsville, WV. 67 Original B/W Photographs. 1966-1979.

Viking Glass Co., New Martinsville, WV. 1974 Catalog.

Viking Glass Co., New Martinsville, WV. "Jewels of Light" by Viking, 1973 Catalog.

Viking Glass Co., New Martinsville, WV. Supplement to the Viking 1982 Catalog to the Trade. 1982.

Westmoreland Glass Co., Grapeville, PA. Paneled Grape pattern illustrated, 1955 Catalog.

Westmorland Glass Co., Grapeville, PA. "Westmorland Glass Company Handmade Reproductions of Choice Pieces of Early American Glass." 1950.

Westmoreland Glass Co., Grapeville, PA. 1955 Catalog, No. 500.

Westmoreland Glass Co., Grapeville, PA. 1974 Catalog Supplement.

Westmoreland Glass Co., Grapeville, PA. 1976 "Treasured Gifts" Catalog.

Westmoreland Glass Co., Grapeville, PA. 1983 color Catalog.

Wright, L.G. Glass Co., New Martinsville, WV. 1970 Catalog Supplement.

Wright. L.G. Glass Co., New Martinsville, WV. 1971 Catalog.

Wright, L.G. Glass Co., New Martinsville, WV. 1974 Master Catalog.

Museum Store/Gift Catalogs

Metropolitan Museum of Art, New York City, NY. 1970, 1971, 1972, 1974, 1977, 1978, 1979, 1980, 1981, 1984, 1985, 1986, 1987.

Smithsonian Institution, Washington, DC. 1978, 1979, 1980, 1981, 1982.

INDEX

Mirror Plate. *See* Galloway, 236
Missouri, 372
Mitre. *See* Sawtooth, 462
Mitre Diamond. *See* Sawtooth, 462
Modiste. *See* New Hampshire, 382
Monkey, 374
Moon and Star, 375
Moon and Star Variant. *See* Jewelled Moon and Stars, 303
Moon and Star Variation. *See* Jewelled Moon and Stars, 303
Moon and Star with Waffle. *See* Shrine, 480
Moon and Star with Waffle Stem. *See* Jewelled Moon and Stars, 303
Moss Rose. *See* Open Rose, 390
Muchness. *See* Minnesota, 370
Multiple Fruits. *See* Strawberry and Currant, 500

Nail, 377
Nailhead, 379
Nailhead and Panel. *See* Finecut and Panel, 212
Nailhead Variant. *See* Spirea Band, 487
Near Slim Ashburton. *See* Ashburton, 26
Nelly. *See* Strigil, 501
Nemesis. *See* Tepee, 508
Neptune. *See* Queen Anne, 428
Nevada, 380
New Century. *See* Delaware, 170
New England Flute. *See* Flute, 225
New England Pineapple, 381
New Floral. *See* Bleeding Heart, 71
New Grand. *See* Grand, 251
New Hampshire, 382
New Jersey, 384
New Jewel. *See* Royal Ivy, 458
New Mexico. *See* Aztec, 35
Newport. *See* Bulls and Daisies, 88
New Pressed Leaf. *See* Pressed Leaf, 416
New York. *See* Manhattan, 348
New York Honeycomb. *See* Honeycomb, 278
No. 1 (Bryce, McKee). *See* Tulip with Sawtooth, 529
No. 3 (McKee and Bros.). *See* Fan with Diamond, 201
No. 3 (O'Hara's). *See* Honeycomb, 78
No. 5 (Adam's). *See* Hidalgo, 273
No. 8 (Kokomo's). *See* Kansas, 306
No. 9 (O'Hara's). *See* Loop, 335
No. 9D (Dalzell, Gilmore and Leighton). *See* Strawberry and Currant, 500
No. 10 (Canton's). *See* Primrose, 418
No. 11 (Indiana Tumbler). *See* Champion, 114
No. 14 (Columbia's). *See* Henrietta, 270
No. 15 (Gillinder and Son). *See* Buckle, Early, 83
No. 17 (Thompson's). *See* Torpedo, 522
No. 18 (Thompson's). *See* Bow Tie, 75
No. 22 (Cape Cod's). *See* Huber, 285

No. 24 (George Duncan's). *See* Quartered Block, 426
No. 24 (U.S. Glass). *See* Paneled Forget-Me-Not, 395
No. 25 (Doyle's). *See* Grape and Festoon, 252
No. 25 (King's). *See* Finecut and Block, 209
No. 25 (Richards and Hartley). *See* Three Panel, 519
No. 28 (Doyle's). *See* Stippled Grape and Festoon, 497
No. 28 (George Duncan's Sons). *See* Tepee, 508
No. 29 (Doyle's). *See* Paneled Forget-Me-Not, 395
No. 29 (Indiana Tumbler). *See* Shuttle, 481
No. 30 (Adam's). *See* Plume, 408
No. 30 (Doyle's). *See* Drapery, 186
No. 30 (Duncan's). *See* Scalloped Six Point(s), 468
No. 39 (George Duncan's Sons). *See* Button Arches, 94
No. 40 (Bellaire Goblet). *See* Honeycomb, 278
No. 42 (George Duncan's Sons). *See* Mardi Gras, 352
No. 50 (Federal's). *See* Dewdrop and Raindrop, 172
No. 50 (Kokomo's). *See* Dewdrop and Raindrop, 172
No. 55 (Richards and Hartley). *See* Question Mark, 429
No. 56 (Gillinder and Sons). *See* Sawtooth, 462
No. 64 (Cape Cod's). *See* Hamilton, 257
No. 67 (Greensburg's). *See* Dewdrop in Points, 173
No. 75 (Dalzell's). *See* Klondike, 315
No. 75D (Dalzell's). *See* Klondike, 315
No. 76 (Doyle's). *See* Triple Triangle, 527
No. 77 (Bryce's). *See* Diamond and Sunburst, 182
No. 77 (Thompson's). *See* Truncated Cube, 528
No. 79 (Bryce's). *See* Chain with Star, 113
No. 80 (Bryce's). *See* Leverne, 322
No. 82 (O'Hara's). *See* Chandelier, 117
No. 85 (Adam's). *See* Valencia Waffle, 535
No. 85 (U.S. Glass). *See* Bleeding Heart, 71
No. 86 (Adam's). *See* Daisy and Button with Thumbprint Panel, 159
No. 90 (George Duncan and Sons). *See* Zippered Block, 566
No. 90 (O'Hara's). *See* Hand, 260
No. 95 (George Duncan and Sons). *See* Gonterman, 245
No. 96 (Cape Cod's). *See* Honeycomb, 278
No. 99 (Richards and Hartley). *See* Daisy and Button with Crossbars, 155
No. 101 (Hobb's, Brockunier). *See* Daisy and Button, 149
No. 103 (Richards and Hartley). *See* Thousand Eye, 514

No. 110 (Federal's). *See* Austrian, 33

No. 124 (Indiana Glass). *See* Daisy and Button with Narcissus, 157

No. 125 (Bryce's). *See* Rose in Snow, 451

No. 130 (Adam's). *See* Thousand Eye, 514

No. 136 (Central's). *See* Honeycomb, 278

No. 139 (Central's). *See* Huber, 285

No. 140 (Adam's). *See* Wild Flower, 544

No. 140 (Central's). *See* Cabbage Rose, 98

No. 140 (Fostoria's). *See* Red Block, 432

No. 145 (Central's). *See* Loop, 335

No. 150 (Duncan's). *See* Frosted Ribbon, 234

No. 151 (Bellaire's). *See* Giant Bulls Eye, 244

No. 157 (Indiana Glass). *See* Bird and Strawberry, 67

No. 157 (U.S. Glass). *See* Giant Bulls Eye, 244

No. 160 (Heisey's). *See* Locket On Chain, 333

No. 175 (Bryce's). *See* Red Block, 432

No. 190 (Richards and Hartley). *See* Kokomo, 316

No. 200 (Indiana Glass). *See* Austrian, 33

No. 205 (Fostoria's). *See* Artichoke, 24

No. 206 (Diamond's). *See* Delaware, 170

No. 209 (Federal's). *See* Stars and Stripes, 492

No. 209 (Kokomo's). *See* Stars and Stripes, 492

No. 250 (Doyle's). *See* Red Block, 432

No. 250 (Pioneer's). *See* Red Block, 432

No. 260 (Bryce's). *See* Finecut and Panel, 212

No. 287 (Northwood's). *See* Royal Ivy, 458

No. 300 (Doyle's). *See* Daisy and Button, 149

No. 301 (Fostoria's). *See* Lorraine, 342

No. 308 (Duncan's). *See* Duncan Block, 187

No. 309 (Duncan's). *See* Duncan Block, 187

No. 315 (Northwood's). *See* Royal Oak, 459

No. 326 (Hobb's, Brockunier). *See* Francesware, 227

No. 328 (Duncan's). *See* Red Block, 432

No. 330 (Hobbs, Brockunier). *See* Hobb's Block, 276

No. 335 (Duncan's). *See* Beaded Swirl, 56

No. 335 (Hobb's, Brockunier). *See* Hexagon Block, 272

No. 339 (Hobb's, Brockunier). *See* Leaf and Flower, 319

No. 350 (Crystal's). *See* Actress, 4

No. 350 (Indiana Tumbler). *See* Cord Drapery, 130

No. 356 (Duncan's). *See* All Over Diamond, 9

No. 360 (Duncan's). *See* Snail, 484

No. 365 (LaBelle's). *See* Bamboo, 41

No. 400 (Duncan's). *See* Three Face, 517

No. 431 (Riverside's). *See* Victoria (Riverside's), 541

No. 436 (Riverside's). *See* Brilliant (Riverside's), 77

No. 450 (Fostoria's). *See* Saint Bernard, 460

No. 456 (Bellaire Goblet). *See* Cottage, 134

No. 484 (Riverside's). *See* Croesus, 135

No. 490D (Dalzell, Gilmore and Leighton). *See* Reverse Torpedo, 436

No. 492 (Riverside's). *See* Empress, 191

No. 500 (Doyle's). *See* Honeycomb, 278

No. 500 (Fostoria's). *See* Atlanta (Fostoria's), 28

No. 500 (King's). *See* King's 500, 309

No. 500 (Richards and Hartley). *See* Cupid and Venus, 140

No. 507 (Kokomo-Jenkins). *See* Paneled Grape, 397

No. 525 (Richards and Hartley). *See* Lion and Cable, 330

No. 544 (Richards and Hartley). *See* Block and Fan, 73

No. 555 (A.J. Beatty). *See* Daisy and Button with V Ornament, 161

No. 555 (Duncan's). *See* Shell and Tassel, 475

No. 558 (Beatty's). *See* Daisy and Button with V Ornament, 161

No. 618 (Fostoria's). *See* Shell and Jewel, 474

No. 623 (Jenkins'). *See* Kokomo, 316

No. 669 (Cambridge's). *See* Feather, 202

No. 676 (Fostoria's). *See* Priscilla (Fostoria's), 422

No. 711 (New Martinsville's). *See* Leaf and Star, 321

No. 720 (Bryce's). *See* Fine Cut, 208

No. 748 (Central's). *See* Log Cabin, 334

No. 775 (Central's). *See* Pressed Diamond, 415

No. 789 (Fostoria's). *See* Wedding Bells, 549

No. 881 (Central's). *See* Red Block, 432

No. 893 (Central's). *See* Red Block, 432

No. 900 (U.S. Glass). *See* Hartley, 264

No. 907 (Model's). *See* Tacoma, 504

No. 1,205 (Heisey's). *See* Fancy Loop, 200

No. 1,205½ (Heisey's). *See* Fancy Loop, 200

No. 1,221 (Beatty's). *See* Texas Bulls Eye, 511

No. 1,255 (Heisey's). *See* Pineapple and Fan (Heisey's), 405

No. 1,903 (Federal's). *See* Stars and Stripes, 492

No. 2,870 (Cambridge's). *See* Inverted Strawberry, 293

No. 4,778 (U.S. Glass). *See* Jacob's Ladder, 297

No. 15,001 (U.S. Glass). *See* O'Hara's Diamond, 387

No. 15,002 (U.S. Glass). *See* Nail, 377

No. 15,004 (U.S. Glass). *See* Barred Oval(s), 48

No. 15,005 (U.S. Glass). *See* U.S. Coin, 532

No. 15,007 (U.S. Glass). *See* Frosted Circle, 230

No. 15,009 (U.S. Glass). *See* Fleur-de-Lis and Drape, 219

No. 15,010 (U.S. Glass). *See* Ribbon Candy, 438

No. 15,011 (U.S. Glass). *See* All Over Diamond, 9

No. 15,014 (U.S. Glass). *See* Heavy Gothic, 268

No. 15,021 (U.S. Glass). *See* Broken Column, 80

No. 15,028 (U.S. Glass). *See* Loop with Dewdrop(s), 341

No. 15,029 (U.S. Glass). *See* Indiana, 291

No. 15,030 (U.S. Glass). *See* Roman Rosette, 449

No. 15,043 (U.S. Glass). *See* Feather Duster, 205

No. 15,046 (U.S. Glass). *See* Shoshone, 478

No. 15,048 (U.S. Glass). *See* Pennsylvania, 402

No. 15,048½ (U.S. Glass). *See* Pennsylvania, 402

No. 15,049 (U.S. Glass). *See* Maryland, 356

No. 15,051 (U.S. Glass). *See* Kentucky, 307

No. 15,052 (U.S. Glass). *See* Illinois, 289

No. 15,053 (U.S. Glass). *See* Louisiana, 343

No. 15,054 (U.S. Glass). *See* Massachusetts, 361

No. 15,055 (U.S. Glass). *See* Minnesota, 370

No. 15,056 (U.S. Glass). *See* Florida, 222

No. 15,057 (U.S. Glass). *See* Colorado, 125

No. 15,058 (U.S. Glass). *See* Missouri, 372

No. 15,059 (U.S. Glass). *See* California, 101

No. 15,060 (U.S. Glass). *See* Vermont, 538

No. 15,062 (U.S. Glass). *See* Alabama, 7

No. 15,064 (U.S. Glass). *See* Tennessee, 507

No. 15,065 (U.S. Glass). *See* Delaware, 170

No. 15,066 (U.S. Glass). *See* Maine, 346

No. 15,067 (U.S. Glass). *See* Texas, 509

No. 15,068 (U.S. Glass). *See* Connecticut, 128

No. 15,069 (U.S. Glass). *See* Iowa, 294

No. 15,070 (U.S. Glass). *See* New Jersey, 384

No. 15,071 (U.S. Glass). *See* Banded Portland, 43

No. 15,072 (U.S. Glass). *See* Kansas, 306

No. 15,073 (U.S. Glass). *See* Oregon, 391

No. 15,075 (U.S. Glass). *See* Nevada, 380

No. 15,076 (U.S. Glass). *See* Georgia, 242

No. 15,077 (U.S. Glass). *See* Michigan, 366

No. 15,078 (U.S. Glass). *See* Manhattan, 348

No. 15,079 (U.S. Glass). *See* Wisconsin, 559

No. 15,080 (U.S. Glass). *See* Utah, 534

No. 15,081 (U.S. Glass). *See* Wyoming, 562

No. 15,083 (U.S. Glass). *See* Carolina, 109

No. 15,084 (U.S. Glass). *See* New Hampshire, 382

No. 15,086 (U.S. Glass). *See* Galloway, 236

No. 15,092 (U.S. Glass). *See* Star in Bulls Eye, 490

No. 15,093 (U.S. Glass). *See* States, The, 493

No. 15,110 (U.S. Glass). *See* Rising Sun, 444

No. 15,117 (U.S. Glass). *See* Bulls Eye and Daisies, 88

No. 15,118 (U.S. Glass). *See* Cane Horseshoe, 106

No. 15,121 (U.S. Glass). *See* Portland, 413

No. 15,140 (U.S. Glass). *See* Reverse 44, 434

No. 15,160 (U.S. Glass). *See* Bulls Eye and Fan, 89

No. 15,601 (Jefferson's). *See* Galloway, 236

North Pole. *See* Polar Bear, 411

Notched Bulls Eye. *See* Texas Bulls Eye, 511

Notched Rib. *See* Broken Column, 80

Nova Scotia Ribbon and Star. *See* Zippered Block, 566

N.P.L. *See* Pressed Leaf, 416

Nugget. *See* Shell and Jewel, 474

Oak Leaf. *See* Ribbed Palm, 442; Willow Oak, 556

Oaken Bucket. *See* Wooden Pail, 561

Oats and Barley. *See* Wheat and Barley, 553

Octagon Rosette. *See* Daisy and Button, 149

O'Hara Pattern (McKee's). *See* Loop, 335

O'Hara's Diamond, 387

Old Abe. *See* Frosted Eagle, 232

Old Man. *See* Queen Anne, 428

Old Man of the Mountain(s). *See* Viking, 542

Old Man of the Woods. *See* Queen Anne, 428

Olive. *See* Blackberry, 46

One Hundred and One. *See* One-O-One, 389

One-O-One, 389

1-0-1. *See* One-O-One, 389

Open Rose, 390

Oregon, 391

Oregon (Richards and Hartley). *See* Skilton, 482

Orient. *See* Shrine, 480

Orient (Bryce's). *See* Buckle with Star, 85

Orion. *See* Cathedral, 111

Oval and Crossbar. *See* Barred Oval(s), 48

Oval and Lincoln Drape. *See* Lincoln Drape, 326

Oval Loop. *See* Question Mark, 429

Owl. *See* Bulls Eye with Diamond Point, 92

Palace (Adam's). *See* Moon and Star, 375; Waffle and Thumbprint, 544

Palmette, 392

Palm Leaf and Scroll. *See* Missouri, 372

Palm and Scroll. *See* Missouri, 372

Paneled Daisy, 394. *See* Amberette, 14

Paneled Forget-Me-Not, 395

Paneled Grape, 397

Paneled Thistle, 398

Panelled Cherry. *See* Cherry Thumbprint, 120

Panelled Daisy. *See* Paneled Daisy, 394

Panelled Daisy and Button. *See* Amberette, 14; Queen, 427

Panelled Diamond Block. *See* Quartered Block, 426

Panelled Diamond Cut and Fan. *See* Hartley, 264

Panelled English Hobnail with Prisms. *See* Mardi Gras, 352

Panelled 44. *See* Reverse 44, 434

Panelled Flower. *See* Maine, 346

Panelled Herringbone. *See* Florida, 222

Panelled Jewel. *See* Michigan, 366

Panelled Oval Fine Cut. *See* Austrian, 33

Panelled Sprig. *See* Sprig, 488
Panelled Star and Button. *See* Sedan, 473
Panelled Stippled Flower. *See* Maine, 346
Panelled Thousand Eye. *See* Three Panel, 519
Panelled Waffle. *See* Waffle, 543
Panelled Zipper. *See* Iowa, 294
Paragon. *See* Cane Horseshoe, 106
Parrot. *See* King's 500, 309
Parthenon. *See* Egyptian, 190
Pavonia, 400
Peacock Eye. *See* Georgia, 242
Peacock Feather(s). *See* Georgia, 242
Peacock Tail. *See* Horn of Plenty, 282
Pennsylvania, 402
Pennsylvania (O'Hara's). *See* Hand, 260
Pennsylvania Hand. *See* Hand, 260
Pepper Berry. *See* Barberry, 46
Petalled Medallion. *See* Brilliant (Riverside's), 77
Picket, 404
Picket Fence. *See* Picket, 404
Pigmy. *See* Torpedo, 522
Pillar. *See* Flat Diamond, 217
Pillar and Cut Diamond. *See* Triple Triangle, 527
Pinafore. *See* Actress, 4
Pineapple. *See* Diamond Point, 177; New England Pineapple, 381; Sawtooth, 462
Pineapple and Fan (Heisey's), 405
Pineapple with Fan. *See* Pineapple and Fan (Heisey's), 405
Pineapple Stem. *See* Pavonia, 400
Pioneer. *See* Westward Ho, 551
Pittsburgh Tree of Life. *See* Tree of Life with Hand, 526
Plain Roman Key. *See* Greek Key, 448
Plain Smocking. *See* Smocking, 483
Plain Sunburst. *See* Diamond and Sunburst, 182
Plain Swan. *See* Swan, 503
Pleat and Panel, 407
Pleat and Tuck. *See* Adonis, 5
Plume, 408
Pointed Bulls Eye. *See* Reverse Torpedo, 436
Pointed Panel Daisy and Button. *See* Queen, 427
Pointed Thumbprint. *See* Almond Thumbprint, 11
Polar Bear, 411
Polar Bear and Seal. *See* Polar Bear, 411
Popcorn, 412
Portland, 413
Portland with Diamond Point. *See* Banded Portland, 43
Portland Loop and Jewel. *See* Loop and Dart with Round Ornament, 338
Portland Petal. *See* Loop, 335
Potted Plant. *See* Flower Pot, 224
Powder Horn and Shot. *See* Powder and Shot, 414
Powder and Shot, 414

Prayer Mat. *See* Good Luck, 246
Prayer Rug. *See* Good Luck, 246
Pressed Diamond, 415
Pressed Leaf, 416
Pride. *See* Leaf and Dart, 318
Primrose, 418
Prince's Feather. *See* Bulls Eye and Fleur-de-Lis, 91; Feather, 202
Princes' Feather. *See* Princess Feather, 419
Princess Feather, 419; Bulls Eye and Fleur-de-Lis, 91
Princeton. *See* Beveled Diamond and Star, 64
Priscilla (Dalzell's), 421
Priscilla (Fostoria's), 422
Prism. *See* Wisconsin, 559
Prism and Diamond Point(s). *See* Prism with Diamond Points, 424
Prism with Diamond Points, 424
Prism and Herringbone. *See* Florida, 222
Prison Window(s). *See* Indiana, 291
Proud Lion. *See* Lion and Cable, 330
Proxy Ashburton. *See* Ashburton, 26
Psyche and Cupid, 425
Purple Block. *See* Barred Oval(s), 48

Quartered Block, 426
Quartered Diamond. *See* Quartered Block, 426
Queen, 427
Queen Anne, 428
Queen's Necklace. *See* Loop and Jewel, 340
Question Mark, 429
Quilted Diamond. *See* Diamond Quilted, 180

R&B Pattern. *See* Stippled Grape and Festoon, 497
R&H Swirl Band. *See* Kokomo, 316
Radiant (Union's). *See* Sawtoothed Honeycomb, 465
Raindrop, 430
Raisin. *See* Ribbed Grape, 439
Rattan. *See* Broken Column, 80
Ray. *See* Ball and Swirl, 38
Rebecca at the Well. *See* Ribbon (Bakewell's), 443
Recessed Pillar-Red Top. *See* Nail, 377
Recessed Pillar-Thumbprint Band. *See* Nail, 377
Red Block, 432
Red Block and Fan. *See* Block and Fan, 73
Red Loop and Fine Cut. *See* New Hampshire, 382; New Jersey, 384
Reeded (New England Glass). *See* Fine Rib, 213
Regal (Bryce's). *See* Paneled Forget-Me-Not, 395
Reverse 44, 434
Reverse Torpedo, 436
Ribbed Asterisk and Concave. *See* Shuttle, 481
Ribbed Bellflower. *See* Bellflower, 60
Ribbed Fingerprint. *See* Broken Column, 80

Stippled Beaded Shield. *See* Locket On Chain, 333
Stippled Chain, 494
Stippled Dahlia. *See* Dahlia, 147
Stippled Daisy. *See* Willow Oak, 556
Stippled Double Loop, 495
Stippled Forget-Me-Not, 496
Stippled Grape and Festoon, 497
Stippled Oval. *See* Egg In Sand, 189
Stippled Panelled Flower. *See* Maine, 346
Stippled Primrose. *See* Maine, 346; Primrose, 418
Stippled Scroll. *See* Scroll, 470
Stippled Star, 498
Straight Huber. *See* Huber, 285
Strawberry, 499. *See* Inverted Strawberry, 293
Strawberry and Bird. *See* Bird and Strawberry, 67
Strawberry and Currant, 500
Stretched Honeycomb. *See* Honeycomb, 278
Strigil, 501
Sultan. *See* Curtain, 144
Sun and Star. *See* Priscilla (Dalzell's), 421
Sunflower, 502
Sunk Daisy and Button. *See* Queen, 427
Sunrise. *See* Rising Sun, 444
Sunshine. *See* Rising Sun, 444
Swan, 503
Swan with Mesh. *See* Swan, 503
Swirl. *See* Feather, 202; Jersey Swirl, 301
Swirl and Ball. *See* Ball and Swirl, 38
Swirl and Diamonds. *See* Jersey Swirl, 301
Swirl(s) and Feather(s). *See* Feather, 202
Swirl and Thumbprint. *See* King's 500, 309
Swirled Column. *See* Beaded Swirl, 56
Swiss. *See* Aegis, 6

Tacoma, 504
Tailsman Ashburton. *See* Ashburton, 26
Tall Argus (Bulbous Stem). *See* Argus, 20
Teardrop and Diamond Block. *See* Art, 22
Teepee/Tee Pee, 508
Tennessee, 507
Texas, 509
Texas Bulls Eye, 511
The Silver Age. *See* U.S. Coin, 532
The Sisters. *See* Three Face, 517
Theatrical. *See* Actress, 4
Thistle, 512
Thistle and Sunflower. *See* Willow Oak, 556
Thousand Eye, 514
Thousand Eye Band. *See* Beaded Band, 53
Thousand Eye Three Panel. *See* Three Panel, 519
Thousand Faces. *See* Honeycomb, 278
Three Face, 517
Three Fates. *See* Three Face, 517
Three Graces. *See* Three Face, 517
Three Knob. *See* Thousand Eye, 514
Three Panel, 519
Three Sisters. *See* Three Face, 517

Thumbprint, 521. *See* Argus, 20
Thumbprint Band. *See* Dakota, 163
Thumbprint Band-Clear. *See* Dakota, 163
Thumbprint Band-Red Top. *See* Dakota, 163
Thumbprint and Prisms. *See* Apollo (Adam's), 17
Thunder Bird. *See* Hummingbird, 287
Tiny Lion. *See* Lion and Cable, 330
Tippecanoe. *See* Westward Ho, 551
Tobin. *See* Leaf and Star, 321
Tooth and Claw. *See* Esther (Riverside's), 192
Torpedo, 522
Tree of Life, 524
Tree of Life with Hand, 526
Trilby. *See* Valentine, 537
Triple Bulls Eye. *See* Waffle and Thumbprint, 544
Triple Triangle, 527
Triple Triangle-Red Top. *See* Triple Triangle, 527
Triple X. *See* Tacoma, 504
Truncated Cube, 528
Tulip. *See* Beaded Tulip, 58; Tulip with Sawtooth, 529
Tulip with Sawtooth, 529
Turkey Track. *See* Yale, 564
Turtle. *See* Garden of Eden, 240
Twin Pear. *See* Baltimore Pear, 39
Twinkle Star. *See* Utah, 534
Two Panel, 531

U.S. Coin, 532
U.S. Portland. *See* Portland, 413
Umbilicated Hobnail. *See* Button Band, 96
Union (New England Glass). *See* Bulls Eye with Diamond Point, 92; Banded Buckle, 42
Utah, 534

Valencia. *See* Artichoke, 24
Valencia Waffle, 535
Valentine, 537
Vandyke. *See* Daisy and Button with V Ornament, 161
Venus. *See* Loop and Jewel, 340
Vermont, 538
Vermont Honeycomb. *See* Vermont, 538
Vernon Honeycomb. *See* Honeycomb, 278
Victor. *See* Shell and Jewel, 474; Shoshone, 478
Victoria (Pioneer's), 539
Victoria (Riverside's), 541
Viking, 542
Vincent Valentine. *See* Valentine, 537
Virginia. *See* Galloway 236; Banded Portland, 43

Waffle, 543
Waffle and Fine Cut. *See* Cathedral, 111
Waffle and Thumbprint, 544
Waffle-Red Top. *See* Hidalgo, 273